PSYCHOLOGY FOR TEACHING

SEVENTH EDITION

PSYCHOLOGY FOR TEACHING

A bear ~~always usually sometimes rarely never always faces the front~~ will not commit himself just now

Guy R. Lefrançois
University of Alberta

Wadsworth Publishing Company
Belmont, California
A Division of Wadsworth, Inc.

Education Editor: Suzanna Brabant

Developmental Editor: John Bergez

Editorial Assistant: Laurie Wiegler

Production Editor: Donna Linden

Designer: Carolyn Deacy

Print Buyer: Barbara Britton

Art Editor: Marta Kongsle

Permissions Editor: Jeanne Bosschart

Copy Editor: Alan R. Titche

Photo Researcher: Sarah Bendersky

Cartoonists: Tony Hall and Jeff Littlejohn

Compositor: Thompson Type,
          San Diego, California

Cover Illustration: Kem Tom
          Santa Barbara, California

Credits

p. 2: © Elizabeth Crews; *p. 4*: © Culver Pictures; *p. 20*: © Jean Gaumy/Magnum Photos, Inc.; *p. 22*: © Cary Wolinsky/Stock, Boston; *p. 56*: © Elizabeth Crews; *p. 58*: © THE FAR SIDE cartoons by Gary Larson reprinted by permission of Chronicle Features, San Francisco, CA; *p. 80*: © Elizabeth Crews; *p. 108*: © Jack Spratt/The Image Works; *p. 132*: © 1986 James Cuebas/Impact Visuals; *p. 134*: © Cornell Capa/Magnum Photos, Inc.; *p. 156*: © Elizabeth Crews/The Image Works; *p. 182*: © 1989 Nita Winter Photography; *p. 220*: © Patricia Ann Schwab/Stock, Boston; *p. 222*: © Michael Siluk/The Image Works; *p. 252*: © Bob Daemmrich/The Image Works; *p. 282*: © Elizabeth Crews/Stock, Boston; *p. 284*: © Jean-Claude Lejeune/Stock, Boston; *p. 312*: © Elizabeth Crews; *p. 323*: © THE FAR SIDE cartoons by Gary Larson reprinted by permission of Chronicle Features, San Francisco, CA; *p. 340*: © Elizabeth Crews; *p. 364*: © Elizabeth Crews; *p. 393*: © 1989 Nita Winter Photography

Printed in the United States of America   34

  2 3 4 5 6 7 8 9 10 — 95 94 93 92 91

Library of Congress Cataloging-in-Publication Data
Lefrançois, Guy R.
    Psychology for teaching : a bear will not commit himself just now
 / Guy R. Lefrançois. — 7th ed.
      p.   cm.
    Includes bibliographical references and index.
    ISBN 0-534-14412-8
    1. Educational psychology.   2. Teaching — Psychological aspects.
3. Learning, Psychology of.   I. Title.
LB1051.L568   1991
370.15 — dc20   90-41634

For my first teacher, my father,
who taught me to love books and learning,
and
For my mother,
who taught me to love people and life.

BRIEF CONTENTS

CONTENTS

PREFACE

This is a basic text in educational psychology. Its emphasis is on presenting the most important and the most educationally relevant psychological research and theory clearly, accurately, and in an engaging way. Its goal is to make you a better teacher.

About the Seventh Edition

This seventh edition presents some important changes from earlier editions. In general, it is more practical — more explicitly oriented toward instruction. It extracts more educational implications from the theories and research it summarizes and provides many classroom examples. It has discarded much of the material that was primarily historical, and most of its references to rats, pigeons, chimpanzees, and other nonhuman creatures have been deleted — save, of course, for wild cows, which are dealt with as necessary.

Changes in this edition of the **Bear** include new or expanded coverage of important concerns, such as learning styles, cooperative learning, learning/thinking strategies, self-efficacy, adult thinking and learning, expert teaching, and the social context of schooling. There is renewed emphasis on the role of knowledge and of learning strategies in empowering students to solve their immediate problems (as well as problems that are ours now but will eventually be theirs). In addition, information is updated throughout the text.

Like its predecessors, **Bear VII** has resisted the urge to become highly prescriptive, still believing that the best teaching decisions are based on sound psychological principles applied with enthusiasm and imagination and tempered with a love of children and of teaching — not on the application of prescriptions copied like recipes from instruction booklets. Teaching and children are too complex for simple recipes.

Considerable effort has been devoted to keeping this text relatively short, as well as motivating, informative, and practical. I hope that as a result **Bear VII** is more teachable, more interesting, and more useful than it was when younger.

About the Bear and Wild Cows

In this book, there are occasional references to a bear and to wild cows. Lest their purpose seem overly mysterious to you — and their inclusion frustrating — let me explain.

In the first edition, subtitled *A bear always faces the front,* the bear was largely whimsy — but not entirely purposeless whimsy. A bear strutting through the pages of a serious textbook was a bit of a jolt. It broke the tedium of uninterrupted academic content; it sometimes made readers smile — or even laugh. And it didn't detract from the serious "nuts and bolts" of the chapters. So the bear continued in all later revisions. Subsequent editions went from a bear *always* facing the front to a bear who *usually, sometimes, rarely,* and finally *never* faced that direction. By the sixth edition, grizzled, battle-scarred, and considerably wiser, the bear had done a complete about-face to *always* face the front once more.

Over the years, the bear has become something more than whimsy, something more than a break: He has become a metaphor. A metaphor is not, of course, a real thing. It is an invention. The bear metaphor was invented as much by readers of earlier editions as by me. Some of these readers have decided that the bear is a metaphor for a teacher, or perhaps for teaching. Others reached different conclusions. All are correct; inventions are never flatly wrong.

The bear, this wonderful metaphoric bear continues in this, the seventh edition. This is a bear who has sniffed the winds of change, who is witness to continuing global conflicts and to some extraordinary social and political events. Sadly, he is also witness to the cumulative effects of disastrous ecological changes. **Bear VII** has seen the invasion of wild cows. Now, in the seventh edition, the bear simply refuses to commit himself to a single posture.

As is explained in the glossary, the bear and the wild cows may be seen as metaphors for two great universals: good and evil. (Few things are entirely good; nor are many entirely evil.)

At another level, the bear and the wild cows — which appear only occasionally in chapter introductions but seldom anywhere else in the text — may be viewed as no more than a piece of whimsy, a tidbit of absurdity, a tiny mockery.

You may choose to completely ignore the bear and wild cows (which need be of no consequence to your performance on exams, to your eventual competence as a teacher, or to your happiness) or you might make them into your own metaphors.*

---

*PPC†: Can you tell us a little more about wild cows?
Author: Not much, but there is a little more in the glossary under the entry *wild cow.* There is also more about the bear in the epilogue on page 395 and in the glossary under *bear.*
†A PPC is a pre-publication critic — one of a number of educational psychologists who read the manuscript before publication. Some of these reviewers' comments are footnoted in the text.

Thank you to

• the people whose ideas are acknowledged in these pages (and to those whose ideas sneaked in unrecognized)
• Richard L. Greenberg, editor for the first bears
• Roger Peterson, Bob Podstepny, Joan Garbutt, and Stephanie Surfus, editors for the middle bears
• Suzanna Brabant, editor for the most recent bears
• Tony Hall and Jeff Littlejohn, cartoonists
• Donna Linden, production editor
• Alan R. Titche, copy editor
• Carolyn Deacy, designer
• Reviewers of the first six editions
• Reviewers of this edition: Steven Banks, Marshall University; Richard Clark, State University of New York at Albany; James Dunn, Cornell University; Janet Moursund, University of Oregon; Dan Rea, University of Wisconsin, Whitewater; Jay Samuels, University of Minnesota; Thomassine Sellers, San Francisco State University; Paul Shore, Moorhead State University; and Sharon Wilson, University of Cincinnati
• Marie, Laurier, Claire, and Rémi, who make it all worth a great deal more than my while.

PSYCHOLOGY FOR TEACHING

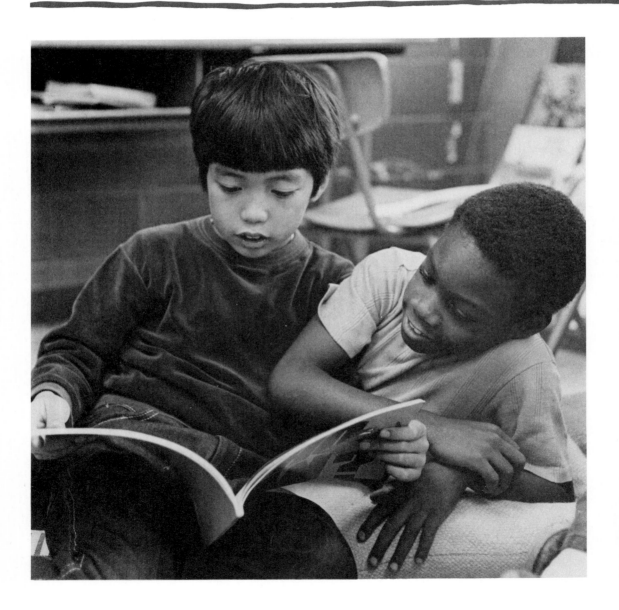

INTRODUCTION

Chapter 1 Psychology and Teaching

*There is only one chapter in Part 1 — only one intro-
duction. It says what psychology is and what educational psychology is. And it presents an overview of
each of the remaining thirteen chapters. These chapters are organized into parts according to their major
emphases. Part 2 presents various explanations of
learning and their educational implications. Part 3
looks at humanism and human development. Part 4
discusses individual differences as they are manifested
in creative behavior, intellectual functioning, behavior disorders, mental retardation, and so on. Part 5
looks at topics important to the teaching/learning
process: motivation, discipline, individualized instruction, and evaluation.*

*And somewhere the subtitle of this book becomes
more significant.*

CHAPTER 1

PSYCHOLOGY AND TEACHING

Thousands . . .
Kiss the book's outside who ne'er look within.
WILLIAM COWPER *Expostulation*

Why, everyone as they like; as the good woman said
when she kissed her cow.
JONATHAN SWIFT *Polite Conversation*

PREVIEW   A preview appears at the beginning of each chapter in this text. Previews are meant to organize and summarize important concepts and to increase the meaningfulness of material that is to be learned — sometimes by stimulating recall of important previous learning, sometimes by providing new information, and sometimes by pointing out relationships. The first chapter is a preview for the remainder of this text. Among other things, it points out that there are some important reasons for taking this course other than the fact that it might be compulsory.

■ *September 1936. Early morning. In the school yard the grass is tall; it has not yet been broken by the trampling of children's feet. The teacher, my father, stands on the steps of the one-room schoolhouse. From there he can see beyond the river toward the hills, and he can watch the trail on which the children will eventually come. It's the first day of school in Pascal, Saskatchewan. And it's also my father's first day as a teacher.*

High above the school, a single V of Canada geese sweeps southward, honking softly. And a bear, a wonderful bear, walks slowly across the school yard, stopping now and again to sniff at something or to wrap his tongue around a sprig of summer clover and ease it gently into his mouth. My father watches the bear. He doesn't know this bear, doesn't understand the meaning of his presence.

But I know the bear. I understand.

The children begin arriving. They are a varied lot: Cree Indians, Métis, Caucasians. They look nervously at the new teacher as they file into the school, carrying their lunchpails. The older children show the younger ones in which of the two cloakrooms, segregated by sex, they are to leave their jackets and their lunches.

They find empty desks and sit timidly, awaiting the voice of this new teacher — this new stomahghee, as the Cree children will call him.

My father, the stomahghee, walks to the front of the class. He turns and faces his pupils. There are forty of them, of many ages and both sexes, with a frightening range of interests, abilities, and prior learning. There is a moment of dizzying panic. What do you say to a new class? What do you do? How do you start teaching?

Would it have helped my father to read this book? Or would its content have been too progressive, too shocking for those distant times?

September 1961. Early morning. It is my first day as a teacher.

I stand for a moment on the steps of what they call a composite high school. I hear no wild geese, and no matter how hard I strain my eyes, I do not see the bear. Not yet. For a moment, however, I think I see a cow. But that cannot be; after all, I am in the city, where we are protected from such things.

Mine is not a single-room school of which I can be master. It has many rooms and many masters and mistresses. But perhaps the fear and the excitement I sense are not very different from my father's feelings so many years earlier. ■

WHY STUDY EDUCATIONAL PSYCHOLOGY?

Would this book have helped me when I began my teaching career? Unequivocally, yes! Because, contrary to what I had hoped, teaching skills turned out not to be hereditary. Even though we can't count on our genes to endow us with teaching ability, we can make use of the information that many other people have developed from their studies and from their own experiences. And we now have a tremendous body of information that can contribute dramatically to the effectiveness of teachers and of schools.

This textbook is your introduction to this information. Its goal is to make you a better teacher. It attempts to do this in two related ways: first, by providing you with important information about the processes involved in learning, organizing, remembering, thinking, solving problems, and being creative; and second, by describing and illustrating practical strategies for facilitating the teaching/learning process. As its title indicates, it presents a psychology for teaching.

PSYCHOLOGY

Psychology* is the study of human **behavior** and experience. It is a large and complex discipline — one that reflects the complexity of human behavior and experience. Some of this complexity is evident in the fact that although all psychologists are concerned with behavior in one way or another, many specialties and divisions have arisen within the field, each concentrating on a specific aspect of the discipline. For example, developmental psychologists look at behavior changes that occur with the passage

---

*Boldfaced terms are defined in the glossary.

of time; clinical psychologists deal with behavioral and emotional problems; and educational psychologists are interested in ways in which psychological knowledge can be applied in the classroom. These are only three of the divisions in psychology; Table 1.1 presents labels and descriptions of several others and provides a clearer picture of the scope of this discipline.

SCIENCE

The psychologist does not study or attempt to understand behavior simply by thinking about the various factors that might be involved in behaving. Rather, psychology as a **science** involves the application of scientific procedures and approaches in an attempt to understand human behavior.

Science is as much an attitude as a collection of methods. As an attitude, science insists on precision, consistency, and replicability. The methods resulting from this attitude consist of rules intended to eliminate subjectivity, bias, and the influence of random factors — in short, rules designed to maximize the extent to which we can have confidence in the conclusions of science. For most of the past century (psychology is approximately one hundred years old), the attitudes and the methods that have governed the psychologist's search for greater understanding of humans and their behavior have emphasized precision, replicability, and objectivity above all else.

Unfortunately for the psychologist, humans possess neither the simplicity nor the predictability of the physical world. The chemist and the physicist, using the same attitudes and scientific methods that the psychologist uses, have been able to discover replicable and precise laws that govern the behaviors of molecules and planets. But the psychologist has been hard-pressed to discover a single precise law governing the behavior of humans (more about laws shortly).

Table 1.1 What psychologists do

Subfield*	Major Concerns and Activities
Clinical	Diagnosing and treating illnesses and disturbances, frequently in a hospital or clinical setting
Counseling and guidance	Evaluating and counseling clients' behavioral, emotional, and other problems not serious enough to require hospital or clinical treatment; also assisting with important decisions (career, marriage, and so on)
Developmental	Studying changes that define growth, maturation, and learning from birth to death; applying findings in education programs
Educational	Researching ways psychology can be applied to teaching and learning; developing and applying learning programs for students
Industrial and personnel	Applying psychology in business and industry; developing and administering tests to evaluate aptitudes; conducting workshops and programs dealing with motivation, management, interpersonal relations, and related areas
Personality	Identifying and describing important, stable characteristics of individuals; developing classification schemes for personality characteristics as well as methods for identifying and assessing these characteristics
School	Identifying individual aptitudes and skills among learners in a school setting; developing and administering tests pertinent to school-related abilities
Experimental, comparative, and physiological	Exploring psychology as an experimental science; conducting research on comparisons among species; investigating physiological functioning as it relates to psychological functioning
Psychometrics	Testing and measuring psychological characteristics and making sense of resulting measures; developing tests and measurement devices
Social	Doing research and consulting on the relationship between individuals and groups

*Not all psychologists fall neatly into one of these categories. Many would consider themselves as belonging to several areas, both by the nature of their interests and by their activities. Others would hesitate to be classified in any of these subfields.

The problem for the psychologist goes beyond the observation that the behaviors of humans are influenced by a tremendous variety of forces — some of which we don't understand at all well (yet). Many aspects of human behavior cannot be measured in the way that the speed, direction, and mass of a planet or molecule can be measured. Nor are changes in human behavior as precise and predictable as are changes in the behavior of physical matter.

However, these observations should not lead you to conclude that we know little, if anything, about human behavior. Nor are they meant to encourage pessimism (although a very slight skepticism might not be entirely inappropriate). Rather, what these observations emphasize is the wonderful complexity of human thought and behavior and consequently the very real difficulties of reducing these events to simple laws and principles.

Facts and Theories

Science, as we have seen, is a collection of methods and attitudes that relate directly to the ways in which we discover and accumulate **facts**. In this context, however, the word *fact* is perhaps too strong; it implies a degree of certainty and accuracy that is not always possible in psychology or education. In these areas, our facts are simply *observations* of events, behaviors, or relationships. The important point is that science insists that these observations be made under controlled conditions so that the same observations can be made by anyone — that is, so that they can be replicated.

Facts (or observations), by themselves, would be of limited value to educators and psychologists if they were not organized, summarized, and simplified. That's where **theory** comes in. In a simple sense, a theory is a collection of related statements whose principal function is to summarize and explain observations. When, for example, I observe that Roland Littlefork repeatedly refuses to join us for our annual fishing excursion, our regular poker games, our Christmas celebration, or our Halloween masquerade, I might develop a theory about his behavior. "I have a theory about Roland," I might say, and everybody would understand what I was trying to say. "He doesn't like social gatherings," I might continue. That, in a nutshell, would be my theory. It summarizes and explains my observations admirably. It is a statement that might be described as a *naive* theory or, as Grippin and Peters (1984) put it, an *implicit* theory. Naive or implicit theories differ from more formal theories in one important respect: Formal theories must be tested. That is, it isn't sufficient simply to assume that the theory accounts for all the important observations and relationships; this must be demonstrably true.

There are many theories in psychology; not all are equally good. Some, for instance, do not reflect the facts very well. Let's say, for example, that Roland Littlefork plays poker regularly with George's group and that he also accepts other social invitations. If this were the case, my theory about Roland's behavior would not fit all the facts.

That it reflect all important facts is only one of the requirements of a good theory. Thomas (1985) suggests a number of others. Specifically, a theory is good if it (1) accurately reflects observations, (2) is expressed clearly, (3) is useful for predicting as well as explaining, (4) is applicable in a practical sense, (5) is consistent rather than self-contradictory, and (6) is not based on numerous assumptions (unproven beliefs).

Of these criteria, one of the most important for the educator is that of predicting. The most useful theories are those that serve not only to explain observations but also to predict events. My naive theory about Roland Littlefork, for example, allows me to predict that he will refuse all social invitations, no matter who issues them. As we saw, however, in this case the prediction is inaccurate because the theory does not account for certain important facts. Presumably, a theory that fits the facts better would lead to more accurate predictions.

A theory, then, is a statement, or more often, a collection of related statements, whose main function is to summarize, simplify, organize, and explain observations and to permit predictions about events relating to this set of observations. Some of these statements may be described as laws, others as principles, and many as beliefs.

Laws, Principles, and Beliefs

Laws are statements whose accuracy is generally beyond question. Physics, chemistry, astronomy, and other natural sciences have discovered numerous important laws ($E = mc^2$, for example). As we saw earlier, however, human behavior is rarely characterized by the regularity and unwavering predictability that characterize laws.

Principles are statements that are probable rather than certain. Unlike laws, they are always open to a degree of doubt, to a certain level of improbability. Accordingly, psychologists' statements about human behavior and experience take the form of principles rather than laws.

Beliefs are statements that are far more private and personal than either principles or laws. Beliefs are our individual convictions, our personal attempts to explain observations. And although they might often be correct, they do not have an important place in the development of formal theory; instead they are the basis of our naive theories (such as that which attempted to explain Roland Littlefork's refusal of my invitations).

Models

There is one additional term that is relevant here: **model**. A model, like a pattern or a blueprint, is a representation of the way things are or of the way they can or should be. As Reese and Overton (1970) point out, models can be very specific and concrete and are often included in, or derived from, theories. For example, there are models of atomic structures, models of the universe, and teaching models.

At a more general level, models can represent our worldviews, including our most basic beliefs and assumptions about human nature. In this sense, each of us has implicit models that govern our view of the world and that guide our perceptions and our behavior. Two such models underlie much of what psychologists think and believe about human beings. On the one hand, the *mechanistic* model reflects the belief that it is useful to think of humans as being very much like machines — predictable and highly responsive to environmental influences. On the other hand, the *organismic* model holds that it is more useful to view humans as dynamic, active, exploring organisms that are more responsive to internal forces than to external stimulation.

In a very real sense, psychological models are metaphors. They don't say "Humans are this or that" so much as "Humans behave *as though* they were like this or like that." Accordingly, models, like theories, cannot be judged in terms of their accuracy so much as in terms of their usefulness.

TEACHING AS PROBLEM SOLVING

In its simplest sense, to teach is to impart skills, knowledge, attitudes, and values. It involves bringing about, or at least facilitating, changes in learners. Teaching can be accomplished by telling and persuading, by showing and demonstrating, by guiding and directing the learner's efforts, or by a combination of these actions. It might involve only the teacher's own resources, knowledge, and skills; or it might rely on professionally prepared materials (films or computer software, for example), resource people, or the combination of talents, skills, and information already present among learners.

Some researchers suggest that it is useful to view teaching as an exercise in problem solving (see, for example, Leinhardt and Greeno, 1986; or Burns and Anderson, 1987). According to this model, teaching involves the ongoing solution of a series of problems. Some problems, such as those relating to specific course or lesson objectives, are clear and obvious. For example, if one of the goals of a lesson in mathematics is for students eventually to learn division, then one problem that requires solution is that of arranging for student experiences that lead to the competency in question. Other related problems are not so obvious. These have to do with managing the classroom environment, monitoring ongoing activities, evaluating and assessing the interest and understanding of individual students, and so on.

It seems that expert teachers develop sequences of routines and strategies that they can apply almost unconsciously as they teach. As a result, much of what they do in the classroom is, in a sense, on "automatic pilot" (Kagan, 1988). They are sensitive to the possibility of restlessness and inattention even before these occur. Not only do they become skilled in recognizing potential problems, but they also become skilled in applying unobtrusive solutions. Automatically — and without breaking the continuity of their ongoing activity — they bring into play new patterns of interaction that serve to shift focus, that draw students back into the flow of activity and rechannel their attention.

The patterns and routines that are such an important part of the classroom involve two different sets of activities: those relating to classroom management and discipline, and those having to do specifically with instructing — with giving students information and establishing learning habits. Accordingly, acquiring these patterns and routines — that is, learning how to teach — requires a wealth of information about both learners and the process of learning. The purpose of this text is to provide you with that information.

But there is more to being an expert teacher than can be learned in one textbook — or even in a dozen texts. Not only do you need information about learners and learning, about human development, and about motivation and interests, but you need to synthesize this information — to understand it, to integrate it with your values, your goals, your personality, and your preferences. Teachers each have their own styles of teaching. No teacher-training program can — or should — make us all alike.

Teaching has often been described as both an art and a science. In fact, some writers argue that expert teaching is a far more artistic activity than we might think. Eisner (1982) suggests that every successful teaching performance can be analyzed not only in terms of the *science* involved in instruction and classroom management, but also in terms of the *art* involved in creating the environment — the context — in which learning occurs.

Although a textbook such as this one is forced to deal with the science rather than with the art, it is worth keeping in mind that we should not resort to art only when science fails; rather, art can and should be an integral part of all classroom activity. Poetry and enchantment can have a place in even the most apparently mundane lesson in an ordinary classroom on a Tuesday. That is one of the things that makes teaching so wonderful.

TEACHING AS EMPOWERING STUDENTS

From the teacher's point of view, then, teaching can be viewed as a problem-solving activity — that is, as an activity that involves the ongoing solution of problems relating to communication, instruction, motivation, classroom management, evaluation, and so on. As is pointed out in the preceding section, one of the major purposes of this text is to provide you with the kinds of information and skills that might be useful in solving problems associated with each of these tasks. In this sense, the text addresses issues relating to the *processes* of teaching.

Another way of looking at teaching is to view it in terms of its objectives rather than its processes. The teacher must be concerned not only with the details of lesson organization and with the hundreds of routines and procedures that contribute to classroom management and effective learning, but also with the goals of the instructional process. What is it that schools ought to accomplish? What are the important objectives of education?

The answers to these questions are fundamental to the teaching/learning process. They determine not only what the *content* of the school curriculum should be, but also what the *goals* of the instructional process will be. Educational goals can be very general (for example, to develop good citizens) or very specific (to teach children to add two-digit numbers). For our purposes, a useful way of looking at educational objectives is to view them in the broadest, most general of all terms: *The goal of education is to* **empower students.**

Literally, *empower* means to give power to—in short, to *enable*. At the most obvious level, education empowers students by enabling them to do things they could not otherwise do. Reading, writing, and arithmetic empower us as surely as do sight, hearing, and our other senses, for while our senses enable us to perceive the world, the "three r's" empower us to deal with it at a very complex, sophisticated level. Without all sorts of school-related knowledge, we would be hard-pressed to function easily and effectively. We need to know a great deal if we are to use our banking machines, understand our instruction manuals, determine how much we owe our governments, read our newspapers, and on and on.

Knowledge of specific things like reading and writing is only one of the sources of empowerment schools bestow. In addition, schools also foster in students both the personal power that comes with social competence and the accompanying feelings of personal confidence, of being a unique and worthwhile individual. It is perhaps a cliché, but no less true for it, that schools must do more than teach subjects; it is far more important that they teach individual students.

Schools provide empowerment not only through the information they impart and the feelings of confidence and personal power they foster, but also through the learning strategies they develop in students. It is becoming increasingly clear, and increasingly true, that because so much information exists in our advanced technological societies, it is impossi-

ble for students to learn more than a fraction of it. And, given the rate at which information changes or becomes obsolete, it would probably be unwise to try. As a result, it is perhaps more important to learn *how* to learn and how to solve problems—to learn what Mulcahy et al. (1990) label *learning/thinking strategies*—than it is to learn only specific items of information. These strategies are the tools of knowing. They are what we use to think, to analyze, and to monitor and evaluate our intellectual activities. They can be applied to all sorts of situations throughout our lives. Accordingly, such strategies are a tremendous source of personal power—of empowerment.

We are a clever species, Nickerson (1986) muses. So smart are we that as a result of our "technological wizardry" we have reached a point at which we can not only destroy everything around us, but ourselves as well. In fact, not only do we have this power, but we are in imminent danger of using it, perhaps without even wanting to. If we are to save ourselves, Nickerson cautions, we must rely not on instinct—as might another animal—but on intelligence. Hence, our ultimate survival depends on how well we can think. That, of course, is another important reason for teaching students how to learn and how to think, to encourage them to be worthwhile human beings whose concerns extend beyond the self to include the well-being of all others.

But we are in danger of moving ahead of ourselves. This chapter is simply an introduction. Later we will speak again of learning/thinking strategies, as well as of morality and ethics and of the personal power of warriors, saints, and others.

A TEACHING MODEL

To simplify without unduly distorting reality, we analyze the teaching process in terms of three stages, each characterized by different demands on the teacher: before teaching, during

The Instructional Process

Before Teaching

1. Establish goals 5, 6, 14*

2. Determine student readiness 6, 7, 8

3. Select instructional strategies; collect required materials 2, 3, 4, 5, 13

4. Plan for assessment and evaluation 14

Teaching

Implement instructional strategies 5, 9, 10, 11, 12, 13

After Teaching

1. Assess effectiveness of teaching strategies 14

2. Determine extent to which goals have been met 14

3. Reevaluate student readiness 7, 9, 14

*Chapters containing relevant information

Figure 1.1   A three-stage model of the teaching process.

teaching, and after teaching. And contrary to what we might immediately assume, the teaching stage is no more important than what occurs before or after it. What we say about each of these stages, here and elsewhere in this text

(see Figure 1.1), is closer to the science of teaching than it is to the art of teaching, a fact that does not make the art any less important.

Before Teaching

In order to be an effective, perhaps even exemplary, teacher, you must make a number of critical decisions before even walking into your classroom and actually engaging in the business of teaching. First you must decide on both the long-range and short-term goals of the instructional process. To determine these goals, you must answer such questions as: What specific learning outcomes are intended and expected? How do these tie in with the broad goals of the educational process in this subject? this grade? this school? this city or county? How do these goals fit in with my values and beliefs? How important are they?

Once you have determined your instructional goals, you must select a teaching strategy to attain these goals, and you must invent, make, or at least collect materials that are useful for teaching. What is required here is not only knowledge of the strategies themselves but also of the skills required to implement them effectively. And, perhaps most important, you must be aware of the extent to which students are *ready* for this specific teaching/learning experience. Student readiness involves a variety of factors, including essential prerequisite knowledge and skills, as well as appropriate motivation. Clearly, students who are eager to learn are most likely to profit from instruction; and just as clearly, students who have already mastered basic knowledge and skills are more likely to attain new instructional objectives. These facts highlight the importance of knowledge about student learning and about human development and motivation.

Our analysis of the teaching process thus far indicates that the preteaching phase involves three steps: setting appropriate goals, determining student readiness, and selecting appropriate instructional strategies. A fourth critical step is planning for assessment: How will you determine the extent to which instructional goals have been met? By what procedures will you evaluate the instructional process itself, as well as changes that might occur among learners? How will the results of your evaluation procedures influence subsequent teaching decisions?

Teaching

The instructional process — commonly called teaching — involves implementing strategies designed to lead learners to attain certain goals. In general, these strategies involve communication, leadership, motivation, and control (discipline or management).

Following an extensive review of research on effective teaching, MacKay (1982) identifies twenty-eight behaviors that most often characterize the teaching strategies of highly effective teachers. MacKay describes these as "suggested" or "recommended" behaviors rather than as the firm conclusions of scientific research. The behaviors are related to four aspects of the teaching process: classroom management and discipline; instructional organization, sequence, and presentation; verbal interaction (communication); and interpersonal interaction. The twenty-eight behaviors are summarized in the box entitled "'Recommended' Behaviors for Effective Teaching." They are well worth thinking about.

After Teaching

The third phase of the teaching process involves assessing the outcomes of instruction in relation to the goals that you set in the preteaching phase. This process of evaluation reveals the effectiveness of your teaching; it might also say a great deal about the appropriateness of your instructional goals, the readiness of your students, the appropriateness of your teaching strategies, and even the relevance and appropriateness of your evaluation procedures.

PSYCHOLOGY AND TEACHING

Psychology's contribution to teaching, viewed within the context of this simple model (preteaching, teaching, and post-teaching activities), is clear. It provides us with answers to such important questions as: How do people learn? How can we use what we know about learning and motivation to increase the effectiveness of our instructional procedures? What do we know about people that might be of value to teachers who face student misbehavior or wish to avoid being faced with such behavior? How can we motivate learners? and a thousand other related questions.

By answering these questions, psychology can make a tremendous contribution to teaching. In fact, when teachers are asked what kind of assistance they require in order to become more effective, the needs they express typically reflect these questions. For example, from a survey of 247 randomly selected elementary school teachers (22 male and 225 female), Moore and Hanley (1982) identified thirteen specific tasks with which teachers felt they could use help (see Table 1.2, p. 17). The need mentioned most often was assistance in helping students become better learners, particularly with respect to acquiring basic skills. Other needs that these teachers expressed had to do with discipline, motivating learners, identifying and developing readiness for learning, and

"Recommended" Behaviors for Effective Teaching

1. Teachers should use a system of rules dealing with personal and procedural matters.

2. Teachers should prevent misbehaviors from continuing.

3. Teachers should direct disciplinary action accurately.

4. Teachers should move around the room a lot (monitoring seatwork).

5. Teachers should handle disruptive situations in a low-key manner (nonverbal messages, proximity, eye contact).

6. Teachers should ensure that assignments are interesting and worthwhile, especially when children work independently.

7. Teachers should use a system of rules that allows students to carry out learning tasks with a minimum of direction.

8. Teachers should optimize academic learning time. Students should be actively involved and productively engaged in learning tasks.

9. Teachers should use a standard signal to get students' attention.

10. Teachers should not begin speaking to the group until all students are paying attention.

11. Teachers should use a variety of instructional techniques, adapting instruction to meet learning needs.

12. Teachers should use a system of spot-checking assignments.

13. Teachers should relate mathematics (or other) games and independent activities to the concepts being taught.

14. Teachers should use techniques that provide for the gradual transition from concrete to more abstract activities.

15. Teachers should use an appropriate mixture of high- and low-order questions.

16. Teachers should be aware of what is going on in the classroom.

17. Teachers should be able to attend to more than one issue at a time.

18. Teachers should facilitate the smooth flow of the lesson or facilitate a smooth transition from one activity to another.

helping students establish realistic goals. Each of these needs falls within the scope of educational psychology.

Educational psychology may be defined as the application of relevant psychological knowledge to educational theory and practice. Accordingly, educational psychology deals with learning processes, human development and motivation, social learning, human personality (particularly in terms of intelligence and creativity), discipline and other facets of classroom management, measuring and evaluating student development and learning, and other related questions. These broad topics, divided into five major units (fourteen chapters), are the substance of this text.

TEACHING AS A CAREER

My father was a teacher for forty-one years. Not all of those years were very easy. For some of the first years he didn't always get paid, and when he did it was never very much. And

19. Teachers' behavior should maintain the pace of the lesson.

20. Teachers should be clear in presentations to the class.

21. Teachers should be able to motivate children.

22. Teachers should provide evidence of caring, accepting, and valuing the children.

23. Teachers should respond accurately to both obvious and subtle meanings, feelings, and experiences of the children.

24. Teachers should direct questions to many different students.

25. Teachers should use techniques such as rephrasing, giving clues, or asking a new question to help a student give an improved response when his or her answers are incorrect or only partially correct.

26. Teachers should use praise to reward outstanding work as well as to encourage students who are not always able to do outstanding work.

27. Teachers should use mild criticism on occasion to communicate expectations to more able students.

28. Teachers should accept and integrate student-initiated interaction such as questions, comments, or other contributions.

Source: Adapted from research on effective teaching by A. MacKay, "Project Quest: Teaching Strategies and Pupil Achievement." Occasional Paper Series, Centre for Research in Teaching, Faculty of Education, University of Alberta, Edmonton, Alberta, 1982, pp. 42–44.

It is worth noting that in a year-long study involving seventy-two teachers of third- and sixth-grade mathematics and language arts, researchers found a positive relationship between student achievement and each of these twenty-eight strategies, except for numbers 1, 4, 7, 9, 11, 13, and 14. However, these seven "recommended" behaviors have been found to be positively related to effective teaching in other studies, notably Evertson, Anderson, and Brophy (1978) and Brophy and Evertson (1974).

many years he had enormous classes — as many as fifty students in an isolated, one-room school, spanning the first through the eighth grades. Nor were the teaching tasks always simple and straightforward; often his beginning students didn't even know English — only French or Cree.

But my father truly loved what he did. He knew how important teaching is, and he was proud to be a teacher. Maybe it was partly because of this that he taught as well as he did. In the end, and in spite of the fact that it was situated in an economically depressed area, his one-room school produced several dozen university graduates, including at least two who earned Ph.D.'s and several who obtained master's degrees.

Teaching *is* important. It's stimulating and exciting, and it can be highly rewarding. But it isn't overwhelmingly lucrative. Nor is it exceedingly easy. It includes a variety of possible sources of stress: pressures to be more effective and *accountable* for the outcomes of the teaching/learning process; drug-related lett, 1988); about a quarter of these male teachers later resume teaching. Not surprisingly, given that many interrupt their careers for childbearing and -rearing, half of all beginning female teachers are no longer teaching within six years. However, almost one-third of these female teachers subsequently return to teaching. Thus, although many beginning teachers abandon or switch their careers, the majority make lifelong careers out of teaching. Many — perhaps most — love what they do.

Teaching *is* important.

SCHOOLING IN A WIDER CONTEXT

Those of us reared in areas where school is universal and compulsory tend to become blasé about its role and its effects on society. We lose sight of the impact of schooling. Perhaps it would be a good thing to remind ourselves occasionally that ours is only one of the world's societies — and it is far from the most populous. Things are not everywhere as they are here; the contrast might highlight some of the differences that teaching and learning can make. Consider, for example, that infant mortality in the United States is now less than 9 per 1,000 (U.S. Bureau of the Census, 1988). In parts of the nonindustrialized world, more than 100 infants per 1,000 die. In fact, more than 15 million of the world's infants die each year *from preventable causes!* Some 4 million die from diarrheal dehydration; almost as many die from vaccine-preventable diseases such as measles and tetanus (Grant, 1986). What does this have to do with education? A great deal. Research makes it clear that exposure to schooling in the Third World is not only related to a much higher probability of infant survival (Levine, 1987), but is significantly related to a reduction in birthrates as well. For example, mothers can be taught the simple hygiene that can prevent diarrhea, and they can be schooled in the inexpensive oral

school problems, including threats of violence; responsibilities associated with large enrollments; and demands resulting from mainstreaming (a policy whereby exceptional children — those who are gifted or talented or disadvantaged — are placed in regular classrooms rather than being segregated). In addition, teaching positions are sometimes difficult to obtain (although at other times there are teacher shortages and positions are abundant).

A relatively large proportion of beginning teachers either do not obtain starting positions or abandon their careers after a few years. Twelve years after they first started teaching, half of all young male teachers have left the teaching profession (Murnane, Singer, and Willett,

Table 1.2 Thirteen tasks for which teachers express a need for help (ranked in order from most important to least important)

1. Developing effective learners and a mastery of the basic skills
2. Guiding children to set up and achieve realistic goals
3. Locating materials and in-service support for more effective teaching
4. Establishing and maintaining discipline
5. Identifying and understanding readiness factors that affect learning
6. Motivating children to learn
7. Designing assessment devices and interpreting the resulting data
8. Supporting teaching and technological methods and materials
9. Understanding interpersonal factors that influence a child's educational goals
10. Developing a greater understanding of human behavior
11. Updating in curriculum content areas and methodologies
12. Improving multipurpose classroom grouping techniques
13. Obtaining administrative assistance with instructional planning

Source: From K. D. Moore and P. E. Hanley, "An Identification of Elementary Teacher Needs. *American Educational Research Journal*, 1982, *19*, 140. Copyright 1982, American Educational Research Association, Washington, D.C.

rehydration therapies that would save large numbers of lives.

It is clear that lack of schooling, illiteracy, poverty, and high mortality go hand in hand. Sadly, in most developing countries, especially in Africa, fewer than half of all children attend school (Tsang, 1988). For those who do attend school, the quality of education is extremely low, dropout rates are high, and the relative cost of education is very high. And although school enrollments in Third World countries have increased approximately fivefold since 1950, lack of funds is seriously curtailing growth of schooling and is having a very significant negative impact on the quality of education (Fuller and Heyneman, 1989).

It may be easy to imagine the impact of a high-quality, universal educational system in some remote Indian or African village; it is not so easy to see its impact closer to home. It might be a valuable exercise to imagine the

eventual effect on our society were we to abandon universal schooling and instead turn our children into the streets.

MAIN POINTS

1. Teaching skills are not hereditary; psychology can contribute significantly to their development.

2. Psychology is the study of human behavior and experience. Various divisions of psychology are concerned with particular aspects of behavior (for example, developmental psychology, clinical psychology, and educational psychology).

3. In psychology, as in most other disciplines, the principal means of discovery and of knowing is *science*. Science is as much an attitude as a collection of methods. It is an

attitude that insists on precision, consistency, objectivity, and replicability. Its methods are designed to ensure these characteristics.

4. Scientific facts are observations that are objective and replicable; theories are statements whose principal function is to summarize and explain related observations; laws are statements whose accuracy is beyond question; principles are statements that are probable rather than certain; and beliefs are private, personal convictions.

5. Models are representations of the way things are or should be. Important models in psychology are the organismic (we are like dynamic, active organisms, responsive to internal forces) and the mechanistic (we are more like machines, highly predictable and responsive to external forces).

6. Given the tremendous complexity and frequent unpredictability of human behavior, the theories and principles of psychology are not simple. In addition, they typically admit more exceptions than do the laws of the natural sciences.

7. Teaching may be viewed as an exercise in problem solving. Expert teachers develop sequences of routines and strategies that allow them to solve or avert many classroom problems almost automatically. These techniques require a wealth of information about students, teaching, and learning, as well as some measure of art.

8. Teaching empowers students (makes them capable) by giving them important information and skills, by fostering in them the feelings of personal power that come with social competence and self-esteem, and by developing in them the learning/thinking strategies that are essential for learning how to learn.

9. A simple but useful model describes the teaching process in terms of activities that occur before teaching (establishing goals, determining student readiness, selecting instructional strategies and collecting necessary materials, and planning for assessment and evaluation); activities that occur during teaching (implementation of teaching strategies); and activities that occur after teaching (assessing effectiveness of teaching strategies, determining the extent to which goals have been met, and reevaluating student readiness).

10. Educational psychology is the application of relevant psychological knowledge to educational theory and practice. Its principal usefulness is to answer such questions as: How do people learn? How can we increase motivation? How can we determine student readiness? What are the best teaching strategies for our objectives?

11. Teaching is not as lucrative as playing baseball or arranging to have wealthy parents. Teaching positions are sometimes scarce, and the demands and stresses of teaching sometimes drive young teachers out of the profession. But many stay and love it.

12. Given that most of us live where schooling is compulsory, it is easy to lose sight of the impact of education on our lives. Conditions in Third World countries underscore the relationship between lack of schooling and poverty, high infant mortality, and other forms of misery.

SUGGESTED READINGS

Educational psychology provides some of the answers — but not all. In his classic article, Coladarci argues that in addition to knowing and implementing the theories and suggestions of educational psychology, the teacher must also innovate and experiment:

COLADARCI, A. P. (1956). "The relevancy of educational psychology." *Educational Leadership, 13*, 489–492.

For a provocative and pertinent discussion of the role of scientific research in the behavioral sciences, see:

McCAIN, G., SEGAL, E. M. (1982). *The game of science* (4th ed.). Monterey, Calif.: Brooks/Cole.

Science is perhaps not the only way of knowing. In books that strive to crack our "cosmic eggs" (disrupt our worldviews) and that appeal to intuition as much as to reason, Pearce argues that science is not even the best way of knowing:

PEARCE, J. C. (1971). *The crack in the cosmic egg.* New York: Fawcett Books.

PEARCE, J.C. (1977). *Magical child.* New York: Bantam Books.

The following little booklet is an attempt to condense the results of educational research and squeeze from it a number of highly practical suggestions for teachers and parents:

U.S. DEPARTMENT OF EDUCATION (1986). *What works: Research about teaching and learning.* Pueblo, Colo.: Consumer Information Center.

A detailed analysis of teaching as a contemporary career, with attention to the goals, functions, and philosophies of schools:

RYAN, K., & COOPER, J. M. (1988). *Those who can, teach* (5th ed.). Boston: Houghton Mifflin.

Bears are rather large, bobtailed mammals. They walk on the soles of their feet; eat flesh, roots, and other vegetable matter; and have five toes on each foot (Cameron, 1956).

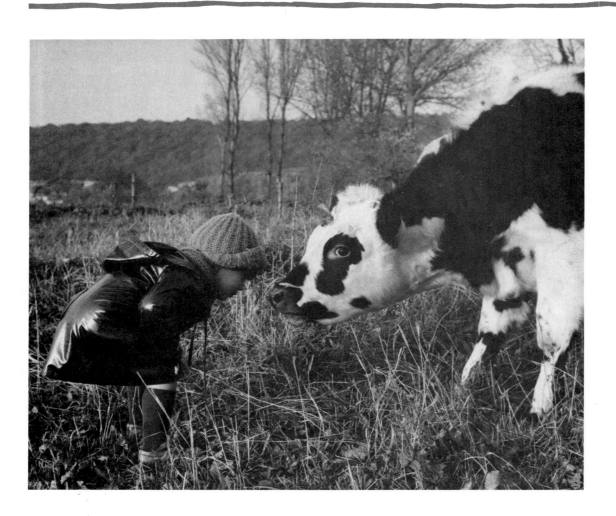

LEARNING

Learning is mostly what the educational process is all about: the learning of skills, of attitudes, of information, and of acceptable social behaviors (and sometimes of those less acceptable). The four chapters in this section address these topics, with particular emphasis on the contributions that knowledge about learning can make to the teaching process.

CHAPTER 2

BEHAVIORISTIC EXPLANATIONS

When I carefully consider the curious habits of dogs
I am compelled to conclude
That man is the superior animal.
When I consider the curious habits of man
I confess, my friend, I am puzzled.

EZRA POUND *Meditatio*

Let such teach others who themselves excel.

ALEXANDER POPE *Essay on Criticism*

A little learning is a dangerous thing
Drink deep or taste not the Pierian spring

ALEXANDER POPE *Essay on Criticism*

PREVIEW For teachers, one of the most important questions about learning is: What conditions lead most effectively to desirable changes in behavior? In other words, how can what we know about learning be applied to instruction? But before we can begin to answer this question, we must look at psychology's explanations of learning. This chapter presents the *behaviorists'* explanations — those that, among other things, concern how behavior is controlled by its consequences. Teachers control some of the consequences of student behavior, and in so doing they indirectly control student behavior. But is it ethical to *control* a person's behavior by manipulating rewards and punishments? This chapter addresses this question as well.

▬ *Last night, inspired perhaps by the winter storm that threatened when I went to bed, I dreamt my truck had stalled in the snow among the aspen. Afraid that I would freeze if I stayed where I was, I stumbled out into the trees.*

But I had no idea where to go, and instantly I could feel the cold seeping into my bones. Desperately I searched the darkness, shivering and afraid. Suddenly I saw a light, and I lurched forward, thinking it would guide me to a house or road. I tried to yell as I struggled through the snow, but no sound would come. Still, the light seemed close, so very close I could almost touch it. It was only a soft glow, as if it were a dim light through a frosted window. . . .

But it was not a light at all. It was only the soft sheen of a cow's eyes. I could see her standing in the snow. I could smell her, too. "A wild cow will watch me die," I thought, feeling strangely humiliated. And I could have sworn the cow took a long pull from a bottle of whisky as I fell into the snow at her feet. . . .

I finally awakened in a tangle of blankets to find that I had left my window unfastened, and a great drift of the coming winter's new snow had been blown across my bed on the chilled teeth of a young blizzard.

It was only a dream. But it reminded me of a winter when I was a boy growing up in a remote area of northern Saskatchewan. It was a long, bitter winter, and more rats than usual moved into our cellar and elsewhere beneath our house.

We trapped them, of course, like we always did, quickly getting rid of all but one of the rats. I never actually saw this rat, but my father did. "He's big," he said. "Biggest rat I ever saw." My fearful childish imagination immediately made him two feet long and gave him a pair of huge fangs. Unkindly, we named him Oscar after one of my uncles.

Oscar seemed to know about traps. He avoided them all, and our vegetables continued to disappear from the cellar at an alarming rate. And sometimes in the stillness of those dark winter nights, I thought I could hear Oscar gnawing against the cold timbers of our house, and I started to fear him. . . .

Insidiously, he began to scurry through my dreams. In the early dreams I caught only fleeting glimpses of him, brown-furred and long-toothed. Later, he strutted more boldly into my dreams, fangs bared, black eyes gleaming malevolently. Finally, he began to chase me. But always, just before he caught me I would awaken, drenched in perspiration, shaking, sometimes even screaming.

Oscar had become a recurring nightmare, and I pleaded with my father to catch him. I knew that if he wasn't caught soon I would awaken one dark night with a rat fastened onto my throat. Or worse yet, I would not awaken.

Finally, my father bought a tube of Rat-Nip, a lethal mixture of warfarin and other things. Oscar ate it; he died.

"See, he's gone," my father announced, holding me up so I could shine the flashlight behind the chimney and see that there was no rat there. This was meant to cure my nightmares.

But it didn't; the rat in my dreams would not leave. How I wished I had a tube of Rat-Nip for him. Or a Skinner box. ▬

LEARNING

With a **Skinner box** I might have trained the rat to press a lever, to genuflect, or to perform some other nonfrightening act. In psychological terms, I might have *conditioned* him — and perhaps rendered him harmless in the process.

Conditioning, which is described in detail later in this chapter, is one form of learning. And learning is mostly what education is all about: Teachers teach and students learn. These are the two sides of the educational coin. (Actually, education has more than two facets; teachers also learn, and students also sometimes teach.)

Learning is the acquisition of information and knowledge, of skills and habits, and of attitudes and beliefs. It always involves a change in one of these areas — a change that is brought about by the learner's experiences. Accordingly, psychologists define learning as *all changes in behavior that result from experience, providing these changes are relatively permanent, do not result simply from growth or maturation, and are not the temporary effects of factors such as fatigue or drugs.*

Not all changes involved in learning are obvious and observable. For example, learning often involves changes in the learner's **disposition** — that is, in the person's inclination to do or not to do something. Hence changes in disposition have to do with motivation. Such changes cannot always be observed by teachers and others but are no less real or important.

Learning involves not only changes in disposition, but also changes in **capability** — that is, changes in the skills or knowledge required to do something (Gagné, 1985). Like changes in disposition, changes in capability cannot always be observed directly. To determine whether or not students' dispositions or capabilities have changed following instruction, teachers must provide them with an opportunity to engage in the relevant behavior. The inference that dispositions or capabilities have changed — in other words, that learning has occurred — will always be based on performance. If instruction affects learners in such a way that their behaviors *after* instruction are observably different from those *before* instruction, we can conclude that learning has occurred.

Although a teacher's estimates of student learning typically are based on student **performance** (actual behavior), all sorts of learning may occur in school without necessarily being manifested in performance. For example, some students learn to like or dislike school, school subjects, teachers, or the sound of amateurish chalk-writing; however, they do not always manifest these *dispositional* changes in their actual behavior. Similarly, students are not always provided with opportunities to display changes in knowledge and skills leading to new *capabilities* — a subject about which we say more in Chapter 14 on measurement and evaluation.

Because learning involves changes in both capabilities and dispositions — changes that will be manifested in performance, given the right situation — we can distinguish among various kinds of learning. For example, learning that involves muscular coordination and physical skills (**motor learning**) appears to be different from learning involving emotions (**affective learning**) or that involving information or ideas (**cognitive learning**). These three distinctions are based on fairly obvious differences among the responses involved. Learning may also be classified by reference to the *conditions* that lead to it — an approach adopted by Gagné (1977a). (See Chapter 5.)

BEHAVIORISM AND COGNITIVISM

Two major groups of theories relate to learning: **behaviorism** and **cognitivism**. Differences between these two groups of **learning theories** center mainly on the questions each tries to answer. Behaviorism tries to explain simple behaviors — observable and predictable responses. Accordingly, it is concerned mainly with conditions (called **stimuli**) that affect organisms and that may lead to behavior, as well as with simple behaviors themselves (**responses**). Behavior-oriented (or *behavioristic*) researchers attempt to discover the rules that govern the formation of relationships between stimuli and responses (the rules of **conditioning**). For this reason, **behavioristic theories** are often referred to as **stimulus-response (S-R) theories**.

In contrast to behaviorism, cognitive approaches deal primarily with questions relating to cognition, or knowing. Cognitive theorists are concerned with how we develop a fund of knowledge and how we eventually develop notions of ourselves as players of what Flavell (1985) calls the "game of cognition." Children's gradual development of an awareness of themselves as *knowers*, their growing awareness of the strategies they can use to acquire and process information, and their ability to direct their efforts and to evaluate their cognitive activities are aspects of **metacognition**. Put another way, *cognition* refers to knowing; *metacognition* refers to knowing about knowing. Cognition-oriented researchers attempt to understand the nature of information — how it is acquired and organized by learners; how it can be recalled, modified, applied, and analyzed; and how the learner understands, evaluates, and controls the activities involved in cognition (see Table 2.1).

This chapter deals with some of the behaviorists' explanations of learning and their implications for teaching. Chapters 3, 4, and 5 look at cognitive explanations. Chapter 6 discusses humanism.

IVAN PAVLOV AND CLASSICAL CONDITIONING

If an infant is repeatedly tossed high in the air by a sadistic psychologist, the infant may well develop a pronounced fear of the psychologist and show evidence of that fear by whimpering, screaming, or attempting to crawl away when the psychologist approaches. To further complicate the matter, if the psychologist yells "Yahoo!" every time the child is hurled upwards, the infant may soon become very frightened when anyone yells "Yahoo!"

This is an easy demonstration to perform, requiring little or no advance preparation, no special equipment, and only a small research grant — and it is a satisfying demonstration, for it illustrates what is generally recognized as one of the simplest forms of animal and human learning. It is an example of **classical conditioning**. The qualifier *classical* is used simply to differentiate between this specific form of learning and other forms of learning loosely referred to as *conditioning* in ordinary speech.

Ivan Pavlov, a Russian physiologist, was one of the first to draw attention to classical conditioning. He had noticed that the dogs in his laboratory began to salivate when they were about to be fed, even before they could see or smell the food. Strangely, they seemed to be salivating at the mere sight of their keeper, or even when they simply heard his footsteps.

This simple observation led Pavlov to a series of well-known experiments. These experiments involved ringing a bell or sounding a buzzer — neither of which ordinarily leads to salivation — and then immediately presenting the dogs with food, a stimulus that does lead

Table 2.1 Three approaches to learning

Theory	Major Focus	Key Variables/Concepts	Representative Theorists	Principal Usefulness for Teachers
Behaviorism	Behavior	Stimuli, responses Reinforcement, punishment Behavior modification	Watson Guthrie Thorndike Skinner	Explains learning of skills and attitudes; emphasizes reinforcement
Cognitivism	Knowing	Decision making Understanding Cognitive structure Perception Information processes Memory	Ausubel Bruner Gagné Piaget Sternberg	Explains development of understanding (meaning); emphasizes importance of meaningfulness and organization
Humanism	The person	Self-concept Self-actualization Self-worth	Maslow Rogers	Focuses on affective development; emphasizes adjustment and well-being.

to salivation. Pavlov soon found that if the procedure was repeated often enough, the bell or buzzer alone began to elicit salivation.

In Pavlov's experiments, the bell is referred to as a **conditioned stimulus** (CS); the food is an **unconditioned stimulus** (UCS); and salivation in response to the food is an **unconditioned response** (UCR), whereas salivation in response to the bell or buzzer is a **conditioned response** (CR). A model (or **paradigm**) of classical conditioning using the psychologist tossing the infant as an illustration is presented in Figure 2.1. In this example, the fact that the psychologist is always present when the infant is thrown in the air serves as a conditioned stimulus. The word *yahoo* is also always present; it, too, may serve as a conditioned stimulus. The fear reaction is the initial unconditioned response, whereas the sensation of being thrown serves as an unconditioned stimulus.

In general terms, a stimulus or situation that readily leads to a response can be paired with a neutral stimulus (one that does not lead to a response) to bring about classical conditioning. Note that this learning is typically unconscious; that is, learners do not respond to the conditioned stimulus because they become aware of the relationship between it and an unconditioned stimulus. In fact, classical conditioning can occur even for responses over which the subject ordinarily has no control. For example, a person can be conditioned to urinate in response to the sound of a bell if a fistula (a tube) is inserted into the bladder, air is pumped in through the fistula, and a bell is rung. After this has been repeated a number of times, the subject will urinate when the bell rings. It is unlikely that this occurs because the subject knows that the bell means air will be blown into the bladder. Likewise, constriction or dilation

Before Conditioning

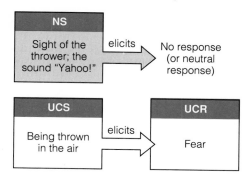

An unconditioned stimulus elicits an
unconditioned fear response

Conditioning Process

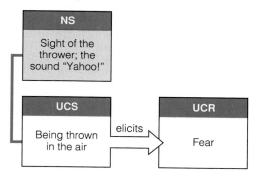

A neutral stimulus is repeatedly
paired with the UCS

After Conditioning

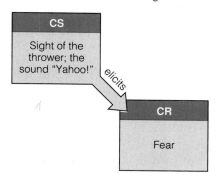

The previously neutral stimulus becomes
a conditioned stimulus eliciting the
conditioned response of fear

Figure 2.1 Classical conditioning. An initially
neutral or pleasant stimulus (NS) is paired with an
unconditioned, fear-producing stimulus (UCS)
so that the subject is eventually *conditioned* to fear
the previously neutral stimulus. Fear is now a
conditioned response (CR) to a conditioned
stimulus (CS).

of the blood vessels can be brought about by
the application of cold or hot packs directly on
the skin. If these stimuli are paired with a neutral stimulus such as a tone, the tone by itself
will eventually elicit vascular constriction or
dilation.

Instructional Applications

The importance of classical conditioning for
teachers is that it is largely through these unconscious processes that students come to dislike schools, subjects, teachers, and related
stimuli—or to like them. Classical conditioning occurs in all schools, virtually at all times,
regardless of the other kinds of learning going
on at the same time. A school subject is a neutral
stimulus that evokes little emotional response
in the beginning, assuming that it is new to the
student. The teacher, the classroom, or some
other distinctive stimulus in the student's immediate environment may serve as a conditioning stimulus. This conditioning stimulus might
be pleasant (a comfortable desk, a friendly
teacher) or unpleasant (a cold, hard desk; a cold,
hard teacher with a grating voice and squeaking
chalk). Following successive pairings of the
subject matter with this distinctive stimulus,
the emotions (attitudes) associated with the
stimulus become classically conditioned to
some aspect of school. In short, students learn
attitudes toward subjects, learning, school, and
so on, largely as a function of classical conditioning. Thus, it is entirely possible to teach
students mathematics while at the same time

Before Conditioning

After Conditioning

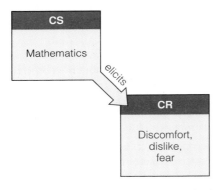

Figure 2.2   Classical conditioning of math phobia.

teaching them to dislike mathematics. Whereas learning mathematics is likely to involve cognitive processes (and perhaps some form of conditioning as well, particularly if repetitive skills are involved), learning to dislike mathematics may involve mainly classical conditioning (see Figure 2.2).

Thus, teachers need to know what is being paired with what in their classrooms, and they need to do whatever they can to maximize the number and potency of pleasant unconditioned stimuli and to minimize the unpleasant.

JOHN B. WATSON AND BEHAVIORISM

Watson is recognized as the founder of the behavioristic movement in psychology, not only because he coined the term (Watson, 1913), but also because he developed its basic concepts. He was greatly influenced by the work of Pavlov and accepted the Pavlovian model of classical conditioning as *the* explanation for learning (Watson, 1916). According to Watson, people are born with a limited number of reflexes; learning is simply a matter of classical conditioning involving these reflexes. Hence differences among people are entirely a function of their experiences — no differences exist initially. This point of view, referred to as **environmentalism**, is discussed in more detail in Chapter 9.

Watson was very determined about rejecting what he called the "**mentalism**" of his predecessors. He intended to rid psychology of such terms as *mind, feeling,* and *sensation* and make it more scientific by reducing it to a study of the observable aspects of behavior. Watson's insistence on precision, rigor, and objectivity greatly influenced the development of psychology in America.

The immense popularity of behaviorism in early twentieth-century American psychology was due both to the scientific spirit of the times and to its just and egalitarian view of humans. If what we become is truly a function of the experiences to which we are subjected, then we are in fact born equal. As Watson declared, any child can become a doctor or a judge. In fact, however, things are not quite that simple: Not everybody can become a doctor or a judge (see Chapter 9).

Instructional Applications: Pairing Stimuli

Watson's view of behaviorism stresses the importance of a rigorous and scientific view of learning and behavior. It also underscores the extent to which teachers can influence learning by controlling the learner's experiences. After all, it is teachers who are largely responsible for determining the stimuli to which learners are exposed and the responses they will make. If we know enough about the conditions that lead to a behavior, Watson informs us, we can not only predict whether the behavior will occur, but can also control its occurrence. More than this, through the careful and scientific pairing of relevant stimuli, we can arrange for specific responses to become associated with a variety of situations.

As we saw earlier, the most obvious instructional implications of a classical conditioning model such as Watson's have to do with how teachers pair stimuli and responses. Teachers, we said, must know what is being paired with what; furthermore, they should attempt to maximize pleasant stimuli and minimize negative ones.

The old adage that learning should be fun is more than a schoolchild's frivolous plea; it follows directly from classical conditioning theory. A teacher who makes students smile and laugh while she has them repeat the 6-times table may, because of the variety of stimuli and responses being paired, succeed in teaching students (1) how to smile and laugh—a worthwhile undertaking in its own right, (2) to associate stimuli such as 6 × 7 with responses such as 42—a valuable piece of information, and (3) to like arithmetic—and the teacher, the school, the smell of chalk, the feel of a book's pages, and on and on.

What does a teacher who makes students suffer grimly through their multiplication tables teach?

EDWIN GUTHRIE AND ONE-TRIAL LEARNING

Conditioning requires the formation of *associations* or links. Accordingly, conditioning theories are sometimes referred to as **association-istic**. As we saw, Watson's model of classical conditioning, like Pavlov's, is based on the belief that associations result from the repeated pairing of stimuli and responses. In contrast, Guthrie's conditioning model is based on the belief that learning (the formation of associations) does not require repeated pairings of stimuli and responses but occurs after a single pairing. In other words, a person who has performed once in response to some stimulation will respond again in an identical fashion if the stimulus is repeated. This belief has come to be known as the **law of one-trial learning**—and, accordingly, Guthrie's theory is referred to as the theory of one-trial learning.

A second law completes Guthrie's learning theory: The strength of the association between the stimulus and response is unaffected by practice. All that practice does is ensure that the response will be performed under a variety of circumstances.

Guthrie explains the formation of a link between a stimulus and a response in terms of "association by **contiguity**." It is because the stimulus and the response are presented in contiguity (simultaneously) that learning occurs. However, stimuli are not always in contiguity with responses, but often precede them. Guthrie gets around this fact by inventing *movement-produced stimuli* (MPS). He argues that the presentation of a stimulus brings about a real but miniature response, which serves as a stimulus for another response, and so on, until the final observable response is emitted. Each of these movement-produced stimuli is in temporal contiguity with the movements that precede and follow it—that is, they occur at the same time. Hence the initial stimulus and the final response are in contiguity.

Guthrie defines learning as the formation of habits—links between a stimulus and a response. **Habits** are acquired through contiguity, require only one presentation of a stimulus followed by the appropriate response, and are as strong after the first pairing as they ever will be. Furthermore, a habit can never be broken.

That is, once an S–R bond has been established (and remember that this happens in *one trial*), it is permanent.

The most obvious criticism of Guthrie's system is that people do not engage in identical behaviors repeatedly, even when they are placed in the same situations. Guthrie's answer to this is simply that the stimulus situation—which is never a single stimulus, but a complex of stimuli—is different if the behavior is different.

A second criticism of Guthrie's system is that habits do appear to be broken. Alcoholics sometimes stop drinking, smokers sometimes give up cigarettes, obese people sometimes lose weight, and schoolchildren sometimes change all sorts of behaviors. Guthrie's rebuttal is that these habits are never broken—they are simply replaced. He describes three methods by which a bad habit can be replaced by a better one. These methods have important practical implications for the classroom and are discussed, with examples, in the following section. A more detailed discussion of techniques for behavior control is presented in Chapter 12.

Instructional Applications: Breaking Habits

According to Guthrie, teachers bring about learning by arranging for desired responses to follow an appropriate stimulus. And to ensure that the response will be well-learned, they can arrange for it to occur in a variety of situations.

Teaching also sometimes requires exchanging undesirable habits for some that are more desirable. Guthrie calls his techniques for breaking habits—that is, for replacing them with more acceptable ones—the **threshold method**, the **fatigue method**, and the **incompatible-stimuli method** (Guthrie, 1935). These can be illustrated by methods of "breaking" a horse (Lefrançois, 1982; see Figure 2.3). In the following discussion, each is illustrated in a classroom situation.

The Threshold Method. This approach involves presenting the stimulus that ordinarily brings about the undesirable response, but presenting it so faintly that it does not elicit the

(a) Threshold

(b) Fatigue

(c) Incompatible Stimuli

Figure 2.3   Guthrie's three ways of breaking habits, illustrated by methods of training a saddle horse. In *(a)* the horse is "gentled" by having progressively heavier weights placed on its back, beginning with a blanket and culminating with a saddle and rider. In *(b)* the horse is "broken" in the traditional sense, being allowed to buck until fatigued. In *(c)* the horse is tied down so that it cannot buck when mounted.

response. Over successive presentations the intensity of the stimulus is increased, but it is always kept below *threshold*. Eventually, if the procedure is successful, the stimulus will have reached full intensity without ever eliciting the unwanted behavior. At that point, the habit may be considered to have been replaced by another, *incompatible* habit — and this incompatible habit may simply be a habit of not responding.

There are many classroom applications of the threshold technique. For example, whenever a new subject or problem is being presented to a class — one that may prove so complex as to be frightening — it is often advisable to present it initially for only a short period of time. Exposure can then be lengthened over successive trials until the subject has lost its ability to frighten. As I have observed elsewhere, this is simply a sophisticated version of grandmother's "don't-throw-him-in-the-water-let-him-get-used-to-it-slowly-damn-it" approach* (Lefrançois, 1982).

The Fatigue Method.

This second technique for breaking habits involves presenting the stimulus repeatedly in order to elicit the undesirable response so often that the individual eventually can no longer respond. At that point the individual performs a different response — perhaps simply not responding. It follows from Guthrie's theory that the most recent response elicited by a stimulus will be learned. Hence, theoretically at least, the undesirable habit will have been replaced.

It is somewhat more difficult to apply the

fatigue method in the classroom. Obviously, many of its potential applications are either barbaric or impractical. A student who is impertinent to a teacher can hardly be made to repeat the impertinence until he is so fatigued that he is forced to cease. Nor can a student who has a habit of fighting with others be compelled to fight until thoroughly fatigued.

The fatigue technique is sometimes used in the classroom in a manner that runs directly counter to sound pedagogical procedures. One example is teachers who ask their less able students to stay in after school and write 200 or 500 times, "I will not throw spitballs at my teacher," or "2 × 2 = 4." Although fatigue may well be involved in the student's behavior, the responses involved are precisely those that the student is *not* to forget.

The Incompatible-Stimuli Method.

This approach involves presenting the stimulus that would ordinarily bring about an undesirable response, but presenting it when the individual is unable, or unlikely, to respond. For example, a teacher who knows that a conventional presentation of a history lesson will put most of the class to sleep can present the lesson in a form that makes sleep difficult. This might be done by using a film or other audiovisual device, by acting out parts of the lesson, by presenting some interesting (and perhaps irrelevant) information, or simply by being especially brilliant, amusing, and informative. The same effect could be obtained by making loud, disharmonious noises at intervals throughout the lesson. Unfortunately, although this might keep the students awake, it would probably not serve to focus their attention in the desired direction.

Some excellent examples of the incompatible-stimuli approach are to have athletes who dislike mathematics do problems involving sports statistics, to have artists who are bored by history study it through art, to have music enthusiasts who have no interest in language study lyrics, and so on.

---

*PPC[†]: "I don't get this. I thought Lefrançois's grandmother was a polite old lady. Should perhaps delete the last two words, damn it."
Author: "She did use that indelicate expression just this once."
[†]For those who missed the Preface, a PPC is a prepublication critic — one of the many educational psychologists who read various editions of the manuscript prior to publication.

EDWARD L. THORNDIKE
AND CONNECTIONISM

In attempting to explain the formation of relationships between stimuli, between responses, or between stimuli and responses, behaviorists can make one of two choices. They can maintain, as did Watson and Guthrie, that the simultaneous occurrence of stimulus or response events is sufficient to bring about learning. This reasoning is ordinarily referred to as a *contiguity* explanation. A second alternative, and one that was explicitly avoided by both Watson and Guthrie, is to explain the formation of S-R bonds by reference to the *effects* of the behavior. This explanation, introduced by Edward L. Thorndike and popularized by B. F. Skinner, is labeled a **reinforcement** approach.

Thorndike defined learning as the formation of connections, or "bonds," between stimuli and responses. Accordingly, he labeled his learning theory **connectionism** (Thorndike, 1949). In his words, learning involves "stamping in" S-R bonds; forgetting involves "stamping them out." Much of the theory deals specifically with the conditions that lead to the stamping in or stamping out of bonds.

Unlike Watson and Guthrie, both of whom believed that contiguity was an accurate and sufficient explanation for learning, Thorndike maintained that it is the *effect* of a response that leads to learning or its absence. Much of his experimental work involved rewarding an animal for a response and then observing what effect the reward had on subsequent behavior (Thorndike, 1911). The classic experiment involved placing a hungry cat inside a cage and dangling a tasty bit of fish outside the cage. To escape from its cell and obtain the fish, the cat had to pull a looped string or perform some other mechanical feat.

The Laws of Learning

From these experiments, Thorndike (1913, 1932, 1933) derived two related conclusions about learning: the **law of effect** and the **law of multiple responses**. These form the basis of his theory.

The law of effect states that responses that occur just prior to a satisfying state of affairs tend to be stamped in (learned); those that occur prior to an annoying state of affairs tend to be stamped out. Thus the law of effect means that learning is a function of the consequences of behavior rather than simply of contiguity. Thorndike later modified this law by asserting that pleasure is more potent for stamping in responses than pain is for stamping out responses. Whereas rewards strengthen behavior, punishment simply leads the learner to do something else.

The law of multiple responses is based on Thorndike's observation that when faced with a difficult problem for which they have no ready solution, individuals will engage in a variety of different responses until one response produces a satisfying effect. In other words, it is through trial and error that problems are solved. As a result of this law, Thorndike's theory came to be known as the theory of **trial-and-error learning**.

A third law, the **law of readiness**, recognizes that certain responses are more or less likely than others to be learned (stamped in), depending on the learner's readiness. Such factors as maturation and previous learning are clearly involved in determining whether learning is easy, difficult, or impossible. This important law provides the basis for Thorndike's definitions of **reward and punishment**. Specifically, it is the learner's readiness that determines whether a state of affairs is pleasant or not. Thorndike maintained that a pleasant state of affairs — a reward — results when a person is ready to do something and is allowed to do it. By the same token, not being allowed to do something when one is ready, or being forced to do something when one is not ready, results in an annoying state of affairs — punishment.

The importance of this law for teaching is readily apparent. It is intuitively obvious that a child who is ready for a specific type of learning is far more likely to profit from such learning experiences than another who is not ready. What is not so obvious is precisely what is involved in being ready. Clearly, there are various types of readiness, some relating to physical maturation, some to the development of intellectual skills and the acquisition of important background information, and some to motivation. Hence, to determine readiness, teachers must have some knowledge of children's emotional and intellectual development — topics covered in Chapters 7 and 8.

Instructional Applications: Rewarding Correct Responses

Thorndike was very concerned with applying his findings to education. He elaborated the instructional implications of his theories in considerable detail, often developing new laws and theories to summarize important principles.

Perhaps most obvious, and most important, are the implications of his belief that learning occurs through trial and error and results from the fact that the eventual correct response is rewarded — and therefore learned or stamped in. This belief leads directly to the principle that teachers and schools need to provide both ample opportunity for students to emit a variety of responses, so that they will eventually arrive at the correct one, and appropriate rewards (satisfying states of affairs) for the correct responses emitted. As we saw, the theory also stresses that rewards and punishments need to be tailored to the situation and to the child, and that, among other things, the child's *readiness* needs to be taken into consideration.

Other instructional implications of Thorndike's theory are to be found in a series of subsidiary laws that are part of the system. For example, the **law of set or attitude** states that people often respond to novel situations in terms of the **sets** or attitudes that they bring

with them. This means that students can be taught that various aspects of a subject are related, and they will then react to new material as though it related to previously learned information. By the same token, students can be given a *set* to proceed as though the best way of learning is through rote memorization.

This law also implies that cultural background and immediate environment not only affect how a person responds but also determine what will be satisfying or annoying. For example, **culture** has determined that academic success will be satisfying — even as the immediate environment sometimes determines that popularity will be more satisfying than academic success.

A second subsidiary law, the **law of prepotency of elements**, recognizes that people respond to the most significant or the most striking aspects of a stimulus situation and not necessarily to the entire situation. Obviously, students cannot and probably should not respond to all of the sights and sounds that surround them at any given moment. Hence teachers must be careful to stress (make *prepotent*) important aspects of the learning situation (for example, by underlining or **boldfacing**, through the use of color, through the use of voice and gestures, through repetition, and so on).

Transfer (sometimes referred to as **generalization**) is one of the important goals of education. It involves emitting a previously learned response in the face of a new stimulus and is illustrated when a child uses a multiplication rule learned in school to determine how many packs of bubble gum a pair of quarters will buy. Thorndike believed that the transference of a response to a new stimulus is a function of the similarity between the two stimuli — hence this subsidiary law is called the **law of response by analogy**. More specifically, he claimed that stimuli are composed of elements and that similar stimulus situations have a number of identical elements. The greater the number of such elements, the more likely the individual is to respond by analogy. This explanation later came to be known as Thorndike's **theory of identical elements**.

Thorndike suggested that teachers can facilitate transfer by pointing out a variety of situations in which a single response (or rule) is applicable. He also emphasized the importance of pointing out *connections* among ideas. These connections, Thorndike insisted, are the basis of knowledge.

BURRHUS F. SKINNER AND OPERANT CONDITIONING

Behaviorists are, by definition, concerned with behavior. They define learning in terms of changes in behavior and look to the environment for explanations of these changes. Their theories are associationistic; they deal with connections or associations that are formed among stimuli and responses. And, as we have seen, these theories make use of one or both of two

principal classes of explanations for learning: those based on contiguity (simultaneity of stimulus and response events) and those based on the effects of behavior (reinforcement and punishment). Pavlov, Watson, and Guthrie are contiguity theorists; Thorndike is a reinforcement theorist. So is Burrhus Frederic Skinner, one of the most influential psychologists of the twentieth century and the originator and chief spokesman of the theory of operant conditioning.

Respondent and Operant Behavior

To begin with, Skinner accepted the existence of classical conditioning. He claimed that many responses, called elicited responses, can be brought about by a stimulus and can become conditioned to other stimuli in the manner described by Pavlov and Watson. He labeled this behavior **respondent** because it occurs in response to a stimulus.

A second, much larger and more important class of behaviors, however, consists of behaviors that are not elicited by any known stimuli

Table 2.2 Classical and operant conditioning

Classical (Pavlovian)	Operant (Skinnerian)
Deals with *respondents*, which are *elicited* by *stimuli* (*reactions to* the environment)	Deals with *operants*, which are *emitted* as *instrumental* acts (*actions upon* the environment)

but are simply **emitted responses** of the organism. These are labeled **operants** because, in a sense, they are operations performed by the organism. Another way of making this distinction is to say that in the case of respondent behavior the organism is *reacting* to the environment, whereas in the case of operant behavior the organism *acts upon* the environment (see Table 2.2).

The distinction between respondent and operant behavior can be clarified further by examining some simple behaviors. Sneezing; blinking; being angry, afraid, or excited; and saying "four" when someone asks what two plus two is—these are all respondents. What they have in common is that they are largely automatic and almost inevitable responses to specific situations. Put another way, they are responses that can reliably be elicited by specific stimuli. Such responses are learned through processes of classical conditioning.

In contrast, driving a car, writing a letter, singing, reading a book, and kissing a baby are generally operants (although these, too, may involve respondents, as when a red light leads me to slam on the brakes). Their common characteristics are that they are deliberate and intentional. They occur not as inevitable responses to specific stimulation but as personally controlled actions (rather than reactions). And they are subject to the laws of operant conditioning.

Operant conditioning, because it does not involve obvious stimuli, is somewhat different from Thorndike's conception of learning and his law of effect. Whereas Thorndike believed that the effect of reinforcement is to strengthen the bond that exists between the stimulus and the response, Skinner declared that not only is the stimulus usually unknown but, in any case, it is irrelevant to the learning. The link is formed between response and reinforcement rather than between stimulus and response. Essentially, all that happens in operant learning is that when an emitted response is reinforced, the probability increases that it will be repeated.

Operant Conditioning

Operant conditioning is most clearly and simply illustrated by reference to a typical Skinnerian experiment with a rat. In this experiment, a rat is placed in a Skinner box, a small, controlled environment (see Figure 2.4). The Skinner box is constructed to make certain responses highly probable and to make it possible for the experimenter to measure these responses and to punish or reward them. For our typical experiment, the box contains a lever, a light, an electric grid on the floor, and a food tray, all arranged in such a way that when the rat depresses the lever, the light goes on and a food pellet is released into the tray. Under these circumstances, most rats will quickly learn to depress the lever, and they will continue to do so for long periods of time, even if they do not receive a food pellet each time they work the lever. Similarly, rats can quickly be trained to avoid the lever if depressing it activates a mild electric current in the floor grid. However, if the electric current is constant and ceases only when the lever is depressed, rats will learn to depress it.

Most of the basic elements of Skinner's theory are evident in this situation. The rat's act of depressing the lever is an operant—an almost random behavior that is simply emitted rather

(a) Light   (c) Bar or lever   (e) Rat
(b) Food tray   (d) Electric grid

Figure 2.4   A Skinner box.
From G. R. Lefrançois, *Psychological Theories and Human Learning* (2nd ed.). Copyright 1982 by Wadsworth, Inc. Reprinted by permission of Brooks/Cole Publishing Company, Monterey, California.

than being elicited by a specific stimulus. The food pellets serve as what Skinner labeled *reinforcement*. Their availability increases the probability that whenever the rat finds itself in this situation, it will saunter over to the lever and depress it.

In general terms, operant conditioning is an increase in the probability that a response will occur again, this increase being a result of reinforcement (about which more is said shortly). Furthermore, Skinner's model of operant conditioning states that the reward, together with whatever **discriminated stimuli***

---

*Also referred to as "discriminative" stimuli; refers to those aspects of a situation (stimuli) that differentiate it from other situations.

were present at the time of reinforcement, are stimuli that, after learning, may bring about the operant. For example, aspects of the sight of the Skinner box from the inside may eventually serve as stimuli for lever-pressing behavior. (See Figure 2.5 for a model of operant learning and Figure 2.6 for some classroom examples.)

Principles of Operant Conditioning

One of Skinner's important concerns was to discover the relationship between reinforcement and behavior and to clarify how behavior is affected by its consequences. The variables he investigated most extensively, together with his major findings, are discussed here.

Reinforcement. Skinner made an important distinction between two related terms: **reinforcer** and *reinforcement*. A reinforcer is a *thing*, or, in Skinnerian terms, a stimulus; reinforcement is the *effect* of this stimulus. For example, candy may be a reinforcer because it can be reinforcing and because it is a stimulus. A piece of candy, however, is not a reinforcement, although its *effect* on a person may be an example of reinforcement.

Although *reinforcement* may be defined in different ways (see, for example, Skinner, 1953), the most widely accepted definition is *any stimulus that increases the probability that a response will occur*. This definition makes it clear that it is the *effect of a stimulus* that determines whether or not it will be reinforcing. Thus, any given situation may be highly reinforcing for one person and highly unpleasant for another. First-grade students may react in a very positive manner when they are presented with little gold stars in recognition of their work. College students whose professor offered them little stars might think, with some justification, that the professor was a little strange.

Skinner differentiated between two major classes of reinforcers: positive and negative.

Before Conditioning

Stimulus Context: Classroom

Response	**Response**	**Response**
Read comic	Attend to teacher	Talk to neighbor

Various responses are emitted
in a certain stimulus context

Conditioning Process

Stimulus Context: Classroom

Response	followed by	**Reward**
Attend to teacher	→	Teacher attention, smiles, praises

One response is systematically reinforced

After Conditioning

Stimulus Context: Classroom

S^D		**Response**
Sight and behavior of teacher in classroom	→	Attentive, on-task behavior

The reinforced response becomes more frequent. Stimuli
accompanying the reward (discriminated stimuli, or S^D)
achieve control over the response

Figure 2.5 Operant conditioning in the classroom. Note that in operant conditioning, unlike classical conditioning, the original response is emitted rather than elicited by a stimulus. In this example, a variety of off-task and on-task behaviors are emitted. Reinforcement leads to the more frequent occurrence of on-task behaviors.

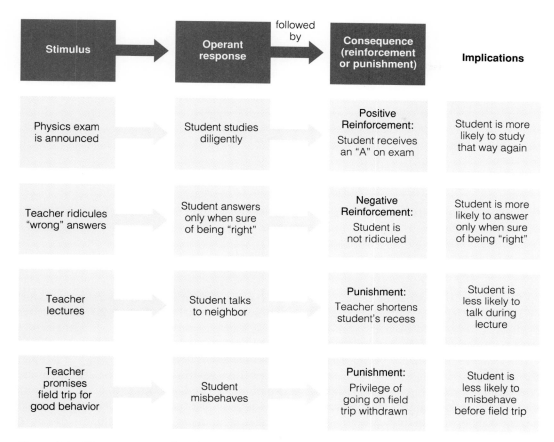

Stimulus Context: Classroom

Stimulus	Operant response	Consequence (reinforcement or punishment)	Implications
Physics exam is announced	Student studies diligently	**Positive Reinforcement:** Student receives an "A" on exam	Student is more likely to study that way again
Teacher ridicules "wrong" answers	Student answers only when sure of being "right"	**Negative Reinforcement:** Student is not ridiculed	Student is more likely to answer only when sure of being "right"
Teacher lectures	Student talks to neighbor	**Punishment:** Teacher shortens student's recess	Student is less likely to talk during lecture
Teacher promises field trip for good behavior	Student misbehaves	**Punishment:** Privilege of going on field trip withdrawn	Student is less likely to misbehave before field trip

Figure 2.6   Classroom examples of operant conditioning. Note that the first two examples (positive and negative reinforcement, respectively) lead to an *increase* in the likelihood of the response. The last two examples (both forms of punishment) lead to a *decrease* in the likelihood of the response. Note also that teachers may inadvertently reinforce maladaptive behaviors (second example).

Each of these may in turn be *primary* or *generalized*. **A primary reinforcer** is a stimulus that is reinforcing without the occurrence of learning. It is ordinarily related to an unlearned need or drive, as, for example, in the case of food: Presumably, people do not have to learn that eating is a good thing.

A **generalized reinforcer** is a previously neutral stimulus that, through repeated pairings with a number of other reinforcers in various situations, has become reinforcing for many behaviors. Prestige, money, and success are examples of extremely powerful generalized reinforcers.

Nature of Stimulus Effect

	Pleasant	Unpleasant
Added to the situation	Positive reinforcement (reward) Louella is given a jelly bean for being "good"	Punishment I (punishment) Louella has her nose tweaked for being "bad"
Removed from the situation	Punishment II (penalty) Louella has her jelly bean taken away for being "bad"	Negative reinforcement (relief) Louella's nose is released because she says "I'm sorry"

(Application of Stimulus)

Figure 2.7   Reinforcement and punishment.

Reinforcers may be positive or negative. A **positive reinforcer** is a stimulus that increases the probability of a response occurring when it is *added* to a situation. A **negative reinforcer** has the same effect as a result of being *removed* from the situation.

In the Skinner box example, food is a positive reinforcer — as is the light. If, however, a mild current were turned on in the electric grid that runs through the floor of the box, and if this current were turned off only when the rat depressed the lever, then turning off the current would be an example of a negative reinforcer.

Reinforcement and Punishment in the Classroom.   In summary, there are two types of reinforcement. One involves presenting a pleasant stimulus (positive reinforcement; **reward**); the other involves removing an unpleasant stimulus (negative reinforcement; **relief**). In the same way, there are two types of punishment, each the converse of one type of reinforcement. On the one hand is the punishment that occurs when a pleasant stimulus is removed (**penalty**); on the other is the more familiar situation in which a noxious (unpleasant) stimulus is presented. Figure 2.7 summarizes these four possibilities.

Positive Reinforcement (Reward).   Examples of positive reinforcement in the classroom are so numerous and obvious as to make citing any one appear platitudinous. Whenever a teacher smiles at students, says something pleasant to them, commends them for their work, assigns high grades, selects someone for a special project, or tells a mother how clever her child is, the teacher is using positive reinforcement. (See Chapter 12 for a more detailed discussion of various kinds of classroom reinforcement.)

Negative Reinforcement (Relief).   Implicit or explicit threats of punishment, failure, detention, ridicule, parental anger, humiliation, and sundry other unpleasant eventualities make up the bulk of the modern, well-equipped teacher's arsenal of negative reinforcers. When these follow unruly, nonstudious, or otherwise unacceptable behaviors, they may be interpreted as punishment (the presentation of an unpleasant stimulus following undesirable behavior). When the threat of these possibilities is removed following acceptable behavior, they provide a clear example of negative reinforcement (the removal of an unpleasant stimulus following desirable behavior). Negative and sometimes maladaptive behaviors, such as the tendency to escape or avoid situations, frequently result from the overzealous administration of negative reinforcement.

Punishment I. The first type of punishment involves presenting a noxious stimulus, usually in an attempt to eliminate some undesirable behavior. A classic example is the use of the lash in one North Carolina school in the year 1848 (see Table 2.3)—a practice that is no longer widely accepted.

Punishment II (Penalty). The second type of punishment involves the removal of a pleasant stimulus. The fairly common practice of detaining students after regular class hours, insofar as it removes the apparently pleasant privilege of going home, is an example of this type of punishment.

Effects of Reinforcement and Punishment. Reinforcement improves learning; it can easily be demonstrated that the behavior of both animals and people can often be controlled through the careful use of reinforcement. That punishment has an equal, if opposite, effect is not nearly so obvious. As Thorndike observed, pleasure is much more potent in stamping in responses than pain is in stamping them out.

In addition to objections based on ethical or humanitarian considerations, there are several other reasons why the use of punishment is an unsatisfactory means of behavior control. Among the most obvious is the fact that because punishment does not ordinarily illustrate or emphasize desirable behavior but simply draws attention to undesirable responses, it is not very useful in a learning situation. A second

Table 2.3 Excerpt from a list of punishments in a North Carolina school, 1848 (Coon, 1915)

No.	Rules of School	Lashes
1	Boys and Girls Playing Together	4
3	Fighting	5
7	Playing at Cards at School	4
8	Climbing for Every Foot Over Three Feet Up a Tree	1
9	Telling Lyes	7
11	Nick Naming Each Other	4
16	For Misbehaving to Girls	10
19	For Drinking Spirituous Liquors at School	8
22	For Waring Long Finger Nails	2
27	Girls Going to Boy's Play Places	2
33	Wrestling at School	4
41	For Throwing Anything Harder than Your Trab Ball	4
42	For Every Word You Miss in Your Heart Lesson Without Good Excuse	1
47	For Going about the Barn or Doing Any Mischief about the Place	7

objection is that punishment is often accompanied by highly undesirable emotional side effects that often are associated with the punisher rather than with the punished behavior. Third, punishment does not always lead to the elimination of a response but sometimes only to its suppression. In other words, a behavior is seldom forgotten as a result of punishment, although it may be avoided—sometimes only temporarily.

A last objection to punishment is a simple, practical one—it often does not work. Sears, Maccoby, and Lewin (1957) report that parents who punish their children severely for being aggressive are more likely than other parents to have aggressive children. And mothers who are unduly punitive when attempting to toilet train their children are more likely to have children who wet their beds. It appears, however, that overpermissive parents are as likely to have problems with their children as are those who make excessive use of physical punishment.

All of which is, indeed, valuable advice, whether it be interpreted by sages or by fools.*

Aversive Control

It should be stressed again that negative reinforcement and punishment describe two very different situations. The two are often confused because each usually involves unpleasant (noxious) stimuli. But whereas punishment results in a reduction in behavior, negative reinforcement, like positive reinforcement, increases the probability that a response will occur. Thus, a child can be encouraged to speak politely to teachers by being smiled at for saying "please" and "thank you" (positive reinforcement). Another child can be beaten with a cane (or threatened therewith) when "please"s and "thank you"s are forgotten (punishment)— with the clear understanding that the cane will be put away only when behavior conforms to the teacher's standards of politeness (negative reinforcement). In the end, both children may be wonderfully polite. But which child, do you suppose, will like teachers and schools more?

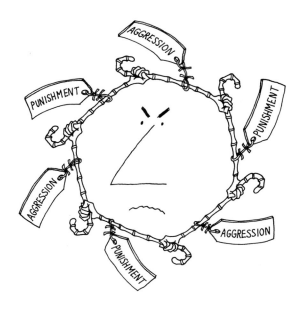

Strange as it might seem, the use of negative reinforcement as a means of control is highly prevalent in today's schools, homes, and churches, as is the use of punishment. These methods of **aversive control** (in contrast to **positive control**) are evident in the use of low grades and verbal rebukes, in threats of punishment, in detention in schools, and in the unpleasant fates that await transgressors in most major religions. They are evident as well in our legal and judicial systems, which are extraordinarily punitive rather than rewarding. Material rewards for being good are seldom obvious, but criminality is clearly punished. In fact, the reward for being good frequently takes the form of not being punished. That, in a nutshell, is negative reinforcement.

It is difficult to determine which is more important in our daily lives—positive reinforcement or negative reinforcement. Nor is it always easy to separate the two in practice, daily life being considerably more tolerant of ambiguity than is psychological theory. Consider, for example, that I work to obtain the

---

*PPC: "Perhaps Lefrançois should point out that the use of punishment is sometimes highly effective and highly appropriate. Or was it punishment that made a fool out of the **bear** who always used to face the front so sagely?"
Author: "I do in Chapter 12. And the bear is too smart to be a fool, although he is not yet a sage."

"good" things in life: food, prestige, power, and a soft, wet kiss. It would seem obvious that I am controlled by positive reinforcement. Or is it true, as my grandmother suggested, that I am really working to prevent hunger, to escape from anonymity and helplessness, and to avoid loneliness?

The issue cannot easily be resolved, but it is worth noting that I am much more likely to be happy if positive rather than negative contingencies control my behavior. Indeed, **avoidance learning** and/or **escape learning** are among the most important consequences of aversive control. A child who performs well in school because of parental and teacher rewards probably likes school; another who performs well in order to escape parental wrath and school punishments will probably have quite different emotional reactions to school and may *avoid* further noncompulsory schooling or might even consider *escaping* from the present situation.

Aversive control of behavior may have one additional, highly undesirable effect. When Ulrich and Azrin (1962) placed two rats in a situation in which they had to turn a wheel to avoid an electric shock, the rodents fell, tooth and nail, upon each other. Although each understood (in a primitive rat way, to be sure) that the source of their pain was the wheel and not the other rat, they insisted on behaving in a most unfriendly fashion.

It should be noted that the most dedicated proponents of applied behavioral techniques and principles strongly advocate the use of positive rather than aversive control methods. This was especially true of B. F. Skinner.

Schedules of Reinforcement

Through experiments with pigeons and rats, Skinner attempted to discover (1) the relationship between the type and amount of reinforcement used and the quality of learning achieved and (2) the relationship between the way reinforcement is administered and learning. The first relationship cannot easily be ascertained because type and amount of reinforcement appear to affect individuals in unpredictable ways. It is clear from numerous experiments that even a very small reward will lead to effective learning and will maintain behavior over a long period. It is also clear that too much reward (satiation) may lead to a cessation of behavior. Several guidelines for the use of reinforcement are presented in Chapter 12. These, however, should be interpreted cautiously.

The second relationship is somewhat easier to determine because it can be investigated directly. The manner in which rewards are administered is usually referred to as the **schedule of reinforcement**. Schedules invariably use either **continuous reinforcement** or **intermittent reinforcement** (also called *partial reinforcement*). In the first case a reward is provided for every correct response (referred to as every trial). In the second case only *some* of the trials are reinforced, in which case the experimenters have two options. They may choose to reinforce a certain proportion of trials (a **ratio schedule**), or they may base their schedule on the passage of time (an **interval schedule**). They might, for example, decide to reinforce one out of five correct responses; or they might reinforce one correct response for every fifteen-second lapse. In either case they have two more options. They might choose to assign reinforcement in a predetermined fashion (**fixed schedule**) or in a more haphazard manner (**random or variable schedule**). Or, to really confuse things in proper psychological fashion, they might combine a number of these schedules and gleefully claim that they are using a mixed or **combined schedule**.

They have no more choices, fortunately . . . except maybe one. It is referred to as a **superstitious schedule** and is explained later in this chapter.

The preceding section may, at first glance, appear somewhat confusing. You are advised

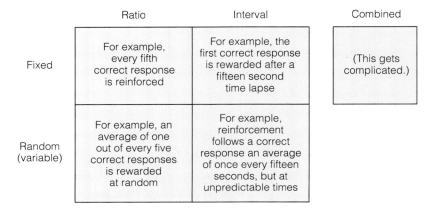

A. Continuous

> Every correct
> response is
> reinforced

B. Intermittent (Partial)

	Ratio	Interval	Combined
Fixed	For example, every fifth correct response is reinforced	For example, the first correct response is rewarded after a fifteen second time lapse	(This gets complicated.)
Random (variable)	For example, an average of one out of every five correct responses is rewarded at random	For example, reinforcement follows a correct response an average of once every fifteen seconds, but at unpredictable times	

Figure 2.8   Schedules of reinforcement. Each type of reinforcement tends to generate its own characteristic pattern of response.

to read it again slowly and consult Figure 2.8. It is really quite simple. Experimenters have two choices: If they choose A, they have no more choices; but if they choose B, they have two new options. Each of these, in turn, offers two further options. And finally, the last four options may be combined.

Schedules and Learning.   Much of Skinner's work was directed toward discovering the relationship between various schedules of reinforcement and one of three measures of learning: **rate of learning, response rate,** and **extinction rate.** Only the most important results of these studies are reported here.

It appears that continuous reinforcement is most effective for increasing the rate of learn-ing. When learning such simple responses as lever pressing, the rat might become confused and would almost certainly learn much more slowly if only *some* of its initial correct responses were reinforced. In terms of classroom practice this means that initial learning, particularly for very young children, probably requires far more reinforcement than does later learning. Students often receive this reinforcement in the form of attention or knowledge that they are performing correctly.

Interestingly, although continuous reinforcement often leads to more rapid learning, it does not usually result in longer **retention** of what is learned. Indeed, the rate of **extinction** for behavior that has been reinforced continuously is considerably faster than for behavior

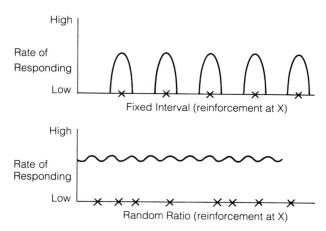

Figure 2.9   Pigeon pecking under two reinforcement schedules.

that has been reinforced intermittently. *Extinction* means the cessation of a response as a function of withholding reinforcement. The extinction *rate* is simply the time that elapses between the beginning of the nonreinforced period and the cessation of behavior.

The use of extinction in schools, often in the form of the withdrawal of attention in the case of unruly, attention-seeking behavior, is widespread and effective. Several illustrations are provided in Chapter 12.

In general, therefore, the best schedule would appear to consist initially of continuous reinforcement, followed later by intermittent reinforcement. Among the intermittent schedules, a random ratio arrangement ordinarily results in the slowest rate of extinction.

The rate of responding can also be brought under the control of the schedule used. Interestingly, the behavior of pigeons and rats often suggests that they have developed expectations about reward. A pigeon that has been taught to peck a disk and is reinforced for the first peck after a lapse of fifteen seconds (fixed interval) often completely ceases pecking immediately after being reinforced and resumes again just

before the end of the fifteen-second interval. If, on the other hand, the pigeon is reinforced on a random ratio basis, its response rate will be uniformly high and constant, often as high as 2,000 or more pecks an hour. (See Figure 2.9.)

Schedules and People.   So! One can reinforce the behavior of rats and pigeons in a variety of clever ways and can note a number of consistent effects that this has on their ludicrously simple behaviors. From this, numerous graduate dissertations and great quantities of published research may be derived for the erudition of the scholars and the amazement of the people.

But what of human beings? How are they affected by schedules of reinforcement?

The answer seems to be: In much the same way as animals. Marquis (1941), for example, investigated the behavior of babies who were fed regularly (fixed-interval schedule) and of others who were fed on demand. Not surprisingly, infants on fixed schedules showed a marked increase in activity just prior to feeding time. Bandura and Walters (1963) make the related observation that behaviors engaged in by young children who desire parental attention tend to be randomly reinforced—and tend, consequently, to be highly persistent. In the same way, the observation that extinction is more rapid in rats following continuous reinforcement appears to be valid for human infants as well (Carment and Miles, 1962; Kass and Wilson, 1966).

There are many examples of the effects of schedules on people's behaviors. The fisherman who goes to the same stream time after time, although he rarely (but occasionally) catches fish, is demonstrating the persistence that results from an intermittent schedule of reinforcement. The small-town student who has been at the top of her classes for eight years, but now, finding herself being outdone in the fierce competition of a new school, ceases to study, may be demonstrating the rapid extinction that follows continuous reinforcement. Knowing how schedules of reinforcement affect people's behaviors can be useful in a variety of practical situations—as the wife who occasionally but not too frequently praises her husband's appearance or his cooking will attest. He may continue to cook and to look good despite long sequences without reinforcement.

Superstitious Behavior. Recall that a fixed-interval schedule provides for reinforcement on the first correct trial after a specified time lapse. In the course of investigating the relationship between schedules of reinforcement and learning, Skinner occasionally used what is actually a fixed-interval schedule of reinforcement that lacks the provision that the learner must perform at least one correct response before being reinforced. This variation is called a *superstitious schedule*. Such a schedule reinforces the learner regularly, no matter what responses are occurring at the time. Consequently it often leads to strange and sometimes highly persistent patterns of behavior wholly unrelated to the reinforcement. Skinner (1948) reported leaving six pigeons on a superstitious schedule overnight. The following morning one bird

was turning clockwise prior to each reinforcement; a second turned its head toward a corner; and two others had developed unnatural swaying motions of the body.

As Skinner (1953) pointed out, it is somewhat more difficult to illustrate superstitious behavior in humans. He maintained, however, that those behaviors that have "accidentally" accompanied reinforcement are more likely to occur again. Skinner's own example is that if a man finds a ten-dollar bill in a park, he may well, the next time he walks in the park, hold his eyes just as he was holding them when fortune struck. Indeed, his entire bearing might closely resemble that which accompanied his good fortune.

There is probably considerable unconscious superstitious behavior in most people. Those who frown, scratch their heads, purse their lips, or chew their hair (it happens) when thinking are not engaging in behaviors directly related to thought processes. But they may be displaying the effects of reinforcement that occurred when they happened to be frowning, scratching, or chewing hair.

Shaping

A Skinnerian psychologist who wished to train a rat to genuflect, turn three somersaults, and then stand briefly on its head with its tail pointing west might approach the rat's cage and watch carefully for the appearance of this complex sequence of operants. When the desired behaviors occurred, it would be a simple matter (theoretically, to be sure) to reinforce the behavior, thus increasing the probability that the sequence would be repeated. Unfortunately, both the psychologist and the rat likely would die of old age before the desired operants appeared.

Another, much better way of teaching rats through the principles of operant conditioning is called **shaping**. Essentially, shaping involves reinforcing the animal for every behavior that brings it slightly closer to the desired terminal behavior. For example, if the objective is to teach the rat to genuflect, the experimenter might initially reinforce the rat every time its front quarters dipped slightly. Later, once the rat had learned to dip reliably and predictably, slight dips would no longer be reinforced, but more pronounced dips would be. And if the reinforcements were accompanied by a distinctive stimulus such as a bell (a *discriminated stimulus*), eventually the rat might genuflect every time the psychologist rang the bell.

For obvious reasons, shaping is also called the **differential reinforcement of successive approximations**. It is one of the most common techniques used in training performing animals. Does it have any relevance to the lives of humans?

Shaping and People. Two related statements may be made about the role of shaping in human behavior. First, the behavior of people is constantly being shaped by its reinforcement

contingencies. Second, people often, and sometimes deliberately, use shaping techniques to modify other people's behavior.

The first statement simply recognizes the fact that a great deal of human behavior is modified by reinforcement. For example, as previously reinforcing activities become habitual and less rewarding, they tend to be modified. A motorcyclist may initially derive considerable reinforcement from the sensation of turning a sharp corner at high speed, but in time the sensation diminishes and the excitement decreases. And as the reinforcement begins to decrease, speed increases, imperceptibly but progressively. This is a clear illustration of shaping as a consequence of the outcome of behavior.

There are many examples of shaping in the classroom. Peer approval or disapproval, sometimes communicated in very subtle, nonverbal ways, can drastically affect a student's behavior. The classroom clown would probably not continue to be a clown if no one paid any attention to her. Indeed, she might never have been shaped into a clown had her audience not reinforced her in the first place.

The second statement asserts that people make direct use of shaping procedures, sometimes consciously, to control the behavior of others. It is well known, for example, that a person's listeners can often direct a conversation by means of deliberate or unconscious signs of interest and approval (or the reverse). Indeed, the susceptibility of human speech to external control through reinforcement has led to a number of studies of verbal conditioning. In these studies a subject is conditioned to utter a preponderance of a specific kind of word in free association (for example, plural nouns; Greenspoon, 1955) as a function of reinforcement. Typically, the experimenter simply says "mm-hm" or makes some gesture of approval such as head nodding whenever the subject emits the desired expression.

Generalization and Discrimination

Two of the most important phenomena in conditioned learning are *generalization* and **discrimination**. Not all situations for which a specific operant is appropriate (or inappropriate) will be encountered by an individual while learning. Yet individuals do respond when faced with new situations. The behavioristic theorist explains this by reference to generalization or discrimination. Generalization simply involves making a response that would ordinarily be made under other, similar circumstances. Discrimination involves refraining from making the response in question because of some difference between this situation and other situations for which the response was clearly more appropriate. For example, children may learn very early in life that they will receive their mother's attention if they cry. This type of behavior is soon generalized from specific situations in which they have obtained their mother's attention to new situations in which they desire her attention. A wise mother can bring about discrimination learning quite simply by not paying attention to her child in those situations in which she does not want to be disturbed. While on the phone, she might completely ignore her child's supplications for attention; soon the child will learn to discriminate between situations in which attention-getting behavior is not reinforced and other situations in which it is more likely to be reinforced.

Instructional Applications: Applying Operant Principles

It is difficult to overestimate the relevance of the principles of operant learning to teaching. Indeed, a classroom is in many ways like a gigantic Skinner box. It is so engineered that certain responses are more probable than others. For example, it is easier to sit at a desk than to lie in one — and it is easier to remain awake when sitting than when lying. And at the front of a million classrooms stand the powerful dispensers of reinforcement — the teachers. They smile or frown; they say "good" or "not good"; they give high grades or low grades; occasionally they grant special favors; and at other times they withhold or cancel privileges. By means of this reinforcement and punishment, they are shaping the behavior of their students.

Drawing an analogy between a classroom, a teacher, and a student on the one hand and a Skinner box, a psychologist, and a rat on the other is somewhat unappealing and perhaps a little frightening (shades of Orwell's *1984*). Yet the analogy is relevant and potentially useful. Indeed, classroom teachers could often profit immensely from the discoveries of experimental psychologists.

One of the first direct results of the application of Skinner's theory to teaching was a renewed emphasis on **programmed instruction** — a topic discussed in some detail in Chapter 13. A second application of the theory to instruction has taken the form of a serious criticism of education and of current teaching methods. In a 1965 article entitled "Why Teachers Fail," Skinner claimed that efforts to improve education seldom involve attempts to improve teaching as such, and that teachers therefore continue to teach the way they themselves were taught. Chief among their methods, for both disciplinary and instructional purposes, are the techniques of aversive control — the use of unpleasant stimuli, often for punishment, but sometimes for negative reinforcement as well.

As alternatives to aversive control, Skinner suggested the obvious — positive reinforcement, together with "attractive and attention-compelling" approaches to teaching. In addition, he presented numerous suggestions for the development of a **technology of teaching** in a book by that title (Skinner, 1968). Interestingly, some ten years later another behaviorist, Fred Keller (1978, p. 53) was to assert: "Never before in the history of mankind have we known so much about the learning process and the conditions under which an individual human being can be efficiently and happily trained." And others, such as Greer (1983), argue strongly that the effectiveness of behavioristic principles for teaching is not equaled by any other approach. The application of these principles requires that teachers become *behavior analysts* — that they dedicate themselves both to identifying and establishing environments that will lead to desirable behaviors and to providing reinforcement contingencies that will serve to maintain these behaviors. The success of such an approach has been demonstrated experimentally numerous times, perhaps most dramatically with mentally retarded, autistic, or other learning-disadvantaged children. A collective label for the application of these principles in education and in therapy is **behavior modification**. Specific behavior modification techniques are discussed in Chapter 12.

BEHAVIORISTIC CONTRIBUTIONS: SUMMARY AND EVALUATION

The pioneering contributions of the behavioral psychologists are difficult to assess; their long-range influence on the development of psychology is still being felt. Watson and Guthrie's insistence on objectivity and rigor is probably their outstanding contribution. These criteria are still a measure of the worth of psychological investigations. In addition, Watson and Guthrie were responsible for elaborating a model of learning that is sufficient to explain at least some animal and human behaviors.

Thorndike's contribution is perhaps more widely acknowledged. He is generally credited with introducing the idea that the consequences of behavior are important variables in learning—an idea that has profoundly influenced the development of psychology.

Admittedly, this book's treatment of these theoretical positions is brief and highly simplified. Only the most striking features of each theory have been discussed. It is possible, nevertheless, to derive a set of general educational implications from this chapter. Keep clearly in mind, however, that these are extremely general principles, that they are merely suggestions, that they are not always compatible with all theories, that they are only *some* of many possible implications, and that they could, in many instances, have been derived from theoretical positions discussed later in this text. In addition, a number of suggestions presented in Chapters 11 and 12 are relevant here.

"To satisfy the practical demands of education, theories of learning must be 'stood on their heads' so as to yield theories of teaching" (Gage, 1964, p. 269). Presumably the same re-sult would be obtained if students were asked to stand on their heads while the theories remained upright. Unfortunately, however, even as extreme a measure as standing these behavioristic theories on their heads would be unlikely to yield *theories* of teaching. On the other hand, they need be tilted only very slightly to produce a variety of *principles* of practical value. Most of these principles and practical suggestions have been mentioned and illustrated earlier in the chapter. For example, the notion that repetition is important for learning follows directly from Thorndike's laws as well as from what is known about classical conditioning. In Thorndike's system, the formation of bonds is a direct function of the number of times a stimulus and a response are paired and reinforced. Even in Guthrie's theory of one-trial learning, repetition is useful; it leads to the learning of the same response in a variety of situations, making the response more available and less likely to be replaced.

The importance of reinforcement is the second of the major instructional implications deriving from behavioristic theories. Skinner and Thorndike each made the principles of reinforcement cornerstones of their systems. And even in Watson and Guthrie's theories, reinforcement may be important.

In the first place, reinforcement may prevent the unlearning of a response by changing the stimulus situation so that the organism is prevented from making another response to the first stimulus. In the second place, Watson's explanation of learning is not really contradicted by a reinforcement principle. In fact, the unconditioned stimulus in a classical conditioning situation serves as a type of reinforcement. Thus, in the classical Pavlovian experiment, the food is a reinforcer. If, after learning has occurred, the conditioned stimulus is presented repeatedly in the absence of the unconditioned stimulus (that is, the buzzer or bell without the food), the dog will eventually cease to salivate in response to the conditioned stimulus. At this point, the conditioned response is said to have been *extinguished*. Specifically, it has ceased to occur as a function of repeated presentations of the conditioned stimulus without presentation of the unconditioned stimulus.

A number of additional suggestions for educational practice can be derived directly from behavioristic theories. For example, the three suggestions advanced by Guthrie for breaking habits can be applied both to classroom learning and to **discipline** problems. (This is discussed and illustrated in Chapter 12.) Watson's emphasis on the pairing of stimuli suggests a particular type of arrangement of cues for learning. This arrangement would present stimuli in such a way as to pair the desired response repeatedly with the appropriate stimulus. Thorndike's consideration of specific pedagogical problems also contains observations of significance to classroom procedures, among which are the following:

1. Punishment is not very effective in eliminating undesirable behavior (Thorndike, 1932).

2. Interest in work and in improvement is conducive to learning (Thorndike, 1935).

3. Significance of subject matter and the attitude of the learner are important variables in school (Thorndike, 1935).

4. Repetition without reinforcement does not enhance learning (Thorndike, 1931).

There are many others, however, who are quick to point out that behaviorism is not a universal cure for all our educational ills. Even if we were to agree that behavioristic principles should be applied whenever possible, we would soon discover that there are countless instances in which they *cannot* be applied very effectively at all. As Walker (1979) points out, teachers seldom control some of the most powerful reinforcers that affect student behavior — for example, peer acceptance and praise, parental approval, and so on. What this means is that teachers are often relegated to using what are, at least for some students, the relatively weaker reinforcers — teacher approval and grades.

A second problem in the universal application of behavioristic principles in teaching is, as Brophy (1983) argues, that most of our instructional problems do not involve establishing a reinforcement schedule so as to *maintain* a desirable response, but instead involve bringing about the response in the first place. This is quite unlike the Skinner-box situation, in which the major problem has been to control and maintain a specific response through the manipulation of reinforcement, and in which eliciting the response is often a minor problem.

That there are problems in applying behavioristic principles and that these principles are not easy solutions for all teaching problems should not blind us to their potential. Some of that potential is discussed in greater detail in Chapters 12 and 13.

BEYOND FREEDOM

If most significant human behaviors are controlled by reinforcement or the lack of it, it follows that most of us are controlled by our environments — that the freedom of which we are so proud is merely an illusion. If I awaken in the morning and decide to brush my teeth, am I really free to make the choice? Can I either brush or not brush according to the whim of the moment? Or am I bound by the dictates of past reinforcement (and/or punishment), real or imagined? A mundane act, surely, that of brushing my teeth; certainly a very insignificant decision, given the cosmic magnitude of other decisions that I can make relative to my destiny.

Here I sit generating yards of words in a rather drab office — an activity that is perhaps of greater magnitude than the mechanical routine of brushing my teeth. But am I free not to be here? Was I free not to walk out of my warm house into a frigid, snowy, 20-below wind, coax my reluctant car to life, and drive through the frozen poplars to this city where my work awaits? I gave it no thought at the time; but if I had, is it not likely that my actions would have been guided by reinforcement contingencies? And if I had decided not to come to work, thereby convincing my neighbors that here indeed is a free man—a man who does what he pleases and a lazy man to boot—is it not true that I would have done so because the consequences of staying home would have seemed to me more pleasant than the prospect of writing to you? My freedom would still have been an illusion, though a comfortable and pleasing one.

In his book dealing with freedom and dignity, Skinner asserted that autonomous man is a myth. "Autonomous man," he explained, "is a device used to explain what we cannot explain in any other way. He has been constructed from our ignorance, and as our understanding increases, the very stuff of which he is composed vanishes" (Skinner, 1971, p. 200). Skinner contended that we are controlled by our environment; but, he reassured us, it is an environment of which we are almost totally in control—or at least an environment that is almost wholly of our own making. There is a fundamental difference between the two. An environment over which we have control implies an environment in which we are free, for we can change the reinforcement contingencies of that environment. An environment of our own making, but over which we have no immediate control, implies an environment in which we are not free. As a species, we may have controlled our own destiny; but as individuals we do not control our own actions.

Skinner discussed at length the possibility of applying a science of human behavior for the benefit of humanity (Skinner, 1953, 1961). Such an application would involve a degree of control over human behavior. It is this aspect of his work that has met with the greatest resistance and has led some to speculate that Skinnerian behaviorism can as easily be made a weapon as a tool. The question is really an ethical and moral one. The science exists, imperfect and incomplete as it is—and it is sometimes used deliberately and systematically. Skinner (1961) described, for example, how advertising uses emotional reinforcement by presenting alluring women in commercials, and how motivational control is achieved by creating generalized reinforcers. A car thus becomes a powerful reinforcer by being equated with sex. He described a society that uses positive reinforcement in the form of wages, bribes, or tips, and that uses drugs, such as "fear-reducers" for soldiers, to control humans.

But all of this began happening before Skinner; and, as he noted, "No theory changes what it is a theory about; man remains what he has always been" (1971, p. 215).

Nevertheless, this description of the human condition has come under severe attack from a wide variety of critics—as Skinner had predicted it would. In essence, he questioned the control exercised by "autonomous" man and demonstrated the control exercised by the environment in an attempt to create a science of behavior. The approach itself brings into question the worth and dignity of people. "These are sweeping changes," Skinner said, "and those who are committed to traditional theories and practices naturally resist them" (1971, p. 21).

The dispute, a very fundamental one in contemporary psychology, is essentially between humanistically oriented psychologists—those concerned more with humanity, ideals, values, and emotions (see Chapter 6)—and experimentally oriented psychologists—those more concerned with developing a relatively rigorous science of behavior. But the two positions are not really incompatible. "Man is much more than a dog," Skinner told us, "but like a dog he is within range of scientific analysis" (1971, p. 21).

Is the fact that I can deliberately choose to lie to you proof that I am free?

MAIN POINTS

1. Learning involves all changes in behavior that result from experience, providing that these changes are relatively permanent, do not result simply from growth or maturation, and are not the temporary effects of factors such as fatigue or drugs.

2. Types of learning can be distinguished in terms of the differences that exist among the behaviors involved (affective, motor, or cognitive) or in terms of the conditions that lead to the learning.

3. Behavioristic theories of learning are concerned with stimulus-response events and with the effects of repetition, contiguity, and reinforcement. Cognitive theories address problems relating to the organization of memory, information processing, problem solving, and metacognition (knowing about knowing).

4. Classical conditioning, described by Pavlov, involves the repeated pairing of a previously neutral stimulus (conditioned stimulus or CS) with an effective stimulus (unconditioned stimulus or UCS) so that the CS eventually brings about a response (labeled a conditioned response or CR) similar to that for the unconditioned stimulus.

5. Classical conditioning is sometimes useful in explaining the learning of emotional responses. Hence it is important for teachers to know what is being paired with what in schools and to maximize situations associated with positive emotions while minimizing those associated with negative feelings.

6. Watson's behaviorism is based on the notion that learning is a function of the classical conditioning of simple reflexes. Watson can be thought of as the champion of the conditioned reflex and of environmentalism — the belief that individual differences are attributable to experiences rather than to genetics.

7. Watson's classical conditioning may be useful for explaining the learning of some attitudes and emotional reactions as well as some simple skills.

8. Guthrie's theory is described as a theory of one-trial learning based on association through contiguity.

9. Guthrie believed that habits can never be broken but can be replaced in one of three ways: the threshold method, the fatigue method, and the incompatible-stimuli method.

10. Thorndike introduced the notion of reinforcement in learning theory through the law of effect, which asserts that responses followed by satisfaction tend to become linked to the stimuli that preceded them.

11. According to Thorndike, learning involves *stamping in* S-R bonds; forgetting involves *stamping out* bonds. Choice of a response is affected by previous reinforcement, but in the absence of previous learning it will take the form of trial and error. Choice of responses attempted may be affected by set, by identical elements in stimulus situations, by classical conditioning, or by prepotent elements.

12. Among the educational implications of Thorndike's theory is his suggestion that

one of the important goals of education is to teach for transfer (generalization) and to stress connections among ideas. He also emphasized the importance of student readiness and of reinforcement, and he recognized the limited effectiveness of punishment.

13. Skinner distinguished between respondent and operant behavior. The primary difference between the two is that the first results from a known stimulus, whereas the second is simply emitted. Respondents are *reactions to*; operants are *actions upon*.

14. The Skinner box is a cage-like device used by Skinner to observe the relationship between behavior and reinforcement — ordinarily in rats or pigeons.

15. The model of operant conditioning maintains that when an operant is reinforced, the probability of its recurrence increases.

16. A reinforcer is any stimulus whose effect is to increase the probability that a response will occur. It may do so by being added to a situation (positive reinforcement; reward) or by being removed (negative reinforcement; relief).

17. Negative reinforcement is *not* punishment. The effect of punishment is to decrease, not increase, the probability that a response will occur. Punishment occurs when a pleasant stimulus is *removed* or an unpleasant one is *introduced* following behavior.

18. Aversive control involves the use of negative reinforcement (often in the form of removal of threats) and of punishment. The emotional consequences of positive control are usually more desirable.

19. Reinforcement may be administered continuously (for every correct response) or in a random or fixed manner relative to a ratio or interval basis (that is, it can be continu-ous, random ratio, random interval, fixed ratio, or fixed interval).

20. In general, continuous schedules lead to faster learning, whereas intermittent schedules result in longer extinction periods.

21. A superstitious schedule of reinforcement is a fixed-interval schedule without the provision that reinforcement will occur only if there is a correct response. It sometimes leads to the acquisition of strange behaviors, both in animals and in people.

22. Shaping may be used to teach animals novel behaviors or to alter human behavior in subtle ways. It involves the *differential reinforcement of successive approximations*.

23. To generalize is to respond to similarities (make the same response in similar situations); to discriminate is to respond to differences (distinguish among situations in which identical responses are not appropriate).

24. Most significant human behaviors are probably of the operant variety. It is partly for this reason that an analogy between a Skinner box and a classroom is not entirely inappropriate.

25. Among the instructional implications that may be derived from these behavioristic theories are suggestions relating to the value of repetition, reinforcement, and punishment, as well as some practical suggestions for breaking habits.

26. There are those who believe that behavioristic principles can provide us with a technology of teaching whose effectiveness is not equaled by any other approach and who lament the apparent reluctance of many educators to apply this technology.

27. There are others who emphasize that the effectiveness of behavioristic approaches is limited, that teachers often control only the

weaker reinforcers, and that many of the problems of instructing (organizing, sequencing, explaining, illustrating) cannot easily make use of behavioristic principles.

28. It is possible that we are not free, that we are controlled by our environment, and that we have only the illusion of freedom.

SUGGESTED READINGS

Among the many attempts to apply learning theories to educational practice, the following three sources have been selected as the most representative and the most practical. Skinner's book is a collection of his papers on teaching; Lefrançois provides a clear explanation of early theories of learning; *and Bell-Gredler presents a useful look at the instructional implications of a variety of psychological theories:*

SKINNER, B. F. (1968). *The technology of teaching.* New York: Appleton-Century-Crofts.

LEFRANÇOIS, G. R. (1982). *Psychological theories and human learning* (2nd ed.). Monterey, Calif.: Brooks/Cole.

BELL-GREDLER, M. E. (1986). *Learning and instruction: Theory into practice.* New York: Macmillan.

Skinner provides a highly readable and important behavioristic estimation of the human condition:

SKINNER, B. F. (1971). *Beyond freedom and dignity.* New York: Knopf.

Hall and Kelson (1959) list exactly 130 subspecies and types of bears, ranging, alphabetically, from Ursus absarokus, *found in 1914 at the head of the Little Bighorn River in Montana, to* Ursus yesoensis.

COGNITION AND MEMORY

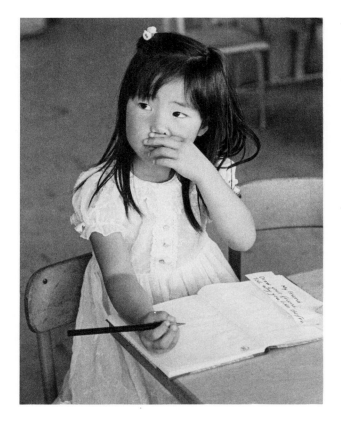

I've a grand mind for forgetting, David.

ROBERT LOUIS STEVENSON *Kidnapped*

The Right Honorable gentleman is indebted to his memory for his jests and to his imagination for his facts.

RICHARD BRINSLEY SHERIDAN *Speech in reply to Mr. Dundas*

PREVIEW Conditioning theories explain how stimuli, responses, and the consequences of behavior can become associated under certain circumstances. Accordingly, these theories are useful in explaining many relatively simple behaviors—and perhaps some complex behaviors as well. But how well do they explain the processes by which you and I can recognize, or at least contemplate, the role of, say, **wild cows** in the grand scheme of things?

■■■ *Wild cows have invaded the bear's forest.* At first light, when he went to the stream, he saw their droppings by the water and he could not bring himself to drink. Now, with heavy heart, he follows their spoor across the forest floor. Wild cows are every bear's nightmare. While we imagine winning lotteries or being hugely loved heroes, bears fantasize about wild-cow alarms that really work. Or, if they are mean-hearted, they dream of wild-cow plagues.*

The bear sees where the bunch of wild cows has crossed the stream. In their spoor, in the trampled beds of wild strawberries and the uprooted clusters of daffodils, he finds confirmation of his greatest fears. He is tempted to stop and weep.

**PPC:* "Maybe this introduction goes too far. After all, educational psychology is a serious subject. Besides, I've never heard of wild cows."
Author: "Dear reader: Your professor is not likely to ask you any questions about this chapter introduction. Those of you who are unrelentingly serious and determined should go immediately to the next section ('Behaviorism and Cognitivism')."
"Dear PPC: Wild cows *are* a real threat, so environmentally unfriendly are they. (If you don't believe this, see the introduction to Chapter 9.)"

Early in the morning, the bear finds the herd. Most of them are lying in a small meadow. They have already filled the first of their stomachs. Now they belch and chew cud. The bear's stomach turns at the stench of the methane gases that fill the air.

It is a pretty, flowered meadow in which the wild cows lie. But the bear knows that the short-lived beauty of spring crocuses does not touch wild cows; nor do the flame-orange, wild tiger lilies. He knows they have no appreciation of sunrises or sunsets; that they are neither awed when the storm clouds gather nor feel joy when the rains rejuvenate the land. They have no sense of mystery or of majesty, these wild cows; they recognize no sacred places. That is the source of the bear's sadness.

The bear lies next to a chokecherry bush on a small rise beyond the meadow. The wild cows are in plain view, but they are downwind, and the smell of their gases is faint. The cows pay no attention to the bear. Some of them play cards while they chew cud; others sip whisky or do their hair. It all looks so harmless, thinks the bear, but he knows it isn't. He knows that if the wild cows are allowed to stay, and if they cannot learn to restrain themselves, there will soon be no more spring clover; no sprigs of fern and tender grasses and sedges through the summer; no wild strawberries and blueberries; no low-bush cranberries, no crocuses, no fish. . . .

"There is no longer room for environmentally unfriendly creatures in our forest," mutters the bear, knowing that they cannot be driven away. And even if they could, they would simply do their environmentally unfriendly things elsewhere, and the problem, and its consequences, would remain unchanged.

Can their behavior be changed through a conditioning process? the bear muses as one of the wild cows throws her cards to the ground and stomps on them in a sudden display of childish rage. Can they be conditioned? the bear wonders. Theoretically, yes, he answers. This would involve reinforcing them for eating in a more restrained fashion, for refraining from lying on beds of clover and wild strawberries, and for changing their toilet habits. But he knows that none of this is likely to work in practice, simply because nobody has sufficient control over the things that reinforce wild cows. Or the things that punish them, either.

"Perhaps the best solution," concludes the bear, "is to reason with them, to get them to understand the impact of their behavior and to espouse values that emphasize the rights of others and the sanctity of the environment."

But don't you think it's a little far fetched to contemplate a cognitive rather than a behavioristic approach with such creatures? ▬

COGNITIVISM

We saw in Chapter 2 that behaviorism, in its simplest sense, is the study of behavior and of the ways in which behavior is influenced by its consequences. In a behavioristic analysis of learning, the primary emphasis is on the external conditions that affect behavior. The typical unspoken assumption is that all learners are initially equal but the conditions to which they are exposed vary. This variance is what accounts for subsequent differences in behavior.

In contrast to behaviorism, cognitivism involves "the scientific study of mental events" (E. Gagné, 1985, p. 4). These mental events have to do with acquiring, processing, storing, and retrieving information. Accordingly, the primary emphasis in a cognitive analysis of learning is on the learner's mental *structure*, a concept that includes not only the learner's previous related knowledge, but also the strategies that the learner might bring to bear on the present situation. In this view, the explicit assumption is that learners are far from equal. It is the individual's preexisting network of concepts, strategies, and understanding that makes experience meaningful.

THE FAR SIDE By GARY LARSON

"Satisfied?...I warned you not to invite the cows in for a few drinks."

※ Cognitivism, Hunt (1989) asserts, is a *perspective* rather than a discipline. It is a way of looking at things rather than a readily identifiable collection of findings. This way of looking at things is characterized by basic underlying beliefs that are apparent in the metaphors of cognitivism.

The Metaphors of Cognitivism

Historically, most scientists have been convinced that the successful completion of their searches would be a literal description of the way things actually are and a mathematically accurate system for relating causes and effects. Initially, there was little reason to suspect that science would one day discover phenomena that could only be described in such nebulous terms as *black hole*, *quark*, *node*, or *schema*. But science did uncover these phenomena and found itself at a loss to describe them literally and exactly; hence these metaphors.

A metaphor is a comparison. It doesn't say, "This is that," but instead it says, "It is interesting, or revealing, or amusing, or intelligent, to look at this *as though it were like* that." Hence a metaphor cannot be judged in terms of whether it is accurate, but only in terms of whether it is useful — or interesting and amusing.

Perhaps more than any other approach in psychology, cognitivism uses metaphors. Its models are not meant to be exact descriptions of functions and processes; instead, they suggest, they compare, they draw analogies. And, as such, they cannot be judged in terms of their accuracy but, like other psychological theories, must instead be subjected to tests of usefulness and consistency.

✳ Cognitivism is defined in terms of cognition. *Cognition*, however, is not a simple concept. Literally, to cognize is to know; hence cognition is knowing. As Neisser (1976, p. 1) puts it: "Cognition is the activity of knowing: the acquisition, organization, and use of knowledge." Or, in Glass, Holyoak, and Santa's words (1979, p. 2): "All our mental abilities — perceiving, remembering, reasoning — are organized into a complex system, the overall function of which is termed *cognition*." What is common to these and other definitions of *cognition* is that they emphasize the role of mental structure or organization in the processes of knowing. In other words, they deal with how mental representations are manipulated (Hunt, 1989). Not surprisingly, then, one of the major emphases of cognitive approaches concerns the ways information is processed and stored. Note how dramatically this departs from the major emphasis of a behavioristic approach, which involves behavior and its consequences.

Cognitivism's concern with information processing is closely related to the development of information-processing machines, more commonly called computers, and specifically to the branch of computer science concerned with *artificial intelligence*. This is the branch of computer science that attempts to make computers smarter. Raphael (1976) suggests that there are several reasons why we might want to make computers smarter. Not the least of these is the fact that a very smart computer can do some marvelous things for us, in the process freeing us to do other, equally marvelous things. But perhaps even more important, especially for those who study intelligence, a truly smart computer might clarify many questions we now have about the workings of our own information-processing systems — our minds. Scientists concerned with the second of these benefits typically use computers in one of two ways: to mimic the functioning of the human mind directly or to generate models of human functioning. In these models, the brain, with its neurons and their networks of interconnections, might be compared to the chips, disks, and the relay systems of computers. Or the processes involved in receiving, organizing, storing, and retrieving information might be compared to the programmed functions of the computer. In that case, it is the program rather than the computer itself that serves as a model for human functioning (Newell and Simon, 1972). (See Figure 3.1.)

The computer is clearly one of the metaphors of the cognitive sciences. This metaphor says, in effect, "It is useful to look at human cognitive functioning as though it were like the functioning of a computer."

More common are approaches that *invent* their own metaphors — that look at cognitive functioning not in terms of something known, such as a computer, but in terms of something that is initially unknown and whose characteristics must therefore be described. They use labels such as "knowledge base," "cognitive strategy," or "schema" for their metaphors. No one has seen a knowledge base, a cognitive strategy, or a schema; they are abstractions, inventions of cognitive theory. But each of these inventions can be described. And, once described, it is possible to say, "Learners behave as though they have a knowledge base and cognitive strategies."

Our current models of cognitive function-

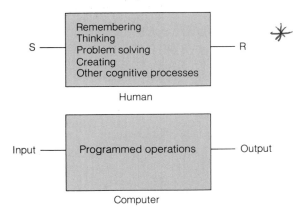

Figure 3.1 A schematic parallel between human cognitive functioning and computer functioning. If S (stimulus) = input and R (response) = output, does it follow that the computer's memory and programs are accurate representations of human cognitive processes? From G. R. Lefrançois, *Psychological Theories and Human Learning* (2nd ed.). Copyright 1982 by Wadsworth, Inc. Reprinted by permission of Brooks/Cole Publishing Company, Monterey, California.

ing—what are termed the *new cognitive sciences*—basically look at three things. First, they look at what Chi and Glaser (1980) call the **knowledge base**—the storehouse of information, concepts, and associations that we build up as we develop from children into adults. Second, they look at **cognitive strategies**—the processes by which information becomes part of the knowledge base, is retrieved from it, or is used. And third, they deal with the individual's awareness of self as a knower and processor of information—with what is termed *metacognition*. We look at each of these aspects of the cognitive sciences in the following sections of this chapter. In Chapters 4 and 5 we look at the tremendous potential contribution of the cognitive sciences to education, especially in developing ways of teaching and improving cognitive strategies.

A BASIC INFORMATION-PROCESSING MODEL

What Simon (1980) describes as the information-processing revolution in psychology, and specifically in learning theory, has led to a widely accepted basic model (Figure 3.2). This model, based largely on the work of Atkinson and Shiffrin (1968), portrays the human information processor in terms of three types of information storage: **short-term sensory storage** (sometimes called **sensory memory**), **short-term memory** (also called **working memory**; Dempter, 1985), and **long-term memory**. Each type of storage is distinct from the others primarily in terms of the nature and extent of the **processing** that information undergoes. In this context, *processing* refers to activities such as organizing, analyzing, synthesizing, rehearsing, and so on. In addition, the three types of storage differ in capacity and in the extent to which their contents are accessible.

The basic information-processing model of cognitive psychology does two related things: First, it provides us with an overall model of human **memory**. Second, it addresses a number of learning-related questions that are critically important for teachers—questions such as, How is information organized and sorted? What teaching and learning methods can facilitate information processing? How can memory be improved?

This basic information-processing model is examined in some detail in the following pages. Bear in mind, however, that what we are discussing is a model—a metaphor. It is not intended to be a literal description of the way things actually are stored in our brains.

Sensory Memory

The information-processing model attempts to represent how we acquire information, how we sort and organize it, and how we later retrieve it. The model is, in effect, a learning and memory model that begins with the raw material of all learning experiences: sensory input.

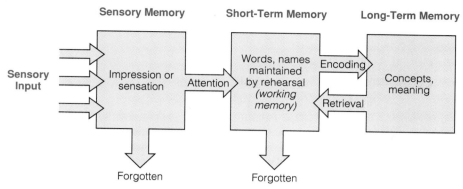

Sensory Memory   **Short-Term Memory**   **Long-Term Memory**

Sensory Input → Impression or sensation → Attention → Words, names maintained by rehearsal (*working memory*) → Encoding → Concepts, meaning → Retrieval

Forgotten

Forgotten

Figure 3.2   The three components of memory. Sensory information first enters sensory memory (*iconic* or *echoic* memory). From there it may go into short-term memory (also called *primary* or *working* memory), where it is available as a name or word (for example) as long as it is rehearsed. Some of the material in short-term memory may then be coded for long-term storage, where it might take the form of concepts. It is important to note that these three components of memory do not refer to three different locations in the brain or other parts of the nervous system but to how we remember — or, more precisely, to how we study memory. Adapted from G. R. Lefrançois, *Psychological Theories and Human Learning* (2nd ed.). Copyright 1982 by Wadsworth, Inc. Reprinted by permission of Brooks/Cole Publishing Company, Monterey, California.

Our sensory systems (vision, hearing, taste, touch, smell) are sensitive to an overwhelmingly wide range of stimulation. Clearly, however, they respond to only a fraction of all available stimulation at any given time; the bulk of the information available in this stimulation is never actually processed — that is, it never actually becomes part of our **cognitive structure**. The label used for this is *sensory memory*, sometimes called *echoic memory* (Neisser, 1976). It refers to the fleeting (less than one second) and unconscious effect on us of stimulation to which we pay no attention.

Note that sensory memory is highly limited, not only in terms of the length of time during which stimulus information is available for processing, but also in terms of the absolute amount of information available. Put another way, sensory memory is no more than the immediate sensory recognition of a stimulus. If, without giving any prior instructions, I read you a list of numbers in a dry, professorial monotone and then ask you to repeat the numbers some ten seconds later, you are not likely to remember very many of the numbers. But if I interrupt my reading and ask immediately, "What was the last number I read?" you will, in all likelihood, respond correctly. In fact, each of the numbers is stored in sensory memory for a very short period of time, but if it is not attended to or processed within a fraction of a second, it will no longer be available.

Short-Term Memory

The information-processing system of which cognitive psychology speaks makes use of a number of different activities with a common goal: making sense of significant sensory input and, at the same time, ignoring or discarding more trivial input. As we have seen, a great deal of sensory input that is not attended to does

Eidetic Images

Sometimes when we remember something, we say, "I can picture it in my mind." But what, exactly, is it that we can "picture"? Most often, psychologists inform us, we see a sort of mental image — an imperfect representation from memory, subject to all the distortions and inaccuracies to which memory is prone. But there are those rare individuals whose mental images are more accurate — they possess **eidetic imagery**.

In effect, an eidetic image is a photograph-like recollection of some stimulus — hence the popular expression *photographic memory*. People who have eidetic imagery are sometimes able to remember with amazing accuracy and detail. For example, in a typical investigation of eidetic imagery, subjects might be shown a picture, such as that reproduced here,* for a brief period, and then asked questions such as: "How many oranges are there in the tree?" "How many stripes are there in the flute player's skirt?" "How many flowers can you see?" Investigations such as these reveal that some degree of eidetic imagery is not uncommon among young school-age children but that it is far less common after adolescence (Ahsen, 1977a, 1977b). These investigations indicate as well that recall based on eidetic imagery is very much like looking at the actual

not go beyond immediate sensory memory. *Paying attention* is, in fact, one of the important activities of our information-processing system. It is the means by which input is transferred from sensory to short-term storage — hence the importance of getting students' attention if teaching is to be effective.

In essence, short-term memory consists of what is in our immediate consciousness at any given time. As Calfee (1981) notes, it is a sort of "scratch pad" for thinking; it contains all that is in our immediate awareness. For this reason, short-term memory is often called *working*

memory. The label draws attention to the function of this level of memory rather than simply to its duration.

One of the important characteristics of short-term memory is that it is highly limited in capacity. Following various memory experiments, Miller (1956) concluded that its average capacity is around seven discrete items (plus or minus two); that is, our immediate conscious awareness is limited to this capacity, and as additional items of information come in, they push out some that are already there.

Short-term memory lasts a matter of sec-

6	6	8	0
5	4	3	2
1	6	8	4
7	9	3	5
4	2	3	7
3	8	9	1
1	0	0	2
3	4	5	1
2	7	6	8
1	9	2	6
2	9	6	7
5	5	2	0
x	0	1	x

picture. Those so gifted continue to "see" the picture after it is removed. When they are asked how many flowers they can see, their eye movements are similar to the eye movements of someone actually looking at the picture.

Eidetic imagery, contrary to popular opinion, does not usually present any advantage in school-related learning tasks, because it seldom involves any transference to long-term mem-

ory. In fact, the eidetic image is seldom available for recall even an hour later; typically, it fades within minutes. There are, however, recorded cases of remarkable, eidetic-like memories that are not subject to the ravages of time. Among these, Luria's (1968) description of a young Russian known to us only as S is perhaps the best known. S went to Luria, a psychologist, because he was bewildered and confused. His mind was such a jumble of sights, sounds, and colors that he had difficulty following ordinary conversations. S's problem, quite simply, was an absolutely remarkable memory. On one occasion, Luria presented S with the array of numbers shown here.[†] After spending three minutes examining the table, S was able to reproduce the numbers flawlessly in forty seconds. Within fifty seconds he read off each of the four-digit numbers forming

the first twelve horizontal rows, as well as the two-digit number in the last row. But what is even more remarkable is that even after several months had elapsed, during which time the table was never again presented, S could still reproduce it flawlessly (although he took somewhat longer to "reimagine" the array).

But memories such as S's are exceptionally rare. Most of the memories with which teachers deal are more ordinary.

*Photo of *The Dream* by Henri Rousseau. 1910. Oil on canvas, 6′8½″ × 9′9½″. Collection, The Museum of Modern Art, New York. Gift of Nelson A. Rockefeller. Reprinted by permission.
[†]Table from *The Mind of a Mnemonist: A Little Book About a Vast Memory* by A. R. Luria, translated from the Russian by Lynn Solotaroff. Copyright 1968 by Basic Books, Inc., Publishers. Reprinted by permission of Michael Cole and Jonathan Cape Ltd.

onds (not minutes, hours, or days) and appears to be highly dependent on rehearsal; that is, for items to be maintained in short-term storage, they must be repeated (consciously thought about). In the absence of repetition, they quickly fade — generally before twenty seconds has elapsed.

The apparent limitations of short-term memory are not nearly as serious as they might at first seem. Although we cannot easily attend to more than seven discrete items, a process called **chunking** dramatically increases the capacity of short-term memory. In effect, a *chunk* is simply a grouping of related items of information. Thus, a single letter might be one of the seven items held in short-term memory, or it might be chunked with other letters to form a single word — which can, in turn, be one of seven items in short-term memory. To illustrate this phenomenon, Miller (1956) uses the analogy of a change purse that can only hold seven coins. If it holds seven pennies, its capacity is only seven cents. But if it holds seven quarters, seven fifty-cent pieces, or even seven gold coins, its capacity increases dramatically.

In summary, short-term memory is the ongoing availability of a small number of items, or chunks, of information in conscious awareness. Without continued rehearsal, these items are generally lost from memory within twenty seconds. The great usefulness of short-term memory is that it enables us to keep information in mind long enough to make sense of sequences of words and directions, to solve problems, and to make decisions.

Educational Applications of Short-Term Memory. The most common measure of short-term memory is to have subjects repeat a sequence of unrelated single-digit numbers they have just heard. This task is, in fact, common to a number of intelligence tests. Under these circumstances, adults and adolescents typically remember six or seven items (or sometimes even nine or more). In contrast, six-year-olds are not likely to remember more than two or three.

These differences may be highly important for teachers. It may well be, as Siegler (1989) suggests, that certain problems are very difficult or impossible for younger learners simply because they cannot keep in mind enough relevant information at one time — as might be the case, for example, if a young child were asked to add several numbers at once. Case et al. (1988) argue that one of the most serious limitations on the young child's ability to understand and solve problems is simply a limitation in the number of items that can be retained in working memory for immediate availability.

Teachers have two possible courses of action in such cases. If much of the young child's cognitive limitations result from limited short-term memory capacity, teachers can either: (1) wait for appropriate changes in memory before progressing to more demanding tasks, or (2) take steps to improve the child's memory.

In practice, teachers most often resort to the first alternative; they simply wait for the child to mature. Recently, however, growing evidence suggests that it might be possible to teach certain aspects of cognitive strategies —

such as rehearsal — that are important for short-term memory. (More about this later.)

Long-Term Memory

The type of memory that is clearly of greatest concern to educators is long-term memory. Long-term memory includes all of our relatively stable information about the world — all that we *know* but that is not in our immediate consciousness. In fact, one of the important distinctions between short-term and long-term memory is that short-term memory is an active, ongoing, conscious process, whereas long-term memory is a more passive, unconscious process. Accordingly, short-term memory is easily disrupted by external events — as we demonstrate every time we lose our "train of thought" due to some distraction. In contrast, long-term memory cannot easily be disrupted. If you know the capital of Finland today, you are likely to know it tomorrow, next month, and even next year.

As noted earlier, we transfer information from sensory storage to short-term storage through the process of *attending*, and we maintain it in short-term memory largely through *rehearsal*. But the transference of material from short-term to long-term memory involves more than simple rehearsal: It involves **encoding**, a process whereby meaning is derived from experience. To encode information is to transform or abstract it — to represent it in another form. Encoding clearly involves information processing, an event that can occur at different levels. Craik and Lockhart (1972; Cermak and Craik, 1979), originators of the **levels of processing** model, suggest that memory results specifically from the level to which information is processed. Information that is not processed leaves only a momentary sensory impression (sensory memory); information that is merely rehearsed is available for seconds (short-term memory); and information that is processed to a greater degree finds its way into long-term memory. But not all material in

Table 3.1 Three levels of memory

	Sensory	*Short-Term*	*Long-Term*
Alternate Labels	Echoic or iconic	Primary or working	Secondary
Duration	Less than 1 second	Less than 20 seconds	Indefinite
Stability	Fleeting	Easily disrupted	Not easily disrupted
Capacity	Limited	Limited (7 ± 2 items)	Unlimited
General Characteristics	Momentary, unconscious impression	Working memory; immediate consciousness; active, maintained by rehearsal	Knowledge base; associationistic; passive, the result of encoding

long-term memory is processed to the same level. If, for example, subjects are asked to learn and remember a word, they can process it át a very superficial level, paying attention only to its physical appearance. At a somewhat deeper level, they might pay attention to the word's pronunciation. And at the deepest level, they would take into account the word's meaning — a process called *semantic encoding*. (Table 3.1 summarizes the characteristics of all three levels of memory.)

Cognitive Models of Long-Term Memory. One of the earliest models of long-term memory was described by Koffka (1935). It viewed the mind as something like a catalogue or a motion-picture camera that records a sequential representation of all our experiences. From this representation, we later withdraw isolated memories as we need them, providing they have not been eradicated in the meantime. The fundamental characteristic of this model of memory is that it is *nonassociationistic*; that is, it views memory as consisting of isolated bits of information recorded sequentially.

Almost without exception, contemporary models of memory are *associationistic*. They are based on the fundamental notion that all items of information in our memories are associated

in a variety of ways. And it is precisely because of these associations that we are able to recall things as impressively as we can. Unlike computer memories, which typically work on the basis of location (items are "addressed" in terms of location), our human memories seem to be addressed by content. Thus a computer can retrieve and analyze information once it knows the particular place in storage that needs to be searched. In contrast, we need only know *what* to look for, rather than *where*, in order to find it.

Speculation concerning the nature of the associations that define human long-term memory have led to a number of abstract models and labels for describing memory. These models are essentially cognitive; that is, they relate to associations based on meaning or significance, rather than to behavioristic associations (for example, repetition and contiguity). This, of course, does not mean that repetition and contiguity are irrelevant. As Calfee (1981) points out, we know that the more often we encounter an idea or an experience, the more likely it is to be richly represented in memory and easily available. Similarly, experiences and ideas that often are encountered together are far more likely to be associated in memory. But what the cognitive, association-

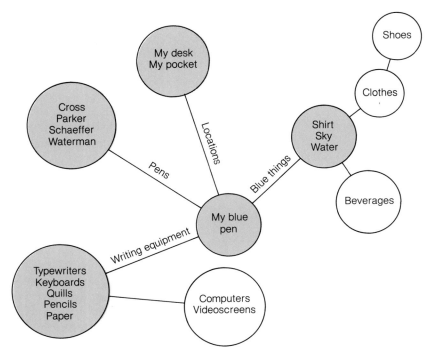

Figure 3.3 A model of a metaphor. Frame or node theory suggests that we remember abstractions — meanings and associations rather than specifics. Thus, my blue pen is depicted as a node embedded in a complex web of abstractions (for example, "blue things"), each of which relates to many other nodes that are not shown here. The complex of associated nodes is sometimes labeled a *frame*. From G. R. Lefrançois, *Psychological Theories and Human Learning* (2nd ed.). Copyright 1982 by Wadsworth, Inc. Reprinted by permission of Brooks/Cole Publishing Company, Monterey, California.

istic model stresses is that many ideas that are not presented frequently or in contiguity will be related in memory because of some association that has to do with their meaning.

Among the various metaphors for items in long-term memory are such terms as *nodes, schemata, scripts, frames, networks, categories, coding systems,* and *subsumers.* Some of these terms are defined and described in detail in the next chapter; several are described here to clarify the associationistic nature of long-term memory.

A *node* is literally a knot, a juncture, or a complication. As a metaphor for human memory, a node may be viewed as an intersection or juncture of concepts, ideas, or thoughts. It is simply a term for whatever it is that we can represent in our minds and that we are able to store and remember. Its essential characteristic is that it represents not only ideas or thoughts, but also the relationships among them. And terms such as *schema, frame,* or *network* are sometimes used to label the organization of memory. Thus a frame or schema might be defined as a metaphor that represents how ideas or concepts (nodes) might be associated (see Figure 3.3). As Bransford (1979) argues, frame or schema models are actually models of the structure of knowledge. What cognitive psychology provides for us is a theory or model of what the educated mind is like.

Generative Versus Reproductive Memory.
One of the important characteristics of long-term memory is that it appears to be partly constructive or *generative*, rather than *reproductive*; that is, what is remembered is often a distortion of what was originally learned. In recalling a scene from a movie, for example, we tend to remember some of the major elements and to "fill in" whatever is missing. Thus, at least to some extent, we construct as well as reproduce; this is one reason why even "eyewitnesses" cannot always be believed. Loftus (1979) had subjects view a film in which a sports car was involved in an accident, and subsequently asked them a series of questions about the accident. Some subjects were asked, "How fast was the sports car going when it passed the barn while traveling along the country road?" Other subjects were asked instead, "How fast was the sports car going while traveling along the country road?" When subjects were later asked whether they had seen a barn, 17 percent of those who had earlier been asked the first question *claimed to remember* seeing one; fewer than 3 percent of the others *actually remembered* a barn!

As a result of this and a host of related studies, Loftus argues that much of what we remember has been modified by intervening events and dulled by the passage of time. In the end, perhaps fewer than half of us will be able to identify the thief; even fewer will remember the color of his hair or eyes. And some of us will remember things that we have never even experienced!

MEMORY PROCESSES

A number of important processes are involved in capturing a sensory impression and maintaining it in immediate awareness or transferring it to long-term storage from which it can later be retrieved. Because these processes have to do with knowing, they are *cognitive processes*. Three of the most important are rehearsal, elaboration, and organization. In addition, a number of specific strategies can be used with each process (Horton and Mills, 1984).

Rehearsal, as we saw, is important in maintaining material in short-term memory (immediate consciousness), as well as in transferring it to long-term storage. To rehearse is to repeat. At a simple level, for example, rehearsal involves nothing more complex than naming something over and over again (repeating "seven-two-seven-five-five-five"). Most preschool children do not rehearse spontaneously and cannot easily be taught to do so (Flavell, 1985).

Elaboration is a cognitive process whereby material is extended or added to (elaborated) in order to make it more memorable. One way of elaborating material is to associate mental images with items to be remembered. Higbee (1977) suggests that because our memories are highly visual (photographs are more easily remembered than paragraphs), the use of mental images is an important aspect of most mnemonic systems (systems for remembering). Some of these systems are described later in this chapter.

Sometimes elaboration involves forming associations between new material and material that is already well known. Research suggests that elaborations that relate to meaning are highly memorable. For example, when Bradshaw and Anderson (1982) asked subjects to recall sentences such as "The fat man read the sign," those who had elaborated the sentence to something like "The fat man read the sign warning of thin ice" performed significantly better than those who had not elaborated. Before age 12, children do not deliberately elaborate to improve recall (Justice, 1985).

Organization as a memory process has to do with grouping, arranging, sorting, and relating material. Chunking—the placing of material into related classes—is one example of organization. Similarly, arranging material according to some logical system is an example of organization (for example, the characteristics of long-term memory on the one hand and those of short-term memory on the other).

The organizational strategies that are so important to long-term memory can be either extremely complex or very simple. What most of them have in common, however, is that they are based on our recognition of similarities and differences. Humans (and perhaps other animals as well, although it is difficult to be certain) seem to have a tendency to see similarities and differences (as well as other relations) and to generalize from them. Put another way, we seem to be information-processing organisms whose function it is to make sense of all the data that surround us. One of the important methods we use for making sense of the world is to extract common elements from various experiences, thereby arriving at concepts or ideas that we can remember (Hintzman and Ludham, 1980).

In addition to this apparently natural tendency to look for relationships, there is evidence that many of our organizations of related concepts or ideas (many of our frames or schemata) result from the application of strategies we have *learned*. More than this, as we become aware of various strategies that we can use to make sense of the world (and to learn and remember), we also become aware of ourselves as organisms capable of learning and remembering. Not only do we learn things, but we also learn about learning. Put another way, we develop *metacognitive* skills.

METACOGNITION

Young children are far less able to organize material than are older children and adults. More than this, they are less aware of the importance of doing so. They are not yet reflective about themselves as knowers and have not yet recognized the special skills that allow them to extract information, to organize, to learn, and, later, to remember. Put another way, they know far less about knowing; they understand less about understanding (Flavell, 1985). In the current jargon, they have not yet developed the skills of **metacognition** or **metamemory**.

Metacognition is knowing about knowing. Similarly, metamemory involves knowing about remembering. Because knowing necessarily involves remembering, metacognition includes metamemory.

The skills of metacognition allow us to monitor our progress when we try to understand and learn something. They provide us with ways of estimating the effects of our efforts, and they allow us to predict the likelihood of being able to remember the material later. Metacognitive knowledge tells us that there are ways of organizing material to make it easier to learn and remember; that some rehearsal and review strategies are more effective for one kind of material than another; and that some forms of learning require the deliberate application of certain strategies, whereas others don't.

As we noted earlier, metacognitive skills seem to be largely absent in young children. This doesn't mean that they make no use of cognitive strategies; it simply means that they are not aware of them and do not apply them consciously. By the same token, young children are far less able to monitor, evaluate, and direct their own learning. In most instances, they don't realize that there are strategies that might make it easier to learn and remember. When Moynahan (1973) asked young children whether it would be easier to learn a categorized list of words or a randomly ordered list, children below third grade chose either list with approximately equal frequency. In contrast, older children almost invariably chose the categorized list; they knew more about knowing.

We appear to have a tendency to extract generalities from experience, as well as to learn how to learn and remember. As we learn how to learn, we begin to see ourselves as players of Flavell's (1985) game of cognition, and we become aware of an increasing number and variety of strategies that can make us better players of this game. The object of the game of cognition is not to beat someone at something. Winners of this game are those who are successful in making sense of information and who can recall and use it effectively.

Some people play the game of cognition badly. They learn and remember with difficulty; much that they encounter is bewildering and frustrating. Others play the game very well. They learn rapidly and with apparent ease; their understanding is often startling.

One of the differences between those who play the game of cognition well and those who play it less well may have to do with how clearly each understands the process of learning and remembering — in other words, it has to do with metacognitive skills. It may be that those who play the game best are those who have learned more about learning and who are better able to apply what they have learned. In addition, the difference between the two may, at least in part, be a difference in cognitive strategies.

COGNITIVE STRATEGIES

Simply defined, cognitive strategies are the tools of intellectual activity. With respect to a school situation, E. Gagné (1985, p. 33) defines cognitive strategies as "goal-directed sequences of cognitive operations that lead from the student's comprehension of a question or instructions to the answer or other requested performance."

There are different kinds and levels of cognitive strategies, some of which appear to develop naturally. Many, however, are learned in schools, sometimes as a result of direct tuition, but more often simply as a result of repeated exposure to certain types of problems that require specific types of strategies. In fact, one of the important functions of schools is to provide learners not only with content, but also with knowledge about ways of organizing, analyzing, synthesizing, evaluating, creating, and so on (Gagné and Dick, 1983). In other words, schools teach much more than content; they also teach students how to learn and remember — they teach cognitive strategies. Historically, most of this teaching (and learning) has occurred incidentally, in the course of teaching other things. Recently, however, a number of concerted attempts have been made to develop programs designed specifically to teach cognitive strategies. Several of these programs are reviewed in some detail in Chapter 5.

Cognitive strategies allow us to learn, to solve problems, to study, and to understand. The strategy itself has little to do with the content of what is learned. It is a generalized approach, a "contentless" series of tactics or procedures (Gagné and Briggs, 1983). Accordingly, attempts to teach cognitive strategies are sometimes quite abstract and generalized, although they need not be. Indeed, Bransford et al. (1986) suggest that teachers relate cognitive strategies to specific subject areas and show students the importance of these techniques for solving problems in their own lives.

Learning/Thinking Strategies

The teaching/learning process has two broad classes of goals. Weinstein and Mayer (1986) describe these as goals relating to the products of learning and goals relating to the process of learning. Goals that relate to the products of learning are the *what* of the instructional process — the information being taught. Goals that have to do with the process of learning are the *how* of learning — the skills and strategies that can be used in acquiring and processing content; that is, they deal with *learning to learn*.

Cognitive psychology's most important current contribution to educational psychology is a renewed emphasis on the second of these major goals: learning to learn. There is little doubt, as is pointed out in Chapter 5, that what Mulcahy et al. (1986) call **learning/thinking strategies** can be taught systematically and deliberately — that they need not be acquired haphazardly and incompletely, solely as a function of repeated practice with different classes of problems.

The phrase *learning/thinking strategy* is preferable to the expression *cognitive strategy* in this context. It is a broader term, including not only specific strategies such as rehearsing or elaborating, but metacognition as well. In addition, it emphasizes that the strategies and processes involved in learning to learn are the very same processes that we ordinarily define as thinking. Put another way, learning/thinking strategies are the learner's information-processing/thinking tools.

And what, you may ask, are these learning/thinking strategies?

Researchers have identified many specific learning/thinking strategies. Weinstein and Mayer's (1986) description of eight categories of what they term *learning strategies* is one of the most useful and logical descriptions of what we refer to here as *learning/thinking strategies.**

Recall from earlier sections of this chapter that our basic information-processing model (the memory model) describes three main processes or activities involved in maintaining material in short-term memory and encoding and transferring it to long-term memory: rehearsal, elaboration, and organization. There are learning strategies, Weinstein and Mayer tell us, for each of these processes. Some are very basic; others are more complex. Accordingly, there are basic rehearsal strategies, complex rehearsal strategies, basic elaboration strategies, complex elaboration strategies, basic organizational strategies, and complex organizational strategies. And, in addition to these six classes of learning strategies, there are comprehension-monitoring strategies, which are essentially identical to what we have described as metacognitive skills, and affective and motivational strategies, which direct our attention, maintain our interest, and help us to relax and control impediments to learning and thinking (such as test anxiety).

Table 3.2 summarizes these eight classes of learning/thinking strategies and gives a simple example of each.

Educational Applications of the Cognitive Perspective

As we saw in Chapter 2, the behavioristic approaches to learning in humans lead to a number of instructional recommendations. Among other things, such approaches emphasize the importance of reinforcement, and they attempt to sort out the particular kinds and schedules of rewards and punishments that are most effective in the classroom. Later (in Chapters 12 and 13, for example), we will see that behaviorism has also led to very specific techniques for behavior modification.

At first glance, the educational implications of the cognitive perspective seem quite different from those of behaviorism. After all, cognitivism is concerned much less with behavior, stimuli, rewards, and punishments than with *thinking*. It asks, how do children become thinkers? and how can we make better, more critical, more creative thinkers of them?

The cognitive perspective suggests a two-pronged answer to these important questions. First, learners must develop an awareness of themselves as thinkers/learners/information processors; and second, they must develop and practice the approaches and strategies involved in critical, creative, and effective thinking and problem solving. Put another way, the cognitive perspective argues that learners must develop metacognitive skills as well as appropriate cognitive strategies. These are the skills involved in learning to learn.

As we noted earlier, schools have tradition-

PPC: "Terms such as *cognitive strategies, metacognition, intellectual skills, learning/thinking strategies,* and *metacognitive strategies* are used in different ways in the literature. This can be very confusing. Maybe the bear could straighten things out, once and for all."
Author: "Perhaps not once and for all, but for the time being, see the box entitled 'Sorting It All Out Cognitively.'"

Table 3.2   Categories of learning/thinking strategies

Basic Rehearsal Strategies	Simple repetition: "*amo, amas, amat, amamus, amatis, amant*"
Complex Rehearsal Strategies	Highlighting all the important points in a text
Basic Elaboration Strategies	Forming mental images or other associations such as "Men very easily make jugs serve useful nocturnal purposes" (the first letter of each word stands for a planet in the solar system)
Complex Elaboration Strategies	Forming analogies, paraphrasing, summarizing, relating
Basic Organizational Strategies	Grouping, classifying, ordering
Complex Organizational Strategies	Identifying main ideas; developing concept-summarizing tables such as this one
Comprehension-Monitoring Strategies	Self-questioning; reciting main points; setting goals and checking progress toward those goals
Affective and Motivational Strategies	Anticipating consequences of academic success (for example, a scholarship); deep breathing and other relaxation activities; positive thinking

Source: Based on C. E. Weinstein and R. E. Mayer. "The Teaching of Learning Strategies." In M. C. Wittrock (ed.), *Handbook of Research on Teaching* (3rd ed.), New York: Macmillan, 1986, 315–327.

ally devoted the bulk of their formal efforts to teaching specific curriculum content; the learning of cognitive strategies and the development of metacognitive awareness have been largely incidental—and sometimes accidental. Recently, however, an increasing number of researchers have developed programs designed specifically to develop cognitive skills in learners. Many of these programs are designed both to make students aware of the existence of cognitive strategies and to teach them to monitor and evaluate their use of these strategies. Such programs advocate a variety of approaches to teaching, including group learning (for example, cooperative learning), individual instruction (for example, teachers' questions designed to foster specific thinking skills), modeling procedures (in which, for example, a cognitive strategy is verbalized as it is being executed),

and various programs in which learners are trained in the use of specific strategies (see, for example, Mulcahy et al., 1990). These programs are described in some detail and evaluated in Chapter 5.

TEACHING FOR RETRIEVAL

Several characteristics of long-term memory are of particular significance for teachers. Material that is meaningful is learned more easily and remembered for longer periods of time than insignificant material. In much the same way, events that are particularly striking tend to be recalled more easily and more clearly (Bower, 1981). Less striking events can be recalled easily over long periods of time if they

Sorting It All Out Cognitively

The following are some common, educationally relevant terms in the new cognitive sciences:

Metacognition

Knowing about knowing; our knowledge about our own cognitive processes and about cognitive processes in general. This knowledge permits us to select different approaches for learning and remembering; it allows us to monitor our cognitive activities and assess the likelihood of success; it suggests alternatives when necessary.

Cognitive Strategies

The tools of cognitive behavior; goal-directed sequences of actions such as rehearsing, organizing, or elaborating; what we actually do to learn and remember.

Learning/Thinking Strategies

A global term that includes both metacognitive and cognitive skills; the entire range of activities involved in learning and thinking.

Summary

Learning/thinking strategies include metacognitive and cognitive strategies. Metacognitive skills are executive (control) skills; cognitive skills are non-executive (applied) skills.

Illustration of the Relationships Between Metacognition and Cognition

I decide to learn the meanings of common, educationally relevant terms in the new cognitive sciences (setting a goal of which I suspect I am capable: a metacognitive experience). I begin to read this box (cognitive activity). I stop after two lines; I have a vague feeling that I have missed something (metacognitive experience). I read the lines again (cognitive activity). I sense that I am understanding (metacognition). I continue reading. I repeat each separate definition mentally once or twice (rehearsal, a cognitive strategy). Something tells me I am learning (metacognitive experience). I finish. I look at each term and silently repeat the definition (cognitive action). I am satisfied that I understand and will remember until tomorrow's quiz (metacognition).

are frequently rehearsed. A common psychological expression for the rehearsal of material that has already been committed to memory is *overlearning*. Overlearning serves as insurance against forgetting. Students are often asked to overlearn multiplication tables; some of us overlearn telephone numbers, social security numbers, and similar items.

Whereas short-term memory has very limited capacity, long-term memory stores appear to be almost limitless. As we saw, short-term memory—which frequently is measured by having individuals repeat digits that they have just seen or heard—appears to be limited to seven discrete items of information. Psychological research has not demonstrated that, after a lifetime of learning, our long-term memories become so crowded that we find ourselves incapable of learning new material until we have forgotten some of the old. But what does seem to happen on occasion is that old and new learning interfere with each other, making retrieval difficult. Our problems with memory may be not so much forgetting as not being able to recall. There is a difference.

Other findings from memory research that are important for our purposes are concerned largely with the characteristics of material that can easily be remembered. As noted earlier, organized and meaningful material appears to be easier to learn and remember than disorganized and meaningless material. Similarly, visual material has an impact on memory that is seldom equaled by other kinds of materials. Standing (1973) showed subjects 10,000 pictures; later he showed them some of the same pictures paired with pictures the subjects had not seen. Subjects were able to recognize as many as 90 percent of the pictures they had already seen. It is not surprising that most of the powerful memory aids described later in this chapter make extensive use of visual imagery.

WHY WE FORGET ✳

Knowledge of the characteristics of long-term memory can be of considerable value for teachers; so too can knowledge of why we forget and of what can be done to impede the process. Although no one knows precisely what the physiology of memory is or what happens when forgetting takes place, a number of theories have been advanced to explain these processes.

Fading

One theory holds that material that is not brought to mind frequently enough (that is not used) tends to fade from memory. I know at this moment that the oldest recorded age at which a woman has given birth to a live infant is fifty-seven. This fact was brought to my attention as I perused *The Guinness Book of World Records* in search of a record that I might break. Unless I review this information again, or have it brought to mind by someone or something, I probably won't remember it next year at this time. It will have faded.

Distortion

Not only does material fade from memory with the passage of time, but that which doesn't fade entirely is often distorted. In Ausubel's (1963) terminology, the material becomes *subsumed* under other material, becomes similar to it, and in the end becomes indistinguishable from it. It is now difficult for me to remember a specific sunset accurately; I have seen so many that even the most striking ones have become distorted until, in my memory of sunsets, there isn't a single one that looks very different from any other. It's sad but true. My sunrises fare better (probably because I haven't seen as many). The notable unreliability of eyewitnesses (Loftus, 1979) is another illustration of memory distortion.

Suppression

It appears that people tend to forget events that are particularly unpleasant. One explanation for this phenomenon derives from the work of Sigmund Freud, who maintained that unpleasant memories filter into the subconscious mind, where the individual is not aware of them even though they continue to have some effect on the person's emotional life. Suppression theory is partially supported by the observation that many mothers don't remember very clearly how painful giving birth is.

Interference

The most popular theory of forgetting, one that has direct relevance for teachers, says that interference from previous or subsequent learning is an important cause of forgetting. When previous learning interferes with present recall,

proactive inhibition is said to occur; **retroactive inhibition** takes place when subsequent learning interferes with recall of previous learning. Teachers often have difficulty remembering the names of new students, especially if they have been teaching for a long time and have known many students with similar names. It becomes easy to confuse old names with new but similar faces. By the same token, once teachers have learned the names of all their current students, they sometimes find it difficult to remember the names of students from years past. The first case illustrates proactive inhibition; the second, retroactive inhibition.

Poor Retrieval

Some psychologists maintain that forgetting can often be accounted for by the inability to retrieve from memory rather than by simple memory loss, distortion, suppression, or interference. In other words, individuals appear not to remember simply because they are unable to find a way of recalling an item of information from memory; presumably they do not possess good retrieval cues.

EDUCATIONAL IMPLICATIONS OF THE THEORIES OF FORGETTING

In summary, information may be forgotten because it has faded through disuse; because it has been distorted, suppressed, or interfered with; or because the individual does not have the proper retrieval cues. One of the important functions of a teacher is to transmit information, attitudes, and skills that will not all be forgotten. Knowledge of why people forget can help in this task.

If students forget because of disuse (fading theory), teachers can provide repetition and review to remind them of important items and to bring about overlearning. Similarly, the effects of distortion can be partially overcome by being careful to emphasize the most important and distinct (the most *memorable*) aspects of a situation.

Suppression theory does not suggest any simple educational applications. It is to be hoped that you will not provide your students with experiences that need to be suppressed. In any case, you would probably be ill-advised to attempt to prevent suppression or to bring back to memory those experiences that have been suppressed.

Allowing time to elapse between lessons and organizing them to make use of similarities and differences may help overcome the effects of interference. And organizing material may partially overcome the retrieval problem, particularly if the organization facilitates the identification of relationships.

Among the most important suggestions for increasing recallability of information are those relating to the use of similarities and differences among items of information, a topic touched upon in the section on generalization and discrimination in Chapter 2. These topics are frequently treated under the heading of *transfer* (or *generalization*); the term refers to the effects of old learning on new learning. Transfer can be either positive or negative. Positive transfer occurs when previous learning facilitates new learning; it is sometimes clearly evident in learning second languages. It is considerably easier, for example, to learn Latin if you know French than if you know only English; the similarities between French and Latin facilitate positive transfer. Negative transfer occurs when previous learning interferes with current learning; it is very similar to proactive interference. Negative transfer occurs, for example, when you or I go to Bermuda, rent a motor scooter, and discover that all the traffic is on the wrong side of the street.

One of the obvious ways of teaching for positive transfer while at the same time eliminating negative transfer is, as was suggested above, to relate new material to old material, emphasizing similarities and differences. The similarities should facilitate positive transfer; knowledge of differences should minimize negative transfer.

SPECIFIC MEMORY AIDS

In addition to these general approaches, there are a number of well-known techniques for improving memory, most of which are simple illustrations of some of the learning/thinking strategies described earlier and summarized in Table 3.2.

Many memory aids, or mnemonic devices, make use of specific retrieval cues. Rhymes, patterns, acronyms, and acrostics are common mnemonic devices. "Thirty days hath September . . ." is a simple rhyme without which many of us would not know how many days hath November. Similarly, the year in which Columbus sailed the ocean blue is nicely recalled by the little rhyme. The number "five million, five hundred fifty-one thousand, two hundred twelve" is considerably more difficult to remember than the number 555-1212; "triple five, double twelve" may be even easier. The mnemonic aid of chunking makes use of patterns.

Acronyms are letter cues that help to recall relatively complex material. NATO, U.N., and UNESCO are popular acronyms. ROY G. BIV is another acronym, made up of the first letters of the words for the ordered colors of the visible light spectrum. Acrostics are similar to acronyms, except that they generally make use of sentences in which the first letter of each word represents an item of information to be remembered. Without the bizarre sentence "Men very easily make jugs serve useful nocturnal purposes," I would have considerable difficulty recalling the planets in order from the sun. "Every good boy does fine" is meaningful to beginning music students.

A number of more complex mnemonic techniques have been described in detail by Higbee (1977) and are reviewed briefly here. All have one thing in common: They make extensive use of imagery. Recall that visual material appears to have a greater impact on memory and can be retrieved much more easily than most nonvisual material.

The simplest of these techniques is the **link system**. It requires the subject to visualize the item to be remembered and to form a strong visual association (link) between it and other items to be remembered. It is easily illustrated with reference to a grocery list. (Once you have mastered this system, you need never write a grocery list again.) Suppose the list contains the following items: bread, salt, ketchup, dog food, and bananas. Visualize the first item. The picture that comes to mind first should be concentrated on because it is likely to come to mind again when you think of bread. It might be bizarre, or it might be a simple image of a plain white loaf or slice of bread. Now visualize the second item, salt, and form a visual link between the first image and the second. You might, for example, see a slice of bread perched delicately on a large silver saltshaker. The saltshaker is dripping with ketchup being poured from a bottle held by a hungry dog with a banana in its ear. In most cases, you need not spend more than a few seconds with each image, nor should these be rehearsed while you are learning the list.

The link system works amazingly well, although it has disadvantages. One is that it is sometimes difficult to remember the first item on the list. In that case, it might also be impossible to remember any of the other items because they are linked one to the other. This problem can be overcome by forming a visual association between the first item and a setting that is likely to remind you of the item. You might, for example, see the loaf of bread reclining in a grocery cart. A second disadvantage of the link system is that if one of the items is not recalled, none of the subsequent items is likely to be recalled.

A variation of the link system, the **loci system**, overcomes this second disadvantage. In effect, in the loci system you simply form associations between items to be remembered and places that are very familiar to you and that can therefore be visualized very clearly. Rooms in a familiar house make good loci (*locus:* Latin, meaning "place"). A grocery list such as that given above can quite easily be "placed" in the rooms of a house simply by forming strong visual images of the objects, one in each of the rooms. The advantage of this system is that if you cannot remember what you placed in the hallway, you can always go to the bathroom.

A third mnemonic system, the **phonetic system**, is by far the most powerful, although it requires considerably more effort. Indeed, if you master this system, you could become a professional mnemonist. At the very least, you will impress your grandmother. The phonetic system allows an individual to recall items in order; backwards; by twos, threes, fours; or perhaps even more impressive, to recall any specific item (for example, the fourteenth item listed).

The first step in learning the system is to make an association between numbers and consonants. (Vowels do not count in the system.) Traditionally, the number 1 is represented by a letter such as *t* or *l*, because each has a single downstroke; the number 2 might be represented by an *n*, because it has two downstrokes; 3 is *m* and 9 is *p* because each member of the pairs resembles the other. Once you have associated a letter with each digit, you can then form words that represent numbers. Thus the number 13 might be *tam, tome,* or *team* (remember, vowels do not count); the number 21 might be *nut* or *net*; and so on. The next step is simply to form a strong visual image of each of the words that correspond to numbers (1 through 25, for example). Having done so, you can stand on stage and have your audience describe or show you twenty-five items, which are recorded in order by your assistant, on a large

chalkboard that remains out of your sight. By forming strong visual associations between each of these items and your number-linked words, you can then recall all twenty-five items in any order, or any specific item by its number of appearance. For example, if the twenty-first item the audience displays is a shoe, you visualize a shoe caught in a net (*net* representing 21).

This must have some classroom implication. Surely.

MAIN POINTS

1. Some of our learning involves apparently random behaviors (trial and error) and resulting reinforcement and punishment; behaviorism studies this type of learning. However, much of our learning seems to be guided by strategies, patterns, and hypotheses, as well as by a recognition of (or a search for) order and meaning in our experiences; these are the concern of cognitive psychology.

2. Cognitivism is a perspective whose primary emphasis is on the mental events involved in knowing, acquiring information, solving problems, and remembering.

3. Cognitive psychology is a psychology of metaphor. Its models are not intended to be literal descriptions of the way things are but simply useful representations.

4. To cognize is to know; hence cognitive psychology deals with knowledge and with knowing and is necessarily concerned with perceiving, organizing, thinking, and remembering. In essence, it looks at three things: the knowledge base (storehouse of information); cognitive strategies (processes used in learning and thinking); and metacognition (awareness of the self as a knower; capacity to understand and monitor cognitive processes).

5. Computers present a useful analogy or metaphor for human cognitive functioning. The branch of computer science concerned with parallels between computer hardware or functioning and human neurological structure or functioning is called *artificial intelligence*.

6. One of the basic models of cognitive psychology describes the learner as an information-processing and storage system. This model includes three levels or types of storage: sensory memory, short-term memory, and long-term memory.

7. Sensory storage involves no more than the immediate, momentary availability of sensory data for processing and perhaps for longer-term storage. All the sensations to which we are not presently attending go in and out of sensory storage in a matter of a fraction of a second. Sensory memory is unconscious.

8. Material to which we attend is processed into short-term storage, where it is maintained for perhaps as long as twenty seconds. The principal processing or control function that occurs at this level is rehearsal (repetition). Without rehearsal, material fades very quickly from short-term memory. Short-term memory is immediate in consciousness or awareness and is also called *working memory*.

9. Short-term memory appears to be limited to seven (plus or minus two) discrete items. However, its absolute capacity can be quite large in view of the fact that each of these seven items might consist of "chunks" of related material.

10. The short-term memories of young children are limited (to two or three items before age 6 as compared with seven plus or minus two items for adolescents and adults). This may explain some of children's difficulties in understanding and solving problems.

11. Material is transferred from short-term to long-term memory through a process called *encoding*. Essentially, encoding involves transforming or changing and is defined in terms of the processes by which we abstract generalities and derive meaning from our experiences.

12. Craik and Lockhart's levels-of-processing theory suggests that the extent and duration of memory result from the level to which information is processed. Thus, we are not conscious of material that is not processed, and it remains in sensory storage for only a fraction of a second; material that is attended to and rehearsed is held in short-term storage for a matter of seconds; and material that is encoded finds its way into long-term memory. Encoding might occur at a superficial level (paying attention to the structure of a word, for example), or at a deeper level (taking into account the meaning of a word—termed *semantic encoding*).

13. A traditional model of memory portrays the mind as a catalogue or motion-picture-like recording of a sequence of experiences. This model is nonassociationistic. Contemporary models of long-term memory are associationistic; they hold that material in memory is organized according to relationships—that everything in memory is associated with something else.

14. Terms such as *node, frame,* or *schema* are metaphors for the organization of knowledge (or, alternately, for the organization of memory).

15. Long-term memory does not simply reproduce events or images as a photograph does, but instead generates or constructs as a painter does. It often forgets or distorts

events that have happened, and it sometimes recalls events that have not.

16. Three important processes are involved in capturing a sensory impression and holding it in consciousness or encoding it for long-term storage: rehearsal (repetition); elaboration (extending); and organization (relating; sorting).

17. We not only learn things, but we also learn about learning. Knowledge about our own cognitive processes is termed *metacognition*. The skills of metacognition allow us to direct, monitor, evaluate, and modify our ongoing learning and thinking.

18. *Cognitive strategy* is one label for the tools of cognitive behavior. When schools teach students *how to learn* (as opposed to teaching them the *what* or the content of learning), they teach cognitive strategies.

19. The term *learning/thinking strategy* emphasizes that strategies are involved in thinking as well as in learning. Weinstein and Mayer describe eight classes of learning/thinking strategies: the first six are rehearsal, elaboration, and organizational strategies for either basic or complex problems; the last two are comprehension-monitoring strategies (strategies of metacognition) and affective (motivational) strategies.

20. Cognitivism asks, How do children become thinkers? How can we make better, more critical, more creative thinkers of them? Part of its answer is: By making them aware of themselves as knowers and information processors (metacognitive skills), and by teaching them specific cognitive strategies (for example, how to rehearse, organize, monitor, and so on).

21. Useful strategies for teaching for retrieval often emphasize meaningfulness, organization, visual imagery, rehearsal, and overlearning.

22. Theories of forgetting maintain that information is forgotten because it is unused, distorted, suppressed, or interfered with, or because the individual has a poor retrieval system.

23. Theories of forgetting suggest that teachers should both emphasize distinct and important aspects of situations and stress similarities and differences in order to minimize interference and maximize transfer.

24. Mnemonic devices include rhymes, patterns, acrostics, and acronyms. More complex mnemonic techniques are the link system, the loci system, and the phonetic system. Each of these is based on the principle that visual imagery is an extremely powerful aid to memory.

SUGGESTED READINGS

A short but excellent introduction to cognitive psychology is presented in:

MAYER, R. E. (1981). *The promise of cognitive psychology*. San Francisco: Freeman.

Ellen Gagné's book is a clear and detailed description of contemporary cognitive psychology and its implications for education. The author looks at the application of cognitive science in specific subject areas:

GAGNÉ, E. D. (1985). *The cognitive psychology of school learning*. Boston: Little, Brown.

Several chapters in the third edition of the Handbook of Research on Teaching *are relevant to cognitive psychology — especially the chapter by Claire F. Weinstein and Richard Mayer:*

WITTROCK, M. C. (Ed.). (1986). *Handbook of research on teaching*. New York: Macmillan.

A summary of research and theory on memory in childhood is presented in:

BRAINERD, C. J., & PRESSLEY, M. (Eds.). (1985). *Basic processes in memory development: Progress in cognitive development research*. New York: Springer-Verlag.

Fascinating accounts of the unreliability of eyewitness testimony are contained in:

LOFTUS, E. F. (1979). *Eyewitness testimony.* Cambridge, Mass.: Harvard University Press.

A highly readable, informative, and practical discussion of memory and mnemonic aids is provided in:

HIGBEE, K. L. (1977). *Your memory: How it works and how to improve it.* Englewood Cliffs, N.J.: Prentice-Hall.

Sternberg's highly readable book presents some of the flavor of current interest in cognitive strategies and includes various suggestions for improving intelligence:

STERNBERG, R. J. (1986). *Intelligence applied: Understanding and increasing your intellectual skills.* New York: Harcourt Brace Jovanovich.

The Esquimaux believe that the soul of a wounded bear tarries near the spot where it leaves its body. Many taboos and propitiatory ceremonies are observed with regard to the slaughtering of the carcass and the consumption of the flesh (Engel, 1976, p. 69).

APPROACHES TO COGNITIVE LEARNING IN SCHOOLS

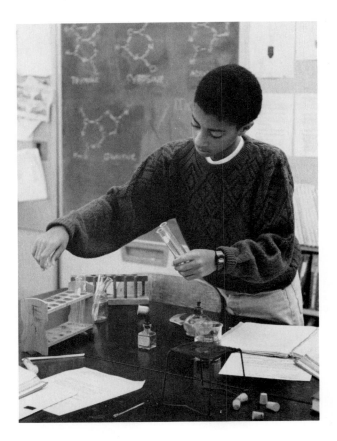

Some folks are wise, and some are otherwise.

TOBIAS SMOLLETT *Roderick Random*

If a little knowledge is dangerous, where is the man who has so much as to be out of danger?

THOMAS HENRY HUXLEY *Science and Culture*

PREVIEW Decision making, problem solving, analyzing and synthesizing, evaluating, and other manifestations of the *cognitive* functions that are involved in what we ordinarily think of as *thinking* — these all qualify as higher mental processes. This chapter discusses higher mental processes and presents two theoretical approaches to cognitive functions. Each leads to explicitly different instructional implications. Bruner's theory argues for discovery-oriented learning; Ausubel's makes a strong case for a more didactic approach. The merits of each are examined.

■ *Just when it looked like it would disappear at the end of the tunnel, the fat blue one turned, opened its great red mouth and, with an awesome crunch and a huge belch, swallowed me whole.*

My son, who was then seven, thought this was very funny. But when he started down the same tunnel, he quickly found himself wedged between another of the blue ones and three of the smaller, cow-like yellow ones. I saw him hesitate momentarily as the red mouth opened. "He's a goner too," I thought. But quick as an instant, he whirled behind the great blue monster and, before it could turn on him, pricked its scaly hide with his lance. It deflated at once with a loud "Chleb" (a sort of reverse belch), spraying the tunnel with a fine bluish mist that hid the cows and allowed my son to escape into another room. There he soon encountered an army of three-legged things, each with a huge menacing eye and a single claw. Defying all odds, the boy leapt boldly over the first thing, scurried between the legs of the second, and ran

smack into the third. Cackling insanely, it reached out with its single claw, grabbed him by the seat of the pants, and lifted him high in the air, holding him there, wriggling and screaming, until another of the fat, waddling, blue things appeared. Then it tossed him, almost carelessly it seemed, spinning through the air and into the huge red mouth. "Belch!"

Another nightmare? No. Just a new computer game that we had purchased earlier that day and were now trying to learn — he because he enjoys playing these games, and I because surely an educational psychologist can squeeze out one or two lessons from learning a new computer game.

My first step in learning this game was to sit and read the directions — completely, carefully, and with the full benefit of years of experience in reading and following directions. My son's first step was to take the controls, start the game, and promptly get himself devoured by the blue thing with the red mouth — again and again and again, each time with a great crunch and a roaring belch. Distracted by this gruesome sound, I escaped to my study, where I could concentrate more easily. "Grip the control in either the right or left hand," I read, "and move the lever in any direction. Note how Varvok goes up, down, left, or right. Now spin the lever to make Varvok turn. See how his lance always points in front of him. To thrust with the lance, press the 'Fire' button on your control." And on and on, through more than a dozen pages describing how each of the creatures in the Caves of Zarool can move, in what way each is dangerous, and how each can be avoided, slain, or transformed into an ally. "Varvok's mission," the instructions informed me, "is to reach Zarool and slay him before he can finish his new formula, which will turn the moon into chocolate pudding and darken the Earth's nights."

"I will gladly make chocolate pudding of him," I chortled as I returned to the computer.

"What you have to do is get to the guy in the cave, Zarool," I explained as I took the controls. "You get past the blue ones by jumping behind them and spearing them, and you can jump over the yellow ones. The red ones throw big blobs of pudding, which you have to dodge unless you can get your spear into them. And the green ones . . . Here's a blue one. Watch as I spin. . . ."

"Chleb!" ▬

KNOWING

Sometimes there is clearly more involved in *knowing* than is made possible by reading, understanding, and remembering. The Caves of Zarool are a case in point. Although I *knew* with utmost clarity and precision the nature of each of Zarool's creatures—how each moves, attacks, destroys, and can itself be avoided, attacked, or destroyed; although I knew the sequence of obstacles that Varvok must surmount in order to reach Zarool; and although I knew Zarool's only weak point (his right heel—like Achilles)—still, I apparently did not really know how to play the game. Yet my seven-year-old son, who had not read the directions and who therefore began to play the game from a totally different knowledge base, could nevertheless slay blue monsters, leap over the bristling, one-eyed, clawed ones, dodge through great clouds of flying puddings, and, in the end, threaten Zarool's very existence.

"Perhaps," I thought, ever the psychologist, "he has learned through trial, error, and reinforcement! And I have learned exactly the same thing, but cognitively to begin with!" For example, his moves were clearly influenced by reinforcement (escaping from a creature or slaying it) and punishment (being captured, eaten, squished, chained to a cave wall, or other-

wise disposed of). In addition, there appeared to be a great deal of trial and error involved in the learning, particularly in the early stages when he had little idea what the object of the game was or what obstacles there might be to attaining success. Surely this is an excellent example of learning through trial and error.

But as I watched him play and learn this game, it soon became apparent that real life is seldom as simple as our theories, and that there might be more to my son's learning of the Caves of Zarool than can easily be explained by means of simple behavioristic theories. True, his behaviors continued to be responsive to the obvious rewards and punishments inflicted on poor chewed-up Varvok; but they also appeared to be guided by his increasing recognition of the strategies and patterns governing the behaviors of the various enemies. "Why did you move there?" I asked once, and he quickly answered, "Because I think they always come in threes, the orange ones, and right after is another of the big blues and I can get behind it if I go that way. It's a lot like the Big Bang." Apparently his learning involved a search for regularities (patterns and strategies); the generation of hypotheses ("If I move this way . . ."); and generalization from previous knowledge ("This is like the Big Bang"). In other words, his learning was at least partly cognitive.

EXPLAINING COGNITIVE LEARNING

As we saw in Chapter 3, cognitive approaches to human behavior stress the importance of the learner's previous knowledge and skills. Unlike behaviorism, which tends to view all learners as initially equal—as equally susceptible to the effects of the consequences of behavior—cognitivism emphasizes that we often derive different *meanings* from experience and that we consequently learn different things.

Common to most cognitive theories is the basic assumption that the learner is an actual processor of information. Accordingly, these theories attempt to analyze learning in terms of what is often labeled **cognitive structure**. At a simple level, cognitive structure is the content of the mind. It includes concepts, relationships that the learner establishes among concepts, and strategies used in abstracting concepts and in organizing them in long-term memory. Terms such as *schema* or *script* are often used to describe cognitive structure.

Schemata and Scripts

Cognitive theorists strongly emphasize that knowledge does not exist in a vacuum — that rather it depends on relationships. As E. Gagné (1985) puts it: "All of a person's declarative knowledge can be conceptualized as a large network of interrelated propositions." In this context, **declarative knowledge** consists of all the facts we have learned and all the experiences we have had. In short, declarative knowledge involves knowing that something is the case. Declarative knowledge is contrasted with **procedural knowledge**, which involves knowing how to do something (that is, knowing a procedure for doing something). Procedural knowledge, too, derives its meaningfulness from interrelationships (Anderson, 1983).

The idea that knowledge consists of networks of relationships is not new. Recall from Chapter 3 that our contemporary models of long-term memory are invariably associationistic; that is, they are models of *relationships.* What is new, however, is the recent upsurge of interest in exploring this idea in an effort to understand how we learn and know things and how we think. Thinking, according to this approach, involves the manipulation of what is represented mentally. In other words, it involves manipulating and forming relationships among items of information (Hunt, 1989). This chapter simplifies and illustrates this central idea and looks at some of its educational implications.

First, to simplify. Why do we say that knowledge and understanding depend on interrelationships among items of information? What does this concept mean?

Consider the following passage:

If the balloons popped, the sound wouldn't be able to carry since everything would be too far away from the correct floor. A closed window would also prevent the sound from carrying, since most buildings tend to be well insulated. Since the whole operation depends on a steady flow of electricity, a break in the middle of the wire would also cause problems. Of course, the fellow could shout, but the human voice is not loud enough to carry that far. An additional problem is that a string could break on the instrument. Then there would be no accompaniment to the message. It is clear that the best situation would involve less distance. Then there would be fewer potential problems. With face to face contact, the least number of things could go wrong. (Bransford and Johnson, 1973, pp. 392–393)

If you find this passage confusing and unclear, don't despair; so does almost everyone else. It's a frustrating experience because the language is clear and simple, the sentences are short and straightforward, none of the concepts is very difficult — yet the whole thing makes no sense.

Turn now to Figure 4.1 and glance at the illustration.

Now the passage makes sense. Why? Simply because the illustration provides a framework within which to understand; it activates what a number of cognitive psychologists refer to as a **schema** (plural: *schemata*).

Schemata are metaphors for cognitive structure and functioning. They are like clusters of related items of knowledge that define concepts. They are what we know about things. For example, schemata relevant to understanding the "balloon" passage include, among other things, our knowledge that balloons filled with lighter-than-air substances will rise, our recognition of the musical equipment involved, and certain assumptions about the intentions and motives of the serenader and the "serenadee." Note that each of these concepts is defined by one or more

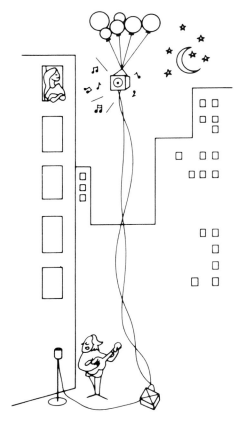

Figure 4.1 From J. D. Bransford and M. K. Johnson, "Consideration of Some Problems in Comprehension" (p. 394). In W. G. Chase (Ed.), *Visual Information Processing*. Copyright 1973 by Academic Press. Reprinted by permission of Academic Press, New York and J. D. Bransford.

relationships (for example, the relationship between weight and falling or rising, the relationship between musical sounds and a guitar, and so on).

One aspect of schemata that is important for learning and remembering real-life things is called a **script**. Schank and Abelson (1977) describe scripts as that part of cognitive structure that deals with routines and sequences. We all

know countless routines, countless scripts. We know, for example, that a sensible way of dressing is to put on undergarments, socks, shirts, pants, and shoes, more or less in that order. This is a verbal description of a common script. For dressing on a day like today in this somewhat harsh climate, I added putting on a parka and gloves to my script—in that order. Had I wanted to be creative this morning and alter my script (perhaps reversing it and beginning with gloves), I might have found dressing considerably more difficult and time-consuming. And I would have had to wear my socks over my shoes and my shorts over my jeans, in which case I would probably not have been courageous or foolish enough to visit the two schools where I was scheduled to observe a pair of student teachers.

Scripts, like schemata, deal with relationships. A script is, in a sense, an expression of sequential relationships. Scripts and schemata clearly have their uses. Nevertheless, they are still only metaphors that need to be made more concrete for our purposes.

Educational Applications of Cognitive Approaches

Cognitive approaches emphasize how information is processed. Accordingly, these approaches look at how we derive information from the environment; how we organize and interpret this information, teasing out relationships in order to abstract meaning from our experiences; how we organize and store meaning; and how our thought processes make use of what we have stored.

From the educator's point of view, these concerns translate directly into a renewed emphasis on cognitive strategies and a recognition of the importance of relationships among items of information. Specifically, they suggest two things: First, the school's curriculum (and the teacher's presentation of that curriculum) needs to be organized to reveal and emphasize important relationships; and second, the school should pay systematic and deliberate attention to developing strategies that are involved in perceiving, interpreting, organizing, analyzing, evaluating, storing, and retrieving information.

A number of cognitively based theories reflect these two educational applications especially clearly. Among them are the theories of Jerome Bruner and David Ausubel. In many important ways these theories are similar, although they use different terms to describe the units and processes of cognitive organization.* There is, however, one important respect in which the theories are dramatically different from each other: Bruner advocates that learners be guided toward organizing material for themselves, once they have been provided with opportunities to discover relationships. In contrast, Ausubel argues that in most cases the teacher can organize the material and present it to the student in relatively final form. In other words, Bruner is a strong advocate of **discovery learning**; Ausubel argues for **reception learning**.

BRUNER'S THEORY: CATEGORIZATION

Cognitive psychology, as we already learned, assumes that the learner is an *active information processor*. It asks how the learner derives information from the environment, how information is organized and interpreted, and how it is used. Jerome Bruner's theory provides one set of answers for these questions — and for many other questions as well. The emphasis in the following sections is on those aspects of his work that form a relatively unified theory of thinking. (For more information, see Bruner, 1973, and Bruner, Goodnow, and Austin, 1956.)

Thinking and Categorization

In everyday terms, to conceptualize is to think. In more psychological terms, to conceptualize is to form or to be aware of concepts. A **concept** can be defined as an abstraction that represents objects, experiences, or ideas having similar properties. *Purple* is a concept; it represents all wavelengths that are interpreted as similar because of their physical properties (as perceived by humans). *Human* is a concept that relates to all organisms that have two legs, two hands, binocular vision, and the ability to speak — in other words, to all organisms that are similar in specified ways. Note that *concept* is a concept that has to do with relationships.

Bruner uses the term **conceptualization** synonymously with the term **categorization**. To *categorize* is to form concepts. In other words, a **category** is a concept. In one sense, it is a representation of objects or events that have similar properties. For example, *bird* is a category that represents animals with feathers, wings, two legs, and beaks. In another sense, a category is a *rule*. It is a rule for classifying things as being equivalent — because whenever two objects are placed in the same category, the implication is that they are in some ways equal. Two objects that are placed in the category *bird* are equivalent in the sense that they each have feathers, wings, two feet, and one head. Indeed, they are both birds — and one bird equals another in terms of "birdness." In other words, they are *related*.

---

*PPC: "Wouldn't the bear find life a lot easier if all cognitive theorists agreed to use the same clearly defined vocabulary, rather than so many insisting on inventing their own meanings or, perhaps worse, their own terms? Weren't *schema* and *schemata* and *script* and *cognitive structure* enough — do we also need *coding systems* and *operations* and *categories* and *subsumers* and on and on?"
Author: "Yes and no; no, those terms aren't enough, and yes, we need a variety of terms. Besides, the bear is an old bear; he's seen much jargon come and go. 'The meaning is in the *meaning*,' he says, 'not in the jargon. Do you get my meaning?'"

Categories and Attributes

As a rule, a category specifies the important characteristics of the objects or events that it comprises. The category *bird* may be described as a set of four rules, as follows:

1. In order to be a bird, an object must have feathers, two legs, one head, and so on.

2. The head must be attached somewhere above the shoulders; the wings must be symmetrical and rest one on either side of the body; the feet must be in contact with the ground when the beast is standing; and so on.

3. Even if the object has only one or two feathers, it might still be a bird.

4. In order to be feathers, objects must possess certain characteristics. Heads are defined by specific properties, and legs must also conform to certain standards.

These four groups of rules may be more generally described in terms of the conditions they specify relative to **attributes** and **values**

(Bruner, Goodnow, and Austin, 1956). An *attribute* is a property or characteristic of an object or event. It is a property that can vary from one object to another and that can therefore sometimes be used in defining a category. *Values* are the variations that are possible for an attribute. For example, the attribute *red* can vary continuously from a yellowish orange to deep carmine; the attribute *sex*, on the other hand, ordinarily varies dichotomously — it is either male or female.

Categories, as rules, specify:

1. the attributes an object must possess

2. the way in which the attributes will be combined

3. the importance of various attributes, singly or in combination

4. the acceptance limits for values of the attributes

The list of rules presented earlier in relation to the category *bird* illustrates these four general specifications for membership in categories.

Whenever an attribute is used as part of the definition for a category, it is said to be a **criterial attribute**. Obviously, not all of an object's properties are essential for its placement in a category. One bird may have tufts of feathers on the back of its head; another may be completely bald. Yet both are birds. Therefore the *location* of feathers is irrelevant for the category *bird*.

Categorization and Human Functioning

Bruner suggests that our interaction with the world always involves categories. Activities such as **perception**, conceptualization, and decision making can all be described in terms of the formation and use of categories, which are not only useful but essential to understanding and dealing with the world. To simplify, categorization achieves at least five things for us (Bruner, Goodnow, and Austin, 1956).

First, categorization reduces the complexity of the environment. When we can respond to different objects as though they were the same, what would otherwise be an extremely bewildering array of isolated objects or events becomes much simpler. A large group of people can be considered a collection of arms, legs, mouths, and so on; but in addition it is something as simple as a crowd.

Second, categorizing permits the recognition of objects. Indeed, Bruner goes so far as to say that it is only through the use of categories that an object will be recognized. If it does not fit in any way into a category, then it cannot be identified; nor can the perceiver's experience of it ever be communicated. It is, in the words borrowed by Bruner, "doomed to be a gem serene, locked in the silence of private experience." In effect, an object is recognized because it is *like* other objects of its class. A pen is identified as a pen not only because it is elongated and because it can be used to make marks on papers and walls, but principally because it is, in these and other respects, like all other objects that are arbitrarily called *pen*.

Third, categorization reduces the necessity for constant learning. It does this by making it possible for individuals to go beyond the information given, an act that not only leads to the identification of an object but also permits making inferences about the object (Bruner, 1957a). Thus, every time you see an object as simple as a piece of chalk, you don't have to learn all over again that this object is chalk, that it is light and not very palatable, and that it can be used to draw lines on an object called a chalkboard. You need see only a small piece of chalk lying on a chalkboard ledge in order to leap immediately beyond this simple perception, identify the object, and make a host of inferences about its qualities and functions.

The fourth achievement of categorization is that it provides direction for activity. We don't know how to behave toward an object unless we can first categorize (and therefore recognize) it. Obviously, the act of running from an angry bear follows from the recognition that this is indeed not only a bear, but an angry one. Even such a mundane act as putting on a shoe demands that the object be recognized as a shoe. For this particular act, the ability to recognize a foot is also helpful.

Finally, categorizing permits individuals to relate objects and classes of events. This, again, serves to reduce the complexity of the environment.

Coding Systems and Cognitive Structure

Not all categories are at the same level of generality. There are, on the one hand, highly specific categories that are defined by relatively detailed descriptions of their members' attributes. Such concepts as *pear, apple, lemon,* and *orange* are highly specific. On the other hand, there are the much more general (the Brunerian term is *generic*), and consequently more inclusive, categories, such as *consumables*. Generic categories include more specific categories. For example, the generic class *consumables* includes pears, apples, lemons, and oranges. In between

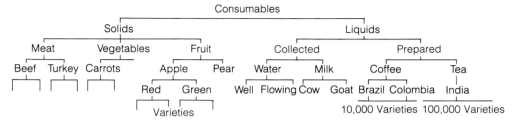

Figure 4.2   A coding system.

the two there may be many other categories, each becoming more inclusive as it becomes more generic and less defined by specifics. Figure 4.2 presents a simplified example of a **coding system** composed of categories at various levels of generality. A coding system is, in a sense, Bruner's metaphor for cognitive structure.

The formation of generic codes is important because of their role in cognitive processes such as remembering, discovering, and learning. Bruner argues that in order to remember something, it is often sufficient to recall the coding system into which it falls. Remembering, for example, that a substance called baloney (also spelled as though it were really bologna) is a meat enables us to remember that it is edible because that is one of the characteristics of this coding system. Similarly, being told only that a banana is a fruit amounts to being told that it may be edible, that it grows, that it originates from a seed, and so on. This example also illustrates the role of coding in discovery and in transfer. Imagine, for example, a group of naive explorers who find a banana. Because they do not know what it is, they cannot categorize it. (More precisely, because they cannot categorize it, they do not know what it is.) But because a banana bears a vague resemblance to an orange (*very* vague), the explorers can tentatively place it in the category *fruit*. "Maybe this is a fruit," one says. And then they become discoverers by virtue of being able to use this coding system, for they now can say, "If it *is* a fruit, it may be edible." Being re-

sourceful, as explorers are, someone may then devise a direct test of that hypothesis.

Coding systems are related not only to discovery but also to transfer (applying previously learned responses in new situations). Clearly, placing a new object in a coding system facilitates transfer in that it not only allows the new object to be related to others, but also suggests responses toward it.

In Bruner's system, thinking (conceptualization) and perception are assumed to involve identical processes of categorization. Bruner makes no clear distinction between the two — except to claim that conceptualization is somewhat more removed from immediate sensation than perception is. For the sake of clarity, however, the point can be made that perceptual processes, as described in this section, are concerned primarily with the identification of stimulus input.

Bruner's theory clearly states that to identify an object is to place it in the appropriate category. Misperception is therefore a function of improper categorization. To perceive correctly requires not only learning the appropriate category but also knowing what cues to use to place objects in that category. In addition, it is helpful to know what objects are most likely to occur in the environment. In other words, students will not recognize a piece of chalk until they have learned what chalk is (learned the category) and until they have learned that shape and color are good cues for categorizing chalk. If, furthermore, they know that chalk often is

Theories as Coding Systems

Coding systems are not limited to such obvious hierarchical arrangements as that shown in Figure 4.2. In a sense, language itself is a coding system consisting of rules governing the use of symbols. Similarly, theories are coding systems invented to enable us to go beyond the information given. Consider, for example, the theory of operant conditioning. Any situation involving reinforcement or learning can be subsumed under this particular coding system. A teacher who wants a student to learn some specific content need not have taught this content to others to develop a strategy for bringing about the learning, but can simply generalize from the knowledge that reinforcement leads to learning. In effect, teachers can devise strategies based on an implicit coding system that might be represented as in the diagram below. Note that the representation serves as a summary of some of the important features of operant conditioning theory. Note also that operant theory in this schematic representation is really a subset of the larger set, behavioristic theory (which in turn is really a subset of the more inclusive set, learning theories, which in turn fits into the general field of human psychology, which is part of the behavioral sciences, which are in turn part of the natural sciences, and so on). In short, it is possible to conceive of all knowledge as being arranged in coding systems that are related one to the other. The extent of their relatedness, their clarity, and their comprehensiveness is directly related to the ease with which an individual can make intuitive leaps among disciplines. Viewed in this way, coding systems are maps of our minds.

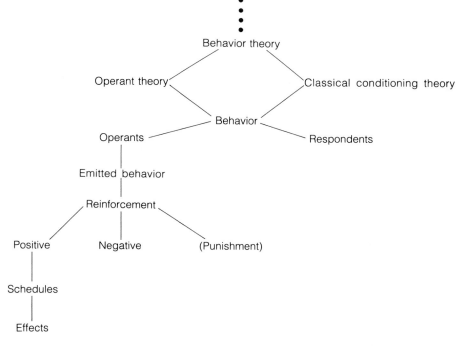

Schematic Representation of Part of a Coding System

found lying peacefully on the ledges below chalkboards, they are very likely to recognize a piece when they see it. Their recognition would be less immediate if they saw the chalk lying on their dinner plates instead.*

Summary of Bruner's Theory

Bruner's cognitive theory describes learning and perception as information-processing activities that reflect our need to simplify and make sense of the environment. These activities involve the formation of categories (concepts) that result from the abstraction of commonalities among events and experiences. From these abstractions, we derive implicit rules that allow us to categorize (conceptualize) the world and discover a wealth of relationships among concepts. Bruner's metaphor for these relationships is called a *coding system* — a hierarchical arrangement of concepts of increasing (or decreasing) generality. Thus, our long-term memories — our relatively permanent store of knowledge, strategies, impressions, and so on — can be seen as a complex, highly associationistic arrangement of categories (concepts) and coding systems (see Table 4.1).

AUSUBEL'S THEORY: SUBSUMPTION

David Ausubel (1963, 1977) has advanced a cognitive theory of learning that is specifically intended to deal almost exclusively with what he calls *meaningful verbal learning*. More important from the point of view of educational psychology, Ausubel's work consists of a search for the "laws of meaningful classroom learning."

---

*PPC: "Unless, of course, they were in the habit of eating chalk for dinner."
Author: "Yecch!"

Table 4.1 Summary of Bruner's metaphors for perception and cognition

1. Thinking, learning, and perceiving involve learning rules for classifying things as equivalent (*categorizing*).

2. Categorization simplifies the environment, allows us to recognize objects and ideas, eliminates the need to relearn constantly, gives direction and purpose to our behavior, and permits us to relate classes of objects and events.

3. Categories may be related to each other to form larger classes of increasing inclusiveness (increasing generality) in what are called *coding systems*.

4. Inventing these more general categories within coding systems is important for learning, for remembering, and for discovering and generating new information.

Meaning

According to Ausubel, an object has meaning when it elicits an image in the "content of consciousness" as a result of being related to something already known. Similarly, a concept acquires meaning when it is related to an idea that is already present in the mind. In other words, for a stimulus or concept to have meaning, there must be something in the learner's *cognitive structure* to which it can be related. For example, the word *car* has meaning for an individual only when it can be related to a mental representation of what cars are.

Cognitive Structure

Cognitive structure consists of more or less organized and stable concepts (or ideas) in a learner's "consciousness." Much like Bruner's, Ausubel's metaphor for cognitive structure assumes that this organization is hierarchical, with the most inclusive concept at the apex and increasingly specific concepts toward the base. Therefore, instruction should proceed from the most general and inclusive toward details of specific instances. This is somewhat like Bruner's notion that teaching should follow a sort of "spiral" curriculum in which the "big idea" (the most general concept) is presented first and then systematically revisited, perhaps over a period of years, at increasingly more complex levels of abstraction. The fundamental difference between Bruner and Ausubel, with respect to their instructional theories, is that Ausubel argues that learners should be provided with preorganized information, whereas Bruner maintains that students should be presented with specifics and allowed to discover their own organization (their own coding systems). The merits and implications of these views are examined later in this chapter.

Subsumption

The most important concept in Ausubel's description of cognitive structure is that of **subsumers** and the process of **subsumption**. A *subsumer* is a concept or an idea — or, to use other terms, it is something similar to what is meant by *schema* or *coding system* or *category*. Subsumers and subsumption are Ausubel's metaphors for what is learned and for the process of learning. The advantage of these terms is that they lead us to think of cognitive structure as a type of organization in which higher-level concepts incorporate or include (subsume) other ideas. It is then appropriate to describe learning and forgetting in terms of a process of subsumption.

To subsume is to incorporate meaningful material into existing cognitive structure. More simply, to subsume is to learn, and the meaningfulness of what is learned is a direct function of the appropriateness of the existing subsumers. A subsumer is appropriate to the extent that it can provide a conceptual framework for the material being learned. Totally unfamiliar

material — unfamiliar because there is nothing like it in existing cognitive structure — is meaningless. Highly familiar material is, by the same token, highly meaningful.

Derivative and Correlative Subsumption. Subsumption may take one of two forms. If the new material is so similar to existing structure that it could have been derived directly from it, **derivative subsumption** is said to take place. If, however, the new material requires an extension of structure because some of it is entirely new, **correlative subsumption** occurs.

Although Ausubel's theory relates specifically to meaningful verbal learning, the principal difference between derivative and correlative subsumption can be illustrated by reference to a nonverbal learning situation involving curves. If you drive down an unfamiliar road that has many new curves, it is likely that each of these will be so similar to other curves you have known that you can subsume them easily and quickly. They are *meaningful* for you. Even if you come across a very different curve — for example, a "pigtail" turn (one of those simultaneously curving and elevating artificial ramps that is sometimes found on mountain roads) — it may also be meaningful for you but in quite a different way. The first kind of curve involves derivative subsumption because it can be clearly understood in terms of previous knowledge; the second requires correlative subsumption because it is partly new. One important difference between the two processes is that the learning involved will be remembered for different lengths of time.

Remembering and Forgetting

Within Ausubel's system the ability to remember is a function of whether or not new material can be dissociated (separated) from existing structure. After learning (subsumption) takes place, the newly subsumed material becomes increasingly like the structure into which it was incorporated — in Ausubel's terms, it loses its

Zebras and Asses

As part of a science lesson, a teacher wishes to familiarize her students with the many breeds of cows. Her students already know what cows are; they also know colors. But they do not know that an Aberdeen Angus is a sleek-looking black cow. She tells them so. Is this likely to be meaningful learning? What type of subsumption is involved?

This same teacher now wishes to teach her class what a zebra is. She tells them what it is; she compares it with horses, donkeys, mules, and — being resourceful — asses; she then shows them a picture of a zebra. What type of subsumption is involved here?

Why would the simple statement that a zebra is a herbivorous, black and white African animal be almost meaningless for urban, North American children who have never seen a zebra in books or on television?

A ZEBRA IS A HERBIVOROUS BLACK AND WHITE AFRICAN ANIMAL

---

dissociability. And when it has finally reached the point of zero dissociability, it can no longer be recalled. Again in Ausubel's terms, it is said to have undergone **obliterative subsumption**. In short, learning involves derivative or correlative subsumption; **forgetting** involves obliterative subsumption. And derivative and correlative subsumption may be further differentiated in terms of the speed with which they reach zero dissociability (obliterative subsumption, or forgetting). Very familiar material is forgotten most quickly because it is already very much like the subsuming structure. On our hypothetical road, an ordinary curve cannot be recalled even one minute after it has been passed. In contrast, unfamiliar material is remembered longer, as in the case of the "pigtail" turn. Whereas derivative subsumption occurs quickly but leads to rapid forget-

ting, correlative subsumption may require more time for the actual learning but is retained for a longer period of time. For a summary of Ausubel's theory, see Table 4.2.

DISCOVERY VERSUS RECEPTION LEARNING

Instructional implications can be derived from any theoretical position that deals with human learning. In some cases the implications are vague and remote; in the theories of Bruner and Ausubel, however, they are explicit. The following discussion of the implications of each of their positions takes the form of an examination of a long-enduring educational controversy between those who believe in teaching by discovery and those who do not.

Table 4.2 Summary and translation of Ausubel's theory of meaningful verbal learning

1. Subsumption may be *derivative* or *correlative*.	Learning (subsumption) involves either (a) relating new material to previously learned, highly similar material (derivative subsumption), or (b) extending previous knowledge to similar but new material (correlative subsumption).
2. Subsumption leads to a *hierarchical arrangement* of knowledge, from most general to most specific.	Learning leads to the meaningful elaboration of cognitive structure.
3. Remembering is *dissociative subsumption*.	Remembering requires being able to separate new learning from old.
4. Forgetting involves *zero dissociability*, or *obliterative subsumption*.	Forgetting occurs when material can no longer be differentiated from what is already in the mind.

Discovery Learning: Bruner

Consistent with his theoretical framework, Bruner strongly advocates the use of discovery in schools. *Discovery learning* can be defined as the learning that takes place when students are not presented with subject matter in its final form but rather are required to organize it themselves. This requires learners to discover for themselves relationships that exist among items of information.

In Bruner's theory of categorizing, discovery is the formation of categories or, more often, the formation of coding systems, which are defined in terms of relationships (similarities and differences) that exist among objects and events.

The most important and most obvious characteristic of a discovery approach to teaching is that it requires far less teacher involvement and direction than most other methods. Note, however, that this does not imply that the teacher ceases to give any guidance once the initial problem has been presented. As Corno and Snow (1986) point out, teachers can offer a continuum of guidance (their phrase is *teacher mediation*) by adapting their teaching to differ-

ent students and different purposes. At one extreme, too little or no mediation can leave students without the means for discovery; at the other extreme, constant teacher direction and guidance may remove all opportunity for self-direction and discovery.

The advantages of a discovery approach, claims Bruner, are that such learning facilitates transfer and retention, increases problem-solving ability, and increases motivation (Bruner, 1961a).

Conditions That Facilitate Discovery Learning. According to Bruner, four sets of conditions contribute to discovery learning and, consequently, to the formation of generic codes: set, need state, mastery of specifics, and diversity of training.

Set refers to a predisposition to react in certain ways. A discovery-oriented person is one whose customary approach to a problem is to look for relationships among items of information. Obviously, one way of affecting set is through instructions. For example, a student can be encouraged to memorize subject matter as though it consisted of isolated bits of information simply by being told to do so. The same effect can also be produced by testing only for knowledge of isolated items of information. This is what Marton and Säljö (1984) call the *surface approach* to teaching and learning. It focuses on memorizing facts, completing tasks, and passing tests. On the other hand, students can be encouraged to look for relationships among items of information either by being instructed to do so or by being told that they will be examined on their understanding of these relationships. This is Marton and Säljö's *deep approach*. It focuses on relationships and on understanding.

Need state is the level of arousal, excitation, or alertness of the learner. Bruner contends that a moderate level of arousal is more conducive to the formation of generic codes than is either an excessively high or low level.

The degree of **mastery of specifics** refers to the extent of the learner's knowledge of specific relevant information. Bruner argues that discovery (which is really the formation of generic codes) is not an accidental event. It is more likely to occur when the individual is well prepared. The wider the range of information learners possess, the more likely they are to find relationships within that information. Bruner's fourth variable, **diversity of training**, is related to this. Bruner argues that a learner who is exposed to information in a wide variety of circumstances is more likely to develop codes to organize that information.

Specific Educational Recommendations. Bruner's plea for the use of discovery-oriented techniques in schools is advanced in several articles and books. Among them is *The Process of Education* (1961b), which includes the following suggestions for educational practice:

1. ". . . the curriculum of a subject should be determined by the most fundamental understanding that can be achieved of the underlying principles that give structure to that subject" (p. 31).

Bruner argues that knowledge of underlying principles and of the structure of a subject facilitates the formation of generic coding systems because these are based on organizing principles. For example, it is much easier to arrive at a concept that relates aspen, birch, and alder once it has been discovered that they are all deciduous hardwoods. Indeed, it is the "peopleness" of individuals, the "treeness" of trees, and the "birdness" of birds that allows them to be reacted to in similar ways and that permits going beyond the information given. Bruner argues that unless the organization of the curriculum is such that it facilitates the formation of structure (coding systems), it will be learned with difficulty, it will not lend itself to transfer, and it will be remembered poorly.

2. ". . . any subject can be taught to any child in some honest form" (p. 52).

Bruner's critics have been quick to point out that not every subject can be taught to children of any age. For example, proportion probably cannot be understood by a four-year-old. Bruner's reply to this is that we should look at the possibility of teaching *aspects* of any subject at any age level. Perhaps some aspects of proportion *can* be taught to a four-year-old. The important question is: How can teaching be made effective for very young children? Bruner's (1966) answer is that the form can be simplified and the mode of presentation geared to the simplest representational systems available. Because children progress from motor or sensory (**enactive**) representation to that in the form of relatively concrete images (**iconic**), and finally to abstract (**symbolic**) representation, it follows that the sequence in teaching should be the same. In other words, if it is possible to present a subject so that a child can first experience it, then react to a concrete pre-

Guided Discovery

Some school subjects lend themselves more readily to discovery-oriented techniques than do other subjects. For example, some (though by no means all) scientific principles can be discovered by students in guided discovery situations in which sufficient background information and the appropriate experimental equipment are provided. Similarly, children on field trips can discover a variety of phenomena, although understanding and interpreting these phenomena (and even noticing them in the first place) often require considerable guidance.

The beginning teacher should not make the mistake of assuming that teaching through discovery implies letting students go out on their own with no more than the simple instruction, "Discover." Not only must the processes of discovery be taught — through experience as well as through more didactic procedures — but the student must frequently be given guidance while in the process of discovering. The guidance need not ruin the discovery or destroy its magic.

Even such prosaic subjects as geography can be taught through discovery. Bruner (1961a) describes how a class of elementary-school children is led to discover important geographical features. Among other things, they are asked where they would establish a settlement if they were exploring an area for the first time. Their reasons for settling in certain areas rather than others gradually lead them to "discover" that major settlements should be at the confluence of rivers and near natural harbors. Thus, studying geography becomes an activity of discovering relationships between the environment and humans rather than simply of memorizing maps and related data.

Can the principle of the combustion engine be discovered by an eighth-grade class? Yes, it can. What might be the major features of a guided discovery lesson that you could design for this purpose?

---

sentation of it, and finally symbolize it, that is the best instructional sequence.

3. A spiral curriculum that develops and re-develops topics at different grades is ideal for the acquisition of generic codes.

    Bruner argues in several places (1961b, 1966) that spiral curricula are ideally suited to the development of coding systems. First, such a curriculum organizes subject matter according to principles, and it usually presents them systematically from simplest to most complex. This progression parallels the development of coding systems. Second, a spiral curriculum involves the sort of repetition that is useful for forming coding systems. To begin with, learners are exposed to the most general, most inclusive idea, and then to a series of specific, simple instances of concepts. As they discover relationships among these concepts, they form the coding systems that are highly conducive to transfer, recall, and discovery.

4. ". . . a student should be given some training in recognizing the plausibility of guesses" (p. 64).

    In this connection Bruner speaks of the intuitive leap — the educated guess, which is something more than a blind attempt but something less than going beyond the information given. The latter involves making predictions on the basis of what is known about similar instances. An intuitive leap is less certain than that. Bruner argues persuasively that to discourage guessing is to stifle the process of discovery.

5. Aids to teaching (audiovisual, concrete, and so on) should be used.

One reason advanced to support this recommendation is that audiovisual aids provide students with direct or vicarious experiences and thus facilitate the formation of concepts. This relates directly to Bruner's suggestion that the best instructional sequence is often one that progresses in the same direction as the child's representation of the world does — that is, from enactive to iconic to symbolic.

Expository Teaching: Ausubel

David Ausubel is an outspoken defender of expository teaching. Part of his defense is contained in the following passage:

Beginning in the junior high school period, students acquire most new concepts and learn most new propositions by directly grasping higher-order relationships between abstractions. To do so meaningfully, they need no longer depend on current or recently prior concrete-empirical experience and hence are able to bypass completely the intuitive type of understanding reflective of such dependence. Through proper expository teaching they can proceed directly to a level of abstract understanding that is qualitatively superior to the intuitive level in terms of generality, clarity, precision, and explicitness. At this state of development therefore, it seems pointless to enhance intuitive understanding by using discovery techniques. (Ausubel, 1963, p. 19)

Ausubel argues not only that expository teaching *can* lead to a high level of understanding and generality, but also that discovery approaches are extremely time-consuming without being demonstrably superior. In a review of the literature on discovery learning, Ausubel and Robbinson (1969) conclude that research supporting such learning is virtually nonexistent. "Moreover," they state, "it appears that enthusiasts of discovery methods have been supporting each other by citing one another's opinions and assertions as evidence and by generalizing extravagantly from questionable findings" (1969, p. 494).

Ausubel's emphasis on expository teaching and its outcome, *reception learning*, stems in part from the fact that most classroom learning seems to be of that type. In addition, meaningful verbal learning, with which his theory deals, occurs mainly in the course of expository teaching. He argues that this type of learning is not passive — nor does it stifle creativity or encourage rote learning. Indeed, meaningful verbal learning is anything but rote. It involves relating new material to existing structure, whereas rote learning involves ingesting isolated bits of information.

Ausubel advances some general recommendations for the planning and presentation of subject matter. These take the form of a discussion of the variables involved in subsumption: **advance organizers**, discriminability, and meaningfulness.

Advance Organizers. **Advance organizers** are complex sets of ideas or concepts given to the learner *before* the material to be learned is presented. It is meant to provide stable cognitive structure to which the new learning can be anchored (subsumed). Another function of an organizer is to increase recall (prevent loss of dissociability). The use of advance organizers is called for, then, under two circumstances: The first is when students have no relevant information to which they can relate the new learning; the second is when relevant subsuming information is already present but is not likely to be recognized as relevant by the learner (Ausubel and Robinson, 1969).

Grippin and Peters (1984) describe four characteristics of advance organizers. First, advance organizers are presented before the lesson. Second, they are designed to bring to mind prior knowledge that is relevant to the lesson (to activate related subsumers). Third, advance organizers are presented at a higher level of abstraction than the material presented later. Put another way, advance organizers ordinarily consist of *subsuming* concepts, which are, by definition, more generic than *subsumed* concepts. Finally, advance organizers make explicit the connection between prior knowledge and the lesson to be presented.

Ausubel describes two different types of organizers — one to be used when the material is completely new and the other when it is somewhat familiar. The first is termed an **expository organizer** because it presents a description or exposition of relevant concepts. The second is called a **comparative organizer** because it is likely to make use of similarities and differences between new material and existing cognitive structure.

An expository organizer in a lesson on gold, for example, might describe the general, defining characteristics of metals before the lesson on the specific qualities of gold. The organizer is intended to provide concepts (subsumers) to which the new material can be related.

There are a number of examples of comparative organizers in this text. Many of these take the form of brief introductory sections that compare material about to be presented with material previously discussed (behaviorism versus cognitivism, for example). Some of the chapter previews are organizers of this kind. Recall that at the beginning of this chapter we associated Bruner with discovery learning and Ausubel with reception learning before actually discussing their theories — another advance organizer. Of necessity, a textbook is primarily expository (although parts of it may lead to a type of guided discovery) — hence the frequent use of organizers in most textbooks.

In the classroom, teachers sometimes unconsciously make use of something very much like advance organizers when they summarize earlier lessons before beginning a new presentation. However, these summaries often fail to make the connection between new and old learning sufficiently explicit; nor are they abstract enough to qualify as advance organizers in the sense in which Ausubel uses the expression. A summary is often simply a summary — an accounting of the things that have been taught before. An advance organizer is more abstract; it draws from previous learning an idea — a concept — that is general enough to subsume the new material to be taught. Consider the following classroom exchange.

"Boys and girls," the teacher asks, *"why are turbo-charged WZ 222A's so expensive?"*

"'Cause everybody wants one," says Jack.

"'Cause there's not enough for everyone who wants one," says Sally.

"Right. Right," the teacher confirms. *"You're both right."*

"Too much demand," Jack elaborates.

"Too little supply," elaborates Sally.

"Supply and demand," summarizes Willy.

"Supply and demand," echoes the teacher. *"Keep that in mind, boys and girls. If nobody wants a thing, or if there's a lot of it, it won't cost very much. Consider this wonderful textbook. Everybody wants it, so it costs an arm and a leg! Supply and demand. Now, today we're going to talk about gold! Pretty exciting stuff, gold! And pretty expensive. Is that because of supply? demand? something else? Let's see what we can find out. . . ."*

The lesson goes on. Notice that it was preceded by a single, very abstract concept: the principle of supply and demand. Notice, too, that there is a promise to relate this concept to the question that constitutes the substance of today's lesson: Why is gold so expensive? The students have been reminded of a single, abstract, highly generic, stable concept upon which to anchor their new learning.

Research that has examined the effectiveness of advance organizers has often used

A Speech Guaranteed to Impress Educators

Bruner's writings lend themselves particularly well to pre- and postdinner speeches before parent-and-teacher organizations, school superintendents, and other groups of educators. This is partly because there is widespread conviction that any approach to education that is not discovery-oriented must be passive, benchbound, meaningless memorization. In case you should ever be asked to present a talk to an eager group of educators, the following is offered as an introduction to one of the most stirring after-dinner speeches of this decade:

Mr. Mayor, Mrs. West, Mr. Two-lips, ladies and gentlemen. It is my very great pleasure to have been invited to speak to you this evening on the occasion of the publication of my book. I feel a little like a cow as I stand before you — heh! heh! — you know, the cow who turned to the farmer one cold winter morning and said, "That's what I appreciate, a warm hand." Heh! Heh! (Pause for laughter.)

But all joking aside, ladies and gentlemen, I will speak to you of a very serious topic: the education of our children — our little Franks, our John Georges, our Johnny Wests. These are our most prized assets. They are the children with whose minds we must be so careful. We must develop and expand those minds; we must increase their intellectual potency; we must teach them creative (emphasis here) ways — I repeat, creative (emphasis again — perhaps pause for a short burst of spontaneous applause). . . . Yes, we must teach them creative ways of solving the problems they will face in this difficult world. We must teach them to appreciate their knowledge. And what better way of doing this than to allow them to discover that knowledge? Discovery, ladies and gentlemen, discovery is the means whereby we shall open up the wondrous storehouse of treasures that a child's mind can be, and whereby we shall teach our children to value the mind, since it is personally their own. And what can be more uniquely personal of all that children know than that which they have discovered for themselves? (Pause for a long round of applause, nodding your head gravely and sagely as you do so.) A great author by the name of Lefrançois once said that learning that is not discovery-oriented (gesture dramatically throughout this line) must be benchbound, meaningless, passive memorization — and that is the truth! (End the line pounding the lectern with your fist and pause again for applause.) [You are invited to complete this speech for yourself.]

---

organizers much like this one, sometimes presented in the form of a written paragraph, sometimes described by the teacher, sometimes elicited from students. Typically, the subsequent performance of a group of students who were given advance organizers is compared with that of a control group given the lesson without the advance organizer.

The results of much of this research are not entirely clear. Some researchers have found that advance organizers provide no measurable advantage (for example, Clawson and Barnes, 1973); others report significant positive effects (for example, Gabel, Kogan, and Sherwood, 1980). White and Tisher (1986) note evidence suggesting that students who lack relevant prior knowledge are most likely to benefit from the use of advance organizers, and that this may well explain the contradictions among studies. In addition, the fact that teaching strategies

Another Speech Guaranteed to Impress Educators

Ausubel's work also lends itself well to speeches before groups of educators. It is particularly well documented and is characterized by both reason and passion. In the event that the reader is a proponent of expository, as opposed to discovery, methods, the following introduction to a rousing Ausubelian speech is provided:

Mr. Mayor, Mrs. West, Mr. Two-lips, ladies and gentlemen. At the end of this evening, ladies and gentlemen, I shall turn to you like a cow on a cold winter morning and say, "That's what I really appreciate, a warm hand." Heh! Heh!

But enough levity. For these are serious times in which we live. A great writer by the name of Lefran-çois — I'm sure you're all familiar with his work — this great man wrote: "We have amplified our capabilities to the point where a mushrooming technology is consuming the resources of our planet and replacing them with garbage. Individuals can, in their wisdom, speak of Utopia and environmental control; but the human race often appears to be a bunch of blundering idiots." (Pause for an ovation.)

These are indeed serious times in which we live. That's why, ladies and gentlemen, it is so terribly important that we give our children the best of all possible educations. This is no time for fads. This is a time for proven methodology! (Pause again for a satisfying burst of applause, nodding in wisdom as you do so.

Now continue emphatically.) While one's educational convictions should be argued with passion, it seems a sensible requirement that they also be informed with reason.* And those who would have us believe that children can effectively and efficiently learn in schools if they are allowed to discover for themselves are not tempering their arguments with reason. (Pause for applause.) They are, in fact, unreasonable! (Pound the lectern at this point, and pause for the cheering that will follow.) [You may wish to complete this and submit it to an oratorical contest.]

*This sentence is from Ausubel and Robinson, 1969, p. 478.

---

such as these do not always lead to immediately measurable effects should not be taken as clear evidence that they are a waste of time. Many of the good things teachers do are never measured — and perhaps they should not be.

Perhaps, just perhaps, the long-term effects of a single propitiously presented advance organizer might become apparent years later when the student, now a grown-up, correctly answers the 20-million-dollar question on a television game show!! Or maybe the long-term effects will become evident in the bankrupt investor's recollection that gold is not really a very useful metal, that the demand for it is rather artificial, and that the supply is quite abundant.

Discriminability. In Ausubel's theory, a major variable in determining the stability of what is learned is the discriminability of the new material from previous learning. Ausubel defines retention in terms of the ease with which new learning can be dissociated from old learning. He observes that information closely resembling previous knowledge (derivative subsumption) is quickly forgotten (zero dissociability), whereas dissimilar input (correlative subsumption) tends to be retained longer

Meaningless Learning

"Learning involves the subsumption of meaningful material within existing cognitive structure through derivative or correlative means." This particular pearl of psychological wisdom is undoubtedly meaningful to you, but only because you know through previous learning what derivative and correlative subsumption are, what meaningful material is, and what type of beast cognitive structure is. Attempting to teach what learning is to a group of people who do not already know each of these terms would be quite fruitless if the above sentence were used. In short, the learning would be meaningless.

It is remarkably easy for teachers to fall into the trap of asking students to learn material that is meaningless for them because they do not have the required background information. One widely cited example of this is the use of white, middle-class-oriented readers for children from nonwhite, poor neighborhoods, or, as was the case in the Arctic until recently, for Eskimo children. The Eskimo children, who had never seen a city, an au-

tomobile, a telephone, or an indoor toilet, were asked to learn to read sentences similar to "John goes for a drive," "Firemen, policemen, and college professors are our friends." (Now, of course, many Eskimos have satellite dishes and access to hundreds of television channels, so that their cultural isolation has been much reduced.)

Do you remember learning that a demagogue is "an unprincipled politician who panders to the emotions and prejudices of the populace"? That the center of the earth is "in a stage of igneous fusion"? That the closest star is "several billion light-years away"? How meaningful was this information?

(higher dissociability). It follows from this that teaching techniques that highlight the *differences* between new material and old learning will lead to longer retention. At the same time it is still necessary to relate the new to the old in order to facilitate subsumption. Hence comparing information in terms of similarities and differences should help both learning and retention.

Finally, Ausubel suggests that the stability and clarity of the subsuming idea are directly related to the ease with which new material can be both incorporated with it and dissociated from it.

Making Learning Meaningful.

Ausubel's emphasis on reception learning as opposed to discovery learning is partly based on his belief that the most desirable kind of learning is "meaningful" as opposed to "rote." This does not mean that discovery techniques do not lead to meaningful learning. However, Ausubel believes that expository approaches have some advantages, especially in terms of the efficient use of the learner's time.

Meaningfulness is defined in terms of the relationship between new learning and existing cognitive structure (knowledge). This definition has a number of implications for teacher behavior, some of which are suggested by the preceding discussion on advance organizers. To begin with, meaning may derive directly from associations that exist among ideas, events, or objects. Obviously, however, this meaning is not present unless the learner is aware of the association. For example, students can quite easily learn to pronounce and spell words that do not relate to any of their existing ideas and thus are meaningless to them. It seems clear that a new concept will have meaning if it relates to both the learner's past experiences and other ideas currently being learned.

The important point is that meaning is not an intangible property of objects or concepts themselves. Ausubel contends that no idea, concept, or object is meaningful in and of itself;

it is meaningful only in relation to a learner. The implication for teaching, therefore, is that the teacher should present no new material until the learner is ready to understand it. And understanding requires appropriate cognitive structure. Consequently, much of the teacher's effort should be directed toward providing the student with background information, frequently through the use of advance organizers.

RECONCILING DISCOVERY AND RECEPTION APPROACHES

It is not difficult to reconcile the two apparently divergent views presented in this chapter; they are not nearly so different as their juxtaposition here might make them seem. In fact, in many ways they are simply different emphases. Neither is necessarily superior to the other, and neither needs to be used to the exclusion of the other. Clearly, both have their uses.

Even Ausubel suggests that discovery learning can be useful (Ausubel and Robinson, 1969). For example, it can be used with younger learners who do not yet have a large store of information to which new learning can be related. When this is the case, expository approaches are not always highly meaningful.

Discovery can also be used to test the meaningfulness of new learning. For example, learners might be asked to generate (that is, *discover*) instances in which some new learning might be applicable — for example, a new principle in arithmetic. In fact, Ausubel argues that discovery learning is essential in problem solving if students are to demonstrate that they *understand* what they have learned. Furthermore, says Ausubel, there are indications that information that is discovered rather than presented in final form might generalize more readily to new situations. In addition, discovery approaches might be more motivating than expository approaches, and self-learning might be more intrinsically satisfying.

Although Ausubel accepts the usefulness of a discovery approach in some instances, he remains a strong advocate of expository teaching. He argues that most learning is of the reception variety and that any alternative would be highly inefficient in terms of the time involved, the cost incurred, and the benefits that accrue to the learner. Relatively little school learning can be discovered by a student, says Ausubel, not only because it would take too long, but also because students are not always capable of discovering much that is significant. Even subjects that apparently lend themselves to discovery approaches can often be mastered as well and faster if the information is given to the learner in relatively final form. Ausubel believes that after the age of eleven or twelve, the learner possesses enough background information to understand many new concepts very clearly if they are explained simply. At this age, Ausubel contends, asking a student to "discover" is largely a waste of time.

The Conclusions of Research

Because a number of studies have attempted to compare discovery-oriented and reception-oriented approaches to teaching and learning, it should be possible to evaluate the two without relying solely on opinion, conjecture, or theoretical speculation. However, that is not really the case because the research does not consistently support one approach over the other and is often confusing and contradictory. Why? Partly because different studies often use different criteria for assessing the effectiveness of different approaches. For example, some studies look at speed of learning; others are concerned with retention; some attempt to assess transfer; and others look at affective or motivational changes in learners.

Another reason why the conclusions of teaching-outcome studies are sometimes contradictory is that it is often impossible to control (and therefore to equate or compare) the approaches used in different studies — or some-times even within a single study. Not only are students and classes dramatically different from one another, but so too are teachers. A well-prepared expository lesson might be extremely effective when presented by Mr. Joneskowski, but the same lesson presented by Ms. Rudifesk might be short of ordinary. By the same token, one fifth-grade class might respond exceptionally well to a discovery lesson, whereas another might be totally confused by the same lesson presented by the same teacher.

Studies that have attempted to evaluate the effectiveness of a single approach (rather than comparing two different approaches) have not led to very clear conclusions either. Among these are a large number of studies that have looked at the contribution of advance organizers to learning, retention, and transfer. Grippin and Peters (1984) point out that about half these studies indicate that the use of organizers makes a significant difference; the other half find that learning is just as effective without the use of organizers. Clearly, however, *good* organizers are more often effective than not.

Mayer (1979) suggests that the most effective organizers are those that (1) allow the student to generate all or most of the logical relationships in the material to be learned, (2) point out clear relationships between familiar and less familiar material, (3) are relatively simple to learn and use, and (4) are used in situations in which the learner would not spontaneously use an organizer, perhaps because of inexperience or inability to recall relevant information.

The effectiveness of discovery approaches has also been researched. Here, too, there is often confusion and contradiction, resulting in part from inconsistent definition, inappropriate measurement, and uncontrolled (and often uncontrollable) differences among teachers and students. However, even strong advocates of other approaches generally concede that discovery approaches can be highly effective in a variety of circumstances (see, for example, Corno and Snow, 1986).

What, then, should the teacher conclude?

Should teachers use mostly discovery or mostly expository approaches? The simple answer is that the question is not as simple as it sounds, nor are the choices as clear. A good teacher will, of course, use both.

Disturbing as it might be for those who prefer the uncomplicated comfort of a black or white position, in a great many instances it is impossible to use only one instructional approach to the complete exclusion of others. Johnny, intensely motivated to discover the mating habits of that noble barnyard fowl, the turkey, runs to the local library and finds a learned exposition on the turkey. From this exposition he learns a bewildering amount. *Discovery* learning? In contrast, Frank's teacher, a recent reception-learning convert, presents a brilliant exposition of the mating habits of turkeys to his benchbound students. During the course of this exposition, it occurs to Frank that turkeys have been unnecessarily and unjustly demeaned in recent times, as is evident in the popular expression, "You turkey!" In the course of his inspired musings, he discovers that there is little reason not to rank turkeys with eagles as birds worthy of our respect and admiration. *Reception* learning?

The confusion arising from these illustrations may be lessened by the realization that learning is what students do and teaching is what teachers do. A teacher who emphasizes discovery will try to arrange the teaching/learning situation so that students are encouraged to experiment, to think, to gather information, and, most important, to arrive at their own organization of that information. Teachers who emphasize expository teaching will be more concerned with organizing information so that it is immediately meaningful for students and therefore becomes a stable part of their existing cognitive structure. In the end, however, it is the student who learns. And, in spite of a teacher's emphasis, students may discover new information and new relationships for themselves, or they may discover no more than a structured exposition ready to be learned and assimilated as is.

General Instructional Applications

The juxtaposition of apparently opposing points of view is sometimes a useful teaching device. It highlights differences and, if Ausubel is correct, makes the points of view more memorable — more easily dissociated from each other.

But there is also a disadvantage to this approach: It exaggerates differences and masks similarities. It leaves the student of education with the impression that the points of view are more different and the theorists more adamant in their beliefs than is actually the case.

This chapter is a case in point. Juxtaposing the theories of Bruner and Ausubel has underlined the differences between them — especially the discovery-versus-reception debate. At the same time, this approach has perhaps glossed over important points of agreement between them — especially the conviction of each that the key to successful cognitive processing is to be found in the learner's organization of knowledge. Both positions are, after all, unwaveringly cognitive. Both present a very similar view of the learner as an active, information-processing organism for whom the environment is meaningful to the extent that new input can be related to existing cognitive structure. Furthermore, the descriptions that each theory provides of the formation of cognitive structure are very similar, even though their language is different (categories and coding systems on the one hand; subsumers and subsumption on the other). And, as we have seen, in the final analysis discovery and reception learning are not totally incompatible approaches to teaching and learning. As described by Bruner and Ausubel, each is intended to lead to the acquisition of meaningful concepts; to maximize transfer, retention, and motivation; and to reduce the extent to which school learning is a passive exercise in rote learning.

Empowerment.   It is worth repeating again the one-sentence summary of one of the most important of educational objectives, which was first presented in Chapter 1: *The goal of education is to empower students.* As we saw, to empower is to enable, to give power. At a simple level, education empowers students by providing them with skills and knowledge that enable them to do important things they could not otherwise do (for example, read newspapers, write love poems, add up the money in one's pocket or purse, and so on). At a deeper level, education empowers by contributing to the development of cognitive content and intellectual processes; that is, it empowers by teaching people actual things (content) as well as by teaching them how to think (process). (There is more about teaching thinking and related topics in Chapter 5.) And finally, education empowers by developing in students the sort of power that comes with feelings of social, intellectual, and personal competence.

Misconceptions and Their Effects on Learning.   Cognitive psychology's attention to how the student learns and understands has led to some important discoveries about the ways students think. For example, it seems that many students (and many teachers as well)

sometimes find it very difficult to understand what might otherwise be relatively simple concepts and principles, simply because they have learned, and incorporated into their cognitive structures, certain very stubborn *misconceptions* that interfere with learning (sometimes referred to as *alternative conceptions*, a less negative term). Evidence suggests that more than three-quarters of fifth-grade students believe that eyes actually *see* objects — rather than responding to reflected light that travels in straight lines and bounces off various objects (Anderson and Smith, 1984). Similarly, elementary-school children who readily state that the earth is round often have a very different conception of what a round earth means than you or I might have (Nussbaum, 1979). Some see it as a flat, round thing, something like a cookie, perhaps surrounded by water; others conceive of the earth as a huge globular object with the ground near the bottom of the globe, the sky at the top, and air in between. In much the same way, some teacher trainees report that the insulating coating on electrical wires is designed to keep electrons from escaping from their pathway (West, 1988). And Lockhead (1985) found that over three-quarters of college students don't really understand ninth-grade algebra, even if they can correctly manipulate algebraic symbols and equations.

These and a large number of related studies have been concerned primarily with what students don't know — or, more precisely, with what they *think* they know that is not only fundamentally incorrect, but is also such a basic part of cognitive structure in specific subjects like physics or mathematics that it interferes with learning. Ramsden (1988a) reports numerous studies that indicate how persistent these misconceptions are.

Among the implications of these studies is the need for teachers to be aware of their students' naive and misleading beliefs and to take pains to correct them (Calfee and Drum, 1986). Advance organizers, questioning, verbalizing solutions to problems, and related activities might be used for this purpose. The important point is that teachers cannot assume that all learners are at the same level. Some may not understand new material at all, and those who do understand might understand in very different ways. Why? Because, in Ausubel's terms, each has a slightly (or dramatically) different organization of relevant subsuming concepts to which to relate new learning — or, in Bruner's terms, because the coding systems into which new material is incorporated are different.

More generally, understanding often depends on prior knowledge (what the cognitivists term *cognitive structure*). For some learners, essential background information or prerequisite skills and knowledge may be absent; for others, naive and incorrect conceptions may interfere with new learning.

Ramsden (1988b) suggests that today's teacher needs to adopt a *relational* view of teaching. This view emphasizes that learning is about changing conceptions rather than simply about the addition of more facts. Accordingly, teachers need to be concerned as much with the processes of learning — with learning how to learn — as with its content. They also need to focus on the relationship between the subject matter and the learner rather than simply on the relationship between teaching methods and test performance. In Nickerson's (1988) words, ". . . it should be the goal of education to help people become competent knowers, thinkers, and learners" (p. 34). Or in Bruner's (1985) words: "The salvation is in learning how to go about learning. . . ." (p. 8). Much of the next chapter deals with precisely this topic.

MAIN POINTS

1. Cognitive theories stress the importance of the individual learner's cognitive structure. They are particularly concerned with how information is processed, organized, and recalled.

2. Cognitive theorists think of knowledge as consisting of vast networks of relationships. Declarative knowledge consists of all the facts we have learned (things that are or have been); procedural knowledge involves knowing how to do something.

3. Schemata are metaphors for cognitive structure and functioning. They may be thought of as clusters of knowledge that define concepts. Scripts are the aspects of schemata that deal with routines and sequences.

4. Cognitive psychology's principal tenets suggest that (1) the curriculum needs to be organized to reveal and emphasize relationships, and (2) schools should pay deliberate attention to developing strategies for organizing and using knowledge.

5. Bruner's learning theory is a theory of *categorization* in which a category is a concept or a rule. In its capacity as a rule it specifies the properties (attributes) an object must possess to be included in the category.

6. Categorization reduces the complexity of the environment, makes possible the recognition of objects, and eliminates the necessity for constant learning. In addition, it permits an individual to go beyond the information given.

7. Hierarchical arrangements of related categories are referred to as coding systems. A coding system is so arranged that the most generic category is placed at the top of the hierarchy, whereas the more specific categories form its base.

8. Coding systems are important for retention, discovery, and transfer. Perception involves categorizing in the same way as conceptualization does. To perceive accurately requires not only having appropriate categories, but also knowing what cues to use for placing objects in those categories.

9. Ausubel's theory is a cognitive attempt to explain meaningful verbal learning. It is concerned largely with arriving at laws of classroom learning.

10. Ausubel defines meaning as involving a relationship between new material and old material (cognitive structure). Cognitive structure consists of hierarchically organized concepts (*subsumers*) arranged much as categories are arranged in Bruner's coding systems.

11. To learn is to subsume material to existing cognitive structure. This may take the form of deriving material from preexisting structure (derivative subsumption), or it may involve material that is an extension of what is already known (correlative subsumption).

12. Loss of ability to recall is *obliterative subsumption*. It occurs when new materials can no longer be dissociated from cognitive structure (zero dissociability).

13. Discovery approaches to instruction require the learner to structure information by discovering the relationships that exist among concepts or principles. In expository teaching (reception learning), the material is presented in final form.

14. Bruner, an advocate of the discovery approach, argues that discovery leads to the formation of codes that are more generic and that therefore lead to higher degrees of transfer and longer retention. It also increases motivation and leads to the development of problem-solving skills.

15. Discovery learning (and the acquisition of generic codes) is affected by four general conditions: *set* (predisposition to learn in a given way); *need state* (degree of arousal); *mastery of specifics* (amount and detail of learning); and *diversity of training* (variety of conditions under which learning takes place).

16. Bruner presents arguments in favor of a spiral curriculum, the teaching of difficult subjects in simplified but honest form to younger students, the organization of a curriculum around themes or underlying principles, the encouragement of plausible guesses, and the use of aids in teaching.

17. Ausubel argues that discovery learning is highly time-consuming and often impossible.

18. The most important instructional technique based on Ausubel's theory is the use of advance organizers — highly generic concepts presented before the lesson, designed to bring to mind relevant prior knowledge, and intended to clarify the relationships between new and old learning.

19. Discovery methods and expository teaching are not mutually exclusive. Both are useful. Ausubel suggests that discovery may have advantages for teaching in the early grades, for testing meaningfulness and problem solving, for ensuring transferability, and for establishing intrinsic motivation.

20. In the end, teaching is what teachers do and learning is what students do. Discovery teaching does not always lead to discovery learning. Nor does expository teaching always lead to reception learning.

21. Although Bruner and Ausubel present points of view that are opposite in many respects, both present a fundamentally cognitive view of the learner as an active, information-processing organism whose efforts to derive meaning from the environment are closely related to the development of associated networks of concepts. Their recommendations for instruction are intended to lead to the acquisition of meaningful concepts, to maximize transfer, retention, and motivation, and to reduce passive rote learning.

22. An important objective of education is to empower students by providing them with knowledge, skills, and confidence.

23. Occasionally, what students *don't* know, or the inaccurate and misleading things they are

convinced they do know, interfere with learning and understanding new principles and new information; hence the importance of advance organizers, questioning, and other approaches in ensuring that all learners have appropriate cognitive structure (that is, appropriate prerequisite knowledge and skills) for new learning.

24. "The salvation is in learning how to go about learning" (Bruner, 1985, p. 8).

SUGGESTED READINGS

Original sources are among the best references for approaches to learning theory such as Bruner's and Ausubel's. The following references are clear presentations of Bruner's theories and educational recommendations:

BRUNER, J. S. (1957). On going beyond the information given. In *Contemporary approaches to cognition.* Cambridge, Mass.: Harvard University Press.

BRUNER, J. S., GOODNOW, J. J., & AUSTIN, G. A. (1956). *A study of thinking.* New York: Wiley.

BRUNER, J. S. (1961). *The process of education.* Cambridge, Mass.: Harvard University Press.

BRUNER, J. S. (1966). *Toward a theory of instruction.* Cambridge, Mass.: Harvard University Press.

The psychological theories of Ausubel are best explained in:

AUSUBEL, D. P. (1968). *Educational psychology: A cognitive view.* New York: Holt, Rinehart & Winston.

An excellent collection of articles dealing with the application of cognitive research in teaching, and especially in teaching science, is:

RAMSDEN, P. (1988). Studying learning: Improving teaching. In P. Ramsden (Ed.), *Improving learning: New perspectives.* London: Kogan Page.

The much feared grizzly bear (Ursus horribilis) *weighs around 900 pounds at maturity. Many "experts" consider the grizzly to be a species of the brown bear* (Ursus arctos). *The grizzly's prodigal strength is attested to by the fact that one bear moved an 850-pound trap one quarter of a mile and then escaped* (Soper, 1964).

LEARNING AND INSTRUCTION

Sciences may be learned by rote, but Wisdom not.
LAURENCE STERNE *Tristram Shandy*

"Contrariwise," continued Tweedledee, "if it was so, it might be; and if it were so, it would be: but as it isn't, it ain't. That's logic."
LEWIS CARROLL *Alice Through the Looking-Glass*

PREVIEW Part of this chapter serves as a major summary of much that has preceded it. Robert Gagné's description of learning categories can be interpreted as a hierarchical arrangement of learning theories, from simplest to most complex. But the usefulness of his approach is not so much that it integrates a great deal of information, but that it presents specific suggestions about the conditions under which each type of learning can be facilitated. The rest of the chapter deals more specifically with learning to learn.

■ *I don't know for a fact that my father actually wanted me to be a teacher. But I do know that as my taste for misbehavior blossomed, he despaired that I could ever become anything of value. I suspect that my mother, too, almost gave up hope during those times.*

But I was not always disordered, undisciplined, and confused. There was a time, early in my childhood, when I was as exemplary a child as one could reasonably wish for. It was then, I think, that my father thought I might be a teacher. And that was perhaps why he presented me with my first formal opportunity to instruct when I was just a skinny seven-year-old.

It all began with John George, a Cree boy who attended the rural school where my dad taught. When John George first came to school, he was a withdrawn boy who spoke no English or French and whose habits were not always the same as ours.

On his first day at school, in the middle of the morning, John George felt the call of nature, left his desk, and walked slowly to the far corner of the schoolyard. There, to our roaring amusement as we watched through the windows, he squatted and attended to that call. At that moment, as I recall, a bear strolled across the pasture just beyond the schoolyard. He seemed to be walking on a cow path.

My father, a resourceful and very capable teacher, rushed to the corner of the yard and tried to explain to John George, using various interesting gestures, that the little edifice in the other corner was equipped to handle problems like the one the boy had just solved. But there are some signs that are not universally understood by frightened six-year-old boys whose pants have settled around their ankles.

Later that day, my dad made me a teacher. "Show him where it is and what it's for," he said.

I did. ■

INSTRUCTION DEFINED

Unfortunately, "showing them" is not all there is to teaching. First, as Gagné (1977a) points out, it is necessary to get the learner's attention. And having done that, the teacher must make certain that the learner's objectives are appropriate, that relevant prerequisite skills are present, and that the "showing" is done in the best way possible. Learners must then be given opportunities to perform, must be given feedback on their performance, and must be helped to increase retention and transfer of what they have learned.

This analysis of the instructional sequence suggests a useful definition: **Instruction** consists of an arrangement of events that are *external* to the learner and that are designed to facilitate the internal processes of learning (R. Gagné, 1985). Put another way, to instruct is to exercise control over some of the learner's experiences in a deliberate and thoughtful attempt to influence learning. What I did with John George is clearly an example of highly effective instruction. But it is only a tidbit of instruction—not an elaborate instructional scheme from which you might take notes and learn.

According to Glaser and Bassok (1989), a comprehensive instructional theory must pay attention to at least three important aspects of the teaching/learning process: (1) describing the desired outcomes of the learning process—the knowledge and skills that learners are to acquire, (2) analyzing the preinstruction state of the learner's knowledge and skills, and (3) suggesting the means by which the learner can be guided to make the transition from the preinstruction state to the desired outcomes of instruction.

As we saw in Chapter 1, the desired outcomes or objectives of education can be expressed in very broad terms, such as "The goal of education is to develop decent, worthwhile citizens" or "The goal of education is to empower students." Although general statements of objectives such as these are useful in guiding the development of curriculum and in influencing the behavior of administrators and students, they are not nearly so useful in the day-to-day business of teaching as are more specific instructional objectives.

INSTRUCTIONAL OBJECTIVES

Instructional objectives are statements about the type of performance that can be expected of students once they have completed a lesson, a unit, or a course. It is important to note that objectives do not describe the course itself but instead describe the intended *performance* of students. Because performance implies behavior, the phrase *behavioral objectives* is often used interchangeably with *instructional objectives*.

In recent years a renewed emphasis on the use of instructional objectives in schools has become apparent. This emphasis stems not only from the recognition of their importance in teaching, but also arises from a growing concern with what is called "teacher accountability." The phrase implies that teachers should in some way be held accountable for their performance in the classroom — accountable perhaps to students, perhaps to parents, but most certainly to the administrative authorities who hire and fire them.

Unfortunately (or perhaps fortunately), there is no easy way of assessing teacher performance per se, although attempts have been made to assess teachers' basic competence. For example, in 1986 some 210,000 teachers in Texas were administered a specially developed test of basic communication skills (Texas Examination of Current Administrators and Teachers, or TECAT). The test was designed to identify teachers whose basic literacy was so poor that they could not justifiably be classed as anything but incompetent. Shepard and Kreitzer (1987) report that, following a massive preparatory program involving workshops, review courses, and study books, almost 97 percent of the teachers passed the test on the first administration, and 99 percent had passed after a second examination. But 1,950 educators who were unable to pass the test lost their jobs; this number represents fewer than 1 percent of all teachers who took the test. (Interestingly, some 8,000 teachers and administrators did *not* take the test but still retained their positions.) Of the 1,950 individuals who failed the test, 887 had held academic positions (principals, superintendents, and teachers of academic subjects) and 1,063 had held nonacademic positions (including teachers of physical education, industrial arts, music, art, English as a second language, and health, as well as school counselors).

Shepard and Kreitzer (1987) estimate the total cost of test development, teacher preparation, and test administration and scoring at more than $35 million. Among the unexpected effects of this testing program was significant demoralization of teachers, many of whom objected to the implicit questioning of their competence and the largely negative portrayal of teacher competence widely disseminated by the media. Furthermore, the questionable validity of the test and the fact that considerable effort and expense were devoted to remediation *before* teachers took the test detract considerably from its usefulness. It is perhaps revealing that as of this writing, the test has not been readministered, and no other school jurisdiction has undertaken a similar, massive screening of teacher competence.

Although it is easy to understand the administration's and the public's wish to monitor teacher behavior and its effects more closely, it is also easy to understand why a large number of teachers are reluctant to conform to increasing demands for manifested competence. Some subjects are more difficult than others to teach and to learn; some students learn more slowly or more rapidly; and some teachers are better than other teachers at their profession.

One way of increasing and monitoring teacher responsiveness to parental and administrative expectations is through the widespread requirement that teachers specify instructional objectives for their courses. But this is not the most important reason for using instructional objectives; their contribution to good teaching is even more important.

Mager's Instructional Objectives

Mager (1962) has described in detail the characteristics of useful instructional objectives. First, the objectives must specify clearly what the learner must be able to *do* following instruction. An instructional objective is a statement of the instructor's goals in behavioral terms — that is, worded in terms of the actual, observable performance of the student. This type of instructional objective serves not only as a description of course goals, but also as a guide for instructional strategy. Furthermore, it serves as a guide for evaluation of student and teacher performance, about which more is said in Chapter 14.

Consider the following statements of instructional objectives:

1. The student should understand evolutionary theory.

2. The student should be able to state the two Darwinian laws of evolution and give examples of each.

Mager argues that the second objective is more useful than the first for several reasons. The second objective specifies exactly what students must *do* to demonstrate that they have reached the course goal; it provides the teacher with specific guidelines for determining whether course goals have been reached; and it suggests what must be taught if course goals are to be reached. The first statement, because of its use of the ambiguous term *understand* and the global phrase *evolutionary theory*, does none of the above. It is clearly open to misinterpretation. Similarly, such terms as *know, appreciate,* and *master* are rarely found in the kind of objectives Mager recommends unless the nature of knowing, appreciating, or mastering is also clearly spelled out.

A second quality of meaningful instructional objectives is that they often establish specific criteria of acceptable performance. Consider the following statements:

1. The learner will be able to translate a simple passage from French to English.

2. The learner will be able to translate a simple passage from French to English without the use of a dictionary. The passage will be taken from the prescribed text, and the

translation will be considered correct if there are no more than five errors for each 100 words of text and acceptable if the translation is completed in no more than twenty minutes for each 100 words.

The second statement is more precise than the first, and again it is more useful for both the instructor and the learner. It specifies not only the nature of the expected behavior but also the constraints under which it is to be performed to be considered acceptable.

Writing good instructional objectives is a time-consuming task. However, carefully prepared objectives can be of tremendous assistance to teachers in planning instructional strategies and in evaluating both their own performance and that of their students. In addition, if statements of behavioral objectives are given to each student at the beginning of courses, units, or lessons, they can be of tremendous value to the learner. In Mager's words, "If you give each learner a copy of your objectives, you may not have to do much else" (1962, p. 53).

Other Views on Instructional Objectives

Not all educators agree that Mager's approach to instructional objectives is the best of all possible approaches. A number argue that the use of performance-oriented objectives presents several definite disadvantages. For example, Eisner (1967) suggests that strict adherence to behavioral objectives restricts the development of curriculum, discourages other important learning outcomes, and fails to recognize that attitudes are among the most important outcomes of instruction. Accordingly, he argues that a teacher's instructional objectives should include not only performance objectives of the kind described by Mager, but also **expressive objectives**. Expressive objectives involve a conscious recognition by the teacher that the visible and measurable outcomes of a learning experience are not the only outcomes of that experience (and, in many cases, not always

the most important). For example, a reading teacher not only should intend to teach reading (an outcome that can easily be expressed in terms of Mager's instructional objectives) but also should try to instill positive attitudes toward reading (an outcome less easily expressed in Mager's terms).

Another viewpoint on instructional objectives, advanced by Gronlund (1972, 1975), is particularly relevant here. To begin with, Gronlund agrees that Mager's emphasis on very specific, performance-oriented objectives is both appropriate and effective for simple skills and for content areas that can be described in terms of specific items of information. Such emphasis is considerably less appropriate, however, for more complex subjects and more advanced cognitive behaviors. For these, Gronlund (1972) suggests that teachers express primary objectives in general rather than specific terms. Each primary objective should then be elaborated in terms of more specific learning outcomes, or, in many cases, in terms of examples of behaviors that would reflect the primary objective.

There is a fundamental difference between these examples of behaviors and Mager's instructional objectives. Mager's objectives specify actual behaviors that constitute instructional objectives in and of themselves. Gronlund's examples, however, are not objectives per se but are instead *examples* of the type of *evidence* that a teacher can look for to determine whether or not the primary objective has been attained. This approach, as is shown in the examples that follow, may be used to describe expressive objectives as well. For instance, the primary objective might be the development of a certain attitude; specific behaviors would serve as evidence of attainment of that attitude. (Figure 5.1 summarizes the differences among these three viewpoints.)

To illustrate and clarify the preceding passage, consider the following objectives for a poetry unit. Objectives based on Mager's approach might include such statements as:

Eisner: "Expressive"	Gronlund: "General and Specific"	Mager: "Behavioral Objective"
Students develop an understanding of everyday uses of multiplication in our society	Primary objective: The student understands how to perform simple multiplication. Specific learning outcomes: a. can define what multiplication means, in his or her own words b. can define relevant terms such as "multiplier" and "product" c. can solve problems	The student can solve nine out of ten multiplication problems of the type "5 x 4 = ?"

Affective ⟶ General ⟶ Specific

Figure 5.1   Different types of instructional objectives.

1. The student should be able to name the titles and authors of five poems in the unit.

2. The student should be able to recite, with no more than three errors, ten consecutive lines from a single poem in the unit.

Eisner's expressive objectives might center on the desirability of having a student develop positive feelings for poetry and/or for specific poems and poets:

1. The student should develop an appreciation for the Romantic poets.

Finally, Gronlund's objectives might begin with an expressive objective such as the preceding one and then elaborate further with one or more of the following behavior examples:

1. The student chooses to read (or write) poetry during a free reading period.

2. The student attempts to evaluate poetry as being good or bad (or to compare different poems).

In summary, each of these three approaches to the formulation of instructional objectives has its advantages and disadvantages. Mager's approach emphasizes specificity and objective behaviors and is particularly useful for simple

skills and factual content areas. Eisner's approach recognizes the importance of affective outcomes of instructional procedures. Gronlund's suggestions are useful for more complex subject areas and for higher-level intellectual processes and can also be used to formulate expressive objectives. There is clearly room for each of these in the conscientious teacher's repertoire.

CATEGORIES OF LEARNING OUTCOMES

The formulation of instructional objectives is not simply an intriguing (or not-so-intriguing) exercise foisted upon teachers-in-training by unsympathetic instructors. Among other things, formulating instructional objectives clarifies for the teacher what should be taught, why it needs to be taught, and in many cases how it should be taught. In addition, clear statements of the expected outcome of the teaching/learning process (in other words, clear statements of instructional objectives) give students a standard against which to match their eventual performance. As Robert Gagné (1985) notes, informing learners of instructional objectives gives them an expectation about their performance. Eventual confirmation of this expectation is a powerful source of intrinsic reinforcement.

Formulating objectives is not a simple armchair exercise that can be performed equally well by idiots and by teachers. Indeed, in a striking number of instances, teachers might devise far more useful and appropriate objectives. And one of the reasons why they might do so is particularly relevant here: A teacher might reasonably be assumed to have knowledge concerning the types of learning in which it is possible and wise for humans to engage. If we could (or should) engage in only one type of learning, such as classical conditioning, then an instructor's objectives should involve no more than classical conditioning outcomes, and corresponding instructional procedures should be based directly on what is known about classical conditioning. Fortunately (or unfortunately),

we are far more complex than this, and we engage in a wide variety of types of learning, each of which is important. This section examines a categorization of learned human behaviors advanced by Robert Gagné. It is similar to that of Bloom et al. (1956), which is discussed in Chapter 14.

R. Gagné (1985) classifies learned human capabilities into five major domains: intellectual skills, verbal information, attitudes, motor skills, and cognitive strategies. These five domains represent, in effect, outcomes of the learning process. The practical usefulness of Gagne's instructional theory* derives largely

---

*Some writers, including Robert Gagné (Gagné and Dick, 1983), refer to this theory as the "Gagné-Briggs theory" following a major book by these two authors (Gagné and Briggs, 1983).

from his analysis of the conditions most conducive to learning the capabilities represented by each of the five domains. Knowledge of these conditions, although still incomplete and speculative, can be of tremendous value in suggesting appropriate instructional strategies. Accordingly, each of these categories is described in the following sections, together with the conditions believed to be conducive to their learning.

Intellectual Skills

As Gagné uses the phrase, **intellectual skills** refers to the outcomes of learning. In one sense, these skills are the outcomes of the learning processes described by the learning theorists discussed in earlier chapters of this book. Thus, intellectual skills include both the effects of classical conditioning and more complex outcomes, such as the learning of discriminations, rules, and concepts.

Discrimination Learning.

Learning various discriminations involves acquiring the ability to differentiate among similar inputs in order to respond correctly to those inputs.

One condition necessary for the learning of discriminations is the presence of the related individual sequences of responses. These sequences are often called **chains**. Several other conditions are also important. To begin with, each of the stimuli that is to be discriminated must be presented in order to elicit the chain appropriate for it. Both confirmation (reinforcement) and repetition also appear to be important in ensuring that the discrimination will not be forgotten due to the interference of other, related learning. Moreover, to reduce interference, measures should be taken to emphasize the discriminability of stimuli.

As a simple example of discrimination learning in schools, consider the task of teaching students to discriminate (tell the difference)

between the letters *p* and *b*. Recall that one of the conditions necessary for discrimination learning is the presence of the related individual chains. In this case, these consist of the students' being able to say "b" or "p." Also, the individual chains must be repeated and reinforced, and distinctions among them must be highlighted. For example, the teacher might draw attention to the most obvious differences between the two letters and might also invent certain mnemonics that highlight these differences (for example, *b* looks like a boot and is also the first letter of that word).

Discrimination learning is complex, but it is prevalent in much school learning. Among other things, it is involved in learning to make different responses to printed letters, numbers, or words; in learning to differentiate among classes of things; and in learning to identify similar objects.

Concept Learning.

Although discrimination learning and concept learning both involve responding to similarities and differences, it is generally true that discrimination is concerned more with differences, whereas concept learning is concerned more with detecting similarities. At a simple level, a concept is a notion or an idea that reflects the common characteristics of related events or objects. In Bruner's terms, a concept (*category* is an equivalent term) is a rule for treating things as though they were in some ways equivalent.

Cognitive theories are clearly among the most appropriate psychological theories to explain the learning of concepts. In Bruner's theory, for example, concept learning involves forming categories on the basis of what is common to different events. Not surprisingly, Robert Gagné suggests that repeated experience with situations and events that present examples of the concept in question is one of the important external conditions that facilitate the learning of concepts. As an illustration, he describes a simple procedure whereby a child can be taught the meaning of the concept *odd*. Essentially, the procedure involves presenting the child with a series of three objects; two of them are identical, the other is odd. The procedure continues with a variety of groups of objects and might involve placing a tangible reward (candy, for example) under the odd object or simply reinforcing the child verbally for selecting correctly. Subsequently the teacher verifies the child's grasp of the concept by asking for additional examples.

The importance of concept learning can hardly be overemphasized. Concepts are essential elements of our thought processes; they are the substance of our views of the world; they enable us to make sense of both the world and our own behaviors. In Bruner's terms, they reduce the complexity of the environment; they make it possible to generalize, to make decisions, and to behave appropriately.

Rule Learning. In spite of the fact that concepts (or categories or nodes, if you prefer those terms) are fundamentally important, they are not sufficient. Clearly, students cannot be presented with all the different instances for which they will need a response. For example, if one of the instructional goals of a mathematics program is that students should be able to subtract 1,978 from 2,134, from 7,461, from 1,979, and so on, each of these instances need not (and probably cannot) be taught separately. Instead, a concept or a combination of concepts is used. This combination of concepts takes the form of a rule (which Gagné defines as a combination of two or more concepts). Rules reflect that which is systematic and predictable, thereby enabling us to respond to different situations in similar, rule-regulated ways. Spoken language offers numerous illustrations of rules. A child who says, "He jumps, cats jump, men jump, and rabbits jump" is obviously applying the rule that a verb preceded by a plural subject does not ordinarily end in *s*.

In discussing the external conditions that facilitate the learning of rules, Gagné suggests that instruction is typically verbal (Gagné and Briggs, 1983). In this case, the purpose of the instruction is usually to remind the learner of relevant concepts as well as to highlight important relationships among these concepts. As an illustration, Gagné and Briggs (1983) describe a situation in which a teacher presents students with a list of words, such as *made, fate, pale*; has them pronounce these words; and points out to them that the first vowel in each has a "long" sound. Following this, students are asked to pronounce *mad, fat,* and *pal*; then the instructor points out that the vowel has a "short" sound and also verbalizes the relevant rule. Alternately, the teacher might simply present a variety of examples and encourage learners, perhaps through appropriate questioning, to discover the rule for themselves. As Gagné and Briggs point out, whether a Brunerian type of discovery learning is involved or whether the learning is more like Ausubel's reception learning depends largely on the amount of instructional guidance provided.

The educational implications of rule learning are considerable, particularly in view of the fact that much of what is learned in school consists of rules. Consider even as simple a statement as "Mammals give birth to live young." The idea that mammals do indeed give birth to live young can only be understood if the concepts of mammals, birth, and live young are meaningful and if the verbal chain involved conveys that meaning. The sentence "Mammals give birth to live young" is really a verbal expression of a rule. In addition, rules are what permit us to solve problems. In fact, Gagné refers to problem solving as a category of "higher-order rules." *Problem solving* refers to the thinking out of a solution to a problem by combining old rules in order to form new ones. It is the main reason for learning rules in the first place.

Numerous examples of problem solving can be drawn from the daily activities of ordinary people. Whenever no previously learned rule is appropriate for the solution of a problem, problem solving may be said to take place (providing, of course, that the problem is in fact solved). A child who is learning to tie a shoe may combine several rules in order to succeed. The idea that laces go into holes and the notion that intertwined laces tend to cling together are rules that may be combined to form the higher-order rule: "Laced shoes with intertwined laces may be considered tied." Gagné (1977a) draws some less mundane examples from mathematics (show that $21(a + b) = 21a + 21b$), and from creative problems such as Maier's (1930) pendulum problem. (Maier's problem involves constructing an apparatus that can be used to mark the floor at a designated point in a room; the subject is provided with poles, wire, chalk, and several clamps.)

A condition clearly necessary for problem solving is the presence of the appropriate rules in the learner's repertoire. Gagné also describes some external conditions that appear to be useful for problem solving:

1. Verbal instructions or questions may be used to elicit the recall of relevant rules.

2. The direction of thought processes may also be guided by verbal instructions.

Summary of Intellectual Skills. The preceding discussion of Robert Gagné's classification of intellectual skills shows how educational implications are derived from learning theory. For example, knowledge of the conditions that facilitate learning suggests specific instructional strategies.

Gagné (1968, 1977b) points out that many school subjects consist of a hierarchy of information or skills such that in order to understand higher levels, it is necessary to have mastered a number of subordinate capabilities. It follows that instruction must proceed from the subordinate to the final task. The validity of this observation is perhaps clearest in subjects such as

mathematics, in which solving higher-level problems requires mastery of a variety of subordinate skills.

Just as knowledge within a given content area may be described in terms of a hierarchical arrangement of subordinate capabilities, so may classes of learning skills. The learner must master lower levels before progressing to higher ones. In a nutshell, problem solving depends upon rules, which are derived from concepts, which require as prerequisites the learning of discriminations. Discriminations depend upon either verbal associations or motor chains, both of which are derived from stimulus-response connections.

The instructional implications of this position can be summarized as follows:

1. Content in a given area should be arranged in hierarchical fashion so that simpler abilities and concepts necessary for later learning are mastered first.

2. Instructional goals should be analyzed in terms of the types of learning involved in their attainment. Instructional procedures should then be premised on knowledge of the *conditions* required for those types of learning.

Next we turn to the remaining four major domains of learned capabilities as classified by R. Gagné (1985). Each of these is also important in schools, and the acquisition of each can be facilitated through manipulation of conditions external to the learner. First we discuss verbal information.

Verbal Information

A great deal of the school learning that is of most direct concern to teachers takes the form of verbal information. In effect, verbal information is nothing more or less complicated than what is generally described as **knowledge**. An identifying characteristic of verbal information is that it can be expressed as a sentence, or that it implies a sentence. Thus the statement "Individuals of *Ursus arctos* are the true bears" and the single word *bear* are both expressions of verbal information; both presumably have meaning for whomever expresses them. This does not mean that verbal information is always learned and stored verbally. Much of our verbal information is derived from pictures and illustrations, perhaps from visions and dreams, but surely from our own behavior and that of others, as well as from the countless observations that we make in the course of our daily activities.

Robert Gagné describes the three principal functions of verbal information as follows: First, specific items of verbal information are frequently required for the acquisition of other verbal information. It is clear that the sentence "Turkeys are noble" will remain meaningless until the learner understands what the words *turkeys* and *noble* mean. Both these items of information are examples of verbal information.

Second, verbal information is very often of immediate practical value; more than that, it is indispensable to ordinary conversation. The names of objects, their relationships and uses, their meanings — all represent items of verbal information. Without a body of common verbal information, not only would we be incapable of communicating verbally with each other, but we would find ourselves quite confused by such simple things as traffic signals and all the other trappings of our cosmopolitan societies.

The third important function of verbal information is that it makes thinking possible. It is little wonder that schools devote so much time and energy to deciding what bodies of knowledge (verbal information) should be transmitted to students and how they can best be transmitted.

Many of the conditions that Robert Gagné describes as desirable external conditions for the acquisition of verbal information are similar to those described by Ausubel and are validated by more recent cognitive research (see, for example, Glaser and Bassok, 1989). Thus, Gagné mentions the importance of advance organizers and meaningful context. In addition, verbal information can often be made more meaningful through use of photos, charts, illustrations, and other pictorial representations. Other useful instructional strategies are intended to ensure that learners pay attention and to facilitate recall and generalization. Thus, variations of tone and emphasis in oral presentation, the use of attention-compelling instructional aids such as slides and films, and other stimulus variations can serve important functions as attention-directing and motivating features of the instructional process. (See Chapter 11 for a more complete discussion of motivation in the classroom.)

Attitudes

Educators throughout the world have a number of grand goals: We want to develop students who love life and learning; who respect the people, institutions, and ideas that we respect; and who want to be good citizens. In short, we want to develop students with positive attitudes. In fact, however, our educational systems teach attitudes only incidentally; they are aimed more toward teaching motor skills, verbal information, intellectual skills, and, to some extent, cognitive strategies. Why? Because an attitude is not an easy thing to teach, for it is a personal affective (emotional) reaction. In brief, an **attitude** is a positive or negative predisposition that has important motivational components. A positive attitude toward school, for example, implies not only liking school, but endeavoring to do well in school, to be liked by teachers, and to conform to the explicit and implicit goals of the school.

At a simple level, attitudes are affected by reinforcement. Students who have been most successful in school usually have more positive attitudes toward school than those who have not been successful (that is, have not been reinforced). And although this observation is, in fact, obvious, teachers do not always behave as though they were fully aware of it. If you want your students to have positive attitudes toward whatever it is you are trying to teach them, it is imperative that they meet with success (reinforcement) rather than failure, particularly in their initial encounters with you and the subject you are teaching.

Gagné (1974) refers to Bandura's description of imitative learning as one of the principal indirect methods for teaching attitudes (see Chapter 12). Steps in the instructional sequence include: selecting an appropriate model, preferably one with whom the student identifies (teachers are powerful models); arranging for the model to display personal choices reflecting the attitudes to be established; and drawing attention to the model's consequent reinforcement. If, for example, a teacher describes some

small act of honesty that she engaged in and for which she was subsequently reinforced either directly or simply through "feeling good" about her behavior, she has gone some distance toward developing positive attitudes toward honesty in her charges. Lest this sound too simplistic, however, let me hasten to point out that attitudes are subtle, pervasive, and powerful predispositions to think, act, and feel in certain ways; they are established in many ways and places (out of school as well as in it); and they are not nearly as easy to modify as the preceding discussion might imply.

Motor Skills

Motor skills are the many skills in our repertoires involving the execution of sequences of controlled muscular movements. Writing, typing, driving, walking, talking, dancing, and digging holes for outdoor toilets are motor skills. Some of these are important for school; others aren't. They can be taught through appropriate verbal instructions and demonstration (for example, "This is how you should sit in front of your computer . . . address the ball . . . grasp the shovel . . . hold the pencil . . . point your nose"); and they are perfected primarily through practice. Like other skills, motor skills are highly susceptible to reinforcement. Not only is reinforcement involved in determining whether a learner is likely to want to acquire a skill (in other words, whether or not the learner's attitude will be positive), but it is intimately involved in determining how well and how rapidly the skill will be learned and perfected. A word processor would learn very slowly if he could not see the results of his work. Not only could he not correct his mistakes, but he would receive little reinforcement for a good performance.

Cognitive Strategies

Our intellectual functioning is guided by complex, highly personal strategies. These strategies govern how we pay attention, how we go about studying and organizing, and how we analyze, synthesize, and recall. In a sense, they result from the development of the elusive capabilities involved in learning how to think, to create, to discover, and to remember.

A Review of Terms in Cognition. The terms *cognitive strategy* and *metacognition* are important in current educational research. To clarify these concepts, this section presents a brief review of definitions and distinctions made in Chapter 3 (where these concepts are discussed in more detail).

Metacognitive skills involve knowing about knowing. As we develop, we arrive at an implicit understanding of some of the processes involved in learning, organizing, and remembering; we develop notions of ourselves as knowers—as players of what Flavell (1985) calls the "game of cognition." And we develop notions about whether we are good or bad players of this game, as well as notions about how we can and should control our activities to become better players. Sternberg (1983) refers to these metacognitive skills as *executive skills*; they are the skills involved both in setting goals and in monitoring, controlling, and evaluating intellectual activity, much as an executive might set company goals, establish policies, direct employee activities, monitor company functioning, and so on.

Cognitive strategies are the procedures that are used in learning, solving problems, and remembering. Unlike metacognitive skills, they have little to do with monitoring, controlling, directing, or changing ongoing cognitive activity. They are, in effect, the tools of cognitive activity—the strategies that are actually applied. They are Sternberg's (1983) *nonexecutive skills*. Specifically, they include the skills of elaboration, rehearsal, and organization (Weinstein and Mayer, 1986).

Robert Gagné's use of the expression *cognitive strategy* is somewhat more global than this, for it includes aspects of both metacognitive and cognitive strategies. Thus, he defines cognitive strategies as "the skills by means of which learners regulate their own internal processes of attending, learning, remembering, and thinking" (1985, p. 55). He also refers to these skills as "executive" processes. In short, he defines cognitive strategies as others have defined metacognitive skills. At the same time, he presents several examples of cognitive strategies that involve procedures used in actual learning (the use of mnemonics, for example), rather than self-monitoring, executive processes. Thus, Gagné's use of the phrase *cognitive strategy* is essentially identical to our use of the expression *learning/thinking strategy*—a global expression that includes both metacognitive (executive) and cognitive (nonexecutive) skills and has the advantage of reflecting the entire

Table 5.1 Robert Gagné's five major domains of learning outcomes, some illustrations, and some suggestions pertinent to the instructional process

Outcomes of Learning (Major Domains)	Examples	Suggested Conditions for Facilitating Outcomes
1. Intellectual skills		
Problem solving (Higher-order rules)	Learner determines optimal order of topics in an instructional sequence through experimentation	Review of relevant rules; verbal instructions to aid in recall of rules; verbal instructions to direct thought processes
Rules	Learner demonstrates that metals expand when heated and contract when cooled	Learner is made aware of desired learning outcome; review of relevant concepts; concrete examples
Concepts	Learner classifies objects in terms of size (shape, function, position, color)	Examples presented; learner actively involved in finding examples; reinforcement
Discriminations	Learner distinguishes among various printed letters of the alphabet	Simultaneous presentation of stimuli to be discriminated; reinforcement (confirmation); repetition
2. Verbal information	Learner recalls information in writing or orally	Advance organizers; meaningful context; instructional aids for motivation and retention
3. Cognitive strategies	Learner devises personal strategy for remembering complex verbal material	Frequent presentation of novel and/or challenging problems
4. Attitudes	Learner selects among a choice of activities (subjects, teachers, schools)	Models; reinforcement; verbal guidance
5. Motor skills	Learner writes (swims, walks, runs, flies)	Models: verbal directions; reinforcement (knowledge of results); practice

range of activities involved in learning and thinking.

Summary of Gagné's Learning Outcomes

Table 5.1 summarizes Robert Gagné's classification of learning outcomes and of external conditions that appear to facilitate these outcomes. Knowledge of both conditions and outcomes can be of considerable value in helping teachers arrive at appropriate and effective instructional strategies. But the learning sequence is, in many respects, much more complex than our somewhat simplified discussions might imply. Gagné (1974) recognizes this greater complexity in a model of the act of learning, presented in Figure 5.2. This model takes into consideration the importance of motivational and attention-compelling factors, as well as retention and transfer.

Motivation Phase
EXPECTANCY

Apprehending Phase
ATTENTION;
SELECTIVE
PERCEPTION

Acquisition Phase
CODING;
STORAGE ENTRY

Retention Phase
MEMORY
STORAGE

Recall Phase
RETRIEVAL

Generalization Phase
TRANSFER

Performance Phase
RESPONDING

Feedback Phase
REINFORCEMENT

Figure 5.2   The phases of an act of learning and the processes associated with them.
From R. M. Gagné, *Essentials of Learning for Instruction.* Copyright © 1974 by The Dryden Press. Reprinted by permission of CBS College Publishing.

EFFECTIVE TEACHING

However intriguing and fascinating learning theories might be, for our purposes they are quite useless unless we can find some way of using them to increase the effectiveness of our teaching.

Some Implications of Learning Theory

Robert Gagné's ideas, summarized in the preceding sections, are an excellent example of how learning theory can be related directly to educational practice. For every type of learning, Gagné describes instructional procedures that might be important. In addition, his classification of learning outcomes takes into account each of the varieties of learning discussed in earlier chapters (classical conditioning, operant conditioning, and cognitive learning), thus serving as a summary of those chapters.

The recent educational literature abounds with other examples of how findings and theories about learning can be translated into instructional practice. In fact, Glaser and Bassok (1989) note that research on instruction can no longer be easily separated from research on cognitive processes.

What kind of research is this?

There is a great deal of it, spanning a wide variety of age and grade levels and involving many subjects and instructional procedures. As a result, it is not easily described or summarized. For our purposes, however, the most important research is that which has looked at the effects of specific, theory-derived instructional procedures on the performance of learners. Often, the research has involved elaborate, relatively long-term experimental, school-based programs. Some of these are described later in this chapter. (Also see Rosenshine and Stevens, 1986, or Glaser and Bassok, 1989, for summaries and reviews.)

More important, what does the research tell us?

Many things, Alexander and Judy (1988) claim, among which are two findings they describe as "undisputed facts." First, the more the learner knows about a specific subject (that is, the more *domain-specific* knowledge there is in the individual's cognitive structure), the better the learner will understand and remember. Second, learners who are most adept at monitoring and controlling their cognitive activities typically do better than other learners who are less skilled players of Flavell's (1985) game of cognition.

These two "undisputed" findings have profound implications for teacher behavior. The finding about those with the greatest amount of domain-specific prior learning (as opposed to more general information) highlights the importance of advance preparation for learning. It also emphasizes the cumulative and hierarchical nature of much of our learning, and it lends support to the contention that both lessons and curricula need to present material so that new understanding builds on a firm existing base of knowledge and skills. It makes no difference whether we use the language of a Bruner (numerous, varied instances of concepts need to be presented so that the learner can discover generic coding systems that will permit *going beyond the information given*); of an Ausubel (learners need to be given — and reminded of — stable, relevant subsuming concepts so that there will be something in cognitive structure to give meaning to new learning and to which new learning can be firmly anchored); or of a Robert Gagné (the content in any given subject area needs to be hierarchically presented so that essential subordinate skills and understanding are available). In the final analysis, the instructional implications of each of these differently worded, and somewhat jargon-laden, parenthetical statements are much the same: Understanding depends very much on what we already know. It isn't a particularly startling revelation, but it is a fundamentally important one.

The second of Alexander and Judy's (1988) "undisputed" facts — that learners who are best at monitoring and controlling their cognitive strategies perform better — also has clear instructional implications: Specifically, if it is possible to teach the skills and strategies of thinking, then teachers should do so. The final section in this chapter, "Teaching Thinking," deals with precisely this topic.

In addition to these two findings (which relate to the role of previous learning in the accumulation of understanding and to the role of self-monitored cognitive strategies), cognitive research on learning presents several other findings that are relevant to instruction. Among these, Shuell (1986) includes cognitive psychology's emphasis on the *active* nature of learning (in contrast to a more passive view that stresses the importance of response consequences) and its concern with comprehension (rather than simply with performance). Another important line of cognitive research, discussed in Chapter 4, deals with the role of the learner's preconceived and often incorrect notions. As Nickerson (1988) notes, "an approach to instruction that ignores [learner misconceptions] is likely to fail" (p. 35).

Conclusions of Research on Effective Teaching

Rosenshine and Stevens (1986) summarize a number of experimental studies that have looked at the effectiveness of theory-generated instructional programs in schools. In general, these studies show that is is possible to train teachers to follow specific instructional procedures and that students exposed to experimental programs often outperform comparable control groups on a variety of measures.

The studies reviewed by Rosenshine and Stevens (1986, p. 377) suggest that effective teaching is characterized by a number of behaviors that can be taught and encouraged in teachers. Specifically, the most effective teachers, with respect to teaching *well-structured* subjects, are those who:

1. start their lessons with a brief review of prerequisite learning

2. begin by stating the lesson's goals

3. present material in small steps, allowing for student practice between steps

4. give explicit and detailed instructions and explanations

5. allow all students to practice lessons actively

6. ask many questions to check for student understanding, and obtain responses from all students

7. provide students with immediate guidance for initial practice

8. provide systematic feedback and correct students' errors as they occur

9. provide clear and explicit instructions for seatwork and monitor student performance as necessary

Rosenshine and Stevens caution that these teaching procedures do not apply to all students at all times. As noted above, they are most applicable to well-structured content for which it is possible to break the presentation into small steps, provide detailed and explicit instructions, allow for student practice with immediate corrective feedback, and so on. But when the lesson deals with more abstract, less-structured content (such as morality and ethics, creative writing, politics, and so on), different teaching approaches are necessary.

TEACHING THINKING

Alexander and Judy (1988) found that those who possess *strategic* as well as domain-specific knowledge make the best learners. Strategic knowledge deals with how to do things: how to solve problems; how to learn and memorize; how to understand; and, perhaps most important, how to monitor, evaluate, and direct these activities as they occur. It is, using the terms we used earlier, *procedural* rather than *declarative* knowledge.

Can students be taught these strategic or procedural skills? Can they be taught how to think and learn?

In a word, yes.

Benjamin Bloom (1984) believes that one of the important current challenges of educational research is to discover instructional procedures that are as effective with entire classes as one-to-one tutorials are with single students. His review of the literature finds that a one-to-one tutorial is by far the most effective method of instruction currently available. In fact, if given good tutoring, the average student can be expected to achieve at somewhere around the ninety-eighth percentile in a group of comparable students taught in a conventional classroom setting. In other words, in a tutorial situation, an average student will outperform 98 percent of students in ordinary classrooms! The potential for higher achievement is apparently there; only the method is lacking. Finding that method (or methods) is the challenge.

Learning How to Learn

One response to Bloom's challenge can be seen in the contemporary cognitive sciences, with their emphasis on identifying cognitive strategies and developing methods for teaching them. One of the major contributions of a cognitive orientation is an emphasis on the processes involved in learning rather than simply on the products of learning. Students are expected to do far more than simply learn; they are expected to learn how to learn.

Learning how to learn in schools is not, of course, entirely new. What is new is our attitude toward what it is that makes learning difficult or easy. Traditionally, we have simply assumed that the most important factor in learning is inherited or natural intelligence — recognizing, of course, that motivation, persistence, and other similar factors are important as well. Recently, however, our conceptions of intelligence have begun to change dramatically. We have begun to accept the view that the important components of intelligent activity are cognitive functions that are largely acquired, not inherited.

Sternberg's (1985) contextual and componential theory of intelligence is a case in point. Intelligence, he informs us, consists of three separate components: **metacomponents, performance components**, and **knowledge-acquisition components**. The metacomponents are the executive skills; the performance components include cognitive functions (non-executive skills) used in carrying out an intellectual task; and the knowledge-acquisition components are skills used in acquiring new information.

Haywood and Switzky (1986) make a similar point. Intelligent behavior, they assert, requires two things: native ability (what we think of as innate intelligence) and cognitive functions. The important point is that, whereas native ability is, by definition, genetic and therefore unmodifiable except by extreme measures, cognitive functions are acquired. Does it not follow that if they are learned, they can also be taught?

The simple answer is yes. And there is increasing evidence that this learning need not occur only incidentally — or even accidentally — as a by-product of school activities whose purposes are far removed from teaching students how to learn. A mushrooming new field of research involves looking for ways in which students can be taught not only the cognitive skills of rehearsing, elaborating, and organizing, but also the metacognitive skills involved in monitoring their own levels of comprehension and in making other important "executive" decisions about their cognitive activities. Psychologists are being increasingly successful in discovering the rules, the strategies, and the objectives of this game of cognition that all of us are called upon to play. And, as a result, today's students may be far better players tomorrow than they would otherwise have been.

Researchers who have developed and investigated programs designed specifically to teach students how to learn and think have emphasized a variety of skills. Nickerson's (1988) review suggests that there have been at least seven identifiable emphases:

1. basic operations such as classifying or generalizing

2. domain-specific knowledge

3. knowledge about reasoning principles such as logic

4. knowledge about informal principles of thinking that might be used in problem solving

5. metacognitive knowledge

6. values such as fairness and objectivity

7. personal beliefs (for example, about problems, about the world, about causes, and about the role of luck and effort)

These different emphases have led to the development of a variety of programs for teaching thinking. Several of these are described briefly in the following sections.

Dansereau's Metastrategies

Dansereau and his associates have developed a program designed to teach a number of general cognitive strategies to college students (Dansereau, 1985). These strategies are applicable primarily to verbal learning and are divided into two groups: primary and support strategies.

Primary strategies are information-processing skills for learning, storing and retrieving, and deriving meaning from textual material. They consist of such activities as using visual imagery, summarizing, paraphrasing, analyzing questions, and using context to facilitate recall. Support strategies are involved in maintaining an appropriate mind-set for learning and remembering. They include such metacognitive activities as setting goals, arranging schedules, monitoring comprehension, and self-evaluation.

A general program for studying devised by Dansereau and his associates is based directly on their analysis of metastrategies (strategies of metacognition). It is called MURDER, an acronym for the following sequential procedure: set your Mood; read for Understanding; Recall; Digest information (a procedure that involves recalling correctly, rehearsing, organizing, and storing); Expand knowledge (involves elaboration through a process of self-inquiry); and Review mistakes. MURDER is a somewhat more complex process than might be implied by this brief description. For example, a number of specific tactics are taught and practiced in connection with each of the major steps in the program (relaxation techniques associated with mood setting, and imaging strategies associated with recall, for example). Studies of this program at the college level have generally shown increases in measures of cognitive functioning.

Feuerstein's Instrumental Enrichment

In practice, intelligence is most often assessed in terms of performance on tests that reveal how much a person has benefited from past experience. According to Reuven Feuerstein (1979), whose work is primarily on the topic of mental retardation, such tests represent a static rather than a dynamic view of intelligence; they reveal what the child has done rather than what the child can do in the future. They do not assess learning potential.

More useful measures of intelligence, Feuerstein argues, would do more than reflect what the child has done in the past; they would provide some estimate of capacity for benefiting from future experience. To this end, he has developed the Learning Potential Assessment Device (LPAD), which focuses on intellectual functioning — on cognitive processes — rather than simply on whether the child can answer correctly within a given time limit. The test allows the examiner to actually teach the child, to offer hints and clues, and to direct and help. Described as a dynamic rather than a static measure, it makes it possible both to identify

strengths and detect absent or deficient cognitive functions. In Feuerstein's (1980) terms, it permits the construction of a "cognitive map" of the learner, which can serve as the basis for analyzing the cognitive functioning of what he calls "retarded performers" and as a blueprint for remediation.

Among Feuerstein's greatest contributions is the development of a complex and far-reaching series of activities and exercises designed to improve cognitive functioning. This program, Feuerstein's Instrumental Enrichment (FIE, sometimes abbreviated simply IE), is based squarely on the assumption that motivates all the learning-to-learn research: namely, a strong belief in cognitive modifiability.

A logical outgrowth of the LPAD, the FIE program is largely content-free; that is, it attempts to teach cognitive functioning rather than academic content. It uses a series of progressively more abstract paper-and-pencil exercises designed to help students identify strategies used in thinking and to encourage them to become aware of their use of those strategies. In all, there are more than 500 pages of exercises — enough for a one-hour daily lesson over the course of several years.

Even though the FIE program was initally developed for use with "retarded performers" (Feuerstein deliberately avoids the term *mental retardation*), he argues that its principles are applicable to a wide range of ages and subjects. Use of the FIE program requires that teachers be specially trained.

Initial evaluation of the FIE materials involved a longitudinal experiment in which performance-retarded adolescents exposed to the FIE program were compared with similar adolescents in a more conventional, content-oriented enrichment program. Results were highly positive (Feuerstein, 1980).

Subsequent research in a number of countries, including Canada, the United States, Venezuela, and Israel, has been summarized by Savell, Twohig, and Rachford (1986). Although many of the studies they reviewed do not report clearly positive results — usually because of experimental-design inadequacies (such as lack of a control group) or shortcomings in applying the program — they nevertheless conclude that FIE has generally positive results. The most commonly reported cognitive gains are on nonverbal measures of intelligence and involve students 12 to 18 years old. Teachers in the most successful FIE programs had typically been given at least one week of training before the program, and students who were most likely to gain had been exposed to a minimum of eighty hours of FIE instruction. Gains were most likely to occur when FIE had been taught in conjunction with subjects of significant interest and importance to students.

SPELT

Another large-scale cognitive program is Mulcahy and associates' Strategies Program for Effective Learning/Thinking (SPELT) (Mulcahy, Marfo, and Peat, 1985; Mulcahy et al., 1986). Described as a learning/thinking instructional program, SPELT is designed for use with children performing over the entire range from learning-disabled to gifted. Like FIE, it focuses on process rather than content. SPELT, unlike many other cognitive development programs such as Dansereau's metastrategies and FIE, is aimed at elementary and junior-high-school students rather than adolescents or college students.

One important difference between SPELT and FIE is that SPELT is what Derry and Murphy (1986) call an *embedded* rather than a *detached* program. A detached program such as FIE or Dansereau's metastrategies is presented separately, as an addition to the school's regular program. In contrast, an embedded program occurs in the context of ongoing curricular activity. Embedded programs have the advantage that they may enhance the student's perception of the relevance of the program and

may also increase the generalizability of what is learned. In addition, financial and logistic considerations make it far easier to introduce a program that does not require a separate allocation of time.

SPELT has three major characteristics. First, its overriding goal is to involve the student actively in the learning process. It attempts to make students increasingly aware of their own cognitive processes and is geared toward discovery rather than reception learning.

The second characteristic is that SPELT requires active teacher participation in identifying and discovering strategies as well as in devising methods for teaching them. Initially, teachers are presented with tested strategies and methods; following continuing in-service training, they are encouraged to develop their own.

Third, SPELT is designed to encourage students to recognize and generate their own cognitive strategies; that is, students are expected to become increasingly aware of their own intellectual processes and to become actively involved in developing and improving these processes. In short, they are encouraged to recognize and develop the tools they use in playing the game of cognition.

The learning/thinking strategies developed and emphasized in SPELT cover the range of strategies described by Gagné, Sternberg, Weinstein and Mayer, Feuerstein, and others — for example, general problem solving, math and reading strategies, memory strategies, study skills, test-taking strategies, mood-setting strategies, and general metacognitive strategies such as comprehension monitoring. In addition, special effort is made to develop social problem-solving strategies.

Implementation of SPELT occurs in three overlapping phases. In the first phase, students are taught a number of learning/thinking strategies by teachers trained in using and teaching these strategies. Instructional procedures in this phase are direct and teacher-controlled. Their basic elements include motivating students, modeling the strategies, providing memorization and practice drills with feedback, and evaluating student learning. The goal of this phase, as expressed by Peat, Mulcahy, and Darko-Yeboah (1989), is metacognitive empowerment—a condition that comes about as students become increasingly aware of the existence of cognitive strategies and of the contribution their systematic use can make to learning and problem solving.

The objectives of the second phase are to maintain the use of strategies learned in the first phase, to begin to evaluate the effectiveness of these strategies, and to modify and extend them to different content areas. The principal instructional method is no longer one of direct tuition, but rather one of facilitating the application of previously learned strategies to new situations (teaching for transfer). The instructional method is now *Socratic* rather than direct; that is, students are encouraged to extend and apply strategies through an interactive question-and-answer process. Among the teacher's guidelines for questioning are the following: start with what is known, ask for more than one reason, ask students to describe steps in their reasoning processes, formulate general rules from specific cases, provide counterexamples or extreme cases, probe for differences among cases, and ask students to make predictions (Mulcahy et al., 1990).

In the third phase of the SPELT program, the learner is encouraged to generate new cognitive strategies and to monitor and evaluate them. The principal instructional method continues to be that of Socratic dialogue. In contrast with the first phase, learning at this level is largely student- rather than teacher-controlled.

The SPELT program was evaluated during a three-year project involving some 900 gifted, average, and learning-disabled students in grades 4, 5, 7, and 8. Results were positive, especially for learning-disabled students and most notably at the fourth-grade level, at which reading comprehension and comprehension-monitoring skills improved most dramatically.

Gifted students also benefited significantly. Use and awareness of cognitive strategies improved at all grade levels and for all groups. In addition, parents, teachers, and administrators responded very favorably to the program. A year after termination of the experimental project, more than 85 percent of the teachers reported that they continued to use aspects of the program in their teaching.

A Conclusion

Dansereau's metastrategies, Feuerstein's Instrumental Enrichment, and Mulcahy et al.'s SPELT are only three of a large number of learning/thinking programs currently being developed, modified, and evaluated (see, for example, Nickerson, 1988). Two things seem clear at this point: First, our attempts to teach students how to think and how to learn are not always as deliberate and as focused as they might be; and second, systematic programs can significantly improve learning and thinking for a variety of individuals and in many different contexts.

Although it would be premature to suggest that teachers should now begin using this or that program for this or that purpose, it is not at all premature to repeat many education critics' claim that the schools have not always done very much to teach thinking and learning skills. The contemporary cognitive sciences are based on the assumption that much more can be done. Perhaps they are also showing us how.

MAIN POINTS

1. To instruct is to exercise control over events *external* to the learner in order to facilitate the *internal* process of learning.

2. A comprehensive instructional theory pays attention to the desired outcomes of the learning process, the preinstruction state of the learner with respect to these outcomes,

and the procedures by which the learner can make the transition from the preinstruction state to the desired outcomes.

3. Mounting concern with teacher accountability is sometimes manifested both in attempts to assess teacher competence and in the relatively general requirement that teachers make their instructional objectives explicit.

4. Statements of instructional objectives should specify both what the learner must do and the criteria of acceptable performance. They may be highly performance-oriented and specific (Mager); more expressive (affective; Eisner); or both general and specific (Gronlund).

5. Gagné classifies learning outcomes into five major domains: intellectual skills, verbal information, cognitive strategies, attitudes, and motor skills.

6. Intellectual skills are hierarchically arranged in the sense that higher-level skills depend upon lower-level skills. Intellectual skills include the learning of discriminations, rules, and concepts.

7. Discriminations result from the ability to respond differentially to similar stimulus input.

8. Concepts result from the ability to respond to similarities and are best explained by reference to cognitive theories.

9. Rules, which are statements of relationships among concepts, enable us to predict and organize. Single rules may be combined to form higher-order rules, which may be used to solve complex problems.

10. Verbal information includes what we commonly refer to as knowledge. Such information can be expressed in sentence form and is indispensable to conversation and other ordinary daily activities. Ausubel's theory deals extensively with verbal learning.

11. Attitudes are affective predispositions to make certain choices or to behave in certain ways, given a choice of behaviors. They therefore have important motivational properties.

12. Motor skills involve the execution of controlled sequences of muscular movements, such as in typing or writing.

13. Cognitive strategies are an important learning outcome in Robert Gagné's theory. He defines the term to include both metacognitive (executive) and cognitive (nonexecutive) skills. Metacognitive skills such as comprehension monitoring relate to knowing about knowing; cognitive skills are what we actually do when we learn, think, and remember — rehearsing or elaborating, for example.

14. Gagné's classification of the outcomes of learning provides a useful organizational framework for summarizing many of the learning theories discussed earlier. In addition, his description of the conditions that might facilitate these learning outcomes suggests a global theory of instruction.

15. Two findings from cognitive research have important implications for effective teaching: (1) The more background knowledge a learner has about a subject, the more effective the learning (domain-specific knowledge), and (2) learners who are most skilled at monitoring and controlling their use of cognitive strategies learn and solve problems (use strategic knowledge) most effectively.

16. Cognitive research also emphasizes the active nature of learning and the importance of comprehension. It also stresses the importance of the learner's preconceived notions (which are often misconceptions).

17. The most effective teachers with respect to well-structured material are those who: (1) begin by reviewing (often using advance organizers); (2) state goals clearly at

the beginning; and (3) present material in small, detailed, and explicit steps with both ample opportunity for practice and systematic feedback during the lesson and during seatwork.

18. Bloom's challenge is to find an instructional method(s) as effective for an entire class as a one-on-one tutorial is for a single student. Cognitive strategies research directed toward teaching thinking (or learning to learn) may be a step in that direction. This research is based on the assumption of cognitive modifiability—that is, the notion that cognitive functions are acquired and can be taught.

19. Dansereau's metastrategies approach to teaching thinking is a detached program (separate from ordinary curriculum content) that attempts to teach primary strategies (those used for learning, storing, and retrieving) and support strategies (those involved in maintaining mind-set for learning) to college populations. MURDER (Mood, Understand, Recall, Digest, Expand, Review) is a Dansereau metastrategy.

20. Feuerstein's Instrumental Enrichment (FIE) program is based on the Learning Potential Assessment Device (LPAD), which attempts to assess the retarded performer's highest potential for achievement rather than simply the extent to which the learner has profited from past experience. The LPAD makes it possible to develop a cognitive map of the learner that indicates deficits in cognitive strategies. The FIE program is designed to remediate these deficits.

21. The FIE consists of paper-and-pencil exercises directed toward the development of several cognitive strategies. The program is intended for use primarily with adolescents with performance deficits (below-average intelligence, or normal intelligence with learning disabilities or cognitive deficiencies).

22. The Strategies Program for Effective Learning/Thinking (SPELT), developed by Mulcahy and associates, is an embedded program (designed for use within the context of ordinary curriculum content) intended for elementary and junior-high-school students. In encourages teachers and students to identify and generate cognitive strategies. In addition, it presents approaches for developing teaching/learning strategies in a variety of areas (general problem solving, social problem solving, math, reading, studying, test taking, mood setting, and general metacognitive strategies).

SUGGESTED READINGS

Gagné's classification of human learning and his explanation of the conditions required for the various types of human learning are succinctly explained in the following books. (The second and third are particularly useful for teachers.)

GAGNÉ, R. M. (1985). *The conditions of learning* (4th ed.). New York: Holt, Rinehart & Winston.

GAGNÉ, R. M. (1974). *Essentials of learning for instruction.* Hinsdale, Ill.: Dryden Press.

GAGNÉ, R. M., & BRIGGS, L. J. (1983). *Principles of instructional design* (3rd ed.). New York: Holt, Rinehart & Winston.

Feuerstein's Instrumental Enrichment program is best described in the following book:

FEUERSTEIN, R. (1980). *Instrumental enrichment: An intervention program for cognitive modifiability.* Baltimore: University Park Press.

The following articles present general overviews of current research in cognitive-strategies training:

NICKERSON, R. S. (1988). On improving thinking through instruction. In E. Z. Rothkopf (Ed.), *Review of research in education* (Vol. 15). Washington, D.C.: American Educational Research Association.

GLASER, R., & BASSOK, M. (1989). Learning theory and the study of instruction. In M. R. Rosenzweig & L. W. Porter (Eds.), *Annual Review of Psychology*, 40, 631–666.

Bear, give up your humility. You are not a humble beast. You think your own thoughts. Tell them to me (Engel, 1976, p. 131).

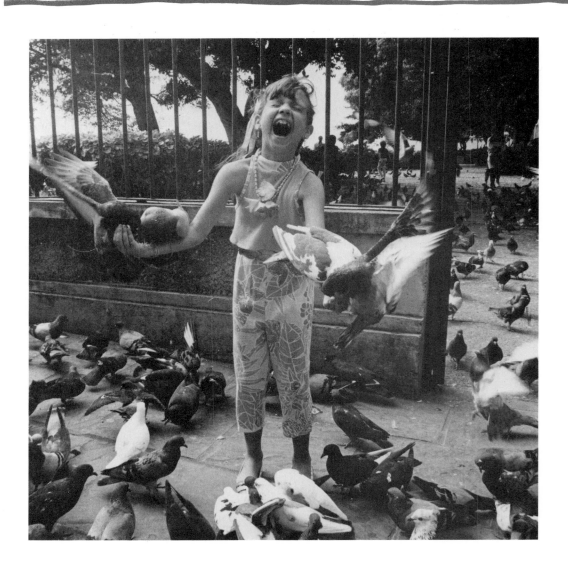

HUMANISM AND HUMAN DEVELOPMENT

We are not products of a single blueprint, put through the same assembly line and appearing identical and fully formed, ready to learn, on the educational scene. Rather, each of us is a unique model — a function of different genetic recipes and different environmental forces. And although educators are well aware of this, our psychologies and our approaches to education have sometimes been accused of mechanizing and dehumanizing the student. Chapter 6 presents a strong plea that we humanize education and recognize the uniqueness and value of every person, and it offers some suggestions about how this might be accomplished. Chapters 7 and 8 look at the processes and forces of human development and at the educational implications of our knowledge in this field.

HUMANISM AND TEACHING

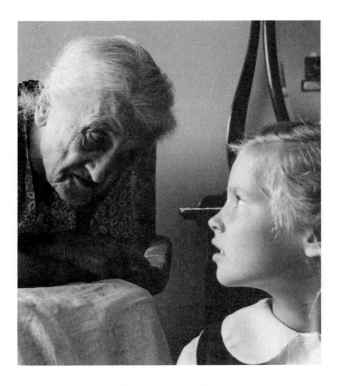

I am going to where life is more like life than it is here.

SEAN O'CASEY *Cock-a-Doodle Donkey*

There is surely a piece of divinity in us, something that was before the elements, and owes no homage unto the sun.

SIR THOMAS BROWNE *Religio Medici*

PREVIEW Humanism objects to what is sometimes interpreted as the mechanistic, dehumanizing, and inhumane emphases of "traditional" approaches to psychology and education. It urges adoption of new attitudes, concepts, and approaches in these fields. This chapter describes the fundamental characteristics of humanistic approaches to understanding people and to teaching. The most important point it makes is that humanism and behaviorism are not necessarily incompatible. You can be all the good things that humanism implies and still make use of the knowledge offered by other approaches.

▬ When I was a young student, newly initiated into the secrets of psychology, I believed that psychologists had devious ways of peering into our minds and that they could, if they cared to, easily uncover all sorts of dark secrets hidden therein. That, of course, had nothing to do with my interest in studying psychology.

I also believed, in those naive years, that there was very little about human and animal behavior that a clever psychologist could not explain to everyone's satisfaction. And so, as a budding psychologist, I brought explanations home to my grandmother. I told her why pigs lie in their muddy wallows on hot summer days; why chickens crow at the opening of new days and roost at their closing. I explained to her why cows always go into the same stall and why horses stand with their backs to winter storms.

But she saw no magic in my explanations, my grandmother. "I too, if I were a pig, would enjoy lying in the mud," she said. "And if I were a chicken I would crow in the morning and roost at night."

"But . . ."

"And if I were a cow," she continued, keeping me from telling her how she was not invalidating my explanations at all, "if I were a cow, I would be a wild cow. I would not go into stalls."

"But the point," I said (brilliantly, I thought), "is that you are not a pig, a chicken, or a cow. You're a people, and we have explanations for that too!" Quickly I launched into a wonderful behavioristic explanation of Frank's fear of cats and Louise's embarrassing attachment to the tattered remnants of a dirty-green baby blanket.

"But," countered my grandmother, "what about why Frank isn't scared of dogs and he was bitten about eight times? And cats hardly ever bit him. And what about how Louise doesn't even like any other blankets or pillows? And why doesn't Lucy like her baby blanket?"

A practiced skeptic, my grandmother could always ask questions more rapidly than I could answer them. And although I had enough of the beginnings of some answers to eventually convince her that Skinner, Freud, Piaget, and others each had important and useful things to say about Frank's fear of cats and Louise's love of a dirty rag, there was no way I could ever convince her that they or I knew more about Frank or Louise than she did.

As my grandmother so pointedly put it, "I personally know pigs that do not care to wallow in mud, chickens that neither roost nor crow, cows that insist on parking where their spirits urge them, and horses so contrary that they will face whichever way they bloody please."

My grandmother was a humanist. ▬

HUMANISTIC PSYCHOLOGY

Humanistic psychology is concerned with the uniqueness, the individuality, the *humanity* of each individual. It is an orientation that readily admits that some people smile when they wallow in mud, some turn up their noses but endure the embarrassment, and others find such behavior quite unacceptable. In more human terms, it is an orientation based on the fundamental observation that although we might resemble each other in many important ways, each of us is quite different from every other. Our uniqueness is our "self." And *self* is the most central concept in humanistic psychology.

Three different passages in this text (in Chapter 1, the Epilogue, and here) make the point that a science of humans tends to dehumanize people. This point is especially appropriate here because the approach discussed in this chapter attempts to *humanize* people.

The conflict between humanistic and more behavioristic approaches to education is a profound ideological conflict. It is based on orientations that are fundamentally different in terms of their most basic beliefs and attitudes toward human beings. In a nutshell, what humanists object to is what they see as the *technological* orientation of behaviorism. In its most extreme form, this technological orientation asserts that there are certain identifiable teaching *processes* that, when used with such and such a type of student for such and such a kind of content, will predictably result in the attainment of specific, previously identified, and clearly intended objectives.

Humanists object strongly to this *process-product* orientation. As Shulman (1986) observes, they see it as focusing too strongly on techniques that "should" be practiced by teachers and as placing far too much emphasis on the measurable outcomes of the teaching/learning process, especially in terms of gains on standardized tests. They are alarmed that the conclusions and recommendations of process-product research have often been used by school author-

ities as a basis for evaluating school systems, teachers, and teaching.

The humanistic view emphasizes two things: the uniqueness of the pupil and the autonomy of the teacher. If teaching is both an art and a science — as we claimed in Chapter 1 — humanists are on the side of art, and behaviorists are on the side of science.

But before we rush forward to describe what it is that the humanists have to say, it is important to note that our use of terms in this section, and in much of this chapter, is almost shamefully loose and general. Real life is not so simple. Behaviorists are not often as technologically oriented as an exaggerated humanistic description of their views might suggest; nor are all process-product researchers behaviorists. In fact, later in this chapter we look at two very important and very specific instructional methods (one based on learning styles and the other on cooperative learning), each of which reflects much of the humanist's concern with the individual and with emotional growth, but each of which is fundamentally concerned with *both* the processes and the products of instruction. The results of process-product research do not really suggest that teachers should ideally be quasi-robotic, classroom mechanics who repair cognitive and behavioral deficits and impairments, and produce wonderful little academic achievers.

Keep in mind that most educators do not fall neatly into either the humanist or behaviorist camp. Most are quite eclectic; they borrow from here and there.

So what we do in this chapter is stretch the truth on two counts: We exaggerate the differences between humanism and behaviorism, and we pretend that all that is not clearly humanistic is, by default, behavioristic. Exaggeration can be a useful pedagogical device — so long as you are not deceived.*

PPC: "This is an important point. Perhaps you should repeat it."
Author: "Okay. 'Exaggeration can be a useful pedagogical

ROGERIAN PHENOMENOLOGICAL THEORY

As an introduction to humanism, we look first at a summary of those aspects of the writing of Carl Rogers that deal with personality and behavior; then we look at several approaches to education that reflect humanistic orientations. (Rogers is among the most influential theorists in this area; Abraham Maslow, another important humanist, is discussed in Chapter 11.)

Rogers's writings are based not so much on objective data as on the answers to such questions as: What do individuals think about the world? How do they feel? How do they perceive their relationships to others? Thus, Rogers's theory contrasts sharply with the more rigorous approaches of other theorists. And it provides the teacher with a different way of looking at and communicating with students.

Different terms are used to describe the various emphases of Rogerian theory. The first, **person-centered therapy** (also called **client-centered therapy**), describes several aspects of the system. It indicates, first, that the theory is a therapeutic one; that is, it is designed to be useful to a counselor who deals with behavioral and emotional problems. Second, the label highlights the major difference between this and other approaches to **counseling**—namely, that the counseling procedures revolve around the person. It proposes person-centered as opposed to **directive therapy**. The counselor's role is accordingly deemphasized; instead of giving advice or solving problems *for* clients,

the therapist sets the stage so that clients themselves define their problems, react to them, and take steps toward their solution. (The process is actually much more complex than it may seem from the preceding statements; see Rogers, 1951.)

The second term is **phenomenology**, a term that denotes concern with the world as it is perceived by an individual, rather than as it may actually be. Rogerian theory is phenomenological in that it is concerned primarily with the individual's own view of the world—that is, with the world as a person sees it rather than as it appears to others.

The third term is **humanism**. Humanism in literature, philosophy, and psychology has historically been concerned with human worth, with individuality, with humanity, and with the individual's right to determine personal actions. Accordingly, the development of human potential tends to be highly valued while the attainment of material goals is deemphasized. Rogers's description of self-actualization as the end toward which all humans strive is a clear expression of humanistic concerns. In addition, his encouragement of person-centered therapy is compatible with the humanist's emphasis on self-determination. Indeed, the question of self-determination versus external control, together with a consideration of the ethical and practical problems of applying a science of behavior, was the subject of a debate between Rogers and B. F. Skinner (1956).

The Behavior-Control Debate: Rogers vs. Skinner

The central issue in this debate concerns the application of behavior-control techniques for personal control in social groups, for educational procedures, and for control by governments. Skinner argued strongly for abandoning techniques of aversive control (see Chapter 2) and for consciously and openly applying techniques of positive control toward the betterment of society. (This topic was the subject of

device—so long as you are not deceived.'"

PPC: "That's not what I meant. Can you make the point in a different way, to make it more memorable?"

Author: "Okay. Real life is seldom like the simple black-and-white pictures that we draw to depict our little theories and our precious ideological stances. We are still like children using crude wooden pencils. In our drawings we miss all the color, most of the nuances, and thousands of other poses that we could have drawn. We draw only frozen stick-men and stick-women, but we think we have drawn something with a soul."

his novel, *Walden II* [1948], an account of a fictitious society developed through the application of a behavioral technology.) But, claims Rogers, Skinner underestimated the problem of power by making the false assumption that techniques of social control will be used in the better interests of society. Furthermore, he failed to specify goals for this behavioral technology. Rogers dismisses Skinner's claim that if behavioral scientists experiment with society, "eventually the practices which make for the greatest biological and psychological strength of the group will presumably survive" (Skinner, 1955, p. 549). Rogers argues instead that a society's goals should be concerned primarily with the process of "becoming," with achieving worth and dignity, with being creative — in short, with the process of **self-actualization.**

The debate resolves no issues. It is a conflict between a position that favors human control (for our benefit) through the thoughtful application of a science of behavior, and another position that seems to assert that science should enhance our capacity for self-determination.

Principles of Rogers's Theory

In the eleventh chapter of *Client-Centered Therapy* (1951), Rogers presents an integrated account of his position in the form of nineteen propositions. The most important of these are summarized below. (Also see Table 6.1.) An understanding of these principles is important for comprehending the rationale underlying the various approaches to humanistic education described later in this chapter.

1. *Every individual is the center of a continually changing world of experience.* This, the fundamental assertion of the phenomenologist, recognizes two features of human functioning that are particularly important for the teacher. First, it states that for any individual, the significant aspects of the environment consist of the world of private experience. Second, it implies not only that the individual's phenomenological world is

private, but also that it can never be completely known by anyone else. Consider, for example, the simple complaint of a child to his mother in the unreal space that follows waking up from a nightmare: "Mama, I'm scared." The fear that the child expresses is a real and significant aspect of his world, and his mother may draw on her own stored-up memories of past fears in order to imagine how her son feels; but she cannot really *know* his fear. The phenomenological world is private.

2. *The organism reacts to a field as it is experienced and perceived. This perceptual field is, for the individual, reality.* This proposition makes the point that reality *is* the **phenomenal field** (the individual's immediate consciousness), and because this field is defined in terms of the individual's private experience, reality is also private. Therefore what is real for one individual is not necessarily real for another. Indeed, much of the disparity in behavior among people in similar circumstances can be attributed to the fact that their concepts of reality differ. A student who likes her teacher, no matter how unbearable that teacher appears to other students, has a likable teacher in her phenomenal field — and her behavior toward that teacher will reflect this reality. This is why it is important for a teacher to understand that students perceive their worlds in different ways. It is no accident that the teacher who seems to understand students best is often described as empathetic (able to intuit how others feel).

3. *The organism has one basic tendency and goal — to actualize, maintain, and enhance the experiencing organism.* It is neither necessary nor useful to list a variety of needs, drives, or goals to account for human behavior; we strive for only one goal — self-actualization. Rogers admits that "it is difficult to find words for this proposition" (1951, p. 488). Indeed, having found the central word, *self-actualization*, he is now left with

the problem of defining it. One definition is that self-actualization involves becoming whatever one can become through activities determined by oneself (Maslow, 1970). In other words, to actualize oneself is to develop one's potentialities.

Rogers attempts to clarify this definition by describing some characteristics of the process of self-actualization. It is, first, a directional process in the sense that it tends toward maturation, increasing competence, survival, reproduction, and so on. Interestingly, all these are *goals*; each has, at some time, been described as a more or less important motivation-related objective of human functioning. For Rogers, however, these goals are merely tendencies that characterize an overriding process.

Self-actualization is also directional in that it is assumed to move toward increasing "self-government, self-regulation, and autonomy." At the same time it moves away from "heteronymous control, or control by external forces" (Rogers, 1951, p. 488). This is one reason for the basic incompatibility of behavior control in a Skinnerian sense with the process of growth in a Rogerian sense.

In summary, Rogers believes that humans have an inner, directing need to develop themselves in the direction of healthy, competent, and creative functioning. This notion is absolutely basic to an understanding of the humanist's view of people as essentially good and forever striving toward a better state. It leads logically to the Rogerian belief that occasional less-than-healthy functioning is a result of the environment. This idea is not new; Jean-Jacques Rousseau proclaimed it in the eighteenth century.

4. *The best vantage point for understanding behavior is from the internal frame of reference of an individual.* This is so because the individual's reality is private and personal. Rogers claims that much of our inability to under-

stand behavior results from our failure to recognize that responses are meaningful only from the individual's own point of view. As an illustration, he explains that the explorer who describes the "ridiculous foods" and "meaningless ceremonies" of a primitive people can label them "ridiculous" or "meaningless" only from the perspective of his own culture. Because the individual's world is private, complete understanding can be obtained only through communication. Not surprisingly, the major emphasis of person-centered counseling (and of student-centered teaching) is to facilitate communication by reducing defensiveness and encouraging openness so that both the counselor and the client can understand the client's field more clearly.

5. *As a result of interaction with the environment, and particularly as a result of evaluational interaction with others, the structure of self is formed. The self is an organized, fluid, but consistent conceptual pattern of perceptions of characteristics and relationships of the "I" or the "me," together with values attached to these concepts.* As we receive feedback about ourselves from others, we incorporate this information into our concept of self. Most children receive signs at a very early age from parents and others indicating that they are lovable and good. Consequently, notions of themselves as being good become part of their perceived selves. In the same manner, a child may learn that he is "cute" from the comments of others; he may also learn that he is anything but cute ("My, my, look at that kid's nose, will you!"). As a result of receiving high grades, a student may develop a concept of self that includes the belief that she is intelligent. Conversely, she may come to think of herself as being stupid if the information she receives is negative.

Two important sources of information are related to the development of the self. The first is the child's *direct* experiences —

Behavior Control à la Rogers

As an alternative to Skinner's behavioral technology, Rogers proposes the following five-point model for the control of human behavior (Rogers and Skinner, 1956, pp. 1063–64):

1. It is possible for us to choose to value humanity as a self-actualizing process of becoming; to value creativity and the process by which knowledge becomes self-transcending.

2. We can proceed, by the methods of science, to discover the conditions that necessarily precede these processes and, through continuing experimentation, to discover better means of achieving these purposes.

3. It is possible for individuals or groups to set the conditions, with a minimum of power or control. According to present knowledge, the only authority necessary is the authority to establish certain qualities of interpersonal relationship.

4. Exposed to these conditions, individuals become more self-responsible, make progress in self-actualization, become more flexible, and become more creatively adaptive.

5. Thus such an initial choice would inaugurate the beginnings of a social system or subsystem in which values, knowledge, adaptive skills, and even the concept of science would be continually changing and self-transcending. The emphasis would be upon the human being as a process of becoming.

---

experiences of being loved and wanted and of feeling good as a result; experiences of being hurt and the consequent realization that the self does not like to be hurt; experiences of gratification (for example, eating) together with the realization that gratification is pleasant. These direct experiences lead to the development of an awareness of self. The child also experiences self-related events *indirectly* and often distorts these experiences in the awareness of self. The child who has learned through direct experience that she is lovable, but who is told by her mother, "I don't like you when you do that," may introject an image of not being liked in her perception of herself.

Indeed, many of an individual's direct and indirect experiences are incompatible and lead to conflicting notions of the self. Consider, for example, the student whose indirect experiences have led him to believe that he is academically gifted (that is, his mother has often said to him, "you're academically gifted, son") but who constantly fails in school. The resolution of this conflict may take several forms. One, of course, involves accepting the direct evidence and concluding that he is not especially brilliant. An alternative would be for him to accept the introjected value and distort his perception of direct experience. He might, for example, conclude that he is, indeed, quite brilliant but that his teachers do not like him. Or he might seek additional information to resolve the dilemma. Rogers suggests that the seeds for later maladaptive behavior are often found in the early failure to resolve the conflicting pictures of self that emerge from directly experienced and introjected values.

6. *Most of the ways of behaving that are adopted by the organism are those that are consistent with the concept of self.* Consider, for example, the man who thinks of himself as a gifted orator and who has been invited to address the local chapter of the Ear Realignment and Onion Society (EROS). This proposition predicts clearly that, in line with his image of self, this individual will accept the invitation. By the same token, a man who thinks of himself as inhibited and verbally inept would be likely to turn down such an invitation. In both these cases, and indeed in most instances of human behavior, the activity selected is compatible with the self-image.

Consider what happens, however, when the image of self is somewhat distorted — when, for example, the person who believes himself to be a gifted speaker has derived this notion not from direct experience (that is, applause following past orations) but from the words of his wise and ancient grandmother: "You shpeak zo vell, Ludwig, you mus be a gud spichmak-errr." In line with his self-image, he accepts the invitation; but as the day approaches, he becomes afraid — not *consciously*, but *organically*. This individual may suddenly find himself physically ill in a literal sense. How can a sick man be expected to address a large audience of ear realigners and onion lovers? Indeed, to refuse to do so, *when ill*, is quite congruent with this man's image of self-as-great-orator. In Rogers's words, "The behavior which is adopted is such that it satisfies the organic need, but it takes channels which are consistent with the concept of self" (1951, p. 588). This — the organism's attempt to satisfy a "real" need that is not consistent with the image of self — is assumed to be one of the primary sources of neurotic behavior in humans.

Evaluation of Rogerian Phenomenology

To summarize: Many aspects of Rogers's views of behavior are intuitively correct. It seems obvious that each individual perceives the world in a manner not experienced by anyone else. It also seems obvious that to understand others completely, it may be useful to adopt their points of view. Admittedly, however, some aspects of the propositions are not so obvious, and the meanings of terms such as *self-actualization* are not always clear. Nor are Rogers's conclusions about human behavior necessarily as general as he implies.

Rogers's approach is clearly "soft-nosed"; it is not based on rigorous, replicable research. Nevertheless, its merits in the progress of science may be considerable; even very speculative theorizing can sometimes generate fruitful ideas. Also, the theory has had considerable impact on counseling and teaching.

The important question now should not be, Is this a correct view of humanity? but rather, Is this a useful way of looking at humanity? It is — and so are other positions.

Instructional Implications of Rogerian Theory

In line with their basic beliefs, humanists such as Rogers, Maslow (1970), and Combs (1965) present a strong plea for **student-centered teaching**. They advocate a philosophy of teaching in which students are given a far more important role in curriculum decisions than has traditionally been the case. They argue, as well, that teachers should be learning facilitators rather than didactic instructors, and that in order to be successful as learning facilitators they must be trained to be sensitive and caring, genuine and empathetic.

Not surprisingly, humanistic approaches to education emphasize healthy social and personal development and, at the same time, deemphasize rigorous, performance-oriented, test-dominated approaches to subject matter. They strongly advocate providing students

Table 6.1 Major characteristics of human personality according to Rogers (1951)

1. Reality is phenomenological.	The significant aspects of reality consist of the world of private experience. Our realities are therefore completely individualistic. They can be *intuited* but not *known* by others.
2. Behavior is motivated by a need to self-actualize.	Each of us has a basic tendency to strive toward becoming a complete, healthy, competent individual through a process characterized by self-government, self-regulation, and autonomy.
3. Behavior occurs within the context of personal realities.	The best way to understand a person's behavior is by attempting to adopt his or her point of view; hence humanism emphasizes the importance of open communication.
4. The self is constructed by the individual.	We discover who we are on the basis of direct experiences and on the basis of beliefs and values that are introjected into our self-concepts by people who communicate to us what we are.
5. Our behaviors conform with our notions of self.	In general, we select behaviors that do not contradict who and what we think we are.

with experiences of success rather than failure; their orientation is toward discovery rather than reception learning. The humanistic view of human functioning accepts individuals for what they are, respects their feelings and aspirations, and holds that every person has the right to self-determination. Such a view of the student would, indeed, lead to child-centered schools.

But the child-centered school is not concerned solely with the emotional and personal development of the child—although it sometimes seems that way, partly because its emphasis *is* on affective growth and partly because this aspect of the humanistic movement has been exaggerated as a reaction against more behavioristic approaches. Most humanistic programs, several of which are described next, are responsive to the important requirements of curricula. After all, even the most self-actualized of individuals may still need to be able to read, write, and name the major capitals of Europe. Indeed, becoming self-actualized—

that is, becoming all that one can and should be—may well depend on both knowledge of the three r's and the wealth of cognitive and metacognitive strategies that our new cognitive instructional sciences use to build their programs. Clearly, cognitive concerns can also be part of a thoughtful, humanistic approach to teaching.

HUMANISTIC MOVEMENTS IN EDUCATION

The thinking exemplified in humanistic theory has become part of the so-called **third-force psychology**—the other two forces being behavioristic S-R theory and Freudian theory. Most proponents of third-force psychology have not put forth psychological theories, however. Rather, they represent a movement pervaded by two beliefs: (1) the uniqueness and importance of the human individual and (2) a strong reaction against overly mechanistic and dehumanizing approaches to understanding humans.

The humanistic movement in psychology has a corresponding movement in education, represented by such writers as Kohl (1969), Dennison (1969), Simon et al. (1972), Gordon (1974), Postman and Weingartner (1971), Holt (1976), and many others, and by a variety of unconventional, alternative approaches to education such as free schools, open classrooms, process education, and community-centered education. The rationale for these methods is based on (1) a genuine concern for the welfare of children and a firm belief that this approach is better for that welfare, and (2) the conviction that current methods of schooling leave much to be desired. Thus, in his description of an alternative to traditional schooling, Dennison (1969) speaks of the profound beneficial effects of that alternative on the *lives* of students. He also criticizes (very politely) the "military discipline, the schedules, the punishments and rewards, the standardization" of more conventional approaches (p. 9). His book, however, like many similar books, is not in itself a criticism of existing educational methods, but rather an attempt to describe an approach that might be better. "There is no need to add to the criticism of our public schools," Dennison informs us. "The critique is extensive and can hardly be improved upon" (p. 3).

Principles of Humanistic Education

The concerns of humanistic education and those of the more traditional schools are basically compatible. All schools are concerned with the present and future welfare of students; all recognize the worth and the rights of the individual; all pay lip service to such human and humane values as openness, honesty, selflessness, and altruism. The conflict between humanistic and traditional approaches exists whenever the pressure of large numbers, regimentation, anonymity, and competition for academic success leave little time and energy for unpressured communication, for the exploration of values, or for the development of affect and self. As was noted earlier, however, nothing prevents you from being a humanistic teacher in a traditional classroom situation.

Humanistic approaches to education are highly varied, although the current literature suggests that they have a number of things in common. Knowledge of these commonalities might be of value for teachers. More detailed information than can be included here might be of even greater value; hence the extensive list of suggested readings at the end of this chapter.

Most humanistic approaches share a number of common emphases (see Table 6.2). Chief among them is a greater attention to thinking and feeling than to the acquisition of knowledge (see, for example, Simpson and Gray, 1976). In this respect they are sometimes quite different from more traditional approaches. Postman and Weingartner (1971), advocates of a "soft revolution," present a number of provocative suggestions for effecting change in the direction of greater freedom and creativity. Many of their suggestions are intended for students rather than for teachers, however, and many are more radical than is typical of the humanistic literature in general.

A second common emphasis of humanistic approaches is on development of notions of self and individual identity. Representative of this emphasis are books by Borton (1970), Satir (1972), and Purkey (1984). Borton presents a highly humanistic, three-phase teaching model designed to identify student concerns, so that students might be reached as individuals and still taught in a systematic fashion compatible with traditional schools. Labels for these three phases form the title of Borton's book: *Reach, Touch, and Teach*. Purkey, also concerned with the developing self-concepts of students, draws an interesting and useful distinction between teachers (and teacher behaviors) that are *inviting* and those that are *disinviting*. One of his major premises is that there are more students who are disinvited than disadvantaged; disinvitation is often communicated to the child through apparent teacher indifference and through failure

Disinvited Students

Purkey (1984) presents a strong argument for the encouragement of teacher behaviors that *invite* students to see themselves as valuable, responsible, worthwhile, and important people. It would be naive to assume that all teachers have attitudes toward students that lend themselves to *inviting* behaviors. Below is a sample of experiences that are clearly *disinviting* in that they label students as irresponsible, incapable, or worthless — and sometimes all three (from Purkey, 1984).

The teacher said I didn't want to learn, that I just wanted to cause trouble.

She told the class we were discipline problems and were not to be trusted.

The teacher put me out in the hall for everyone to laugh at.

They put me in the dummy class, and it had SPECIAL EDUCATION painted right on the door.

The teacher said to me in front of the whole class: "I really don't think you're that stupid!"

When the principal hit me he said it was the only language I understood.

She said I was worse than my brother, and I don't even have a brother.

My name is Bill Dill, but the teacher always called me "Dill Pickle" and laughed.

I transferred to a new school after it had started. When I appeared at the teacher's doorway, she said, "Oh, no, not another one!"

---

to respond to students as people. A teacher invites students by communicating to them (in any of numerous different ways) that they are valuable, able, and self-directed, and by expecting behaviors and achievements that are compatible with their worth and their self-directedness — in short, by having and communicating highly positive feelings about students. Examples of disinvitations are listed in the box entitled "Disinvited Students."

A third major emphasis is on communication. Gordon's (1974) Teacher Effectiveness Training (TET) program illustrates this emphasis. It presents teachers with specific advice on methods of bringing about good teacher-learner relationships, and it is based on the notion that teachers should be taught the principles and skills of "effective human relations, honest interpersonal communication, [and] constructive conflict resolution" (1974, p. ix).

A final emphasis shared by most humanistic approaches is the recognition and development of personal values. Students are encouraged to know themselves and express themselves, to strive toward feelings of self-identity, to actualize themselves. Simon, Howe, and Kirschenbaum (1972), for example, present teachers with seventy-nine specific strategies aimed at the elaboration and clarification of values in students.

These four common emphases — affect, self-development, communication, and values — lend themselves to a number of instructional methods more readily than do the more traditional emphases on mastery of academic content, good citizenship, and sportsmanship. Thus, group-process approaches, rooted in the sensitivity-group and encounter-group movements (sometimes referred to collectively as "growth groups"), are common instructional

Table 6.2   Common emphases of humanistic approaches to education

1. Affect	Much greater emphasis on feeling and thinking and less on the acquisition of information
2. Self-Concept	Explicit concern with the development of positive self-concepts in children
3. Communication	Attention to the development of positive human relationships and honest interpersonal communication
4. Personal Values	Recognition of the importance of personal values, and an attempt to facilitate the development of positive values

approaches in humanistic education. In groups, students can be encouraged to express their feelings more openly, to discover and clarify these feelings, to explore interpersonal relationships, and to articulate their personal value systems. Various communication games can be used to enhance the genuineness and openness of interpersonal relationships. Role-playing games also offer a way of exploring emotions and human relationships.

General descriptions of humanistic classrooms are often of limited value to the prospective teacher, particularly in relation to the nitty-gritty of classroom activity. Such descriptions pay less attention to the details of the instructional process than to the personal qualities of teachers and to teacher attitudes toward children. In short, although advocates of humanistic approaches to teaching present appealing and sometimes highly convincing arguments for humanizing the teaching/learning process, they too often leave the novice teacher woefully short of methods and strategies. Unfortunately, they also often leave the novice with the impression that the traditional classroom and the more humanistic classroom are quite incompatible and that the latter should replace the former.

Perhaps the most important contribution humanistic concerns can make to teacher preparation is in the realm of attitudes rather than methods. The humanistic educator strives to-

ward a real caring for people, toward open and effective communication, and toward genuineness, empathy, and warmth. But these are vague terms, and vagueness is not what we need; we need examples and methods.

In the final sections of this chapter, we look at three alternatives to traditional education. The first — open education — is most concerned with the affective (emotional) development of students, and, by that token, is most clearly humanistic. The other two alternatives — learning-styles approaches and cooperative learning — although also driven by some of the humanist's concerns for the individual, retain some emphasis on academic and cognitive growth.

THREE HUMANISTIC CLASSROOM APPROACHES

We all know what traditional classrooms are like; most of us have been through them. And most of us, given that we are here in this rarefied academic atmosphere — you there and me here — have not been treated too badly by this thing called "traditional education."

But that alternatives exist is what this chapter is all about. In the following sections we look at three of them.

The Open Classroom

Several decades ago, a phenomenon called *open education*, or the *open classroom*, became something of a North American fad. The open classroom differs from the traditional classroom in a number of important ways. First, the principal goals of open education are not the kinds of goals — specifically, individual growth, critical thinking, self-reliance, cooperation, and a commitment to lifelong learning — that are ordinarily sought in traditional classrooms (Walberg, 1986). Second, in open education, the most important person is the student, not the teacher. And third, the open classroom typically does not adhere to the same curriculum-bound, age-/grade-locked system that typifies the traditional school, but is instead far more informal.

The flavor of open education is perhaps best conveyed by Dennison's (1969) description of an open classroom. He describes an approach that emphasizes student-centered and intensive but relaxed teacher-pupil contact (made possible in his example by the fact that the teacher-pupil ratio was extremely low). It is an approach that deemphasizes schedules — following Rousseau's notion that time is not meant to be saved but to be lost (Dennison, 1969, p. 13). The philosophy of open education, as expressed by Dennison, is that a school should be concerned with the lives of its children rather than with education in a narrow sense; that abolishing conventional classroom routines can lead to important insights about the roles of emotions and other features of the human condition; and that running an elementary school can be a very simple thing once it is removed from "the unworkable centralization and the lust for control that permeates every bureaucratic institution" (p. 9).

It is impossible, in this short section, to fully convey the atmosphere that permeates the type of school of which Dennison speaks (at least to convey it as he has in his own words). Indeed, it seems futile and perhaps misleading to describe such a school as one that has no administrators, no report cards, no competitive examinations, and extremely modest facilities; where every child is treated with "consideration and justice"; where the unfolding lives of the children are the primary concern. Whereas this is an accurate description of the school, it is only a partial description. As Kohl (1969, p. 15) points out, it is difficult to say exactly what an open classroom is. Similarly, it is difficult to say what freedom is or to draw the line between chaos and student-determined order, between rebelliousness and the legitimate expression of individual rights, between nonproductive time-wasting and the productive waste (or use) of time for noncurriculum-defined activities.

Open education is now rare in North America. Interestingly, however, most of the many studies that evaluated this approach and compared it with more traditional approaches found that open education was usually effective in reaching its most important goals; that is, students exposed to open classrooms typically had better self-concepts and were more creative and cooperative (see, for example, Horwitz, 1979). However, these gains were usually at the expense of academic achievement as defined by more traditional measures.

The Learning-Styles Approach

In discussing traditional education, Dunn and Griggs (1988) claim: "The system works well for some, but not for others" (p. 1). Why?

Because, Dunn and Griggs explain, some students do not learn at all well in the morning but perform very well in the afternoon. Some work well in bright, noisy environments; others do their best work in quiet places with subdued lighting. Some excel with highly structured, teacher-directed instructional methods; others do far better in informal, unstructured environments. Some students need and want to be told what to do, and when and how to do it; others perform best when working on their own initiatives. In short, each student has a personal and unique **learning style**.

Unfortunately, traditional schools do not often take individual learning styles into account. As a result, they reward students whose personal styles happen to match that for which the traditional school was designed — and, by the same token, they unwittingly punish those whose rhythms are sounded on a different drum. Students whose biological rhythms make it difficult to concentrate in the morning must nevertheless come to school and sit through the same offerings as everyone else. Those who respond best to visual stimuli — or to tactile stimulation — are forced to listen as much as those who are more responsive to auditory stimuli. Children with shorter attention spans are compelled to sit as long as those who are not so easily distracted.

This situation is not fair, argue Dunn and Griggs; it is not an optimal learning situation. Schools, they insist, must take into account these fundamentally important differences in learning styles. But how?

First, schools need to develop a profile of each student's learning styles. A number of instruments are available for this purpose, including Gregorc's (1982) *Style Delineator* and Renzulli and Smith's (1978) *Learning Styles Inventory*. The Gregorc instrument provides a measure of perceptual strengths (how people obtain information, including a concrete/abstract dimension) and differentiates among learners on the basis of their predispositions toward reason, emotion, and intuition. It also looks at the individual's preferred ways of dealing with and ordering information.

The Renzulli and Smith inventory is designed to help teachers customize their instructional procedures to match individual learners' attitudes toward such common instructional procedures as lectures, simulations, discussions, projects, games, drills, recitations, peer teaching, independent study, and programmed instruction.

Identifying individual learning styles is only the beginning; dramatic changes are required in schools and in teacher behavior if schools are to be truly responsive to students'

individual differences. Dunn and Griggs (1988) visited ten schools where attention to learning styles had become the determining factor in educational offerings. Although there were many differences among these schools, a number of things were common to many of them. A description of these is, in a sense, an idealized description of a humanistic school.

This idealized school gives learners an almost staggering assortment of options. It allows children to work alone on soft carpets or to work in groups at conference tables. It provides highly structured teacher-presented lessons, peer teaching, programmed instruction, computer-assisted instruction, and self-learning. It rotates presentation of core subjects so that they are offered at all times of the day, including early in the morning and later in the afternoon. It allows students to take examinations and do projects at times that are compatible with their biological rhythms.

The idealized humanistic, learning-style-driven school is identifiable not only by its attention to differences among individual learners, but also by its values and objectives. Far more than the traditional school, it stresses student involvement at all stages of learning, and it emphasizes problem solving and creativity.

Finally, this idealized school's most common instructional technique, especially for presenting new material, is a highly participatory, cooperative, small-group approach that is sometimes called **circles of knowledge**. This approach is described in the next section, which discusses cooperative learning.

This brief description of the translation of learning-styles information into classroom practice cannot do justice to the complexity of the topic. There is no single, best program that we can describe simply and accurately; programs continue to change and develop. As we noted, most require very profound changes in schools and in teachers, and the changes required must be continual. They involve experimentation in and modification and clarification of programs, as well as refocusing of objectives and of efforts, and on and on.

We cannot, as of this writing, begin to evaluate the effectiveness of this approach, other than very tentatively. Dunn and Griggs (1988) report that in the ten learning-styles-driven schools they visited, learners performed exceptionally well on a variety of measures of academic performance. Some had won national awards and many had succeeded in passing subjects they had previously failed. And most said they liked — no, *loved* — school.

Perhaps when the bear is a very, very old bear, history will look back and say, "Hey, that learning-styles stuff just before the turn of the millenium was another one of those educational fads, like open schools and teaching machines." Or maybe, just maybe, history's judgment will be: "Hey, just before the millennium — that's when it all started."

Cooperative Learning

According to Johnson et al. (1984), teachers have three basic choices: "In every classroom teachers may structure lessons so that students are in a win-lose struggle to see who is best. They can also allow students to learn on their own, indi-vidually, or they can arrange students in pairs or small groups to help each other master the assigned material" (p. 1).

Unfortunately, these authors claim, most students see schools as competitive because that is how grades are typically assigned. Not everyone can do very well; in order to achieve at the highest level, students must compete with, and outachieve, the others. And when schools are not competitive, they are most often individualistic; that is, students are urged to work toward the attainment of their own individual goals — without help, proudly and independently!

A simple way of distinguishing among these three alternatives is in terms of rewards (Bossert, 1988). In a *cooperative* situation, the individual is rewarded in proportion to others in the group; in a *competitive* situation, individual rewards are inversely related to those others receive; and in an *individualistic* situation, there is no relationship among individual rewards.

Occasionally some schools present a few activities that are cooperative. Only very rarely do schools and teachers make cooperative learning a fundamental part of their instruction.

Schools that do, claim Schniedewind and Davidson (1988), are humanistic schools because cooperative learning is essentially a humanistic approach to education. It combines the cognitive and affective aspects of learning, and it emphasizes participation and active engagement, both of which are humanistic concerns. But perhaps more than other explicitly humanistic approaches, cooperative learning also stresses academic achievement and clearly defined curricular goals. In most schools that use cooperative-learning methods, students do not have the unstructured freedom that they might be given in an open classroom; nor does the system cater to their personal strengths and preferences as it might in a school organized to respond to individual learning styles.

The Rationale for Cooperative Learning. Why is it important to learn to cooperate? Advocates of this approach present a variety of reasons. Among the most compelling is the nagging suspicion that it is our only hope for salvation — that if we do not learn to cooperate, we and our planet are doomed.

There are other reasons why we must learn to cooperate — if survival does not seem sufficiently important, or if our doom seems too distant, or if we simply prefer not to think about it. Cooperation, Bossert (1988) tells us, is the cornerstone of modern democracy. Nations cannot be governed without cooperation among leaders; cooperation is essential for political and economic survival.

At a more immediate level, teaching cooperation in the schools might do much to reduce student dependence on teachers and to decrease divisiveness and prejudice among students. Cooperative learning, Johnson et al. (1984) claim, may resolve two important crises: declining academic performance and pervasive feelings of alienation, isolation, purposelessness, and social unease among students.

Cooperative Learning Defined. Cooperative learning occurs when students work together to achieve a common goal. Unlike competitive learning, rewards depend not on doing *better than* someone else, but on doing *well with* someone else.

Although there are a variety of approaches to cooperative learning in the classroom, most have a number of features in common (Johnson et al., 1984). To begin with, cooperative learning requires *face-to-face interaction* among group members. Second, the relationship among group members can be described as one of *positive interdependence*; that is, members must cooperate in allocating resources, assigning roles, and dividing labor if they are to achieve their goals. Third, cooperative learning usually assigns some degree of *individual responsibility* for sharing, cooperating, and learning. Accordingly, various techniques are used to ensure that goals and rewards are contingent on the performance and contribution of all group members. Finally, cooperative learning involves the use of *interpersonal and small-group skills*, such as those involved in taking turns, facilitating, collaborating, and so on.

Cooperative Learning Activities. Bossert (1988) describes a large number of cooperative group activities that have been developed and used in schools. They have a variety of names, including learning together, student team learning, and jigsaw. A more generic label for these cooperative approaches is *circles of knowledge* or *circles of learning*. Although each activity is distinct from the others, all share the common features described earlier, the most important of which is the interdependence of group members.

In *learning together*, groups of four to six students are given a lesson or worksheet that they must learn or complete together. Members must help each other to ensure that everyone learns the lesson or completes the assignment. Members of each group are also encouraged to help other groups once they have completed the assignment. Praise is given for cooperating and finishing the assignment. In this approach, there is no competition among groups.

In the various forms of *student team learning*, individual groups are teams that compete against one another. For example, groups might be assigned lessons or worksheets, which they cooperatively complete or learn, or they might be asked to help one another prepare for quizzes. Points are awarded to each team on the basis of group performance. In variations of this approach, teams compete against one another in academic games or in a variety of achievement tests.

In *jigsaw*, the material to be learned is divided into separate units. Individual members of the group are then given separate parts of the whole to learn, and they must teach what they learned to other members of the group. No one member is given sufficient information to solve the problem at hand or complete the assignment in question, but when all the information is put together — *Voilà!** The jigsaw is complete.

Implementation of Cooperative Learning Techniques. The techniques just described are only a few of the many that have been developed and evaluated. For those interested in still more approaches, the "Suggested Readings" section at the end of this chapter lists important sources of information.

Unlike the learning-styles approach, cooperative learning does not require a major restructuring of the school day or a reordering of curriculum offerings. Whereas the learning-styles approach attempts to cater to individual differences in learning styles and learning preferences, cooperative group methods typically include all students simultaneously. In fact, one of the advantages of cooperative approaches is that they foster cooperation among students with different strengths and weaknesses, and perhaps those of different ethnic backgrounds, ages, and sexes.

PPC: "Ha! Ha! A bilingual bear!"
The Bear: "But of course!"

Cooperative learning techniques are most often introduced as an adjunct to regular classroom offerings. In a typical situation, they might be used for sixty or ninety minutes a day. However, the most vocal advocates of this approach recommend that as much as 70 percent of class time should involve cooperative activities, with 20 percent devoted to individualistic approaches and only 10 percent to competitive activities (Johnson and Johnson, 1975).

Although cooperative approaches normally make up only a small part of the total curriculum, their implementation usually requires careful preparation of material. Depending on the specific approach used, the teacher will need to prepare worksheets, questions, resource materials, and so on, all carefully structured to foster cooperation while promoting learning.

Evaluation of Cooperative Learning. How well do these cooperative techniques work? Johnson et al. (1981) analyzed 122 studies that had examined cooperative learning. Most of these studies contain direct comparisons between specific cooperative approaches and traditional classroom instruction. Johnson and colleagues conclude that cooperative learning leads to *better* achievement at virtually all grade and age levels studied and for all subjects. They suggest that increases in achievement occur because group discussion and cooperation promote discovery, lead to the development of higher-quality cognitive strategies, increase motivation to learn, promote overlearning through repetition, increase comprehension by requiring students to teach each other, enrich the learning experience by blending students of a variety of ability levels and experiences, and promote highly positive relationships among group members. This last statement is also supported by results of a study involving a school with a mixture of Jewish and Middle-Eastern students (Sharan and Shachar, 1988), in which students exposed to a cooperative approach not only performed better academically than those exposed only to a traditional approach, but also displayed far fewer signs of ethnic tension in their language.

In general, the research reviewed by Bossert (1988) supports this positive evaluation. Cooperative learning approaches most often result not only in measurably superior academic performance, but also in higher motivation, greater interest in school, and better relations among students. He suggests, however, that the positive academic effects of cooperative learning may be partly due to the fact that lessons are typically more highly structured and more systematic, rather than simply to peer interaction.

Does this mean that all teachers and schools should now become cooperative — that is, *entirely* cooperative?

Bossert (1988) advises caution. Even though it seems clear that cooperative approaches have substantial academic and social benefits, they also have some disadvantages. For example, low-achieving students are sometimes embarrassed by their performances and ashamed of the fact that they lower the group's score. As a result, they may become progressively reluctant to participate in cooperative activities as their motivation and self-concepts deteriorate. The long-term effects of this situation might be lower achievement for these students — and perhaps lower achievement for their groups as well.

Bossert also cautions that those who advocate that cooperative techniques should be the dominant feature of classroom activity may be overlooking the possibility that one of the reasons cooperative learning is effective is precisely because it presents a clear contrast to conventional classroom procedures. The shifts in attention and in procedures required of students serve to increase concentration, to motivate, and ultimately to enhance performance. But if all or most classroom activity were cooperative, these shifts might not occur, and performance might not improve so dramatically — if at all.

Finally, Bossert argues that even though it is important for children to learn to cooperate with one another, it is also important to learn competitive and individualistic skills.

SOME REACTIONS TO HUMANISTIC EDUCATION

To the extent that humanistic education represents concern for the individual lives and self-concepts of students and concern for the healthiest and happiest development of human potential, it is beyond reproach. All teachers *must* be humanistic.

However, humanistic education too often appears to deal with vague qualities and speculative conclusions. Terms such as *authentic, open, real, genuine, fully functioning,* and *meaningful* are often largely meaningless. How do you distinguish between an authentic experience and one that is not authentic? Between a genuine teacher and an imposter? Between a fully functioning student and one that is only three-quarters functioning? Unfortunately, although these terms are vague, they seem to represent good things and are therefore highly appealing. Equally unfortunate, the things they represent cannot be easily defined or measured, and as a consequence the evidence upon which advocates of humanistic reforms base their arguments is not always very convincing.

Perhaps the most telling criticism of general humanistic approaches to teaching is that most are highly dependent upon the personal qualities and skills of individual teachers. More-conventional approaches to classroom practice are, in this respect, much more "teacher-proof."

These criticisms are not entirely fair, however. They apply primarily to global approaches to humanistic education, such as those represented by "open" (or what have sometimes been called "free") schools. As we saw earlier, research evidence suggests that although students who emerge from these schools appear to be more creative and more cooperative and have better self-concepts, these gains typically come at the expense of academic achievement. A large-scale evaluation in the United States found that these students performed more poorly than comparison groups on almost all achievement measures (Kennedy, 1978). Perhaps it is not surprising that most of these schools have now closed.

These criticisms—of vagueness, overattention to affective growth, and disregard of both standard curricula and cognitive development—are not relevant with respect to two expressions of humanistic concerns detailed in this chapter: learning-styles-oriented schools and cooperative learning. As we saw, both these approaches have been seen to lead to superior academic achievement. Interestingly, among the important techniques of learning-styles schools are the group methods that define cooperative learning.

It is extremely important to bear in mind that humanism is not a specific educational technique, in spite of the fact that it manifests itself most clearly in specific techniques. In effect, humanism is an educational philosophy characterized by the sorts of admirable attitudes toward students and toward educational goals that should be characteristic of all teachers. These attitudes, as mentioned earlier, are not subject to the same criticisms that have been applied so generously to specific humanistic approaches to education. In the end, it may not be important to copy the models or take the advice presented by the more visible of humanistic educators. What is important is that you genuinely care about students as people.

THE LAST WORD— FROM WATSON!

It may seem strange to conclude a discussion of humanism by referring to the recognized initiator and principal spokesman of the position usually considered most directly opposed to humanism. Interestingly, however, some of the

writings of John B. Watson describe a very humanistic society. Some six decades ago, Watson concluded a book with a section entitled "Behaviorism as a Guide for All Future Experimental Ethics" (Watson, 1930, pp. 303–304):

Behaviorism ought to be a science that prepares men and women for understanding the principles of their own behavior. It ought to make men and women eager to rearrange their own lives, and especially eager to prepare themselves to bring up their own children in a healthy way. I wish I could picture for you what a rich and wonderful individual we could make of every healthy child if only we could let it shape itself properly and then provide for it a universe in which it could exercise that organization—a universe unshackled by legendary folklore of happenings thousands of years ago; unhampered by disgraceful political history; free of foolish customs and conventions which have no significance in themselves, yet which hem the individual in like taut steel bands. I am not asking here for revolution; I am not asking people to go out to some God-forsaken place, form a colony, go naked and live a communal life, nor am I asking for a change to a diet of roots and herbs. I am not asking for "free love." I am trying to dangle a stimulus in front of you, a verbal stimulus which, if acted upon, will gradually change this universe. For the universe will change if you bring up your children, not in the freedom of the libertine, but in behavioristic freedom—a

How Should I Teach?

The school system that hires you (and that also can fire you) will almost inevitably operate within a relatively well-defined set of regulations governing the conduct of teachers in classrooms, prescribed curricula, reporting and testing procedures, disciplinary actions, and so on. Yet, in the final analysis, you alone will determine your approach to teaching. No person should be forced to violate personal conviction. And if you firmly believe in the importance — even the sanctity — of the right of all students in your care to be treated as human beings and to be allowed to develop in such a way as to enhance their human qualities, it might happen that you will be frustrated by the system (or by your interpretation of that system) and that you will look for alternatives. In that case you would be well advised to read some of the references annotated at the end of this chapter.

---

freedom which we cannot even picture in words, so little do we know of it. Will not these children in turn, with their better ways of living and thinking, replace us as society and in turn bring up their children in a still more scientific way, until the world finally becomes a place fit for human habitation?

MAIN POINTS

1. Humanistic psychology is concerned with the uniqueness, the worth, and the dignity of the self. It presents an ideological conflict with behaviorism, objecting to the apparent technological orientation of behaviorism. It also objects to the school's emphasis on academic achievement and its neglect of affective growth.

2. Carl Rogers's theory may be described as phenomenological in view of its concern with what is termed the *phenomenal* as opposed to the *real*. The phenomenal world is the environment as it is perceived by one individual.

3. The theory is also humanistic, particularly in terms of its concern for the individual and its belief that self-actualization is a prime motivating force.

4. Rogers's notions regarding the desirability of self-determination are opposed to Skinner's expressed concern with control through the application of a science of behavior (namely, the principles of operant learning).

5. Rogers summarizes his theory of behavior and personality in the form of nineteen propositions. The substance of the most important of these is contained here in points 6 through 9.

6. An individual's real world is the phenomenal world (what a person perceives). Only the individual can fully know it.

7. The direction (purposiveness) of behavior is determined by a tendency toward self-actualization.

8. One way of defining self-actualization is to say that it involves a continuing effort to achieve the maximum development of an individual's potential. The process is assumed to be related to healthy and creative functioning.

9. The development of the "self" results from interactions with the world (direct experience) and from values about the "me" that are borrowed from the actions of other people (indirect experience). Occasionally

the values derived from these two sources are incompatible and result in conflict.

10. The most important education-related implication of Rogerian theory is that in order to promote full, healthy functioning, schools should be student-centered. The instructional procedures that Rogers sees as best for these schools are discovery-oriented.

11. The major emphases of humanistic approaches are the development of self, the clarification of values, openness, honesty, and self-determination.

12. Open education is most concerned with the affective growth of students — with critical thinking, self-reliance, and commitment to learning. It is student- rather than teacher-centered. Research suggests that graduates of open schools may be more creative, more cooperative, and have better self-concepts — but they usually fare less well on traditional academic measures.

13. Learning styles are individual preferences and strengths as they relate to the best conditions for learning (for example, morning vs. evening; visual, auditory, or kinesthetic; individual vs. group; structured vs. unstructured; and so on).

14. Learning-styles-driven schools develop profiles for individual students and attempt to match instructional methods, curriculum offerings, scheduling, and other aspects of instruction to each learner's personal style. Accordingly, they present a wide array of options for each student. Their most common instructional technique is a highly participatory, small-group, cooperative learning approach.

15. Students in learning-styles schools appear to do very well on standard academic measures.

16. Cooperative learning involves small-group techniques structured so that learners are rewarded for the group's results but are nevertheless individually responsible for learning and for helping other members of the group learn. It is characterized by face-to-face interaction, positive interdependence, individual responsibility, and the use of interpersonal and small-group skills.

17. Some techniques for cooperative learning (sometimes collectively labeled *circles of learning*) include *learning together* (pure cooperation, in which members of groups work together to achieve a common goal but do not compete with other groups); *student team learning* (in which groups are teams that compete against each other); and *jigsaw* (in which each member of a group is given only part of the information required to solve a problem or learn a lesson, so that members must share if the group is to complete its assignment successfully).

18. Evidence suggests that cooperative learning techniques lead to superior academic achievement, very high motivation, and the enhancement of social skills. These positive effects may be due in part to both the greater curriculum structure required for cooperative learning and the contrast these approaches present to the traditional classroom. There is a danger, however, that poor achievers may be embarrassed at their performance and ashamed that it lowers the group's scores, and that their self-concepts, motivation, and subsequent performance may suffer.

19. General humanistic approaches to education are often highly dependent upon individual teachers' qualities, and sometimes use vague and speculative terms.

20. Humanism in education is less vulnerable to criticism as an attitude or philosophy than as a technique — and as an attitude it is perhaps more valuable to teachers. In this sense, all teachers should be humanistic.

SUGGESTED READINGS

Rogers's attempt to apply his theories and beliefs to education is expressed in:

ROGERS, C. R. (1969). *Freedom to learn.* Columbus, Ohio: Merrill.

Additional insight into humanistic psychology is provided by interviews with Maslow, Murphy, and Rogers in:

FRICK, W. B. (1971). *Humanistic psychology: Interviews with Maslow, Murphy, and Rogers.* Columbus, Ohio: Merrill.

Two intriguing and stimulating first-person accounts of alternatives to traditional education are detailed in:

DENNISON, G. (1969). *The lives of children: The story of the First Street school.* New York: Random House (Vintage Books).

KOHL, H. R. (1969). *The open classroom: A practical guide to a new way of teaching.* New York: Random House (Vintage Books).

Among numerous humanistic books for teachers and students are the following:

BORTON, T. (1970). *Reach, touch, and teach: Student concerns and process education.* New York: McGraw-Hill.

PURKEY, W. W. (1984). *Inviting school success: A self-concept approach to teaching and learning* (2nd ed.). Belmont, Calif.: Wadsworth.

SIMPSON, E. L., & GRAY, M. A. (1976). *Humanistic education: An interpretation.* Cambridge, Mass.: Ballinger.

The learning-styles approach to education is well described in:

DUNN, R., & GRIGGS, S. A. (1988). *Learning styles: Quiet revolution in American secondary schools.* Reston, Va.: National Association of Secondary School Principals.

The book by Johnson et al. is an excellent description of cooperative learning and of a number of different schools that use this approach. Rhoades and McCabe present a brief and useful guidebook for the teacher wishing to initiate cooperative activities in the classroom. The Schniedewind and Davidson book contains a large number of cooperative activities designed to foster feelings and attitudes — like racial tolerance — that might contribute to world peace. And the Slavin et al. book is a collection of articles reporting on a variety of cooperative learning experiments in different schools and for different subjects.

JOHNSON, D. W., JOHNSON, R. T., HOLUBEC, E. J., & ROY, P. (1984). *Circles of learning: Cooperation in the classroom.* Alexandria, Va.: Association for Supervision and Curriculum Development.

RHOADES, J., & MCCABE, M. E. (1985). *Simple cooperation in the classroom.* Willits, Calif.: ITA Publications.

SCHNIEDEWIND, N., & DAVIDSON, E. (1988). *Cooperative learning, cooperative lives: A sourcebook of learning activities for building a peaceful world.* Dubuque, Iowa: Brown.

SLAVIN, R., SHARAN, S., KAGAN, S., HERTZ-LAZAROWITZ, R., WEBB, C., & SCHMUCK, R. (Eds.). (1985). *Learning to cooperate, cooperating to learn.* New York: Plenum.

The Laplanders venerated the bear and called it the Dog of God. The Norwegians called it "the old man with the fur cloak" (Engel, 1976).

CHAPTER 7

HUMAN DEVELOPMENT: AN OVERVIEW

The childhood shews the man,
As morning shews the day.
JOHN MILTON *Paradise Lost*

As for being a General, well, at the age of four with
paper hats and wooden swords we're all Generals.
Only some of us never grow out of it.
PETER USTINOV *Romanoff and Juliet*

PREVIEW It seems clear that in order to teach children effectively it is useful to understand them. Certainly, in training our dogs we have found it helpful to have some knowledge of the ages at which they are most likely to profit from our efforts, as well as of the methods to which they are most likely to respond. But even with dogs we have found remarkable individual differences, not only among different breeds, but also among individual dogs within a single breed. So it is with children. This chapter presents a selective summary of some of the most important findings and concepts in the study of child development. It is important to keep in mind, however, that our discussion is necessarily limited to that mythical but convenient invention, the "average child." Your children are not likely to be "average"; they will need to be understood as individuals. Nevertheless, knowledge of the average may prove very valuable in understanding the individual.

■ *When I was still very young, my father took me to my first fair. It completely overwhelmed me. I had never before heard such an assortment of noises; I had not smelled a fair's peculiar combination of smells; I had never seen such a riot of color and movement. Nor had I ever tasted cotton candy or candied apples, or touched an elephant. And I don't think I had ever actually seen a wild cow. But what most impressed me about the fair was the "freak" show we attended at the end of the day. There I saw a man swallow an incredibly long and sharp sword without cutting himself, and a woman who allowed herself to be sawed in half inside a box and then was magically put together*

again. Later, a midget stuffed flaming balls in his mouth and then spit them out, black and smoking; and a woman with tattoos over every inch of her body, or so she said, thrilled me with her display. For weeks after, I could talk of little else. I now knew that there were things in this world that those less fortunate than I—those who had not actually seen them—would not believe existed.

I am still fascinated by fairs, freaks, and fools.* When the fair came to our town one summer, I quickly offered to take my youngest, who was then seven years old. He was not overly enthusiastic, but I knew that this was partly because he likes to watch television on Saturdays and partly because he didn't yet know how wonderful fairs are.

So we went to the fair. And, to paraphrase an old song, all the wonderful things were there.

But my son didn't see them! He seemed unmoved by the sights, the sounds, the smells, and the tastes. And when we stood in front of the sideshow tent, listening to a man with a splendid voice urging us to come in and see the woman with the two heads, the woman with the skin of an elephant, the largest man in the whole world, and the one-handed midget concert pianist, my son didn't even look skeptical. He just looked bored.

"This is it," I said. "This is really what fairs are all about! Wait till you see this." And I dragged him into the tent in the wake of my enthusiasm.

---

*PPC: "I don't think you should make fun of those less fortunate. One of them might be offended."
Author: "I mean *fools* in the sense of *clowns.* I used the term because of the alliteration. Besides, few of the other kinds of fools would actually read a book like this."

Later that night, when we talked about the fair, I discovered that my son had not seen a woman with the two lovely heads or a strange woman with the soft gray folds of elephant skin. All he had seen was an unfortunate one-headed woman with a hint of a second head where her right ear should have been and another pathetic woman with a revolting skin disease. Nor had he seen a giant with a great rumbling voice. Instead he had watched an unhappy, grotesquely obese man walk painfully across a barren stage, making plaintive breathing noises as he moved. And he had not heard heart-rending sonatas played by the one-handed midget; all he had heard were a handful of sad notes played on a tinny miniature piano.

And I had always thought there was magic in the fair. But he and I are from different worlds. His is far less naive than mine. Television, among other things, has seen to that.

But where can he find magic these days? ▬

CONCEPTS IN HUMAN DEVELOPMENT

Developmental psychology looks at changes that occur between conception and death. It tries to describe human characteristics at different ages, to identify predictable differences among different ages and sexes, and to explain the processes that account for developmental changes. To simplify, developmental psychology describes what it is like to be a seven-year-old, how seven-year-olds might be different from fourteen-year-olds, how seven-year-olds got to be the way they are, and how and why they will continue to change. This information is obviously crucial to teachers, who must always be concerned with students' readiness, interests, and capabilities. Unfortunately, however, the information that developmental psychology provides us is not always simple and straightforward; it often must be qualified, and it is subject to a great many exceptions. Each of us is, after all, individual and unique.

One of the factors particularly important to the developmental psychologist is the place and time in which individuals are born and raised. My son and I are clearly a case in point. We are, as I have said, of different worlds — of different contexts. As developmental psychologists would say, we are of different cohorts.

A **cohort** can be described as a group of individuals who were all born within the same period of time — say the 1940s or the 1960s. Thus, a cohort is initially of a fixed size and composition, and it cannot grow in size after the time period that defines it has elapsed. Instead, with the passage of time its size decreases as members die. And some predictable patterns of changes occur in a cohort. For example, the proportion of males to females changes because males tend to die sooner than females throughout the world. Although there are 105 males born for every 100 females, the numbers of each still alive by early adulthood are approximately equal. And by age 65, only 69 males are still alive for every 100 females. These predictable changes clearly have implications for understanding the lives of men and women.

From developmental psychology's point of view, the most important thing about a cohort is not that it includes only individuals who were born at the same time, but rather that these individuals have had a similar sequence of historical influences in their lives, particularly if their geographical, social, and other circumstances are also similar. And in interpreting the conclusions of developmental psychology, we must keep in mind that many of these conclusions are based on research conducted with a small number of cohorts — often only one — and that they might not be valid for other cohorts.

This chapter gives a brief overview of some of what is known or suspected about human development. The next chapter deals with cognitive and social development.

To clarify the issues involved in this discussion, four terms need to be defined: *growth, maturation, learning,* and *development*.

Growth refers primarily to physical changes, such as increases in height and weight. These changes are quantitative rather than qualitative; that is, they are changes in quantity or amount rather than transformations that result in different qualities.

Maturation, a somewhat less precise term than growth, is used to describe changes that are relatively independent of the environment. These changes are assumed to be closely related to the influences of heredity. In most areas of development, however, there is a very close interaction between heredity and environment. For example, learning to walk depends on the maturation of certain muscle groups and on increasing control over their movements (maturational developments), as well as on the opportunity to practice the various skills involved (environment, learning). An important illustration of maturation is the changes in early adolescence that lead to sexual maturity (*puberty*) — changes collectively labeled *pubescence*. Although their onset seems to be affected by environmental conditions (menarche — the onset of menstruation — occurred progressively earlier between 1850 and 1970, apparently because of nutritional factors; see Frisch and Revelle, 1970), the changes of pubescence are largely genetically programmed.

Learning is defined in terms of actual or potential changes in behavior as a result of experience. Thus, all relatively permanent changes in behavior that are not the result of maturation or of external factors whose effects are unrelated to environment (such as the temporary effects of drugs or fatigue) are examples of learning.

Development can be defined as the total process whereby individuals adapt to the environment. This process involves growth, maturation, and learning.

THE NATURE OF HUMAN DEVELOPMENT

This section briefly summarizes important knowledge in developmental psychology. The summary takes the form of eight principles of development, each of which can be viewed as a concluding or explanatory statement. These principles are not an exhaustive summary of all of developmental psychology; rather, they have been selected largely for their relevance to the teaching/learning process.

Influences on Development: "Nature and Nurture"

1. *Development is influenced by both heredity (nature) and environment (nurture).* We know, for example, that nature (heredity) is responsible for many of our physical characteristics, such as hair and eye color, facial features, and, to some extent, height and weight. But even here, the influences of heredity are not entirely simple and straightforward. Although some characteristics (for instance, hair and eye color) do appear to be entirely under the control of our genes (Waddington, 1975), other characteristics (for instance, height and weight) clearly are also influenced by environmental factors.

The situation is far less clear in terms of personality and intellectual characteristics than in terms of physical characteristics. Thus, it has been extremely difficult to determine how important qualities such as intelligence and creativity are influenced by heredity, and the extent to which they can be modified by the environment. In attempting to clarify this question, many studies have focused on identical twins because, as Gould notes, they are "the only really adequate natural experiment for separating genetic from environmental effects in humans . . ." (1981, p. 234). This is because identical (monozygotic) twins are genetically identical, a condition that is not true for any other pair of humans, including fraternal (dizygotic) twins. Therefore, if intelligence is genetically determined, identical twins should have almost identical intelligence test scores (almost but not exactly identical because we cannot measure intelligence completely accurately). But if intelligence is largely a function of the environment, ordinary siblings and fraternal twins should resemble each other about as closely as identical twins — and far

Category		Correlation coefficient 0.0 0.1 0.2 0.3 0.4 0.5 0.6 0.7 0.8 0.9	No. of groups studied
Unrelated people	Reared apart		4
	Reared together		5
Foster parent-child			3
Parent-child			12
Siblings	Reared apart		2
	Reared together		35
Two-egg twins	Opposite sex		9
	Like sex		11
One-egg twins	Reared apart		4
	Reared together		14

Figure 7.1   Correlation coefficients for intelligence-test scores from fifty-two studies. The high correlation for identical twins shows the strong genetic basis of measured intelligence. The greater correlation for siblings or twins reared together, compared with those reared apart, supports the view that environmental forces are also important in determining similarity of intelligence-test scores. Adapted from L. Erlenmeyer–Kimling and L. F. Jarvik (1963), "Genetics and Intelligence: A Review," *Science, 142*, 1478. Copyright 1963 by the American Association for the Advancement of Science. Used by permission.

more closely than identical twins who are brought up in separate homes.

Figure 7.1 presents a summary of studies of the relationship between intelligence and genetic relatedness. What does this figure reveal? First, note that the correlation coefficient (a measure of relationship that ranges from − 1 to + 1) for intelligence-test scores is lowest for those who are least alike genetically (unrelated persons) and becomes progressively higher as the degree of genetic similarity increases. Intelligence is clearly influenced by heredity.

Note too, however, that the correlations also increase with degree of environmental similarity. Thus, identical twins reared together are more alike in measured intelligence than are those reared apart. Similarly, fraternal twins, who are no more alike genetically than are other siblings, nevertheless manifest higher correlations — presumably because their environments are more alike than are those of most siblings. After all, fraternal twins are of exactly the same age and are often exposed to the same experiences at about the same time.

The conclusion? As we stated at the beginning of this section, *development is influenced by both heredity and environment*. The two interact in complex and not clearly understood ways to determine what you and I become. What is most important about this principle, from the educational point of view, is that many of our characteristics *can* be influenced by the environment. And although there is relatively little that we can do about heredity at this point, much of the environment still remains under our control. (See Chapter 9 for further discussion of the roles of heredity and environment relative to intelligence.)

Differential Growth Rates

2. *Development takes place at different rates for different parts of the organism.* This is not intended to mean that the left foot grows rapidly for a short while, then the right foot, and then one arm. It does mean, however, that various parts of the body, as well as some aspects of personality and cognitive and perceptual ability, grow at different rates and reach their maximum development at different times.

The development of cognitive ability and personality traits has been shown to be governed by this principle. Bloom (1964) found that each personality trait has a characteristic growth curve. By the age of two and a half,

humans have reached half their future height. Half of a male's aggressiveness toward others is thought to be established by age 3, and much of our intellectual potential has already been developed by age 6,* a fact that may be partly related to how and when the brain grows.

Investigations of brain development reveal several interesting and important facts. First, most of the **neurons** (nerve cells) that make up the human brain are formed during the prenatal period, although some additional neurons may form in the first few months after birth (Rosenzweig and Leiman, 1982). At birth, the infant's brain weighs approximately one-quarter of what it will weigh at its maximum, which is reached at about age 25. Most of the increase in

---

*Statements such as these are hypothetical approximations at best and refer to variation rather than to absolute amount. The important point is simply that major personality and intellectual characteristics appear to be strongly influenced (and perhaps partly determined) by early childhood experiences.

brain weight between birth and adulthood seems to be caused by the growth of axons and dendrites (the elongated portions of the nerve cell, which permit neural transmission) and by myelination (the growth of a protective covering around the axon).

Second, brain growth also seems to be subject to varying rates. The brain does not grow at a uniform rate between conception and birth, nor between birth and adulthood. Instead, it appears to grow in spurts. These growth spurts are reflected by increases in cranial (head) circumference. Examinations of head measurements have led Lewin (1975) to believe that there is a dramatic spurt in brain growth during the later stages of fetal development. Evidence suggests that this period of rapid brain development is a critical period during which the effects of malnutrition can be especially severe — as can also be true during the first few months of infancy, during which there is a continuation of the growth spurt (Parmelee and Sigman, 1983). It is not surprising that in the majority of the world's undeveloped nations, where malnutrition is most prevalent, scientists have noted smaller-than-average head circumference among children (Winick, 1976).

Epstein's (1978) examination of head-circumference data leads him to the conclusion that significant and distinct spurts in brain growth take place during four periods between birth and adulthood: two to three months; two to three years; six to eight years; and fourteen to sixteen years for males and ten to twelve years for females. He notes as well that these spurts occur during periods that correspond closely with periods of major cognitive change according to Piaget's theory (described in the next chapter) and suggests the possibility that physical changes in the brain that accompany these growth spurts make cognitive development possible. Evidence to substantiate this supposition or to corroborate the consistency and significance of changes in cranial circumference is still scarce.

Another observation related to the principle of differential growth rates is **lateralization** — a term that refers to the fact that the two lateral halves (hemispheres) of the brain are somewhat specialized. For example, in the majority of individuals (95 percent of right-handed people and 70 percent of left-handed) the left hemisphere controls speech and other language functions, reason, and logic. And in the majority of people the right hemisphere is more concerned with the spatial and the temporal — for example, art and music — as well as with emotions. Thus, individuals who are logical are sometimes described as left-brain-oriented; those who are more intuitive and artistic might be referred to as right-brained (see Figure 7.2).

A number of researchers and theorists point out that our current educational practices emphasize left-brain functions, as is reflected in our preoccupation with verbal learning, mathematics, science, and logic (see, for example, Sonnier, 1985). Our schools neglect right-brain functions, they claim. Hence we should change our educational fare and philosophy to educate both halves of our students' brains. The phrase **holistic education** has been coined to represent this point of view. Unfortunately, investigating the dual function of the brain has proven difficult, and much of what passes for information in this area may be more speculation than fact.

To summarize the second principle briefly: Development is not a uniform process for all features of an organism. The description of growth curves for development has led Bloom (1964) to postulate a law that, if valid, is of major importance for education. It is given here as principle 3.

Timing of Environmental Influences

3. *Variations in environment have greatest quantitative effect on a characteristic at its period of most rapid change, and least effect on the characteristic at its*

Left Hemisphere Functions

language

writing

logic

math

science

sequential

organization

Right Hemisphere Functions

spatial organization

perception

aesthetics

art

music

dance

fantasy

Figure 7.2 Dominant abilities of the right and left hemispheres. How accurate is this "division of labor"? Kinsbourne and Cook (1971) describe a simple experiment to illustrate right and left hemisphere functions. They have a person balance a wooden dowel on the index finger of first the right hand and then the left. For right-handed individuals, balancing is easier on the right hand. But when the person is asked to speak while balancing the dowel (speech is a left-hemisphere function), balancing time decreases for the right hand but increases for the left.

period of least rapid change (Bloom, 1964, p. vii). This principle is most clearly illustrated with respect to physical growth. It is evident, for example, that changes in environment are not likely to affect the height of subjects over age 20. On the other hand, dietary changes for children under age 1 could conceivably have a more significant effect on future height.

This principle also holds with respect to intellectual development. As mentioned earlier, brain growth seems highly vulnerable to malnutrition during a growth spurt, especially during prenatal and early postnatal development. In addition, there is evidence that cognitive development may be most sensitive to environmental influences earlier rather than

later in life. A well-known study that illustrates this effect examined intelligence-test scores of American blacks living in Philadelphia (Lee, 1951). Of two groups of blacks who had been born in the South, one had moved to Philadelphia before first grade, and the second had moved at fourth grade. The first group showed much greater increases in intelligence-test scores than the second. In addition, the greatest changes occurred during the first few years. A third group of blacks, born and raised in Philadelphia, scored higher than the other two groups at all grades (see Figure 7.3).

Additional evidence suggesting that the timing of environmental influences can be very important is found in language acquisition:

Infants and young preschoolers can easily learn two or more languages simultaneously and well, whereas adults experience far more difficulty and far less success.

To summarize: There are periods of rapid development of specific kinds; during these periods, environmental influences are strongest. The implications of this principle for education are twofold: Educators need to identify periods of greatest and least rapid change, and they need to arrange for relevant experiences during periods of most rapid change. This line of thinking is illustrated in preschool programs such as Project Headstart, in which disadvantaged children are provided with experiences designed to allow them to catch up with more advantaged children. Although initial evaluations of these programs were not always very positive (see, for instance, Bronfenbrenner, 1977), much of the pertinent research suffered from the fact that it is extremely difficult to measure many of the important positive changes that can result from these programs. Typically, for example, research looks at obvious things such as achievement on standardized tests but fails to take into account important social and emotional events, such as changes in self-concept, motivation, and so on.

Barnett and Escobar (1987) present a summary of some twenty studies that have investigated the effects of preschool intervention and the economic benefits of intervention in relation to its cost (in the jargon of the age, what economists call *cost-effectiveness*). They conclude that many of these studies provide credible evidence indicating that early intervention with disadvantaged children is not only educationally and socially beneficial, but also economically sound.

Sequential Development

4. *Development follows an orderly sequence.* In fetal development the heart appears and begins to function before the limbs reach their final form; the lips and gums form prior to the nasal pas-

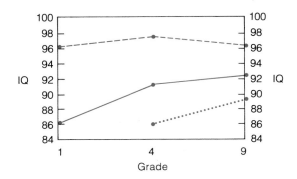

Figure 7.3 Changes in intelligence-test scores on measures obtained in first, fourth, and ninth grades for black students born and raised in Philadelphia (dashed line), those born in the South who moved to Philadelphia in the first grade (solid line), and those who did not move to Philadelphia until the fourth grade (dotted line).
Adapted from E. S. Lee, *American Sociological Review*, 1951, p. 231. Copyright 1951 by the American Sociological Association. Used by permission of the author.

sages; the tail regresses before the permanent tooth buds are formed; and so on.

In motor development, children can lift their chins from a prone position before they can raise their chests; they can sit before standing; they can stand before creeping; and they can creep before walking (Shirley, 1933).

In intellectual development, the same principle can be seen to apply, although the sequences are less obvious and the stages less distinct. Piaget's theory (see Chapter 8) is based on the assumption that human development is characterized by distinct sequential stages. Piaget's analysis of the changes in children's play behavior is one example of sequential development. The illustration deals with the changing relationship between children and game rules — a progression that Piaget describes as comprising two aspects, both of which exhibit the orderly sequence of principle 4. On the one hand is the child's actual behavior in game situations; on the other are verbalized notions of rules. These do not necessarily agree.

Table 7.1 Piaget's description of children's understanding and use of rules

Approximate Age	Degree of Understanding	Play Behavior
Before 3	No understanding of rules	Do not play according to any rules
To 5 or so	Believe rules come from God (or some other high authority) and cannot be changed	Break and change rules constantly
To 11 or 12	Understand social nature of rules and that they can be changed	Do not change rules; adhere to them rigidly
After 11 or 12	Complete understanding of rules	Change rules by mutual consent

In the first stage, lasting until about age 3, children do not understand the concept of rules and play as though there were none. Their play is "free play" in the sense that it is unencumbered by notions of what is permitted and what isn't.

During the second stage, lasting until age 5 or so, children have begun to imitate aspects of the rule-regulated play of adults, but the rules by which they play are idiosyncratic and constantly changing. They make rules up as they go along. But if asked about rules, they describe them as being external and unchangeable.

In the third stage (until age 11 or 12), children realize that rules are inventions that can, in fact, be changed. But their play behavior is again a contradiction of their beliefs; now they follow rules rigidly, seldom (if ever) changing them. It is not until the fourth stage (beyond age 11 or 12) that their play behavior finally reflects their understanding of the function of rules. Now, although they play according to rules, they occasionally change them by mutual consent. (See Table 7.1.)

The understanding of rules is only one small aspect of development that follows an orderly and predictable sequence. Piaget's investigations, described in detail in Chapter 8,

suggest that notions of reality, logical reasoning, understanding of time and space, and a wealth of important cognitive and perceptual events are sequential and predictable.

The observation that much of development follows an orderly and predictable sequence is especially valuable for teachers, who need to be concerned with the readiness of students. Teachers need to know when specific cognitive and perhaps metacognitive skills develop if they are to present children with tasks that are not impossible for them but are challenging enough to be interesting and to promote growth. As is made clear in the next chapter, it may also be extremely important to understand the factors that enhance—or that retard—development.

Developmental Stages

5. *Development may be described in stages.* Most developmental theories are in fact stage theories; that is, they describe important developmental events in terms of age-defined stages. Stage theories are based on the understanding that although development is generally a relatively smooth, ongoing process, distinct and important changes nevertheless occur in a predictable sequence.

Stages are very useful. They give us convenient places to "hang" our facts; they simplify our understanding, help our organization, and facilitate recall. They have been used extensively by such theorists as Freud, Erikson, and Piaget. The interesting point is that the stages used by these theorists are not parallel; they are all expressions of different points of view, and they all describe different features of child development. Therefore, even though it might appear reasonable to say that development proceeds in stages, it must also be made clear that any such stages are invented by theorists to clarify and order their observations.

One set of stages is Piaget's. It describes intellectual development:

Stage	Age
1. Sensorimotor	0–2 years
2. Preoperational	2–7 years
3. Concrete operations	7–11 years
4. Formal operations	11–15 years

A less forbidding, more intuitive classification is Hurlock's:

Stage	Age
1. Prenatal	Conception–280 days
2. Infancy	0–10 or 14 days
3. Babyhood	2 weeks–2 years
4. Childhood	2 years–adolescence
5. Adolescence	13 (girls)–21 years
6. Adolescence	14 (boys)–21 years

Stage theories are important for teachers because they provide information about the sequence of human development, about the most likely behaviors of children in different stages, and perhaps about the factors that facilitate transition from one stage to the next. We consider these matters again in the next chapter.

Correlation vs. Compensation

6. *Correlation, not compensation, is the rule in development.* There is a popular notion that contradicts this principle. According to this notion, individuals who are intellectually gifted are, of course, not nearly so well endowed in other areas. The "egghead" is believed to be a blundering social idiot; he is certainly unattractive and frail; his vision is weak; he is completely useless at any kind of task requiring even the smallest degree of dexterity; his breath smells; and his teeth are crooked. The athlete, a handsome and virile brute, is remarkably stupid; he spells his name with difficulty; he cannot write a check without a lawyer to correct it; he reads very simple comic books and laughs uproariously at very unfunny events.

These stereotypes do not represent reality. Rather, the person who excels in one realm is more likely to excel in others, an observation supported by data from studies by Terman et al. (1925). The corollary is that people who are below average in one area tend to be below average in other areas as well — and this too is true. Although there are obvious exceptions to this principle, it nevertheless serves as a useful guide in understanding the overall development of children.

Rate of Development

7. *Development usually proceeds at the rate at which it started.* A child who learns to walk and talk at a very early age is more likely to be highly intelligent as an adult than is a child who begins developing more slowly. Data to support this contention are relatively difficult to find because early measures of intelligence are notably unreliable. However, Bloom (1964) surveyed a large number of studies that, taken as a whole, suggest that human characteristics are remarkably stable. In other words, there is relatively little change in the rate of development after the initial period of rapid development that characterizes most physical and intellectual qualities.

Individual Differences

8. *There is a great deal of variability among individuals.* This is related to the high plasticity of the human being, to different genetic characteristics, and to the effects of different environments

on children. It remains true, nevertheless, that valid generalizations about children as a group can be made. But — and this is extremely important — these generalizations apply to children as a group and not to any specific individual child. There is no normal, average child; the "average child" is a myth invented by grandmothers and investigated by psychologists.

The preceding developmental principles constitute an overview and summary of some educationally relevant statements that can be made about developmental processes. Even though they do not suggest highly specific instructional implications, they can nevertheless provide teachers with general concepts that might be useful for understanding students better.

There is, of course, far more to human development than can be summarized in eight principles. From the teacher's point of view, the aspect of development that is absolutely central to the teaching/learning process is intellectual development, which is dealt with in Chapter 8. Two additional topics of particular importance for teachers are language development and moral development. We turn to these next.

LANGUAGE DEVELOPMENT

Our ability to communicate through **language** is one of the things that clearly separates us from other beasts — and not simply because language makes it possible for us to communicate with one another at levels of abstraction that we suspect are beyond the imaginations and the capacities of these other beasts. Language separates us from wild and domestic beasts in at least two other related ways: It provides us with a means for storing our knowledge and wisdom, and it allows us to *transform* that knowledge. More than this, language is what makes possible the universality of meanings and the sharing of human experience. And because it is the chief medium of instruction in schools, its importance can hardly be overestimated.

Language and Communication Distinguished

Language is not synonymous with **communication**. Animals communicate, but they do not have language. A dog who gets its master's attention, walks to its dish and barks, looks its master in the eyes, and then begins to growl is communicating very effectively. Animals that are not domesticated also communicate. Pronghorn antelope convey alarm by bristling their rump patches; white-tailed deer, by flagging their long tails. Pheasants threaten rivals by crowing; elk, by bugling; and moose, by grunting. Hebb (1966) refers to this type of behavior as communication through reflexive activity. The behavior of the dog described above, however, is an example of purposive communication — but it is still not language.

To communicate is to transmit or convey a message, which requires a sender and a receiver. To communicate through language is to make use of *arbitrary* sounds, gestures, or symbols in a purposive manner to convey meaning. Further, the use of language involves sounds or other signs that can be combined or transformed to produce different meanings. A parrot, for example, can mimic a word or even a phrase and can be taught to speak a phrase so that its utterance will appear purposive. A parrot that says "You bore me" after a guest has been talking incessantly for two hours may appear to be using language in a purposive manner. But the parrot is not using the phrase with the intention of communicating meaning and cannot transform the phrase with the intention of communicating a different meaning. That would be the use of language as opposed to reflexive communication.

The Early Development of Language

In the course of babbling, infants may emit every sound used in all of the world's languages. How these sounds become organized into the meaningful patterns of language is still a matter of some speculation.

One relatively reasonable and clear account of early language learning can be based on an operant conditioning model. This explanation maintains that while babbling, a child emits wordlike sounds, which tend to be reinforced by adults. As the frequency of these specific sounds increases, parents or siblings may repeat the child's vocalizations and thus serve as models for the child. Eventually, through reinforcement, children learn to imitate the speech patterns of those around them. Were it not for this imitation and reinforcement, frequency and variety of speech sounds would probably decrease. This is borne out by the observation that deaf children make sounds much like those made by normal children until around the age of six months; after that they utter few sounds, and not many of these are repetitive.

Note that even though reinforcement may be a relatively good explanation for the early learning of speech sounds (**phonology**) and simple meanings (**semantics**), it is not an adequate explanation for either the rapidity with which children learn language or for the acquisition of complex **syntax** (sentence formation rules), **grammar** (rules of word classes and functions), and **pragmatics** (implicit rules governing conversation — for example, who should speak and when, and the meanings of pauses, intonations, gestures, and so on). These — phonology, semantics, syntax, grammar, and pragmatics — are the elements of language.

Researchers who have looked at the origins of language have been particularly interested in infants' first sounds and gestures and the interactions of infants and their caretakers. It seems clear that the ability to use and understand words develops through a complex series of such interactions, which Bruner (1983) labels the *language acquisition support system (LASS)*. Among other things, this system involves learning how to make eye contact, how to direct attention through eye movements, and how to emphasize and communicate meaning through facial and other bodily gestures.

For convenience and simplicity, the learning of language can be considered a series of stages. One useful account is Wood's (1981) outline of six stages, summarized in Table 7.2.

The prespeech stage spans most of the first year of life. Significant speech-related developments during this period include the devel-

Table 7.2 Stages of grammatical development in children

Stage of Development	Nature of Development	Sample Utterances
1. Prespeech (before age 1)	Crying, cooing, babbling	"Waaah." "Dadadada."
2. Sentence-like word, or holophrase (by 12 months)	The word is combined with nonverbal cues (gestures and inflections).	"Mommy." (meaning: "Would you please come here, Mother.")
3. Two-word sentences (by 18 months)	Modifiers are joined to topic words to form declarative, interrogative, negative, and imperative structures.	"Pretty baby." (declarative) "Where Daddy?" (question) "No play." (negative) "More milk!" (imperative)
4. Multiple-word sentences (by 2 to 2½ years)	Both a subject and predicate are included in the sentence. Grammatical morphemes are used to change meanings ("ing" or "ed," for example).	"She's a pretty baby." (declarative) "Where Daddy is?" (question) "I no can play." (negative) "I want more milk!" (imperative) "I running." "I runned."
5. More complex grammatical changes and word categories (between 2½ and 4 years)	Elements are added, embedded, and permuted within sentences. Word classes (nouns, verbs, and prepositions) are subdivided. Clauses are put together.	"Read it, my book." (conjunction) "Where is Daddy?" (embedding) "I can't play." (permutation) "I would like some milk." (use of "some" with mass noun) "Take me to the store." (use of preposition of place)
6. Adult-like structures (after 4 years)	Complex structural distinctions made, as with "ask-tell" and "promise."	"Ask what time it is." "He promised to help her."

Source: Based in part on B. S. Wood, *Children and Communication: Verbal and Nonverbal Language Development* (2nd ed.), © 1981, p. 142. Reprinted by permission of Prentice-Hall, Inc., Englewood Cliffs, New Jersey.

opment and refinement of gestures and noises such as cooing, babbling, and crying, largely through infant-caretaker interaction.

The second stage involves the appearance of what Wood calls the **holophrase**, or sentence-like word. This usually occurs by the age of twelve months. Although the child's utterances consist of a single word at a time at this stage, the meanings of the words plus nonverbal cues are sufficiently detailed that an adult would require an entire sentence to say the same

thing. For example, the holophrase "cat," uttered in an unmistakably imperious tone by my nephew Eskabar, means very clearly, "Fetch me my orange tabby-cat, Boris Lefrançois, or I will wail very shrilly and loudly!"*

PPC: "Perhaps the author should choose an example that would be less likely to offend his relatives."
Author: "Good idea. That's why I've changed my nephew's name to Eskabar here. Boris, the cat, doesn't read."

More on Language Acquisition: LAD

The operant-conditioning model advanced to explain children's acquisition of language is partly correct, but it is also inadequate. The incredible rapidity with which children acquire syntax and grammar during their third and fourth years, coupled with the fact that they make only a fraction of all the mistakes that they would be expected to make if they were learning through reinforcement alone, makes it unlikely that operant conditioning is the complete explanation. And the nature of their errors frequently reveals that the errors result not so much from lack of proper models or lack of reinforcement, but rather from the application of rules that they have derived unconsciously without direct adult tuition. The irony is that their application of the rules themselves is correct, but our language presents so many exceptions that children cannot simply apply these rules universally; they must also learn the exceptions. Thus children who say "I eated," "I was borned," "I dood it," and "I runned fast" are displaying that they are fine grammarians, even if they have not completely mastered the language.

Noam Chomsky (1957, 1965), a noted linguist, has attempted to explain children's development of language. His conclusion, simplified, is that the child's rapid acquisition of an incredibly complex syntax can be explained only on the basis of prewired (innate) neurological mechanisms. In other words, the child is neurologically predisposed to learning the forms of a language. Chomsky calls this neurological predisposition a language acquisition device (*LAD* for short—hence Bruner's use of the expression LASS). Note that LAD and LASS, in this context, are not *real*, observable things; they are simply useful metaphors.

Two-word sentences (the third stage), made up primarily of modifiers joined to nouns or pronouns, appear by the age of eighteen months. At this stage, speech is still highly telegraphic; that is, complex meanings are squeezed into simple, and sometimes grammatically incorrect, two-word utterances. For example, the sentence "Mummy gone" may mean something as complex as "My dear mother is currently on a business trip in Chicago."

The fourth stage, multiple-word sentences, is reached between ages 2 and 2½. Sentences may now be five or more words in length. Although they continue to be telegraphic, they make use of more grammatical variations to express different meanings, and they typically consist of appropriate subjects and predicates.

Between ages 2½ and 4, children learn to use progressively more complex grammatical structures (the fifth stage), culminating in adult-like structures in the late preschool years.

It is important to note that although ages are assigned to each of these stages, they are only approximations based on the average performance of large groups. Here, as in all other areas of human development, it is normal for some to display a behavior earlier and others later. An average is not an expression of normality in the sense that those who deviate from it are abnormal; it is simply a mathematical indication of a point around which a population is distributed.

Language and Intelligence

The **correlation** (see Chapter 9 for an explanation of this term) between verbal ability and measured intelligence is very high. This may be partly because most measures of intelligence are verbal — they require that subjects at least understand verbal directions. In many cases, subjects are asked to make oral or written responses. In addition, many of these tests measure the extent and sophistication of vocabulary. On the one hand, then, the very nature of intelligence tests probably accounts for at least some of the high correspondence between language and intelligence. On the other hand, the fact that verbal ability is given such a central role in these tests is an indication of its importance in our definitions of intelligence (see Chapter 9).

THE ROLE OF LANGUAGES IN EDUCATION

In 1982, almost 75 percent of the school-age population in the United States was white; Hispanic children accounted for only 10 percent of school-age children. However, projections are that by the year 2020, the percentage of white school-age Americans will have decreased to about 50 percent. Approximately half the remainder — that is, one out of every four children — will be Hispanics. The rest will be blacks (about 16.5 percent of school-age children) and other races (Pallas, Natriello, and McDill, 1989).

These projections are tremendously important for American education because, if they are accurate, they will in all likelihood be reflected in dramatic changes in the school. Whereas in 1982 the majority of American schoolchildren spoke English — the dominant, standard, majority language — by 2020 English may not be nearly so dominant. By the same token, Spanish and so-called nonstandard forms of English, such as *Black English*, will have become far more common. What are the implications of these changes?

Nonstandard Languages

The languages that most majority-group people understand, speak, and read are referred to as **standard languages**; they are viewed as correct, acceptable language forms against which other forms of the same language can be compared. And the often-explicit assumption that we make is that language forms that are nonstandard are inferior to the standard language. The varieties of English spoken by many American blacks, by Americans of Hispanic origin, by French Canadians, and by natives (Indians) of both countries are cases in point. We generally assume not only that these forms of language are inferior, but also that they are responsible for the frequent schooling problems experienced by those less proficient in standard English. However, the most plausible explanation for the poorer performance of those who speak a nonstandard English may not be that their language is less complex, less sophisticated, and less grammatical, but simply that it is different. Because instruction in schools typically occurs in standard English and because evidence of achievement requires understanding of and expression in standard English, these children are clearly at a disadvantage (Baratz, 1969).

What, if anything, can — or should — be done to enhance the child's sophistication in the use of standard language? The first part of the question is simple; the second isn't. Several things *can* be done. One of the obvious solutions is to emphasize standard English both in the home and in the school—an approach that is clearly favored by many middle-class blacks as well as whites. The argument is that most commerce both outside and inside school is carried out in standard English, and that therefore those children who do not learn standard forms of the dominant language will be at the same disadvantage outside school as they are in school. Another solution is to allow black children to use their nonstandard dialects, at least part of the time, in schools (Seymour, 1971). This would require that teachers also develop some proficiency in the nonstandard language.

What *should* be done is another matter. Such issues cannot always be resolved through either research or reason alone.

Bilingualism and Language Immersion

Research suggests that one of the best ways of learning a second language is not to take occasional lessons, private instructions, expensive audio- or videotape courses, or concentrated study, but to become immersed in the language. In essence, **language immersion** involves entering an environment in which only the language that is to be learned is spoken. And there is ample evidence to suggest that if this occurs early enough (soon after the first language is firmly established), children can painlessly learn a second language and perhaps even a third and a fourth.

Language immersion programs in school are a recent, mushrooming phenomenon in Canada, where French immersion programs are very widespread. Similarly, Spanish immersion programs are common in California. Most of these immersion programs begin in preschool settings and continue through the elementary grades. For example, the French immersion program in which my 13-year-old is enrolled began when he was in kindergarten.

Teachers and teacher assistants speak only French in the first year of this program; that is, French is taught not as a separate subject but is simply the language through which the regular curriculum is taught. In the second year (first grade), English is introduced for perhaps 10 percent of the school day. The percentage increases each year, until by sixth grade half of the school day is conducted in English and half in French.

Research leaves little doubt that immersion programs are extremely effective in teaching a second language (for example, Genesee, 1983, 1985). Participants quickly reach high levels of proficiency in understanding and speaking the second language, as well as in reading and writing, although the majority do not reach as high a level of proficiency as native speakers. In addition, perhaps only a small number will ever become what Diaz (1983) calls balanced bilinguals (individuals who are equally proficient in both languages). However, as Genesee (1985) points out, the language deficiencies of immersion students do not appear to interfere with their functional use of the second language. In addition, these students typically perform as well as students in conventional English programs in academic subjects such as mathematics, science, and social studies, as well as on measures of social and cognitive development. If the immersion program is entirely in the second language and students have not yet received instruction in English language arts, they do not, of course, do as well on measures of English literacy. But Genesee (1985) reports that within one year of receiving English instruction, they perform as well as children in monolingual English programs.

Effects of Learning a Second Language. Unfortunately, learning a second language is not always an entirely positive experience. Lambert (1975) coined the expression *subtractive bilingualism* to describe the situation in which learning a second language has a negative influence on the first. *Additive bilingualism* describes the opposite situation.

Research indicates that the circumstances under which learning a second language is most likely to be a negative experience involve minority-group children whose first language is a minority language. In such instances, the second language—the dominant, majority language—is extensively reinforced in the mass media and in society, whereas the minority language is not. This may be the case, for example, for French-speaking children in Canada or Hispanics in the United States who learn English as a second language in school. Because television and other media (and perhaps most community transactions) use English, the first language receives little support and reinforcement outside the home—and perhaps not even in the home. As a result, the first language tends to be given less-valued social roles and is used at a less advanced level (Landry, 1987). Moreover, models of the minority language are often poor models of that language. Thus the Spanish or the French spoken at home might be more colloquial—less developed in terms of vocabulary, liberally sprinkled with English expressions, grammatically incorrect, and characterized by idiosyncratic pronunciation (Carey, 1987). And if the minority language is not part of children's schooling, they are unlikely to learn to read and write it. Ultimately, their first-language proficiency may be largely oral.

Learning a second language most often has a positive effect on children when the language learned is a minority language. This would be the case, for example, for English-speaking American or Canadian children enrolled in Spanish or French immersion programs. Growing evidence suggests that such programs are not only successful in developing a high level of proficiency in the second language, but they also contribute to general academic achievement (Bialystok, 1988). In addition, they frequently strengthen the first language (Cummins and Swain, 1986).

There are, of course, numerous exceptions to these simple generalizations; real life is rarely as simple as our interpretations of research might suggest. But given the probability that our conclusions are more often correct than incorrect, there may be merit in Cummins's (1986) recommendation that the primary language of instruction for minority-group children be the minority language—and that the majority language be presented as a second language. And if our demographic projections are accurate, these issues may be far more pressing by the year 2020.

KOHLBERG'S MODEL OF MORAL DEVELOPMENT

Many decades ago Piaget (1932) interviewed children to ask them about rules and laws, right and wrong, and good and evil. To no one's great surprise, he discovered that very young children do not operate within limitations imposed by abstract conceptions of right and wrong, but respond instead in terms of the immediate personal consequences of their behavior.

A very young child's morality is governed by the principles of pain and pleasure. Accordingly, children consider good those behaviors that have pleasant consequences, (or at least do not have unpleasant consequences). Piaget's label for this initial stage of moral development is *heteronomy*. During this stage the child responds primarily to outside authority, which is the main source of rewards and punishments. This initial stage is followed by the appearance of more autonomous moral judgments. During the stage of *autonomy*, behavior is guided more and more by internalized principles and ideals.

Some three decades after Piaget, Kohlberg (1964) undertook detailed longitudinal investigations of moral beliefs and behaviors, eventually arriving at a detailed description of three sequential levels of moral orientation, each of

Table 7.3   Kohlberg's levels of morality

Kohlberg identified levels of moral judgment in children by describing to them situations involving a moral dilemma. One example is the story of Heinz, a man whose wife is dying but might be saved if given a drug discovered by a local pharmacist, who charges such an exorbitant price that Heinz can't pay. Should he steal the drug?

Level I: Preconventional	Stage 1: Punishment and obedience orientation	"If he steals the drug, he might go to jail." (Punishment.)
	Stage 2: Naive instrumental hedonism	"He can steal the drug and save his wife, and he'll be with her when he gets out of jail." (Act motivated by its hedonistic consequences for the actor.)
Level II: Conventional	Stage 3: "Good-boy, nice-girl" morality	"People will understand if you steal the drug to save your wife, and they'll think you're cruel and a coward if you don't." (Reactions of others and the effects of the act on social relationships become important.)
	Stage 4: Law-and-order orientation	"It is the husband's duty to save his wife even if he feels guilty afterwards for stealing the drug." (Institutions, law, duty, honor, and guilt motivate behavior.)
Level III: Postconventional	Stage 5: Morality of social contract	"The husband has a right to the drug even if he can't pay now. If the druggist won't charge it, the government should look after it." (Democratic laws guarantee individual rights; contracts are mutually beneficial.)
	Stage 6: Universal ethical*	"Although it is legally wrong to steal, the husband would be morally wrong not to steal to save his wife. A life is more precious than financial gain." (Conscience is individual. Laws are socially useful but not sacrosanct.)

*Stage 6 is no longer included among Kohlberg's stages because none of his sample reached it. However, it is still described as a *potential* stage.
Source: Based on L. Kohlberg (1971, 1980).

which is divided into two stages (see Table 7.3). In principle, these stages are similar to Piaget's description of a progression from heteronomy to autonomy, although they are considerably more detailed. Each of the levels and stages is described briefly here.

Level I: Preconventional

At the earliest level, children respond primarily in terms of the immediate hedonistic consequences of their behaviors and in terms of the powers of those who have authority over them.

Preconventional reasoning may take two forms, described by Kohlberg as Stages 1 and 2.

Stage 1: Punishment and Obedience Orientation. Behavior is designed to avoid punishment. The child believes that obedience is good in and of itself. Evaluation of the morality of an action is totally divorced from its more objective consequences, but instead rests solely on its consequences to the actor. Behavior for which one is punished is, *ipso facto*, bad; that for which one is rewarded must necessarily be good.

Stage 2: Instrumental and Hedonistic Orientation. This is the beginnings of reciprocity ("Do for me and I will do for you"). The reciprocity characteristic of this stage is strikingly practical. Children will do something good for others only if they expect it to result in someone's doing something good for them in return. Their moral orientation remains largely hedonistic (pain- and pleasure-oriented).

Level II: Conventional

Conventional morality is a morality of conformity: Behaviors that are good are those that maintain established social order. This level reflects the increasing importance of peers and of social relations and is expressed in two stages.

Stage 3: "Good-Boy, Nice-Girl" Morality. Children judge their actions largely in terms of their role in establishing and maintaining good relations with authority and with peers. Approval is all-important and is assumed to be the result of "being nice."

Stage 4: Law and Order. Morality is characterized by blind obedience. What is legal is, by definition, good. And the good person is the one who is aware of rules and obeys them unquestioningly.

Level III: Postconventional

At the highest level of moral reasoning, the individual makes a deliberate effort to clarify moral rules and principles and to arrive at self-defined notions of good and evil.

Stage 5: Morality of Social Contract. This stage retains an important element of conformity to laws and legal systems, but with the important difference that legal systems are interpreted as being good to the extent that they guarantee and protect individual rights. The individual can now evaluate laws in terms of social order and individual justice and is capable of reinterpreting and changing them.

Stage 6: Universal Ethical. The final stage of moral development is characterized by individually chosen ethical principles that serve as major unifying guides to behavior. Individual moral principles are highly abstract rather than concrete. They are not illustrated by the Ten Commandments, for example, but are implicit in deep-seated convictions that guide behavior — for example, beliefs in justice or equality.

Kohlberg's Model Evaluated

Kohlberg's (1971) early research suggested that a child's progression through these stages is sequential and universal; that is, all children were assumed to progress through all stages in the same sequence. This did not mean, however, that all individuals eventually reached the sixth stage (self-determined principles) and that adults operated only on that level. In fact, a reanalysis of Kohlberg's original data using more careful criteria found that only one-eighth of subjects (in their twenties) seemed capable of fifth-stage judgments. The same analysis found no evidence whatsoever of sixth-stage judgments (Colby and Kohlberg, 1984). Subsequently, Kohlberg has dropped the sixth stage from his description of moral development.

There have been criticisms of Kohlberg's stages. For example, Holstein (1976) found that many subjects skipped stages, reverted apparently randomly to earlier stages, or otherwise responded in ways that provided little evidence of stages. In addition, Holstein's female subjects often expressed moral judgments that appeared to be systematically different from those of male subjects. Furthermore, there is often such a lack of consistency among responses given by the same subject for different moral dilemmas that subjects cannot always be described as operating at one level rather than another (Fishkin, Keniston, and MacKinnon, 1973).

What this evidence suggests is that moral judgments depend not only on the ages of subjects, but also on a host of other variables, including the intentions of the transgressor, previous experiences in similar situations, and the social, material, or personal consequences of the behavior (Eisenberg-Berg, 1979; Suls and Kalle, 1979).

Apart from the observation that progression through stages of moral development might not be as predictable and as systematic as Kohlberg suggested, Gilligan (1982) suggests that this research has at least two other important weaknesses. One is that Kohlberg's subjects were all males — and, as noted earlier, there is evidence of some sex differences in morality; the other is that the moral dilemmas that Kohlberg used may not always be immediately meaningful in the lives of children. It may be that our responses to hypothetical moral dilemmas ("What would you do if you were at war and you had the opportunity to shoot an enemy soldier who hasn't seen you and is unlikely to?") will be quite different from our actual behaviors, if we ever must in fact make a choice.

In an attempt to examine morality in women by means of meaningful moral dilemmas, Gilligan interviewed a sample of pregnant

women struggling with a decision concerning abortion. All twenty-nine women in the sample had been referred by a counseling clinic for pregnant women. Twenty-one of these women subsequently had an abortion, four had their babies, one miscarried, and three still remained undecided throughout the duration of the study. In fact, however, it is not so much the decision itself (to have or not to have the baby) that reflects level of moral development as the reasons for the decision.

Gilligan identified three stages in the women's moral development. In the first stage the woman is moved by selfish concerns ("This is what I need . . . what I want . . . what is important for my physical/psychological survival"). In the second stage there is a transition from selfishness to greater responsibility toward others. This change is reflected in reasoning that is based not on simple, selfish survival, but on a more objective morality (notions of what is right and wrong; specifically, a growing realization that caring for others rather than just for self is a form of "goodness"). The third stage reflects what Gilligan labels a "morality of nonviolence" toward self and others. This level of morality is reflected in the fact that the woman will now accept sole responsibility for her decision and that she bases this decision on the greatest good to self and others. The best moral decision at this level is the one that does the least harm to the greatest number of those for whom the woman is responsible.

In summary, Gilligan describes adult female moral development in terms of three stages beginning with a selfish orientation, progressing through a period of increasing recognition of responsibility to others, and culminating at a level at which moral decisions reflect a desire to treat the self and others equally — that is, to do the greatest good (or the least harm) for the greatest number. At each of these three levels, what women respond to most when initially considering their moral dilemmas are the emotional and social implications of their decision for the self, and subsequently implications for others as well as for self. In contrast with Kohlberg's description of a male moral progression that moves from initial hedonistic selfishness toward a greater recognition of social and legal *rights*, Gilligan describes a female progression from selfishness toward greater recognition of *responsibility* to self and others.

Put another way, one of the important differences between male and female morality (as described by Kohlberg and Gilligan) is that moral progression in males tends toward the recognition and use of "universal ethical principles"; in contrast, women respond more to considerations of fairness and equality for self and others.

Additional corroboration of these sex differences are implicit in the fact that a number of studies have found that girls frequently reach Kohlberg's third stage, morality of good relations, earlier than boys and remain at that level long after boys have gone on to the fourth stage, morality of law and order (see, for example, Turiel, 1974; Gilligan et al., 1971). One plausible explanation for this observation is that girls are more responsive to social relationships, more concerned with empathy and compassion, and more in touch with real life and less concerned with the hypothetical (Holstein, 1976). In contrast, boys are more concerned with law and order, social justice, and the abstract as opposed to the personally meaningful dimensions of morality.

Educational Implications of Moral Development

Knowledge of the progression of moral development can be of value to the teacher in several ways. First, knowing how and why children judge things to be morally right or wrong relates directly to the types of rationalizations a teacher might offer children in exhorting them to "behave" and/or not to "misbehave." There is evidence, for example, that rationalizations that stress the object — "the toy might break" — are more effective for younger children than rationalizations that are more abstract — "you should not play with toys that belong to other children" (see Chapter 12). By extrapolation, the types of rationalizations that might be offered adolescents would be quite different from those offered younger children. Also, the most meaningful rationalizations for girls might stress social relationships, empathy, and responsibility; the most meaningful rationalizations for boys might stress legal rights and social order.

A second application of knowledge of moral development is the actual teaching of morality. Unfortunately, little research has been devoted to the question of whether or not moral development can be promoted or accelerated in children. This is partly because early studies (Hartshorne and May, 1928, for example) found little correspondence between actual behavior and moral and religious training. Specifically, these investigators found that immoral behaviors such as cheating were much less affected by religious training, apparent strength of conscience, and other abstract signs of "moral goodness" than by the probability of being caught. Given these widely accepted and highly pessimistic findings, it is not surprising that schools have traditionally paid little attention to the deliberate inculcation of virtues. However, Fodor (1972) has found that children identified as delinquents operate at a much lower level on the Kohlberg scales than nondelinquent children. And Kohlberg and Candee (1984) found that children at the higher stages of moral reasoning are more likely to be honest and to behave "morally." In other words, there does appear to be some correspondence between level of moral orientation and actual behavior. If this is the case, anything that the schools can do to promote progression through these stages might contribute directly to classroom control and indirectly to the development of better individuals.

What, precisely, can be done? Unfortunately, suggestions remain rather abstract (perhaps Bear VIII will be more concrete). Kohlberg (1964), for example, suggests that even though the content of moral rules can be taught, the attitudes necessary for behavior at each level result from a complete process of cognitive development and cannot themselves be taught. In addition, as Peters (1977) points out, Kohlberg's theory deals with the cognitive aspects of moral development, but it does not consider the affective components of morality. Hence the theory itself does little to clarify the types of feelings that ought to be fostered if children are to develop morally. But Peters and other researchers have attempted to clarify this matter.

Peters (1977) argues that caring for others is perhaps the most important attitude involved in progressing from primitive levels of morality to self-determined principles. Similarly, McPhail, Ungoed-Thomas, and Chapman (1972) have developed a teaching program for adolescents designed to foster empathy and concern. Sullivan (1977) argues that the dimension of "care" often appears to be lost in contemporary society. He argues as well that the type of moral training most often characteristic of established, orthodox religions appears to serve as a motivator for attaining higher levels of moral reasoning (Sullivan and Quarter, 1972; Sullivan, 1977). Oser (1986) presents a strong argument for the use of a discursive approach whereby issues of morality and values are discussed, examined, and challenged, and in which attempts are made to resolve moral conflicts.

In general, then, the implication of these findings and speculations is that teachers ought to attempt to develop in children care and concern for others and to encourage and reward behaviors that reflect virtues ordinarily associated with caring.

More concretely, Hoffman (1976) suggests four different kinds of experiences that can foster altruistic and caring behavior in children, some of which may suggest worthwhile classroom activities:

1. Situations in which children are allowed to experience unpleasantness rather than being overprotected

2. Role-taking experiences in which children are responsible for the care of others

3. Role-playing experiences in which children imagine themselves in the plight of others

4. Exposure to altruistic models

MAIN POINTS

1. Developmental psychology is concerned with the changes that occur between conception and death. It looks at characteristics at different ages, at predictable differences among age and sex groups, and at the processes that account for developmental change.

2. A *cohort* is a group consisting of individuals who were born during the same time period and who therefore are subject to the same historical influences. Conclusions that are valid for one cohort are not necessarily valid for others.

3. *Development* can be viewed as comprising all changes attributable to maturation, growth, and learning. *Maturation* refers to a natural unfolding, whereas *learning* refers to the effects of experience. *Growth* is defined by physical changes.

4. Development results from the interaction of *heredity* and *environment*, although the extent of the contribution of each is difficult to determine. Investigations of twins and

of other pairs of individuals of varying degrees of genetic relatedness indicate that heredity contributes significantly to the development of measured intelligence.

5. Development takes place at different rates for different features of the organism. A case in point is the human brain, which at birth weighs approximately one-quarter of what it will weigh at adulthood. The brain seems to grow in spurts, with a major spurt occurring just before and just after birth (considered a critical period during which malnutrition can have serious consequences).

6. *Brain lateralization* is the functional specialization of the cerebral hemispheres. The left hemisphere is concerned primarily with reason, language, and mathematics; the right, with intuition, music, and art. Advocates of *holistic education* believe that conventional education is left-brain-oriented — that we do not teach the whole brain.

7. Environmental changes are most effective during the period of fastest growth and least effective during slowest growth. In practice, this principle favors early intervention, particularly with respect to such things as language development.

8. Development follows an orderly sequence, although the age at which various events occur can vary considerably from one child to another.

9. Development may be described in terms of arbitrary stages. These inventions are useful for organizing our observations about children.

10. *Correlation*, not compensation, is the rule in development.

11. Development usually proceeds at approximately the rate at which it started.

12. In spite of the generality of our developmental principles, there is considerable variation among different individuals.

13. The ability to use language for purposive communication is one of the things that most clearly separates us from other animals.

14. The elements of language are phonology (speech sounds), semantics (meanings of sounds), syntax (sentence formation rules), grammar (word classes and functions), and pragmatics (implicit rules governing conversation).

15. The early development of language is thought to depend upon a complex network of caretaker-infant interaction, which includes learning how to make eye contact, how to direct attention through eye and body movements, the meanings of expressions and gestures, and so on. Bruner labels this network of interactions a *language acquisition support system (LASS)*.

16. Six stages in the development of language, according to Wood, are prespeech (before age 1; cooing and babbling); sentence-like word, or holophrase (by age 1); two-word sentence (by eighteen months); multiple-word sentences containing subject and predicate (ages 2 to 2½); more complex sentences and grammatical changes (by age 4); and adult-like structures (age 4 onward).

17. *Nonstandard languages* (different dialects of the dominant language, such as Black English) often place children at a disadvantage because school success typically requires a high level of proficiency in the dominant language.

18. Language immersion programs appear to be among the most effective means of learning a second language. Evidence suggests that most immersion students develop a high degree of proficiency (although not perfection)

in the second language and perform equally well in other subjects, including measures of literacy in the dominant language once it has been introduced and studied.

19. Learning a second language sometimes has a negative effect on knowledge of the first language (an effect termed *subtractive bilingualism*), especially for minority-group children who learn the dominant, majority language as a second language. For native speakers of the dominant language, learning a second language is most often an *additive* experience that results in a relatively high level of proficiency in both languages.

20. Moral development in boys seems to proceed from a preconventional level (characterized by hedonistic concerns and obedience to authority) to a conventional level (characterized by conformity and a desire to maintain good relationships). The postconventional level (characterized by attention to individual rights and the development of individual principles of conduct and beliefs) is seldom, if ever, reached.

21. Moral development in girls seems to be tied more to social responsibility, empathy, and social relationships than to law and social order. It proceeds from a level of selfishness, through a level of increasing acceptance of social responsibility, and finally to a level of nonviolence in which the greatest good is to do the least harm to the greatest number of people socially linked to the individual.

22. Knowledge of moral development might be of value in helping teachers determine the types of rationalizations most likely to be effective with different children. In addition, it might be possible to foster moral growth through systematic educational programs.

SUGGESTED READINGS

For further elaboration and greater clarification of the developmental principles outlined in this chapter, you might consult the following textbooks:

LEFRANÇOIS, G. R. (1990). *The lifespan* (3rd ed.). Belmont, Calif.: Wadsworth.

LEFRANÇOIS, G. R. (1989). *Of children: An introduction to child development* (6th ed.). Belmont, Calif.: Wadsworth.

Language development is described in considerably more detail in:

WOOD, B. S. (1981). *Children and communication: Verbal and nonverbal language development* (2nd ed.). Englewood Cliffs, N.J.: Prentice-Hall.

The following are two good sources of information on moral development. The first describes Kohlberg's recent revisions of his theory; the second focuses on the role of social interaction in the development of morality:

KOHLBERG, L. (1980). *The meaning and measurement of moral development.* Worcester, Mass.: Clark University Press.

KURTINES, W. M., & GEWIRTZ, J. L. (Eds.). (1987). *Moral development through social interaction.* New York: Wiley.

The following is a readable collection of articles on the separation of functions between the right and left cerebral hemispheres and on the need for more right-brain-oriented instructional procedures:

SONNIER, I. L. (Ed.). (1985). *Methods and techniques of holistic education.* Springfield, Ill.: Thomas.

A clear and interesting analysis of gender roles, of gender-role biases in television programs, and of the relationship between the two, is presented in:

DURKIN, K. (1985). *Television, sex roles and children: A developmental social psychological account.* Philadelphia: Open University Press.

Folklore has it that many years ago in Switzerland, bears were worshipped because the faithful believed that they were descended not from Adam and Eve but from the bear (Engel, 1976).

CHAPTER 8

COGNITIVE AND SOCIAL DEVELOPMENT

*The parent who could see his boy as he really is
would shake his head and say: "Willie is no good:
I'll sell him."*

STEPHEN LEACOCK *The Lot of the Schoolmaster*

*Youth will be served, every dog has his day, and
mine has been a fine one.*

GEORGE BORROW *Lavengro*

PREVIEW Of the theories that have attempted to explain human development, two broad groupings are especially important for teachers. One group deals with social learning, especially the effects of models on the behavior of children and adults; the other deals with cognitive (intellectual) development. This chapter describes these theories (specifically, those of Bandura and Walters, Piaget, and Vygotsky) and considers their educational implications.

■■ *My Aunt Lucy has many theories. She is forever saying, "I have a theory about that" — and if anyone cares to listen, she will explain.*

Most of her theories are simple explanations for common observations. They account for the greening of mosses and the disposition of wild cows; they explain the productivity of her garden and the superiority of cats. She has theories relating to fluctuations in populations of fish; theories that foretell the harshness of winters, the likelihood of pregnancy, the probability that it will be a boy this time — and if it is, that he will certainly have a long nose. Or else the father isn't you know who.

And, of course, she has a theory of child development. "You know, I have a theory about children," she informed me when I told her about the book I was writing for you. I was hardly surprised.

"Take Luke, for example," she continued quickly, having long since learned that one of the best ways of gluing people to their seats is to forge ahead without hesitation. Besides, Luke, her son, has always been one of her favorite topics.

"Luke, if I say so, turned out pretty good. No trouble like, say, Robert. I know you guys don't talk about Robert any more since the last time, but you

know why he turned out that way. . . ." I could feel her warming up. She has always loved dragging the bones out of that old closet.

"It started when he was young. Everything starts then, when you're young. It started that time your grandpa brought Nesbitt home. You know about Nesbitt?" She looked at me, hesitating, suspecting perhaps that she was telling me something I wasn't supposed to know. I already knew, but she told me again about Nesbitt, who had punched cows in Montana, shot grizzlies in Alberta, and, one drunken night, wrecked a tavern in Saskatchewan. From there, Nesbitt went to jail and stayed just long enough to learn to like it and to invent all sorts of creative ways of being sent back.

My grandfather and Nesbitt had fought in a war together. They were friends. But when my grandfather brought Nesbitt home that night, he didn't know that Nesbitt was about to execute one of his clever plans to return to jail. That my grandfather joined him for a short while was purely a case of mistaken identity and bad luck.

"And if it hadn't been for Nesbitt, you can bet that Robert would be on stage today — probably in Europe, the way he plays that grand piano. But just that one time, he met Nesbitt and he became his hero, and look how it turned out. That's why, with Luke, the first thing I made sure of was that we always had the priest home for supper every Saturday. And every new teacher that ever came here — we took their side right off so Luke would have a decent hero. And we had every teacher over for supper too. And see, it worked. That's my theory. One important hero. Good or bad, that's it."

"But," I interrupted politely, "How about the — "

"I know," she cut me off, "I figured you'd ask that. You didn't think I'd have an answer. You go to school a couple years and all you learn is to ask questions you don't think other people can answer."

"But you don't know what I was going to say."

"Yes I do. And the answer is simple. The reason you didn't turn out as bad as you should have—yet, and mark my word when I say yet—is that you're a bit of an exception. You don't exactly fit my theory." ▬

THE NATURE OF SCIENTIFIC THEORY

I do not fit my Aunt Lucy's theory. There probably are many of us who don't fit her theories very well. However, some of us do, because my aunt's theories, like scientific theories, stem from observations—and some of her observations *are* accurate. But the big difference between my aunt's observations and those of scientists is that we can have more faith in scientific observations because science demands that observations be made with precision and objectivity that are beyond the patience of naive theorists like my aunt.

Not only do we know that the observations of science are usually more objective and precise than those of untrained observers, but we know as well that the conclusions and generalizations of social scientists are more likely to apply to a greater number of individuals. Whereas my aunt can, with profound conviction, base her conclusions on a single isolated instance, science insists on samples that are large enough and representative enough to justify generalizing conclusions.

One final, important difference between my aunt's naive theories and those of science is that my aunt does not habitually take random or chance factors into account. Science, on the other hand, is guided by a mathematically precise model of probability. Accordingly, science is far more likely than my aunt to admit that certain outcomes and observations are due to chance (or at least to unknown factors), rather than to specific things like the manipulations of an experimenter or the presence of a priest or a teacher at Saturday night dinners.

As we saw in Chapter 1, a theory is a collection of related statements whose principal function is to summarize and explain observations. It is, in a sense, an invention designed to make sense of what we know or suspect. In addition, a good theory allows us to make predictions. Accordingly, we judge theories on the basis of how well they reflect the facts, how consistent and logical they are, how useful they are for explaining and for predicting, and how practical they are in suggesting how to solve problems or simply how to behave in certain situations.

In this chapter we look at several theories that attempt to explain social and cognitive development in the school-age child and that have important educational implications.

SOCIAL LEARNING AND IMITATION

In psychology, the phrase **social learning** is often used without precise definition, as though everybody intuitively knows exactly what it means and all agree about that meaning.

Not so. In fact, the term is used in two distinct ways. For some writers, it seems to mean all learning that occurs as a result of, or involves, social interaction. Others use the term to signify the type of learning that is involved in finding out what sorts of behaviors society accepts and expects, as well as those that are unacceptable. This difference in meanings is essentially a distinction between process and product. In other words, *social learning* might refer to the way in which learning occurs (that is, through social interaction) or to what is learned (the product: acceptable behaviors). In this section we speak briefly of the product before looking at several theories more concerned with the process of social learning.

Socially acceptable behavior varies both

from culture to culture and from group to group within a single culture. Thus it is socially acceptable for students in some Asian countries to bow to their teachers and to offer them gifts. In most Western countries, a student who habitually bowed to teachers and offered gifts might embarrass both self and teacher.

Similarly, socially acceptable behavior is often a function of age and of sex. Thus young children are not expected to address teachers and other adults by their first names; they are expected to learn and obey an assortment of unwritten rules of respect and of social distance. In much the same way, there are behaviors that are socially expected — hence culturally appropriate — for males but not for females, and vice versa. The learning of such gender roles is discussed in some detail later in this chapter.

The point of these illustrations is that social learning does not involve simply learning a set of behaviors that *are* acceptable; it also involves learning under what conditions they are *not* acceptable. In other words, effective social learning involves a great deal of generalization and discrimination.

Probably one of the most important tasks of the home in the early years of a child's life, and of the school in later years, is to foster the development of appropriate behaviors — a process called **socialization**. This process involves transmitting the culture of a society to children and teaching them behaviors appropriate for their sex and social circumstance.

The central question from a developmental point of view is, How does the child learn socially acceptable behaviors? A number of answers have been given to this question. The concept most common to these answers is *imitation*, the process of copying the behavior of others. Put simply, learning through imitation, sometimes referred to as **observational learning**, involves acquiring new responses or modifying old ones as a result of seeing a model do something. According to Bandura (1969), the processes involved in imitation are "one of the fundamental means by which new modes of

behavior are acquired and existing patterns are modified . . ." (p. 118).

It is largely through the processes of social learning and imitation that fads and expressions sweep through countries: Overnight (almost), men begin to wear their hair long or short; short skirts are in, then out, then in . . . ; everyone is saying "yeah" or "outasight"; things are "cool" or "neat" and people are "beautiful."*

But these are trivial matters in the grand scheme of more cosmic events — although how to dress and what to say are by no means trivial in our more private, less cosmic, worlds. Social learning theory explains much more than our fads and expressions — as is made clear by the theory we look at next.

THE SOCIAL LEARNING THEORY OF BANDURA AND WALTERS

The social learning theory advanced by Bandura and Walters (1963) and by Bandura (1969, 1977) is based in part on a model of operant conditioning. But perhaps more important, it recognizes the fundamental importance of our ability to symbolize, to imagine, to ferret out cause-and-effect relationships, and to anticipate the outcomes of our behaviors. Accordingly, it is as much cognitive as behavioristic. The environment clearly affects our behavior, Bandura informs us; there is little doubt that we engage in many behaviors because of the reinforcing consequences of so doing. But reinforcement does not control us blindly; its effects depend largely on our awareness of the relationship between our behavior and its outcomes.

---

*PPC: "Your faddish words are now a bit outdated. How about 'totally' or one of the other valley-girl expressions to add to the list?"
Author: "This is no longer a real young bear. He has almost stopped trying to keep up with fads. But he still thinks valley-girl talk is like awesome and vertical and totally tubular. You know? He has humongous appreciation for valleys, for sure."

As Bruner (1985) points out, it is not re-inforcement that leads to or affects behavior directly, for reinforcement occurs *after* the behavior (sometimes considerably after). Rather, it is the individual's anticipation of conse-quences that immediately affects learning and behaving.

Our ability to symbolize and to anticipate is reflected not only in the fact that we can imagine the consequences of our behavior and therefore govern ourselves accordingly, but also in the fact that we deliberately arrange our environments so as to control some of the con-sequences of our actions. As Bandura (1977) puts it, "By arranging environmental induce-ments, generating cognitive supports, and pro-ducing consequences for their own actions, people are able to exercise some measure of con-trol over their own behavior."

Put another way, environments — espe-cially the reinforcing and punishing aspects of environments — have a real and important role in determining behavior. At the same time, the individual controls the effects of the environ-ment by choosing environments and behaviors and through such cognitive factors as the ability to anticipate outcomes of behavior. Accord-ingly, one of Bandura's labels for his theory is **reciprocal determinism**. This concept is a far cry from the type of environmental control to which some of the so-called "radical behavior-ists" sometimes seem to think we are subject.

The Theory Summarized

Bandura's position can be summarized in three statements:

1. Much human learning is a function of ob-serving the behavior of others or of such symbolic models as fictional characters in books or or television programs.

2. It is probably correct to assume that we learn to imitate by being reinforced for doing so, and that continued reinforcement maintains imitative behavior.

3. Some aspects of imitation, or observational learning, can therefore be explained in terms of operant conditioning principles (see Chapter 2).

The following questions, directly related to these statements, are particularly relevant:

1. How prevalent is observational learning?

2. What are the sources of reinforcement in observational learning?

3. What are the possible results of this kind of learning?

4. What are the processes involved in obser-vational learning?

Some answers to these questions follow.

The Prevalence of Imitation

Copying the behavior of others is a widespread phenomenon that is perhaps more obvious among nontechnological societies. For exam-ple, Bandura and Walters (1963) cite an illustra-tion of imitation among the Cantalense. In their culture, a young girl is given miniature work-ing replicas of all the tools her mother uses: broom, corn-grinding stone, and so on. From the moment she can walk she follows her mother and imitates her actions. There is little or no direct teaching. Most of the significant social learning accomplished by Cantalense girls results from direct imitation.

Another culture in which learning occurs through observation is that of the Canadian Ojibwa Indian, who, until the turn of this cen-tury, depended almost exclusively upon trap-ping, hunting, and fishing. In Ojibwa tribes, young boys followed their fathers around trap lines as soon as they were physically able. For the first few years they simply observed — again, there was no direct teaching. When the boy was old enough, he would fashion his own weapons and traps and set his own snares as he had seen his father do. Whatever he bagged would be brought back to his father's lodge. If he had a sister, she would have learned how to prepare hides, meat, and fish; how to make clothing; how to erect shelters; and how to do the many other things she had seen her mother doing. Now, if she were old enough, she would take care of her brother's catch, prepare his meals, and make his clothing.

In more technological societies such as ours, it is usually not possible to provide children with miniature working replicas of the tools used by their parents—nor is it possible for children to observe their parents at work. It would appear, then, that observational learning, although of some academic interest, could hardly be of much practical value for teachers. This notion, however, is false. The reason has to do with the meaning of the term *model*.

Models

The term *model* may refer to an actual person whose behavior serves as a stimulus for an observer's response, or it may, as is more often the case in our society, refer to a **symbolic model**. These include such things as oral or written instructions, pictures, mental images, cartoon or film characters, religious figures, and, not the least important, the content and characters in books and television. Such models are probably more prevalent than real-life models for children in a technological society. This contention is not to deny that peers, siblings, and parents serve as models, or that teachers and other well-behaved people are held up as **exemplary models**. ("Why don't you behave like Dr. Lefrançois? See how nicely he sits in church with his eyes closed. He's praying for us, dear man.") It is probably true that much social learning involves direct observation of real-life models.

Animals, like people, appear to be susceptible to the effects of imitation. Among the many studies that support this contention is that of Herbert and Harsh (1944), who demonstrated that cats can learn remarkably rapidly after watching other cats perform learning tasks.

Some animals also appear to imitate humans. When monkeys or chimpanzees are reared in human families, they typically adopt many human behaviors (Kellogg, 1968). Do people also imitate animals? Is proof in the affirmative to be found in the observation that people can be squirrelly, can act like mules, occasionally go ape, are called pigs or turkeys, or sometimes behave like the south end of a northbound horse? No. But that we imitate each other, and that we learn from books, television, and other symbolic models is clear. Why?

Sources of Reinforcement in Imitation

An easy answer to the question, Why do people imitate? is simply that they imitate because to do so is reinforcing. The next question is not quite so simple: What are the sources of reinforcement in imitation?

Imitation is reinforced in three ways. The first, **direct reinforcement** of the learner by the model, is most applicable to the early learning of children. It is not uncommon to hear parents exclaim over the behavior of their child simply because "he's doing it just like Daddy!" Nor is it uncommon to hear a child draw his parents' attention to the fact that he *is* doing it just like Daddy—and that is pretty strong evidence that the child has learned to expect reinforcement from the model.

A second source of reinforcement is the consequences of behavior, particularly if it is socially acceptable behavior that is instrumental in attaining a goal. Even though a child may learn to say "milk" partly as a function of imitation and partly as a function of her model's reinforcing her, she is not likely to go on saying "milk" unless someone gives her milk when she says it. It is in this sense that the consequences of behavior learned through observation can be reinforcing.

A third type of reinforcement is termed **vicarious reinforcement**. It involves deriving a kind of secondhand—hence vicarious—type of reinforcement from observing someone else perform a behavior. It is as though the observer assumes that the model does something because he or she derives reinforcement from that behavior. Therefore, in the observer's logic, anyone else engaged in the same behavior would receive the same reinforcement.

Interestingly, vicarious reinforcement can lead an observer to engage in even ineffective behavior over a prolonged period of time. The fact that the behavior is maintained despite an apparent lack of direct reinforcement is evidence that some sort of vicarious reinforcement is involved. In fact, studies have shown that the administration of reward or punishment to a model has an effect on the behavior of observers similar to that which the direct administration of the reward or punishment would have. One such study (Bandura, 1962) involved exposing three groups of children to three different models. All models behaved aggressively toward an inflated plastic doll. The first model was rewarded for so doing, the second was punished, and the third received neither positive nor negative consequences. Subsequently, the model-rewarded group behaved significantly more aggressively than the model-punished group. The effect of reward and punishment on the models was transferred vicariously to the subjects.

The Effects of Imitation

Superficially, imitation seems to consist of little more than copying the behavior of a model. A closer examination of the responses involved, however, suggests that there are three categories of imitative behavior (Bandura and Walters, 1963; Bandura, 1977): the *modeling effect*, the *inhibitory-disinhibitory effect*, and the *eliciting effect* (see Table 8.1).

The **modeling effect** involves the acquisition of new responses. The **inhibitory-disinhibitory effect** involves the **inhibition** or the **disinhibition** of deviant responses, usually as a result of seeing a model punished or rewarded for the behavior. The **eliciting effect** involves

Table 8.1   Three effects of imitation

Modeling Effect	Acquiring *new* behavior as a result of observing a model
Inhibitory-Disinhibitory Effect	Ceasing or starting some *deviant* behavior as a result of seeing a model punished or rewarded for similar behavior
Eliciting Effect	Engaging in behavior *related* to that of a model

behavior that is neither novel for the observer nor deviant; it is manifested when the observer engages in behavior related to (but not identical to) that of the model.

The Modeling Effect.   Whenever an observer acquires a new behavior as a result of seeing a model emit that behavior, the modeling effect is illustrated. The acquisition of novel aggressive responses has been extensively studied in laboratory situations (Bandura, 1962; Bandura, Ross, and Ross, 1963). Subjects have usually been nursery-school children. The typical experiment involves exposing the subjects to a real-life model or a cartoon or filmed model engaged in novel aggressive behavior directed toward a large inflated plastic doll. The model might punch the doll, strike it with a hammer, kick it, or sit on it. Control groups are exposed to the same model sitting quietly with the doll. The results of experiments such as this almost invariably illustrate the modeling effect. Children exposed to aggressive models are not only more aggressive than control groups when left with the dolls, but they also usually demonstrate imitative aggressive responses that are, in all likelihood, novel to them.

These experiments involve eliciting aggressive behavior in laboratory situations. The **aggression** is directed at an inanimate object. It might be argued that this is a far cry from aggression against real people in real life. Ethical considerations, however, prevent the use of babies rather than dolls in these experiments. It is therefore very difficult to illustrate the acquisition of meaningful aggressive responses experimentally. However, studies of the effects of televised violence on children's behavior suggest that it may increase aggression in children, especially if the violence is realistic rather than slapstick (as in cartoons). But the extent and nature of the effects depend also on the child's personality and maturity (Collins, 1983). Similarly, prosocial television programs can sometimes have a positive effect on behavior (Cook et al., 1975).

Many other behaviors are also transmitted through imitation and are examples of modeling. The initial learning of socially appropriate behavior in primitive cultures such as that of the Cantalense or Ojibwa people provides one illustration. The learning of a language is also an example of modeling. This is especially obvious in the case of adults learning to speak a foreign language by imitating a teacher or an audiotape.

The Inhibitory-Disinhibitory Effect. This effect of imitation is particularly important for people who are concerned about deviant behavior. The inhibitory effect is the suppression of deviant behavior in an observer, usually as a result of seeing a model punished for engaging in the same behavior. The disinhibitory effect is the opposite; it occurs when an observer engages in previously learned deviant behavior, usually as a result of seeing a model rewarded (or at least not punished) for the same behavior.

As experimental evidence of disinhibition, Bandura and Walters (1963) cite studies in which viewing films led to aggression in children; the aggressive responses were not novel but were previously learned behaviors that had been suppressed. Evidence from this research indicates that exposure to aggressive models may have a disinhibitory effect on young observers. Typically, the number of aggressive responses manifested by members of experimental groups is significantly higher than the number engaged in by the control groups. Also, the Bandura (1962) study that looked at the effects on observers of punishment or reward of the model showed that punishing a model inhibited similar behavior in observers and that rewards had an opposite, disinhibiting effect.

A related finding from the Bandura (1962) study is especially striking: When observers were themselves offered rewards for behaving aggressively, all differences between the groups were wiped out! Now those who had been exposed to models who were punished for being aggressive nevertheless behaved as aggressively as those whose models had been rewarded for being aggressive. This observation is especially important in explaining why punishing those who misbehave often fails to discourage other transgressors. One of the reasons for punishing criminals is the hope that others will take heed and cease committing crimes. In other words, the intention is to inhibit criminal behavior by punishing a model. It follows from the Bandura experiment, however, that as long as subjects have their own incentives for criminal behavior, the model may just as well be rewarded as punished, as far as deterrence is concerned.

A series of sobering experiments illustrates that socially unacceptable behavior in adults can be disinhibited through the use of models (Walters et al., 1962; Walters and Llewellyn, 1963). These studies were modeled after the well-known Milgram (1963) obedience studies in which college students willingly administered what they thought were extremely dangerous, high-voltage electrical shocks to other students, simply because they had been told to do so by an experimenter. Results of the Milgram studies have often been cited to explain various wartime atrocities perpetrated by apparently normal and gentle people who claimed they were simply obeying some powerful authority.

In the studies conducted by Walters and his associates, adult subjects were asked to participate in an experiment dealing with memory. Subjects were first shown one of two films: The first group saw a scene from the film *Rebel Without a Cause* in which two youths engage in a fight with knives; the second group saw adolescents engaged in artwork. All subjects were then asked to help with another experiment. This one involved administering a series of shocks to students in order to study the effects of punishment on learning. The student subjects involved in this learning experiment were actually confederates of the experimenters. The adults, who were the actual subjects, were made to sit in the confederate's chair and were administered one or two mild shocks so that they would know what the punishment was like. They were then seated at a control panel that consisted of two signal lights (one red and one green), a dial for selecting shock intensities, and a toggle switch for administering the shock. Instructions were simply to administer a shock whenever the red light went on, because it indicated that the subject had made an error.

These studies indicated that exposure to films with aggressive content significantly increases aggressive behavior, as revealed in the number and intensity of shocks the subjects were willing to give. (The students did not actually receive any shocks, because one electrode was always disconnected before the experiment.)

The results of studies such as these, if they can be generalized, may be important for interpreting and predicting the probable effects of television violence — particularly in view of the fact that preschoolers spend more than one-third of their waking time watching television (Winn, 1985).

The Eliciting Effect. A third effect of imitation involves eliciting responses that do not necessarily precisely match those of the model (although they might) but that are related to the model's responses; that is, they belong to the same class of behavior. For example, a man might serve as a model of generosity if he works hard for civic organizations, at church activities, and at school functions. A number of his neighbors might be moved by his example to be generous in different ways. One might give money to local charities; a second might donate a prize for a church raffle; a third might give freely of advice. None of these observers imitates the model's behavior precisely, but each of them emits a response that is related to it in that it involves being generous.

Another illustration of the eliciting effect is the herd behaviors that are sometimes apparent in crowds at sporting events. One person's applause might elicit applause from the entire crowd; or one person's booing and hissing might elicit similar behavior from others. Similarly, when people begin to rise for the national anthem, the same behavior may be elicited in a great many who are not immediately aware of why they are standing. In each of these illustrations of the eliciting effect, no new behavior is involved (as is the case in the modeling effect), and the behavior in question is not deviant (as it is in the inhibitory-disinhibitory effect).

The Processes of Observational Learning

Although reinforcement is implicated in learning through imitation, Bandura (1977) makes it clear that the effects of models are largely a result of what he refers to as their *informative function*. In other words, from observing models we learn cognitively not only how to do certain things but also what the consequences of our actions are likely to be.

According to Bandura (1977), four distinct processes are involved in observational learning: attentional processes, retention processes, motor reproduction processes, and motivational processes (see Figure 8.1).

Attentional Processes.   It is clear that we are not likely to learn very much from models unless we pay attention to the significant features of the behaviors we want to learn. Clearly, many of the behaviors in which our models engage have no value for us; therefore we pay little attention to them and do not learn them. For example, when I lived with my grandmother as a young adolescent, I was quite passionately interested in, among other things, trapping and snaring wild things for food and money. And when I had the opportunity to go out into the woods with the renowned trapper,

George Ahenikue, I watched his every move like a hawk — how he walked, how he looked around, how and where he stopped, how he fashioned his sets and arranged his snares. These behaviors had very high value for me.

But when I caught one of the rabbits who stupidly blundered into my snare, I paid little attention to the way my grandmother disjointed, sauteed, and stewed the beast; I just sat at the table and licked my chops in anticipation. The culinary preparation of the rabbit held no interest for me, although I relished the final result.

It wasn't until many years later, when I had a rabbit to prepare in my own kitchen, that I realized how little I had learned from my grandmother of the mysteries of the kitchen. Although I had watched her prepare dozens of rabbits, the behavior had not been sufficiently valuable for me to pay attention.

So I called my grandmother and I asked her about the stewing of snowshoe hares and jackrabbits, and she explained. Her explanation was every bit as much of a model as her behavior might have been years earlier (had I been paying attention), but it was a symbolic model.

In addition to the affective and functional value of the behavior being modeled, a number of other factors affect attentional processes. These include the distinctiveness, the complexity, and the prevalence of the stimuli. Also, a number of characteristics of the learner are important, including arousal (motivation), perceptual set (readiness to observe), and history of previous reinforcement.

Retention Processes.   Just as we must pay attention if we are to learn, so too must we remember what we have observed. Because the effects of imitation are usually delayed rather than immediate, we need some way of symbolizing, understanding, and organizing our observations.

According to Bandura (1977), observational learning involves two types of representation systems: visual (his term is *imaginal*) and verbal. For example, to learn a complex motor

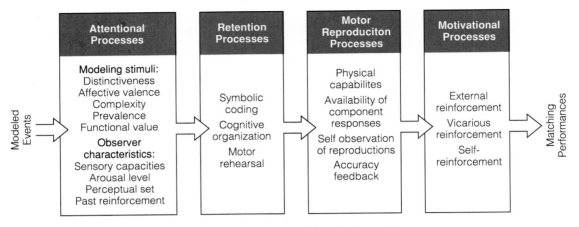

Figure 8.1 Component processes governing observational learning in social learning theory.
From A. Bandura, *Social Learning Theory*, © 1977, p. 23. Reprinted by permission of Prentice-Hall, Inc., Englewood Cliffs, New Jersey.

skill, it is sometimes useful to observe a model closely and store a visual sequence of the behavior. It is then possible to rehearse the desired behavior mentally. Bandura (1977) cites research indicating that mentally rehearsing a complex motor sequence (as in high jumping, diving, or gymnastics, for example) can significantly improve performance. He suggests that the best way of learning from a model is to organize and rehearse the observed behavior cognitively, and then act it out.

Motor Reproduction Processes. Acting out a modeled behavior involves transforming symbolically represented (mentally visualized or imagined) actions into physical movements. Being able to do so successfully, of course, depends on essential physical capabilities; clearly, some of us will never be able to jump very high no matter how many models we observe. Accurate motor reproduction of an observed behavior depends also on the individual's ability both to monitor attempted reproductions and to use motor feedback to make corrections. Imitations of motor behavior are seldom perfect the first time—they must be refined. A coach might demonstrate repeatedly how a batter

should stand, how she should hold the bat, how she should distribute and shift her weight, what her eyes and toes should do. But in the end, the truly good batter will have refined and perfected her batting through a long succession of trials (motor reproductions). These, however, are not blind trial-and-error reproductions repeated until the right one is accidentally found. Rather, they are carefully modeled trials that are evaluated and slowly modified as a function of feedback involving, among other things, how often contact is made with the ball, how far the ball goes when it is hit, and whether the coach smiles or frowns while watching the batter.

Motivational Processes. Much of what people observe and potentially learn is never manifested in their behavior. George Ahenikue, for example, was an important model for me with respect to setting snares for snowshoe hares; he knew a dozen clever little tricks for ensnaring them. I emulated as many of these tricks as I could. But he also knew a fantastic trick for blowing his nose. I have little doubt that I learned it; I remember it very clearly. But I don't do it. Ever. Put another way, I have *acquired* the behavior but do not *perform* it.

The distinction between *acquisition* and *performance* is important in social learning theory because, as we have noted, much of what is observed and presumably acquired is never performed. Whether or not the modeled behavior will ever be performed is a function of reinforcement or, perhaps more precisely, of anticipated reinforcement.

In summary, observational learning begins with a modeled event (perhaps a real-life model doing something, a verbal or symbolic model, or a combination of these) and culminates in some sort of matching performance on the part of the observer. Four processes intervene between the presentation of the model and the appearance of the modeled behavior. First, the observer must pay attention; second, the observer must represent the observed behavior cognitively, store it, and perhaps rehearse it; third, if the observer has the required capabilities, he or she reproduces and refines the observed behavior; and fourth, given appropriate motivational conditions (defined primarily in terms of anticipated reinforcement), the observer performs the learned behavior.

INSTRUCTIONAL IMPLICATIONS OF SOCIAL LEARNING

The greatest advantage that learning by imitation has over other forms of learning is that it provides a complete behavioral sequence for the learner. There is no need for successive approximations, for trial and error, or for association by contiguity. Nobody would put a person behind the wheel of a car and allow the person to learn to drive by trial and error alone. One might, on the other hand, teach driving to someone by presenting one or more models: exposure to a person driving, a driving manual, or a series of oral instructions. In this, as in many other types of learning, it would be foolhardy to permit people to learn only by doing.

A careful analysis of the processes involved in social learning suggests a number of considerations that might be important for teaching.

For example, many of the factors associated with attentional processes (such as distinctiveness of stimuli, the learner's arousal level, history of past reinforcement, and so on) are at least partly under teacher control. Similarly, teachers can provide direction and opportunity for the activities involved in retention and in reproduction. And because the effects of reinforcement depend on our awareness of the connection between our behavior and its consequences, teachers can also exercise considerable influence on motivational processes.

The deliberate use of social learning theory for changing and controlling behavior (sometimes included under the general term **behavior management**) presents yet another important educational implication, considered in Chapter 12.

GENDER ROLES

Social learning, as we have seen, deals with both the *processes* by which behaviors are acquired and the behaviors themselves. One especially important class of social behaviors are **gender roles**.

A *gender role* (also called a *sex role*) is a *learned* pattern of behavior based on gender. Thus, there are masculine roles and feminine roles. In essence, these roles are defined in terms of the behaviors, personality characteristics, and attitudes that cultures find appropriate for each sex. The learning of behaviors suitable for one's gender is called **sex typing**.

That gender roles are largely learned becomes evident when we observe other cultures in which males and females sometimes behave (and think and feel) in ways very different from males and females in our society. For example, in her investigations of three New Guinea tribes, Margaret Mead (1935) found a tribe, the Mundugumor, in which both men and women were ruthless, aggressive, and in other ways highly "masculine" (by *our* definition). In a second tribe, the Arapesh, both sexes were warm, emotional, noncompetitive, and unaggressive —

in other words, both men and women were highly "feminine." And a third tribe, the Tchambuli, illustrated what Mead described as a "genuine reversal of the sex attitudes of our own culture" (p. 190).

The Nature of Male and Female Roles

When young children in our culture are asked which personality characteristics are masculine and which are feminine, they typically have no problem in creating similar lists of characteristics for each gender. Not only do they agree as to what boys and girls should be like, but they often agree, as well, that masculine traits are more desirable, as is shown dramatically in the "sex-change" study conducted by Tavris and Baumgartner (1983).

The study is simple and straightforward. Boys and girls were asked: "If you woke up tomorrow and discovered that you were a girl (boy), how would your life be different?" "Terrible," the boys answered. "That would be a catastrophe." "A disaster." "I would immediately commit suicide." "I would be very depressed." But the girls responded very differently. "Great," they said. "Now I can do what I want." "Now I can play sports." "Now I can be happy."

When, half a decade later, Intons-Peterson (1988) replicated this study using the same sex-change question, she reported no major changes and no surprises. Boys still responded very negatively to the thought of becoming female. They saw girls as more passive, weaker, more restricted in their activities, more emotional, and burdened by menstruation. And although most females are content with their gender, the majority nevertheless respond to the sex-change question by describing what they see as the highly positive aspects of being male. They view males as more active, less concerned with appearance, more aggressive, more athletic, and better able to travel and develop a career.

Parents, too, agree concerning proper behavior for boys and girls. In general, they feel that boys should be more aggressive, more boisterous, more adventurous, and less emotional, and that girls should be more passive, more tender, more emotional, and less boisterous (Holland, Magoon, and Spokane, 1981).

In recent decades, there has been a strong reaction against the basic inequities of these roles and the stereotypes they foster, as well as against the injustices of traditionally male-dominated societies — societies that continue to favor males in spite of some notable progress toward sexual equality in recent years. For example, although the number of women working outside the home has increased dramatically — 56.6 percent of all adult women in the United States in 1988 compared with 13 percent in 1960 (Women's Bureau, 1982; U.S. Dept. of Labor, 1988) — female occupations are still not on a par with male occupations in terms of status, prestige, or income. Average income for females is approximately 65 percent that of males (*Edmonton Journal*, 1989). And in 1981, women with four years of college could expect to earn less than men who had quit school after eighth grade (Tittle, 1982).

Determinants of Gender Roles

Lynn (1974) suggests that three important factors are involved in determining sex roles: genetic (or biological), family-based, and cultural factors.

Genetic contributions to sex typing are evident in innate tendencies for the sexes to act, think, or feel differently. And although considerable evidence (including cross-cultural comparisons such as Mead's investigation of the three New Guinea tribes) suggests that many of the most obvious components of gender roles appear to be environmentally determined, there is nevertheless some rather compelling evidence that suggests that certain aspects of male-female differences have a biological basis. This is most notably true of aggression, for example, for which four separate lines of evidence support the notion of a genetic influence. First, greater aggressiveness is often found in males at a very young age, before the time that environmental influences would be expected to have had a significant impact. Second, greater male aggressiveness is common among most cultures, Mead's testimony notwithstanding.* Third, most species of nonhuman primates (baboons, apes, chimpanzees) exhibit more aggressiveness among males than females. And fourth, injections of male hormones, particularly testosterone, can significantly increase manifestations of aggression; in fact, injections of testosterone in pregnant mothers have been shown to increase the subsequent aggressiveness of their female infants (Money and Erhardt, 1972).

However, in spite of the probable genetic contributions to greater aggressiveness in males, family and other cultural influences are also of significance. Considerable evidence suggests, for example, that parents treat manifestations of aggression differently in their male and female children, encouraging it in the former and discouraging it in the latter (Russell and Ward, 1982). Similarly, teachers *expect* more aggressiveness in boys and are more likely to tolerate and even encourage it. In much the same way, we expect more emotionality from girls and consequently tolerate and encourage it in ways that we would find less appropriate for boys.

The Reality of Gender Differences

We have noted that parents, children, and society in general assume that there are differences in male and female roles. Most can describe the nature of these differences with little difficulty.

But just because our naive psychologies agree does not mean that they are always correct.

Following a review of research on gender differences, Maccoby and Jacklin (1974) suggest four areas in which gender differences are consistently found. First, females excel in verbal ability, particularly in the early grades; second, males excel in mathematical ability; third, males have greater spatial-visual ability (evident in geographic orientation, for example); and fourth, males are more aggressive. In addition, there is some evidence that males are more achievement-oriented than females (Horner, 1969).

But as we noted, there is contrary evidence, much of which suggests that when early experiences are similar, many of these male-female differences disappear (Tobias, 1982). Furthermore, even when differences are found, they tend to be very modest and far from completely general (Deaux, 1985). Shepherd-Look (1982) reports that research now finds only trivial male-female differences in verbal performance, except among underprivileged populations. And Jacklin (1989) points out that differences in mathematics achievement are more closely related to students' anxiety about math, parents' stereotyped views of expected male-female performance, and the perceived value of the subject than to gender. In fact, a number of studies done in Hawaii report results that are directly opposed to those most often reported in North America. In those studies girls typically perform better than boys on standardized mathematics tests (Brandon, Newton, and Hammond, 1987).

Implications of Gender Roles for Teachers

Teachers do, however, need to take some differences between the sexes into consideration. That some of these differences are not inevitable and that many are unjust might, in the final analysis, be quite irrelevant to the immediate business of being a teacher. Although teachers need to treat all children equally fairly, this does

---

*In this connection, it is perhaps worth noting that following several years of interviewing many of the tribes that Mead interviewed, and following a painstaking analysis of her writings, Freeman (1983) suggests that much of her data is worthless — that she was so anxious to demonstrate the truth of her fundamental belief in the power of environments that she often overlooked evidence contrary to her beliefs and perhaps exaggerated evidence that she found more agreeable.

not mean that all children need to be treated in exactly the same manner. If girls are less interested than boys in violent contact sports, it might be more than a little foolish to insist that they don shoulder pads and participate in the school's football games. And if their interest in the opposite sex manifests itself earlier, and if it sometimes expresses itself in different ways, that too needs to be taken into consideration. At the same time, however, there is a sometimes desperate need for teachers to be aware of and to eliminate the many flagrant and subtle instances of sex bias that still permeate our attitudes, our books, our schools, and our society.

COGNITIVE DEVELOPMENT

The social learning theory described in this chapter is a somewhat cognitive theory with behavioristic roots, evident in the fact that its principal explanatory concept is reinforcement. The theory's cognitive orientation is manifested both in Bandura's emphasis on the importance of the learner's awareness of the connections between behavior and its outcomes and in the inclusion of concepts such as symbolic models, cognitive organization and rehearsal, and vicarious reinforcement. It is referred to as a social learning theory because it is mainly concerned with learning that occurs within the context of social interaction.

A number of developmental theories are concerned primarily with cognitive rather than social learning. Flavell (1985) suggests that all of these current explanations of cognition can be reduced to two points of view: the information-processing approach and the approach of Jean Piaget and related theorists (sometimes referred to as the neo-Piagetians). The information-processing approach is primarily concerned with processes involved in memory: deriving information, abstracting, sorting, organizing, analyzing, and retrieving, for example. We looked at this approach in Chapter 3.

Piaget's approach looks at how the child's interaction with the environment leads to the development of cognitive abilities and cognitive structure. It places far more emphasis on the developmental aspects of cognition than do most information-processing approaches. However, the two are very closely related.

The remainder of this chapter looks at cognitive development. It pays particular attention to Piaget's theory, which is the most influential child-development theory of this century, and it looks as well at Vygotsky's theory.

One of the intriguing and difficult things about studying children is that we cannot subjectively verify the inferences we make about them. We all have some intuitive notions about how adults feel and think. But we don't have any idea how children feel and think — and such ideas, in any case, can be verified only in very indirect ways.

Jean Piaget developed a method for studying children that permits the investigator to be both flexible and relatively precise. This, in fact, is one outstanding feature of his work. The technique, known as the **méthode clinique**, is an interview approach. The experimenter has a clear idea of the questions to ask and of how to phrase them, but many of the questions are determined by the child's answers. Hence, the technique provides for the possibility that the child will give unexpected answers and that further questioning will lead to new discoveries about thinking.

BASIC PIAGETIAN IDEAS

Piaget's theory is contained in more than thirty books and several hundred articles. Its scope is extremely broad.* It would be highly presumptuous to attempt to reduce the entire system to a single chapter. Our discussion here is something less than highly presumptuous — only some aspects of the theory are discussed.

---

*Throughout a large part of his career, Piaget's closest associate and collaborator was Barbel Inhelder, who coauthored a large number of their publications and was sole author of many other books and articles.

Consistent with his early training in biology, Piaget's approach to the study of children stems very directly from a biological orientation. His theory is much easier to understand when viewed from that perspective. Biologists have two overriding interests, each of which can be expressed in the form of a question:

1. What are the characteristics of organisms that enable them to adapt to their environments?

2. What is the simplest, most accurate, and most useful way of classifying living organisms?

Interestingly, the biologists' questions can also be asked about people, specifically:

1. What are the characteristics of children that enable them to adapt to their environment?

2. What is the simplest, most accurate, and most useful way of classifying or ordering child development?

Piaget's answers for these two questions form the basis for his entire system. The answers are therefore very complex in detail, but in principle they can be simplified.

Assimilation and Accommodation Permit Adaptation

The newborn child is a remarkable little sensing machine. Almost from birth, it can detect sounds, odors, sights, tastes, and touches; it can respond by squirming and wriggling, by crying, by flinging its limbs about and grasping things, and by sucking.

But can it think? Does it have a store of little ideas? Of budding concepts? We can't answer these questions very easily; the neonate doesn't communicate well enough to tell us. But Piaget tells us that the child probably does not have ideas or concepts — does not think — in the sense that we ordinarily define these terms. In brief, the newborn does not have a store of memories or hopes or dreams — does

not have a fund of information about which, and with which, to think.

But what this little sensing machine does have are the characteristics necessary for acquiring information. Flavell (1985) describes these characteristics somewhat like this: First, in order for the human system to acquire as much information as quickly as it does, it must be naturally predisposed to process an extraordinary amount of information, even when there is no tangible reinforcement (such as food) for doing so; that is, the system must be mainly *intrinsically* motivated — it must derive satisfaction from its own functioning and from its gradual acquisition of information.

Second, the human information-processing system must be preset to focus on the most informative — and therefore the most cognitively useful — aspects of the environment. Accordingly, the system must respond most strongly to novelty, surprise, and incongruity. It should search out the unexpected, for it is in the unexpected that the greatest amount of new information can be found. Similarly, it should be pretuned to attend to speech sounds and to make the hundreds of subtle distinctions that are so important in learning a language.

The human newborn that Jean Piaget describes is exactly such a system. It continually seeks out and responds to stimulation, and by so doing it gradually builds up a repertoire of behaviors and capabilities. The system is initially limited to a number of simple reflexive behaviors, such as sucking and grasping. Rapidly, however, these behaviors become more complex, more coordinated, and eventually purposeful. The process by which this occurs is **adaptation**. And, to answer the first question posed just before this section began, adaptation is made possible through the twin processes of **assimilation** and **accommodation**.

Briefly, *assimilation* involves making a response that has already been acquired; *accommodation* is the modification of a response. Or, to put it another way, to assimilate is to respond in terms of preexisting information; it often involves ignoring some aspects of the situation in order to make it conform to aspects of the child's mental system. In contrast, to accommodate is to respond to external characteristics; as a result, it involves making changes in the child's mental system.

Imagine, if you will, an infant lying idly in her crib, not doing anything in particular. Now she waves her little hands seemingly haphazardly in the air, and one of them comes in contact with a pacifier that is fastened to her shirt by means of a safety pin and a length of purple ribbon. Her hand closes immediately around the familiar object, raises it into the air, and brings it unerringly to her mouth, which has already opened in anticipation and which closes greedily around the rubber end of the pacifier. Suck! Suck! Suck!

According to Piaget, there are *schemata* involved here — a primitive mental representation of the infant's knowledge of pacifiers, including information concerning their suitability as objects to be grasped, to be transported toward the mouth, and to be sucked. The pacifier is being assimilated to these schemata; it is being understood and dealt with in terms of previous learning.

Imagine, now, that a generous grandmother replaces the infant's familiar old pacifier with a brand new one — one of those with the patented Easy Suck bulb on one end and the patented Easy Grab plastic knob on the other. The infant swings her tiny arms around again, until one pudgy little hand accidentally strikes the new object. Her hand closes on it at once; that's what hands are for. And again, her mouth begins to open; that's one of the important ways of exploring the world. Besides, in the very beginning, what can't be sucked isn't all that valuable in any case.

But the Easy Grab knob is too large and the little girl's grip inadequate, and the new pacifier squirts away.

"Here, sweetie," the grandmother purrs, shoving the object back into the child's hand. Now the infant's grip is rounder, more secure; subtle changes have occurred in the positioning of the fingers and in the pressure of the palm.

In Piaget's terms, she has begun to accommodate to the characteristics of this new object. She has adapted. As a result, the mental system — the arrangement of schemata — has changed in subtle ways.

Assimilation and accommodation are the processes that make adaptation possible throughout life. Note, however, that they are not separate and independent processes. All activity, Piaget maintains, involves both assimilation and accommodation. We cannot begin to make changes in schemata — to accommodate — without first having some basis for responding — that is, without having relevant previous learning to which we can assimilate new situations. Thus, all accommodation requires assimilation. At the same time, all instances of assimilation involve some degree of change to schemata, no matter how familiar the situation or how well-learned the response — even if the change is no more significant than that the response will be a tiny fraction better learned and more readily accessible in the future. In Flavell's (1985) terms, assimilation and accommodation are simply two sides of the same cognitive coin; both always occur together.

Human Development Consists of Stages

The answer to the second question can only be outlined here; the details are given later in this chapter. Piaget conceives of human development as consisting of a series of stages, each characterized by certain kinds of behaviors and certain ways of thinking and solving problems. Piaget's descriptions of what he terms the "broad characteristics of intellectual functioning" constitute his answer to the second question. Put very simply, Piaget's theory classifies human development by describing the characteristics of the child's behavior at different ages. This description can be valuable in helping teachers understand their students; it is, in a sense, a description of how cognitive structure develops and changes.

PIAGET'S COGNITIVE STRUCTURE

In our earlier discussions of information processing and related cognitive theories, we saw that one of the principal tasks of these theories is to describe both how we process perceptual input to derive meaning from it and how we organize resulting meanings into long-term memory. In effect, the organization of our long-term memories defines what is meant by *cognitive structure*. Recall that terms such as *subsumers, schemata,* and *coding system* serve as metaphors to label the concepts and associations that make up long-term memory and that are the substance of cognitive structure.

Piaget, too, is a cognitive theorist. His principal interests relate to the origins of cognitive structure—specifically, to its development from birth to adulthood. For Piaget, as for other cognitive theorists, *cognitive structure* can be defined as those properties of intellect that govern behavior. These properties are *inferred* rather than *real*—that is, a cognitive structure can neither be isolated and looked at nor described in concrete terms. It is, after all, a metaphor.

In very young children, structure can be defined in terms of reflexes because these are the first "governors" of behavior. Piaget labels each reflex a **schema** (pl.: schemata). Schemata become more firmly established as children assimilate objects to them, and schemata change as children accommodate to objects. A schema is usually named for the activity it represents. For example, there is a sucking schema, a looking schema, a reaching schema, a grasping schema, and, unfortunately, a wailing schema. Structure in later stages of development, usually after age 7 or 8, is defined in terms of less overt acts. By this age, children have internalized activities; that is, they can represent activities in *thought*. In addition, thought is subject to certain rules of logic. These rules, which are discussed in connection with the stage of concrete operations, define the term **operation**.

Structure governs behavior, and changes in behavior define stages of development; therefore, Piaget's description of development is really a description of cognitive structure at different ages. The details of these developmental changes are discussed next (see Table 8.2).

Sensorimotor Intelligence: Birth to Age 2

Piaget labeled the first two years of life the period of **sensorimotor intelligence**. It seemed to him that until the child develops some way of representing the world mentally, intelligent activity must be confined to sensorimotor functions. The child's world at birth is a world of the here and now. Objects exist when they can be seen, heard, touched, tasted, or smelled; when they are removed from the child's immediate sensory experience, they cease to be. One of the child's major achievements during this stage is the acquisition of what Piaget calls the **object concept**—the notion that objects have a permanence and identity of their own and that they continue to exist even when they are outside the child's immediate frame of reference.

Piaget (1954) devised an interesting and easily replicated experiment to trace the development of the object concept. It involves showing a bright, attractive object to an infant and then hiding it. At the earliest level, children will not even look for the object; it does not exist when they can no longer see or touch it. Later they will begin to search for the object if they saw it being hidden. It is usually not until around age 1 that children will search for an object they have not just seen.

There is no language early in the sensorimotor period, but there is the beginning of symbolization. Piaget suggests that the internal representation of objects and events is brought about through imitation. Thought is defined as internalized activity; it begins when children can represent to themselves (in a sense, imitate) a real activity. The first step in this process of internalization involves activities relating to objects or events that are in the child's immediate

Table 8.2 Piaget's stages of cognitive development

Stage	Approximate Age	Some Major Characteristics
Sensorimotor	0–2 years	Motoric intelligence World of the here and now No language, no thought in early stages No notion of objective reality

Preoperational
  Preconceptual
  Intuitive
	2–7 years
	2–4 years
	4–7 years
		Egocentric thought
		Reason dominated by perception
		Intuitive rather than logical solutions
		Inability to conserve

Concrete operations	7–11 or 12 years	Ability to conserve Logic of classes and relations Understanding of numbers Thinking bound to concrete Development of reversibility in thought
Formal operations	11 or 12–14 or 15 years	Complete generality of thought Propositional thinking Ability to deal with the hypothetical Development of strong idealism

presence. At a later stage, that of **deferred imitation**, the child can imitate in the absence of the object or event. This internal imitation is a symbolic representation of aspects of the environment. It is also the beginning of language because eventually words will come to replace more concrete actions or images as representors. And, as Hunt notes (1961, p. 262):

The more new things an infant has seen and the more new things he has heard, the more new things he is interested in seeing and hearing; and the more variation in reality he has coped with, the greater is his capacity for coping.

In other words, the amount and variety of stimulation a child receives are instrumental in determining adaptation.

Among important accomplishments of the sensorimotor period is the acquisition of internally controlled schemes — the establishment of controlled internal representations of the world. In other words, by age 2, children have made the transition from a purely perceptual and motor representation of the world to a more symbolic representation. They have begun to distinguish between perception and conceptualization, but they will not perfect this distinction until much later.

A second accomplishment is the development of a concept of reality. Much of a child's development can be viewed in terms of how he or she organizes information about the world. It is evident that this information will be very much a function of what the child thinks the world is. As long as children do not know that the world continues to exist by itself, they are not likely to have a very stable representation of it. Or perhaps it would be more accurate to say that as long as children do not have a stable representation system for the world, they cannot conceive of it when they are not actually experiencing it. In either case, the development of some notion of object constancy is absolutely essential for the child's further cognitive development.

A third accomplishment of this period is the development of some recognition of cause and effect. This is a logical prerequisite for the formation of intention, because intention is seen in behavior that is engaged in deliberately because of its effect. Piaget sees intention as being inseparably linked with intelligence; for him, intelligent activity is activity that is, in fact, intentional.

Although these accomplishments describe the child at the end of the period of sensorimotor intelligence, they are not the general characteristics of that period. Those are implicit in the label given to the stage—sensorimotor. In general, the first two years of a child's life are characterized by an enactive (Bruner, 1966) or motor representation of the world. The next stage progresses from the perceptual-motor realm to the conceptual.

The Preoperational Period: Ages 2 to 7

The preoperational period is so called because children do not acquire operational thinking until around age 7. Before that age their fum-bling attempts at logic abound with contradictions and errors.

The period of **preoperational thinking** is often described in terms of two substages: the period of preconceptual thought and the period of intuitive thought.

Preconceptual Thought: Ages 2 to 4.   The period of **preconceptual thinking** is preconceptual not in the sense that children fail to utilize concepts, but rather that the concepts they use are incomplete and sometimes illogical. Piaget illustrates this by describing his son's reaction to a snail. He had taken the boy for a walk one morning, and they had seen a snail going north. This humble creature had occasioned an expression from the child that can be imagined to have been phrased in the following manner:

"*Papa! Cher Papa! Mon cher Papa!*" (Swiss children like their fathers.) "*Papa! Papa! Papa!*" he repeated. "*Voici un escargot.*"

To which Piaget probably replied, "*Mon fils, mon fils, mon cher fils! Oui, mon fils, c'est un escargot!*"

It was an interesting conversation, as father-and-son conversations go, but it was not remarkable. It happened, however, that a short while later they chanced upon another snail, whereupon the boy again turned to his father and said, "*Papa! Cher Papa! Mon cher Papa! Mon Papa! Voici encore l'escargot! Regarde! Regarde!*"*

This, Piaget says, is an example of preconceptual thinking. The child does not yet understand that similar objects define classes (all snails are snails) but are not identical (snail A is not snail B). In the same way, a child who is shown four different Santa Clauses in four different stores all on the same day, and who still thinks there is *one* Santa Claus, is manifesting preconceptual thinking. She evidently knows something about the concept "Santa Claus," for she can recognize one; but she does not know that objects with similar characteristics can all belong to the same class yet each have an identity of its own. A young child who sees another child with a toy identical to one he has at home can hardly be blamed for insisting that he be given back *his* toy.

Another feature of thinking in the preconceptual stage is called **transductive reasoning**. Whereas inductive reasoning proceeds from particular instances to a generalization, and deductive reasoning begins with the generalization and proceeds toward the particulars, transductive reasoning goes from particular instances to other particular instances. It is not a logical reasoning process, but it does occasionally lead to the correct answer. Consider, for example, the following transductive process:

A gives milk.
B gives milk.
Therefore, B is an A.

If A is a cow and B is also a cow, then B *is* an A. If, however, A is a cow but B is a goat, then B is not an A. Surprising as it might sound, children do appear to reason in this way, as is evident when a child calls a dog "kitty" or a stranger "Daddy."

PPC: "Should this be translated?"
Author: "Dad! Dear Dad! My dear Dad! Dad! Dad! Dad! Here is a snail."
"My son, my son, my dear son! Yes, my son, it is a snail!"
"Dad! Dear Dad! My dear Dad! My Dad! Here is the snail again! Look! Look!"

Intuitive Thought: Ages 4 to 7. After age 4, the child's thinking becomes somewhat more logical, although it is still largely dominated by perception rather than reason. It is labeled **intuitive thinking** because intuition, which is governed by perception and egocentricity, plays an important role in the child's thinking. Piaget describes, for example, the answers given by children for this simple problem: Two dolls are placed side by side on a string. One is a girl doll, the other a boy. A screen is placed between the child and the experimenter, who are facing each other. The experimenter holds one end of the string in each hand in such a way as to hide the dolls behind the screen. The child is asked to predict which doll will come out first if the string is moved toward the right. Whether or not the child is correct, the boy doll is moved out and then hidden again. The question is repeated; again the boy doll will come out on the same side. This time, or perhaps next time, but almost certainly before very many more trials, the subject will predict that the *other* doll will come out. Why? "Because it's her turn. It isn't fair." This experiment clearly illustrates the role of **egocentrism** in the child's problem solving at the intuitive stage—the problem is interpreted only from the child's point of view.

An example of the role of perception is provided by the following experiment: A child is asked to take a bead and place it in one of two containers. As she does so, the experimenter places a bead in another container. They repeat this procedure until one of the containers is almost full. To confuse the child, the experimenter has used a low, flat dish, whereas the child's container is tall and narrow. The question asked is: "Who has more beads, or do we both have the same number?" The child will probably say that she has more because they come up to a higher level, but she also might say that the experimenter has more because his cover a wider area. In either case she will be answering in relation to the appearance of the containers. This reliance on perception, even when it conflicts with thought, is one of the major differences between children and adults.

Another striking characteristic of children's thinking during the intuitive period is their inability to classify. Although they can group objects in simple collections, they cannot nest these collections one within another; that is, they cannot reason about two classes if one is part of the other. The following classical Piagetian experiment illustrates this. A five-year-old child is shown a collection of wooden beads, of which ten are brown and five are yellow. He acknowledges that all the beads are wooden, but when asked whether there are as many, fewer, or the same number of brown beads as wooden beads, he says there are more. Piaget's explanation of this phenomenon is simply that asking children to consider the subclass destroys the larger class for them. In other words, children at this level understand that classes may contain many different but similar members (they would not make the preconceptual "escargot" error), but they do not yet understand that classes can be "nested" one inside the other in hierarchies (as the class of brown beads is nested within that of wooden beads, each being separate but related).

The child's problem solving in this period is largely intuitive rather than logical. Whenever possible, mental images rather than rules or principles are used in arriving at answers. A striking illustration of this is provided by asking five- or six-year-old children to solve the rotated-bead problem: Three different-colored beads are placed on a wire, and the wire is then inserted into a tube so that the child can no longer see them. She knows, however, that the red one is on the left, the yellow in the middle, and the blue on the right. She is then asked what the order of the beads will be if the tube is rotated through 180°, 360°, 540°, 720°, and so on. Younger preoperational children are likely to be thoroughly confused by the question; older children will solve it correctly so long as they can imagine the actual rotations — but they will *not* apply any rule to the solution of the problem (odd versus even number of turns, for example).

In summary, the thought processes of the intuitive period are egocentric and dominated by perception. In addition, the ability to classify or apply rules of logic for problem solving has not yet been acquired. A final, very significant difference between thought at this period and thought during the subsequent period of concrete operations is that only in the latter stage does the child acquire the ability to conserve. (See Figure 8.2 for a summary of preoperational thought.)

STOP! It would probably be wise for the reader who is not already familiar with Piaget to stop at this point. If you have available an electroencephalograph, a cardiograph, a thermometer, and a pupillometer (or any other graph or meter), these should be connected and read at once. Alpha waves, together with decelerated heart rate, abnormal temperature, and reduced pupil size are symptoms of imminent **jargon shock**. This condition in advanced stages can be extremely detrimental to concentration and learning. Several hours of sleep or some other amusement may bring about a significant improvement.

If you don't have any of this sophisticated electronic gadgetry readily available, you can substitute a hand mirror. Hold the mirror up to your face and look at your eyes. If they are closed, you are probably in the terminal stage of jargon shock.*

Concrete Operations: Ages 7 to 11 or 12

An *operation* is a mental activity — a thought, in other words — that is subject to certain rules of logic. Before the stage of concrete operations, children are described as preoperational not because they are incapable of thinking, but because their thinking exhibits certain limitations. These limitations are related to children's reliance on perception, intuition, and egocentric tendencies rather than on reason.

But with the advent of **concrete operations,**

---

*PPC: "Are you serious?"
Author: "If you need to ask, yes."

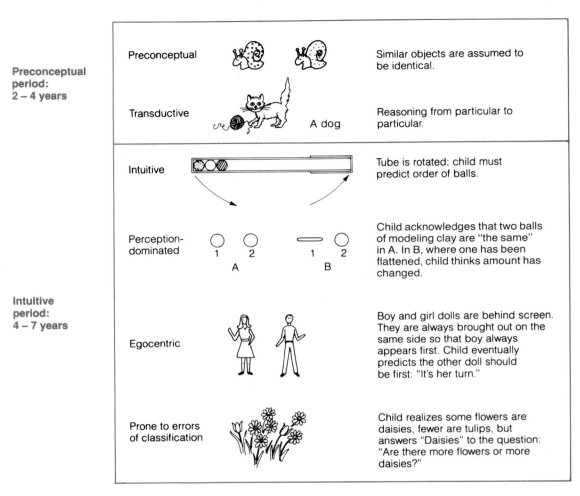

| Preconceptual | Similar objects are assumed to be identical. |
| Transductive | A dog | Reasoning from particular to particular. |

Intuitive	Tube is rotated; child must predict order of balls.
Perception-dominated	1 2 A — 1 2 B	Child acknowledges that two balls of modeling clay are "the same" in A. In B, where one has been flattened, child thinks amount has changed.
Egocentric	Boy and girl dolls are behind screen. They are always brought out on the same side so that boy always appears first. Child eventually predicts the other doll should be first: "It's her turn."
Prone to errors of classification	Child realizes some flowers are daisies, fewer are tulips, but answers "Daisies" to the question: "Are there more flowers or more daisies?"

Intuitive
period:
4 – 7 years

Figure 8.2   Some characteristics of preoperational thought.

children make a fundamentally important transition from a prelogical form of thought to thinking characterized by rules of logic. The operations that define thought at this stage apply to real, *concrete* objects and events—hence the label. Concrete operations are distinguished most clearly from the preoperational period by the appearance of one group of capabilities: the ability to conserve.

The Conservations.   **Conservation** is "the realization that quantity or amount does not change when nothing has been added to or taken away from an object or a collection of objects, despite changes in form or spatial arrangement" (Lefrançois, 1966, p. 9). In the experiment cited earlier, in which children are asked whether the two containers have the same number of beads, the children do not demonstrate conservation until they realize that the numbers are equal. A correct response to a conservation problem not only marks the end of the preoperational period, but also signals the beginning of concrete operational thought. It is a direct manifestation of a number of rules of logic that now govern and limit the child's thinking.

Among these rules are **reversibility** and **identity**. The rule of *reversibility* specifies that for every operation (internalized action) there is an inverse operation that cancels it. *Identity* is the rule that states that for every operation there is another that leaves it unchanged. Both reversibility and identity can be illustrated by reference to the number system. The operation of addition can be reversed (and nullified) by subtraction (for example, $2 + 4 = 6$; $6 - 4 = 2$). The identity operator for addition is 0 (that is, $2 + 0 + 0 + 0 = 2$); for multiplication it is 1 ($2 \times 1 \times 1 \times 1 = 2$).

The relevance of the operational rules to the thinking of a child at the concrete-operations stage can be illustrated by reference to any of the conservation problems. The child who has placed one bead in a tall container for every bead placed by the experimenter in a flat container, and who now maintains that there is the same number in each despite their appearances, may be reasoning as follows: (1) If the beads were taken out of the containers and placed again on the table, they would be as they were before (reversibility); or (2) nothing has been added to or taken away from either container, so there must still be the same number in each (identity).

There are as many conservations as there are perceptible quantitative attributes of objects. There is conservation of number, length, distance, area, volume, continuous substance, discontinuous substance, liquid substance, and so on. None of these conservations is achieved before the period of concrete operations; even then, some (volume, for example) will not be acquired until very late in that period.

The experiments are interesting, and the results are often very striking. Several experimental procedures for conservation are described in Figure 8.3, together with the approximate ages of attainment.

One of the intriguing things about conservation is that preoperational children can be made to contradict themselves many times

without ever changing their minds. After the experiment on conservation of liquid quantity, for example, the experimenter can pour the water back into the original containers and repeat the question. The subject now acknowledges that they have the same amount — but the moment the water is again poured into the tall container and the flat one, the decision may be reversed.

In addition to conservation, children acquire three other abilities as they come into the stage of concrete operations: the abilities to classify, to seriate, and to deal with numbers.

Classification.   To classify is to group objects according to their similarities and differences. The **classification** process involves incorporating subclasses into more general classes, all the while maintaining the identity of the subclasses. This process leads to the formation of what Piaget calls **hierarchies of classes** (Piaget, 1957b). An example is given in Figure 8.4 (p. 208). The preoperational child's inability to deal with classes was illustrated in the experiment involving the ten brown and five yellow wooden beads. Recall that at that stage the child thought there were more brown than wooden beads even while acknowledging that all the beads were wooden. The child no longer makes this error after reaching concrete operations.

Seriating.   The ability to order objects in terms of some attribute is essential for an understanding of the properties of numbers. One experiment that Piaget conducted to investigate the understanding of **seriation** involves presenting children with two corresponding series: one containing dolls, the other canes. The problem is simply to arrange these as shown in Figure 8.5 (p. 209). When the objects are presented in random order, preoperational children cannot arrange a single series in sequence. Typically, they compare only two objects at a time and fail to make an inference that is almost essential for the solution of the problem. This inference is that if A is greater than B, and B is greater than C, then A must be greater than C. Preoperational children do not hesitate to put C

1. Conservation of number (age 6 or 7)
Two rows of counters are placed in one-to-one correspondence between the experimenter (E) and the subject (S):

0 0 0 0 0
0 0 0 0 0

One of the rows is then elongated or contracted:

0 0 0 0 0
0 0 0 0 0

S is asked which row has more counters or whether they still have the same number.

2. Conservation of length (age 6 or 7)
E places two sticks before the subject. The ends are aligned:

S is asked if they are the same length. One stick is then moved to the right:

The question is repeated.

3. Conservation of substance or mass (age 7 or 8)
Two modeling/clay balls are presented to S. She is asked if they have the same amount of modeling clay in them. If S says no, she is asked to make them equal. (It is not at all uncommon for a young child simply to squeeze a ball in order to make it have less modeling clay.) One ball is then deformed.

or

or

S is asked again whether they contain the same amount.

4. Conservation of area (age 9 or 10)
S is given a large piece of carboard, identical to one that E has. Both represent playgrounds. Small wooden blocks represent buildings. S is asked to put a building on his playground every time E does so. After nine buildings have been scattered throughout both playgrounds, E moves his together in a corner.

S is asked whether there is as much space (area) in his playground as in E's.

5. Conservation of liquid quantity (age 6 or 7)
S is presented with two identical containers filled to the same level with water.

Figure 8.3   Experimental procedures for conservation of six physical attributes.

One of the containers is then poured into a tall, thin tube, and the other is poured into a flat dish.

S is asked whether the amount of water in each remains equal.

6. Conservation of volume (age 11 or 12)
S is presented with a calibrated container filled with water,

and two identical balls of modeling clay. One is squished and placed into the container; the other is lengthened.

S is asked to predict the level to which the water in the container will rise if the longer piece of clay replaces the squished piece.

before A if they have just been comparing B and C.

Numbers.   The ability to deal with numbers is simply a by-product of classification and seriation activities. A number involves classes in the sense that it represents a collection of objects (cardinal property of numbers); it involves seriation in the sense that it is ordered in relation to larger and smaller numbers (ordinal property of numbers).

To summarize, children at the stage of concrete operations can apply rules of logic to classes, to relations (series), and to numbers. In addition, their thinking has become relatively decentered; that is, it is no longer so egocentric or so perception-bound. They are still incapable, however, of applying rules of logic to objects or events that are not concrete. In other words, they deal only with the real or with that which they are capable of imagining. Their ready answer to the question, "What if Johnny West had a short nose?" is "Johnny West does *not* have a short nose!"

Formal Operations: Ages 11 or 12 to 14 or 15

The final stage in the development of thought structures is labeled **formal operations** — *formal* because the subject matter with which children can now deal may be completely hypothetical, and their thinking may involve a *formal* set of rules of logic.

An example of the difference between the thinking of a child at the formal-operations level and at the concrete level is provided by an item from Binet's reasoning test. The item deals with abstract relations. Edith is fairer than Susan; Edith is darker than Lilly; who is the darkest of the three? (If the reader has difficulty with this . . .) The complexity of this problem does not reside in the fact that it involves seriation (because seriation has already been mastered in the stage of concrete operations) but is due, instead, to the nature of the events that are to be ordered.

If Edith, Susan, and Lilly were all standing in front of a ten-year-old subject, the subject could easily say, "Oho! Edith is fairer than Susan, and she is darker than Lilly—and Susan is the darkest." When the problem is not a *concrete* but rather a *verbal* one, however, it becomes insoluble until the child can handle propositions logically.

A second experiment that illustrates a distinction between formal and concrete thinking involves a number of colored disks. If subjects are asked to combine each color of disk with every other in all possible ways (that is, by twos, threes, and so on), a complete and systematic solution will not be achieved until the formal-operations stage. Before this stage, the child will arrive at a large number of combinations but will not do so systematically, and will therefore not exhaust all the possibilities. Piaget refers to the thought processes involved in the solution of this and of similar problems as *combinatorial thinking*.

The development of formal operations in the schoolchild is of particular significance because before this stage the child will understand many concepts incompletely or not at all. Such concepts as proportion and heat (see Lovell, 1968) are ordinarily beyond the comprehension of a child at the level of concrete operations.

An important feature of formal operations that results from the child's ability to deal with the hypothetical is an increasing concern with the ideal. Once children are able to reason from the hypothetical to the real or from the actual to the hypothetical, they can conceive of worlds and societies that, hypothetically, have no ills. Having just discovered this boundless freedom of the mind to envisage the ideal, adolescents create their Utopias and rebel against the generation that has as yet been unable to make its Utopias realities.

Beyond Formal Operations

For a long time, developmental psychologists believed that the major intellectual changes of human development occur between birth and

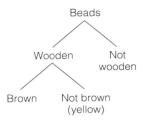

Figure 8.4   A hierarchy of classes.

the end of adolescence. This model held that after adolescence there is a long period of relatively little change, a sort of plateau. This plateau is eventually followed by gradual decline in old age.

Piaget's description of intellectual development reflects this long-prevalent model. Thus, he describes intellectual growth in terms of changes reflected in identifiable stages. The last of these stages, formal operations, is a stage descriptive of adolescents; beyond that—nothing. . . .

But what of adults? Is adulthood merely a plateau followed by inevitable decline? Are no more positive changes possible?

The simple answer is no; we have invented a new model. Now we believe, with good evidence, that important, positive changes come in adulthood—although these changes are not characteristic of everyone. Indeed, formal-operations thinking is not characteristic of all adolescents, or even of all adults. For some, thinking remains at the concrete stage all their lives; for others, thinking never even progresses beyond the intuitions of the preconceptual level.

But the truly adult thinker, Basseches (1984) informs us, does not think like the schoolchild or the adolescent. Cognitive development, Basseches insists, continues after adolescence. But this kind of development does not tend toward progressively more sophisticated forms of logic; instead of becoming more logical—more unwaveringly rational—thinking becomes more relative, more attuned to conflict, and more sensitive to moral, ethical, social, and political realities. It is a form of

Figure 8.5   Two ordered series.

thinking that Basseches terms more *dialectical*. Dialectical thinking struggles to create meaning and order by resolving conflict. The dialectical thinker is always aware of other possibilities and recognizes that no solution is necessarily absolute and final.

Labouvie-Vief (1980) agrees. Formal logic, she informs us, might be entirely appropriate for some of the problems that children face, especially in schools. But it might be inadequate and perhaps even largely irrelevant for many of the problems that adults face. The most logical solution may well be entirely wrong, entirely inappropriate. Mature reasoning requires "concrete pragmatics"; that is, it must take into account what will work and what is acceptable—what is, in other words, *pragmatic* (Labouvie-Vief, 1986). The thinking of the truly wise person is not bound simply by logic—which is not to say that it is illogical. Instead, it is sensitive to a wide range of possibilities; it considers implications; it factors in social and moral realities.

In summary, Basseches, Labouvie-Vief, and others concerned with the intellectual growth of adults claim that Piaget's model is not adequate for describing adult thought processes. According to these theorists, adult cognitive growth may take the form of learning new ways to resolve a wide range of personal problems that could involve relationships, artistic activities, business transactions, religion—indeed, all of life. They argue that adult thinking is more sensitive to and tolerant of ambiguity and contradiction, and that it is more likely to bring into play a variety of factors (for example, morality, social and political implications, economic considerations, and so on) in addition to simple logic.

PIAGET EVALUATED: THE CONTRIBUTIONS OF THE NEO-PIAGETIANS

Although Piaget's stature in developmental psychology is probably unequaled, he nevertheless has a number of critics. Among the standard criticisms are that he has not used sufficiently large samples, sophisticated analyses, or adequate controls. The validity of these criticisms can be assessed by determining whether or not replications support his findings.

Of the many hundreds (or thousands) of studies that have attempted to replicate Piaget's findings, a majority provide at least some evidence that the sequence of intellectual stages is very much as Piaget described, especially the sensorimotor period. However, many of these studies have found that North American and European children often reach Piaget's stages earlier than he had thought—although less privileged groups might reach them later (see, for example, Dasen, 1977).

There is somewhat less agreement with respect to sequencing and descriptions of major stages in later childhood and adolescence than there is for earlier stages. Here, there are two major criticisms: The first is that Piaget has drastically underestimated the cognitive achievements of the preschool child; the second is that he has overestimated the formal-operations capabilities of adolescents (and even of adults).

With respect to the first criticism, the neo-Piagetians* are widely agreed that it is inappropriate and misleading to refer to the preschool child's mind as preconceptual, preoperational, or prelogical (see, for example, Case, 1985; Gelman, 1982; Flavell, 1985). Their research suggests that a number of very significant cognitive achievements of this period were underemphasized or simply overlooked by Piaget. Among these are monumental advances in the child's ability to represent symbolically and to discover relationships among ideas. And perhaps the clearest illustration of children's very impressive abilities with respect to discovering and working with relationships is their understanding of numbers.

Gelman (1982) and colleagues (Gelman, Meck, and Merkin, 1986) have identified two kinds of knowledge about numbers that appear during the preschool period. The first kind is *number abstraction skills*. They give the child an understanding of number, or quantity—how

many things there are in a collection of, for example, baby mice in one's pockets. A number of principles underlie number abstraction skills. These include the *one-on-one principle* (if you're going to count mice, you must assign one, and only one, number to every mouse that is to be counted); the *stable-order principle* (the correct order for counting is one, two, three, four . . . and not one, three, four, two . . .); the *cardinal-order principle* (the last number assigned is the one that indicates the quantity of the collection); the *abstraction principle* (absolutely anything and everything can be counted); and the *order irrelevance principle* (the order of counting is irrelevant to the final outcome of the counting operation).

These five principles relate to number abstraction skills; they have to do with how to count, what to count, and what it means to count. Children as young as two or three years of age often behave as though they understand these principles very clearly, even though they might still make mistakes (often very systematic errors) in their counting. The second kind of knowledge about numbers that appears during the preschool period relates to *numerical reasoning principles*. This is the knowledge that permits the child to reason about or predict the outcome of simple numerical operations such as adding to or taking from.

Number abstraction and numerical reasoning are important and complex cognitive activities. They serve as dramatic illustrations of the cognitive achievements of the preschool child, in sharp contrast to Piaget's description of the intuitive, egocentric, perception-dominated, prelogical, preoperational child.

Some criticism of Piaget's stage of formal operations has been based on the observation that many people do not manifest such thinking during adolescence or even beyond (Papalia, 1972; Rubin et al., 1973). Piaget (1972) has conceded that this stage may be less general than he originally had thought.

Another criticism of formal operations relates to errors that Piaget apparently made in his use of models of logic to describe adolescent

---

*The neo-Piagetians are so called because their research stems largely from Piagetian ideas.

thought. Chief among his critics in this matter is Ennis (1976, 1978), who argues that Piaget's use of propositional logic involves redundant and unnecessary concepts, misuses the concept of propositions itself, and contains some errors of logic.

Fischer and Silvern (1985) argue that the evidence now available from neo-Piagetian research suggests a reformulation of developmental stages into eight levels (Fischer and Silvern consider *level* a more "modest" term than *stage*). The first four levels span infancy and are very similar to Piaget's description of the stages of sensorimotor development; a single level (relations of a few representations) covers the entire preconceptual period; two levels cover concrete and formal operations, respectively; and a final level occurs in late adolescence. Some researchers also suggest that an additional level follows adolescence (for example, Arlin, 1975; Riegel, 1973).

In evaluating the importance and seriousness of these criticisms, it is important to keep in mind that Piaget's theory, like other theories, is simply a metaphor. Specifically, Piaget presents a philosophical/biological metaphor intended to explain intellectual adaptation through the growth of intellectual capabilities and functions. Many of the criticisms of his theory stem from a misunderstanding of the basic metaphors and intentions of the theory, and from too narrow an application of its principles. In the final analysis, it may not be fundamentally important to the basic metaphor that some of the observations upon which it is based are inaccurate or that there are errors of logic, interpretation, or emphases in its description. Its explanatory strength and its practical utility may be far more important.

EDUCATIONAL IMPLICATIONS OF PIAGETIAN THEORY

Piaget's theory is a monument of cognitive-theory building in child development and has had (and continues to have) a profound im-

pact on educational practices. Its most useful instructional applications relate to three topics: instructional theory, the acceleration of development, and the derivation of specific principles for teaching.

Instructional Theory

Case (1975) advances an interesting proposal for combining Robert Gagné's learning model with Piagetian theory to design instruction that will take into account the learner's cognitive level. Recall that Gagné's model is premised on the notion that learning involves a hierarchical process, such that higher-order skills and concepts are built upon subordinate capabilities. Hence, instruction based on this model always begins by analyzing what is to be learned and ordering content into a hierarchy of tasks—a process called **task analysis**. Case argues that careful task analysis can reveal why certain tasks are too difficult—for example, for preoperational children—and might also suggest ways in which tasks can be structured to be more compatible with the student's developmental level. Although Case's suggestions for combining the models of Gagné and Piaget are still highly abstract, the potential of these suggestions is intriguing.

Can Development Be Accelerated?

This question was of little direct concern to Piaget. He was concerned more with describing specific details of growth than with the factors that cause developmental changes. By implication, however, his theory supports the belief that a rich background of experiences should lead to the earlier appearance of more advanced ways of thinking.

Direct attempts to accelerate development have generally been aimed at the teaching of conservation behavior to young children. The results of the many studies on this subject are contradictory. Early attempts to teach conservation were not often successful (see, for example, Smedslund, 1961a–e). What appears to be one of the easiest teaching tasks possible — simply convincing a five-year-old child that an amount of modeling clay does *not* change unless something is added to or taken away from it — is next to impossible. And although several systematic training procedures have succeeded in accelerating the appearance of conservation behavior in young children, no evidence has yet been provided to indicate that this has a generally beneficial effect on other aspects of intellectual functioning (see, for example, Lefrançois, 1968; Côté, 1968).

As Nagy and Griffiths (1982) conclude, "attempts to prescribe instructional strategies that accelerate intellectual development have borne little fruit" (p. 513). What is not clear is whether the general failure of these attempts is due to the fact that intellectual development cannot easily be accelerated or to the fact that we simply do not understand enough about the nature of intellectual development to devise more appropriate strategies.

Instructional Principles

Although Piaget's research has stimulated a great deal of thinking among educators, it is still true that much research needs to be undertaken to determine the best way of applying his findings to actual classroom practice and curriculum development. A number of preschool programs have been based on Piaget's writings (see, for example, Kamii, 1972; Weikart et al., 1969; Weber, 1970). Their impact is still limited, and the final evaluation is pending.

Beard (1969) attempted to derive educational implications from Piaget's work. She cites four main areas of development during the school years to which Piaget has drawn particular attention: the function of language, the formation of concepts, the translation of concrete experiences into symbolic forms, and the development of logical thinking. In each of these areas, Piaget's findings have definite, although general, implications.

To the extent that language facilitates and guides thought processes, children should be given opportunity to interact verbally not only with teachers but also with one another. To the extent that concepts arise from sensing and acting upon the environment, children should be involved in numerous real and relevant activities. Insofar as development proceeds from activity to the apprehension of the concrete and finally to the symbolic, a reasonable argument can be advanced for structuring curricula from activity to the concrete and finally to the symbolic (just as Bruner advocates proceeding from the enactive to the iconic to the symbolic). And, to the extent that teachers understand the progression of logical thought forms from the beginning to the end of the school years, they can provide activities that are appropriate to the child's developmental level but that, on occasion, are challenging enough to require that the child make some accommodations (modifications in responses).

These general instruction-related observations have been made more specific by a number of writers, including Athey and Rubadeau (1970), Ginsberg and Opper (1979), Phillips (1969), and Furth (1970), among others. The following sections present brief summaries of these principles. They are not intended as a collection of recipes for classroom practice, but rather as guiding principles for developing your own recipes.

Understanding Child Thought. Although it has always been recognized that there are some important differences between children and adults, Piaget, more than anyone, has demonstrated precisely what some of these differences are. When a child says that there is more water in a tall container than in a short, flat one, she truly *believes what she is saying*. When a row of disks is made shorter than a corresponding row, and the child changes his mind and says that now there are fewer disks in that row, he is *not really contradicting himself* because he sees no error and therefore no contradiction. When a second-grade student becomes completely confused by a verbal seriation problem — for example, "Frank Twolips has a shorter nose than Johnny West, and Johnny West has a longer nose than John George. Who has the longest nose?" — she is not being unintelligent.

These and other discoveries about the world of the young child should help teachers both to accept more easily the limitations of children's thought and to communicate more effectively with children.

Providing Activity. The ability to deal with classes, relations, and numbers results from the activities of combining, separating, and setting up correspondences among real objects during the preoperational stage. Because children's natural methods of learning and of stabilizing what they know involve activity, much class-room learning should also involve activity. For Piaget, activity is not only physical activity but *internalized*, mental activity as well. The point of this principle is twofold:

1. Provision should be made for a relatively large amount of *physical* activity in school, but obviously *mental* activity should be provided as well.

2. Provision should be made for relating learning to real objects and events, especially before the formal-operations stage.

Providing Optimal Difficulty. Assimilation and accommodation are the child's two ways of interacting with the world; all activity involves both. Assimilation occurs when new objects or events can be reacted to largely in terms of previous learning; accommodation involves modification or change. Assimilation requires that a situation be somewhat familiar: accommodation will take place only if the situation is, at the same time, somewhat strange. Therefore, what is required is an optimal discrepancy between new material and old learning. (This point is also made by other theorists — for example, Ausubel and Bruner.) By knowing a student's

level of functioning, a teacher can more effectively and realistically determine which learning experiences are best for the individual.

Knowing Children's Limitations. A teacher needs to be aware of the limitations of children at different ages. Concepts of proportion cannot easily be taught to seven-year-old children — nor can conservation of volume be taught to five-year-olds. Even if this statement were proven false, it would probably still be true that the amount of time required to teach five-year-olds conservation of volume might have been better spent teaching them to read. This is particularly true because they would probably acquire conservation of volume by themselves, but they would be less likely to learn to read without instruction.

Providing Social Interaction. One of the chief factors in making thought more objective is social interaction. The egocentric point of view of the young child is essentially one that does not recognize the views of others. Through social interaction the child becomes aware of the ideas and opinions of peers and adults. Piaget contends that the socialization of thought, the development of moral rules as well as game rules, and even the development of logical thought processes are highly dependent on verbal interaction. The implication for teaching is that instructional methods should provide for learner-learner as well as teacher-learner interaction.

Assessing Student Readiness. Detailed accounts of Piaget's experimental procedures and findings provide the classroom teacher with many informal and easily applied suggestions for assessing students' thought processes. It is not particularly difficult or time-consuming, for example, to ascertain whether a child has acquired conservation of number or the ability to seriate. Both these abilities are important for early instruction in mathematics.

Researchers have developed several scales to assess Piagetian concepts in children (for example, Pinard and Laurendeau, 1964; Goldschmid and Bentler, 1968; Uzgiris and Hunt, 1975). However, none of these scales has been widely used or standardized.

VYGOTSKY'S SOCIAL-COGNITIVE THEORY

Bandura's social learning theory describes how children learn and how their behavior is shaped by exposure to both people and symbolic models. Piaget's theory shows how the child's mind develops through interaction with the environment. Bandura emphasizes social development; Piaget, cognitive development. Vygotsky's position, summarized briefly in this final section, emphasizes both.

The Man and His Ideas

A quick look at current writings in human development might make one think that Lev Vygotsky is a contemporary theorist. Almost all major textbooks, for example, have at least one or two references to him. And there are a significant number of new books dealing with his work, as well as new translations of his own books (for example, Wertsch, 1985; Vygotsky, 1986). But he is not contemporary in a literal sense; he has been dead for more than half a century (he died of tuberculosis in 1934 at the age of thirty-eight). And although he was already a major intellectual force in the Soviet Union by the time he was twenty-eight, his work was not well known outside that country until much later. It is interesting to contemplate what his contributions and his stature might have been had he lived as long as Piaget, who died in 1980 at the age of eighty-four.

Three underlying themes unify Vygotsky's rather complex and far-reaching theory. The first theme is the importance of culture; the second is the central role of language; and the third is what Vygotsky labels the zone of proximal growth. We look at each of these briefly.

The Importance of Culture

Vygotsky makes an important distinction between what he calls *elementary* mental functions and *higher* mental functions. Elementary functions are our natural, and therefore unlearned, capacities, such as attending and sensing. In the course of development, these elementary capacities are gradually transformed into higher mental functions such as problem solving and thinking, largely through the influence of culture. It is culture, after all, that makes language possible; and it is social processes that bring about the learning of language (referred to as *signs*). Language, or signs, ultimately make thought possible. Thus, during the *preverbal* stage of development, the infant's intelligence is a purely practical, purely natural capacity that is closely comparable to that of apes.*

The Role of Language

Not only does language make thought possible, but it also regulates behavior. Vygotsky (1962) describes three stages in the development of these roles of language. He labels them in terms of three functions of speech: social, egocentric, and inner.

Social speech (or external speech) emerges first. The most primitive form of speech, its function is largely to control the behavior of others (as in "I want juice!") or to express simple and sometimes poorly understood concepts.

Egocentric speech is predominant between ages 3 and 7. It serves as a bridge between the primitive and highly public social speech of the first stage and the more sophisticated and highly private inner speech of the third stage. During this stage, children often talk to themselves in an apparent attempt to guide their own

---

*PPC: "How about bears? What is their intelligence like?" *Author:* "They are possessed of a great wisdom, tempered by a savage cunning. They are accomplished dialectical thinkers, both pragmatic and poetic. They are pensive and somber, jovial and — in truth, Vygotsky does not say."

Table 8.3   Vygotsky's theory of the role of language

Stage	Function
Social (external) (*to age 3*)	Controls the behavior of others; expresses simple thoughts and emotions
Egocentric (*3 to 7*)	Bridge between external and inner speech; serves to control own behavior, but spoken out loud
Inner (*7 onwards*)	Self-talk; makes possible the direction of our thinking and our behavior; involved in all higher mental functioning

behavior. For example, they might speak about what they are doing as they do it. Unlike older children, however, they are likely to say things out loud (externalize) rather than silently, as though they believed that if language is to direct behavior, it must be spoken.

Inner speech is silent self-talk. It is characteristic of older children as well as adults. It is what William James (1890) called the stream of consciousness. Our self-talk — our inner speech — is what tells us that we are alive and conscious. It permits us to direct our thinking and our behavior. More than this, it makes all higher mental functioning possible (see Table 8.3).

The Concept of a Zone of Proximal Growth

Higher mental functioning involves activities such as thinking, perceiving, organizing, and remembering. These functions originate in social activity and are inseparably linked with language, which is also a social phenomenon. In a very real sense, these higher mental functions define intelligence.

One of Vygotsky's strong interests was in maximizing intellectual development. Like Feuerstein (see Chapter 5) he was far less interested in measuring past accomplishments or in assessing current levels of functioning than in arriving at some notion of potential for future development. Every child, he maintained, has a sphere or a zone of current capabilities — in Vygotsky's words, a **zone of proximal growth**. Take, for example, two five-year-old children, who can both, under normal circumstances, answer questions that other average five-year-olds can also answer. Their mental ages might be said to correspond to their chronological ages, and their intelligence would be described as average. But if, when prompted, one of these children could successfully answer questions corresponding to a mental age of seven but the other could not, it would be accurate to say that the first child's zone of proximal growth is greater than the other's (that is, it spans a wider range of higher functions). This is, in fact, the concept that underlies Feuerstein's assessment of "retarded performers."

EDUCATIONAL IMPLICATIONS OF VYGOTSKY'S THEORY

Several educational implications can be derived from this brief overview of some of Vygotsky's principal theoretical beliefs. First, the theory highlights the importance of language in the development of higher mental functions. Vygotsky believed very strongly that language is a social and cultural phenomenon that is centrally involved in the development of thinking. Accordingly, schools can perhaps do a great deal to enhance the development of cognitive processes by paying special attention to the development of language facility.

Second, the theory stresses that cognitive development is profoundly influenced by the cultural and social environments. Specifically, to the extent that the environment requires that the child perform at a level slightly in advance of current developmental level, progress will be enhanced. In this connection, Vygotsky suggests that the level at which instructions and questions are phrased is extremely important. These, he argues, should be sufficiently ahead of the student's developmental level that they present a genuine intellectual challenge.

In summary, Vygotsky's social-cognitive developmental theory underscores the role of culture and its most important invention, language, in the development of higher mental functions. Without culture, he argues, our intelligence would be comparable to that of apes* — hence the fundamental role of education is cultural transmission.

We knew that. But we were perhaps not entirely aware of the theoretical underpinnings of this belief.

Do bears have a culture? Do wild cows?

MAIN POINTS

1. A theory is a systematic attempt to organize and interpret observations. It is an invention that cannot easily be judged in terms of accuracy and truthfulness, but rather in terms of how well it reflects the facts, how consistent it is, and how useful it is for explaining and predicting.

2. *Social learning* refers to (1) learning that occurs in a social context — a process; and (2) the learning of social rules and conventions, of what is acceptable and what isn't — a product. Socially accepted behaviors vary from culture to culture and from one situation to another within the same culture.

3. Most theories of social learning assume that *imitation* is a central process in determining behavior.

4. Bandura's observational learning theory is based on the effects of reinforcement, on the observer's awareness of the connections between behavior and outcomes, and on the observer's ability to symbolize. It is a theory of *reciprocal determinism* (the environment determines behavior, but the individual chooses and alters the environment).

5. The term *model* refers to a person who serves as an example for another and to symbolic models (highly prevalent in technologically advanced societies), which include oral and written instructions, fictitious characters in books or films, television, and so on.

6. Sources of reinforcement in observational learning include direct reinforcement by the model, reinforcement as a consequence of behavior, and vicarious reinforcement (when the punishment or reward an observer thinks a model has received affects the observer's behavior).

7. Three effects of imitation include the *modeling effect* (the learning of novel responses), the *inhibitory-disinhibitory effect* (deviant behavior is disinhibited or suppressed, usually as a function of response consequences to the models) and the *eliciting effect* (the emission of responses that are related to those made by the model but that are neither novel nor deviant).

8. The effects of models are brought about largely through their *informative* function. They show us what to do, how to do it, and the most likely consequences of doing it.

PPC: "And bears?"
Author: "And perhaps to bears, too."

9. Four processes are involved in observational learning: *attentional processes* (the observer directs attention to those aspects of the model's behavior that are distinct and that have high functional and affective value); *retention processes* (the observer symbolizes observations visually or verbally, stores them, and perhaps rehearses them mentally); *motor-reproduction processes* (the observer acts out the imitated behavior and refines it on the basis of feedback); and *motivational processes* (what has been learned may be manifested or not, depending on the learner's motivation — an *acquisition-performance* distinction).

10. Gender roles are learned patterns of culturally approved masculine and feminine behaviors. The process whereby gender roles are learned is called *sex typing*. Gender roles appear to be a combined function of genetic, family-based, and cultural forces.

11. Traditional gender roles, which might be changing slowly, reflect males as more aggressive, more boisterous, and more adventurous than girls. Both boys and girls tend to prefer male to female roles.

12. Sex differences, which typically have both genetic and environmental roots, are sometimes evident in the greater aggressiveness, visual and spatial ability, and mathematical ability of males and in the greater verbal ability of females. However, differences in mathematics and in verbal achievement are increasingly trivial, nonexistent, or opposite to those expected.

13. Sex differences in abilities are too trivial and too inconsistent to be of any importance to teachers. What is important is that teachers be sensitive to both the interests of boys and girls and to the many instances of sexual bias that still permeate society.

14. Piaget's theory stems partly from his biological orientation and focuses on cognitive development. It describes the characteristics of human behavior that permit adaptation, and it classifies important intellectual events in terms of sequential developmental stages.

15. The newborn infant is an intrinsically motivated information-processing machine that pays attention to the most informative aspects of the environment. It acquires information and adapts through the joint processes of assimilation (making already acquired responses; making environmental stimulation conform to mental structure) and accommodation (modifying responses; making mental structure conform to environmental demands).

16. Piaget describes development as proceeding through four major stages. The *sensorimotor period* (birth to two years) is characterized by a motor representation of the world. Among the child's major achievements during this period are the development of language, the development of the *object concept*, the development of internally controlled representational schemes, and the recognition of cause-and-effect relationships.

17. The *preoperational period* (two to seven years) is divided into two substages: the preconceptual (two to four years; reasoning is characteristically transductive — it proceeds from particular to particular) and the intuitive (four to seven years; reasoning is egocentric, perception-dominated, and intuitive).

18. The stage of *concrete operations* (seven to eleven or twelve years) is marked by the appearance of thought processes that are subject to some logical rules (identity, reversibility, and compensation, for example) evident in the development of concepts of conservation (the realization that certain qualities of objects, such as weight or volume, do not change unless matter is added or subtracted).

19. In addition to conservation, three new abilities mark the period of concrete operations:

the ability to classify, the ability to order, and the ability to deal with numbers.

20. During the *formal-operations stage* (eleven or twelve to fourteen or fifteen years), the child becomes freed from concrete objects and events and can now deal with the hypothetical. This ability is advanced as one of the reasons for the idealism of adolescence.

21. Researchers such as Basseches (dialectical thinking) and Labouvie-Vief (pragmatic reasoning) argue that although formal operations may be appropriate for problems requiring nothing but logic, mature adult reasoning is more sensitive to and tolerant of ambiguity and contradiction and is more likely to consider the practical, social, ethical, and personal implications of decisions.

22. Although replications of many of Piaget's experiments have tended to confirm the general sequence of stages up to formal operations, a number of these replications (sometimes using simpler or clearer problems) report that important concepts are often attained at younger ages.

23. Evidence presented by researchers who replicate and extend Piaget's work (sometimes called *neo-Piagetians*) suggests that Piaget overlooked or underemphasized some important cognitive achievements of the preschool period (for example, the number-abstraction and numerical-reasoning skills described by Gelman) and that Piaget's stages should perhaps be reformulated into more general levels.

24. Case has advanced ideas for using Piaget-based indicators of intellectual maturity as guides for the hierarchical analysis of learning tasks within the framework of Gagné's instructional theory.

25. Attempts to accelerate development by teaching Piagetian concepts have met with relatively little success. The reason may be that the treatments used have been inadequate because we know too little about in-

tellectual development or that the ordinary course of cognitive development cannot easily be affected by contrived experiences.

26. Among the principles for teaching that can be derived from Piaget's work are the following: Teacher recognition of differences between children and adults can enable the two to communicate more effectively. Instructional procedures should provide opportunities for student activity. There is an optimal level of difficulty for new learning, which can be determined on the basis of what the student already knows. A teacher should be aware of the limits of children's abilities; some concepts are too difficult at certain ages. Social interaction is an important variable in the development of thought and should be provided in schools.

27. Vygotsky's social-cognitive theory stresses the importance of culture and of its principal invention, language. Without culture, our intellectual functioning is limited to ape-like, *elementary mental functions*; given culture and language, we become capable of *higher mental functions* involved in thinking, reasoning, remembering, and so on.

28. The child progresses through three stages in developing language functions: *social speech* (also termed *external speech*), which is predominant before ages 3 or 4, involves the use of speech largely to control others or to express simple, poorly understood concepts; *egocentric speech* (ages 3 to 7 or so), which is *self-talk* that is spoken out loud and that has a role in controlling and directing the child's own behavior; and *inner speech*, marked by unspoken verbalizations that control thought and behavior.

29. Vygotsky's *zone of proximal growth* is the child's potential for development from the current level of mental functioning. Vygotsky emphasizes the importance of assessing potential rather than simply measuring past accomplishments or current level of functioning.

30. Vygotsky's theory presents a strong argument for language-related activities in schools and for instruction at the upper edge of the student's zone of proximal development—that is, for challenging instructional materials and methods.

SUGGESTED READINGS

The social development theory of Bandura and Walters is presented in the following:

BANDURA, A. (1977). *Social learning theory.* Morristown, N.J.: General Learning Press.

BANDURA, A., & WALTERS, R. (1963). *Social learning and personality development.* New York: Holt, Rinehart & Winston.

Although Piaget's books are relatively difficult reading and are more suitable for the advanced student than for the novice, the following is something of an exception. It is of particular value in understanding the logical thought processes of children in the concrete-operations and formal-operations stages:

INHELDER, B., & PIAGET, J. (1958). *The growth of logical thinking from childhood to adolescence.* New York: Basic Books.

The following is a highly readable and excellent analysis of cognitive development; it deals in some detail with Piaget's theory, as well as with current developments in information processing and metacognition:

FLAVELL, J. H. (1985). *Cognitive development* (2nd ed.). Englewood Cliffs, N.J.: Prentice-Hall.

A comprehensive account of Vygotsky's theory is:

WERTSCH, J. V. (1985). *Vygotsky and the social formation of mind.* Cambridge, Mass.: Harvard University Press.

Delayed implantation is one of the common features of brown and polar bears, badgers, mink, and a small number of other animals. The fertilized egg does not become implanted in the uterine wall shortly after conception, but may remain dormant for weeks and sometimes months. Although delayed implantation clearly has survival value, ensuring that the young will be born at the optimal time of the year, the mechanisms which delay embryonic development and later serve to trigger it are not understood (Matthews, 1969).

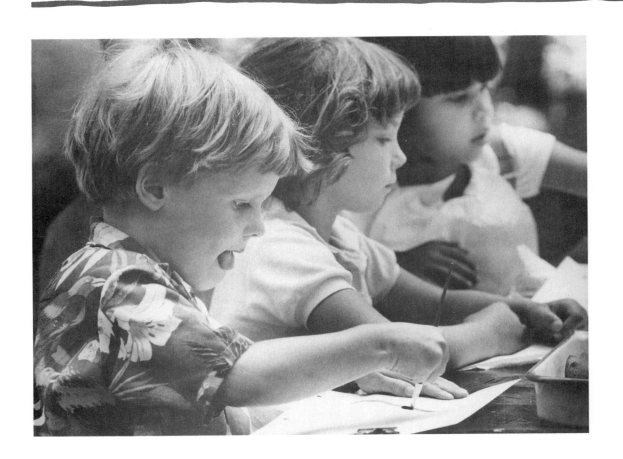

INTELLIGENCE, CREATIVITY, AND EXCEPTIONALITY

Last week I observed one of my student teachers during a reading period with an ordinary, reasonably bright, third-grade class of students. Reasonably bright — some were far more, and others far less. And so, even in this very ordinary class, the students had been separated into two groups for reading instruction. In more extraordinary and less homogeneous classes, the need for grouping students becomes even more apparent, and the implications of grouping may also become more apparent. Chapters 9 and 10 address these concerns and the dimensions of exceptionality, paying particular attention to creativity, intelligence, mental retardation, and current trends and issues in special education.

INTELLIGENCE AND CREATIVITY

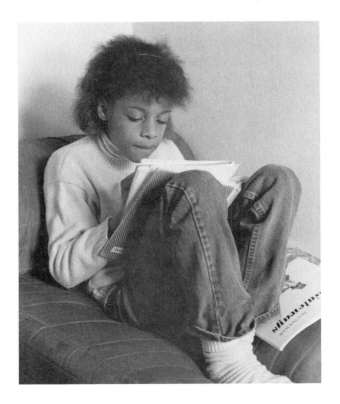

*I will not Reason and Compare:
my business is to Create.*
WILLIAM BLAKE *Jerusalem*

Since when was genius found respectable?
ELIZABETH BARRETT BROWNING *Aurora Leigh*

PREVIEW Intelligence and creativity, those nebulous and ill–defined characteristics, are among the most prized of our "possessions" — and perhaps among the most useful as well. This chapter examines the meanings of these terms, the forces that shape the qualities they represent, and some of the methods that have been devised to assess them. In addition, the chapter looks at the relationship between creativity and intelligence. Is it possible to be creative but stupid? To be intelligent but totally devoid of creative talent?

■ *The wild cows are back! They haven't been around much since Chapter 3, but now they have appeared again, perpetrating their environmental atrocities willy-nilly through the forest and even in streams and lakes. These wild cows do things unmentionable in polite textbooks, and other things that we can mention only in passing.*

For example, they insist on building themselves fires on chilly evenings. As a result, they are rapidly depleting the world's forests. They don't really need the fires to keep warm, given that each has a heavy hair-coat; the fires are merely a wild-cow indulgence. But they think that denuding the forests will make grazing easier and more economical. Wild cows scarcely notice immediate things like the scarcity of songbirds. How can they be expected to notice more distant things, like the fact that the planet's oxygen supply is no longer being replenished, that the ozone layer is thinning, and that the earth is warming up and the oceans expanding? How can they be expected to realize that one day there will no longer be any forests in which they can run amok?

That isn't all. Wild cows have recently decided that it is clever to use hair sprays from cans that have chlorofluorocarbon propellants. These sticky sprays set their hair-coats in rigid patterns. They think this makes them look sweet. "It's a bloody affectation," says the bear. "Ugly, stupid wild cows. Don't they know what it does to the atmosphere?"

Today's trendy wild cow is no longer satisfied simply to eat and chew cud and run amok. Now when she is done with her cud, she lounges about sipping her whisky — from styrofoam cups! This, of course, is after she has pillaged and soiled the bear's table. And when she has had enough whisky, she throws her cup away in nonbiodegradable plastic garbage bags. "For spite," the bear claims. "Wild cows have no interest in keeping their garbage out of the forest!"

And perhaps worst of all, wild cows emit great clouds of methane gas as they forage and run amok. Some even smoke cigars, spewing streams of "cigarrous" sulphides into the atmosphere, leading to "cigarrous" rains, resulting eventually in "cigarrous" fish. But do wild cows care about such things? Not much.

To quote the bear again, "Bloody wild cows!"

It really upsets the bear that wild cows are not concerned about their behavior. Sometimes he remembers the songs of birds he no longer hears, and he weeps. "It's those damn wild-cow philosophers," he moans. Wild-cow philosophers reassure the populace with meaningless axioms, like "Every problem contains its own solution!" As a result, wild cows believe that the technology they worship will solve the world's problems when those problems are serious enough to require solution. In the meantime, they continue to use Styrofoam cups and hair sprays, to wear their Dynel wigs and plastic false eyelashes, and to enjoy their cigars and whisky.

Wild-cow philosophers are wrong, insists the bear. This problem does not contain its own solution. Technology's values, he says, are driven too much by economics. And even if this weren't true, he argues, the wild cows have gotten us into a mess that technology is not likely to resolve.

*"Our creativity and our intelligence are our only hope for salvation," the bear says. "But first, we must get rid of wild cows."** ▬

INTELLIGENCE EXAMINED

The second most frequently used and least understood term in education is **intelligence**; first place goes to the term *creativity*.

I once interviewed a number of people to discover the common meaning of intelligence, if it has a common meaning. Surprisingly, there is more agreement among nonexperts than among so-called experts. The question asked was simply, "How can you tell whether or not someone is intelligent?" Most nonexperts (service station attendants, ticket sellers, fans at hockey games, and undergraduate students) gave some variation of the following answer: "Intelligent people are the ones who do well at school." Presumably, then, unintelligent people would be those who do less well at school. The experts (educational psychologists!), in contrast, had a variety of beliefs about intelligence. When pressed to answer the simple question, "How can you tell whether or not someone is intelligent?" a few replied that intelligent people would do well on school achievement tests. Others said that intelligence would

be reflected in performance on intelligence tests. A number of experts also discussed some of the definitions given in the following section.

Psychometric Definitions of Intelligence

1. "Intelligence is what the tests test" (Boring, 1923, p. 35).

2. "The global and aggregate capacity of an individual to think rationally, to act purposefully, and to deal effectively with his environment" (Wechsler, 1958, p. 7).

3. Intelligence A: "The innate potential for cognitive development." Intelligence B: "A general or average level of development of ability to perceive, to learn, to solve problems, to think, to adapt" (Hebb, 1966, p. 332).

4. To Hebb's definition, West and MacArthur (1964) added another dimension, labeled Intelligence A': "The present potential of an individual for future development of intelligent behavior, assuming optimum future treatment adapted to bring out that potential" (p. 18).

The first definition (that is, what the tests measure) is not meant to be facetious. It is at once an admission that *intelligence* is an extremely difficult concept to define and an assertion that intelligence tests are useful, provided they are related to success on tasks requiring intelligence. Whatever they measure can then be called intelligence, even if its exact nature is unknown.

The second definition ("global and aggregate capacity") defines intelligence in terms of clear thinking, purposeful activity, and effective interaction with the environment. Wechsler sees intelligence as a "global" capacity. This view is advanced in distinction to the view held by Spearman (1927) and Thurstone (1938), among others, that intelligence is not a single

---

PPC: "What is all this about wild cows? What does it mean? Why is the author doing this?"
Editor: It's clearly a metaphor. Fortunately, your author has responded to this inquiry — in the glossary, under **wild cow**. Check it out."

trait but instead consists of a number of separate abilities or factors. Guilford (1959), whose work is reviewed later in this chapter in the section on creativity, advances a similar view.

The third and fourth definitions make some useful distinctions among different types of intelligence. As Vygotsky (1986) points out, people are born with different *potentials* for development — what Hebb calls "intelligence A." However, conventional measures of intelligence assess "intelligence B" — *current* level of development — rather than intelligence A. Inferences about potential are then based on measures of current performance. In contrast, Vygotsky's approach to measuring intelligence, as well as Feuerstein's (1980), gives test subjects hints and suggestions to determine maximum potential performance.

In another approach, Cattell (1971) makes an important distinction between two kinds of intelligence. On the one hand, certain capabilities seem to underlie much of our intelligent behavior. Cattell calls these basic capabilities, which are essentially nonverbal and are unaffected by culture or experience, **fluid abilities**. Such measures as general reasoning, memory, attention span, and analysis of figures reflect fluid abilities.

In contrast with fluid abilities is a grouping of intellectual abilities that are primarily verbal and that are highly influenced by culture, experience, and education. These **crystallized abilities** are reflected in vocabulary tests, tests of general information, and arithmetic skills. Not surprisingly, performance on crystallized measures tends to increase with age, sometimes into very old age (Horn and Donaldson, 1980). In contrast, fluid abilities seem to be more dependent on physiological structures and more susceptible to the ravages of age; they typically show declines in old age (Horn, 1976).

How, then, should we define intelligence? Is it what the tests test? A global and aggregate sort of thing? A two-sided thing involving what is potential as well as what is actual? A different two-sided thing involving relatively "pure" capabilities on the one hand and capabilities that are highly affected by experience on the other? Perhaps we should use a combination of all these definitions. As Vernon (1969) observes, when we speak of intelligence, we often mean any one of three things, or a combination thereof: a genetic capacity (presumably reflected in fluid intelligence or in Hebb's intelligence A); a test score (derived from any of a large number of different intelligence tests); or observed behavior (reflected in Hebb's intelligence B).

An Information-Processing View of Intelligence

Wagner and Sternberg (1984) suggest that there are basically three different views of intelligence. They label the first the *psychometric* view. Historically, it has been the most common approach to understanding intelligence, and it is well illustrated in the preceding section on definitions of intelligence (and in later sections dealing with various tests as well). *Psychometrics* refers to the measurement of psychological functions; hence, the psychometric view of intelligence is that which is based on a measurement approach.

The second view is Piaget's. This perspective sees intelligence as an active process involving progressive adaptation through the interplay of assimilation and accommodation. The results of intelligent activity are manifested in cognitive structure. The principal characteristics of cognitive structure change with age; the changes are the essential features of Piaget's developmental theory.

The third view of intelligence is the information-processing view to which we alluded in Chapter 3. We look at it in more detail in this section.

Briefly, the information-processing view of intelligence stresses the importance of the strategies and processes involved in knowing. Accordingly, it is a cognitive perspective. In its simplest form, this perspective maintains that one of the important components of intelligent activity are cognitive functions. And most important from the teacher's point of view is the widely held belief that these functions are largely acquired. As was discussed in Chapter 5, functions that are acquired (that is, functions that are learned) can be taught. That, in a nutshell, is the rationale underlying the cognitive-strategies programs or learning/thinking-strategies programs currently being developed and tested.

A good representative of the information-processing approach to intelligence is Sternberg's (1984a, 1984b, 1986) contextual and componential theory. The theory is contextual in that it defines intelligence in terms of adaptation to a particular environment. In Sternberg's words, intelligence is the "purposive selection and shaping of and adaptation to real-world environments relevant to one's life" (1984a, p. 312). One of the important features of this definition is that it emphasizes the individual's control over the environment. It says, in effect, that intelligent individuals exercise control over their environments not only by changing and

molding significant aspects of them, but also by selecting them in the first place. Thus, it would be quite stupid (or at least moderately unintelligent) of someone who is tone-deaf to select a career in music or for someone who suffers from severe vertigo to buy a home high on a cliff.

How can we measure contextual intelligence? One way, Sternberg suggests, is simply to ask people what is considered intelligent and stupid in their culture. After all, contextual intelligence is simply an indication of how well a person adapts in a specific environment — and people who live in that environment may be expected to be the best sources of information concerning what is required for effective adaptation. Not surprisingly, an analysis of the responses of people in North American cultures to the question of what makes up intelligent behavior reveals that there are three broad groupings of abilities that best describe intelligent people: practical problem-solving ability, verbal ability, and social competence. In other cultures, responses might be different.

One of the advantages of a contextual view

Intelligence in Other Species

We generally assume that of all animals on earth, we are by far the most intelligent and the most inventive. As evidence, we point proudly to our increasing mastery of nature, and we contrast with this the perennial struggle for survival of those less gifted than we are.* So viewed, we appear to be the creature that has adapted best to the environment — and this, the ability to adapt, is an accurate and useful definition of intelligence.

Ironically, we — the self-designated *wise* ones — do not have the largest brain of the earthly species. Indeed, the adult male brain weighs a mere three and one-quarter pounds. The

female brain weighs approximately 10 percent less — not even three pounds. This, compared with the thirteen-pound elephant brain or the brain of a whale, which in some cases weighs nineteen pounds, is relatively unimpressive. However, given the strong likelihood that the absolute weight of the brain is less related to intelligent behavior than is the ratio of brain to body weight, we still retain the advantage. Our brain-to-body-weight ratio is approximately 1 to 50; that of the whale and elephant approaches 1 to 1,000. However, some small monkeys have even better brain-to-body-weight ratios — as high as 1 to 18. But in these cases, the absolute size of the brain is so small that it probably cannot do much more than handle simple physiological functioning.

The dolphin, on the other hand, is not inordinately large; in fact, it often weighs no more

than an adult man. Yet its average brain weight is a full three and three-quarters pounds. This fact has led to a great deal of speculation and research on the dolphin's intelligence — research that has not yet succeeded in determining how intelligent the dolphin really is.

Although a fairly accurate ranking of species in terms of intelligence may be based on their brain-to-body-weight ratios, such a crude indicator of intelligence does not appear to be of any real value in gauging the subtle but significant differences that exist between geniuses and less gifted individuals within the human species. For this, instruments labeled "intelligence tests" are commonly used. Not only are these tests generally unsuitable for nonhumans, but they also are often suitable only for very specific groups within the human species.

*And we point, less proudly, to our dwindling supply of irreplaceable resources, to our idiotic penchant for polluting the environment, to our unreasoning failure to control our numbers, and to the increasing risk of nuclear self-annihilation.

---

of intelligence is that it highlights the importance of the individual's success in coping with the ordinary demands of life in the social and physical context; that is, it removes intelligence from the realm of the abstract and theoretical and brings it to a more concrete, more easily understood level. But this view also has a number of disadvantages. First, it is too inclusive. Because all adaptive behaviors are intelligent, then almost all behaviors are potentially intel-

ligent (even if they are perhaps somewhat stupid in one context, they may be adaptive in some other context). Second, the contextualist view does not adequately describe the processes and structures that underlie intelligence; instead, it describes intelligence in terms of the characteristics and effects of behavior.

As a response to these weaknesses, Sternberg (1986) has proposed a componential theory of human intelligence (mentioned briefly in

A Contextual Subtheory

Intelligence is adaptation to real-world environments and involves selecting and shaping the environment

A Componential Subtheory

Metacomponents
Executive skills involved in planning, monitoring, and evaluating cognitive activity

Performance Components

Processes actually used in carrying out tasks, such as encoding, inductive reasoning, remembering

Knowledge Aquisition Components

Processes used in acquiring new information, such as separating important from unimportant information (selective encoding), relating items of information (selective combination), and comparing new information with old (selective comparison)

Figure 9.1   Sternberg's information-processing view of intelligence consists of three related subtheories. The first two, the contextual and the componential, are represented here; the third relates intelligence to experience with different tasks.

Chapter 5). This theory identifies three separate components of intelligence (see Figure 9.1). First are the components involved in metacognition—that is, in planning, monitoring, and evaluating cognitive performance. These are labeled **metacomponents**. They include what Sternberg also calls executive skills—those used in making decisions about what cognitive activities to use and in monitoring and evaluating the results of these ongoing activities. Conventional measures of intelligence typically do not measure metacomponents.

Second, there are **performance components**. These are processes that are actually used in carrying out tasks. They include inductive reasoning, encoding, analyzing, remembering, paying attention, and so on. Note that these processes are what Cattell defines as *fluid abilities*. They appear to be relatively independent

of experience and more dependent on innate factors. Sternberg suggests that a number of conventional intelligence tests that measure fluid intelligence can also serve as good measures of performance components.

The third of Sternberg's three components of intelligence are the **knowledge-acquisition components**. Sternberg (1984c) identifies three processes that are important for acquiring new information: *selective encoding* (separating relevant from irrelevant information), *selective combination* (combining selected information with other information so as to make it meaningful), and *selective comparison* (deriving meaning from new information by relating it to previous learning).

In summary, there are three separate views of intelligence. The psychometric view looks at intelligence as a phenomenon that is evident in the individual's performance on tasks assumed to require intelligent behavior and that can therefore be measured by a carefully selected assortment of these tasks. Piaget's view describes what he terms *intelligence in action*. He sees intelligence as an ongoing adaptive process involving the interplay of assimilation and accommodation and resulting in the gradual development of cognitive structure. And the information-processing view is concerned with the cognitive processes that underlie intelligent behavior. As an example, Sternberg presents a contextualist definition of intelligence (intelligent behavior is behavior that is adaptive in a particular context) and argues that intelligence consists of three components. Metacomponents have to do with metacognition (planning, organizing, monitoring, and selecting processing strategies); performance components are processes that are actually used in carrying out a task (encoding, inductive reasoning, and so on); and knowledge-acquisition components have to do with acquiring new information (separating the important from the unimportant, relating items of new information, and comparing new information with old knowledge).

From the teacher's point of view, intelligence is an important concept both to the extent that it relates to school achievement and to the extent that it may sometimes require teachers to modify their instructional strategies. And from a practical point of view, teachers will most often obtain evidence of intelligence from the actual performance of their students and somewhat less often from more formal measures of intelligence.

Intelligence and Achievement

The Concept of Correlation.
Correlation is a frequently used term that is not always clearly understood — hence this brief introduction that is meant to clarify your understanding of sections that follow.

Two or more **variables** (properties that can vary) are correlated if there is some correspon-

dence between them. Size of shoe is correlated with size of sock; income is correlated with standard of living; size of house is correlated with number of windows; and drunkenness is correlated with alcohol consumption. These are all examples of **positive correlation**: As one variable increases, so does its correlate. The inverse relationship, labeled **negative correlation**, can also hold: Number of wild animals is correlated with number of people; amount of pollutants in water is correlated with number of fish; and sobriety is correlated with alcohol consumption. In each of these cases, as one variable increases, the other decreases; therefore each is an example of *negative correlation*.

The index (or coefficient) of correlation most often used ranges in value from -1.00 to $+1.00$. Each extreme indicates perfect correlation, whereas 0 indicates complete lack of relatedness (see Figure 9.2). The symbol used for a correlation coefficient is usually r.

It is important not to make an inference of causality solely on the basis of correlation. Even though any two variables that vary together are correlated, variation in one does not necessarily *cause* the other to vary. It is true, for example, that there is a very high positive correlation between the number of liquor outlets in urban areas and the number of churches in those same areas. However, some people would prefer to think that one does not cause the other.

Measuring Intelligence and Achievement.
One of the assumptions underlying the construction of most intelligence tests is that intelligence is related to successful performance of school tasks. It is not surprising, therefore, that these tests correlate relatively highly with measures of school achievement. In fact, intelligence tests and achievement tests both measure the same sorts of things — that is, both measure the effects of previous learning (achievement), and both typically are highly verbal. The principal differences between the two are that intelligence tests sample from a wider range of behaviors and (to some degree) emphasize the ability to apply knowledge and skills to new

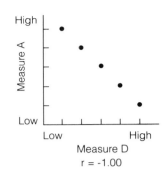

Figure 9.2 Representations of correlation (*r*), which indicate the extent to which two measures tend to vary together. The *direction* of the relationship (positive or negative) is shown by the *sign* of the correlation coefficient (plus or minus). The *strength* of the relationship is indicated by the *magnitude* of the correlation coefficient: The closer *r* is to ±1, the stronger the observed relationship; the closer it is to 0, the weaker the relationship. In this example, scores on Measure A correlate perfectly with scores on Measures B and D and not at all with scores on Measure C.

problems; in contrast, achievement tests tend to be limited to specific content areas or subjects.

Conventional intelligence tests, particularly the kinds of paper-and-pencil group tests that are most commonly used in classrooms, do *not* measure innate capacity except by very remote inference; that is, psychologists sometimes make the inference that those who do well on these tests have higher innate capacity for learning than those who do less well. In fact, however, what the tests actually provide is a measure of the learning experiences that subjects have had, as well as a crude measure of how much they have profited from these experiences. Vygotsky (1986) and Feuerstein (1979) both argue that in order to measure learning potential, subjects must be placed in situations in which they must learn rather than in situations in which their past learning is tapped — hence the use of hints and clues in Feuerstein's measurement of aptitude called the Learning Potential Assessment Device (LPAD).

In view of the close relationship between what achievement and intelligence tests mea-

sure, it is not surprising that the correlation between the two ranges from .30 to .80 over a large number of studies (Tyler, 1965). It would appear, then, that knowledge of a student's score on an intelligence test may be of considerable value to a teacher. Unfortunately, as is pointed out later in this chapter, intelligence test scores are not usually very valuable in predicting how an individual will perform. Their results are notably unreliable: Scores fluctuate widely for the same individual from one test to another, and for any individual they may not accurately reflect future or past performance. However, they can be of considerable value in predicting how well *groups* of students are likely to do. Accordingly, they are often used for grouping students for instruction and counseling purposes. Keep in mind, however, that intelligence is only one of the factors that correlates with school success. Previous success is an even better predictor of future success.

Myths Concerning IQ. Teachers who make use of intelligence tests should be aware of their limitations and of the myths that frequently surround the concept of **intelligence quotient (IQ)**.

First, it is widely assumed that all individuals have an IQ — an assumption that is implicit in the question "What is your IQ?" or the expression "My IQ is . . ." It is also assumed that IQ is constant because it is a magical (or sometimes not-so-magical) number *possessed* by someone. The fact is, the numerical index of intelligence known as the IQ is simply a score obtained by an individual in a specific testing situation and on a specific "intelligence" test. Intelligence tests have (a sometimes disputable) **validity**. A test is valid to the extent that it measures what it claims to measure; hence, an intelligence test is valid if it measures intelligence and nothing else. In addition, none has perfect **reliability**.* The accuracy (reliability) with which intelligence tests measure whatever it is that they do in fact measure varies considerably. This variation, technically known as the error of measurement, is such that any teacher looking at a specific intelligence quotient should reason: "This score of 130 means that this student probably has a measured IQ that ranges somewhere between 120 and 140."

Second, it is also widely believed that IQ is highly related to success. However, Thorndike and Hagen (1977) and Cohen (1972) point out that although the correlation between intelligence test scores and school achievement is substantial, previous achievement correlates even more highly with future achievement than does IQ. In addition, the correlation is considerably higher for some subjects (those requiring verbal or numerical skills) than it is for others. Hence the IQ is not necessarily related to success; it depends on the field in which success is being measured.

Third, intelligence tests measure relatively limited kinds of abilities — typically the ability to work with abstract ideas and symbols. They seldom tap interpersonal skills, athletic ability, creativity, and a variety of other desirable human attributes. As Weinberg (1989) notes, they do not reveal many important things about human cognition. For example, most measures of intelligence do not tell us anything about social intelligence, motivation, adaptive skills, or emotion.

Finally, intelligence tests are culturally biased; that is, they tend to favor children whose backgrounds are similar to that of the sample that was the norm for the test. In North America that sample has usually consisted of white, middle-class children, a fact that explains why the majority of intelligence tests are unfair for a variety of minority groups. However, the most recent revisions of such tests as the Stanford Binet and the Wechsler have expanded their standardization samples to include minority groups in a representative way. Accordingly, they are now fairer to minorities.

A number of other tests — none of them widely used in practice, though some are used more extensively in research — attempt to minimize cultural bias. Such tests, sometimes labeled *culture-fair*, or, more accurately, *culture-reduced*, are typically nonverbal. They attempt to tap intellectual functions through problems involving pictures or abstract designs (for example, the Ravens Progressive Matrices Test). One important approach to overcoming some of the cultural biases in testing is Mercer's **SOMPA** (1979, Mercer and Lewis, 1978), which is described later in this chapter.

INTELLIGENCE TESTS

A wide variety of intelligence tests are available, most of which yield a score referred to as the IQ. The average IQ of a randomly selected group of people on most tests is around 100. Approximately two-thirds of the population score between 85 and 115. About 11 percent score above 120, and 1.6 percent score above 140.

---

*See Chapter 14 for a discussion of reliability and validity.

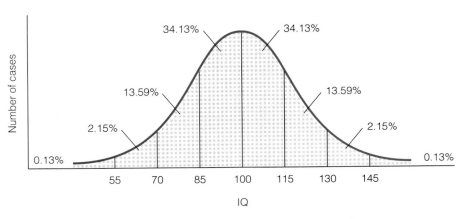

Figure 9.3 A normal curve depicting the theoretical distribution of IQ scores among humans. (Average score is 100; 68.26 percent of the population score between 85 and 115; only 2.28 percent score either above 130 or below 70.) Actual scores for a population may vary somewhat from this theoretical distribution.

Figure 9.3 depicts the distribution of measured intelligence in a normal population.

There are two general types of intelligence tests: group and individual. The former are administered simultaneously to a group of test subjects; the latter require individual administration. Typically, **group tests** are paper-and-pencil tests. There are many more of them than there are individual tests, probably because group tests are inexpensive and widely used. Unfortunately, their validity and reliability are very poor. **Individual tests**, in contrast, are much more expensive in terms of both equipment and administration time. The scores they yield are sometimes more reliable, however, and they often provide greater insight into the functioning of the subject's mind. They are particularly valuable in diagnosing specific learning problems in children. It is relatively rare, for example, to find school systems that base decisions to put students in "special" classrooms simply on a group assessment. Typically, an individual assessment is required after initial screening with a group measure, partly to determine whether the test has been fair to the student.

Group tests can usually be administered and scored by any reasonably competent classroom teacher. However, the administration of individual tests, with few exceptions, requires a great deal of training and skill. Brief descriptions of some of the most commonly used individual and group tests are given below. For more information, consult *Tests in Print* (Mitchell, 1983).

Individual Intelligence Tests

Peabody Picture Vocabulary Test Revised (PPVT–R). This is among the most easily administered and scored individual intelligence tests. It is an untimed test, usually requiring fifteen minutes or less per subject. It consists simply of having the subject point to the one picture out of four that represents a word that has been read by the examiner. There are two forms of the test (L and M), each consisting of 175 words (plates) arranged from easiest to most difficult. After six consecutive incorrect answers the test is discontinued. An intelligence score can then be computed on the basis

Table 9.1 The Wechsler Intelligence Scale for Children (WISC-R)

Verbal Scale	*Performance Scale*
1. *General information*. Questions relating to information most children have the opportunity to acquire.	1. *Picture completion*. Child indicates what is missing on pictures.
2. *General comprehension*. Questions designed to assess child's understanding of why certain things are done as they are.	2. *Picture arrangement*. Series of pictures must be arranged to tell a story.
3. *Arithmetic*. Oral arithmetic problems.	3. *Block design*. Child is required to copy exactly a design with colored blocks.
4. *Similarities*. Child indicates how certain things are alike.	4. *Object assembly*. Puzzles to be assembled by subjects.
5. *Vocabulary*. Child gives meaning of words of increasing difficulty.	5. *Coding*. Child pairs symbols with digits following a key.
6. *Digit span*. Child repeats orally presented sequence of numbers, in order and reversed.	6. *Mazes*. Child traces way out of mazes with pencil.

of the subject's age and the level of the last correct response.

Revised Stanford-Binet. This is one of the best-known and most widely used individual measures of intelligence. A relatively high degree of training and competence is required to administer it. It consists of a wide variety of different tests graded in difficulty so as to correspond to various age levels. It yields a score that can be converted to an IQ. The most recent revision of the Stanford-Binet (4th ed.; Thorndike, Hagen, and Sattler, 1985) yields scores in four separate areas: verbal reasoning, quantitative reasoning, abstract/visual reasoning, and short-term memory. It also provides a composite score that is described as a measure of "adaptive ability" and is interpreted in much the same way as an IQ.

Wechsler Intelligence Scale for Children Revised (WISC-R). This individual test is sim-ilar to the Stanford-Binet, but it is somewhat easier to administer. It also yields scores on a number of specific tests (for example, vocabulary, block design, digit span) and two major "intelligence" scores — one verbal and one performance. These can be combined to yield what is referred to as a full-scale IQ score. There is an adult version of this test (WAIS-R — Wechsler Adult Intelligence Scale Revised), as well as a preschool version (WPPSI — Wechsler Preschool and Primary Scale of Intelligence). Various subtests of the WISC-R are described in Table 9.1.

System of Multicultural Pluralistic Assessment (SOMPA). In several instances in this chapter, the point is made that many intelligence tests are unfair to those from ethnic and social groups outside the white middle-class majority. Indeed, a variety of court decisions in the United States have recognized this fact. For example, in *Diana* v. *California State Board of*

Education, twelve Mexican-American children claimed that they had been improperly placed in classes for the mentally retarded on the basis of testing that was conducted in a language other than their native one. Specifically, these children had been administered standard English versions of the Wechsler scales and of the Stanford-Binet. The judgment — in favor of the plaintiffs — ordered that the children be retested by someone fluent in Spanish, that greater emphasis be placed on nonverbal parts of the tests, and that new tests be developed for Spanish-speaking children.

This and a number of related court cases have had several effects on testing in schools. One not entirely beneficial effect has been to discourage the use of tests. It is probably a lot better to rely on tests, however biased they might be, than to rely on the judgments of teachers and other professionals who are not allowed the assistance of test results. Biases in tests are fixed and therefore perhaps detectable and measurable; human biases are no less real, but they are more subtle — and therefore harder to detect and control.

The second effect of these court cases has been to stimulate the development of new tests and new approaches to testing. Among these new approaches is Mercer's SOMPA (Mercer, 1979; Mercer and Lewis, 1978, 1979). The SOMPA consists of a battery of ten separate individual measures. These measures reflect assessments in three areas, which Mercer refers to as models: the medical model, the social-system model, and the pluralistic model. Measures relating to the medical model attempt to determine whether the child is biologically normal. These measures include tests of visual and auditory acuity, measures of physical dexterity and motor coordination, and indexes of health and physical development. Measures relating to the social-system model are intended to discover whether the child is socially "normal" — that is, whether the child behaves in expected ways in social situations. The WISC-R and a test labeled the Adaptive Behavior Inventory for Children (ABIC) are used to measure functioning in the social system. Mercer's assumption is that children who fall in the bottom 3 percent of the WISC-R will not behave as expected in school. In her terms, their *school functioning levels* will be abnormally low.

The pluralistic model is of particular interest because it considers the child's cultural and social background in attempting to determine the probability of his or her success in school. The principal measure used here is the WISC-R, administered in the usual fashion but normed with an entirely new set of subjects. Specifically, Mercer administered the WISC-R to a California standardization sample consisting of 456 blacks, 520 Hispanics, and 604 whites. As expected, Hispanics and blacks scored significantly lower than the white groups — 91.9 and 88.4 were the average full-scale IQs for Hispanics and blacks, compared with 103.1 for the whites. Combining these norms with information relating to the child's family (family size, family income, family structure, and socioeconomic status), Mercer developed a formula for predicting the likelihood of the child's success in school. This prediction, labeled an estimated learning potential (ELP) score, is *pluralistic* in that it attempts to take into account social and ethnic background as well as measured potential.

Although the SOMPA attempts to fill a real need in aptitude testing of cultural and social minorities, it is open to a number of serious criticisms. Sattler's (1982) criticisms include the following: the California sample is not nationally representative; there is little substantial evidence that predictions based on the SOMPA are more valid than those based solely on the WISC-R; and there is some question concerning the wisdom of using a medical model at all in making educational decisions until we have substantive evidence that the model contributes in useful ways to our predictions and to remediation of problems.

Group Intelligence Tests

Draw a Person Test. This is an interesting measure of intelligence developed by Goodenough (1926) and later revised by Harris (1963) and Naglieri (1988). It is based on the assumption that children's drawings reflect their conceptual sophistication. The child is simply asked to draw the best person possible; no time limit is imposed (see Figure 9.4). Drawings are scored primarily on the basis of detail and accuracy according to a well-defined set of criteria. Tables for converting raw scores to IQ scores are provided.

Cognitive Abilities Test (CogAT). This is a widely used, multilevel, paper-and-pencil test suitable for grades 3 through 13. It yields three scores — verbal, quantitative, and nonverbal — as well as a composite IQ score. The test includes tables for converting individual scores to percentile scores based on the performance of other children at the same grade level. (A percentile indicates the percentage of cases that fall at or below a given point. For example, a student who scores at the 75th percentile has performed as well or better than 75 percent of students in the same grade.)

Otis-Lennon School Ability Test. A test designed to assess school-related ability, the Otis-Lennon consists of five levels of items suitable for grades 1 through 12. Items are intermingled (for example, vocabulary, reasoning, and numerical and other items are presented in mixed order) and are presented in order of increasing difficulty. The test yields a single standardized score labeled a *school ability index* (SAI).

Uses of Intelligence Tests

Although still used in many school systems, intelligence tests are no longer routinely administered to all students everywhere. This is

a   b

Figure 9.4 Two examples of the Goodenough-Harris Drawing Test. Both subjects were boys aged 10¾ years. The raw scores and IQ equivalents, respectively, for the drawings are (*a*) 41 and 110; (*b*) 4 and 54. The child who drew *b* also had a low Stanford-Binet IQ score.
From B. D. Harris, *Children's Drawings as Measures of Intellectual Maturity*. © 1963 by Harcourt Brace Jovanovich, Inc. Reproduced by permission of the publisher.

partly because of a strong antitest movement among parents and others, and partly because of a growing recognition of the potential weaknesses and abuses of testing. Chief among the purposes for which intelligence tests are used are counseling, career guidance, class placement, and diagnosis for remedial or enrichment purposes. There is little doubt that when skillfully administered and intelligently interpreted, they can be of considerable value for any and all of these purposes. Unfortunately, however, they are not always skillfully administered and intelligently interpreted.

A number of very important cautions should be kept in mind when interpreting the results of intelligence tests. Some of these have already been mentioned, but they are summarized again here:

1. The validity and reliability of *all* measures of intelligence are less than perfect. What this means, quite simply, is that an intelligence test provides a general and imprecise index of what its makers consider to be intelligence. If Johnny's measured IQ today is 120 and Frank's is 115, it would be foolish in the extreme to conclude that Johnny is more intelligent than Frank and that he should therefore be granted the privilege of studying with the Orioles rather than with the White-Breasted Kites. It might well be that Johnny's measured IQ next month would be 110 or that Frank's measured IQ on another test today would be 130. It is, in fact, precisely the relative imprecision of measured IQ that has served to justify the secrecy that sometimes surrounds the IQ. Unfortunately, the concept of IQ is not at all well understood by parents; perhaps even more unfortunately, it is often not well understood by educators.

2. Measured IQ does not predict academic success nearly as well as is generally assumed. Recall that past success is usually more highly correlated with later success than is measured IQ (Cohen, 1972). Hence teachers would be well advised *not* to base their expectations of success for individual students *solely* on information derived from intelligence tests.

3. Intelligence, as it is measured by available tests, is not a fixed and unchanging characteristic. This observation is particularly true of tests administered in the preschool period. As the child's age increases, however, measured IQ becomes increasingly stable (Bloom, 1964). This does not necessarily mean that it then predicts academic success more accurately. In addition, a high correlation can still admit numerous individual exceptions. In other words, even though measured intelligence of children at

age 9 serves as a good predictor of IQ at age 15, a number of high-scoring nine-year-olds may score relatively low at fifteen. The opposite is equally true.

In practice, what these cautions mean is that teacher decisions based on test results should be tentative and subject to continual review; that students should not be labeled on the basis of limited and changing samplings of their behavior; and that, in short, good sense should prevail here as it should elsewhere.

DETERMINANTS OF INTELLIGENCE

Intelligence is like a disease: It doesn't just happen; it is caused. It is probably obvious that the causes of intelligence are also the causes of stupidity, for one is the absence of the other. The assumption that human characteristics result from the interplay of heredity and environment is discussed in Chapter 7. As we saw there, the debate has by no means ended, although a great deal of evidence has been gathered on both sides. Heredity versus environment is clearly no longer an either-or question.

The Rubber-Band Hypothesis

Probably one of the better analogies advanced to describe the relative influence of heredity and environment is Stern's rubber-band hypothesis. It compares innate potential for intellectual development to a rubber band. Intelligence at any time is reflected by the length of the band. Obviously, a short piece (poorer genetic background) can be stretched; with a great deal of effort it can be stretched a long way. The forces that exert the pull on the band, or that fail to, are environmental. Hence genetic and environmental forces interact in such a way that less environmental stimulation may be required for average development if genetic endowment is high. The reverse is also true. One of the functions of schools is to "stretch rubber bands" (see Figure 9.5).

In connection with the rubber-band hypothesis, research indicates that the band (manifested intelligence) can be stretched more easily at younger ages. Recall the Lee (1951) studies, mentioned in Chapter 7, which found that black children who had moved north at the youngest ages showed the least intellectual deficit relative to whites who had been born and brought up in more advantageous environments. Recall, too, Bloom's (1964) related assertion that the environment will have the most profound effect on a trait during its period of most rapid growth. The implication for educational practice points directly to the advisability of providing stimulating environments for children at the youngest possible age.

Additional evidence of the validity of these observations has been provided by Jensen (1977) in studies of decrements in measured IQ, apparently as a function of environmental impoverishment. Large samples of black and white schoolchildren in rural Georgia were tested between ages 5 and 18. Results indicated that measured verbal and nonverbal IQ declined significantly between ages 5 and 16 for children whose environments could be described as deprived. Children in more advantageous environments exhibited no comparable decrements. Jensen's explanation, labeled a *cumulative deficit* hypothesis, maintains simply that environmental deprivation has a progressive and cumulative effect on measured intelligence such that decrements in IQ increase with age. It might well be that in the same way that poor environments have a progressively deleterious effect, enriched environments have a progressively beneficial effect. Put more simply, a rubber band is easier to stretch when it is new and highly elastic; with increasing age, it becomes less elastic, perhaps more brittle, and apparently less susceptible to forces that might initially have served to stretch it.

Figure 9.5 The Stern hypothesis: Individuals with different inherited potentials for intellectual development (genetic endowment) can manifest below-average, average, or above-average intelligence as a function of environmental forces.

The Effect of Families

Some evidence suggests that family size and birth order are important factors in determining manifested intelligence of children. Many years ago, for example, Galton (1869) observed a preponderance of firstborn children among the great scientists that Britain had produced. Since then, many studies have revealed that firstborn and only children (who are necessarily also firstborn) speak more articulately and at a younger age than later-born children (Koch, 1955), score higher on measures of intellectual performance, have a higher need for achievement (Altus, 1967), perform better academically (Zajonc, 1976), and are more likely to attend college and to achieve eminence (Velandia, Grandon, and Page, 1978).

A closer examination of birth-order data suggests, however, that the contribution of birth order to such things as academic achievement or intelligence is negligible at best; at worst, birth order may make no contribution whatsoever. Following a massive investigation of 9,000 high-school graduates and their brothers and sisters (more than 30,000 subjects), Hauser and Sewell (1985) found that birth order made absolutely no difference. They did find, however, that size of "sibship" (number of brothers and sisters) has a negative impact on schooling. In other words, the larger the family, the more likely that academic achievement will be lower.

The relationship between family size and academic achievement, as well as that between family size and performance on intelligence tests, has been corroborated in a number of studies. In an attempt to explain these relationships, Zajonc (1975, 1976, 1986) and Zajonc and Markus (1975) suggest that one of the important influences on intellectual development is the intellectual climate of the home. Furthermore, they provide a simple formula, based on the **confluence model**, for determining the approximate intellectual climate of a home.

According to this model, each family member is assigned a value related to age: Parents are worth thirty points each; newborn infants, zero; and all other children, values that range between zero and thirty. The index of intellectual climate is then calculated by averaging values assigned to each individual in the family. For example, a firstborn child is born into an intellectual climate valued at thirty plus thirty (when there are two parents) plus zero (for the infant), divided by three (this equals twenty, for those whose calculators are not functioning). A child born later or born into a large family in which there are many young children would be born into a family with a lower index of intellectual climate. The Zajonc-Markus model predicts, simply, that measured intelligence for large groups will be related to the intellectual-climate index. And there is, in fact, some evidence that this is the case (see, for example, Grotevant, Scarr, and Weinberg, 1977).

Do these observations support the notion that family size and birth order are among the important influences on intelligence? Zajonc and Markus argue yes (1975); however, more recent analyses suggest that they are only partly correct.

Most evidence does not question the conclusion that family size correlates inversely with measured intelligence (larger families equals lower intelligence), although this correlation is not always very high or very general. What is often questioned, however, is whether the most important variable is family size. In one of several large-scale and systematic investigations of this type, Page and Grandon (1979) found pretty much the same correlations that Zajonc and Markus and others had previously reported. But they also found that when the variables of social class and race were included, correlations of these factors with manifested intelligence were even more significant than that of family size. Put more simply, in most studies that found a high correlation between family size, birth order, and intelligence, researchers did not consider the fact that large families tend to be more common in lower social classes, in certain ethnic minorities, and among those who are less well educated. And perhaps the "intellectual climate" in large families is more a function of ethnic, social, and educational variables than of family size per se.

The most reasonable conclusion at this point is probably that many variables are influential in determining intellectual development. Among the important variables are genetic forces (over which we have relatively little control) and such environmental variables as parent-child and sibling interactions. These environmental variables appear, in turn, to be influenced by factors such as family size, which also reflects ethnic and social variables.

Experience and Intelligence: A Debate

The most important question from an educator's point of view is, Can intelligence be *increased* through the manipulation of experience? A sample of the research relevant to this question, and relevant to the general nature-nurture question, is summarized below in the form of an imaginary debate between John Watson (a champion of environmentalism) and Francis Galton (who believed that intelligence is entirely inherited). The debate is replete with glaring anachronisms. In order to know all that they claim to know, Galton and Watson would both have to be over 100 years old.

Galton: My dear Watson, if you will simply open your mind to the problem, I can demonstrate for you beyond any doubt that heredity is the most powerful factor in development. As I said in 1869, "I have no patience with the hypothesis occasionally expressed, and often implied, especially in tales written to teach children to be good, that babies are born pretty much alike. . . ."

Watson: Give me a dozen . . .

Galton: You have said that before. Consider, if you will, the numerous twins studies that have been performed. As you know, **identical twins** are genetically exactly alike, whereas **fraternal twins** are as dissimilar as any two siblings. Burt's (1958) famous study shows that the intelligence-test scores of identical twins, whether reared together or apart, display considerably higher correlation than the scores of fraternal twins. I have no doubt that if we had more reliable measures of intelligence, the correlations would be higher still. Bloom (1964, p. 69) has summarized this study, along with four others. They all show the same thing.

Watson: Whoa now! That is a highly prejudiced interpretation. If you look at the Newman, Freeman, and Holzinger study (1937) — and that one too is included in Bloom's summary — if you look at that study, you'll see just where environment comes in. Why do you suppose it is that the correlation for twins reared together is *always* considerably higher than for twins reared apart? Ha! What do you say to that?

Galton: I say that studies involving the measurement of intelligence in people are highly suspect. Now take rats, for example.

Watson: That is irrelevant!

Galton: It is not! Now you just hold on and listen here for a minute. Tryon (1940) did a fascinating study and it will prove you wrong. Do you know it?

Watson: You mean Tryon's study?

Galton: Yes.

Watson: No.

Galton: I thought not. You don't read much, do you? You're just a popularizer. What Tryon did was take 142 rats and run them through a seventeen-unit maze nineteen times. The brightest rat made, I forget . . . about twenty errors [actually, he made exactly fourteen] and the dullest made 200 errors. [Again Galton is wrong. The dullest rat made 174 errors.] The brightest rats were then bred with each other, whereas the dull males were given dull females. That usually happens to people, too. Heh! Heh!

Well, after repeating the same procedure for only eight generations, a remarkable thing began to happen. The dullest rats in the bright group consistently made fewer errors than the brightest rats in the dull group. In other words, the brightest rats in the dull group were duller than the dullest rats in the bright group — or the dullest rats in the bright group were . . . you know. Imagine what we could do with people. John Humphrey Noyes would have done it if the American government hadn't outlawed polygamy. [John Humphrey Noyes set up a religious, communal, free-love group in Oneida, New York, in the late nineteenth century. He practiced selective breeding with the aim of producing a super-race, but had to disband the group when polygamy was outlawed in the 1880s.]

Watson: So that's the kind of ridiculous evidence you base your eugenic movement on. [*Eugenics* is the term given to the practice of selective breeding.] Let me tell *you* about a rat study, seeing as you're the one who brought it up. Hebb (1947) and Krech, Rosenzweig, and Bennett (1960, 1962, 1966) provide evidence that randomly selected rats can be significantly affected by environment. In the first case Hebb (1947) showed that rats reared as

pets did better than laboratory rats on maze tests. Krech, Rosenzweig, and Bennett (1962) even changed the brain chemistry of rats by enriching their environments. And if you don't think that's enough evidence, consider Heyns's (1967) work in South Africa. He's been affecting the intelligence of babies by using vacuum cleaners.

Galton: Whoa, there, whoa! Vacuum cleaners! You're going a little far.

Watson: That's what you think. It was reported in *Woman's Own* (Feb. 4, 1967).

Galton: You read *Woman's Own*?

Watson: My wife does. Anyway, what Heyns did was set up a decompression unit using a vacuum cleaner motor. He put this plastic bubble-like thing over the woman's abdomen and sucked the air out. It relieves all kinds of aches and pains and makes babies brighter, too.

Galton: It sounds like a gimmick to me. Jensen (1968) reviewed the research, and he concluded that there is a powerful genetic factor in the determination of intelligence.

Watson: Well, the optimistic point of view for a teacher to have is certainly mine. You can't do anything about genetics, but you can alter the environment . . . and that's what schools should be doing. That's what acceleration is and television for kids and books and . . .

Galton: Don't get carried away, Watson. Your point of view might be more optimistic, but it's less accurate. I'm a scientist, not a philosopher.

(The argument ends with Watson's wife calling him in to wash dishes.)

But the debate continues, although most scientists now believe that both heredity and environment are important, that their relative influences cannot easily be separated, and that the important question in any case is not *what* the effects of these factors might be, but rather *how* they affect intelligence (Anastasi, 1958).

All of which is far from simple.

Finally, it should always be kept in mind that the grand conclusions of social science are most often based on the average performance of large groups of individuals. Invariably within these groups are many individuals whose behavior contradicts the conclusion at every turn. In other words, there are geniuses among large families and among all social and ethnic groups, even as there are fools, morons, and idiots everywhere.*

CREATIVITY

A great deal of attention has been devoted to the subject of creativity in the past several decades, particularly following the work of J. P. Guilford (1950, 1959, 1962). However, the central question in creativity research and speculation—What is creativity?—remains largely unsolved. Few people agree on an answer.

While conversing with George Bernard Shaw, his biographer Stephen Winsten (1949) alluded to the proverbial "hair's breadth" that separates genius from madness: "The matter-of-fact man prefers to think of the creative man as defective, or at least akin to madness," Winsten said. To which Shaw replied, "Most of them are, most of them are. I am probably the only sane exception" (p. 103).

Although we no longer fear the creative person as openly as we might once have, uneasiness and uncertainty remain. Are creative people nonconformists, eccentrics, radicals, and fools—or are they ordinary people? The answer is probably that there are some of both, but that there really is no mystical or magical quality about creativity. Like intelligence, it is a quality of humans and of human behavior—a quality possessed by everyone. Just as very low

intelligence is stupidity, so very low creativity is ordinariness. There are few geniuses as identified by tests of intelligence; there are also few very highly creative people.

Creativity Defined

Creativity has been variously defined. The following are three of many possible definitions:

1. Creativity involves fluency, flexibility, and originality (Guilford, 1959).

2. Creativity is "the forming of associative elements into new combinations which either meet specified requirements or are in some ways useful. The more mutually remote the elements of the new combination, the more creative the process of solution" (Mednick, 1962, p. 221).

3. Creativity results in "a novel work that is accepted as tenable or useful or satisfying by a significant group of others at some point in time" (Stein, in Parnes and Harding [eds.], 1962, p. 86).

Consider these three cases:

1. René Choumard is a resident of a remote rural area. For the past three years he has been sitting on the porch of his dilapidated shack, knitting himself purple mittens with no thumbs. He talks to himself incessantly about everything he has ever seen or done. Is he creative?

2. Joseph Lalonde is René's neighbor. Joseph is the local wit. His humor is also local humor. His jokes are expressions of associations between extremely remote ideas. They are never funny. Is Joseph creative?

3. In the course of routine procedure in a laboratory, a scientist accidentally spills a small amount of chemical into a large vat filled with 700 gallons of sweet cream. The cream immediately turns into four cows

---

PPC: "Is the bear a cynic? Does he mean this?"
Author: "Older bears are often cynical."

(a reversal phenomenon). Is this scientist creative?

In the first case, René was creative according to Guilford. His behavior was original and he manifested remarkable verbal fluency and flexibility. He was not creative, however, according to Mednick and Stein. Joseph, in contrast, fulfilled Mednick's criteria for creativity — highly remote associations satisfying his own specifications. It could even be assumed that he was original, fluent, and flexible. But he did not produce anything "tenable or useful or satisfying." The scientist, however, did. Yet he did not behave in an original fashion, but rather in a clumsy fashion — nor did he make any remote associations whatsoever.

This discussion is intended to highlight the confusion that makes the assessment of creativity extremely difficult. The problem is partly resolved by accepting that *creativity* is, in fact, a global term, and that it does not necessarily represent only one event or quality. If we distinguish among the creative process, the creative product, and the creative person, many of the contradictions implicit in earlier formulations disappear. René, then, is a creative person who doesn't produce anything; Joseph uses a creative process, but also produces nothing creative; and the scientist neither is creative nor uses a creative process, but he produces something valuable.

These distinctions, although useful, solve only part of the problem because they are not reflected in current attempts to measure creativity. The inference continues to be made, at least implicitly, that creative personalities and processes can be judged on the basis of products that are deemed to be creative.

From an educational point of view, it is important to be able to define creativity in order to make it possible to identify and select students for special programs. Accordingly, many school systems lump together various categories such as *creative, talented,* and *gifted* under a single label (such as *talented and gifted* or simply

gifted) and provide specific criteria for identifying students who belong to this group. The most often used criterion is, not surprisingly, measured intelligence expressed in the form of an IQ — and the most common cutoff is 130; that is, all students whose measured IQ is 130 or more would qualify as gifted (Humphreys, 1985). (Programs for the gifted are reviewed briefly in the next chapter.)

There are a number of problems associated with defining creativity or giftedness solely (or even primarily) in terms of intelligence (Hoge, 1988). In the first place, as is shown in a later section, independent measures of creativity do not correlate at all well with measured intelligence. In the second place, given the rather unimpressive validity and reliability of our current intelligence tests, their use for selecting students for special programs is often unfair. On the other side of the coin, however, these tests may be considerably fairer than teachers who are forced to rely only on their intuitive judgments.

One interesting approach to defining creativity and giftedness is taken by Gardner (1983), who speaks of seven largely unrelated kinds of intelligence: linguistic, logical and mathematical, visual and spatial, musical, bodily-kinesthetic, interpersonal, and intrapersonal. He believes that creativity (or giftedness) can occur in any one of these domains and that it represents the highest level of functioning in each. Thus, it is possible to be highly gifted in one aspect but not in any other — as may be evident among the musically or the scientifically gifted. Wallach (1985) has a similar point of view, arguing that creativity can be manifested in excellence in any specific domain.

The argument that creativity is largely domain-specific is not shared by all researchers. Many believe that although giftedness is often manifested in one domain rather than another, there are certain general underlying qualities that make it possible for the creative person to be described as *generally* creative. And perhaps it is possible to measure these qualities.

Table 9.2   Sample answers and scoring procedure for one item from a test of creativity

Item	How many uses can you think of for a nylon stocking?
Answers	* wear on feet
	§†* wear over face
	* wear on hands when it's cold
	†* make rugs
	* make clothes
	§†* make upholstery
	†* hang flower pots
	* hang mobiles
	§†* make Christmas decorations
	†* use as a sling
	†* tie up robbers
	§†* cover broken windowpanes
	§†* use as ballast in a dirigible
	†* make a fishing net
Scoring	* Fluency: 14 (total number of different responses)
	† Flexibility: 10 (number of shifts from one class to another)
	§ Originality: 5 (number of responses that were unusual, or occurred less than 5 percent of the time in the entire sample)

Measuring Creativity

One of the simplest (and most unreliable) ways of identifying creative talent is to have teachers rate students. Gallagher (1960) cites research indicating that teachers miss approximately 20 percent of the most highly creative students. Another simple method is to have individuals rate themselves. Taylor and Holland (1964) suggest that this may be one of the most effective techniques.

A more popular method is that proposed by Guilford (1950) and developed by Torrance (1966, 1974). The *Torrance Tests of Creative Thinking* continue to be used in current research (see Diaz, 1983), although the volume of research on creativity appears to have declined dramatically since the late 1960s. These tests are based on the assumption that creative ability comprises several separate factors, among which are fluency, flexibility, and originality. Tasks have been designed that encourage the production of a variety of responses, which can then be scored in terms of these and other factors. One such test is the Unusual-Uses Test, in which subjects are asked to think of as many uses as they can for an ordinary object, such as a brick or a nylon stocking. Responses are counted to arrive at an index of fluency. Flexibility is measured by counting the number of shifts between classes of response. For example, a brick might be used for building a house, a planter, a road, and so on. Each response scores for fluency but not for flexibility. A shift from this category of uses to one involving throwing the brick would illustrate flexibility. Originality is scored on the basis of the number of responses that are either statistically rare or are

Measured Intelligence

	High	Low
Divergent Thinking (Creativity) — **High**	high control over their own behavior; capable of adult-like and child-like behavior	high internal conflict, frustration with school, feelings of inadequacy; can perform well in stress-free environment
Divergent Thinking (Creativity) — **Low**	addicted to school, strive desperately for academic success; well liked by teachers	somewhat bewildered by environment; defense mechanisms include intensive social or athletic activity; occasional maladjustment

Figure 9.6 Characteristics of children identified as high and low on measures of intelligence and of divergent thinking (creativity). Based on studies reported by Wallach and Kogan, 1965.

judged unusual by the experimenter. A statistically rare response might be one that occurs less than 5 percent of the time. (See Table 9.2.) A related test is the Product Improvement Test, which requires subjects to think of as many ways as possible to improve a toy that is shown to them.

THE CONNECTIONS BETWEEN CREATIVITY AND INTELLIGENCE

A classic study highlighting the distinction sometimes assumed to exist between creativity and intelligence is that reported by Getzels and Jackson (1962). They found that creative students were not necessarily the most intelligent, despite the fact that they achieved as well in school as those who were more intelligent. (Interestingly, however, the creative students were not as well *liked* by the teachers.) The study can be interpreted as implying that a relatively weak relationship exists between creativity and intelligence. It should be pointed out, however,

that the subjects were selected from a private high school in a large U.S. city. The mean IQ rating in that school was 132. The mean IQ for the group designated as "High Creative, Low IQ" was a more-than-respectable 127. With such a limited range in intelligence-test scores, it is doubtful that any relationship would be found, even if it existed. In addition, the general findings of the study are probably not generalizable beyond this highly select group.

A related study (Wallach and Kogan, 1965) also identified four groups of students classified as high or low on intelligence and creativity, respectively. The purpose of this study was to identify characteristics that might be different among the four groups. Results of the study are summarized in Figure 9.6. They indicate that highly creative but less intelligent students are most frustrated with school and that highly intelligent but less creative students are addicted to school and well liked by their teachers. Keep in mind, however, that these four groups represent extremes of measured intelligence and creativity. The vast majority of students are not extreme. In addition, these general descriptions of school adjustment and personality characteristics are just that — general descriptions. Even with groups as highly select as these, there are numerous individual exceptions.

No conclusive statements can yet be made concerning the correlation between creativity and intelligence. Torrance states, for example, that "if we were to identify children as gifted simply on the basis of intelligence tests, we would eliminate from consideration approximately 70 percent of the most creative" (1962, p. 5). A number of investigators, however, maintain that there is a high correlation between creativity and intelligence, as well as among creativity, playfulness, and fantasy (Kogan, 1983).

GUILFORD'S MODEL OF THE INTELLECT

J. P. Guilford's (1959, 1967) model of the intellect is an interesting and unusual representation of intellectual functioning. It is relevant both to intelligence and creativity. The model is organized around three main aspects of human functioning: **operations**, **products**, and **content**. A specific ability involves a combination of all three. There are 120 abilities (see Figure 9.7).

1. *Operations.* An operation is a major intellectual process. The term includes such activities as knowing, discovering, or being aware (cognition); retrieving from storage (memory); generating multiple responses (divergent thinking); arriving at a single, accepted solution (convergent thinking); and judging the appropriateness of information or decisions (evaluation).

2. *Content.* An operation is performed upon certain kinds of information. This information, or content, may be figural, symbolic, semantic, or behavioral. Figural content is concrete information, such as images. Symbolic content is information in the form of arbitrary signs, such as numbers or codes. Semantic content is information in the form of word meanings. And behavioral content is nonverbal information involved in human interaction — for example, emotion.

3. *Products.* Applying an operation to content yields a product — the form that information takes once it is processed. Products include single, segregated items of information (units); sets of items grouped by virtue of their common properties (classes); connections between items of information (relations); organizations of information (systems); changes of information (transformations); and extrapolations or predictions from information (implications).

The two operations that have stimulated the most research and interest are convergent and divergent thinking. These are also the two operations most closely related to creativity and intelligence. **Convergent thinking** involves producing one correct solution to a problem; it is a crucial factor in intelligence testing. **Divergent thinking** involves producing multiple solutions or hypotheses; it is central in the creative process. The phrase *divergent thinking* is often used as a synonym for *creative thinking*.

Guilford's model is another example of a theoretical position based on the assumption that intelligence is not a single trait but a collection of separate abilities. This viewpoint resolves the apparent contradiction among some of the studies that have examined the relationship between creativity and intelligence. If intelligence is defined in terms of the entire structure, and if creativity involves only some of the 120 abilities described in the model, it is inevitable that there should be some correlation between the two. At the same time, it is also

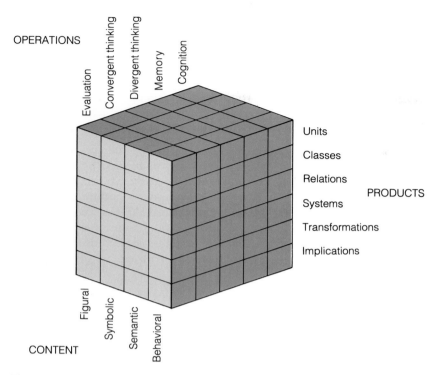

OPERATIONS

Evaluation
Convergent thinking
Divergent thinking
Memory
Cognition

Units
Classes
Relations
PRODUCTS
Systems
Transformations
Implications

Figural
Symbolic
Semantic
Behavioral

CONTENT

Figure 9.7 In Guilford's model, intelligence comprises 120 separate abilities, each of which represents a combination of a specific operation, content, and product.
From J. P. Guilford, "Three Faces of Intellect," *American Psychologist*, Vol. 14, 1959, pp. 469–479. Copyright 1959 by the American Psychological Association and reproduced by permission.

inevitable that this correlation will vary from very low to very high according to the individual's pattern of abilities.

Guilford's model of the intellect has a number of important implications for the teaching/learning process. To begin with, the model draws attention to both the complexity of intellectual processes and the variety of forms in which these processes can be expressed. By so doing, it highlights the crucial role that the instructional process can play in intellectual development. If, for example, teachers always require that students *remember* content as presented, then only memory operations are being emphasized. And if, as is often the case, only

semantic content is involved, then figural, symbolic, and behavioral content are being overlooked.

In short, consideration of this model makes it apparent that the classroom teacher and the educational process bear considerable responsibility for the intellectual development of students, and that this development may well be shortchanged if only the traditional, highly limited operations, products, and content are attended to. Although schools have traditionally fostered the development of a variety of abilities in children — providing repeated practice in psychomotor skills, mathematics, verbal skills, social skills, and so on — teachers have not always systematically attended to the development of some of the more complex abilities, such as those involved in creative thinking (divergent thinking), evaluating, arriving at implications, and so on. Programs designed to foster learning/thinking strategies are an attempt to correct this failure.

It is alarming to note that the school dropout rate of gifted adolescents is often higher than that of the general population (McMann and Oliver, 1988). There are a number of possible reasons for this, including the frustration that may result from the fact that school programs may not permit adequate expression and development of special abilities. In addition, Kanchier (1988) suggests that the expectations that gifted adolescents have of themselves — and that others have for them — may affect some of them negatively.

Current educational practice and beliefs typically insist that identifying and teaching those who have disabilities requires special training. But, it is sad to note, we are strangely ambivalent about what should be done to identify and teach those who are highly gifted.

There is an important distinction to be made between *inherent* and *functional* abilities. There may be many Raphaels, Da Vincis, Mozarts, and Einsteins unrecognized and undeveloped, disguised as ordinary people, totally unaware of their inherent abilities. Only in the right circumstances and with the right environmental demands will these talents become functional. And on a perhaps less glorious and less dramatic but no less important scale, it is largely to the extent that schools demand evaluation, implication, divergent thinking, and so on that these abilities will be transformed from inherent to functional.

MAIN POINTS

1. Intelligence generally implies a capacity for adapting well to the environment, but it is defined in different ways: in terms of what intelligence tests measure; as a global quality that governs our ability to act purposefully and rationally; as a two-component quality consisting of innate potential and current level of functioning; and as a three-component quality consisting of innate potential, current potential, and current level of functioning.

2. Cattell describes *fluid abilities* (basic, nonverbal, and unaffected by experience) and *crystallized abilities* (primarily verbal, highly influenced by culture and education). Crystallized abilities tend to increase with old age; fluid abilities are more susceptible to physiological disruption and tend to decline with age.

3. There are three basic views of intelligence: the psychometric (based on measurement concepts), the Piagetian (based on interaction between the person and the environment through assimilation and accommodation and resulting in the elaboration of cognitive structure), and the information-processing view (based on processes involved in knowing).

4. Sternberg's information-processing view of intelligence includes a contextual subtheory (intelligence is defined in terms of adaptation to a specific environmental context) and a componential subtheory. The three components that make up intelligence are metacomponents (executive processes involved in selecting cognitive activities, monitoring them, and evaluating their results), performance components (activities actually used in carrying out cognitive tasks), and knowledge-acquisition components (activities involved in acquiring new information).

5. A correlation coefficient is an index of relationship between variables. It is a function of covariation — not of causal relatedness. The ordinary index (r) varies from -1.00 to $+1.00$.

6. Intelligence tests typically correlate quite well with school achievement measurements, partly because both measure similar things (aptitude, achievement, and verbal sophistication). Intelligence tests are more general and emphasize the ability to apply skills and knowledge in new areas.

7. Conventional measures of intelligence do not measure innate capacity (except by inference); instead, they provide a measure of the extent to which the individual has profited from past learning experiences.

8. Among the limitations of intelligence tests and of the concept of IQ are the following: Tests are less than perfectly valid (do not always measure only what they purport to measure) or reliable (do not always measure consistently); previous achievement is an even better predictor of school success than is measured intelligence; intelligence tests typically do not tap a number of important qualities, such as interpersonal skills, creativity, and athletic ability; and many intelligence tests are biased against social and ethnic minorities.

9. Intelligence tests usually yield a score referred to as an *intelligence quotient* (IQ). It ranges from perhaps 50 to 160 on some tests. The average IQ of an average population is around 100.

10. Two types of instruments are commonly used to measure intelligence: group tests (usually of the paper-and-pencil variety; can be administered to large groups at one time) and individual tests (can be administered to only one person at a time). Individual tests require trained testers, consume a great deal of time, and are consequently far more expensive; however, they are also more valid and reliable for important educational decisions.

11. Widely used individual tests include the Peabody Picture Vocabulary Test–R, the revised Stanford–Binet, and the Wechsler scales.

12. The SOMPA (System of Multicultural Pluralistic Assessment), developed by Mercer, is a collection of ten measures relating to a medical model, a social-system model, and a pluralistic model. It attempts to assess biological and social normality and to derive an estimated learning potential (ELP) score on the basis of WISC-R scores normed on ethnic minority samples, taking into account important family variables.

13. Group intelligence tests include the Draw a Person Test, the Cognitive Abilities Test (CogAT), and the Otis-Lennon School Abilities Test.

14. Both creativity and intelligence appear to be a function of an interaction between heredity and environment. Family size and configuration also play a role, as do ethnic background and social class. None of these factors necessarily *cause* high or low intelligence; they are merely related to manifested intelligence.

15. The rubber-band hypothesis summarizes the relationship of heredity, environment, and intelligence by comparing innate potential for learning to a rubber band: It can be stretched by a good environment, but it will shrivel in a poorer environment. In this analogy, the final length of the band (after it has been stretched by experience) reflects measured intelligence.

16. Although birth order has sometimes been associated with intelligence and academic achievement (firstborns and only children are favored), the weight of the evidence suggests that observed effects are the result of family size and related social and ethnic factors rather than of birth order. Zajonc explains the observation of higher intelligence among individuals from smaller

families in terms of his *confluence model*, which describes the intellectual climate of the home in terms of its membership, with older individuals (parents and siblings) adding significantly to the intellectual climate of the home and younger children subtracting from it.

17. *Creativity* is defined in various, apparently contradictory ways. Much of the contradiction disappears when the creative product, process, and person are considered separately.

18. Creative, talented, and gifted individuals are often identified in terms of performance on measures of intelligence (for example, an IQ of 130 or more). Gardner suggests that there are seven unrelated kinds of intelligence (linguistic, logical and mathematical, visual and spatial, musical, bodily-kinesthetic, interpersonal, and intrapersonal) and that creativity is simply the highest level of functioning in any one (or more) of these domains.

19. Creativity can be measured by using teacher or pupil ratings or by using some of the tests developed for this purpose. Chief among these tests are the Torrance Tests of Creative Ability.

20. Creativity and intelligence may or may not be highly related. It is likely that relatively high intelligence is required for superior creative effort. Above a certain point, however, personality and social factors are probably more important than purely intellectual ones.

21. Guilford's model describes human intellectual functioning in terms of *operations* (major intellectual processes such as knowing and remembering), which are applied on *content* (cognitive information in the form of numbers, symbols, or words, for example) to yield a *product* (the result of processing information, describable in terms of forms such as units, classes, relations, or implications). The model yields 120 separate abilities.

22. *Divergent and convergent thinking* are two important operations in Guilford's model. Divergent thinking relates to creativity; convergent thinking is more closely related to the types of processes required for successful performance on intelligence tests.

23. Teachers and schools bear important responsibility for some aspects of intellectual development.

SUGGESTED READINGS

The following two books present an important information-processing view of intelligence:

STERNBERG, R. J. (1985). *Beyond IQ: A triarchic theory of human intelligence*. New York: Cambridge University Press.

STERNBERG, R. J. (1986). *Intelligence applied: Understanding and increasing your intellectual skills*. New York: Harcourt Brace Jovanovich.

For a sensitive look at giftedness and numerous practical suggestions for fostering excellence in the home and the school, see:

CLARK, B. (1983). *Growing up gifted: Developing the potential of children at home and at school* (2nd ed.). Columbus, Ohio: Merrill.

Current thinking and research in creativity are summarized in:

BRUCH, C. B., ET AL. (Eds.). (1981). *The faces and forms of creativity: Proceedings of the First National Conference on Creativity and the Gifted/Talented*, March 21–22, 1980, Houston, Texas. Ventura, Calif.: Ventura County Superintendent's Office.

Guilford's structure of intellect is described in the following article, which has been reprinted in countless books of readings and in his 1967 book:

GUILFORD, J. P. (1959). Three faces of intellect. *American Psychologist, 14*, 469–479.

GUILFORD, J. P. (1967). *The nature of human intelligence.* New York: McGraw-Hill.

A book that describes some common psychological tests and provides some interesting case studies is:

SIEGEL, M. G. (1987). *Psychological testing from early childhood through adolescence: A developmental and psychodynamic approach.* Madison, Conn.: International Universities Press.

A second book that provides detailed information on a variety of intelligence tests and other standardized tests is of particular value for teachers of exceptional children:

SATTLER, J. M. (1982). *Assessment of children's intelligence and special abilities* (2nd ed.). Boston: Allyn and Bacon.

During hibernation, all the metabolic processes are slowed to an absolute minimum. The animal is exceedingly torpid, and approaches death as closely as possible without actually dying. Bears do not truly hibernate, although they do "den-up" during severe weather   (Matthews, 1969).

ADAPTING TO STUDENT DIFFERENCES

How dull it is to pause, to make an end,
To rust unburnished, not to shine in use!
As tho' to breathe were life.

ALFRED, LORD TENNYSON *Ulysses*

Ah, yes! I wrote the "Purple Cow" —
I'm sorry, now, I wrote it!
But I can tell you anyhow,
I'll kill you if you quote it!

GELETT BURGESS *Burgess Nonsense Book, The Purple Cow*

PREVIEW   Teachers too often define their roles as involving little more than is explicit in prescribed curricula. They see themselves as sources of information and students as the recipients. Chapter 6 urged a greater recognition of the student as a person and highlighted the importance of teacher behaviors and attitudes in the student's development of self-concepts and attitudes. This chapter presents specific suggestions for increasing the basic abilities, skills, and attitudes that are inherent in creativity and intelligence. Although the fundamental psychological characteristics of creativity and intelligence probably cannot be taught directly (intelligence cannot be *taught*), certain behaviors and attitudes that relate to the characteristics *can* be. In addition, this chapter looks at individual differences as they are reflected in exceptionality and at their implications for the classroom teacher.

■   *"Suppose," my father said, "suppose you have a wild cow . . . no, make that a demented goose. . . ." Some of us chuckled a bit, squirming forward in our seats to get closer and not miss anything. My father often began his lessons that way, especially when we were hot and sweaty and unsettled from recess. All he had to say was something like "suppose" — a rich word, pregnant with implications — and we would collectively draw a quick breath and listen for what was to come next. And when, in the same short sentence, he would wave in front of us an image like that of a wild cow or a demented goose, he had us — attention riveted, unwavering.*

"A demented, cross-eyed goose," he continued.

"A goose with a completely unnatural passion for Ford cars." Robert tittered suddenly, loudly, perhaps knowing or suspecting something about demented geese or unnatural passions of which the rest of us were not yet aware.

"Now suppose this crazed goose is flying along at 30 miles an hour and looks down and sees that he just happens to be over a nice Ford that's going in the same direction, only at 20 miles an hour. Well, the goose is tempted to go right down and get closer to this Ford." Robert tittered once more.

"But," my father continued, "when the goose looks out in the distance with his crossed eyes, he sees another Ford exactly 120 miles away. The second Ford is coming directly toward the first one at a steady speed of 40 miles an hour.

"Well, our mad goose immediately leaves the first Ford and flies directly toward the second one at 30 miles an hour; and when he gets to the second Ford, he remembers the first, changes his mind, and turns right around. Without slowing down a bit, he flies right back to the first Ford. Well, as I told you, this goose is a little strange, so when he gets back to the first Ford, he turns around again and flies right back to the second, always at 30 miles an hour and always without slowing down — back and forth and back and forth, honking insanely and looking in both directions at once with his crossed eyes, until finally the two fine Fords run right smack into each other!

"The question is," my dad announced into the expectant silence — and we knew that we had again been seduced into a math problem — "the question is, how far will that goose have flown before the two cars run into each other?"

Stan raised his hand at once. "I know the answer! Can I tell it?"

"Just write it down and hand it to me." We knew that Stan's answer would be correct, although I couldn't understand how he could have figured it out so fast. Most of the rest of us struggled with the problem, writing numbers, dividing, multiplying, drawing lines, trying to figure out how many turns the goose would make, how much shorter each one would be. For his part, Robert drew exquisite replicas of two Ford cars, one in each of the bottom corners of a sheet of paper. Then he sketched a clearly delirious cross-eyed goose in one upper corner, drew a line from that corner to the other, curved the line down and back part of the way, curved it back again (but a shorter distance this time), and continued doing this, back and forth, until he had drawn what looked like a continuous series of diminishing S's down to the bottom center of the page. He then measured this line with a ruler and a string and announced, "Three hundred and seventy-four miles—give or take a few." There was something about demented geese that Robert apparently did not know. ▬

THE TALENTED AND
THE GIFTED

"That is an excellent goose!" my dad announced. He seemed truly proud, as if he were somehow responsible for the fact that Robert could draw and paint so well. "May I show it to the others, even if the goose didn't fly quite 374 miles?"* And even Robert was proud. One of my father's greatest gifts as a teacher was that he recognized gifts and talents in others, and that he encouraged those attributes and made their owners feel proud.

Education does not always recognize giftedness and talent. One of the problems is that historically, with some notable exceptions, most school jurisdictions have not offered special programs for gifted children. And those

that have were never quite certain about which children to include in these programs. As Adamson (1983) notes, our "fuzzy" concept of giftedness might include superior academic achievement, high measured intelligence, exceptionally rapid learning, evidence of a single extraordinary ability or talent, or combinations of these.

Giftedness Defined

The concept of giftedness was clarified somewhat in 1969, following the passage of U.S. Public Law 91-230. A section of this law (Section 806) relates directly to the gifted and talented and includes the following definition:

Gifted and talented children are those . . . who by virtue of outstanding abilities are capable of high performance. These are children who require differentiated educational programs and/or services beyond those normally provided by the regular school programs in order to realize their contribution to society.

The law goes on to state that capacity for high performance may be defined in terms of demonstrated achievement and/or potential for achievement in one or more of the following aptitudes and abilities:

1. General intellectual ability

2. Specific academic aptitude

3. Creative or productive thinking

4. Leadership ability

5. Visual and performing arts

6. Psychomotor ability

Estimates are that somewhere between 3 and 5 percent of the school population might be considered gifted on the basis of these criteria (Marland, 1972). However, special programs are provided for nowhere near this proportion of students.

Defining giftedness and establishing criteria for admission to this group is particularly important when special programs are available

---

*PPC: "How far *did* the goose fly?"
Author: "I don't remember. But I could figure it out. Now, to reach the second Ford the first time . . ."

for gifted and talented children. The definition and criteria we use determine which children will be eligible for special programs. By the same token, they determine which children are *not* eligible — that is, they implicitly label a large group of children "not gifted." There are, as Hoge (1988) notes, important ethical and equity issues here, particularly in light of the fact that there are serious problems with the procedures used to identify gifted children.

In practice, those who are gifted are typically identified through their performance on group intelligence tests, through teacher nominations — usually as a function of superior achievement in schools — and perhaps through an individual intelligence test. But a great deal of ambiguity and confusion surrounds the use of intelligence tests. As we saw in Chapter 9, what these tests measure isn't entirely clear; what we do know is that they tell us very little about some important things, such as motivation, persistence, and other personality variables. And they don't measure very accurately.

In effect, then, what happens in practice with respect to identifying gifted children often does not reflect official definitions of giftedness. In the majority of cases, general intellectual ability and academic achievement are taken into consideration, but these are only two of the six criteria identified by U.S. Public Law 91-230. Although special talents and abilities in the other four criteria (creative ability, leadership qualities, talents in visual and performing arts, and psychomotor ability) may influence teacher nominations, they are seldom part of formal identification procedures.

Many researchers have attempted to develop assessment procedures and definitions of giftedness that reflect these concerns, Renzulli (1986), for example, defines giftedness in terms of a variety of characteristics. Renzulli's *Scale for Rating Behavioral Characteristics of Superior Students* gives teachers a preliminary instrument for identifying gifted and talented students. Such instruments are essential if teachers and administrators are to identify candidates for special programs fairly and adequately.

Programs for the Gifted

Subsequent to the passage of PL 91-230, a massive survey of programs for the gifted and talented was undertaken in the United States. The survey, which involved thousands of parents and educators, revealed several things. One was that the education of the gifted and talented was typically perceived as a very low-priority issue: Only twenty-one states had any legislation to provide facilities for the gifted, and in most cases this legislation represented intent rather than concrete action. Another revelation was that those programs that did exist typically did not reach the gifted and talented from ethnic and social minorities, and that there were some serious problems in identifying the gifted and talented (Marland, 1972).

A similar survey, conducted some six years after the passage of PL 91-230, found that all but eight states had some type of legislation concerning programs for the gifted and talented. However, the majority of states still provide services to relatively small numbers of children in this category. In fact, only eight states have programs for more than half of their gifted and talented children — a situation that may be attributed to lack of funding, lack of trained personnel, and lack of widely accepted procedures and criteria for identifying the gifted and talented (Council for Exceptional Children, 1978). Sadly, an observation made by Terman et al. (1925) over six decades ago might still be true today: When comparing potential and achievement, we find that the most "retarded" group in our schools is the highly gifted.

There are two approaches to educating the gifted: **acceleration** and **enrichment**. The terms are essentially self-explanatory. Programs that *accelerate* simply move students more rapidly through the conventional curriculum, exposing them to the same material as other students. Programs that *enrich* provide gifted students with additional and different school experiences in an attempt to deepen and broaden their knowledge and capabilities.

The enrichment approach is well illustrated by Renzulli's (1977) *enrichment triad model*, also called the *revolving door model* (Renzulli, Reis, and Smith, 1981). This model advocates selecting gifted individuals on the basis of three characteristics: high academic ability, high creative potential, and high motivation. No rigorous cutoff scores are used; instead, all students whose achievement or apparent potential places them in the upper 25 percent of students in the school are designated as talented. Any of these students may then enter enrichment programs, and drop out of them, as they wish (hence the "revolving door"). The programs vary according to the expressed interests of the students. When they identify a project and commit themselves to it, they are allowed to enter a resource room and work on the project.

The acceleration approach is perhaps best illustrated by Stanley's (1976) *radical acceleration model*, developed primarily for students gifted in mathematics. It attempts to compress the ordinary curriculum so as to enable gifted individuals to master a course of studies in a fraction of the time ordinarily required. Subsequently, many of these accelerated youngsters are enrolled in university-sponsored courses for additional acceleration.

The relative merits of acceleration and enrichment have long been debated among educators. One of the most common arguments against acceleration is that it might be harmful to move students much beyond their social and psychological levels of development. Educators have been concerned that one of the effects of accelerating gifted students might be that they would eventually no longer "fit in" socially with their peers — a possibility that might have harmful consequences. Interestingly, the most common argument *for* enrichment is precisely the argument used *against* acceleration; that is, educators simply assume that enrichment will not have the same social and psychological implications as acceleration. After all, enrichment does not remove gifted children from their age and grade levels as does acceleration; it simply provides them with an opportunity to deepen and broaden their knowledge at each level.

Horowitz and O'Brien (1986) point out that research has not yet established that one of these methods is superior to the other. It does seem clear, however, that most acceleration programs do not lead to negative social or emotional consequences (Janos and Robinson, 1985). And it may well be that the best programs are sufficiently flexible that they can include both acceleration and enrichment according to the needs of the learners.

Torrance (1986) describes a number of additional approaches to the education of creative and gifted learners, some primarily involving enrichment, others emphasizing acceleration. One approach is **mentoring**, a procedure whereby gifted students are given the opportunity to develop a special relationship with an individual who serves as a sort of intellectual and psychological guide. In one investigation of creativity, Torrance (1984) found that students who had mentors benefited significantly in terms of creative achievement.

Another approach to the education of the gifted involves self-directed and independent study, often using learning/thinking strategies of the kind mentioned in Chapter 5. Some self-directed study programs use **individual education plans** (IEPs), individually designed for students according to their special needs and talents. IEPs are widely used for learning-disabled children, their use having been mandated in the United States by a 1975 law (PL 94-142). Torrance (1986) notes that IEPs are becoming more popular for use with gifted children, for whom the plans usually involve a combination of approaches and materials such as self-directed study, mentoring, enrichment, perhaps acceleration, and programs for development of learning/thinking strategies and motivation.

In addition to these approaches to the education of the gifted, a number of schools cater solely to these children, as do Saturday and summer programs and a variety of community or university enrichment programs. Some of their offerings can sometimes be included in IEPs designed for gifted children.

In spite of these special programs, many gifted and talented children — like many whose gifts and talents are *less* than average — are in regular classrooms and lack access to any formal "special" education. This does not mean, however, that there is nothing that teachers of regular classrooms can (or should) do for them. In fact, as we discuss later in this chapter, mainstreaming legislation now makes it mandatory for many children who would otherwise receive special instruction to spend most of their time in regular classrooms. It has therefore become necessary for teachers in regular classrooms to learn about exceptionality and about what they can do for these children. Many of the suggestions included in this chapter are appropriate for both ordinary students and for those who are more extraordinary.

PROMOTING CREATIVITY

An assumption implicit in this chapter is that being creative is a good thing. The validity of this assumption is not usually questioned. It is true, nevertheless, that were it not for our tendency to create, to innovate, and to change, much of the social unrest characteristic of this age and many of our more serious national and international problems would not exist. At the same time, however, were it not for our creativity, we would still be living in caves and killing wild animals to survive (or being killed by them). As the world's problems multiply, the need for creativity becomes ever more pressing and more apparent — as does the need for teachers to learn how schools can contribute to the development of creativity in students.

After you have been teaching for a while, it might be a good idea to pause and ask yourself what it is that you have been teaching. If you are honest (as most teachers are), you will prob-

ably find that you have been teaching information relating to one or more conveniently labeled and categorized bodies of knowledge that we call subjects, and perhaps a number of practical skills such as reading, writing, and manipulating numbers. You might also note that some of your students, some of the time, have also begun to learn how to understand and appreciate, how to analyze and synthesize. Some will show signs of being able to compare and summarize, will perhaps even know how to interpret and criticize, find and test assumptions, and observe and classify.

Sadly, however, unless you are one of those rare teachers who have taken pains to work toward these ends, or unless you are part of one of the many ongoing experimental projects designed to develop learning/thinking strategies (see Chapter 5), most of this learning will have occurred incidentally — almost accidentally. In spite of the fact that we have long paid lip service to the desirability of developing creative and thinking skills in students, schools have paid little attention to programs deliberately designed to foster these skills. In fact, we have naively assumed that the abilities involved in creating and thinking are largely innate. Worse yet, we have assumed that systematic exposure to increasingly large bodies of information and increasingly difficult problems and concepts would automatically develop the ability to think. With respect to creativity, we have been less certain; we have preferred, instead, to assume that some have it and others don't. At the same time, we have assumed that the worst thing a teacher might do with respect to creativity is to stifle it, and that the best thing a teacher might do is *not* stifle it.

But there *are* specific things teachers can do to foster creative thinking. Interestingly, many relevant programs and suggestions were first developed in industry, which has long been concerned with creativity. Its emphasis, however, has been less on the development of creative *people* than on the production of creative *things* or *ideas*. Fortunately, the techniques that have been shown to contribute to creative production also seem to enhance creativity in people. Next we examine some of these techniques.

Brainstorming

The most common group approach for solving problems creatively is probably Alex Osborn's (1957) **brainstorming**. This is a technique based on the principle of deferred evaluation — in essence, producing a wide variety of solutions while deliberately suspending judgment about the appropriateness of any of them. This is an extremely difficult thing for inexperienced problem solvers to do, but it seems to be highly conducive to production of creative ideas. Parnes (1962) reports, for example, that individuals working alone produce from 23 to 177 percent more good-quality solutions when deferring judgment than when simply following instructions to "produce good ideas." Delaying evaluation allows much greater scope in the responses emitted. Evaluation during production has a dampening effect on both groups and individuals.

In a brainstorming session, several rules are followed closely:

1. Criticism of a contributed idea is absolutely barred (deferred evaluation).

2. Modification or combination with other ideas is encouraged.

3. A large quantity of ideas is sought.

4. Unusual, remote, or wild ideas are sought.

A brainstorming session may last for two or more hours. It usually involves anywhere from five to twelve people who often come from a wide variety of backgrounds. If the members of the group are new to brainstorming, the leader begins by explaining the procedural rules. The specific problem of concern is then described for the group, and the session begins. Ideally, it is a free-wheeling, wide-ranging affair, with ideas coming very rapidly from all sources. All forms of evaluation are forbidden. Evaluative comments such as "that sounds good" or "no, that won't work," ridicule, laughter, or nonverbal expressions of either admiration or disgust are stopped immediately. Habitual offenders may even be removed from the group.

During the course of a brainstorming session, a number of specific aids to creativity are used. The most common of these are lists of ways to deal with problems. Parnes (1967) has adapted one such list from Osborn's (1957) book. The items in Parnes's list, including examples of responses to a general classroom discipline problem, is presented below. The examples are not necessarily solutions; they are the kind of suggestions that might be offered in a brainstorming session.

1. *Put to other uses.* The class might be used as something other than a learning situation. For example, it might be given the responsibility of entertaining the school at a social evening.

2. *Adapt.* Adaptation involves using ideas from other sources; perhaps the class could be run like a factory, like a prison, or like a playground.

3. *Modify.* Modification suggests changing the composition of the class, changing teaching methods, or changing the approach to discipline problems. This list could suggest possible forms for changes to take.

4. *Magnify.* Class size could be increased, as could number of teachers, number of as-signments, or magnitude of punishment or reinforcement.

5. *"Minify."* Class size could be decreased, as could number of assignments, number of reprimands, or number of school days.

6. *Substitute.* A new teacher might be substituted, the entire class might be exchanged, or a few members of the class might be replaced by students from other classes.

7. *Rearrange.* The physical setup of the room could be changed, or the seating plan could be rearranged to separate troublemakers. Perhaps the desks should all face the rear.

8. *Reverse.* The previous idea came one point too early. However, the teacher might face the front as a sort of reversal. Another reversal would be to have the students take turns teaching.

9. *Combine.* A combination of the previous suggestions might provide a solution. Or the teaching/learning function might possibly be combined with other functions, such as entertainment, problem solving, or discussion of noncurricular topics of interest.

Several other lists have been developed. All are designed to stimulate the production of ideas. If the brainstorming session slows down, the leader will often make suggestions based on such a list: "How can we modify this?" "Magnify it?" — and so on. The suggestions are evaluated only after the session.

Research has shown that simply by being involved in brainstorming sessions, people may increase their scores on tests designed to measure creativity (Anderson, 1959; Haefele, 1962).

The uses to which brainstorming can be put in a classroom are infinite. Quite apart from facilitating creative behavior, it can be used to solve numerous day-to-day classroom problems, particularly in this age of participatory democracy. There is no reason why students and teachers cannot or should not use it to produce suggestions for planning courses and assignments, for conducting social and athletic events, or for involving themselves in local, national, and international projects.

The Gordon Technique

A slight modification of brainstorming, the **Gordon technique**, is based on the work of William J. J. Gordon (1961), who developed a process called "operational creativity." The major difference between the Osborn and the Gordon approaches is that the former presents the participants with a complete, detailed problem, often before the session itself, whereas the latter presents them only with an abstraction. For example, if the problem is one of parking cars in New York, the leader of a Gordon group might begin by saying, "The problem today is one of storing things. How many ways can you think of for storing things?" I have used this example as an illustration in several classes. Below is a list of some ways in which college students responded to this question:

1. Put them in bags.
2. Pile them up.
3. Put them in rows.
4. Can them.
5. Put them on hangers.
6. Convey them on belts to storage areas.
7. Cut them up.
8. Fold them.
9. Put them in your pocket.
10. Put them in boxes.
11. Disassemble them.
12. Put them on shelves.

After a time, the leader of the group begins to narrow the problem down. The next step might be to say, "The things to be stored are quite large." Later, more restrictions will be specified: "The objects cannot be folded or cut up," and so on.

One advantage of the Gordon technique is that presenting an extreme abstraction of a problem may lead to many ideas that would not ordinarily be considered for solutions — such as, for example, the idea of storing cars by hanging them. The idea of hanging would probably not come easily in relation to parking cars; but in relation to the question of storing things, it is a relatively ordinary suggestion. Consider, also, the idea of moving objects to storage areas on conveyer belts. This one might have merit!

Morphological Analysis

This procedure, described by Osborn (1957) and Arnold (1962), was originated by Fritz Zwicky of Aero-Jet Corporation. It involves dividing a problem into a number of independent variables, thinking of as many potential solutions as possible for each one, and then combining the results in all possible ways. Arnold illustrates **morphological analysis** using the problem of developing a new type of vehicle. Three different aspects of this problem are (1) the type of vehicle, (2) the type of power, and (3) the medium in which the vehicle will be

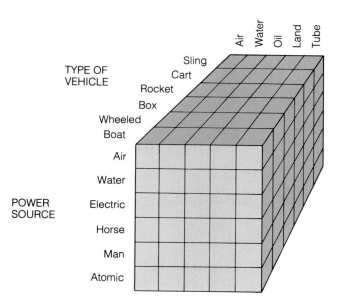

MEDIUM

TYPE OF VEHICLE

Sling
Cart
Rocket
Box
Wheeled
Boat

Air
Water
Electric
Horse
Man
Atomic

POWER SOURCE

Air Water Oil Land Tube

Figure 10.1   A model of morphological analysis for the "problem" of developing a new vehicle. One hundred eighty possible "solutions" are shown.

used. Each of these aspects lends itself to various solutions. For example, the type of vehicle might be a cart, a sling, a rocket, a box, and so on. Figure 10.1 presents 180 possible solutions for the problem; there are thousands more. Some of these have already been invented; some are completely impractical; others might be worth pursuing. Imagine, for example, a sling-type vehicle, drawn by horses, going through oil; or imagine an atomic-powered rocket going through a tube.

CNB Method

Haefele (1962) describes what he calls the *collective notebook* (CNB) method, which can be used in a factory (or probably anywhere else). It consists of presenting a problem, together with some possible solutions, on the first page of several notebooks. These notebooks are then distributed to everyone in the factory. As individuals arrive at possible solutions for the problem, they write them down or diagram them in their books. At the end of a specified period of time, the notebooks are collected and potential solutions are evaluated. The originators of worthwhile ideas are rewarded.

One argument advanced in favor of the notebook method is that it allows more time for incubation. Worthwhile ideas may occur to people at strange times—sometimes in the middle of the night, in the bathtub, in court, or even in school. If a person has a notebook handy, the pearl may be recorded for posterity.

CBB Method

The *collective bulletin board* (CBB) method is a combination of brainstorming and the CNB method designed for use in a classroom.

One of the major advantages of group brainstorming over an individual method such as the CNB is that it allows members of the group to profit from one another's ideas. One of its major disadvantages is that the more vocal and uninhibited members of the group will often monopolize the proceedings. The collective bulletin board allows individuals to benefit from one another's ideas in an environment that is more conducive to expressing their own ideas. It consists of placing a description of a problem and possible solutions on a bulletin board in a classroom, rather than placing them in a notebook. Students are then encouraged to add their own solutions to the board and to adapt the ideas already on it. The CBB method was used over a ten-week period with two different classes. At the end of that time, participants in the CBB program did significantly better on tests of creative thinking than did comparable control groups (Lefrançois, 1965).

Lateral Thinking

According to de Bono (1970), if you want to dig a hole deeper, it is necessary to dig vertically. If, however, the object is to have a hole that, so to speak, covers different ground, then you have to dig laterally. In the same way, if the object is

to discover more about something or to arrive at a conventional, accepted, "convergent" solution to a problem, **vertical thinking** is entirely appropriate; but if the object is to find unusual, divergent, creative solutions for problems, **lateral thinking** is indicated. de Bono argues that lateral thinking is a way of using the mind that *leads* to creative thinking and to creative solutions, but that it is not the same thing as creative thinking. He maintains that although lateral thinking is closely related to insight, creativity, and humor, these last three can only be prayed for, whereas lateral thinking can be developed deliberately. Accordingly, he has devised a program for teaching lateral thinking, as well as one designed just to teach thinking (de Bono, 1976).

Unlike brainstorming and other techniques designed to foster creative behavior, de Bono's program for teaching lateral thinking does not require students to solve specific problems; instead, it encourages them to develop new ways of approaching all problems. More precisely, it attempts to teach lateral rather than vertical approaches. Many of the exercises in de Bono's program are similar to items used on various tests of creativity. Students might be presented with various geometric designs, for example, and asked to describe them in as many ways as possible. Other activities are designed to encourage students to ask why, to suspend judgment, to identify and challenge assumptions, to brainstorm, to produce analogies, and so on.

Throughout, emphasis is on creating new ideas and challenging old ones, but care is taken to assure that the learner does not overemphasize the negation of the old. Negation, de Bono says, is one of the principal techniques in vertical thinking, for such "logical" thinking is based on negation and selection, with the major role being played by rejection — hence, the centrality of a word such as *no* in logical (vertical) thinking.

Lateral thinking does not have a central word — that is, it didn't. In addition to offering a large number of exercises, de Bono also presents his students with a new word, *po*, intended to be to lateral thinking what *no* is to vertical thinking. The word *yes* is clearly unsuitable, for it implies uncritical acceptance. But the word *po* is entirely suitable; it means nothing and everything. It is a word that permits us to do or say anything, a word that requires no justification, a word that, in de Bono's words, is the laxative of language and thinking. More simply, *po* is neither an affirmation nor a negation; it is simply an invitation to think laterally. As such, it is an invitation to examine, challenge, modify, combine, brainstorm, or analogize. *Po* might have some place in your teaching.

IMPLICATIONS OF RESEARCH ON PROMOTING CREATIVITY

The preceding section has discussed various techniques developed largely in industry and designed specifically to lead to the production of ideas of real and immediate industrial value. One fairly obvious implication of this work is that the techniques themselves are valuable and could be a part of instruction in problem solving, perhaps even in elementary grades. A second, less obvious implication is that creative

behavior in students can be increased by having them participate in creative problem-solving exercises. (See the suggested readings at the end of this chapter for helpful references.)

Clearly, however, encouraging creativity in students needs to go far beyond occasionally making use of specific techniques developed for this purpose. Lowe (1983) suggests that creative teaching and learning stem from a belief in the importance of self-initiated learning, from flexible and nonauthoritarian instructional methods, and from approaches that value reasoning, questioning, and the manipulation of ideas and materials. More generally, creativity is fostered by teachers who have an attitude that recognizes and encourages individuality and creativity in students, by a culture that rewards rather than punishes those who produce with originality, and by a classroom climate that promotes rather than stifles expressions of creativity.

Classroom Climate and Creativity

A question of immediate practical interest for educators is the extent to which the atmosphere of a classroom relates to creative behavior in students. In one of several studies that have dealt with this question directly, Haddon and Lytton (1968) contrasted two types of schools, which they labeled *formal* and *informal*. The formal schools were characterized by an authoritarian approach to learning and teaching, whereas the informal schools tended to emphasize self-initiated learning and greater student participation. Not surprisingly, students in informal schools consistently did better on measures of creative thinking than did students of comparable intelligence and socioeconomic status who attended the formal schools.

One important aspect of classroom climate is the extent to which students perceive school activities as cooperative or competitive. In this connection, Adams (1968) reports that students tested under noncompetitive conditions scored higher on tests of spontaneous flexibility than did those tested under competitive conditions.

Further, if the examiner was warm and receptive, students did even better. These findings have since been corroborated in a large number of more recent studies, twenty-eight of which are reviewed and summarized by Slavin (1980). Among other things, the studies indicate that cooperative teaching methods (in which students work in small groups and receive rewards based on group rather than individual performance) lead to "increased student achievement, positive race relations in desegregated schools, mutual concern among students, student self-esteem, and other positive outcomes" (p. 315). (See Chapter 6 for a detailed discussion of cooperative learning.)

Teacher Attitudes and Creativity

Some evidence suggests that humanistically oriented approaches to teaching are more likely to lead to creativity among students. Research reviewed in Chapter 6, for example, indicates that open education often leads to higher creativity scores, but it also often leads to lower scores on standardized achievement tests. Similarly, Turner and Denny (1969) found that warm, spontaneous, and caring teachers are more likely to encourage creative behavior in their students than are teachers characterized as highly organized and businesslike.

It should be kept in mind, however, that humanistic concerns and attitudes are not clearly and irrevocably incompatible with businesslike approaches to learning. The important variables are probably not specific teaching methods so much as teacher attitudes and other personality characteristics.

Torrance (1962) gives a list of suggestions for teacher attitudes and behaviors designed to promote creativity in students. Consider how each might be implemented in the classroom:

1. Value creative thinking.

2. Make children more sensitive to environmental stimuli.

3. Encourage manipulation of objects and ideas.

4. Teach how to test each idea systematically.

5. Develop tolerance of new ideas.

6. Beware of forcing a set pattern.

7. Develop a creative classroom atmosphere.

8. Teach children to value their creative thinking.

9. Teach skills for avoiding peer sanctions.

10. Give information about the creative process.

11. Dispel the sense of awe of masterpieces.

12. Encourage self-initiated learning.

13. Create "thorns in the flesh" (that is, awareness of problems).

14. Create necessities for creative thinking.

15. Provide for active and quiet periods.

16. Make available resources for working out ideas.

17. Encourage the habit of working out the full implications of ideas.

18. Develop *constructive* criticism — not just criticism.

19. Encourage the acquisition of knowledge in a variety of fields.

20. Develop adventurous-spirited teachers.

In contrast with these behaviors and attitudes that might foster creativity, Hallman (1967) lists some common inhibitors of creativity:

1. Pressure to conform

2. Authoritarian attitudes and environments

3. Rigid teacher personality

4. Ridicule and sarcasm

5. Overemphasis on evaluation

6. Excessive quests for certainty

7. Hostility toward divergent personalities

8. Overemphasis on success

9. Intolerance of play attitudes

It follows that if these behaviors discourage creativity, then their opposites might promote it. This list suggests what *not* to do — as opposed to Torrance's list, which suggests what a teacher *should* do. Both, taken in combination, can serve as useful guides for teacher behavior.

Conceptual Models and Creativity

Education, we argued in Chapter 1, must do far more than simply teach facts and procedures. Students should not only learn; they should also learn *how* to learn. Although they need to accumulate facts and formulas, they should also grow in their ability and in their willingness to think. One of the grand goals of all education, we insisted, is to *empower* students; that is, students should be given the skills, the attitudes, and the information that will enable them to deal most effectively with life — that will *empower* them to solve their problems (as well as yours and mine).

To be truly empowered, students must also be creative. Mayer (1989) asks the question, "What can be done to empower students to be creative when they are faced with problems?" (p. 43). One important answer, he claims, can be found in the use of conceptual models as an instructional technique.

A conceptual model is a verbal or graphic presentation designed to assist the learner in developing a clear and useful mental representation of whatever is being studied. It is, as Mayer (1989) puts it, a special form of advance organizer of the kind we discussed in connection with Ausubel's theory (see Chapter 4).

Figure 10.2 is an example of a conceptual model that includes the most important elements required to understand how radar functions. Students who were allowed to examine this model for one minute before a short lecture

1. TRANSMISSION: A pulse travels from an antenna.

2. REFLECTION: The pulse bounces off a remote object.

3. RECEPTION: The pulse returns to the receiver.

4. MEASUREMENT: The difference between the time out and the time back tells the total time traveled.

5. CONVERSION: The time can be converted to a measure of distance because the pulse travels at a constant speed.

Figure 10.2   A conceptual model of how radar functions.
Adapted from R. E. Mayer (1989), "Models for Understanding." *Review of Educational Research, 59,* 1, 43–64. Copyright 1989 by the American Educational Research Association. Reprinted by permission of the publisher.

on radar later recalled 57 percent more of the important concepts than did students who had been given the lecture without the model. Perhaps more important, students who had examined the conceptual model were able to produce 83 percent more correct solutions for problems that required *transferring* what they had learned to new situations. Put another way, these students were able to use what they had learned *creatively* in the sense that they could then apply it to new situations.

Mayer (1989) cites a number of other studies that support the argument that conceptual models significantly increase students' creative solutions of problems not presented in the initial lesson. In addition, models of this kind increase recall of important concepts, although they tend to decrease rote, or verbatim, recall. Like Ausubel's advance organizers, conceptual models provide the learner with important concepts that organize previous learning and that provide essential elements of cognitive structure to which new material can be related.

From the teacher's point of view, it is important to know both how to devise models and which models are most likely to be effective. Mayer (1989) describes a number of characteristics of good conceptual models.

First, such a model is *complete* in the sense that it contains all essential aspects of a system, so that the learner sees and understands how the system works. At the same time, the model needs to be both *concise* (so that it doesn't overwhelm with detail) and *coherent* (so that it makes sense). The model must be *concrete* in that it deals with events and functions that are familiar to the learner, but it also needs to be *conceptual* in that it deals with meaningful ideas. It goes almost without saying that it must also be *correct*, and finally, a good conceptual model must be *considerate* in that it takes into consideration the learner's sophistication and level of understanding.

Clearly, there might have been better terms with which to describe the characteristics of conceptual models most likely to lead to understanding and creativity; but note that in the alliteration is a useful mnemonic.*

Research with conceptual models suggests that they can be particularly effective in science, especially when there is a need to explain how a system (such as radar) works. Mayer (1989) suggests that visual models are also highly effective for organizing and recalling lists.

Conceptual models of this kind, like Ausubel's advance organizers, seem to work best when presented before or early in the course of the lesson. Their effectiveness is reduced or nonexistent if they are used later.

Finally, and significantly, conceptual models do not necessarily work for all students and in all situations. They work best for students who have the least amount of prior knowledge or the lowest aptitude for the lesson in question. For higher-aptitude students, use of a conceptual model does not significantly increase retention of concepts or ability to generate creative solutions for subsequent transfer problems. This, Mayer suggests, may be because higher-aptitude students often bring with them relatively sophisticated *a priori* conceptual models with which the teacher's simpler models might conflict.

Teaching Styles and Creativity

The use of conceptual models as advance organizers reflects a particular kind of teaching style. In a global sense, a teaching style is an identifiable and related group of teaching activities. Thus researchers speak of styles that reflect specific ways of instructing (for example, the lecturing style, the questioning style, the role-playing style). Or they speak of styles that reflect the teacher's predominant relationship with students or the major roles that each assumes (for example, authoritarian vs. democratic; teacher-centered vs. pupil-centered; traditional vs. progressive). Research has also examined several broad classifications, such as formal-informal styles or direct-indirect styles.

Although teaching style often reflects a teacher's personality, it also reflects many other

---

*PPC: "I'm not sure all students will understand this. Even those who know what alliteration is may not c the relevance of this sentence. Do you get it?"
Author: [Groan.]

factors, including personal philosophy, educational goals, the influences of teacher-training programs, maturity, wisdom, and the use of inspiring or less inspiring textbooks. Nor do most teachers invariably display only a single style. For example, most use a variety of instructional procedures and choose different ones depending on the lesson being taught, who the learners are, the amount of preparation time and the resources available, and other factors. However, many teachers have a definite tendency to be more formal than informal (or vice versa) or to use more-direct rather than less-direct approaches to instruction.

From the teacher's point of view, it may be important to know the likely effects of these different styles on student achievement, on student motivation, and on the development of the skills and attitudes related to being thoughtful and creative.

Formal-Informal Styles. One of the broadest classifications of teaching styles describes *formal* and *informal* styles (Bennett, 1976). Teachers whose styles are most formal teach each subject separately, emphasize individual rather than group work, assign class seating, restrict student movement, emphasize assessment and achievement, and make extensive use of extrinsic motivation. Those whose styles are more informal tend to integrate subjects, provide students with considerable freedom in determining their activities, typically allow students to select their seating, do not emphasize tests and academic achievement, and tend to rely on instrinsic motivation. Put another way, open education, described in Chapter 7, reflects a highly informal teaching style. In contrast, much of traditional education has been characterized by more formal teaching styles.

Do these styles significantly affect student achievement? Research suggests that they do. As we saw earlier, in our evaluation of the effects of open education (Chapter 7), formal styles are associated with higher academic achievement than are informal styles. However, informal styles may be associated with higher levels of creativity.

Direct-Indirect Styles. Flanders (1970) describes two types of teacher-learner verbal interaction that define *direct* and *indirect* teaching styles. The direct style is in some ways much like the formal style just described. Teachers whose behavior reflects this style *direct* classroom activity: They lecture, elaborate their opinions, give directions, and criticize or justify on the basis of their authority and that of others. In contrast, the indirect teaching style involves asking questions rather than providing information, and it is characterized by an acceptance of the student's feelings and attitudes, by the encouragement of student-initiated behaviors and opinions, and by the solicitation of ideas from students. Flanders's analysis of teacher-student classroom interaction led him to conclude that the direct style predominates in approximately two-thirds of all classrooms.

Research that has evaluated both direct and indirect teaching styles reports mixed results — perhaps, as Silvernail (1979) notes, because using verbal interaction alone to evaluate teaching style oversimplifies a very complex situation. In some situations and for some students, a direct style may be best; in different situations or for different students, indirect styles may be superior.

In spite of these ambiguous conclusions, a number of specific characteristics of teaching styles are clearly related to the outcomes of the educational process. As we have seen elsewhere in this text, such things as praise, feedback, criticism, advance organizers or conceptual models, classroom climate, and cooperative reward structures are all importantly related to student achievement, and perhaps to creativity and thoughtfulness as well.

Teacher expectations, too, may be related to student behavior. It is to this subject that we turn next.

THE EFFECTS OF
TEACHER EXPECTATIONS

In tracing the history of the use of **placebos** in medicine, Shapiro (1960), describes the discovery of a toothache cure by Professor Ranieri Gerbi of Pisa. It seems that in 1794 Professor Gerbi discovered that a small worm, later named *Curculio antiodontaligious*, could cure toothaches and prevent their recurrence for at least a year. The treatment involved crushing the worm between the thumb and the forefinger and applying it gently to the sore tooth. Gerbi made such wild claims for his worm cure that a special committee was set up to assess their validity. This committee later reported that of hundreds of toothaches studied, a full 68.5 percent were relieved by the worm. What is most astounding is that these "cures" occurred despite the fact that the chemical composition of the worm could not account for its effectiveness. The worm cure illustrates a self-fulfilling prophecy.

A striking illustration of this same phenomenon is provided by the schoolteacher who found on his desk a list of IQ scores for the students in his class. He copied them down in his record book for future reference. During the course of that year, the teacher often noticed how well the students with high IQs did when compared to those with low IQs. At the end of the year, being a good, industrious, and well-educated teacher, he computed a correlation coefficient for IQ and achievement scores, and found that the correlation was .80. In order to show how well he had taught, he brought this information to his principal. It was with some embarrassment that he learned that no IQ tests had been given to his class; the list of scores that he had found was nothing other than locker numbers.*

It would appear from these anecdotes that **expectations** can be instrumental in determining the outcomes of behavior. It has been intuitively suspected for some time that school achievement, and performance on less intellectual tasks as well, could probably be affected by communicating high expectations to students, verbally or nonverbally. What does the research tell us?

The classical study of the effects of expectations is that reported by Rosenthal and Jacobson (1968a, 1968b). The study took place in "Oak School"—a lower-middle-class institution. Teachers in this school were told that they were participating in the validation of a new test designed to predict academic "blooming." They were informed that children, particularly slow achievers, often show sudden spurts in their intellectual development, and that the new test could identify these "spurters." But the tests that the Oak School children were given were actually only intelligence tests (the Flanagan Tests of General Ability). The tests were administered in the spring, and the teachers were given information the following September, ostensibly about the test results. They were casually given the names of students designated "late spurters" but actually chosen randomly from the student body. This group comprised about 20 percent of the school population. The only difference, then, between the "spurters" and the control groups was that the teachers had reason to expect increased performance on the part of the "spurters."

Amazingly, their expectations were fulfilled. What is more surprising is that not only did academic achievement—which is to some degree under teacher control—increase, but so did intellectual ability as measured by the Flanagan tests. The most dramatic "spurts" were for first-grade students, probably the ones who had the greatest room for improvement. In addition, indications are that intelligence is more malleable at an earlier age (see Chapter 7).

The results of the Rosenthal and Jacobson study were later questioned by many reviewers

---

PPC: "Is this a true story?"
Author: "No. Well, maybe. Yes."

(see Wineburg, 1987; Rosenthal, 1987). In particular, critics question the analyses used, alleging frequent misjudging, misrecording, and misrepresentation of data. Furthermore, numerous attempted replications have failed. But a number of reviewers have not been entirely negative.

Brophy and Good (1974) reviewed sixty attempted replications and concluded that many were confusing and inconclusive and that none provided strong evidence of results as dramatic as those first reported by Rosenthal and Jacobson. But, they hasten to point out, many of these studies reveal quite consistent patterns of expectations among teachers, and these expectations are probably linked in important ways to such crucial things as the student's self-concept and self-esteem, as well as to achievement.

Similarly, Braun (1976) reviewed a wealth of teacher-expectation literature and also found remarkably consistent patterns of teacher expectations. Specifically, it seems that teachers often develop more positive expectations (with respect to academic achievement) for children who come from higher socioeconomic backgrounds, who are obedient and compliant, who are attractive, and who sit close to the teacher and speak clearly. And there is evidence, as well, that expectations might be communicated in subtle but measurable ways. For example, Brophy and Good (1974) report that some teachers pay less attention to lower achievers, give them less time to answer questions, and are more likely to criticize their answers than identical answers given by higher achievers.

Other investigations continue to clarify the conditions under which teacher expectations develop and the effects they might have on the teaching/learning process. For example, Rolison and Medway (1985) found that both the type of label applied to the student and the information the teacher has about the student's recent performance are important in determining teacher expectations. Teachers had higher expectations for students labeled *learning-disabled* than for those labeled *mentally retarded*;

they also had higher expectations for students whose recent performance showed an ascending rather than a descending pattern. Babad (1985) reports a significant bias in the grading of worksheets by teachers relative to whether or not teachers believe the work to have been done by excellent or weak students.

Implications of Research on Expectations

Obviously, the conclusion that teacher expectations undeniably and consistently affect pupil behavior is not fully warranted by the evidence. It appears, nevertheless, that teachers do develop expectations and that these may be important (see, for example, Means et al., 1979).

In the first place, high achievement may well be no more affected by increased expectations than is low achievement. For ethical reasons, this contention cannot be investigated experimentally because, if it were correct, the result would be to depress performance. Anecdotal observations support it, however. Consider the plight of slum children entering school. It is not at all unlikely that the teacher's expectations of low achievement for these children will be at least partly responsible for their inferior performance. Obviously, however, teachers cannot honestly expect high achievement from every student. Nevertheless, they should guard against the stereotype that associates children of less advantaged backgrounds with lower achievement. This precaution could prevent much educational injustice.

In the second place, the effect of teacher expectations need not be restricted to a few students. Conceivably, it can include the whole class. It is relatively simple, particularly when there are multiple sections of one class, for the teacher to communicate to the students that this is the best class she has ever taught. The effect can be quite remarkable.

Third, expectations manifested in the teacher's behavior vis-à-vis the student (in terms of classroom interaction or grading, for example) may be important in the student's motivation. Bardwell (1984) found that simply by stating an optimistic expectation, teachers significantly increased students' performances.

EXCEPTIONALITY

Some people, in one or more ways, are different from the normal, average individuals who account for most of our population. Some are far more intelligent, far more creative; others are endowed with superior motor skills or outstanding physical appearance; members of yet another group are socially gifted. These are individuals for whom the label *exceptional* is appropriate.

Unfortunately, there is another dimension of exceptionality — one that includes those less intelligent, less creative; those with physical and motor disabilities; those with emotional and adjustment problems. In short, the term *exceptional* applies equally to those to whom "nature and nurture" have been noticeably generous and to those to whom they have been much less kind.

Exceptionality in each of these three areas — the cognitive, the physical, and the social-emotional — ranges continuously from some point just noticeably beyond the average to the furthest extreme in either direction. People at the extreme of the negative end include, for example, the severely mentally handicapped, those with severe multiple physical disabilities (such as being blind, deaf, and quadriplegic), and those with serious emotional disorders (such as schizophrenia).

Of more immediate concern to the ordinary classroom teacher are those whose exceptionality is less marked, but who are nevertheless in need of special educational services. The role of the ordinary teacher (as opposed to the "special" teacher) in these cases might simply involve initial identification of a problem and referral to the proper source for further diagnosis. In an increasing number of instances in the United States, however, it will also involve providing special services within the context of the regular classroom, particularly since the passage of Public Law 94-142 in 1975. In attempting to redress some of the injustices that have sometimes existed in the treatment of exceptional children, this law requires, among other things, that school jurisdictions provide special services for qualified children in the "least restrictive environment" possible (Macmillan, Keogh, and Jones, 1986). In many instances, this environment has been judged to be the regular classroom; hence an increasing number of teachers must now deal with exceptional children. And it has consequently become doubly important that all teachers at least be familiar with the dimensions of exceptionality and with the rudiments of special-education programs.

In addition to the provision for education in the "least restrictive environment," Public Law 94-142 brought about three other significant changes in the schools' treatment of exceptionality (Macmillan, Keogh, and Jones, 1986). First, it established the exceptional child's right to due process. In practice, this means that classification and placement procedures are open to examination, that all school records are accessible to parents or other legal guardians, and that appeal and independent evaluation procedures are available for all children.

Second, PL 94-142 attempts to protect children against biased and discriminatory testing. In effect, this means that placement would seldom, if ever, be based on the results of a single test. It means, as well, that testing must be carried out in the child's dominant language.

Third, PL 94-142 mandated the use of individual education plans (IEPs). In an attempt to bring about greater accountability on the part of school jurisdictions, the law requires educators to provide written plans for each exceptional child. The IEP must specify objectives, the specific services to be included, a schedule of services, and evaluation procedures to be used in assessing the program's effectiveness.

For obvious reasons, PL 94-142 is often described as the Bill of Rights for the Disabled. But even though it has done a tremendous amount in reducing bias and unfair practices in the treatment of exceptional children, it has also presented some real difficulties of interpretation and implementation for educators. IEPs, for example, are difficult and time-consuming to prepare and are therefore extremely costly, and they have not proven very popular (see, for example, Zigler and Muenchow, 1979). Nor is it always easy or even possible to find tests for specific forms of exceptionality or to find tests in the child's native language. In addition, the law's most obvious practical manifestation—mainstreaming—has not been entirely without controversy.

Mainstreaming

The label used to describe the placement of exceptional children in ordinary classrooms, rather than in segregated classrooms devoted exclusively to "special" children, is **mainstreaming**. The mainstreaming movement is a direct result of the passage of PL 94-142. In addition, it resulted from at least two other related events in the field of special education. The first involves the recognition—both by individuals and, not infrequently, by courts of law—that many individuals who had been labeled *emotionally disturbed* or *mentally retarded* and who had therefore not been admitted into regular classrooms were indeed capable of learning and functioning effectively when given access to these classrooms. At the same time, a relatively new classification of student was introduced: the learning-disabled. This category, often loosely defined, generally includes individuals who do not have obvious disabilities (blindness, deafness, or mental handicaps, for example) and have therefore not been eligible for special classes but have not functioned well in regular classrooms.

Thus, there is, on the one hand, a recognition that some "special" children have been mislabeled and that, even if they have not been mislabeled, they can benefit from regular classroom experiences. On the other hand, educators now recognize that there are a number of children in regular classrooms for whom special attention would be highly desirable.

And the upshot of all of this is that teachers prepared to promote creativity and thinking among ordinary and gifted students (as well as to teach them all manner of other things) must now be able to identify and help those who are deprived as well as those who are more ordinary or more gifted.

Dimensions of Exceptionality

Exceptionality, as we saw, has two dimensions: One is exemplified by those who are more intelligent, more gifted, more creative than average; the other includes those with one or more handicaps. PL 94-142 provides an important official definition for the term *handicapped*: "Handicapped children means those evaluated as being mentally retarded, hard-of-hearing, deaf, speech impaired, visually handicapped, seriously emotionally disturbed, orthopedically impaired, other health impaired, deaf-blind, multihandicapped, or as having specific learning disabilities, who because of these impairments need special education and related services" (U.S. Office of Education, 1977, p. 42478).

The following sections examine exceptionality of three major kinds—physical, cognitive (intellectual), and social (emotional)—with special emphasis on cognitive exceptionality, which often is more relevant for the regular classroom teacher (see Figure 10.3). Teachers who major in special education would be expected to know much more than can be included in these few pages.

Physical Exceptionality. At one extreme among the physically exceptional are those who are endowed with superior capabilities that might be manifested in athletic skills and in other activities requiring motor coordination, strength, rhythm, and so on. At the other

	"Normality"	
Exceptionality (negative)		Exceptionality (positive)

Physical

Visual impairment Hearing impairment Cerebral palsy Other physical loss, injury, or disease	Superior athletic ability Superior sensory ability

Social-Emotional

Autism Schizophrenia Hyperkinesis Conduct disorders (aggressiveness, delinquency, withdrawal, severe shyness)	Invulnerability Leadership

Intellectual

Mild, moderate, severe, and profound mental handicaps Learning disabilities	Giftedness Superior intellectual, creative, and motivational qualities

Figure 10.3   Dimensions of exceptionality.

extreme are those with physical disabilities, sensory deficits, cerebral palsy, or a number of diseases that might or might not lead to problems in school. Among these, blindness and deafness may require special assistance beyond the capabilities and resources of the regular classroom teacher. On occasion, however, corrective devices (glasses and hearing aids) and special learning aids (large-print books, for example) can be used together within the regular classroom in compliance with mainstreaming regulations.

Social-Emotional Exceptionality.   At the positive end of this dimension of exceptionality are those more socially adept, better adjusted,

more immune to the stresses and tensions of life than are ordinary individuals. These exceptional individuals often go unrecognized and unheralded, although they might on occasion be envied.

At the other extreme are those variously described as "behavior-disordered," "emotionally disturbed," or "socially maladjusted." What these labels have in common is that each describes individuals who are troubled and often unhappy, and who are also usually a source of trouble for teachers, peers, parents, and others (Whelan, 1978). Estimates of the prevalence of emotional disorders vary from 2 to 20 percent of the total school population, depending on the criteria used and on whether both mild and more severe cases are included (Kelly et al., 1977).

For the most severe manifestations of emotional disturbance (for schizophrenia, for example), institutional care is generally required. In many cases, however, children who might be described as suffering from emotional disorders continue to function in regular classrooms. For instance, hyperkinesis (commonly called hyperactivity) does not generally require special services outside the school, although it is often treated medically. A variety of personality and conduct disorders (sometimes manifested in lying, cheating, extreme insolence, and other socially maladaptive behaviors) occasionally present serious management and teaching problems for teachers. In most cases, however, such students remain in regular classrooms, barring some major transgression of school regulations or some criminal activity that might lead to expulsion from school and/or to detention in an institution for juvenile offenders.

Intellectual Exceptionality.   On the one hand are the gifted and creative, about whom we spoke earlier in this chapter; on the other are children who have significant difficulty in learning some, if not all, of the things learned relatively easily by others. This dimension of exceptionality includes two important categories: the mentally handicapped (or retarded) and the learning-disabled.

Mental retardation is defined by the American Association on Mental Deficiency (AAMD) as follows: "Mental retardation refers to significantly subaverage general intellectual functioning resulting in or associated with concurrent impairments in adaptive behavior and manifested during the developmental period" (Grossman, 1983). Figure 10.4 presents some commonly used classification schemes for mental retardation. Note that the labels are based primarily on performance on standard measures of intelligence, most commonly the Stanford–Binet. In practice, approximately 1 percent of the general population appears to be mentally handicapped — when level of adaptive behavior is taken into account (Mercer, 1979). This is why it is so important to take adaptation into consideration (Edgerton, 1979).

The causes of mental retardation are so varied that classification is almost always done in terms of degree rather than cause. Among these causes are cerebral injury, chromosomal aberrations and defects such as Down's syndrome, maternal infections at critical periods of fetal development, and so on.

The largest group of retarded children (approximately 75 percent) are only mildly handicapped. Very few of these children are identified as intellectually impaired until they have been in school for a period of time. Most are eventually capable of academic achievement at approximately the sixth-grade level. These children are often described as the educable mentally handicapped and usually are mainstreamed.

A second group, the moderately handicapped, comprise another 20 percent of the retarded. They are sometimes described as trainable and are capable of learning to talk and to walk, although their motor coordination is generally markedly inferior to that of normal children. Most moderately mentally handicapped children are eventually placed in special schools.

Severe and profound mental impairment are generally associated with very limited motor learning — virtually no communication skills in the case of profound impairment and only rudimentary skills for the severely impaired — and institutionalization throughout life. In the case of profound retardation, institutional care is usually of a custodial nature, involving feeding and clothing.

Whereas intellectual impairment usually affects all areas of cognitive functioning, a second class of cognitive exceptionality manifests itself in only a few areas of functioning — and frequently, only in one. This class includes children who, in the absence of any perceptible

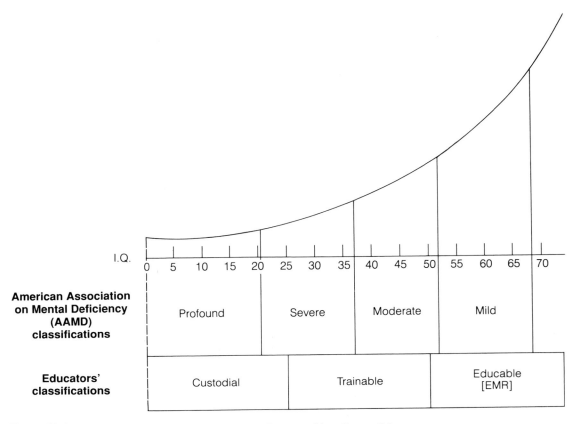

Figure 10.4 Two common classification schemes for mental handicaps. (Note that these classifications are based entirely on measured IQ. In practice, adaptive skills would also be taken into account.) The AAMD classifications shown here are based on the Stanford–Binet or Cattell tests. The Wechsler scales have a different distribution and therefore different cutoff points: 55–69, mild; 40–54, moderate; 25–39, severe; below 25, profound.

physical or emotional disturbance, nevertheless experience significant difficulty in learning specific skills. These children are sometimes described as suffering from a learning dysfunction, hyperactivity, cerebral dysfunction, minimal brain damage, perceptual handicaps, dyslexia, perceptual disability, or simply as being slow learners.

Ross (1976) notes that most of these terms are nonspecific, are often confusing, and are sometimes meaningless. Largely for this reason, Samuel Kirk proposed the term **learning disability** in 1963. It soon became widely popular and is now used to describe a variety of conditions, including academic retardation; specific learning problems associated with single subject areas, such as reading or arithmetic, and manifested in uneven patterns of development; some central nervous system dysfunctions; and all other learning problems not due to mental retardation, environmental disadvantage, or emotional disturbance (Morsink, 1985).

The identifying characteristic of *learning disabilities*, according to government regulations, is a significant discrepancy between IQ and achievement caused by problems in such basic psychological processes as remembering or perceiving. Children whose ability to learn is *generally* depressed or who suffer from environmental deprivation, emotional problems, or sensory defects are specifically excluded from the category of the learning-disabled. But, as Shepard, Smith, and Vojir (1983) found following a survey of 800 children classified as learning-disabled, many supposedly learning-disabled children have characteristics that do not conform to the definitions found in government regulations. In fact, more than half this sample had emotional disorders, mild retardation, or specific language problems; they should not have been classified as learning-disabled. Unfortunately, this misclassification may lead to the use of inappropriate treatment strategies with some of these children. It will almost certainly confound the results of research designed to investigate the incidence of learning disabilities and the effectiveness of various treatments.

Given this evidence of widespread faulty classification, it is perhaps not surprising that the number of children identified as learning-disabled more than doubled between 1978 and 1983 (Kavale and Forness, 1985). The learning-disabled now make up roughly two-thirds of all students requiring special education in the United States — almost 4 percent of the total school population.

In most instances, learning disabilities are treated in the context of the regular classroom, often with the help and advice of learning-disability specialists. Here, as in other areas of exceptionality, the onus of initial identification rests with the classroom teacher.

Identifying Exceptional Children

Macmillan and Meyers (1979) note that mild mental retardation, learning disabilities, and emotional disturbances are seldom identified before the child goes to school. A number of stages appear to be common in the identi-

fication of each of these manifestations of exceptionality.

Initially, these children begin school as ordinary students. Some will achieve at a sufficiently deficient level that they may be kept in first grade an extra year, a practice that seems to be more common for the mildly retarded from lower socioeconomic backgrounds (Mercer, 1973).

The next stage described by Mercer begins when the teacher realizes that the child has not progressed sufficiently to be promoted to the next grade. At this point, the decision is made to refer the child for further diagnosis. In some cases, the child may simply be promoted to the next grade — an action that is called a *social promotion*, and reflects the school's reluctance to separate children from age peers.

Lynch et al. (1978) provide a number of suggestions to help teachers in the early stages of tentative diagnosis — when the important decision is whether or not professional assessment is warranted. First, teachers are urged to learn to observe carefully in order to identify children who seem "difficult," hard to get along with, or slow. Having identified these children, teachers can then attempt to determine what might work with them and can try several different approaches. Frequently, it turns out that there *is* no problem.

Second, Lynch et al. suggest that teachers ask themselves key questions such as: Does the child learn so slowly, or is the child's adaptive behavior (ability to use language, to play with other children, and to be reasonably independent) so poor that the child cannot participate fully with the other children?

Third, and very important, teachers must be careful to distinguish between exceptionality and simple cultural differences. Very intelligent children whose dominant language and values are significantly different from those of the mainstream can sometimes appear less than normally bright.

Fourth, just as it is important to distinguish between the culturally different and those in need of special education, it is also important to

Identifying Exceptionality

Some extremes of exceptionality are obvious and can easily be detected by parents and others not specifically trained in such things. However, most instances of exceptionality are not extreme, and their diagnosis and assessment is often difficult.

Although the final diagnosis and assessment of an exceptionality that requires special intervention are almost invariably made by a professional, initial identification of those in need of further evaluation is often made by parents or teachers — and sometimes by the individual concerned. It is useful to know what to look for. At the same time, parents and others need to be extremely cautious in their tentative judgments of exceptionality, especially in cases in which children (and sometimes adults) experience mild problems with subjects such as reading or arithmetic. It is extremely easy to misinterpret a common learning problem as evidence of a learning disability or mental retardation.

The following are some of the symptoms parents and teachers might notice. Further assessment and evaluation, or referral, can usually be provided by school psychologists.

Cerebral Palsy

Diagnosis should be made by a physician. Symptoms can include any, none, or most of the following and can range from very mild to very severe:

uneven gait

jerky movements

speech problems

rigidity

drooling

balance problems

uncontrolled fluttering movements

involuntary facial gestures

shaking movements

possible convulsions

Epilepsy

Diagnosis requires medical assessment. Observable symptoms are seizures. In *petit mal*, seizures are momentary lapses of attention lasting only seconds and may be accompanied by fluttering of the eyelids and suspension of activity. *Grand mal* seizures (also called fits, attacks, or convulsions) may involve sudden stiffening, falling, thrashing around, and moaning. Seizures may last only a few seconds and seldom more than five minutes. Seizures that last longer require urgent medical attention.

Hearing Problems

frequent earaches

inattentiveness

speech problems

high volume on TV or radio

failure to respond

discharge from one or both ears

child turns head to listen

speaks in abnormally loud voice

Vision Problems

rubbing of eyes

redness of eyes

headaches

difficulty seeing chalkboard

squinting

high sensitivity to light

holds material close to see

Schizophrenia

Requires psychiatric diagnosis. May be characterized by one or more of the following:

aloofness

refusal to cuddle

self-injurious behavior (head banging, for example)

no verbal communication

repetitive behaviors (twirling, rocking, for example)

abnormal object attachments

insensitivity to pain

poor balance

withdrawal

extreme distress when faced with change

high sensitivity to pain

poor coordination

Attention Deficit Disorder with Hyperactivity

Also called *hyperactivity* or *hyperkinesis*. Primarily a male disorder. May be characterized by one or more of the following:

incessant physical activity (running, climbing, walking, jumping, skipping)

difficulty in sustaining attention

discomfort at sitting still or being inactive

impulsivity

difficulty taking turns

low frustration tolerance

forgetfulness

Conduct and Personality Disorders

These disorders require psychological or psychiatric assessment. They span a wide range of behaviors and symptoms, some of which might include the following (note that only extreme and persistent manifestations of these

behaviors would be considered disorders):

high aggressiveness and hostility

extreme withdrawal and social isolation

extreme shyness

lying

stealing

temper tantrums

highly negative self-concept

Mental Handicaps

Diagnosis and assessment require administration of individual intelligence tests by a trained psychologist. Most obvious feature is deficient ability to learn, ranging from mild to severe. Defined in terms of significantly subaverage performance on intelligence tests (below IQ 70) and deficits in adaptive behavior. Early symptoms of moderate to severe handicaps include:

significant developmental lag in learning to crawl, walk, and talk

failure to learn developmental tasks such as eating, dressing, tying shoes

poor motor coordination

markedly inferior verbal skills

Mild retardation is not ordinarily detected before school age; once in school, the child

may show the following symptoms:

significant difficulty in learning

problems with short-term memory

language deficits

motor problems

short attention span

Learning Disabilities

Identification and assessment are difficult even for trained professionals. Learning disabilities may be manifested in:

uneven pattern of academic achievement

academic retardation

learning problems not related to intelligence or environmental disadvantage

specific learning problems in language-related subjects or arithmetic

erratic spelling

frequent failure to recognize simple words

confusion of letters or numbers

persistent difficulty with simple arithmetic computations

inattentiveness, impulsivity, mood shifts

poor visual memory

recognize normal individual differences in temperament, motivation, interests, and so on. And teachers must always be aware of the possibility that difficulties between themselves and certain children might have to do with differences in personal style rather than with specific failings in the children.

Once teachers have determined that there is a real possibility of a problem requiring special attention, the next stage is to obtain professional help. Subsequent diagnosis — typically undertaken by professionals — usually involves assessments using prescribed instruments. Following diagnosis, remedial action will depend on the specific diagnosis, especially for learning disabilities, for which remedial prescriptions are based on as detailed a diagnosis as possible (Arter and Jenkins, 1979). And most children diagnosed as having mild mental retardation, an emotional disturbance, or a learning disability will continue to attend regular classes, although they may also be segregated for group or individual special services. (See box entitled "Identifying Exceptionality.")

Trends and Controversies in Special Education

Perhaps the most notable trend in special education in recent years is the gradual shift of the responsibility for the special care of exceptional children from institutions designed specifically for that purpose to institutions that have much broader functions. Thus, hospitals and schools are rapidly assuming many of the responsibilities that were once the sole province of asylums and other institutions with more euphemistic labels. The most dramatic manifestation of this trend in schools is the mainstreaming movement, which, as noted earlier, is at least in part a result of court decisions and legal action. Following implementation of major laws in California, for example, between 14,000 and 22,000 children were moved from institutions to regular classrooms (Bancroft, 1976).

The mainstreaming trend is not without controversy, however. Early research called into question the effectiveness of special classrooms for mildly retarded children and was partly responsible for the mainstreaming movement (Dunn, 1968). But subsequent research has not always confirmed these earlier findings. Although some children do not fare as well in special classrooms, others seem to do much better (see, for example, Budoff and Gottlieb, 1976; Semmel, Gottlieb, and Robinson, 1979). And there is mounting evidence that the self-concepts and social adjustment of children who are mainstreamed are more positive than those of segregated children (Macmillan, Keogh, and Jones, 1986). In general, however, learning-disabled students have lower self-concepts than do average children, whether or not they are mainstreamed (Chapman, 1988).

No matter how this very real controversy is resolved, Public Law 94–142 — based as it is on the doctrine of least restrictive alternative — now requires that exceptional children be placed in as nearly normal an environment as possible. Thus mainstreaming is mandated by law.

A second controversy in special education concerns the use of labels and is manifested in an antilabeling trend. Common arguments insist that labels are often unfair (given the social and cultural biases of intelligence tests), that they lead to lower expectations and thus present an additional disadvantage to those who are labeled, and that there is a remarkable lack of homogeneity among those who are given identical labels. (Macmillan and Meyers, 1979). In addition, there is a growing tendency to treat disabled children as quantitatively rather than qualitatively different from normal children. The use of generally pejorative labels is clearly incompatible with this trend.

A final trend, noted in the preceding chapter, relates only indirectly to special education. It is a growing movement away from the routine use of tests in schools — a movement based in part on a more public recognition of the inadequacy of many tests, of their occasional unfairness and unreliability, and of the extent to which they sometimes constitute an invasion of privacy. Following litigation in which petitioners successfully argued that decisions based on intelligence tests had been unfair to plaintiffs, many school jurisdictions have wholly or largely abandoned the use of tests other than in special circumstances. Although it is perhaps too early to determine what the final implications of this trend will be for special education, it is not unlikely that it will affect the ease and confidence with which the classroom teacher can recognize instances of mild retardation and/or learning disabilities. At the same time, however, it might also eliminate a number of premature and false diagnoses.

MAIN POINTS

1. Giftedness has sometimes been defined as superior academic achievement, high measured intelligence, exceptionally rapid learning, evidence of a single extraordinary ability, or a combination of these.

2. U.S. federal regulations define the talented and gifted as children who are identified by professionals as being capable of high performance by virtue of outstanding capabilities that might be reflected in general intellectual ability, specific academic aptitude, creative or productive thinking, leadership, artistic talent, or psychomotor ability.

3. The two main approaches to educating the talented and gifted are acceleration, in which students progress through the conventional curriculum at an accelerated pace (for example, Stanley's *radical acceleration*); and enrichment, in which students explore the conventional curriculum in greater depth and breadth (for example, Renzulli's *revolving door model*).

4. Other approaches to educating the gifted include mentoring, self-directed and independent study, the use of individual education plans (IEPs), the establishment of

special schools, and the provision of special out-of-school programs and courses.

5. Brainstorming groups are composed of small numbers of people who are encouraged to think up as many wild ideas as they can for solving a specified problem. The key to the production of worthwhile ideas in a brainstorming session is *deferred evaluation*.

6. The *Gordon technique* is a slight modification of Osborn's brainstorming that begins with an abstraction of the problem. *Morphological analysis* involves dividing a problem into its attributes and brainstorming each of these. The *CNB (collective notebook) method* consists of presenting participants with notebooks, on the first page of which a problem is presented, together with participants' possible solutions. The *CBB (collective bulletin board) method* combines the CNB method and brainstorming.

7. de Bono presents a number of practical suggestions for developing skills involved in lateral (creative) and vertical (logical) thinking.

8. Classroom climate is related to creative behavior. Students in formal schools have lower scores on creativity measures than do their counterparts in informal schools; warm, receptive teachers are more likely to encourage creativity; and severe competition is detrimental to creative performance.

9. Torrance, Hallman, and Taylor and Williams provide useful lists of do's and don't's for promoting creative behavior in students.

10. Conceptual models (verbal or graphic presentations preceding a lesson, much like Ausubel's advance organizers) that present important underlying concepts completely, concisely, coherently, concretely, conceptually, considerately, and correctly are associated with superior retention of

important concepts and superior ability to transfer the concepts to new situations.

11. Teaching styles are related groups of teaching activities. Formal styles (structured, teacher-controlled, achievement-oriented, emphasizing individual work) often lead to higher academic achievement. Informal styles (student-centered, integrative, intrinsically motivated — characteristics of open classrooms) are frequently associated with lower academic achievement and are sometimes associated with higher creativity and motivation. Results of research comparing direct styles (teacher-controlled, lecture-dominated, authority-driven) with indirect styles (student-centered, question-oriented) are somewhat ambiguous.

12. There is disputed evidence suggesting that teacher expectations can serve as self-fulfilling prophecies. As such, they may increase scores on tests of academic achievement, of intelligence, of physical performance, and probably of creativity as well. It is also possible that low expectations can have the opposite effect.

13. Teachers appear to develop more positive expectations for students from higher socioeconomic levels, for obedient children, for students with the most positive labels (for example, "learning-disabled" rather than "mentally retarded"), and for those who sit front and center and speak clearly. These expectations might be communicated to students, partly because teachers often pay less attention to lower achievers, give them less time to answer questions, and are more critical of their answers.

14. *Exceptionality* describes significant deviation from the norm in cognitive, social-emotional, or physical functioning. It can be either positive (associated with superior functioning) or negative (related to deficits in functioning).

15. In addition to mandating education in the "least restrictive environment" (main-streaming, in other words), Public Law 94-142 attempted to establish the child's right to due process (classification and assessment procedures and all school records open to parents and subject to appeal and independent evaluation); to protect children from biased and discriminatory testing (more than one assessment procedure must be used, and tests must be presented in the child's native language); and to assure that all children in need of special programs are given systematic programs with clear goals and built-in evaluation procedures (individual education plans, or IEPs).

16. *Physical exceptionality* may be manifested in exceptional athletic ability, for example; or, at the other extreme, it may be manifested in a variety of sensory or motor impairments, physical disabilities, diseases, and so on.

17. *Social-emotional exceptionality* in its negative sense includes manifestations of emotional disturbance, behavioral disorders, and hyperkinesis, among others. All but the most severe forms of social-emotional exceptionality are ordinarily dealt with in the regular classroom.

18. Mental retardation is characterized by a marked depression in general ability to learn and may vary from mild to profound. Learning disabilities generally refer to more specific learning impairments, often manifested in difficulties with reading or arithmetic.

19. Initial identification of exceptionality is often made by classroom teachers after the child has begun school. Mild retardation and learning disabilities are seldom diagnosed before this time.

20. Among the trends in special education are those related to mainstreaming, labeling, and testing. Whereas there is a movement toward mainstreaming, there are corresponding movements away from labeling and routine testing.

SUGGESTED READINGS

The following two references should be of particular value for teachers concerned with the creative behavior of their students. The first has been translated into many different languages and continues to be very popular. The second is a practical aid for use in the classroom. It consists of a collection of carefully researched activities designed to enhance creative behavior in students.

OSBORN, A. (1957). *Applied imagination*. New York: Scribner.

PARNES, S. J., NOLLER, R. B., & BIONDI, A. M. (1977). *Guide to creative action* (revised edition of *Creative behavior guidebook*). New York: Scribner.

A very practical booklet that looks at teaching styles and at the effects of such variables as praise, feedback, criticism, and questioning, is:

SILVERNAIL, D. L. (1979). *Teaching styles as related to student achievement*. Washington, D. C.: National Education Association.

A highly controversial book by Rosenthal and Jacobson presents a provocative, though perhaps biased, view of the possible effects of expectations on academic achievement.

The feelings generated by reading the book should probably be tempered by following it with the Wineburg article.

ROSENTHAL, R., & JACOBSON, L. (1968). *Pygmalion in the classroom: Teacher expectations and pupils' intellectual development*. New York: Holt, Rinehart & Winston.

WINEBURG, S. S. (1987). The self-fulfillment of the self-fulfilling prophecy: A critical appraisal. *Educational Researcher*, 16, 28–37.

A clear and comprehensive introduction to the field of special education is provided by:

BERDINE, W. H., & BLACKHURST, A. E. (1985). *An introduction to special education* (2nd ed.). Boston: Little, Brown.

The following are practical sources of information for teachers of exceptional children:

KROTH, R. L. (1985). *Communicating with parents of exceptional children: Improving parent-teacher relationships* (2nd ed.). Denver: Love Publishing.

MANDELL, C. J., & GOLD, V. (1984). *Teaching handicapped students*. St. Paul, Minn.: West.

STEVENS, S. H. (1984). *Classroom success for the learning disabled*. Winston–Salem, N.C.: John F. Blair.

In the summer, a bear's heart normally beats approximately forty times per minute. In winter, when the bear is denned-up, heart rate may drop as low as ten beats per minute. Amazingly, extreme cold rouses the bear as readily as does warmth. If this were not the case, many bears would freeze to death, for it is necessary for the bear to awaken and warm up when the temperature drops too low. (Matthews, 1969).

INSTRUCTIONAL LEADERSHIP

The nitty-gritty of classroom practice requires a great deal more than what we have gleaned from educational psychology and reported in the preceding chapters. Among other things, it demands of the teacher interpersonal and management skills of the highest order; it requires patience and imagination, a measure of genius and a touch of humility, enthusiasm and warmth, and other good things often more characteristic of angels than of teachers. The four chapters in Part 5 discuss these and related topics.

MOTIVATION AND TEACHING

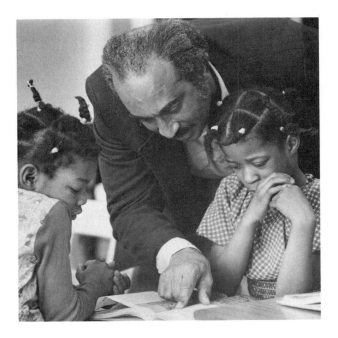

Boredom is a sign of satisfied ignorance, blunted apprehension, crass sympathies, dull understanding, feeble powers of attention and irreclaimable weakness of character.

JAMES BRIDIE *Mr. Bolfry*

Persons attempting to find a motive in this narrative will be prosecuted; persons attempting to find a moral in it will be banished; persons attempting to find a plot in it will be shot.

MARK TWAIN *Huckleberry Finn*, Introduction

PREVIEW   My grandmother, an astute observer of human affairs, spent much of her knitting and quilting time in quiet contemplation of human motives. "Why do geese go south and ravens stay?" she would wonder as her needles clicked. "Why did René go out in the storm?" "Why did Frank get so excited about it?" "Why doesn't Robert want to go to school anymore?" This chapter might have been of some value to her, although the questions it examines are surely no more important than the questions she asked. But it does provide some answers for why we do or don't do things and some suggestions for teachers whose role in motivating students can hardly be overstated.

■■■ *I was an excellent student during most of my elementary schooling. In those years only a few things could distract me from my studies — things such as the sight of a bear through the school windows, or sometimes a brief glimpse of a wild cow. Although I didn't yet know either of them for what they are, on those rare occasions when I did see one or the other my concentration invariably suffered for days afterwards.*

Later I discovered other distractions: Martha, Gloria, . . . many others, I think. These discoveries came before the turbulent years, during a time when adults could still be amused at our puppy-like behaviors. "Puppy love," they called it. But with the coming of the turbulent years, I found the lovely Clarisse. When my grandmother first noticed me turning my mongrel eyes on Clarisse, she apparently decided it was not puppy love, and she was cautious and watchful rather than amused.

But I was unaware of her concern. By then I was absolutely smitten with a dog-like (though not puppy-like) devotion to this wonderful creature. I followed her around the school yard constantly, at what I thought was a discreet distance; I admired her while she ate her lunch, sometimes imagining myself to be a cucumber sandwich or a pickle; I gazed longingly at her back when she stood at the chalkboard declining copulative verbs. That's when I first noticed that she had trouble with her verbs. I didn't; I knew copulative verbs inside out.

"I'll help you with your grammar," I blurted out. At last I had spoken the line I had rehearsed over and over. "If you want, that is." I added. "At my grandma's after school."

"'Kay."

She had said yes! I couldn't believe it! But when I broached the subject with my grandmother, she was not so agreeable.

"No!" she announced very firmly in response to my suggestion that I might take Clarisse into my room, where I usually studied. "No, that wouldn't be right. Right here in the kitchen would be fine."

"All I want is a quiet place with no distractions so that I can teach her some verbs," I insisted.

"I won't distract you at all," my grandmother said. "And it's not that I don't trust you. It's just not right. People would wonder about your motives."

"My motives are just to help —"

"Your motives, like everybody else's," my grandmother interrupted, "are selfish. Not that that's bad. Everybody's motives are selfish. All of what I call our creature motives, like for food and drink and you-know-what — they're selfish. I'm not saying, mind you, that you-know-what is your motive for helping Clarisse."

"It isn't for you-know-what. She needs help. That's all."

But my grandmother disagreed at length, citing many convincing instances of behaviors for which motives might seem obvious and scrupulously moral, but which were revealed by careful examination to have baser and far more selfish motives.

"But there are, of course, exceptions," she concluded generously.

"I'm one!" I exclaimed at once.

"I don't think so," she said. "I think you have an ulterior *motive."* ■■

MOTIVES: EXPLANATIONS FOR BEHAVIOR

Ulterior motives — a strange and wicked disorder from which I still suffer. You see, ulterior motives are, by definition, hidden and unknown; they do not show themselves. More than once I have wished that my true motives had been more obvious — had been more apparent to others.

In this chapter we look not at motives that are ulterior, but at those that are more obvious. Motives are what *move* us; they are our reasons for doing the things we do. As Dweck (1986) notes, motives are the causes of all our goal-directed activity. They explain the *why* of our behavior, whereas learning theories are more concerned with the *how* and the *what.*

From the teacher's point of view, the most important motives are those relevant to learning and achievement. The teacher needs to be especially concerned with the reasons why some students expend a great deal of effort in achievement situations and why others don't. It's important to know how teacher behaviors and instructional strategies affect student *interest* (a loose synonym for **motivation**). To the extent that teachers have control over conditions that affect students' motives and behaviors, they have an important responsibility to ensure that each student is treated in the best way possible. Unfortunately, determining what the best treatment is might not be a simple task.

Theorists with different points of view and beliefs tend to approach problems of motivation in different ways. They provide us with different discoveries, different insights, and different tidbits of practical knowledge. Teachers, whose outlooks are sometimes more practical than those of many theorists, need not adopt any single point of view to the exclusion of others. They are free to select and discard according to their needs, their understanding, and their personal styles.

This chapter explores a variety of explanations for human behavior, with special consideration of views that emphasize learning and achievement and that are therefore most useful in the classroom. Initially it touches on some historical approaches to motivation; then it outlines a psychological theory that has physiological underpinnings (arousal theory); and finally it moves on to a series of more detailed discussions of contemporary views of motivation. The contemporary views are organized according to the three major models discussed in earlier chapters: behaviorism, humanism, and cognitivism. Keep in mind that these divisions continue to be artificial and therefore somewhat misleading. As we study them, we sometimes feel compelled to judge them and choose only one among them. But we need to keep in mind that these are simply different orientations — reflections of different worldviews and different underlying emphases and metaphors. One is not correct and the others incorrect; rather, something of each may be useful for our purposes.

HISTORICAL VIEWS OF HUMAN MOTIVATION

History, as is often its custom, can teach us about an assortment of past beliefs, not all of which are very relevant to our current views. Nevertheless, there is often something in these historical views that may be useful to our understanding of human behavior in general, and of children in particular. In the case of the first historical view of human motivation that we'll consider — that concerning instincts — what history can tell us may be more relevant to our understanding of animals.

Instincts

My English Setter was one-and-a-half years old when she gave birth to her first litter. Two hours before the births, she began to tear up newspapers and arrange them in a pile in a secluded corner of the garage. I joined her at this point clad in a clean white shirt and armed with a stack of fresh towels, a pair of blunt scissors, two yards of cord, three human obstetrics textbooks, one veterinary textbook, and a large bottle of liquid depressant (for medicinal purposes).

Two hours later, the first of the little pups emerged, encased in its sac. The bitch turned, began to lick the sac vigorously, broke it, and released the pup. She then cleaned the mucus from its nose, dried its body, stimulated its breathing, and moved it toward a nipple. Three more pups were delivered in the same expert fashion by a bitch who, unlike her master, had never read a medical textbook.

There are many examples of instinctual behavior patterns among animals. The question is, Do people engage in behavior that can be similarly explained in terms of **instinct**?

Among the earliest scientific attempts to solve the problems of motivation were a variety of human instinct theories (McDougall, 1908; Bernard, 1924). *Instinct* was broadly defined to include any type of behavior that seemed to be generally human. For example, Bernard listed some 6,000 human instincts, ranging from the common ones (sexual, maternal, gregarious) to remote inclinations, such as the tendency "to avoid eating apples that grow in one's own garden" (p. 212).

The obvious disadvantage of this approach is that naming an instinct neither explains a behavior nor predicts it. At best, the whole process is entirely circular. If humans make love, it is obvious that we have an instinct for doing so. Why, then, does one make love? Well, because one has this instinct, you see. How do we know that this instinct exists? Well, because people make love. And so on, *ad infinitum*.

Currently, the notion of instinct is applied more to animal than to human behavior, although a related phenomenon, **imprinting**, is sometimes linked to some features of infant development. Imprinting is the appearance of complex behaviors, apparently as a result of exposure to an appropriate object or event (releaser) at a **critical period** in the animal's life. For example, newly hatched ducklings will follow the first moving object they encounter and become attached to it. Fortunately, this object is usually the mother duck. Lorenz (1952) reports, however, the case of a greylag goose that imprinted on him and followed him around like a dog. Much to his embarrassment, when it matured it insisted on foisting its affections on him during mating season.*

Although few complex human behaviors appear to be instinctual in the sense that many animal behaviors are, we may be born with potential instincts that are modified through experience. Perhaps a mother, left to her own devices, would instinctively know how to deliver and care for her child. Perhaps not. In any event, experience, culture, and evolution have so modified our behavior that the question of the existence of human instinct has become largely irrelevant.

Psychological Hedonism

A second historical explanation of human motivation appears to be intuitively true: We act so as to avoid pain and obtain pleasure. This

---

PPC: "Among other demonstrations of undying love, Lorenz's birds persisted in depositing beakfuls of minced worms in his ears. Lorenz didn't reciprocate."
Author: "Yecch!"

In Stinks

It seems that a mother skunk had given birth to identical twin skunks — both female as it happened. Identical twin skunks are extremely difficult to tell apart. Yet this wise mother could always differentiate between her twins, whom she had named, in a moment of whimsy, In and Out. When asked how she managed to tell In and Out apart, she said, sagely, "Instincts."

Instincts are *complex, species-specific, relatively unmodifiable behavior patterns*. The definition is broken down and explained below.

Complex: Because the behavior patterns that fall within the realm of instinct are complex, all simple behaviors are excluded. Thus, blinking in response to air blown in the eye, sucking behavior, and other simple behaviors of which we are capable at birth are not instincts; they are reflexes.

Species-specific: Instincts are not general *across* species, but *within* species. Thus wild ducks are characterized by a migratory instinct and bears by the urge to den-up in winter (except for polar bears).

Relatively unmodifiable: It was long believed that instincts were unaffected by environmental influences because they are largely innate. Research has now shown, however, that instincts can be modified by the environment. Female rats reared in deprived environments do not exhibit the maternal and nesting instincts characteristic of normally reared female rats. It remains true, nevertheless, that instincts are *relatively* unmodifiable.

---

explanation for human behavior is referred to as <u>psychological hedonism</u>. However, psychological hedonism does little to explain behavior because it does not specify those conditions that are pleasurable or painful. Even if it is true that the pain/pleasure principle governs our activities, we can predict and control these activities only if we know what gives pleasure and what gives pain.

Need–Drive Theories

Need-drive theories offer one way to define pain and pleasure. **Needs** are states of deficiency or lack within an organism. **Drives** are the energies or the tendencies to react that are aroused by needs. For example, we have a need for food; this need gives rise to a hunger drive.

If we assume that satisfying needs is pleasant and that a state of need is unpleasant, then the relationship between need theory and psychological hedonism is obvious. The identification and description of needs make clear the nature of pain and pleasure. A list of needs is a list of conditions that, when satisfied, are pleasant, and when unsatisfied are unpleasant.

In a broad sense, needs can be divided into two categories: psychological and physiological. **Physiological needs** are manifested in actual tissue changes; **psychological needs** are more closely related to mental functioning. Other differences exist between the two categories. Psychological needs are never completely satisfied, whereas physiological needs can be. In addition, psychological needs are probably more often learned than are physiological needs. Physiological needs include the need for food, water, sleep and rest, activity, and sex. Psychological needs include the need for affection, belonging, achievement, independence, social recognition, and self-esteem.

Summary and Implications of Historical Approaches to Motivation

Motives are psychology's explanations for behavior. Motivation theories try to explain *why* we do certain things; they provide us with insights about the circumstances under which we will be most interested in doing certain things — and least interested as well.

As we saw, historical approaches to problems of motivation sometimes tried to explain behavior on the basis of genetically ordained, largely unlearned patterns of behavior such as instincts or imprinting. But although these are valuable explanations for a bear's habit of denning up in the winter, they tell us little about why Robert will study all night before his science exam, or about why Sam will watch television instead and will then have to explain how he forgot all about the exam.

Psychological hedonism, too, does not tell us a great deal about Sam or Robert. True, the belief that we do things that we expect will lead to pleasant outcomes — and that we avoid behaviors that lead elsewhere — does little violence to our naive convictions about human behavior. But, as we saw, the belief by itself explains little; we need to know what is pleasant and unpleasant.

Theories about needs and drives begin to spell out some of the conditions and outcomes we find pleasant or unpleasant. We don't need to engage in a great deal of psychological experimentation to realize that people who are hungry and thirsty will go to extraordinary lengths to obtain food and drink. Accordingly, it is important for teachers to be aware of needs in their students. It is obvious, for example, that certain basic biological needs must be satisfied if the teaching/learning process is to be effective. A hungry or thirsty student is almost certain to find concentration difficult to maintain. By the same token, a hungry teacher is probably seldom as effective as a well-fed one. Other basic needs, such as the need for sex, are not likely to present a very serious problem for younger students. Unfortunately (or fortunately, perhaps?) the same cannot be said about adolescents or about teachers — young or old.

Because, in our society, most children's basic needs are adequately taken care of, teachers are not often called upon to walk around with a bag of cookies and a jug of milk. Psychological needs are quite another matter. Recall that these include the need for affection, for belonging, for achievement, for social recognition, and for self-esteem. A useful exercise for a prospective teacher might be to consider what a "bag" filled with the wherewithal to satisfy these needs would look like. Teachers who through their actions can give each student a sense of accomplishment and belonging are probably carrying such a bag.

By now it should be apparent that teachers can use their knowledge of student needs directly for instructional purposes. Obviously, many students can have their needs for achievement and self-esteem (among others) satisfied through school-related activities. Such activities must not be so difficult that success is impossible, nor so easy that success is meaningless. The meaningfulness of these activities, their relevance to the students' lives, and the recognition that students will gain from peers, parents, and teachers are of real importance.

AROUSAL: A PHYSIOLOGICAL/ PSYCHOLOGICAL THEORY

Arousal is both a psychological and a physiological concept. Psychologically, it refers to alertness or attentiveness. It is, in a sense, the individual's degree of wakefulness. At the lowest levels of arousal, the individual is asleep (or in a coma) and is totally inattentive; at higher levels of arousal, the individual is intensely aware and alert; at still higher levels of arousal, the individual might be in a state of panic or shock.

Accompanying these psychological states — ranging from sleep to panic — are underlying physiological changes evident in the functioning of the sympathetic nervous system. At the lowest levels of arousal, respiration and heart rate, brain-wave activity, conductivity of the skin to electricity, and so on, are all at very low levels. But with increasing arousal, respiration and heart rate may increase, the skin's electrical conductivity increases as a function of perspiration, and brain-wave activity changes in predictable ways.

Sources of Arousal

The main sources of arousal are the **distance receptors** — hearing and vision — but arousal may be affected by all other sources of stimulation, including activity of the brain. Level of activation is a function of the impact of all stimuli present at a given time. However, there is no direct relationship between amount of stimulation and arousal level. Some properties of stimuli — meaningfulness, intensity, surprisingness, novelty, and complexity (Berlyne, 1960) — make them more arousal-inducing than others. Therefore, *amount* of stimulation is probably less critical in determining level of activation than the *nature* of stimulation.

Arousal and Motivation

The relationship between arousal and motivation can be seen more clearly in terms of two assumptions, both of which appear to have considerable research support:

1. For any given activity there is a level of arousal at which performance will be optimal. This level will vary somewhat from one individual to another.

2. At any given time, an individual behaves in such a way as to maintain the level of arousal that is most nearly optimal for on-going behavior.

The first assumption simply means that certain activities can best be performed under conditions of relatively high arousal, whereas others are best performed under conditions of lower arousal. Activities such as sleeping or resting, or activities involving routine, habitual responses such as counting one's fingers or driving a car, do not ordinarily require a very high level of arousal. On the other hand, intense, concentrated activities such as taking examinations require higher levels of arousal.

The relationship between arousal level and performance is illustrated in Figure 11.1 (Hebb, 1955). At the lowest level of arousal — sleep — there is little or no response to external stimulation. Try asking a sleeping person what the capital of Saskatchewan is. Ask him again just as he is waking up. He may say "Pardon?" — or he may respond in some less printable manner. As he becomes more fully awake, he may respond correctly (if he knows the answer). If, however, in your zeal for observing the relationship between arousal and behavior you proceed to set your subject's house on fire, awaken him with a bucket of cold water, inform him that his house is on fire, and then ask him what the capital of Iran is, you will probably observe the ineffectiveness of behavior that accompanies excessive arousal.

People under great stress often engage in inappropriate behavior. There are instances of students "freezing" when taking examinations and responding by writing their names several hundred times or by not writing anything at all. There is stage fright, which causes actors to forget their lines and professors to tell lies because they have forgotten the truth (not because they didn't know the truth). There are the tragic examples of panic-stricken people in crowds trampling one another to death in their

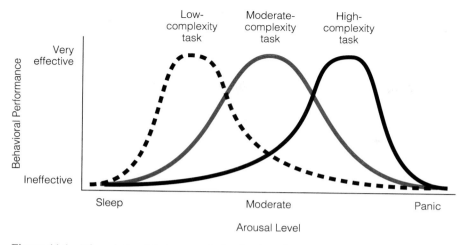

Figure 11.1   The relationship between behavioral performance and arousal level. The level of arousal that is optimal for effective behavior varies with the complexity of the task.

haste to escape danger (Schultz, 1964). There are the studies of Marshall (cited by Bruner, 1957b), who found that fewer than one-quarter of the infantrymen in combat during World War II actually fired their rifles when under heavy fire. Fortunately, the enemy probably did no better.

The second assumption is that people behave so as to maintain their arousal level somewhere near the optimal. In other words, if arousal level is too low, the individual will seek to increase it; if it is too high he or she will attempt to lower it. If this is true, and if we know what factors increase or decrease arousal, we can perhaps explain and predict some behaviors that are not easily explained in other ways. When people experience great fear, their first reaction may well be to flee the object of their fear. The effect, if they succeed in escaping, is to reduce arousal level. When people are bored, their level of arousal is probably too low. They may then engage in more stimulating activity: reading, sports (participating or observ-

ing), or, if they are students, daydreaming. The effect should be an increase in arousal level.

Arousal and Learning

Like effective behavior, maximally effective learning takes place under conditions of optimal arousal. Low levels of arousal are characterized by low attentiveness — a condition that, in a student, rarely leads to effective learning.

An experiment can be conducted by any teacher to illustrate this point. Prepare a good lesson full of content, write it out, and read it to your class very slowly in a soothing monotone. Then deliver the same lesson to another, comparable class in your usual, exciting, stimulating style. Test the relative retention of your two classes. It is little wonder that common synonyms for the term *motivating* are expressions such as *interesting, captivating, arousing, moving, useful, involving, stimulating, compelling, attention-getting, challenging,* and *curiosity-whetting.*

Controlling Arousal in the Classroom

The relevance of arousal theory for education depends on the teacher's control over the variables that affect arousal. Ideally, all students in a given class should be working at their optimal levels. But there are a number of problems. Are all students at the same level? How does the teacher know the level of each student? How can arousal level be changed?

In the first place, all members of a class are probably not at the same level of arousal. In the second place, the teacher doesn't know the exact level of each student. Probably those who are asleep, nearing sleep, or just waking up are at low levels of arousal; those who show signs of panic and impending flight are at higher levels of arousal.

But the really central question for teachers is, How can arousal level be controlled?

We saw that the primary sources of arousal are the distance receptors, but all other sources of stimulation also have some effect. Furthermore, it is less the amount than the intensity, meaningfulness, novelty, and complexity of stimulation that affect arousal. There are other factors as well. Degree of risk or personal involvement is probably directly related to arousal level, as is illustrated by the arousing effects of risk-taking behavior.

Teachers in a classroom are stimuli. They control a very significant part of all the stimulation to which students will be reacting. The intensity, meaningfulness, and complexity of what teachers say, of what they do, of how they look, and of what they write all directly affect the attention (arousal) of their students. They can keep students at an uncomfortably high level of arousal by presenting material that is too complex, and the students may reduce that arousal by ceasing to pay attention. Teachers can also keep students at too low a level of arousal by failing to present meaningful material in a stimulating manner — and again students may cease to pay attention.

Because changes in stimulation are usually arousing, changes in voice should increase student attentiveness. The range of the human voice in terms of tone, volume, and inflection is amazing. Given this range, it is also amazing that some teachers rarely depart from a monotone. A useful exercise for teachers (or prospective teachers) is to tape-record some of their presentations in order to learn how effective their voice changes (if any) are. They might also use a videotape recorder in order to see themselves teaching. Stimuli that emanate from a teacher consist not only of verbal signs, but also of visual ones; changes in appearance, posture, and position, together with the use of expressive gestures, should affect students' arousal levels.

The essential thing for a teacher to remember is that arousal increases in proportion to the intensity, meaningfulness, novelty, and complexity of stimulation. Consequently, *all* changes in teacher behavior that tend to intensify these properties of stimuli may increase attention as well. The key word, without doubt, is *variety*.

A teacher's motivational problems seldom involve too high an arousal level. More often, problems arise because teachers fail to awaken their students sufficiently, or because they actually put them to sleep. What can you do?

1. You can fire a miniature cannon. That is an intense and novel stimulus.

2. You can stand on your head, walk on your hands, jump in the air, and holler "Yahoo!"; or, as one of my colleagues once did before he was dismissed, you can pound your fist on the desk and very quietly say, *"Nghaa."*

3. You can present problems of increasing complexity, interest, and meaningfulness.

4. You can involve students in projects. Personal involvement is accompanied by a risk of personal failure. This is probably arousing.

5. You can read this book for good ideas.

6. You can. . .

You are invited to add to this list. Be aware that even suggestions that seem facetious,

Biofeedback

There are many fascinating and potentially useful experiments related to arousal. Many are lumped under the heading "biofeedback experiments" because they involve providing subjects with instant information about arousal level so the subjects can control their own arousal.

In a typical experiment, subjects are connected to an electroencephalogram recorder, also called a polygraph — or, more popularly, an alpha recorder. Simple alpha recorders differentiate between alpha (normal, resting arousal level) and beta (more vigilant, excited) waves. The object of the experiment is to have the subject control brain functioning in order to increase the proportion of alpha waves. It has repeatedly been demonstrated that this is quite feasible without any direct instructions. Indeed, the procedure used can be explained in terms of an operant conditioning model. Whenever subjects emit a sufficient proportion of alpha waves, a tone is heard. Because they have been told that the object is to keep the tone going as much as they can, the sound serves as reinforcement. Eventually most subjects find that they can reach the "alpha state" much more easily than was originally the case. Interestingly, practitioners of Zen, yoga, and transcendental meditation can, through the practice of their respective meditative techniques, arrive at similar states of low arousal — a condition that is believed to be highly conducive to physical and mental health.

Biofeedback instruments and techniques are currently being used to bring about relaxation, to treat migraine headaches, to deal with mental and emotional problems involving tension and anxiety, and in the treatment and prevention of cardiovascular problems such as hypertension (Parloff, London, and Wolfe, 1986).

whimsical, or absurd can sometimes be related directly to the content of a lesson and can then be used with good results.

Arousal, Anxiety, and Learning

One manifestation of increasing arousal is **anxiety** — a feeling characterized by varying degrees of fear and worry. Research on anxiety and its relationship to learning (and more specifically to performance on tests) dates back more than four decades but has been sporadic and unsystematic throughout much of this time. However, recent years have seen a marked upsurge in research on the nature of anxiety, its relationship to performance, and techniques that can be used to reduce it. A great deal of this research is necessarily of a psychiatric nature, given that anxiety is implicated in a great many mental disorders (American Psychiatric Association, 1980). Research that deals more specifically with anxiety and education is reviewed briefly here.

Among the earliest research on this topic was that undertaken by Sarason (1959, 1961, 1972, 1980). Among other things, this research presents evidence indicating that anxiety related to test taking decreases test performance. This important finding has been well documented by subsequent research. Hembree (1988) summarized 562 separate studies that have investigated what is labeled **test anxiety**. The conclusion is clear, claims Hembree: Test anxiety *causes* poor test performance. In addition, it is related to lower self-esteem. Females tend to be somewhat more test-anxious than males, although their greater anxiety does not manifest itself in lower performance. Research also indicates that in addition to performing less well on tests, highly anxious students do not profit as much from instruction. In other words, anxiety appears to have a detrimental effect not only on test taking, but on learning as well (McKeachie, 1984). This observation is apparently true for a wide variety of instructional methods. However, highly anxious students tend to learn better with the more highly structured instructional approaches, such as programmed learning, computer-assisted instruction, and teacher-directed lessons in which student interaction is not expected or required (see Resnick, 1981).

Attempts to reduce anxiety in students may take various forms. In an extensive review of research on anxiety-reducing techniques, Tryon (1980) concludes that many techniques lead to a reduction in anxiety. These techniques are aimed at changing students' attitudes about their personal competence and at focusing attention on the tasks at hand rather than on feelings of worry. Accordingly, such techniques often take the form of attempting to develop learning/thinking strategies (McKeachie, Pintrich, and Lin, 1985). These techniques contrast sharply with more therapeutically oriented approaches such as systematic desensitization (described in Chapter 12).

Other possibilities for reducing anxiety, suggested by Hill and Wigfield (1984), include a variety of changes in instructional and evaluation procedures. For example, teachers can reduce time pressure on students by providing more time for assignments and tests and by teaching students simple time-management strategies. They can also try to prevent failure by changing the difficulty level of assignments and tests, thereby matching them more carefully to students' skill levels.

Hembree's review of 562 studies indicates not only that many of these approaches are effective in reducing test anxiety, but that improved performance typically follows anxiety reduction. In light of these findings, he argues that tests such as intelligence or standardized achievement measures—and even teacher-made examinations—consistently underestimate the abilities of test-anxious students—at least after fifth grade. Before this time, test anxiety is not ordinarily a very significant factor in test performance.

The implications of these findings are twofold: First, steps should be taken to reduce test anxiety for highly anxious students, both through treatment programs and through changes in test-taking directions. And second, education needs to conduct research to discover ways of preventing test anxiety from developing in the first place.

THREE CURRENT APPROACHES TO MOTIVATION

Motivational theories can be categorized in much the same way as approaches to learning: behavioristic, humanistic, and cognitive. Recall that behaviorism is concerned with how the consequences of behavior regulate and control actions; that humanism is concerned with the autonomy, the dignity, and the worth of the self; and that cognitivism deals with how we know, think, and remember. Accordingly, behavioristic approaches emphasize *extrinsic* or *external motives* such as those having to do with praise and reward; humanistic approaches emphasize the importance of *intrinsic* or *internal motives* such as those related to the need to be autonomous, to develop competence, to actualize potential; and cognitive approaches emphasize the individual's need to know and understand. Next we consider each of these approaches to motivation.

The Behavioristic Approach

Psychological hedonism—the pain/pleasure principle—is a simple summary of the most basic behavioristic motivational principle: We behave so as to obtain pleasure and avoid pain. However, as we saw in Chapter 2, pain and pleasure are subjective emotional evaluations that are not easily admitted into a rigidly behavioristic position. Instead, the behaviorist attempts to identify situations (stimuli) whose effect is to increase the probability of a behavior. These *positive reinforcers* can then be used in various ways to bring about desirable behaviors and sometimes to eliminate those that are less desirable.

Positive and negative reinforcement (and sometimes punishment as well) is used in virtually all classrooms, even by the most humanistic or cognitively oriented of teachers. Teachers praise and admonish students; they give high and low grades; they smile and frown. These and a thousand other indicators of approval or disapproval are examples of reinforcement techniques. As is made clear in Chapter 2 and again in Chapters 12 and 13, there is much in behavioristic theory that can be usefully applied to instruction.

But we are not simply hungry rats in some experiment, Weiner (1984) informs us. If we look into the classroom, we will see that behavior is informed—that it is driven by cognitions and by emotions and that it is both logical and illogical.

It should come as no surprise that current applications of reinforcement theory in the classroom take the student's thinking into account. As Stipek (1988) notes, the most powerful reinforcers for students are stimuli such as *praise*, the effectiveness of which clearly depend on the student's interpretations of teacher behavior.

Praise. Praise is not like food in an empty belly, warm and pleasurable even in the absence of learning. Rather, it is a complex event that says not only, "you have done well," but also, "you have behaved in a socially approved manner." Praise—and its absence, too—gives us fundamentally important information with which to build notions of self. It says things about how worthwhile and competent we are. And, as is made clear shortly, these are fundamentally important concepts in human motivation.

But teachers do not always use praise very well. Brophy (1981) notes that much teacher praise is determined not so much by the student's actual behavior as by the teacher's perception of what the student needs. As a result, praise is often used too infrequently to be very effective; or it is used so often as to be almost meaningless. Praise used in these ways is not clearly contingent upon a specific desired behavior, as a good reinforcer is; nor is it sufficiently credible to be very rewarding.

Brophy suggests that if it is to be effective, teacher praise should not be too frequent, and there are a number of ways in which it can be made far more effective. Most of these suggestions reflect principles discussed in Chapter 2. For example, praise should be contingent upon some specific behavior, it should be credible, and it should be informative. In addition, it should focus on the student's efforts and personal competence. It should *not* be random and unsystematic; nor should it reward mere participation rather than quality of performance. (See Table 11.1 for a summary of Brophy's suggestions.)

Although reinforcement (in the form of praise and otherwise) is used extensively by virtually all teachers, some object to its systematic and deliberate use because they sense that there might be something mechanistic and dehumanizing about the systematic application of rewards and punishments to shape behavior. Others object because they fear that if students are trained to respond too readily to *extrinsic* reinforcers, they might become too dependent

Table 11.1 Guidelines for effective praise

Effective Praise	Ineffective Praise
1. Is delivered contingently	1. Is delivered randomly or unsystematically
2. Specifies the particulars of the accomplishment	2. Is restricted to global positive reactions
3. Shows spontaneity, variety, and other signs of credibility; suggests clear attention to the student's accomplishment	3. Shows a bland uniformity, which suggests a conditioned response made with minimal attention
4. Rewards attainment of specified performance criteria (which can include effort criteria, however)	4. Rewards mere participation, without consideration of performance processes or outcomes
5. Provides information to students about their competence or the value of their accomplishments	5. Provides no information at all or gives students information about their status
6. Orients students toward better appreciation of their own task-related behavior and thinking about problem solving	6. Orients students toward comparing themselves with others and thinking about competing
7. Uses students' own prior accomplishments as the context for describing present accomplishments	7. Uses the accomplishments of peers as the context for describing students' present accomplishments
8. Is given in recognition of noteworthy effort or success at difficult (for *this* student) tasks	8. Is given without regard to the effort expended or the meaning of the accomplishment (for *this* student)
9. Attributes success to effort and ability, implying that similar successes can be expected in the future	9. Attributes success to ability alone or to external factors such as luck or easy task
10. Fosters endogenous attributions (students believe that they expend effort on the task because they enjoy the task and/or want to develop task-relevant skills)	10. Fosters exogenous attributions (students believe that they expend effort on the task for external reasons — to please the teacher, win a competition or reward, etc.)
11. Focuses students' attention on their own task-relevant behavior	11. Focuses students' attention on the teacher as an external authority figure who is manipulating them
12. Fosters appreciation of, and desirable attributions about, task-relevant behavior after the process is completed	12. Intrudes into the ongoing process, distracting attention from task-relevant behavior

Source: From J. Brophy, "Teacher Praise: A Functional Analysis," *Review of Educational Research, 51,* No. 1, 5–32 (p. 26). Copyright 1981 by the American Educational Research Association. Reprinted by permission of the publisher.

on them. And some humanists fear that such students will never learn to listen to their own motives — to their *intrinsic* and fundamentally human urge to excel, to become something worthwhile and actualized.

Humanistically Oriented Motives

Humanistic psychology's concern with the self is especially well reflected in the writings of Abraham Maslow (1970).

Self-Actualization.   Maslow proposes two general need systems: the basic needs and the meta-needs. The basic needs consist of:

physiological needs: the basic biological needs — for example, the need for food, water, and temperature regulation;

safety needs: those needs that are manifested in people's efforts to maintain sociable, predictable, orderly, and therefore non-threatening environments;

love and belongingness needs: the need to develop relationships involving reciprocal affection; the need to be a member of a group;

self-esteem needs: the need for cultivating and maintaining a high opinion of oneself; the need to have others hold one in high esteem.

These needs are hierarchical in the sense that higher-level needs will be attended to only after lower-level needs are satisfied (see Figure 11.2). While people need food they are not likely to be concerned with love or with self-esteem. History provides striking examples of the potency of lower-level needs. In the 1933 famine in the Eastern (Soviet) Ukraine, for example, in which at least 4.5 million people died, more than half the victims were infants. In the words of one of the survivors (*Edmonton Journal,* 1983):

All you think about is food. It's your one, your only, your all-consuming thought. You have no sympathy for anyone else. A sister feels nothing for her brother; a brother feels nothing for his sister; parents don't feel anything for their children. You become like a hungry animal. You will throw yourself on food like a hungry animal. That's what you're like when you're hungry. All human behavior, all moral behavior collapses.

Maslow's basic needs are also termed *deficiency needs* because they motivate (lead to behavior) when the organism has a deficiency with respect to a need (for example, lacks food or water). The meta-needs are termed *growth needs* because they motivate behaviors that result not from deficiencies, but from our tendencies toward growth. All of them will be attended to only after the basic needs are reasonably satisfied. The meta-needs include aesthetic and cognitive urges associated with such virtues as truth and goodness, the acquisition of knowledge, and the appreciation of beauty, order, and symmetry. The highest need in Maslow's system is our tendency toward self-actualization — the unfolding and fulfillment of self.

Recall from Chapter 6 that self-actualization is a process rather than a state. It is a process of growth — of becoming — a process that most humanistic psychologists consider absolutely central to the healthy experience of being human. And although such abstractions as beauty, goodness, truth, and self-actualization are difficult to describe and even more difficult to examine in a scientific way, they do represent motivating concerns and processes for a great many individuals.

Competence Motivation.   White (1959) argues that one of our most important *intrinsic* needs is the need to feel competent. **Competence motivation** is manifested in the child's struggle to perform competently and in the feelings of confidence and worth that accompany successful performance.

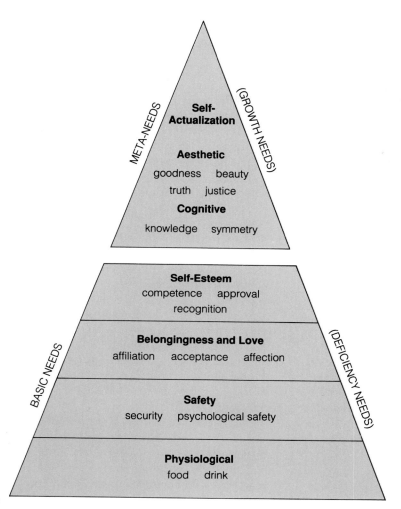

Figure 11.2 Maslow's hierarchy of needs.

White believes that competence motivation is especially important in species such as ours in which individuals are born with so few innate competencies. Unlike the young of many non-human species, our infants cannot run or hide; they cannot feed themselves; they have little recognition of enemies or of danger. Perhaps even more important, they know few of the signals, gestures, and sounds they need to mas-

ter in order to communicate competently. To be human is to learn a thousand competencies.

Competence motivation, suggests White, explains a tremendous range of behaviors engaged in by children. It is the drive for competence — for mastery — that explains curiosity and information-seeking behavior. Competence motivation is evident in the repetitive, circular reactions of Piaget's infant (see Chapter

8); it also explains why schoolchildren practice skills over and over again until they achieve competence.

White explains the child's struggles for competence in terms of the feelings of pride and *efficacy* (personal effectiveness) that result from mastering a skill or understanding a concept. Albert Bandura expands this concept.

Self-Efficacy.   One of the most important aspects of the information we have about ourselves, Bandura (1981, 1986) informs us, concerns our estimates of our personal effectiveness — our **self-efficacy**. The most efficacious people are those who can most effectively deal with situations — in other words, those who are most *competent*. Accordingly, self-efficacy has two related components: The first has to do with the skills — the actual competencies — that are required for successful performance; the second has to do with the individual's personal estimates of competence.

Notions of self-efficacy or competence are especially important in motivating behavior. Schunk (1984) points out that under most circumstances, children (and adults as well) do not spontaneously undertake activities in which they expect to perform badly. Thus, judgments of self-efficacy affect our choices of activities and settings. In addition, they also influence the amount of effort we are likely to expend. Normally, if our expectations of success are high (that is, if our judgments of self-efficacy — of competence — are high), we will willingly expend considerably more effort on a given task. If, on the other hand, our expectations of success are low, we may not devote nearly as much time and effort to the task.

Judgments of efficacy also motivate our behavior by influencing our thoughts and our emotions. Those whose judgments of personal competence are low are far more likely to evaluate themselves negatively and to suffer from poorer self-esteem. Significantly, Coopersmith's (1967) research with adolescent boys indicates that positive self-concepts are closely related to success both in school and in interpersonal affairs.

It follows that highly favorable judgments of competence (high self-efficacy), together with accompanying positive evaluations of the self (positive self-esteem), can be extremely important positive influences on a child's behavior in school. By the same token, low self-efficacy judgments may have highly negative effects. Accordingly, it is very important for teachers to understand the origins of judgments of self-efficacy. Much of what teachers do — and can do — has an effect on self-efficacy.

Bandura (1986) identifies four important influences on a person's judgments of self-efficacy (or personal competence). He labels these *enactive, vicarious, persuasory,* and *emotive influences*.

Enactive influences are evident in the results of the individual's own actions. Whether or not a person is habitually successful in a given task clearly influences personal judgments of competence. Those who are never successful are less likely to have highly positive evaluations of self-efficacy than are those who most often succeed. It does not follow, however, that success is invariably attributed to personal competence — and inevitably results in high self-efficacy judgments. As we see in a later section on cognitive approaches to motivation, some individuals habitually attribute their successes to good fortune or to other factors over which they have no control, rather than to their own competence and effort and intelligence. By the same token, these individuals take little personal blame for their failures, attributing them instead to bad luck (see the later section on attribution theories for more information).

A second influence on self-efficacy judgments is *vicarious* (secondhand); it has to do with observing the performance of others. Clearly, if we see that others around us always produce nicer paintings than we do, we are not likely to develop very high evaluations of our artistic competence. Similarly, children who always receive the poorest grades — or the highest — are being provided with comparative information that might be highly instrumental in determining their judgments of personal worth.

Bandura (1981) suggests that the most important comparisons for making judgments of personal competence are those the child makes with peers. It is not particularly helpful for one's self-concept to perform better than those who are either much younger or are expected to be less competent for other reasons. But it is potentially very helpful to perform as well, or better than, one's peers.

Vicarious sources of influence on self-judgments are most important in competitive school situations — which means, of course, that they are very important in *most* school situations because, as we saw earlier, most are competitive. In more cooperative settings, however, comparisons with peers are not nearly so important.

Persuasion can also sometimes be an important source of information about competence. Those who lack confidence — and whose self-efficacy judgments are therefore presumably low — can sometimes be persuaded to do things they would otherwise be reluctant to do. Implicit in the persuasion ("Come on, Emily, play your bandura* for us") is a positive judgment ("You play your bandura so well, Emily").

The fourth source of influence on judgments of self-efficacy is *arousal*. As we saw in an earlier section of this chapter, arousal describes a physiological and psychological state most clearly apparent in the individual's alertness or vigilance. It ranges from sleep or comatose states to states of very high, intense alertness or even panic. We saw that the relationship betwen arousal and behavior is curvilinear (represented by the inverted U-shaped curves in Figure 11.1). For most behaviors there is an optimal level of arousal at which behavior is most effective; it is less effective if arousal is much above or below this optimal range.

High arousal, Bandura (1986) suggests, can affect self-judgments in different ways. For example, great fear might lead to judgments of very low personal competence. A mountain climber overcome by fear might decide he is incapable of continuing — as might a person about to speak in public. In contrast, great fear might lead a hiker to judge that she is capable of outrunning a bear.

In summary, our feelings of competence are a combined function of the results of our behavior (*enactive influence*: our successes and failures tell us much about how competent we are); our comparisons with others (*vicarious influence*: our performance is as good as, better than, or poorer than that of others); the persuasions of others (*persuasory influence*: when others persuade us, their behavior tells us positive things about our competence); and the intensity of arousal (*emotive influence*: judgments of competence can be raised or lowered by the intensity of an immediate emotional reaction).

Implications of Humanistic Orientations. Humanistic approaches to motivation emphasize internal or intrinsic factors that affect behavior. As we saw in Chapter 6, humanistic schools are child- rather than teacher- or subject-centered. Their emphasis is on affective growth and on the development of self-concept. At the same time, however, humanistic concerns need not be incompatible with more traditional values that emphasize curriculum content and the development of basic skills.

Three educational alternatives that illustrate humanistic concerns are open education,

---

PPC: "I don't get this. Are you trying to make fun of Albert Bandura?"
Author: "Not really. A bandura is an ancient, many-stringed Ukranian musical instrument. It looks a little like what we might imagine an angel's harp to look like."

learning-styles schools, and cooperative learning. Each of these approaches translates into practice some of the educational implications of humanistic approaches to motivation (see Chapter 6 for a discussion of their strengths and weaknesses).

The greatest contribution of humanistic approaches to instructional practice is embodied perhaps less in specific recommendations for the "nitty-gritty" of classroom practice than in teacher attitudes toward students (cooperative learning approaches are an exception). The humanistic educator is a concerned individual who places great value on the personal development of students. Accordingly, self-actualization is one of the important goals of humanistic instruction — as is the concomitant development of positive feelings about the self and about personal effectiveness and competence (self-efficacy).

A Cognitive Look at Motivation

Once again it's important to realize that our categories in psychology are seldom as neat as we would like; the real world is not as simple as the models we invent to represent it. For example, aspects of Bandura's self-efficacy theory and of White's competence motivation theory are every bit as cognitive as they are humanistic; and in some ways they are behavioristic as well. Even though they deal with motives that are intrinsic and that have to do with the self (a humanistic concern), and even though they are also concerned with the effects of success and failure (a behavioral concern), perhaps most importantly they deal with the individual's understanding and awareness (a cognitive concern).

Bandura's theory of self-efficacy (like his theory of imitation described in Chapter 8) gives a very important role to imagination and anticipation. In a very real sense, it is the learner's ability to *imagine and anticipate* success or failure, reward or punishment, pain or pleasure that is fundamentally important to learning and motivation. Not surprisingly, Bandura's theorizing is sometimes labeled *social cognitivism*.

So at this point in our exploration into motivation, we have considered instincts, pain and pleasure, needs, drives, arousal, and self-efficacy. An interesting assortment of explanations for human behavior, what? And valuable explanations, too, as has been shown in this chapter. But their value is limited, and the explanations they offer are only partial.

Most historical accounts of motivation viewed the human organism as a passive being, unmoved and unmoving in the absence of those external or internal conditions that define needs, drives, and arousal levels, that trigger instinctual or primitive learned behavior, or that are clearly associated with pain or pleasure. In other words, psychology has, inadvertently or otherwise, described an organism that is highly *reactive* but considerably less *active* — hence the contention that older theories have painted an overly passive and mechanistic picture of human beings.

The newer approaches are clearly more *cognitive* and *social*. Humans are seen not as the victims of internal or external prods moving them willy-nilly through their daily activities, but as organisms whose ongoing activity is mediated largely by conscious evaluation, anticipation, and emotion. Bolles (1974) makes the point that there are no unmotivated behaviors; thus motivation is not some special force that should be isolated and classified as needs are isolated and listed. It is simply a characteristic of ongoing behavior. The plea of the contemporary cognitive theorist is that psychologists turn their attention to ongoing behavior in natural situations, in the process taking into account what may well be the single most important feature of human motivation: *our ability to delay gratification* (Mischel and Baker, 1975). So much of our behavior is motivated by our anticipations of distant outcomes that the analysis of human behavior in terms of those conditions that seem relevant to the behavior of rats and very young children is often fruitless for schoolchildren and adults. We can delay gratification by virtue of some uniquely human abilities involved in thinking, imagining, and verbalizing. It is through a study of these ongoing cognitive processes that cognitive theorists such as Weiner search for understanding and explanations.

Attribution Theories. Weiner (1974, 1980a, 1980b) begins with the assumption that people attribute their successes and failures to internal or external causes. If I am internally oriented, I might attribute my successes and failures to my ability, to my effort, or to some combination of the two. In any case, I am attributing my performance to causes for which I assume some personal responsibility. If I am externally oriented, I might attribute my performance to factors for which I have no responsibility and therefore over which I have no control; namely, luck or task difficulty. Thus, if I fail, I might assume that the task was too difficult or that I was unlucky (or both); conversely, if I succeed, I might attribute my success to the easiness of the task or to luck (see Figure 11.3). Clearly, there are other causes to which performance can be attributed (mood, illness, or fatigue, for example), but these are more personal, more variable, and not easily amenable to scientific investigation.

The tendency to attribute success and failure to either internal or external causes seems to be a relatively predictable and stable personality characteristic. However, it is less apparent in children under nine years old, who have not yet differentiated between such factors as ability and effort. Nicholls (1978) reports that these children equate effort with intelligence; they believe that smart people are those who work hard (and consequently succeed). At the age of nine or ten the child begins to consider ability as a separate factor that contributes to success. But even at this age, smartness is still equated

Causal Attributions

Figure 11.3   Attributions for success and failure. Our explanations of why we succeed or fail may be internal or external; in addition, they may involve causes that are either stable or unstable.

with hard work. By age 11, however, the child typically shares our intuitive notions about the distinctions among ability, luck, effort, and task difficulty.

Children, Dweck (1986) informs us, seem to behave as though they subscribed intuitively to one of two views of intelligence: the entity theory or the incremental theory. If they subscribe to the entity theory, they behave as though they believe that intelligence is fixed and unchanging. Accordingly, their achievement goals are *performance*-oriented; that is, they will be moved to obtain favorable judgments about their competence (about their ability) and to avoid unfavorable judgments. On the other hand, if they subscribe to the incremental theory, they behave as though they believe that intelligence is malleable. Accordingly, the goals of their achievement-oriented behavior will be *learning* goals rather than performance goals; that is, they will focus on effort and will attempt to increase their competence.

Dweck's analysis of attribution research strongly suggests that students whose basic orientation is toward performance goals (have a view of intelligence as being fixed) need to have

Table 11.2   Achievement goals and achievement behavior

Theory of Intelligence	Goal Orientation	Confidence in Present Ability	Behavior Pattern
Entity theory (Intelligence is fixed)	Performance goal (Goal is to gain positive judgments/avoid negative judgments of competence)	If high	Mastery-oriented (Seeks challenge; high persistence)
		If low	Helpless (Avoids challenge; low persistence)
Incremental theory (Intelligence is malleable)	Learning goal (Goal is to increase competence)	If high or low	Mastery-oriented (Seeks challenge that fosters learning; high persistence)

Source: Adapted from C. S. Dweck (1986), "Motivational Processes Affecting Learning." *American Psychologist, 41*, 1040–1048.

extremely high confidence in their ability to be willing to accept challenges — that is, to be oriented toward *mastery*. Students whose confidence is lower are more likely to be characterized by what Dweck describes as *helplessness*, primarily because they see failure as a direct reflection of their ability. In contrast, students who are oriented toward learning goals (those who view intelligence as malleable) are far more likely to seek challenges and to be persistent; that is, when students view ability as a function of effort, they are more likely to strive toward high achievement because for them, the cost of failure is not as high as it is for those who see ability as fixed and unchangeable. (See Table 11.2.)

Attribution and Achievement Motivation. The implications of attribution theory for understanding student behavior become clearer when considered in relation to what is known or suspected about achievement motivation. Several decades ago, McClelland and his asso-

ciates (1953) began to investigate what appears to be an intuitively valid observation: Some individuals behave as though they have a high need to achieve, to be successful, to reach some standard of excellence; others behave as though they are more afraid of failing than desirous of success. Measures were then devised to identify those with a high need for achievement, those with a low need for achievement, and those with a high need to avoid failure (Atkinson and Raynor, 1978).

The principal measure, still in use, particularly for research purposes, presents subjects with pictures from the Thematic Apperception Test (TAT). Pictures selected typically portray one or more individuals doing something (a boy playing the violin, for example) and ask the subject to describe what is happening in the picture, what has happened in the past, and what will happen in the future. This projective test assumes that individuals project their personal feelings and thoughts into the descriptions. Thus, those individuals for whom

Causal Attributions

Figure 11.4 Relations between causal attributions and feelings associated with success and failure.

achievement is an important motive provide descriptions replete with achievement imagery and themes. A count of these achievement-related references provides a crude measure of achievement orientation. Despite the problems associated with this type of measurement, research indicates that individuals who score high on this test also tend to be the high achievers in school.

Other relevant findings in this subject area are that high need-achievers are typically moderate risk takers. They attempt tasks that are moderately difficult, thus providing themselves with a challenge while keeping their probability of success fairly high (McClelland, 1958; Thomas, 1980). In contrast, low need-achievers typically attempt tasks that are very difficult or very easy. The relevance of this finding was not immediately obvious and did not become obvious until the elaboration of attribution theory. If I attempt a very difficult task and fail, I will probably attribute my failure to task difficulty, a factor over which I have no control; hence, I will assume no personal responsibility and therefore experience no negative affect (emotion). If I am successful, there is

again little positive affect because my success is not due to factors over which I have any control, but to external factors. Moderate risk takers, on the other hand, can attribute success to skill or effort; similarly, they can attribute failure to personal factors. In either case, there is considerably more emotional involvement in the outcomes of their performances. Also, the nature of the emotional reaction is likely a function both of specific attribution and of locus of control (see Figures 11.4 and 11.5).

It appears reasonable to suppose, then, that high need-achievers will tend to be internally oriented, whereas low need-achievers will more likely attribute their performance to external factors. This supposition is, in fact, borne out by research (Greene, 1985; Wittrock, 1986). As is shown in a subsequent section of this chapter, knowledge of the relationship between achievement orientation and causal attribution can be of considerable value to teachers.

Educational Implications.   Assuming that high-achievement needs are desirable, can they be increased in students? Research and common sense agree that they can. Alschuler (1972) and

Locus of Control

	Internal	External
Success	Pride Confidence Competence	Grateful Thankful
Failure	Guilt	Anger Surprise

Figure 11.5 Relations between locus of control and feelings associated with success and failure.

others (for example, McClelland and Winter, 1969; Andrews and Debus, 1978) have devised achievement programs for use in schools and with adults in economically deprived circumstances. In general, these programs provide learners with a series of situations in which they are invited to take risks, make predictions about their performance, modify their predictions on the basis of ongoing feedback, and earn or lose points or token money on the basis of their performance. Among the objectives of these programs are to encourage learners to make use of information concerning their previous performance, to arrive at realistic goals, and to assume personal responsibility for their performance. Indications are that these programs can be quite successful both in increasing measured need for achievement and in improving actual performance (Alschuler, 1972).

A more general educational implication that can be derived from a combined consideration of achievement and attribution theory concerns the structuring of conditions that appear to be related to attribution. Weiner (1980a) suggests that a number of specific factors are involved in an individual's evaluation of causes of success and failure. Clearly, the difficulty of a task might be determined by its objective nature. In practice, however, a student is likely to judge a task difficult or easy on the basis of previous experience with similar tasks and knowledge of other people's successes and failures. Ability is most often inferred from past failures and successes. Effort is judged relatively objectively in terms of time and energy expended on a task, and luck is inversely related to the control subjects assume they have over the outcomes of their behaviors.

A number of attribution-changing programs have been developed and investigated. As Wittrock (1986) notes, the major objective of most of these programs is to move students in the direction of effort attributions; that is, the programs attempt to lead students to the understanding that their successes and failures ought to be attributed to their personal efforts. For example, de Charms's (1972) program attempts to teach students to shift their locus of control from an external orientation — in which they see themselves as helpless pawns who have no responsibility for their own learning and achievement — to an internal orientation, in which they perceive themselves as origins and assume greater responsibility for the outcomes of their behavior. Similarly, a program developed by McCombs (1982) attempts to develop motivation not only by changing the student's attributions to internal causes, but also by teaching cognitive strategies and metacognitive skills (see Chapter 5). It follows that as students become more adept at the management of these skills and strategies (as they learn more about learning), they will also begin to realize that they can exercise a great deal of control over learning and achievement — that it isn't all just a matter of luck and faith.

In most school-related tasks, luck should have little bearing on performance, although there are those students who will invoke that lady repeatedly in any case. They blame her for the fact that they have studied the wrong sections, inadvertently misaligned their answer sheets, or had the misfortune of being presented with inferior teachers. Teachers can exercise some control over the other three major categories to which performance outcomes can be attributed (effort, ability, or task difficulty), but luck can only be left to chance.

It should come as no great surprise that repeated failures are likely to have a negative effect on self-concept and on feelings of competence, and that individuals who have failed more than they have succeeded will be reluctant to attribute their failures to lack of ability. Indeed, it appears reasonable to predict that repeated failures will contribute to external attribution and concomitant feelings of powerlessness. By the same token, repeated successes in tasks of moderate or high difficulty (rather than tasks too absurdly simple) are most likely to lead to positive self-concept, feelings of competence, acceptance of personal responsibility for performance, and high achievement drives.

The key phrase undoubtedly is *personal responsibility*. To the extent that students accept personal responsibility for their performance they will be emotionally involved, success will enhance their self-concepts, motivational forces will be largely intrinsic rather than extrinsic, and the problems of classroom management (discussed in the next chapter) will become interesting pedagogical problems rather than discipline problems.

THE IMPORTANCE OF SELF-EVALUATION IN MOTIVATION

How do you keep students interested? What can the teacher do? What is it important to know?

Big questions, these, with no very short or very simple answers. But we have too little space here to be long-winded and no wish to be complex. So here is only a little bit of an answer.

What *is* important? The student's self-evaluation is one thing that is important. Believing that we are bright and capable—and loved because we are lovable—is fundamentally important to each of us. Most of our lives, Kegan (1982) says, we struggle to be meaningful—to mean something to others. If we mean nothing, that is the measure of our personal worth.

Do teachers affect students' self-evaluations? Clearly, yes. Much of what teachers do—and can do—directly and indirectly influences students' perceptions of their competence and their meaningfulness. But the classroom factors that contribute to these evaluations do not mold them in simple ways. As Marshall and Weinstein (1984) put it, influences are complex and interactive. Often students' self-evaluations are based at least in part on comparisons with other students. But many factors (in complex interaction) are involved in the final evaluation. For example, in most competitive situations, success increases self-evaluations of ability; failure has the opposite effect. But if children are each given different tasks, the opportunity for comparison is much less than if all work on identical tasks. In much the same way, whole-class instructional procedures often provide more opportunity for direct comparisons than do small-group approaches such as those often used in cooperative learning.

In addition, students' self-evaluations clearly depend on the outcomes of their behaviors and on the responses of teachers and others. Other things being equal, success leads to positive self-evaluations more often than does failure. And teacher responses to students are typically loaded with information. Gestures, attention, facial expressions, grades, and verbal comments are just a few sources of information that tell the student, "Gee, you're pretty dumb, kid" (or worse), or that say, "Hey, way to go!"

Unfortunately, not everyone can do very well. In fact, not everyone is equally competent. But, as Marshall and Weinstein (1984) put it, the outcome of social comparisons need not always be negative for low achievers. If teachers and students alike see competence and intelligence as a matter of accumulating skills and knowledge through effort (Dweck's incremental theory), rather than as a fixed, unchangeable quality (entity theory), then those who achieve less well need not suffer from unfavorable comparisons. Teachers who hold these views, claim Marshall and Weinstein, will favor noncompetitive learning, flexible grouping, mastery-oriented learning, and comparisons of a student's current performance with previous performance instead of with the current performance of others.

MAIN POINTS

1. Theories of motivation attempt to answer questions about the initiation, the direction, and the reinforcement of behavior. Obviously, these answers (if available and valid) are tremendously significant for education.

2. Instinct theory as applied to human behavior is largely of historical rather than current interest. Instincts are complex unlearned patterns of behavior common to an entire species (for example, nesting behavior in ducks or rats). Whatever human instincts remain have become so confounded by culture that the concept retains little explanatory value for a study of human behavior.

3. Psychological hedonism recognizes that people usually behave so as to achieve pleasure and avoid pain. Need theories offer one definition of pain and pleasure: The satisfaction of a need (physical or psychological) is assumed to be pleasant; not to satisfy a need is unpleasant.

4. *Arousal* is a concept with physiological and psychological components. Physiologi-

cally, increasing arousal is defined by changes in respiration and heart rate and in brain-wave activity. Psychological signs of increasing arousal include increasing alertness or wakefulness. With excessively high arousal, however, high anxiety and panic may result.

5. The primary sources of arousal are the distance receptors (vision and hearing); secondary sources include all other sensations. The amount, intensity, meaningfulness, surprisingness, and complexity of stimulation are directly related to the level of arousal.

6. The relationship between arousal and motivation is expressed by two assumptions: There is an optimal level of arousal for maximally effective behavior and the individual will behave in such a way as to maintain arousal level at or near the optimal.

7. In general, with increasing arousal, behavior (and learning) becomes more effective until an optimal level of arousal is reached. If arousal continues to increase beyond this point, effectiveness of behavior will decrease, as is sometimes evident in the behavior of people under great stress.

8. The teacher in a classroom can be seen as the source of the stimulation that maintains student arousal at low or high levels. This view has important implications for teacher behavior.

9. Anxiety often has a detrimental effect on student learning and performance. In particular, test anxiety has repeatedly been shown to decrease grades.

10. Not only does high anxiety reduce test performance, but there is evidence to suggest that it reduces effectiveness of learning as well. Accordingly, studies have often found that highly anxious students do better when exposed to instructional methods

that are more structured, less demanding of public interaction, and consequently less anxiety-arousing.

11. Humanistic approaches emphasize intrinsic (internal) motives such as those relating to autonomy, competence, and self-actualization; behavioristic approaches emphasize extrinsic (external) motives such as those relating to rewards and punishments.

12. Praise is an important classroom reinforcer that provides the student with important information about the self. Teachers often use praise infrequently, unsystematically, and more in response to their perceptions of student needs than in response to actual student behavior.

13. Maslow's humanistic theory presents a hierarchical arrangement of need systems, with physiological needs at the lowest level and the need for self-actualization at the highest. The central assumption in Maslow's theory is that higher-level needs will be attended to only after lower-level needs have been satisfied.

14. White believes that competence motivation, manifested in the child's struggles to become competent and to develop accompanying feelings of worth and pride, is very important to school learning.

15. Bandura's self-efficacy motive, similar to White's notions of competence, describes personal estimates of effectiveness. Notions of self-efficacy are important in determining both what behaviors will be undertaken (children are least likely to attempt activities in which they expect failure) and the amount of effort that will be expended (greater if success is anticipated).

16. Judgments of self-efficacy are affected by four influences: enactive influences (successful outcomes of behavior increase positive judgments); vicarious influences (comparisons with others); persuasory influences (persuasion of others informs a person of competence); and emotive influences (high arousal can increase or decrease judgments of self-efficacy).

17. The humanistic educator is especially concerned with both the personal development of students and the enhancement of positive self-concepts.

18. Traditional theories of motivation present a passive view of humans. More "cognitive" theories describe humans as active, exploring, evaluating organisms capable of delaying gratification and of explaining the outcomes of their own behaviors.

19. Weiner's attribution theory of motivation is based on the assumption that individuals attribute their successes or failures to internal (ability and effort) or external (difficulty or luck) factors. Individuals with a high need for achievement tend to attribute their performances to internal factors, thus accepting personal responsibility for their successes and failures. Those with a lower need for achievement are more likely to attribute their performances to external factors over which they have no control.

20. Dweck suggests that children behave as though they subscribe to one of two views about intelligence: the entity theory or the incremental theory. Children who subscribe to the entity theory (intelligence is fixed and unchanging) tend to be oriented toward performance goals intended to produce a good impression (performance reflects directly on personal ability); these children will be mastery-oriented only if their confidence in their ability is very high. If their confidence is lower, they are likely to avoid challenges and to be characterized by helplessness rather than a mastery orientation. Children who subscribe to the incremental theory (intelligence is

highly malleable and increases with effort) are more likely to be oriented toward learning goals, to focus on effort, to seek challenges, and to be mastery-oriented.

21. Achievement motivation (the tendency to strive toward achieving some standard of excellence) and the need to avoid failure appear to be closely related to attribution theory. Students whose need for achievement is high are typically more internally oriented (have an internal locus of control) and consequently are more likely to accept personal responsibility for the outcomes of their efforts.

22. Training programs geared toward increasing achievement orientation have been used successfully in the classroom. Common elements of such programs are that they invite children to take risks, to make predictions about their performance, to modify predictions realistically on the basis of past performance, to establish realistic goals, and to assume personal responsibility for the results of their behaviors.

23. Attribution-changing programs attempt to move students in the direction of making more effort attributions — that is, attributing successes and failures to the results of effort rather than to causes over which the individual has no personal control. One such program, developed by deCharms, attempts to lead students to see themselves as origins (controllers) rather than as pawns (the controlled).

24. Feelings of competence, of self-worth — in short, positive self-concepts — appear to be related to internal sources of attribution and consequent feelings of powerfulness. The key concept with respect to the educational implications of attribution theory is *personal responsibility*.

SUGGESTED READINGS

A practical guide to motivating students in school, with particular attention to the development of achievement motivation, is the following:

STIPEK, D. J. (1988). *Motivation to learn: From theory to practice.* Englewood Cliffs, N.J.: Prentice-Hall.

Fowler's book is of value in understanding the development of motivation theory. Chapter 4, which considers arousal theory in some detail, is especially relevant to the present chapter. The last part of the book contains fourteen of the more interesting and readable articles in motivation theory.

FOWLER, H. (1965). *Curiosity and exploratory behavior.* New York: Macmillan.

For a fascinating account of the effect of high arousal on human behavior, see:

SCHULTZ, D. P. (1964). *Panic behavior.* New York: Random House.

Cognitive theories of motivation are presented clearly at a sophisticated level in the following book:

WEINER, B. (1980). *Human motivation.* New York: Holt, Rinehart & Winston.

McClelland's theories of motivation are described in considerable detail in the following two books. The first, a collection of writings by some of McClelland's most outstanding former students, is both a tribute to McClelland and an elaboration of many of his ideas. The second is a detailed analysis of the relationship between achievement and attribution theory.

STEWARD. A. J. (Ed). (1982). *Motivation and society.* San Francisco: Jossey-Bass.

HECKHAUSEN, H., SCHMALT, H., & SCHNEIDER, K. (1985). *Achievement motivation in perspective* (translated by M. Woodruff & R. Wicklund). New York: Academic Press.

A collection of articles that looks in some depth at motivational issues in the classroom is:

AMES, R., & AMES, C. (Eds.). (1984). *Research on motivation in education* (Vol. I): *Student motivation.* New York: Academic Press.

The brown bear (Ursus arctos) *is still found in small numbers in very limited mountainous areas of western Europe, in Russia, Asia, India, and northern China, as well as in North America. It is extinct in the British Isles (Southern, 1964).*

CLASSROOM MANAGEMENT AND DISCIPLINE

Most people sell their souls and live with a good conscience on the proceeds.

LOGAN PEARSALL SMITH *Afterthoughts*

Few men have virtues to withstand the highest bidder.

GEORGE WASHINGTON *Moral Maxims*

PREVIEW It may not come as a surprise to you that one of the principal reasons for teacher unhappiness and premature retirement is discipline problems. This chapter, one of the more practically oriented chapters in this text, outlines a number of strategies and principles that might be effective in preventing and/or correcting disruptive behavior in the classroom. It looks too at the application of behavior modification in the classroom. The single most important point it makes is that here, as in medicine, prevention is far more valuable than correction.

■■ *In the second grade I tried to make a hole in my rubber eraser by holding a freshly sharpened pencil against it and hitting the pencil with my ruler. This was to be the last of a series of noisy experiments I had undertaken that day. The teacher interrupted me (not for the first time), called me to the front of the class, and administered the strap once on each of my small hands.*

In the fourth grade I was detained after school and asked to scrub the inside walls of the outhouse, where someone had discovered an offensive bit of graffiti penciled above the small hole (there was a larger one). I might have remained convinced to this day that God does watch all transgressors and reports directly to their teachers had I not remembered later that the spelling test we had been given that afternoon had contained most of the words found in the graffiti. In those days I spelled turkey "t-e-r-k-e-e."

In the eighth grade I had to write "I will not squirt ink on Louise" 150 times. I don't remember why I had to write "I will not squirt ink on Louise," though it now strikes me that these words might be a nice title for a song.

In the ninth grade I had to write "I will not write about wild cows or draw their pictures" 250 times. I remember why.

I escaped unscathed from the tenth grade, having fallen in love with a sweet young thing who seemed to prize academic excellence, cooperation, and love of teachers. I cooperated, tried to excel, and almost succeeded in loving my teacher.

In the eleventh grade, I fell out of love and into a small gang of village terrorists. We placed thumbtacks on our teacher's chair, glued her books to her desk, painted her class register, and aimed missiles at her back in between barely suppressed fits of hysterical giggles. Elsewhere we broke light bulbs, "borrowed" horses for insane bareback romps along the lakeshore, and distributed dead chickens on doorsteps in the middle of dark winter nights. Various unimaginative disciplinary measures did little to dampen our enthusiasm, though most of us eventually tired of regular noon-hour and after-school detention.

In the twelfth grade they sent me to a private boarding school — a place for bright kids, I was told, although I did hear one of my cousins remark unkindly, "He's always been a discipline problem." ■■

DISCIPLINE AND MANAGEMENT DISTINGUISHED

Although the term *discipline* is in constant use among teachers, administrators, and students, it is not always the preferred word. Indeed, for quite a number of recent years, the more euphemistic expression *classroom management* has seemed less offensive and has consequently been more in vogue. Part of the reason for this lies in current philosophical movements in education that are perhaps more permissive, more humanistic, and more child-centered than was once the case. It now seems more appropriate to exhort teachers to "manage" their classrooms rather than to "discipline" their students.

One of the more common meanings of the term *discipline* equates it with punishment of various kinds. Recall Thorndike's widely accepted "discovery" that punishment is not nearly as effective for its purposes as is reinforcement for opposite purposes; indeed, punishment does not lead to the extinction of a response but merely to its suppression. It is hardly surprising that educators should have rejected punishment as a control technique. Nor is it surprising that discipline should also have fallen into disfavor, given its apparently close relationship with punishment. However, classroom control and discipline problems remain one of the primary preoccupations of many teachers. Discipline problems are one of the principal reasons for teacher failure and stress (Blase and Pajak, 1985). The contribution of these problems to student failure has not been negligible either—hence their importance in teacher-training programs.

Although the terms *discipline* and *classroom management* are often equated, there is an important distinction between the two. Put simply, **classroom management** refers to the arrangement of classroom activities in order to facilitate teaching and learning; **discipline** refers to teacher actions made necessary by student behaviors that disrupt (or threaten to disrupt) classroom activity. Thus, management and disciplinary acts may occur simultaneously or in close sequence, depending on the requirements of the immediate situation. Accordingly, this chapter discusses classroom management and discipline together. The emphasis throughout is on the practical and ethical aspects of disciplinary and management processes, rather than on the distinctions between the two. As Doyle (1986, p. 394) notes, some educators view management as a prerequisite to instruction—something to "get out of the way so that teaching can occur." Exactly the same thing may be said about discipline—that is, some educators view discipline as something that must be taken care of so that teaching can occur.

Not so. Neither classroom management nor classroom discipline can be "taken care of" and then put aside so that instruction and learning can take place. Rather, both are centrally involved in the ongoing process of teaching.

Definitions of Discipline

Some of the various meanings of the term *discipline* are revealed in the following common statements:

One of the reasons she's a good teacher is that she maintains such good discipline.

They had to be disciplined again after they released the pigeons in the classroom.

Now, Jack, for example, is a well-disciplined young man.

What sort of discipline do you use in your classroom?

A consideration of these statements reveals that *discipline* can refer to the degree of order or control that characterizes a group. Thus, teachers are said to maintain good discipline when their students are obedient and well behaved.

A second meaning relates to the techniques

used to bring about order and control. When teachers are asked to describe the sort of discipline they use, they are being asked to reveal the methods by which they establish order.

A third meaning is self-control. Thus, individuals are described as being highly disciplined when they appear to exercise firm control over their personal activities.

The final, and most common, meaning of the term *discipline* is punishment. When, for example, a teacher proudly claims to have successfully disciplined her class, the most obvious inference is that he has punished them and has thereby succeeded in achieving a higher degree of control. In fact, in the same way that the term *classroom management* has been used as a euphemism for *discipline*, the term *discipline* is often used as a euphemism for *punishment*. In this text, the term *punishment* is used freely. It was defined and discussed briefly in Chapter 2 and is considered in more detail later in this chapter.

For our purposes, *discipline* may be considered a comprehensive term that describes the variety of methods that might be used to maintain a classroom climate conducive to learning and to the healthy personal development of individuals. It includes procedural strategies, instructional strategies, reward and punishment, and all other facets of teacher-learner interaction.

Next we consider some of the ethical issues implicated in discipline, followed by discussions of specific preventive and corrective disciplinary measures.

THE CLASSROOM ENVIRONMENT

To put the subjects of this chapter into perspective, it is important to consider the environment (the context) in which teaching and learning occur — and in which the teacher manages and disciplines.

In the same way that the "average student" is an abstraction that does not exist in the real world, there is no "average classroom." Every classroom is unique. Each has its special blend of personalities that interact with one another, and with the personality and style of the teacher, to create its own dynamic ecology — that is, its own ever-changing environment.

Certain characteristics are descriptive of all classrooms and need to be taken into account in the business of teaching students and managing classrooms. Doyle (1979) describes these characteristics as follows: Classrooms are *multidimensional*. As we have just noted, they include a variety of individuals participating in many different activities and working toward a number of goals. In addition, many of the different events in the classroom are *simultaneous*. Seldom is only one thing happening at a time. Even when they are engaged in direct, whole-class instruction, teachers may recognize different degrees of attentiveness among individual students and different behaviors (or misbehaviors) that may require them to interrupt the instructional process. As they phrase questions, they must also make decisions about who will answer, assess the pace of the lesson relative to existing time constraints, and constantly monitor individual students for signs of inattention or for potentially disruptive behaviors.

Not only are classroom events multidimensional and simultaneous, but they are also *immediate*; that is, many of the events that occur simultaneously in the classroom require immediate teacher response. Decisions must be made and implemented very rapidly if the flow of classroom activity is to remain smooth and purposeful.

Finally, and perhaps most important, given the immediacy, the multidimensionality, and the simultaneity of classroom events, their course at any given moment is highly *unpredictable*.

To manage such an environment — one that demands a continuous, rapid sequence of immediate decisions and is as complex and unpredictable as a classroom — requires a special set of managerial skills. These skills are tempered, of course, by the teacher's personal philosophy and teaching style and should be consistent with sound pedagogical principles gleaned from writings in educational psychology — or from the mutterings of old bears. It is not a simple task.

But it is not a completely overwhelming task either — although it might seem that way to the beginning teacher. Expert teachers do not need to consciously analyze all the elements simultaneously present in the classroom; they don't need to deliberately and sequentially monitor and appraise the immediate activities of each student, responding when necessary and all the while maintaining a wonderful pedagogical flow, never failing to recognize and capitalize on those brief, unpredictable opportunities that recent jargon labels "teachable moments." The expert teacher, Kagan (1988) tells us, does all these things, many of them unconsciously. Such teachers develop sequences of routines and strategies that become almost automatic.

Can the skills and the strategies used by expert teachers be learned?

In a word, Yes. Some of these skills and strategies have been identified, and simply being aware of them might prove very helpful to beginning teachers. For example, certain important pedagogical (instructional or teaching) skills concern sequencing, structuring, and managing the content of instruction. Many of these skills can be gleaned from what psychology knows about learning and development, and many of them are described in the chapters of this text.

But teaching is more than organizing content. Teaching also requires important classroom management skills having to do with paying attention to students and being aware of ongoing classroom events. Copeland (1987), who labels these *multiple-attention* and *vigilance* skills, has devised a computer-simulated classroom in which it is possible to detect and evaluate these skills in teachers and to relate them to what goes on in real classrooms. As we see later in this chapter, some teachers are more "with it" than others; they are more aware of what is going on in their classrooms and are better able to direct the flow of activities to keep students on-task and interested. And as Eisner (1982) puts it, some teachers are more gifted in the "art," although not necessarily the science, of teaching. Such teachers can more skillfully build the classroom environments — the contexts — that are most conducive to learning *and* to happiness — and least conducive to management and discipline problems.

In addition to the artistic, pedagogical, and "with-it-ness" skills that teachers require are a wealth of specific strategies and potential responses to classroom events that can be learned and applied in the discipline and management of classrooms. These strategies and responses are the subject of this chapter.

THE ETHICS OF CONTROL

The term *control* is highly — and unjustifiably — unpopular. Some of its unpopularity can be traced to educational and philosophical writings that have addressed issues of freedom, self-determination, self-worth, individuality, and other humanistic concerns — those often equated with liberal and permissive child-rearing and educational methods. These concerns define much of the spirit of our times; no teacher wants to be "nonliberal" and restrictive. And there is little doubt that the deliberate exercise of control *is* restrictive. Is control therefore unethical?

There is, of course, no simple answer. If there were, there would be little controversy, and behaviorists and humanists would have much less about which to disagree.

Consider, first, that control is not only inevitable but necessary. There is no doubt that teachers, by virtue of their position and by virtue of their duties, have control. Indeed, it is not at all unreasonable to insist, as Marland (1975) does, that the exercise of control is one of the teacher's most important duties. We are not speaking here of a fear-enforced control that might have been characteristic of some of yesterday's schools. Control can be achieved, or at least facilitated, in a variety of gentle ways, some of which can be learned.

Parents too control their children (or at least try), often by setting limits for their behavior. Part of the successful socialization process requires that children be prevented from engaging in behaviors that might be injurious to themselves or to others. Thus, parents do not permit their children to play with dinner as it is cooking on the stove, to insert knives into electrical outlets, to jump off ladders, or to swim in dangerous waters. Less extreme instances of control involve the teaching of socially appropriate behavior, of values and morals — of "shoulds" and "should nots." It is less by accident than by virtue of parental control that children learn not to deface walls, steal other people's property, or kill the neighbor's dog. In short, certain standards of behavior are learned at least partly as a function of parental control. Whether such control involves reinforcement, punishment, models, reasoning, or a combination of these and other strategies cannot hide the fact that control is being exercised.

The classroom situation is not really very different. Teachers have often been described as acting *in loco parentis* — in the place of parents. They are urged to act in all ways as might a wise, judicious, and loving parent. And there is, in fact, no great incompatibility between values held in highest esteem by those who describe themselves as humanistically oriented and the techniques of behavior control that have been described by science. Love, empathy, warmth, genuineness, and honesty can go a long way toward ensuring a classroom climate conducive to learning and development. In spite of these highly desirable qualities, however, discipline problems are not uncommon in classrooms. That teachers should judiciously administer rewards and punishment in an effort to maintain an effective educational environment does not mean that they care less for their students; indeed, it might well indicate that they care more.

PREVENTIVE STRATEGIES IN THE CLASSROOM

In the classroom, as in medicine, there is little doubt that prevention should be valued more highly than correction. And it is reassuring that research is paying increasing attention to the methods by which teachers might prevent the occurrence of discipline problems (see, for example, Doyle, 1986). Perhaps the most important (though not entirely surprising) finding from this research is that the degree of order in a classroom depends far less on the frequency and insistence with which the teacher acts to maintain or restore order than on the nature of ongoing classroom activity. In the current jargon of classroom management, the strength of the primary vector — the principal ongoing stream of activity — is most influential in establishing and maintaining order (Kounin, 1970).

The second most important finding from this research concerns the timing of teacher interventions. The most successful classroom managers are those teachers who seem to anticipate most accurately when misbehaviors are likely to occur and intervene early to prevent them. In addition, the most effective interventions are subtle, brief, and often almost private, and as a result they do not interfere with ongoing classroom activities (Erickson and Mohatt, 1982).

Preventive strategies greatly depend on classroom management — that is, on the arrangement of classroom activities to facilitate teaching and learning. It is not difficult to find advice intended to help teachers manage the classroom in order to avoid discipline problems. Much of this advice is based on the collective experience of successful teachers and on the systematic observation of teachers in their classrooms. For what it might be worth to you, this chapter presents a distillation of such advice. Bear in mind, however, that the teacher's personality is probably the single most important factor in the classroom situation. Students find reasons to like or to dislike teachers in the combination of elusive and abstract qualities that define personality. Some traits can be learned, but desirable personality characteristics cannot, and thus they are not discussed further in this chapter. Not everybody should be a teacher. If you do not genuinely love children, and if they don't like you very much either, . . . please.

Caring for Children

One obvious but highly useful classroom strategy is to memorize pupils' names as soon as possible (Marland, 1975). More important, perhaps, learn as much as you can about individual students. Relevant knowledge can be obtained from conversations with other teachers (but beware of their prejudices and the consequent expectations that you might develop), from records, from involvement in extracurricular activities, and from parents and others. The children you teach should be more than just names and faces. The extent to which you care about them is reflected in the knowledge and understanding that you have of each. And the evidence suggests that the depth of your caring also affects how much they care about you and about each other.

Setting Rules

Classroom management and discipline would be much simpler if we could just give teachers a clear and simple list of rules and regulations that should govern all students in classrooms — complete with prescribed punishments for violation of these rules.

It's not quite so simple. Rules for student conduct are not, and should not be, fixed and absolute. Instead, they must be relative to teachers, to situations, and to students. Because of their different temperaments and styles, not all teachers expect or approve of similar student behaviors. Nor do teachers expect conformity to the same rules among students of widely differing ages and experience. And the rules of conduct imposed in a physical education class are quite different from those imposed during a recitation or a final examination.

In spite of the relativity of rules, research suggests a number of generally valid observations. Probably the most important is that effective classroom management depends to a large extent on the successful establishment of rules and procedures early in the school year (Doyle, 1986). However, because rules are highly relative to situations, they are not usually established formally; that is, teachers seldom tell students that this is a rule and that is a rule and that is another rule and so on. Instead, as Hargreaves, Hester, and Mellor (1975) note, students tend to learn most rules indirectly, often when infractions of those rules occur. Many of the rules are never made explicit but are simply implied by the teacher's interventions.

In contrast, many routines are taught explicitly and directly. Particularly in the elementary grades, such routines are indispensible to the smooth operation of the classroom and govern the activities of teachers and students. They specify where books and supplies are to be kept, how questions are to be asked and answered, how games are to be played, where reading circles are to be placed, and dozens of other details of classroom activity. The establishment of such routines is an important aspect of classroom management that provides a context within which learning can be greatly facilitated.

Routines need to be established early in the school year. As Doyle (1986) observes, the most successful classroom managers are those who, in a sense, hover over activities at the beginning of the year, guiding and directing students until procedures have become routinized and the routines have been learned and accepted by all students. Although rules and routines need to be predictable and consistent, this does not mean that they must always be enforced inflexibly. Even in the highly controlled, one-room bush school that I attended, there were occasions when the "no talking" and "no leaving your desk without permission" rules could be bent and sometimes broken.

I remember this happening one day when a beaver dragged himself across the school yard and the teacher (my father) allowed the entire class to crowd up against the windows and watch. Later that day, he delivered a marvelous lesson on how young beavers are driven from overcrowded lodges and forced to swim across lakes or rivers, or trudge overland, in search of new areas to settle and populate.

For days after that, I kept looking out of the window, hoping to see a beaver. Even now, years later, when I'm bored and tired I sometimes catch myself looking for a beaver through my window. . . .

But there are no places for the beaver here. There is only concrete.

Giving Legitimate Praise

Marland (1975) advises that teachers arrange situations so that they can make frequent but *legitimate* use of praise, and that they observe some simple guidelines concerning the use of praise and criticism. Praise, given its effect on self-esteem and self-concept, should be public. On occasion, it should be communicated to parents and other interested adults as well. Criticism, in contrast, also because of its effects on self-esteem and self-concept, should be given privately.

In addition, both praise and criticism should be specific rather than general. As we saw in Chapter 11, research clearly demonstrates that praise and punishment that are not contingent on behavior or that are not clearly related to a specific behavior are much less likely to be effective. Thus, Marland suggests that a student should not be admonished in general terms such as "Behave yourself" or "Be good." Instead, students should be directed to engage in a specific behavior and given a reason for that behavior. For example, the teacher might say, "Please put down your water pistol and your hunting knife because you are disturbing the class." Presumably, the rule relating to the inadvisability of disturbing the class will already have been explained and justified and the penalties for repeated infraction of that rule will have been made explicit.

Using Humor

The effectiveness of humor is often overlooked by teachers who do not consider themselves spontaneously humorous. And faculties of education have not gone far out of their way to encourage prospective teachers to learn either how to make others laugh or, perhaps most important, how to laugh at themselves. Potentially explosive confrontations can often be avoided by turning aside an implied student challenge with a skillful humorous parry.

Consider, for example, Ms. Howard, who, because of her reputation for maintaining order in the classroom, has been assigned a ninth-grade class that might generously be described as predelinquent. (Less generous descriptions are entirely inappropriate in a textbook as polite as this one.) On the first day of class, she is challenged. One Rodney Phillips, closely modeled after a popular television personality who is himself modeled after a stereotype of the 1950s, finds an excusable error in Ms. Howard's arithmetic computations on the chalkboard. "She can't even add proper and they call her a teacher," he says for the benefit of his classmates. Whereupon Ms. Howard immediately falls to her knees and in an amateurish imitation of the television hero, prays loudly to some undisclosed source to "Make me perfect again like

I used to be!" Laughter that might otherwise have been directed *at* her is now *with* her. Ms. Howard simply has the knack of not taking herself too seriously.

Establishing "With-it-ness"

Kounin (1970) viewed several hundred hours of videotaped classroom lessons in an attempt to identify qualities of teacher behavior that appear to be most closely related to good classroom management. One factor common to most successful teachers was that they seemed to be more aware than less successful teachers of what was going on in their classrooms, of who was responsible for infractions of rules, and of when intervention was necessary. Accordingly, Kounin argues that a quality best described as **"with-it-ness"** is important for maintaining order in the classroom. A teacher who is "with it" knows what is going on and is more likely to be respected by students. Similarly, Kounin found that the most successful teachers were able to handle more than one behavior problem at one time, all the while maintaining the direction and momentum of ongoing classroom activities.

Precisely what with-it-ness is and how it can be developed are important matters for the teacher. Unfortunately, we know little about its development, although we may know more about its nature. Kounin (1970) arrived at teacher with-it-ness scores by looking at how often a teacher successfully directed a student to **desist** — that is, to stop engaging in some "off-task" behavior. Teachers with the highest scores were those whose "desists" were *on target* and *on time* (neither too early nor too late). Teachers who were less "with it" tended to instruct the *wrong* students to desist, or they tended to deliver their desist requests either after an off-task behavior had been going on for some time or too far ahead of its occurrence.

In an attempt to define with-it-ness in concrete terms, Borg (1973) identifies several components of with-it "teacher desist behaviors."

According to Borg, the most with-it teachers suggest some alternative, on-task behavior rather than simply requesting cessation of the off-task behavior, praise on-task behavior while ignoring concurrent off-task activities, and provide descriptions of desirable behaviors or of relevant classroom rules. In addition, the most effective desists are timely (they occur before the misbehavior spreads and/or intensifies) and on target (they are directed toward the principal wrongdoer).

Kounin's (1970) research on teacher with-it-ness led to the conclusion that timely and on-target desists are associated with less deviant behavior in the classroom and more involvement in classroom activities. This conclusion was later corroborated in a study by Brophy and Evertson (1976) and again in research conducted by Copeland (1987). In Copeland's study, teachers interacted with a computer simulation of a classroom situation. The simulation allowed the investigator to assess teachers' *multiple-attention* and *vigilance* skills — described in much the same terms as Kounin's with-it-ness. Teachers were then observed in their classrooms, and measures were obtained of the extent to which their students remained on-task or were disruptive. Copeland reports that the highest on-task scores were associated with high teacher vigilance and attentiveness.

Shaping the Learning Environment

Everything involved in teacher-learner interactions and in the teaching/learning environment can facilitate or impede classroom discipline. Marland (1975) suggests various ways to personalize the learning environment. For instance, there is something impersonal and cold about the traditional, dominating position of the teacher's desk at the front-center of the class. Similarly, student desks traditionally are aligned in straight, even-length rows with uniform spaces front, back, and sides. Eyes front!

Of course, certain definite advantages are inherent in this traditional placement, not the least of which are that there must be some focal point for student attention and that it is considerably easier for students to look to the front to see their teacher than it is to look to the rear. My eleventh-grade teacher moved her desk to the back of the room — not because she was experimenting with ways to personalize the classroom environment, but because she could more easily watch those among us who were dedicated to mischief and other innocent amusements. We suspected as well that she had tired of being bombarded with our crude, elastic-propelled spitballs.

Marland's advice that the learning environment be personalized goes beyond a search for a more "personal" arrangement of desks. It includes as well those small decorative touches that are often more visible in the early rather than the later grades. Posters, charts, wall hangings, and other instructional and/or decorative objects need not be provided solely by the school and by teachers, but might also be provided by students.

Classroom climate is more than the physical environment. As was shown in Chapter 10, for example, creativity appears to be fostered in certain climates (warm, friendly, and so on) and to be impeded in others (cold, authoritarian). So, too, certain classroom climates are more conducive to preventive discipline than others. Glasser (1969), for example, says that discipline problems will be minimized in warm, personal environments in which all students are accepted as capable.

Maintaining Classroom Activity

As we saw earlier, the most important factor in determining classroom order is not the frequency or strength of teacher interventions so much as the nature of ongoing classroom activity; this observation must surely contain an important implication or two for the classroom teacher.

Researchers inform us that there are perhaps eleven (Berliner, 1983), perhaps seventeen (Stodolsky, 1984), or perhaps a less definite number of different classroom activities. These activities include such things as "seatwork," student presentations, small-group activities, discussions, recitations, demonstrations, lectures, giving instructions, tutoring, and so on. In the elementary school an activity typically lasts somewhere between ten and twenty minutes; in the higher grades, an activity often lasts somewhat longer. Between activities are transitions, also sometimes considered a type of activity.

In an extensive study of student involvement (sometimes referred to as "on-task" behavior) and classroom activity, Gump (1969) found that small-group activities led by the teacher brought about the greatest involvement. In contrast, student presentations elicited the least student involvement — at least on the part of nonpresenters. Subsequently, a number of researchers have reported that involvement is lowest when students are doing seatwork and highest when teachers are actively leading the class (see, for example, Ross, 1984; Burns, 1984). Accordingly, disruptions and misbehaviors are most likely to occur during seatwork, during student presentations, and during transitions.

Maintaining Democratic Procedures

Webster (1968) offers a number of principles to guide teachers in their efforts to maintain a non-autocratic form of classroom order. One of the primary goals of these principles is to promote the development of self-discipline in students. The principles themselves are based on what Webster describes as the three r's of good discipline: reason, respect, and relevance. Thus discipline should be reasonable and interpreted as such by students; it should reflect one of the most important of society's values, respect for individuals; and it should be relevant to the behaviors giving rise to disciplinary action. Several of the principles listed by Webster (p. 50) are shown in Table 12.1.

Table 12.1 Webster's principles of nonautocratic order

1. Teachers must make sure that all students understand rules and standards and the reasons for their existence.

2. The first violation of a rule should lead to a warning, a discussion of alternative ways of behaving, and clarification of the consequences of repeated infractions.

3. Teachers should endeavor to discover the causes underlying misbehavior.

4. Whenever possible, teachers should address students in private regarding their misbehavior.

5. Sarcasm, ridicule, and other forms of discipline that lead to public humiliation should be avoided.

6. When teachers make mistakes (if they ever do), they should apologize.

7. The punishment should fit the crime. Minor infractions should not bring about harsh punishment.

8. Extra classwork and assignments, academic tests, and other school-related activities should never be used as a form of punishment.

Even though there is little that is surprising, obscure, or difficult about Webster's advice, it is nevertheless valuable. It is all too easy to act "instinctively" when faced with a discipline problem. And although the teacher's instincts might often be entirely appropriate, there might be occasions when other behaviors would have been considerably more appropriate. Perhaps knowledge of these principles can increase instances of appropriate action.

Creating a Context for Preventive Classroom Management

The preceding sections might seem a little like a catalog from which a clever teacher might select an assortment of tricks and tactics for managing classrooms, all the while keeping students happily on-task. But good teaching is not so simple; in teaching, there are no recipes that, when followed one-two-three, always lead where they are intended.

Good teaching—which implies effective classroom management and discipline—requires far more than the deliberate and judicious application of principles and tactics in specific classroom situations. As we saw at the beginning of this chapter, classrooms are characterized by a multiplicity of often unpredictable events occurring simultaneously; they demand of the teacher an exceptional level of attention and vigilance (with-it-ness). And they require as well an ongoing series of instantaneous decisions and their immediate implementation.

In addition to the ongoing decision making and problem solving that good teaching requires, it also involves a large number of decisions that are made in advance. These might be in response to specific, immediate questions, such as: "What do I teach next?" "What assignments are appropriate for this unit?" "How should I arrange the seats in my classroom?" Or they might be in response to more global questions, such as: "Should I incorporate cooperative learning activities in my classroom?" "Should I involve students in decisions about rules?" "Should I include programs designed to increase prosocial behavior?" "Should I emphasize a whole-class, teacher-directed teaching style?" "Should I implement more small-group learning activities?" And so on.

The important point is that learning, management, and discipline occur in a classroom context that is determined by at least four influences: the blend of students that compose the class, the teacher's beliefs and personality, the teacher's application of the *science* that texts such as this provide, and a measure of *art*.

You may have some control over the third and fourth of these influences, but not over the first two. You cannot easily change your beliefs and personality, and you are not likely to be allowed to select students for your classes. Still, enough is under your control to make the struggle to become the best teacher you can worthwhile. All that relates to good and effective teaching also relates to maintaining classroom order.

CORRECTIVE STRATEGIES FOR THE CLASSROOM

It is clear that even good, effective teachers are sometimes called upon to deal with disturbances and disruptions in the classroom. That this should be the case does not necessarily mean that the teacher is a failure, that the system is at fault, or that teacher-training institutions have been remiss. Although each of these might be wholly or partly responsible, the point is not to lay the blame but to deal with the situation.

In dealing with any disciplinary problem, two concerns are of paramount importance. The first is that the individual not be harmed — that whatever the teacher does is done in the best interests of the student, with full consideration of that person's self-esteem and humanity. The second is that the disciplinary measures invoked should be applied in the interests of the entire group. In short, the teacher as a humanitarian practitioner of skills (with a little art, to be sure) must strike a delicate balance between the well-being of the group and that of the individual. The resolution is not always simple.

A variety of corrective strategies are available to the teacher. Because the immediate objective of corrective discipline is to change or eliminate a particular behavior, these strategies can appropriately be labeled behavior modification techniques. *Behavior modification* refers specifically to strategies predicated on behaviorist learning theory. These include the use of reinforcement, models, extinction, and punishment. Each of these strategies is discussed here with specific reference to discipline problems, as are less behavioristic procedures such as reasoning.

Reasoning

Reasoning is one of the most important alternatives to the more direct forms of corrective intervention. Essentially, to reason is to provide rational explanations; hence reasoning as a corrective strategy involves presenting children with reasons for not engaging in deviant behavior and/or reasons for engaging in some alternative behavior. There is a fundamental difference between saying to a student, "Don't snap your fingers because you are distracting the others and making it difficult for them to study," and saying, "Don't snap your fingers or you will have to stay after school." The first uses reasoning; the second involves a threat of punishment. Note, however, that the first statement, while appealing to reason, might also be interpreted as implying a threat, depending on the child's prior experience with the person attempting the correction. If children have learned through experience that the likely consequences of not acceding to authority's wishes, no matter how reasonably those wishes might be phrased, is some form of punishment, the effectiveness of reason might well be due to the implied threat.

Reasoning is considerably more appealing to parents and teachers than are most other disciplinary alternatives. It seems somehow more human to deal with children on an intellectual level than to deal with them from our positions of power as dispensers of rewards and punishments. And, happily, research and good sense both confirm our suspicions that reasoning can be an effective means of controlling or correcting student behavior.

A number of researchers have investigated the comparative effectiveness of various kinds of reasons that might be given children to prevent them from engaging in some behavior. In a typical experimental situation, children are requested not to play with a toy and are then left alone with that toy; they have no reason to believe that they will be apprehended if they do play with the toy. Investigators give the children specific reasons for not playing with the toy.

Parke (1974) reports that rationales that stress the object ("The toy might break") are more effective for younger children than are more abstract rationales relating to rights of possession ("You should not play with toys that belong to others"). However, Hoffman (1970) found that for older children rationales that emphasize the consequences of their behavior for other people (other-oriented induction) are more persuasive than rationales that emphasize the consequences to the child. In other words, if the experimenter says, "Do not play with that toy because you will make the child it belongs to unhappy," subjects are more likely not to play with the toy than if the experimenter says, "Do not play with that toy because it might break and that would make you unhappy."

Walters and Grusec (1977) also argue that reasoning that arouses empathy for others is usually more effective than reasoning that focuses on personal consequences, particularly after the age of six. Thus, with advancing intellectual and moral development, children are more likely to respond to rationales relating to abstractions and ideals and to become less concerned with immediate objective consequences. This observation is further corroborated by what is known about the sequence of moral development in children (see Chapter 7).

The implications of the foregoing observations are obvious: It is wise to provide younger children with specific, concrete reasons for requests that are made of them. After children have reached school age, however, more abstract rationales are preferable. Perhaps most important, rationales that are other-directed and that consequently arouse empathy for others appear to be most effective.

In addition to humanitarian and ethical considerations that clearly favor reasoning over punishing, reasoning is preferable to punishment for several practical reasons. First, a punishing agent provides a model of aggressiveness for the learner. In effect, the punisher's activities signify that one acceptable method of dealing with difficult situations is through the assertion of power in punitive form. Reasoning provides a rather different model. To reason with a child — to provide a rationale for required behavior — is to say, in effect, that one of the ways of coping with difficulty is the deliberate application of thought.

A second advantage of a reasoning strategy is that such an approach lends itself naturally to the description of alternative acceptable behaviors. In other words, reasoning need not be restricted to providing rationales for why a behavior should *not* be engaged in, but it can also be directed toward explaining why certain behaviors *should* be undertaken. Various forms of altruistic and prosocial behavior (cooperation, sharing, helping) cannot easily be taught by punitive means, but instead lend themselves more easily to the use of models, reasoning, reinforcement, or a combination of these.

Systematic Reinforcement Programs

Applying positive reinforcement to a discipline problem simply requires that the problem be reinterpreted: Instead of focusing on the elimination of undesired responses, the teacher focuses on the reinforcement of the opposite behavior. Consider the example of students who continually disrupt classroom activities in order to gain the teacher's attention. A relatively easy, and often effective, disciplinary measure is to pay attention to those students whenever they are not being disruptive and to ignore them when they are.

Teachers have at their disposal a wide variety of potent reinforcers, not the least important of which are praise, smiles, grades, and attention. When these social reinforcers prove ineffective, more elaborate reinforcement systems can be established. The best-known are token systems whereby students earn points or tokens for good behavior and sometimes lose them for less desirable behavior. The tokens can later be exchanged for tangible rewards.

Psychology journals offer numerous examples of the use of positive reinforcement in the classroom. For example, O'Leary and Becker (1967) describe a study in which a token system of reinforcement was used in conjunction with social approval in order to eliminate deviant responses and encourage acceptable classroom behavior. The subjects were seventeen nine-year-olds. (Although these students were of average intelligence, they had been classified as emotionally disturbed and placed in a special classroom.) The experimental procedure, which lasted for a year, involved writing a number of instructions on the chalkboard (for example, "Desk clear," "Face the front," "Do not talk") and then assigning each student a daily score based on observance of the rules. The scores were entered in a record book on each student's desk and could be totaled and exchanged for small toys and trinkets at any time. Additional reinforcement was provided for each child by the teacher's comments (for example, "I like the way you held your hand up before talking today"). The success of the project was evaluated by comparing incidents of deviant behavior before the program and at its completion. The evidence suggests that it was highly effective.*

Although the effectiveness of reinforcement in establishing and maintaining acceptable behaviors can hardly be disputed, there are a number of problems involved in the systematic use of token systems. The establishment of such a system requires a great deal of time and care and presents some real problems in selecting reinforcers for which tokens can be exchanged. In addition, several studies have found tokens ineffective for some students and distracting for others (Kazdin and Bootzin, 1972). Some students spend so much time counting and sorting their tokens that they experience considerable difficulty attending to the tasks desired of them.

One frequently used alternative to token systems, called the Premack principle, simply allows students who have behaved appropriately (or who have not behaved inappropriately) to engage in some reinforcing activity — one that the child enjoys. Thus, one child might be permitted free time for reading, another for painting, another for running around the gym. (A later section describes the Premack principle in more detail.)

Another interesting alternative is presented by Nay et al. (1976), who used tape to demarcate an area of approximately one square yard around each student's desk. These areas were described as the students' personal spaces, to be named and decorated by them and to be occupied by them alone. The experiment addressed two types of deviant behaviors: leaving one's desk at inappropriate times and speaking out. Unambiguous signals were placed at the front of the class to indicate when leaving one's territory and speaking were not allowed. A red light was the signal prohibiting leaving; a figure with the lips closed signaled 'no talking.' When walking quietly around the room, obtaining

---

*The procedure described here involved both positive reinforcement and extinction. In fact, most programs based on behavior modification make use of a combination of techniques.

supplies, or leaving personal territory for some other reason was permitted, a green light replaced the red light; similarly, when children were permitted to talk quietly, a figure with the lips open was placed at the front. The assumption of the experiment was that being allowed to remain in one's territory is reinforcing, particularly if infractions of rules result in one's removal from that territory. Accordingly, desks were set aside in an area labeled "no-man's land," and children guilty of leaving their seats or of talking when these activities were prohibited were sent to one of these desks for a twenty-minute period. Further infractions in "no-man's land" resulted in a longer exile from home territory. Strikingly, after several weeks, disruptive behavior had virtually been eliminated in a classroom that had previously threatened to pose some severe discipline problems.

In spite of the apparent effectiveness of some systematic behavior modification programs as corrective disciplinary strategies, it should be noted that many of them are difficult or impractical in ordinary classrooms. The intelligent use of praise as reinforcement does not present the same practical problems. However, as Lepper (1981) has demonstrated, the excessive use of reinforcement can have harmful effects on subsequent motivation. In one representative experiment, Lepper and Greene (1975) asked two groups of children to solve a number of geometric puzzles. One group was told that they would be allowed to play with some attractive toys as a reward; the other was also allowed to play with the puzzles, but was not led beforehand to expect a reward. Later, children were observed unobtrusively to see whether any of them spontaneously played with the puzzles, which were freely available in the classroom. As is shown in Figure 12.1, significantly more of those who had not expected a reward continued to be motivated to play with the puzzles.

Why? Lepper and Greene suggest that the most reasonable explanation is a cognitive one. It is important for us to try to make sense of our

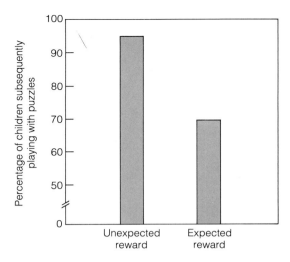

Figure 12.1 Significantly more of the children who had not expected a reward showed intrinsic interest by subsequently playing with the geometric puzzles.
Based on data from M. R. Lepper and D. Greene (1975), "Turning Play into Work: Effects of Adult Surveillance and Extrinsic Rewards on Children's Intrinsic Motivation, *Journal of Personality and Social Psychology, 31*, 479–486.

behaviors—to understand why we do things. Typically, we resort to two classes of explanations for our behaviors: *extrinsic* or *intrinsic* causes; that is, we generally recognize that we do things for certain external rewards (money, prestige, being allowed to play with toys), for internal rewards (satisfaction, sense of accomplishment, personal interest), or sometimes for both internal and external rewards. When external rewards are large and obvious, our motivation becomes largely extrinsic; but when we expect no great extrinsic rewards, we must look to intrinsic causes. Thus, children who expect reinforcement can understand and justify their behavior in terms of extrinsic factors; those who do not expect external rewards must justify their behavior in terms of such things as the pleasure and enjoyment associated with it. Children who do not expect rewards are subsequently more highly motivated (intrinsically motivated) to continue the activity. To the extent that this observation is true, there may clearly be some danger associated with the indiscriminate and excessive use of external rewards — hence the following section, which deals with the judicious use of reinforcment in schools.

Positive Reinforcement

Positive reinforcement is centrally involved in classroom learning. Its systematic application, however, requires that two related questions be answered:

1. Under what stimulus conditions will the desirable response be emitted?

2. What reinforcement will be used?

The first question can be answered in a number of ways. The stimulus conditions may involve special pedagogical devices, such as programs and computers, or common day-to-day classroom routines that involve explaining, asking, showing films, demonstrating, and experimenting.

The second question also gives rise to several answers. Reinforcement can be extrinsic (external) or it can be intrinsic (internal). Obviously, **extrinsic reinforcment** is more likely than **intrinsic reinforcement** to be under the control of the teacher. According to Drabman (1976), the most important and most powerful extrinsic reinforcer in the classroom is teacher attention; others are praise, tokens, stars, grades, and promotion. Intrinsic reinforcement is defined in terms of the satisfaction that the student gets from learning.

Intrinsic Reinforcement. Although intrinsic reinforcement is not under direct teacher control, the teacher can nevertheless structure learning situations in ways that are more or less likely to lead to satisfaction. Presenting students with tasks that are too difficult is not likely to lead to satisfaction with learning.

Likewise, excessively simple tasks are not self-reinforcing.

The teacher's use of external rewards is another source of influence on intrinsic reinforcement. If rewards are initially administered for behaviors related to learning, it follows that the process of learning will acquire the characteristics of a generalized reinforcer. In fact, it is customary in structured teaching programs based on reinforcement principles to use external rewards only in the initial stages of the program (see, for example, Meacham and Wiesen, 1969; Hewett, 1968). It is assumed that intrinsic reinforcement will eventually suffice to maintain the behavior.

Extrinsic Reinforcement. Among the extrinsic reinforcers most commonly used are those mentioned above: attention, praise, tokens, stars, grades, and promotion. Another very important and apparently very effective source of reinforcement is defined by the **Premack principle** (Premack, 1965), which states that behavior that ordinarily occurs very frequently can be used to reinforce less frequent behavior. Parents and teachers use this principle constantly: A child is allowed to play outside *after* eating supper; a student is permitted to read a library book *after* completing an assignment.

Bijou and Sturges (1959) classify extrinsic reinforcers into five categories: consumables, manipulatables, visual and auditory stimuli, social stimuli, and tokens. It is interesting, and potentially valuable, to consider the use of each of these in the classroom. Consumables are relatively inconvenient. A teacher walking around a classroom with a bag of cookies, dispensing them as she observes desirable student behavior, might occasion some concern among parents. Manipulatables, objects such as toys or trinkets, can be used successfully, particularly with young children. Reinforcing auditory and visual stimuli are less likely to be readily available to a teacher. Such reinforcers are signals that have been given reinforcing properties. For example, if a teacher told students that he would ring a bell every time he was happy with them, the bell would be an auditory reinforcer. This is not to be confused with social reinforcers, which take the form of praise, approval, or simply attention, and which are by far the most prevalent and powerful reinforcers available to a teacher. In this connection it should also be kept in mind that peer approval is often as powerful or more powerful a reinforcer than teacher approval. Tokens, check marks, or stars are sometimes used as direct extrinsic reinforcement for desirable behavior. In a token system, it is not uncommon to arrange for tokens to be exchanged for other reinforcers: consumables, manipulatables, or perhaps time for some pleasant activity.

Teachers are not the only ones who have control over reinforcers that are important to the lives and learning of their students. Indeed, parents also are administrators of what can be particularly powerful rewards — and punishments too.

Barth (1979) reviews several dozen studies in which investigators deliberately and systematically enlisted the help of parents in providing reinforcement for school-related activities. These studies involved students in group homes, in special classrooms, and in ordinary classrooms. Reinforcers used varied from tokens and social praise to consumables and special privileges and were administered for an extremely wide range of behaviors. In many cases, money was also used as a reinforcer. For example, students would earn varying amounts of money for different school grades — and sometimes would lose money for failing to complete assignments or for getting low grades.

Taken as a whole, the studies reviewed by Barth indicate that home-based reinforcement can be extremely influential in bringing about measurable and significant positive changes, both in behavior and in academic achievement, for many students in a wide range of subjects and situations.

Seven Principles for Using Reinforcement. Michael (1967) describes seven principles that should be kept in mind when attempting to control behavior through its consequences. Some of these have been discussed earlier, but all are important enough to bear repeating.

The first principle is that the consequences of behavior, whether rewarding or punishing, are defined only in terms of their effect on the learner. Teachers cannot always assume that a stimulus that they consider pleasant for a student will, in fact, strengthen behavior. Peer approval, for example, is generally strongly reinforcing; for a very inhibited student, however, peer approval and the attention it generates may be quite punishing. Nor can a teacher simply ask students what is reinforcing for them, because this might well render some reinforcers almost meaningless. If, for example, students were to indicate that praise was reinforcing, subsequent praise might be interpreted as less genuine and hence would be less reinforcing.

A very useful concept in relation to this first principle (that reinforcement is highly individualistic) is that of the **reinforcement menu**, introduced by Addison and Homme (1966). Based largely on the Premack principle, a reinforcement menu is a list of potentially reinforcing activities from which the student is allowed to select following some behavior that merits reinforcement. Table 12.2 presents one example of a reinforcement menu.

The second principle states that the effects of reinforcement are automatic; that is, the teacher need not explain to students that if they learn well they will receive some specific reinforcement that will then lead them to study even harder. The point is that if students do learn and consequently are reinforced, they will probably study even harder without ever having discussed this marvelous phenomenon with their teacher. However, as Kalish (1981) points out, praise (or punishment) by itself, especially for young children, is not as effective as praise

Table 12.2   A reinforcement menu*

Reward	Cost
1. One free period in the library	10
2. One free period in class	10
3. One day off from clean-up duty	5
4. Lunch with Miss Clements [the teacher]	15
5. Lunch prepared by Miss Clements	25
6. Extra help with one subject	2
7. Get to choose the game for gym	10
8. Get to sit anywhere in class for one day	3

*Members of a fifth-grade class could purchase activities from this menu, using points earned in school-related activities.

accompanied by a description of what was done to deserve praise or by an explanation of why it is deserved.

The third principle stresses that reinforcement or punishment should be related very closely to the terminal behavior. In other words, teachers must have some short-range goals clearly in mind so that they can reinforce behavior that matches those goals.

The fourth principle is that reinforcement should be consistent. This does not mean that reinforcement must occur for every correct response. It does mean, however, that a specific behavior should not be reinforced one time and punished the next.

A related principle, the fifth, is that consequences should follow behavior very closely. Delayed reward or punishment is much less effective than immediate consequences. Adherence to this principle is very clearly one of the major strengths of programmed instruction in which learners receive knowledge of results immediately (discussed in Chapter 13). Another implication of this principle is that the period of time between giving a quiz and returning the results should be kept as short as possible.

The sixth principle, according to Michael, is that the amount of reinforcement necessary for behavioral change is usually underestimated. This is particularly true for the early stages of learning. The sixth principle says, in effect, that reinforcement must be potent. If teacher praise is highly valued by a student, that student will probably require less praise than another who does not value it so much.

The seventh principle relates to the structuring of a learning situation. It maintains that the student's work should be set up as a series of clear steps, each of which can be reinforced. Programmed instruction (see Chapter 13) can meet this requirement much more easily than can a classroom teacher who is responsible for a relatively large number of students.

A simple illustration of the use of rewards in a learning situation was provided by a ninth-grade typing teacher in a remote rural school. The teacher had contracted with the class to give students fifteen minutes of free time if they learned to type at a rate of fifty words per minute. No rural school has since developed a group of such proficient ninth-grade typists. This may have been due to the fact that the students interpreted the contract to mean that the entire class would get fifteen minutes for each typist scoring fifty. On a warm morning in June when the lake lay calm and inviting, we sent the teacher a note informing her that we had earned the entire day. Not a single student showed up in class. Most of us can still type.

Modeling

Teachers make unconscious use of the various effects of models throughout their teaching careers. It is inevitable that they should be models for students and that students should also be models for each other. The deliberate and systematic use of models is perhaps rarer, but it can be highly effective.

Recall that one of the effects of models is the suppression or reappearance of previously suppressed deviant behavior. This effect, labeled the inhibitory-disinhibitory effect (see Chapter 8), apparently occurs as a result of seeing a model being punished or rewarded for deviant behavior. Not surprisingly, the application of the inhibitory effect is extremely common in schools. Often, when a teacher punishes a student in a class, she makes the assumption that other students will inhibit any tendencies that they might have to engage in the punished behavior. Whenever teachers single out for punishment one offender from among a group of offenders, they hope that the effects of the punishment will spread to the remainder of the group. This is why leaders are often punished for the transgressions of their followers. Interestingly, the punishment may have a "secondhand" effect, as does reinforcement. The reinforcement that an observer derives from seeing a model reinforced is termed vicarious reinforcement: the similar effects of punishment could also be termed vicarious.

Using Extinction

Animal studies indicate that responses maintained by reinforcement can usually be eliminated through the complete withdrawal of reinforcement. Thus, a pigeon that has been taught to peck at a disk for its food should soon cease to peck when food is no longer provided as a contingency of disk pecking. In fact, however, many pigeons will continue to peck at the disk indefinitely, even when the pecking no longer leads to reinforcement. A humanist might simply insist that to be a pigeon is to peck, and that a fully actualized pigeon gets high by pecking disks and remains unmoved by the crass material rewards that might move other pigeons. A behaviorist would analyze the situation differently, insisting that a pigeon continues to peck because there is something intrinsically reinforcing about the act of pecking. Whatever the reason might be, it remains true that not all behaviors can be extinguished through the removal of reinforcement. Furthermore, it should be noted that many disruptive behaviors in the classroom are reinforced by peers rather than by teachers. To the extent that teachers are not in control of relevant reinforcers, there is little that they can do to remove them.

More optimistically, some disruptive behaviors appear to be maintained by teacher attention, in which case it might be a relatively simple matter to cease paying attention. However, the matter might not be quite so simple if the behavior in question is highly disruptive of class activities. But there are other alternatives, the most common of which is punishment.

Punishment

Punishment can take a variety of forms. Recall that there are, in principle, two distinct types of punishment: The first involves the presentation of a noxious (unpleasant) stimulus; the second involves the removal of a pleasant stimulus and was illustrated in the Nay et al. (1976) study in which students were removed from their territories for infraction of rules.

Specific punishments used by teachers include facial gestures of disapproval, reprimands, detention, unpleasant activities, time-outs, and, occasionally, physical punishment. There are many passionate objectors to the use of punishment and a number of practical objections as well. At the same time, there is a need to reexamine the effectiveness of various forms of punishment.

The Case Against Punishment.

In addition to some obvious ethical and humanitarian objections to punishment, there are a number of more practical objections. Among these is the observation that punishment by itself draws attention to socially undesirable behavior and fails to illustrate suitable alternatives. Note that punishment used in conjunction with reasoning and other corrective measures need not be subject to the same objection.

Additional evidence suggests that punishment sometimes has effects opposite to those intended. This is particularly obvious when parents or teachers attempt to eliminate aggressive or violent behavior through physical punishment (Sears et al., 1957). In effect, parents who punish violence with violence provide a model of violence for the child—a model that might be interpreted to mean that aggressiveness is permissible under certain circumstances.

Other objections to the use of punishment are described by Clarizio and Yelon (1974,

p. 50) as follows: First, punishment does not eliminate an undesirable response, although it might result in its suppression or in a reduction in its frequency. Second, punishment may have unpleasant emotional side effects that are themselves maladaptive (for example, fear, anxiety, and tension). Finally, punishment is a source of frustration and may therefore lead to other undesirable or maladaptive behaviors.

The Case for Punishment.

Most of the objections just cited apply only to one type of punishment: the presentation of unpleasant stimuli. Furthermore, these objections are most applicable to physical punishment and much less applicable to verbal punishment. The forms of punishment that involve the removal of pleasant stimuli (for example, loss of privileges) are not subject to the same practical and philosophical objections and should be considered legitimate methods by which teachers can maintain the degree of control essential for humane and personal teaching.

The case to be made for punishment can be based on a number of studies demonstrating that punitive methods can be effective in suppressing disruptive and sometimes dangerous behaviors (Parke, 1974). Some situations demand immediate and decisive intervention and do not lend themselves to the more gentle strategies of reinforcement, modeling, and reasoning. A child caught lighting matches and touching them to the draperies may be reasoned with and physically removed; but if he persists in burning the curtains at every opportunity, punishment may well be in order.

Although reinforcement, modeling, and reasoning have proven highly effective for promoting desirable behaviors, it is extremely difficult for a child to learn to recognize unacceptable behaviors simply by generalizing in reverse from situations that have been reinforced (Ausubel, 1958). In many cases, then, punishment of *specific behaviors* can be highly informative. And even though considerable evidence shows that punishment administered by an otherwise warm and loving parent is more effective than punishment administered by a habitually cold and distant parent (Aronfreed, 1968), no evidence shows that punishment administered by a loving parent disrupts emotional bonds between parent and child (Walters and Grusec, 1977).

One of the theoretical objections to the use of punishment is that it does not work—that although it might serve to suppress behavior or reduce its frequency, it does not lead to the elimination (extinction) of a response. Consider, however, that a punisher's intent clearly is to *suppress* a behavior; complete elimination is, in fact, absolutely irrelevant. If Johnny has been punished for burning curtains, we should not dare hope that he will, as a result, have forgotten how to burn curtains. But we are justified in hoping that he will refrain from doing so in the future.

Interestingly, most of the data that we have regarding punishment is derived from animal studies. For obvious reasons, it is easier to do research with animals than with children (although even the lowly rat is now treated with considerably more respect than was once the case). It is possible to administer electric shocks to animals; there are no directly comparable stimuli that can be used with children. Hence, controlled research of the effects of punishment on children typically use such "annoyers" as loud buzzers. Evidence from a number of studies suggests that these annoyers can be effective in suppressing unwanted behavior. (In many of these experiments children are asked not to play with a toy; the buzzer sounds if they do.)

This section is not meant to minimize the dangers of punishment. Several important points need to be made. The most important is that most researchers and theorists remain virtually unanimous in their rejection of physical punishment. Not only is physical punishment a humiliating violation of the person, but it presents a highly undesirable model. If your task were to teach children that the best way of obtaining what they want is by force, then excessive use of physical punishment might well be your best teaching method.

If we do reject physical punishment (in practice, the rejection is very far from complete), a number of alternatives remain. The least objectionable are those involving the withdrawal of reinforcement.

If you are like most teachers, you are likely to make use of both major types of punishment in your classroom: withdrawal of pleasant consequences and the administration of unpleasant consequences. A careful review of the punishment literature and of humanistic counterarguments reveals that three effective forms of punishment that do not have the disadvantages usually associated with punishment are verbal reprimands, time-outs, and response-cost.

Reprimands. Reprimands can be mild or harsh; they can be verbal or nonverbal; and they can be administered by teachers, parents, or peers. A simple "no" is a verbal reprimand; a negative head shake is a nonverbal reprimand.

Reprimands are the most common form of punishment, both in the home and in school. This is not particularly surprising given that reprimands are simply expressions of disapproval. As such, they are available to anyone in power, and they are extremely easy to administer. Furthermore, given our social natures, reprimands can influence us in a way that they cannot influence most animals.

Researchers have compared the frequency of praise and of reprimands by teachers. In a large-scale survey, White (1975) found that the proportion of praise and reprimands changes markedly through school. Praise is more frequent than reprimands during first and second grade; in subsequent grades, reprimands are more common. The actual rate of reprimands through the remaining elementary and junior-high-school grades was approximately one every two minutes but dropped to about half that rate in senior high school. In college, it drops even more drastically. White also found that reprimands are somewhat more common with respect to students of lower ability.

Van Houten and Doleys (1983) reviewed a number of studies that have examined the effectiveness of reprimands and the particular qualities that increase their effectiveness. The majority of these studies found reprimands to be highly effective. Among other things, verbal reprimands that identify the undesirable behavior and provide specific rationales for doing (or not doing) something are more effective than reprimands that simply express disapproval (a point that we stressed earlier). For example, it is more effective to say, "Robert, please do not stick out your tongue because you distract the other children and you confuse me when I'm trying to explain something" than to say, "Don't do that, Robert!"

Investigations of reprimands also reveal that those given at a closer distance are more effective than those given from far away. In a study conducted by Van Houten et al. (1982), students were reprimanded from a distance of 1 meter or 7 meters (approximately 3¼ feet or 23 feet). Tone and intensity of reprimand were kept constant. Reprimands from a distance of 1 meter were more effective.

Research examining the effects of reprimand intensity has produced contradictory results. In one series of studies (O'Leary and Becker, 1968; O'Leary et al., 1974), soft reprimands, audible only to the student being reprimanded, were found to be more effective than loud reprimands, audible to the entire class. However, Van Houten and Doleys (1983) report that higher-intensity (loud) reprimands often are more effective than soft reprimands, and that the O'Leary results might be due not to the intensity of the reprimands but to the fact that soft reprimands were always delivered in closer proximity to the student. In addition, being in close proximity to the student increases the possibility that the teacher will reinforce the reprimand by means of eye contact and other nonverbal gestures that have been found to increase the effectiveness of reprimands.

Whether or not soft reprimands are as effective or more effective than loud reprimands may be less important than some other considerations. Recall the advice given earlier about praise and punishment: Because of the effect on the child's self-concept, praise should be public (loud) and criticism should be private. Also, because reprimands are typically used either to prevent or to stop behaviors that threaten classroom activity, the most successful reprimands consist of simple, unobtrusive squelches such as "shh," "wait," "no," or simply a look or gesture. Reprimands such as these have the advantage of minimizing disruption of the class.

Reprimands of the type discussed in this section are clearly not always appropriate or effective for the most severe instances of disruptive behavior. Those who engage in crimes such as physical violence, robbery, drug use and sale, rape, and vandalism in schools are likely to sneer at gentle reprimands. For these behaviors, more drastic measures are clearly warranted. In most cases, these misbehaviors occur in corridors, lunchrooms, washrooms, and playgrounds rather than in the classroom, and they are sufficiently rare in most schools that when they occur, they are usually dealt with by school administrators. The most common misbehaviors the classroom teacher must deal with on a daily basis are truancy, tardiness, inattentiveness, talking, and forgetting books and assignments (Doyle, 1986). For these misbehaviors, a simple reprimand might suffice — or perhaps a time-out or response-cost procedure might work.

Time-Outs. In a **time-out** students are removed from a situation in which they would ordinarily expect reinforcement and are placed in a situation in which they cannot be reinforced. For example, if classroom activities are such that children *like* to be in class, being removed from the classroom for a time-out may be interpreted as a form of punishment.

Brantner and Doherty (1983) distinguish among three different time-out procedures that the classroom teacher might use. The first involves **isolation**. This is clearly illustrated when a child is physically removed from the area of reinforcement (typically, the classroom; perhaps also the playground, the lunchroom, or the library) and isolated in a different place. Although isolation is not entirely uncommon in schools, it is somewhat controversial because it violates our more humanistic values. It reminds us of the types of seclusion that have sometimes been used with criminals.

A second time-out procedure does not isolate misbehaving children, but simply excludes them from ongoing activities. A common **exclusion** time-out procedure in a school might require a child to sit at the back of the room, facing in the opposite direction or perhaps sitting behind a screen.

The third time-out procedure is labeled **nonexclusion**. In this, the mildest of the three, the child is removed from the ongoing activity (removed from the immediate source of reinforcement) and is required to observe others engaging in the activity. The child might, for example, be asked to stand apart from a game (or at the side of the class) and simply watch.

Following a thorough review of the time-out literature, Brantner and Doherty (1983) conclude that this is an extremely common classroom management device, but that research results are too few and too inconsistent to identify the characteristics of effective time-out procedures. In addition, although time-out procedures are generally effective, they do not always work.

Response-Cost. When students have been given tangible reinforcers for good behavior but stand to lose some of these reinforcers for disruptive behaviors, the loss is referred to as **response-cost**. It too constitutes a mild form of punishment—similar to preventing a child who has misbehaved from watching television. Response-cost systems are frequently used in token-reinforcement programs. An experiment reported by Kaufman and O'Leary (1972) clearly illustrates the difference between a response-cost method and a reinforcement system. The experiment was conducted in two classes in a children's unit of a psychiatric hospital. In one class, students earned points for good behavior (token reinforcement); in a second class, children were awarded all their points at the beginning of a class period and had points subtracted from their total for specific misbehaviors. Although both methods were highly effective in reducing disruptive behavior, neither was more effective than the other.

Pazulinec, Meyerrose, and Sajwaj (1983) report that the majority of studies of the effectiveness of response-cost procedures have found positive results. Not only have such procedures successfully reduced disruptive classroom behavior, but they also have brought about significant increases in classroom achievement and in performance on standardized tests. Among the relative advantages of response-cost procedures for classroom management is the fact that they do not remove the child from the learning situation (as time-out procedures typically do). In addition, they are usually combined with a reinforcement procedure (use of tokens, for example) and can therefore derive benefit from the many advantages of reinforcement.

FROM DISCIPLINE TO MORALITY

The first part of this chapter has intentionally emphasized preventive and management strategies, rather than corrective strategies, in the hope that with proper attention to the aspects of teacher-learner interaction that are conducive to enthusiasm, warmth, and caring, seriously disruptive behavior will be infrequent and the need for corrective action rare. As a result, the teacher may have more time and energy to address the larger but sometimes less visible problems of social adjustment, self-discipline, and moral development.

Rules and standards in a classroom might exist primarily to ensure the order necessary for teaching and learning, but they have other effects as well. School is more than preparation for later life; it is a fundamental part of the child's immediate life. And it is perhaps fortunate that, in many respects, schools mirror the larger society. The penalties for infraction of school rules might not be as harsh as those that apply to the infraction of society's laws, but the rewards for compliance are no less. And although we might strenuously object that schools should not teach compliance, we must nevertheless admit that society would be incredibly more chaotic than it sometimes appears to be were it not for the fact that most of us have learned to live within social, legal, and moral prescriptions, that we have learned how to resolve a majority of our conflicts without resorting to knives, guns, and fists, and that we behave in morally acceptable ways most of the time.

It is probably highly presumptuous, and perhaps not a little remiss, of schools to assume that the development of high moral standards, the internalization of values, and the development of principles and ideals will result incidentally from the experiences that life provides for children — that nothing can, or should, be done deliberately to foster their development. In fact, it is likely that much is accomplished incidentally by wise and sensitive teachers who might accomplish much more were they to address themselves deliberately to the development of character. A grab-bag expression for values, moral strength, principles, and virtues, *character* is an ill-defined and very unpopular term in today's social sciences. Consequently, these sciences have little advice to offer the teacher who might be concerned with more than classroom management and the curriculum-bound teaching/learning process.

Prosocial Programs

Humanistic approaches to education represent several attempts to cater directly to children's social and emotional needs and to help them develop the social skills that are useful and necessary for effective interaction with others. The humanistic emphasis on affective education points clearly in this direction, as do the various group-process approaches that have become popular in humanistic schools. One additional example is described briefly here.

Palmares and Logan (1975) have developed an extensive curriculum, both audiovisual and textual, for conflict management. Essentially, the curriculum is intended to teach children a variety of methods they can use to resolve conflicts. Many of these methods are used spontaneously by children and are learned incidentally as a function of the give-and-take of social interaction. However, a number of children experience more difficulty than others in acquiring these social skills. For these children, the program should prove particularly effective.

Among the conflict resolution skills taught by the program are negotiating, compromising, taking turns, explaining, listening, apologizing, soliciting intervention, using humor, and invoking chance (for example, flipping a coin). Seventeen specific strategies are developed, fourteen of which are primarily positive and clearly useful in adult interaction as well. Three are more negative (violence, flight, and tattling), although they too might occasionally be resorted to.

A more general approach to developing prosocial behavior is illustrated by an experimental program implemented and evaluated during a five-year period in three elementary schools (Solomon et al., 1988). The program emphasizes commitment to accepted and shared values, a sense of community, and the development of concern and care. It includes five separate kinds of activities for students. Among the most important of these are small-group *cooperative activities* of the kind described by Johnson et al. (1984) and intended primarily to develop values associated with fairness, respect, responsibility, and helping one another.

The second aspect of the program, *developmental discipline*, is a student-centered approach to classroom management and discipline wherein students are given an opportunity to participate in formulating and enforcing rules. The emphasis is on understanding the principles that underlie rules, and the goal is to foster student development toward autonomy.

A third component of the Solomon et al. (1988) program involves *activities promoting social understanding* and is exemplified in instances in which the teacher uses classroom situations to discuss and reinforce prosocial values. In addition, role-playing games, formal discussions, books, films, and other activities are used to increase children's sensitivity to one another and to promote tolerance of differences.

Fourth, the program encourages activities that involve *highlighting prosocial values*. For example, teachers are instructed to draw attention to instances of prosocial behavior in the classroom, such as sharing and comforting. Films, books, and other models of prosocial behavior are also used.

The fifth component of this program stresses *helping activities*. It consists of encouraging children to engage directly in prosocial behaviors by helping one another and their community. To this end, "buddy" systems and tutoring programs are set up, and various school- and community-improvement activities are organized.

Evaluation of this program involved making comparisons between students in three experimental schools and comparable students in three other schools. The results? In the authors' words, "[The program] had substantial positive effects on children's interpersonal behavior in the classroom (without impeding their achievement)" (Soloman et al., 1988, p. 545). Children in these programs were found to be more supportive, more cooperative, friendlier, and more helpful toward one another than comparable children not in the program.

Although implementing this program required that teachers undertake week-long training sessions, attend weekly and monthly meetings, and be provided with considerable supportive material, elements of the program can profitably be incorporated into any classroom. As Soloman et al. (1988) note, two very general aspects of life in the classroom seem clearly related to the development of prosocial values and behaviors: One is the establishment of a warm teacher-student relationship; the other is the provision of opportunities for cooperation and collaboration among students.

Intentionally or otherwise, schools do much to teach children how to get along with one another. Unfortunately, students sometimes learn *not* to get along instead. Perhaps if teachers attend to these two things—the teacher-student relationship and interstudent cooperation—schools will intentionally do much more that is positive.

MAIN POINTS

1. The expression *classroom management* is often a euphemism for *discipline*, which may be a euphemism for *punishment*. More precisely, classroom management is the arrangement of classroom activities to facilitate teaching and learning; discipline is the interventions made necessary by student behaviors that disrupt (or threaten to disrupt) classroom activities.

2. The context in which teaching occurs— the classroom—is *multidimensional* (many individuals, many activities, many goals), *simultaneous* (many events occurring at any one time), *immediate* (many events require instant teacher decisions and their implementation), and *unpredictable* (the course of classroom events, given their complexity, cannot easily be predicted).

3. Managing a system as complex as a classroom while maintaining on-task student behavior requires special pedagogical and information-processing (vigilance and "with-it-ness") skills, many of which eventually become unconscious and automatic.

4. Despite some valid ethical and humanitarian objections to control, to the extent that teachers act *in loco parentis* and *care* for their students, discipline is necessary.

5. Research on classroom management indicates that it is the strength of ongoing activity (the primary vector), rather than the frequency and insistence of teacher interventions, that is most important in establishing and maintaining order. Also, timely, sometimes anticipatory, interventions that do not disrupt the flow of classroom activity are most effective.

6. Preventive strategies are of paramount importance in classroom management. These strategies include establishing routines, learning students' names, setting rules, applying rules consistently, arranging frequent occasions for the legitimate use of praise, using humor, having an elusive quality labeled *with-it-ness*, and paying attention to classroom environment and climate.

7. The most with-it teachers are those whose *desists* (instructions to stop some off-task behavior) are timely, on target (directed toward the offender), and informative. *Multiple attention* and *vigilance* are characteristic of with-it teachers and are associated with more on-task behavior and fewer classroom disruptions.

8. Warm and personal classroom environments seem to be associated with fewer discipline problems; similarly, certain types of classroom activities such as teacher presentations or teacher-led small-group activities are associated with fewer disruptions than are other activities such as seatwork and transitions.

9. Webster's *democratic discipline* is based on reason, relevance, and respect guided by a number of obvious but often-overlooked principles.

10. The context or ecology of the classroom is influenced by student blend, teacher beliefs and characteristics, the teacher's application of science, and a measure of art. The third of these is most clearly under teacher control.

11. Corrective discipline is invoked when preventive discipline has not been successful in curbing the appearance of a disciplinary problem. Methods include reasoning, reinforcement, the use of models, extinction, and punishment.

12. Reasoning, often in combination with other disciplinary measures, appears to be a highly effective and humane way of handling classroom problems. Concrete reasons appear to be more effective with younger children; abstract reasons work better with older children. In addition, reasons that appeal to the effect of behavior on others are particularly successful and may be important in developing higher levels of moral orientation.

13. Systematic reinforcement programs in schools typically use positive reinforcement, sometimes in the form of tokens or a combination of teacher praise and other tangible rewards. Some evidence suggests that excessive reliance on external rewards may have a dampening effect on intrinsic motivation as reflected in the student's subsequent interest and motivation.

14. The Premack principle states that behaviors that occur spontaneously and frequently are probably reinforcing and can be used to reinforce less frequently occurring behaviors.

15. Extrinsic reinforcers include consumables, manipulatables, visual and auditory stimuli, social stimuli, and tokens. Teacher

attention is among the most important and the most powerful of reinforcers that are under teacher control.

16. Important principles governing the use of reinforcement in the classroom include these: Reinforcement is individualistic (defined only in terms of its effects on the individual); the effects of reinforcement are automatic; reinforcement and punishment should be consistent, should be related closely to the relevant behavior, and should occur as soon as possible; the amount of reinforcement required should not be underestimated; and student work should be organized in such a way that it is possible to reinforce small steps frequently.

17. A reinforcement menu provides students with a list of reinforcing activities from which they can select according to what they have earned.

18. Models provide children with standards of appropriate behavior. On occasion, punished models may serve to inhibit deviant behaviors as well. Perhaps the most important of classroom models is the teacher.

19. Extinction involves an attempt to eliminate undesirable behavior through the withdrawal of reinforcement. It is frequently inapplicable when teachers do not have control over reinforcement or when reinforcement is intrinsic or unidentifiable.

20. Punishment involves the presentation of an unpleasant stimulus or the removal of a pleasant stimulus as a consequence of behavior. Among objections to the use of punishment are claims that it does not always work, that it presents an undesirable model of violence, that it might have undesirable emotional side effects, and that it might lead to maladaptive behaviors through the introduction of frustration.

21. Research indicates that punishment may suppress undesirable behaviors and that it

may be particularly appropriate in cases in which it is necessary for a child to learn about behaviors that are not permitted.

22. Reprimands (expressions of disapproval, generally verbal but sometimes nonverbal) are among the most common of classroom punishments. Praise is more common than reprimands in the first two grades; reprimands subsequently become more common but decline in frequency after junior high school.

23. The effectiveness of reprimands appears to be related to the extent to which they provide reasonable rationales for doing or not doing something and to the proximity of the reprimander to the reprimanded.

24. Time-out punishment is the removal of a student from a reinforcing situation to another situation in which the same reinforcement is not possible. It might involve isolation (physical removal); exclusion (removal of the child from ongoing activities but not from the classroom); or nonexclusion (removal of the child from the ongoing activity to a place where the child is required to continue observing the activity).

25. Response-cost is a form of punishment in which previously earned reinforcers are removed as a consequence of undesirable behavior.

26. In addition to maintaining classroom order, teachers should also attend to the development of social and affective skills in children. The withdrawn, nonparticipating child is in as much need of help as the rebellious, truculent discipline problem.

27. Humanistic educators suggest that in addition to preventing and correcting problems in students, teachers should also pay attention to students' emotional and moral development, perhaps by using specific prosocial programs and techniques.

SUGGESTED READINGS

The following is a short, highly readable, and very practical discussion of specific methods by which teachers can achieve and maintain a level of classroom control described by the author as necessary for "personal" teaching:

MARLAND, M. (1975). *The craft of the classroom: A survival guide to classroom management in the secondary school.* London: Heinemann Educational Books.

An excellent guide to the application of behavior management principles in the school is Wielkiewicz's book. Especially useful is the second part, which deals with specific applications in such problem areas as hyperactivity, learning difficulties, anxiety and fear, social problems, and so on:

WIELKIEWICZ, R. M. (1986). *Behavior management in the schools: Principles and procedures.* New York: Pergamon Press.

A comprehensive analysis of research on punishment, its effectiveness, and its uses is detailed in:

AXELROD, S., & APSCHE, J. (Eds.). (1983). *The effects of punishment on human behavior.* New York: Academic Press.

A book that can be of tremendous value to those interested in using behavioristic principles to manage their own lives (more specifically, to change behaviors such as smoking or overeating) is the following:

WILLIAMS, R. L., & LONG, J. D. (1978). *Toward a self-managed lifestyle* (2nd ed.). Boston: Houghton Mifflin.

A good introduction to the systematic use of reward and punishment in attempts to change behavior using behavioral "contracting" is provided in:

O'BANION, D. R., & WHALEY, D. L. (1981). *Behavior contracting: Arranging contingencies of reinforcement.* New York: Springer.

For a philosophical, thoughtful, and thought-provoking analysis of the components of education, see Gowin's book. Especially relevant to this chapter are the discussion of governance — the essential exercise of power in a teaching situation — and the assertion that authority based on expertise and the power of knowledge is good, whereas authority based on the position and status of power is not.

GOWIN, D. B. (1981). *Educating.* Ithaca, N.Y.: Cornell University Press.

Bears are extremely confident and capable climbers, particularly when young. With increasing weight, however, they trust only the stoutest of branches, although a fall is not likely to prove disastrous. Polar bears, for example, can climb an almost sheer ice wall, and will then routinely jump down from heights of fifteen to twenty feet. And this in spite of their ponderous weights. One bear reportedly dove more than fifty feet into the water to escape hunting dogs and then set off in the direction of the closest land mass — an impressive twenty-two miles away   (Perry, 1966; Matthews, 1969).

INDIVIDUALIZING INSTRUCTION

Making the Lesson Fit the Student
Programmed Instruction
The Computer and Instruction
Mastery Learning and PSI
Individualizing with IPI and IGE
Individualized Instruction Evaluated
Attribute-Treatment Interaction
Main Points
Suggested Readings

*I am a Bear of Very Little Brain, and long words
Bother me.*

A. A. MILNE *Winnie-the-Pooh*

*Madam, I have been looking for a person who
disliked gravy all my life; let us swear eternal
friendship.*

SYDNEY SMITH *Memoirs*

PREVIEW My *Funk and Wagnall's* tells me that technology is the application of science and of technical advances in industry, the arts, and other fields. Education is presumably among these other fields, and this, the thirteenth chapter, is this textbook's technology chapter. It details the application of science (to the extent that psychology is a science) and of technical advances in the business of educating. Accordingly, this chapter describes programmed instruction, the use of computers in education, and specific teaching techniques founded on distinct theoretical principles.

▬ *Once more, bunches of wild cows trample their way across our pages. They are a preoccupation of the bear, these wild cows. He does not know what to make of them. Their wanton destruction of his world puzzles and angers him. He is frightened for his children. And he is sad, too, that there are so few virgin patches of wild strawberries left, and so few birds to sing while he eats. More and more often he is driven to seek out one of his sacred places, that he might replenish his soul. There are not very many such places left in his world. So many of the places he had thought to preserve untouched — not to forage in or to lie in, but simply as places in which to rejoice — even these sacred places are now overrun by wild cows.*

Today he lies on the ledge just below the crest of the ridge overlooking the valley. It is one of the sacred places the wild cows have not yet despoiled. They have ignored the bear's ledge because they think that no green plants could grow on a slope so steep and so clearly exposed to the heat of the summer sun. They do not yet know of the spring that oozes gently from the ground at the back of the ledge, or of the fiddlehead ferns that line the spring's run.

The bear does not eat these ferns. He sniffs them, and sometimes he licks the dew from their curled heads, but something in his pagan soul prevents him from curling his tongue around their stalks and wrenching them into his mouth. He sees magic in their unfurling and hears poetry in their gracefulness. On his ledge, the bear is a poet; sometimes he can hear the music of the fiddlehead ferns.

But today wild cows are dancing on the floor of the valley below the bear's sacred ledge. They dance in groups of four, tails intertwined, shuffling to and fro in time to the heavy rhythms of the cousset drums. Those who do not dance lounge around the perimeter of the dance area drinking whisky from styrofoam cups and smoking cigars, or they dive and swim in the nearby stream to refresh themselves. A "cigarrous" and methane-gas odor rises from the valley, and the bear is no longer able to smell the ferns or the freshness of his spring. He is no longer a poet.

Unexpectedly, the bear wonders about the taste of wild cow meat. But because he is a vegetarian by choice, the thought is revolting; it makes him ill on his sacred ledge.

The bear is not ordinarily a complainer. True, wild cows make him angry — in his words, "They tick me off, disgusting cows!" — but he is not a complainer; he is a doer!

Suddenly the bear stands on his ledge. "Listen up, cows!" he yells. But the insistent drumming of the coussets and the low mooing of the wild cows, who don't know the lyrics but are simply mooing in accompaniment, drown out the bear's cry.

"Listen up!" the bear roars. Some of the wild

cows turn toward the ledge. They see the bear standing above them, waiting for silence.

The bear is a terrific teacher; he has wonderful presence, and he knows how to handle a class of wild cows. "I have some important things to teach you," he says. The wild cows grow silent. The bear smiles. He will teach them about the world. He will lead them to discover how all things are One. He will instill in them respect for their environment. Eventually, they will be environmentally friendly, these wild cows!!

The bear looks his class over. Where to start? What to do? Clearly, there are some intelligent wild cows here. They have that keen look in their bovine eyes and an especially attentive posture. There is an alertness and a readiness about them.

Sadly, there are others who are neither so intelligent nor so interested. Many have not yet understood the seriousness of the bear's call; they do not sense the strength of his presence. They continue to smoke and drink whisky.

The bear, remarkable teacher that he is, knows at once that not all wild cows can be taught in exactly the same way. ▄▄▟

MAKING THE LESSON FIT THE STUDENT

Some very ordinary classes are a lot like a bunch of wild cows. Some students are bright, alert, inquisitive, and interested; others are less capable or less interested — or both. There are times when, if the lesson does not fit all the students, many may learn, but some will undoubtedly continue to dance and drink whisky — metaphorically, of course. What can an ordinary classroom teacher do to individualize instruction?

One solution is for the teacher to spend time with each student individually, responding to the student's immediate needs and interests, explaining, probing, imparting strategies, and doing other things good teachers do. Unfortunately, teacher-pupil ratios, the time available, and the demands of the curriculum make this a difficult and often impractical solution.

A second solution is to "track" the class.

Tracking involves separating the class into ability or interest groups and then providing different instructional experiences for each group.

Other possible solutions, discussed in some detail later in this chapter, include the use of computers, which can interact with students and can sometimes modify instructional programs according to student responses; specially designed teaching programs (programmed instruction), which can be presented in text form or by means of computers; and any of a number of relatively elaborate, theory-based instructional systems, such as PSI (personalized system of instruction) or IGE (individually guided education).

The Learning-Styles Approach

Another solution, perhaps the one that goes furthest toward making the lesson fit the student, is the learning-styles approach discussed in Chapter 6 (see Dunn and Griggs, 1988). The learning-styles philosophy recognizes that students learn in different ways — that each has a unique learning style. Some students learn well in the morning; others awaken reluctantly and don't function well until later in the day.* Some excel with highly structured, teacher-directed, whole-class approaches; others perform much better with less-structured, self-initiated, individual approaches; and still others achieve better in small-group, cooperative settings. Some students prefer to work in bright, well-lit surroundings, with loud music; others require quiet, more subdued environments. Some learners have a marked preference for the visual or the auditory mode, some respond better than others to praise or criticism, some have longer attention spans than others . . . and on and on.

To truly individualize instruction, advocates of learning-styles approaches argue, it is

---

*PPC: "We'd have a lazy bunch of students if we let them sleep all morning just because that's their learning style."
Author: "The bear is not lazy, but he sleeps all winter. That's his lifestyle."

necessary to develop a profile of each learner. This profile provides a detailed description of strengths and weaknesses, as well as of preferences and dislikes. Schools and classrooms can then be tailored to cater to each individual's style. As we saw in Chapter 6, in practice this approach requires a tremendous assortment of alternatives. Core school subjects must be presented at different times of the day; classrooms must be organized so that individuals can select among small-group, individual, or whole-class approaches; rewards must be restructured so that classrooms include individual, cooperative, and competitive situations; and instructional materials must be developed to appeal to visual, auditory, and kinesthetic sensory modes.

Truly individualizing instruction as completely as is suggested by a learning-styles approach is difficult or impossible for many practical reasons. In most instances, and even if everyone concerned were convinced that this were the best of all possible instructional alternatives, there simply isn't enough time, money, or energy to implement all aspects of the program. But individualization on a more limited scale is possible in virtually every classroom.

Keep in mind that individualization of instruction does not mean that all students work individually at all times throughout the school day. What individualization means is that instructional methods, classroom organization, evaluation procedures, and other components of the teaching/learning process are selected and modified in response to learner characteristics, course and lesson goals, and practical constraints. In practice, this usually means that some students are exposed to different experiences *at least some of the time*; some of these experiences might well be individual, but many will occur in small groups. And even in classrooms in which the teacher individualizes instruction, much can take place in whole-class situations.

Among the instructional methods available to teachers are lecturing, discussing, reciting, questioning, facilitating guided discovery, us-

ing small- or large-group strategies, tutoring, peer teaching, and so on. Each has advantages for different purposes, but even the methods that research has identified as potentially "best" (for example, one-to-one tutoring; Bloom, 1984) cannot, for practical reasons, be used exclusively. Even the methods represented by such global terms as *lecturing, discussing,* and so on are virtually never used to the exclusion of all other methods by any teacher worth even slightly more than his or her salt. Thus teachers do not typically lecture or discuss; they present lessons, an activity that involves talking, listening, questioning, demonstrating, using instructional materials, and sometimes standing on one's ear or nose. These activities might be directed toward an entire class of students (large or small), a single student, or a handful of students; or they might alternate among the various possibilities. And they might occur in connection with any of a number of specific techniques that have been developed to individualize, to systematize, to computerize, and/or to personalize instruction.

Several of these techniques, some derived directly from specific psychological theory and experimentation, are described in the remainder of this chapter: programmed instruction, computer-assisted instruction (CAI), mastery learning, Keller's personalized system of instruction (PSI), individually guided education (IGE), and individually prescribed instruction (IPI). Aspects of the methods and principles of each of these approaches might be profitably incorporated into the increasingly sophisticated arsenal of every contemporary teacher.

PROGRAMMED INSTRUCTION

The term *programmed instruction* can be used in a general sense to describe any organized **autoinstructional device** — that is, any device that presents information in such a way that the learner can acquire it without the help of a teacher. In this sense, textbooks are a kind of programmed material, as are computers. A more specific definition of programmed instruction, however, limits it to material that is specifically designed to be autoinstructional and is arranged according to one of two patterns, linear or branching, or a combination of the two. Skinner (1954) is usually associated with the **linear program**, whereas Crowder (1961, 1963) introduced the **branching program**.

Linear Programs

The Skinnerian or linear program is one in which all learners move through the same material in exactly the same sequence, but they progress at their own rate. Thus does it individualize.

Linear programs are based directly on an operant conditioning model. They present material that leads the student to emit a correct response and that provides reinforcement for that response. In effect, the students' responses are operants, and the knowledge that they have responded correctly is a reinforcer. Accordingly, linear programs have the following characteristics that ensure that a student will almost always answer correctly:

1. The material is broken down into small steps, referred to as **frames**, which are presented in logical sequence. Each frame consists of a minimal amount of information, so that this information can be remembered from frame to frame.

2. Students are required to make frequent responses — usually one in every frame, and often as many as four or five in one frame. They are given **prompts** to ensure that they answer correctly.

3. Linear programs provide immediate **knowledge of results**. Students know at once whether they have answered correctly. This knowledge is assumed to act as reinforcement. Kaess and Zeaman (1960) have demonstrated that positive feedback (that is, knowledge that one is correct) is more effective than negative feedback (knowledge that one is wrong). Because linear programs attempt, through the use of prompts and small frames, to ensure that few errors are made, most of the feedback is positive.

To try your hand at a linear program, see the box entitled, "Piagetian Jargon: A Linear Program" and follow the directions.

Branching Programs

Crowder or *branching programs* present learners with much longer frames than linear programs (sometimes an entire page at a time), and unlike linear programs, they require learners to select from among several alternative answers, rather than making up their own. But the most striking difference between the two is that in branching programs, not all students go through the program in exactly the same way. Students who give all responses correctly go through the shortest possible way. Students who make errors receive remedial instruction and further clarification. Typically, learners who answer incorrectly are sent to a **remedial frame** or sequence of frames and eventually return to the main branch. They then proceed from there (see Figure 13.1). An example of a branching program is presented in the box entitled, "Bear Tracking: A Branching Program."

Usefulness of Programmed Instruction

Instructional programs, as originally conceived and developed, are largely of historical interest only, although some of their principles may be useful in ordinary classrooms. Markle and Tiemann (1974; Markle, 1978) point out that these principles constitute the rudiments of an instructional theory that can be applied to simple tasks of motor learning or to highly complex cognitive learning tasks. The three fundamental concepts of this programmed-instruction theory are active responding, errorless learning, and immediate feedback. Applying these

Piagetian Jargon: A Linear Program

Directions Fold a sheet of paper or use a strip of cardboard to cover the answers, which are given in the right-hand margin. With the answers covered, read frame 1 and write your answer in the blank provided. Move the paper or cardboard down to check your answer before proceeding to frame 2.

1. Jean Piaget has developed a theory that deals with human adaptation. It is a developmental theory of human _____.

   adaptation

2. As children learn to cope with their environment and to deal effectively with it, they can be said to be _____ to it.

   adapting

3. Adaptation therefore involves interacting with the environment. The process of adaptation is one of organism-environment _____.

   interaction

4. One of the central features of Piaget's developmental theory is that it attempts to explain _____ through interaction.

   adaptation

5. Interaction takes place through the interplay of two complementary processes: One involves reacting to the environment in terms of a previously learned response. This process is called assimilation. Assimilation involves a _____ learned response.

   previously

6. Whenever children use an object for some activity they have already learned, they are said to be *assimilating* that object to their previous learning. For example, when Jennifer sucks a pacifier, she is _____ the pacifier to the activity of sucking.

   assimilating

7. Sam is given a paper doll. He looks at it curiously and then puts it in his mouth and eats it. He has _____ the doll to the activity of eating.

   assimilated

8. Assimilation is one of the two processes involved in interacting with the environment. It is part of the process of _____.

   adapting or adaptation

9. Adaptation involves two processes. The first is assimilation. The second is called accommodation. It occurs whenever a change in behavior results from interacting with the environment. Accommodation involves a _____ in behavior.

   change or modification

10. When children cannot assimilate a new object to activities that are already part of their repertoire, they must _____ to them.

    accommodate

11. Johnny West was presented with a very long pacifier on the occasion of his first birthday. Prior to that time he had been sucking a short "bulb" pacifier. The long pacifier matched his nose. He had to elongate his mouth considerably more than usual in order to suck this new pacifier. Johnny West had to _____ to the new pacifier.

    accommodate

12. If Johnny West had been given his old, short pacifier, he could more easily have _____ it to the activity of sucking.

    assimilated

13. . . .

Figure 13.1   A branching program.

principles to classroom practice involves presenting small units of information so as to maximize immediate comprehension and minimize the number of errors students make while learning; providing for continual student involvement through active responding; and providing students with immediate confirmation of correct responses. And although it is very time-consuming to structure lessons in as logical a sequence as programs require, such a sequence can be very conducive to learning.

THE COMPUTER AND INSTRUCTION

The principles of programmed instruction are also increasingly evident in another development—the use of computers in schools, a topic we consider next.

The Computer Revolution

"The computer revolution is upon us!" we are told almost daily—and have been told for some time now. A big word, *revolution*. Small wonder that so many of us should wonder what this computer revolution is, whether it actually *is* upon us, and whether it is good or bad.

Yes, the computer revolution is upon us, according to Alvin Toffler (1980), who earlier (1970) warned us that the coming of this revolution might send many of us into a state of shock. Toffler sees the computer revolution as the third wave in a series of monumental changes that have swept over humanity. The first wave, which occurred more than 10,000 years ago, was the agricultural revolution—a revolution that transformed our hunting and foraging ancestors into domesticators of animals and growers of food, changing the very meaning of what it was to be human in those times. The second wave, far more recent in our history, was the industrial revolution, the ultimate effects of which were to transform our work places, our homes, and the very fabric of our lives. Only history can ultimately tell us how profound will be the effect of the third wave—the computer revolution that is sweeping over us now.

Evidence of the computer revolution is all around us. Some two decades ago I wrote the first edition of this book using a 25-cent ball-point pen and two dozen pads of yellow paper. Now I write to you on a computer linked to a laser printer—and linked as well to a university computer, a library system, and an assortment of data bases. Not that there were no computers then—quite the contrary, there were quite a number; and, surprising as it might seem, in many important ways they were not very different from today's computers in terms of their capabilities. But some important differences between first-generation computers and today's computers account for the revolution. Chief among those differences are the reduced size and price of today's machines, made possible by **microcomputers**—computers so small that their processing units reside on a single, fingernail-size wafer. Now people (and schools) can own personal computers as easily as they can own television sets. In addition, today's personal computer is far easier to operate than its grandparents. It is, in the jargon of the trade, far more "user friendly." Small wonder that personal computers proliferate on the market. But what will their effect be on education?

The Effects of Computers on Education

Computer enthusiasts and other optimists predict sweeping, somewhat radical, and highly beneficial effects of the widespread introduction of computers into schools. Among other

BRANCHING PROGRAM BADLY IN NEED OF PRUNING

things, they see schools becoming a part of large information-exchange and -retrieval systems in which individual students will have virtually instant access to an almost unlimited quantity of high-quality information. Some also predict that smaller, friendlier, more personal schools will again proliferate once the resource disadvantages that sometimes characterize smaller schools disappear with the coming of the computer (Coburn et al., 1982). Some of these enthusiasts insist that problems with reading, writing, and arithmetic will end as people master the new computer skills. Indeed, some go so far as to suggest that many of the ill effects of television will be replaced by the creative activities encouraged by computers, and that family ties will be strengthened as more and more of the third-wave generation are able to work from their homes, linked to their offices (if there still are such things) and to the world via spun-glass fibers, gold filaments, infrared rays, or more mundane telephone lines.

There is, of course, a less optimistic view of the likely impact of computers. This view suggests that our basic computational skills may decline dramatically as computers take care of all our computational needs; that reading skills are likely to suffer as children spend more time being amused by computers and their fantasy games and less time reading; and that violence may increase as a function of computer-based video games whose predominant themes are violent. Others believe that computers are not likely to make knowledge and power more accessible to the masses, but rather to have the opposite effect.

Parsons (1983), for example, argues that according to our best historical evidence, computers are more likely to increase than to decrease the gap between the haves and the have-nots. He also says that computer enthusiasts are sometimes guilty of exaggerating and misrepresenting the benefits of computers in education. For example, he points out that these enthusiasts use the term *interaction* widely and inaccurately. Parsons sees interaction as a "meeting of minds," a sort of sharing of *meaning* (exemplified in conversation or in reading a book). Typically, however, interaction with a computer is quite different: It primarily involves the giving of information. Furthermore, in spite of the fact that computers often are described as "expert" systems of one kind or another, they do not resemble the human experts in most fields (doctors, lawyers, professors, psychiatrists); computers are generally ill-equipped to provide

Bear Tracking: A Branching Program

Objectives: After you have read this program, you should be able to:

1. recognize a forest
2. recognize a bear's tracks
3. recognize a bear
4. recognize a bunch of wild cows
5. run very rapidly in all directions

Note: Because only part of the program is presented here, only the first two objectives can be attained.

Directions: Read each frame very carefully; reread it if it appears confusing. Then select what you think best completes the statement presented, and follow the directions that correspond to that answer.

1. A forest is a collection of trees. It is a large collection of trees, just as a city is a large collection of people. A wood is a small collection of trees, just as a town is a small collection of people. A bush is a collection of small trees. What is a collection of small people? Never mind. Bears are often found in large collections of trees.

   If you were looking for a bear, you would go to:
   (a) a large collection of people.
   (b) a forest.
   (c) an ocean.
   If you answered (a), go to frame 10.
   If you answered (b), go to frame 3.
   If you answered (c), go to frame 7.

2. Correct. Good. Now that you have found a forest, you must find some tracks. Remember, a bear's tracks look like this:

After you have found the tracks, follow them. Somewhere, a bear is standing in them. If you find these tracks:

you should go
   (a) N.
   (b) S.
   (c) E or W.
If you said (a), go to frame 8.
If you said (b), go to frame 12.
If you said (c), go to frame 4.

3. You are correct. Bears are often found in forests. Occasionally, however, bears are also found elsewhere. You should keep this in mind. The best way of finding a bear is to do two things: First, look for a forest; second, look for a bear's tracks. They look something like this:

The best way of finding a bear is to:
   (a) look for an ocean.
   (b) look for its tracks.
   (c) look for a forest.
If you answered (a), go to frame 7.
If you answered (b), go to frame 9.
If you answered (c), go to frame 2.

4. Your answer is incorrect, but it may not be un-wise. If you are afraid of bears, you might even consider going south. Go to frame 12 to see what would happen if you went south.

5. It is obvious that you are afraid of bears. Your instructions are to go directly to your local university library (do not pass Go, do not collect $200, heh, heh). You are asked to read about counterconditioning, paying special attention to systematic desensitization. If you can afford to, you might consider hiring this textbook's author as a therapist. If you can't afford me, hire someone else.

6. Good! Good! You should do something else. But first you must return to the large collection of people. Having done that. . . .

(Now go to frame 13.)

7. You are not paying attention. Go back to frame 1 and start again.

8. Good. You noticed the arrow. You may eventually see a bear. It is interesting, don't you think, that a bear always stands facing toward the front of its tracks, *sniffing around*? This makes it a lot easier to locate. After you have found the bear, you will have to make a decision:

Will you:
(a) stop and pray?
(b) run home?
(c) do something else?
If you said (a), go to frame 11.
If you said (b), go to frame 5.
If you said (c), go to frame 6.

9. That is not correct. If you begin to look for a bear's tracks before finding a forest, you may never find either track or bear. Go back to frame 3.

10. That is not correct. A large collection of people is a city. Bears are not usually found in cities, but they are often found in large collections of trees (forests). You might waste a lot of time looking for bears in cities. Now go back and read frame 1 again.

11. Piety is an admirable quality in a student, but it is not the desired response here. You might seriously consider, at this point, whether or not you really want to track bears. If you are sure that you do, you are instructed to begin with frame 1.

12. Stop! You are going in the wrong direction. A bear faces toward the front of its tracks. This is an important point. Now you may go back to frame 2, or you might want to rest for a minute before continuing. You may do so, but you should probably begin at frame 1 when you are well again.

13. The beginning of this program is included here simply as an illustration of a branching program. Frustrated would-be bear trackers are invited to consult their local library — or you can hire me as a guide (high-quality service at reasonable rates).

us with advice—information, yes, but advice only occasionally.

In the final analysis, these opposing optimistic and pessimistic views of how computers are likely to affect our lives are no more than speculation—based perhaps on reason and probability, but certainly based also on hope and fear. What will come to pass in the end may not be affected a great deal by our often-premature speculations. From the teacher's point of view, given the invasion of the computer into our lives and our schools, what is most important is to understand the uses of the computer that will provide the greatest benefits to students.

Uses of Computers in Education

With their peculiar tendency toward jargon and acronyms, educators have given us a whole series of computer-related expressions: CAI (computer-assisted instruction), CML (computer-managed learning), CBE (computer-based education), CAT (computer-assisted training), CBT (computer-based testing), CBT again (computer-based training), CMI (computer-managed instruction), CMT (computer-managed training), and CAL (computer-assisted learning). Of these, CAI is perhaps the most general term.

Basically, a **computer-assisted instruction** system includes a computing center and a number of student terminals, or it consists of one or more stand-alone units, each with its own computer and terminal. Typically, the learner interacts with the computer program by means of a monitor and a typewriter keyboard or some other control device such as a "mouse" or a "joystick." This physical paraphernalia is collectively labeled **hardware**; the programs, which are really the "brains" of the computer—its information, instructions, and capabilities—are termed **software**, or sometimes courseware.

Computers can assist in schools in a variety of ways, including executing routine clerical tasks such as registering students, storing data, solving scheduling problems, issuing report cards, and so on. Although these are extremely valuable functions, they are associated with the actual business of instruction more remotely than some of the computer's other uses.

How, specifically, can a computer be used to instruct? First, it can be used as a sort of teaching machine—as an ultrasophisticated piece of audiovisual equipment designed to present programs or lessons, with or without the assistance of teachers. The computer is particularly suitable for presenting repetitive, drill-type exercises (in mathematics or language learning, for example), and it can do a great deal to free the classroom teacher for other activities that computers do not do as well.

Happily, however, the computer's uses are not limited to drill and practice exercises but include simulations as well. For example, programs are available that mimic the circulatory system, a chemical laboratory, or the in-flight responses of a Boeing 737. Simulations allow the learner to discover the results of specific responses without the risk and expense of actually performing them. Thus, in using a computer-controlled simulator a pilot can learn that a particularly unlucky combination of aileron and rudder movements can cause a crash—without actually destroying either a multimillion-dollar aircraft or several lives.

At a less dramatic level, a clever simulation of a chemical laboratory might allow students to discover the potentially disastrous effects of combining, chilling, heating, pressurizing, or eating different chemicals, without losing a school building or a human body in the process.

One of the benefits of computer simulation is that it can be used for teaching problem-solving skills. For example, Woodward, Carnine, and Gersten (1988) presented students with a commercial program called Health Ways. This program not only presents information about factors that contribute to health and survival, but also simulates the probable outcomes of different combinations of these factors. The program presents learners with different profiles (basic information about an individual, including age, occupation, heredity, and so on) and asks them to manipulate important variables to increase life expectancy. In the Woodward, Carnine, and Gersten study, students who had used the Health Ways computer program were compared with students in a control group given the same information in a structured teaching format that included enrichment instruction and exercises instead of the computer simulation program. After a twelve-day instructional sequence, members of the experimental group outperformed those in the control group not only with respect to factual knowledge, but also in solving health-related problems.

Another instructional function of computers relates to their impressive information-storage and -retrieval capacities. Accordingly, they can be used extensively to satisfy inquiries. When connected to the appropriate data banks, a computer terminal can give us almost instant access to the most encyclopedic and current information available.

Computers can also be used as a source of advice on career decisions. The great advantage of computers in career guidance is that they can store a tremendous wealth of information concerning career opportunities and requirements that relate to a very rapidly changing job market. Not only can they handle routine career-related questions quickly and efficiently, but they also can be programmed to find relationships between a student's achievement, aptitude, and interests and the likelihood of success in various careers. Stahl (1983) describes a variety of career-advice packages now available in the form of appropriate computer software. Many of these packages contain information on thousands of careers, and an increasing number are designed to run on the personal computers found most commonly in home and school.

A final, very important use of the computer in school is as a tool that can itself be learned and used. This function is well illustrated in the use of computers as word processors, data processors, or sound synthesizers. In each of these cases, the computer becomes a tool to facilitate activities that would otherwise be more time-consuming, more difficult, and sometimes impossible. Another fundamentally important use of the computer as a tool is evident in the learning of programming skills. As Papert (1980, 1987) has shown, these skills can be learned by very young children — children who program computers rather than being programmed by them.

In order to teach young children how to program computers, Papert and his associates have developed a simple computer language, **Logo**, which is powerful enough to let children explore the world of differential equations but simple enough to enable children with no mathematical sophistication whatsoever to explore the world of plane geometry. For this purpose, the program (which can now be run on most of the popular home and school computers) introduces the turtle — a triangular-shaped little creature on the computer monitor that can be moved by means of ordinary words rather than the more abstract and complex terminology of most computer languages. For example, the child simply types the words FORWARD 50 to make the turtle move straight ahead fifty little turtle-steps, dragging a "pen" behind it so that you can see its path; FORWARD 50 RIGHT 90 FORWARD 50 makes it go ahead fifty steps, turn to the right, and go forward another fifty steps at right angles to the first path. It is only a short child-step from here to the design of a complete square, and but one small additional step to learn that all the instructions required for making this square can be shortened because they involve repetition (REPEAT 4 FORWARD 50 RIGHT 90) and can be given a name — such as SQUARE. Subsequently, when the child types SQUARE, the turtle draws a square. The child has easily and painlessly created a simple program.

As the child learns new instructions and continues to "play turtle," the programs can become more complex and the designs of plane geometry more intricate. Playing turtle simply involves imagining how the turtle will respond to all the possible combinations of instructions. Thus can a child learn to program the computer to draw a cartoon figure, a house, a tree, an anything. Thus, too, can the child learn geometry, mathematics, the systematic and clear thinking required to write programs, and other aspects of what has come to be called **computer literacy**. If the effects of the computer revolution are anywhere near the magnitude of the agricultural and industrial revolutions, those who remain computer illiterates may be swept under and drowned by the third wave.

Computer-Assisted Instruction Evaluated

Among the advantages of CAI are the impressive memory capacities of modern computers, the rapidity and accuracy with which they can deliver information, their problem-solving and computation capabilities, and the versatility of their presentation modes. Computers also present a number of advantages not directly related to their role in assisting instruction—advantages that have relatively little to do with how they are used to help in the ordinary business of teaching (and learning) the conventional curriculum. These advantages have to do with the computer's unique qualities and with the cognitive processes it can foster. As Olson (1985) notes, computers are "tools of the intellect" that require a degree of explicitness and precision in the use of language—and, therefore, in thinking—that is not found in ordinary conversation. Computers do not understand ambiguous statements; they are not programmed to guess or to "read between the lines." Instead, they respond logically and rationally. As a result, to be intelligent in the computer society—to be truly computer literate—requires learning how to be completely explicit, context-free, repeat-able, logical, and rational (Calfee, 1985). This type of communication is quite different from our natural, spoken language, which tends to be highly implicit, specific to context, idiosyncratic, and intuitive.

Because of the important differences between computers and other instructional media such as teachers, texts, and television, Salomon and Gardner (1986) caution against attempting to evaluate computer-related instruction by asking such naive and largely uninformative questions as "Does it teach better than . . . ?" The important point in evaluations is the recognition that computers both do things that are different from other instructional methods and do them differently as well. For example, computers allow us to teach programming and perhaps to foster the types of cognitive processes involved in programming. As Linn (1985) puts it, the function of programming courses is to teach problem solving as well as programming. In much the same way, Papert's Logo is designed to teach students how to learn (as well as to teach them Logo). And subsequent assessments reveal that children who became skilled in Logo not only increased their mastery of metacognitive skills, but improved in measured creativity as well (Salomon and Gardner, 1986).

A comprehensive review of evaluations of CAI at the college level looked at fifty-nine separate studies (Kulik, Kulik, and Cohen, 1980). Although this global review does not offer direct comparisons of different CAI programs, it does provide additional evidence that CAI in general produces significant positive changes in both achievement and attitude among college students. It should be noted, however, that these changes are very small. More encouraging is the finding of Kulik and associates that CAI substantially reduces instruction time.

But are we in the midst of a computer revolution in education and in society at large? *Revolution* implies sudden, dynamic, sweeping changes that ultimately transform significant aspects of our lives. Looking back through the ages, social historians have no difficulty identifying and naming revolutions: the agricultural, the industrial, the French. We recognize these revolutions clearly; sometimes we even think we understand them.

But recognizing current social change — or predicting future change — is more difficult. We are too much a part of our cultures to easily sense change in them. Perhaps we are too much part of the change itself.

Computers, Papert (1987) tells us, are a fundamental part of our culture. They are more than simply tools that we can use for various purposes; they change our very way of thinking and acting. We are part of the computer revolution, and as a result, perhaps we do not see it very clearly.

But if a computer revolution is actually happening in education, it certainly doesn't seem very sudden. Laurillard (1988) notes that computers should provide an excellent learning environment for our students, given their amazing powers for storing, retrieving, and processing information and in light of their interactive capabilities. However, in her words, "computer assisted learning has never become a principal teaching method at any level of education" (p. 215).

We have now had a full two decades to examine the use of computers in schools and to incorporate them into our programs, says Laurillard. Yet those who advocate their use must continue to rely on their promise rather than on evidence of what they have done.

But change in education is seldom very rapid — especially from the perspective of those who are part of it. In the end, history might look back and judge that, yes, this was a sudden and most dramatic revolution that produced a truly marvelous outcome. The ultimate contributions of computer-based instructional systems may be even greater than we can yet imagine. It is also possible that historians will look back and say, "There was no revolution of any kind back there near the end of the twentieth century. There was only the rather slow proliferation of that primitive tool they called the computer. Of course, now it's obsolete."

MASTERY LEARNING AND PSI

Programmed instruction — in all of its variations, with or without computers — is but one of the instructional modes that clearly reflect the influence of psychological theory on education. There are more. Among them, perhaps no others have received greater attention than Bloom's suggestions for **mastery learning** and Keller's outline for a **personalized system of instruction (PSI)**, sometimes called the *Keller plan*.

These approaches have a great deal in common. Most important, each is based on a fundamental assumption: There are faster learners and slower learners (Bloom, 1976). Accordingly, aptitude is primarily a function of the speed with which a student acquires information, concepts, or skills. So long as all students receive identical instruction, there will be a high correlation between aptitude and achievement. In other words, with identical instruction, faster students will achieve better and slower students will achieve at a lower level. However, if each student is presented with the most optimal learning conditions, the relationship between aptitude and achievement will be very slight, and most learners will reach the same level. In Bloom's terminology, all learners, provided they are given optimal instruction, will achieve *mastery* of important objectives. If all learners master the same material, differences among them will be minimal, and the relationship of achievement to aptitude will be negligible.

A second assumption, fundamental both to the Keller plan and to Bloom's mastery approach, is that learning requires constant evaluation, not so that the learner can be graded, but to guide the learning/instruction process.

Table 13.1   Basic elements of Bloom's mastery learning

Underlying Assumptions	1. There are *faster* learners and *slower* learners (not *better* learners and *poorer* learners).
	2. Learning requires constant *formative* evaluation, designed specifically to guide the teaching/learning process.
Broad Characteristics of Teaching Methods	1. Instruction is directed toward the attainment of specific, explicit, and previously identified objectives.
	2. Instruction is guided by the results of formative evaluation.
	3. Numerous *corrective* instructional procedures in the form of study sessions, cooperative student groups, individualized tutoring, reteaching, and alternative instructional materials are provided.

This type of evaluation, termed *formative*, is not to be confused with more formal evaluation provided at the end of a unit or course, termed *summative*. Whereas **summative evaluation** is intended primarily to provide a grade, **formative evaluation** is an essential diagnostic tool in the teaching process. And in both Bloom's and Keller's systems, the attainment of a specific grade is not the most important criterion; mastery of course objectives is.

Bloom's mastery learning model is based largely on John B. Carroll's (1963) model of school learning. Simply stated, this model specifies that degree of learning is primarily a function of the time spent learning relative to the amount of time required to learn. Amount of time required is, in turn, a function of both aptitude and quality of instruction received.

Carroll's emphasis is on providing all learners with both high-quality instruction and the time required to learn. His objective is "equality of opportunity," which contrasts with Bloom's objective of "equality of attainment" (Carroll, 1989, p. 30).

Bloom's basic notion is that it is possible to analyze any learning sequence into a number of specific objectives and to teach in such a way that most, if not all, students attain these objectives. Although the teaching methods suggested by Bloom are not fundamentally different from those ordinarily used by teachers, they differ in two important respects: First, they are directed specifically toward the mastery of previously identified objectives; and second, they make extensive use of formative evaluation to diagnose learner difficulties, to suggest modifications in instructional strategies, and to identify subject areas in which more time needs to be spent. A third very important characteristic of Bloom's mastery learning is that it requires the use of a great variety of systematic and deliberate corrective procedures in conjunction with formative evaluation (Bloom, 1987). Among these corrective procedures are study sessions, individualized tutoring, reteaching, students helping each other in small, cooperative groups, and a selection of alternative instructional materials in a variety of forms, such as programs, films, audiotapes, and so on. (See Table 13.1.)

One final characteristic of Bloom's mastery learning is the provision that classes typically progress from one unit to another as a group. This is accomplished by providing enrichment for students who master course objectives first. Thus, the pace of progress through the curriculum is determined largely by those who require the longest time to reach mastery. Ultimately, all students who have mastered course objectives are given A's; those who have not succeeded are given I's (for Incomplete, but meaning "mastery in the making"). No students fail in this system.

The Keller PSI plan is an elaboration of Bloom's mastery learning (Keller, 1968). Originally developed for teaching introductory psychology at the college level, PSI has since been used in a variety of college courses. And although its applicability at the elementary or secondary school level has not been extensively demonstrated, the principles upon which it is based and the methods it suggests might prove useful there as well.

Essentially, a PSI approach requires that the course be broken down into small units, that appropriate instructional materials be developed for each of these units, and that students be allowed to take as much time as necessary to learn each unit. Whenever students feel that they are ready, they are given a short unit quiz, the quiz is marked immediately, and they are told whether they need to spend more time studying the same unit or whether they can proceed to the next unit. At the end of the course, an examination covering all material is given.

Unlike mastery learning, the Keller plan does not advocate the use of traditional instructional methods; nor does it rely as heavily on corrective procedures, although alternative learning materials are available. Instead, the onus for mastering a unit rests largely on the student. In many cases, the unit in question corresponds to a chapter in a textbook and/or to a programmed version of the same material. Tutoring often occurs after a student proctor marks the unit quiz, but it is not an essential part of the course. Nor, indeed, is the traditional lecture. In fact, students attend lectures only *after* they have successfully completed specified units. Lectures are intended to serve as reinforcement for success rather than as a basis for it.

In summary, Bloom's mastery learning and Keller's PSI are designed to provide success experiences for all learners. And although these approaches recognize that there are important individual differences among learners, they contradict the ancient belief that there are good and bad learners — faster or slower, perhaps, but not better or poorer. Accordingly, each approach attempts to provide learning experiences that will optimize the attainment of specific objectives for each learner. Those objectives might be behavioral or performance objectives or a specified score on a quiz.

The advantages claimed for approaches such as these center on the attention that each pays to individual differences in learning rate. Whereas traditional approaches to instruction and evaluation almost necessitate that those who learn more slowly than their age/grade peers will often fail, these highly individualized approaches ensure that almost all students will eventually succeed.

Another possible advantage of mastery approaches is increased student motivation. As Stallings and Stipek (1986) note, repeated exposure to a mastery approach should lead students to the expectation that they will succeed if they work hard enough. It follows that students who are externally oriented may, as a result, eventually become more internally oriented and consequently more willing to accept challenges (see Chapter 11).

INDIVIDUALIZING WITH IPI AND IGE

To individualize teaching is to make it more responsive to the needs and the characteristics of the individual learner. This does not mean that instruction must occur only in a private, individual setting and in a self-paced situation

(Anderson and Block, 1977). The essential requirement is simply that some of the characteristics of instruction (such as level of material presented, mode of presentation, and instructional goals) take into account at least some of the student's characteristics (such as aptitude, interest, and previous achievement). Clearly, programmed instruction, mastery learning, and Keller's personalized system of instruction are not the only approaches to individualizing learning. In this section we look briefly at two other approaches: individually prescribed instruction (IPI) and individually guided education (IGE).

Each of these approaches requires the almost total reorganization of an entire school or, more often, of an entire school system. **Individually prescribed instruction**, for example, is a complex system based on the reorganization of the entire curriculum for each subject into a large number of sequential units, each with its own objectives and test. Students work individually on a unit, making extensive use of written materials. Once they have completed a unit, they take the accompanying test; if their performance is satisfactory, they then proceed to the next unit. Units are essentially ungraded so that a learner can progress as rapidly or as slowly as ability and inclination allow. Thus, at any one time, students in what would otherwise be a single grade might be working at levels that elsewhere would fall within a wide spread of grades (Scanlon, Weinberger, and Weiler, 1970). In fact, IPI's advocates claim that this is one of the chief advantages of the system.

Individually guided education, which originated at the University of Wisconsin in the early 1970s, also requires a reorganization of school systems, for it too is based on the principle of ungraded schools. In addition, it makes use of teams of teachers, extensive workshops to coordinate the objectives and activities of teachers, a systematic program of home and school cooperation, individual programming for students, and ongoing research to develop and improve IGE materials (Klausmeier, Ross-

miller, and Saily, 1977; Haney and Sorenson, 1977). Both IGE and IPI use their own curriculum materials or extensively modify existing materials. Partly for this reason, both can involve considerable expense, particularly in their early stages.

INDIVIDUALIZED INSTRUCTION EVALUATED

Do individualized approaches to instruction work? In a word, yes. But to say that they work better than more conventional approaches all (or even most) of the time would require more convincing evidence than we now have. Approaches such as IGE and IPI, which require extensive reorganization of schools and school systems, cannot easily be compared to more traditional instructional methods. As Walker and Schaffarzick (1974) point out, the "new" approaches are usually slightly superior in some respects, perhaps somewhat inferior in others, and not very different in most.

Investigations of Keller's PSI at the college level and of Bloom's mastery learning primarily in elementary schools have found these approaches to be quite effective, both in terms of reaching course goals and in terms of general attitude toward course work. In a review of studies that have investigated the effectiveness of mastery approaches, Slavin (1987) tells of a number of studies with positive results — and of several that show no advantage for mastery learning. Bloom (1987) suggests that results are usually positive when students make full use of the "corrective feedback" process that is part of formative evaluation.

Kulik, Kulik, and Cohen (1979) analyzed seventy-five separate studies that compared Keller's PSI with conventional approaches (see Figure 13.2 for one comparison). Their conclusion:

The analysis establishes that PSI generally produces superior student achievement, less variation in

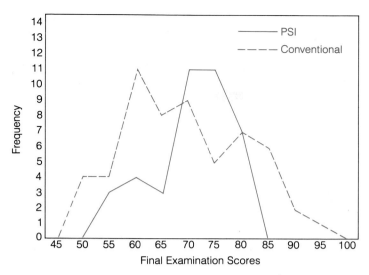

Figure 13.2 Distribution of final-examination averages for forty-eight PSI and forty-eight conventional classes (PSI = personalized system of instruction).
From J. A. Kulik, C. C. Kulik, and P. A. Cohen, "A Meta-analysis of Outcome Studies of Keller's Personalized System of Instruction," *American Psychologist*, 34, 307–318. Copyright 1979 by the American Psychological Association. Reprinted with permission of the authors.

achievement, and higher student ratings in college courses, but does not affect course withdrawal or student study time in these courses. (p. 307)

Lest we madly run off selling another educational panacea, however, it should be noted that PSI and mastery learning have their faults and weaknesses as well, and that not all evaluations are as positive and as optimistic as that of Kulik and associates. For example, a number of researchers have noted that student attrition is often higher with these methods than with more conventional approaches (Robin, 1976). And other critics have observed that an emphasis on the mastery of objectives that all (or most) learners can achieve might, in fact, penalize the fast learner (Arlin, 1984). At best, such a system does not maximize the faster learner's achievement; at worst, it leads to boredom, destroys motivation, and renders meaningless the

assignment of grades because all who work long enough obtain A's. Furthermore, we cannot completely discount the possibility that undue emphasis on specifiable objectives might restrict the teaching/learning process and prevent the occurrence of important incidental learning.

In one of the most comprehensive investigations of individualized instruction in secondary schools, Bangert, Kulik, and Kulik (1983) analyzed and summarized the findings of fifty-one separate studies. Each study had measured the effectiveness of instructional methods involving the division of the curriculum into units, the use of "learning activity packages," students working at their own rate, and formative testing prior to moving to the next level of work. Thus the summary included studies of IPI, IGE, and PSI, among other approaches. The summary indicates that individualized instruction has a modest but positive effect on school achievement in secondary grades, but that it does not affect attitude toward subject matter, self-esteem, or measures of abstract thinking ability.

As Bangert and associates note, the results of this study are very different from those reported by Bloom and associates or those summarized by Kulik and associates (1979). Note, however, that the earlier analysis dealt with research at the college level; this one deals with the secondary-school level. It appears that individualized instruction has far more positive results at the college level than it does in secondary schools — a fact that might be explained partly in terms of the characteristics of college students compared with those of secondary-school students. These characteristics might include greater maturity, greater motivation, better study skills, and more appropriate cognitive strategies.

In summary, individualized instruction is at least as effective as more conventional approaches in secondary schools and often is significantly more effective at the college level. In general, the approaches require considerable effort on the part of schools and teachers with respect to systematizing and simplifying instruction. And they demand that schools and teachers make a conscious effort to specify their immediate goals, and sometimes also their long-range goals. Among their virtues, these approaches provide important experiences of success for learners who might otherwise lack them, by making it possible for learners of all aptitudes to master units and courses. In addition to these and other positive features of systematic individualized instruction, the greatest contribution of this approach may turn out to lie in the impetus it provides for research on attribute-treatment interaction (ATI). Such research is designed to uncover the relationships among specific instructional modes, identifiable learner characteristics, and the attainment of instructional goals. We examine ATI next.

ATTRIBUTE-TREATMENT INTERACTION

Approaches such as Keller's PSI and Bloom's mastery learning are based on the assumption that all learners are capable of achieving the same instructional goals — of mastering relevant instructional requirements. However, they also recognize that some people learn faster than others and that some people learn with less additional help than others. In other words, even approaches that attempt to minimize the importance of differences in learners' characteristics must, in the end, recognize that these differences are sometimes fundamentally important. Other programs, such as learning-styles approaches, are based directly on a recognition of differences among learners. Such programs require information about the relationship between learner characteristics and specific instructional methods — or what is termed **attribute-treatment interaction** (Cronbach and Snow, 1977).

The basic premise of attribute-treatment research is simple: Specific instructional methods are better for students with a particular characteristic, whereas different instructional methods for achieving the same goals might be better for students with other characteristics. Put another way, an attribute-treatment interaction exists whenever the effectiveness of instruction (the treatment) is shown to depend, at least in part, on the learner's characteristics. The ultimate goal of attribute-treatment research is to identify the optimum combinations of attributes and treatments.

Researchers have looked at numerous student characteristics (including anxiety, dependence, conformity, various dimensions of intellectual abilities, and many others) and have attempted to relate these to various instructional methods (such as lecturing, small-group interaction, programs, computers, demonstrations) and to various characteristics of each of these — including, for example, whether the

"So when Farmer Bob comes through the door, three of us circle around and ... Muriel! Are you chewing your cud while I'm talking?"

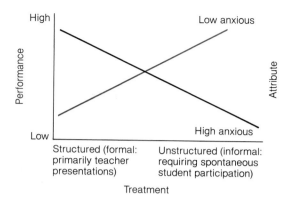

Figure 13.3   A schematic representation of an attribute-treatment interaction — specifically, an interaction between anxiety and degree of structure in teaching method. Note that highly anxious students tend to perform better with more structured approaches, but that the opposite is true of students who are less anxious.

approach is "structured" or "unstructured" (Ross, Rakow, and Bush, 1980; Whitener, 1989).

Although findings from ATI studies are by no means clear and simple, researchers advance several tentative conclusions. One of the most replicated findings is the interaction between anxiety and the degree to which an instructional method is structured or requires active learner participation. Specifically, highly anxious students do better with instructional approaches that do not require a high degree of student interaction but instead are more "teacher-centered" (see, for example, Peterson, 1977; see Figure 13.3). Similarly, there appears to be an interaction between general ability and structure, such that students of lower ability do relatively better with highly structured approaches (such as programmed instruction)

that use small steps together with frequent responding and reinforcement (Swing and Peterson, 1982). This interaction may result in part from the fact that highly structured approaches reduce information-processing requirements — that is, they demand fewer cognitive strategies of the learner (Resnick, 1981).

Whitener (1989) also reports an interaction between prior achievement (as opposed to aptitude) and lesson structure. Highly structured lessons *increase* the difference between high and low achievers; in contrast, self-paced, relatively unstructured lessons tend to *decrease* that difference. In effect, what this means is that higher achievers benefit more than lower achievers from an increase in instructional structure.

In conclusion, then, at least three separate interactions between lesson structure and student attributes have been uncovered by research. Specifically, highly structured approaches benefit students of lower ability, more anxious students, and students whose prior achievement is higher.

Several important cautions are in order. First, these conclusions are extremely tentative at best. Furthermore, simple summaries of complex studies tend to make the results seem far clearer and more definite than they actually are. In fact, the results of research on attribute-treatment interaction are highly inconsistent and often contradictory. As a case in point, consider that two of our three conclusions are almost contradictory: Students of lower ability do better with highly structured approaches, but higher-achieving students also improve more with increasing structure than do students who have previously achieved at a lower level.

It is likely that an accurate description of these interactions would not describe attribute-treatment interactions, but rather attribute-attribute-treatment interactions, or perhaps even more confusing combinations. In other words, it may well be that a characteristic such as anxiety, in combination with a particular level of some specific ability and taking into account prior achievement, might interact with a given instructional method quite differently from the same level and type of anxiety when combined with a different level of the ability or achievement.

Interestingly, when student preferences are taken into account in an attempt to discover the best combinations of attributes and teaching approaches, the picture becomes more confused rather than clearer. For example, research tells us (tentatively to be sure) that students of lower ability tend to perform better in more highly structured classroom environments, but that the opposite is true of higher-ability students (Snow and Lohman, 1984). However, Clark (1982) found that lower-ability students *prefer* unstructured and highly permissive classrooms—perhaps because their lack of achievement is more likely to go unnoticed in this environment. In contrast, better students express a strong preference for highly structured approaches that make it unnecessary for them

to plan and think and that they suspect will make it easier for them to direct their efforts and achieve well. Thus, student preferences directly contradict what research suggests is best for them.

If this sounds impossibly complex to you, do not despair. Its complexity and lack of clarity mean that no very valuable suggestions can yet be derived and applied directly to classroom practice (Pintrich et al., 1986). Besides, as Gagné and Dick (1983) observe, measures of relationships uncovered thus far have been extremely modest. In the end, the most powerful variables related to school achievement continue to be intellectual ability and previous school achievement. Consequently, the most fruitful approach to matching instruction to student characteristics is probably one that takes these two variables into account. And that is what happens, at least to a small degree, when students are sorted into groups on the basis of achievement and sometimes of ability. We should not be misled into thinking, however, that these two variables—achievement and ability—account for most of the variation in observed student achievement. In fact, they account for only about 25 percent of the variation; some of the remaining 75 percent is due to other factors such as home background, type and quality of instruction, and personality characteristics, particularly as they are reflected in motivation and attitudes (Bloom, 1976).

MAIN POINTS

1. A number of different methods are available for dealing with students' individual differences. Among them are increased individual attention and tracking. For practical reasons, these are not always highly effective.

2. Learning-styles approaches to education are among the most highly individualized of instructional approaches. They attempt

to tailor a variety of instructional features — instructional method, timetabling, teaching mode, curriculum, evaluation, and rewards — to individual students' strengths and weaknesses.

3. Programmed instruction and computer-related instruction can also provide opportunities for individualizing instruction, as can such systems as Bloom's mastery learning, Keller's personalized system of instruction (PSI), individually guided education (IGE), and individually prescribed instruction (IPI).

4. A *program* is a sequential arrangement of information in small steps (frames), each of which requires the learner to make a response. Immediate feedback (knowledge of results) serves as reinforcement. Programmed instruction individualizes instruction largely by allowing students to progress at their own rates, and sometimes by providing additional help (remedial frames) for learners who experience difficulty.

5. A *linear program* (Skinner) requires all learners to progress through the same material in exactly the same sequence and to construct their own responses; a *branching program* (Crowder) requires learners to select an answer and then directs them to the next frame on the basis of that answer. Those who make errors are provided with further help.

6. Programs do teach; they often do so most effectively as adjuncts to other methods of instruction. Instructional methods that incorporate the principles of programmed instruction emphasize active responding, "errorless" learning, and immediate feedback concerning the correctness of the learner's responses.

7. The computer revolution, which was made possible largely through the invention of the microcomputer, is evident in the rapid proliferation of microcomputers in our homes, our work places, and our schools.

8. The optimistic view suggests that computers will provide students with immediate access to high-quality information; may lead to smaller, friendlier, and more personal schools; can reduce problems with basic reading, writing, and mathematical skills; and might do a great deal to counter the negative effects of television.

9. A more pessimistic view suggests that computers may lead to a decline in computational and reading skills; might encourage violence; might help widen the gap between the "haves" and the "have-nots"; might lead us to rely on "expert" computer systems whose expertise rests on information rather than on wisdom; and might depersonalize schools.

10. Computers are used in schools to manage instructional programs (data storage and analysis, for example); for computational purposes; as sophisticated "teaching machines" or audiovisual aids to present programs; to simulate the functioning of complex systems; as sources of information; as sources of career-related guidance; or as tools.

11. As tools, computers may be used as word processors, data processors, or music synthesizers. Students can be taught to program them. The resulting *computer literacy* may soon be one of the important goals of the educational process.

12. One additional contribution of the computer is the unique cognitive processes it fosters. These are characterized by an explicitness, clarity, and rationality of expression that far surpass that required for ordinary communication; they are also characterized by a problem-solving, learning-how-to-learn orientation.

13. Bloom's mastery learning is based on the assumption that most learners are capable of mastering important school objectives, but that some people require more time and more nearly optimal instruction than others. Bloom emphasizes that the provision of optimal instruction and time leads to mastery.

14. Keller's personalized system of instruction (PSI), closely related to Bloom's mastery learning, is designed for teaching at the college level. It places the onus for attainment of unit and course objectives primarily on the student. Students are allowed to repeat unit quizzes until they reach a specified performance criterion and then progress to the next unit.

15. Individually guided education (IGE) and individually prescribed instruction (IPI) require the reorganization of entire school systems because both are nongraded approaches. In IPI, the entire school curriculum is divided into small units, each with related tests. Students work individually on each unit and progress to the next whenever they are successful on the accompanying test. In IGE, students also work individually on specially prepared and sequenced material. IGE uses teams of teachers and home and school programs, as well as workshops and research programs designed to improve instructional materials and approaches.

16. Evaluations of major system approaches to individualizing instruction indicate that typically these approaches have moderately positive effects in elementary and secondary schools, but more highly positive effects at the college level.

17. Attempts to individualize instruction have also taken the form of studies of attribute-treatment interactions. Such interactions exist when there is a consistent relationship between the effectiveness of an instructional approach and some identifiable characteristic (or grouping of characteristics) of the learners.

18. The clearest example of an attribute-treatment interaction involves anxiety and instructional structure. Specifically, highly anxious students often do better with structured approaches (programmed instruction or highly didactic teacher presentations in which students are not required to participate extensively). Also, lower-ability students perform better under highly structured conditions, and prior high achievers also do better with increasing structure.

19. Conclusions about attribute-treatment interactions are tentative at best. These interactions are typically very modest. In the final analysis, the two variables that appear to be most highly related to school success are ability and previous achievement.

20. A bear always faces the front of its tracks.

SUGGESTED READINGS

The following book should be of practical assistance to students who wish to explore programmed instruction more carefully:

MARKLE, S. M. (1964). *Good frames and bad: A grammar of frame writing.* New York: Wiley.

The following two sources might be valuable for teachers involved in implementing computers in schools:

COBURN, P., KELMAN, P., ROBERTS, N., SNYDER, T. F. F., WATT, D. H., & WEINER, C. (1982). *Practical guide to computers in education.* Reading, Mass.: Addison-Wesley.

DEAN, C., & WHITLOCK, Q. (1983). *A handbook of computer based training.* London: Kogan Page.

An important vision of the potential of computers in the cognitive development of children is exceptionally well presented in:

PAPERT, S. (1980). *Mindstorms: Children, computers, and powerful ideas.* New York: Basic Books.

Classic references for PSI and Bloom's mastery learning include:

BLOOM, B. S. (1976). *Human characteristics and school learning.* New York: McGraw-Hill.

KELLER, F. S. (1968). Good-bye, teacher. . . . *Journal of Applied Behavior Analysis, 1,* 79–89.

An excellent collection of many of the best of Benjamin Bloom's articles and presentations appears in:

BLOOM, B. S. (1981). *All our children learning: A primer for parents, teachers, and other educators.* New York: McGraw-Hill.

The following booklet is an interesting and potentially useful attempt to translate research about teaching into practical applied principles. It presents forty-one findings, with explanatory comments and practical suggestions relating to each.

U.S. DEPARTMENT OF EDUCATION. (1986). *What works: Research about teaching and learning.* Pueblo, Colo.: Consumer Information Center.

Seals are the staple food of the polar bear. Infant seals are particulary easy to capture when they are still in the aglos *(calving dens). The aglo is a small ice cave hollowed out by a mother seal and accessible only from the water. It is covered with a three- to five-foot layer of snow and a thick cover of ice. The polar bear can scent* aglos *from a remarkable distance. Having found one, the bear rapidly excavates the overburden of snow with quick blows of paws, and then attempts to break through the ice by rearing up and smashing downward with both front paws. If the ice is too thick, the bear may move back a short distance, run toward the* aglo, *leap high in the air, and come thundering down with all four paws, crashing noisily through the ice. It is then a simple matter to reach inside and pull out the squirming infant (Perry, 1966).*

MEASUREMENT AND EVALUATION

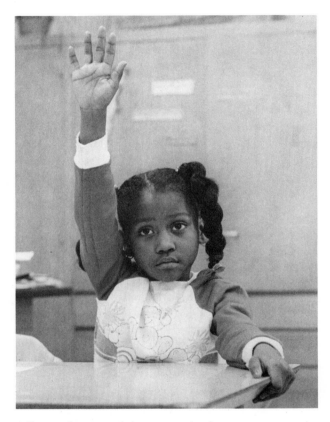

All animals are equal, but some animals are more equal than others.

GEORGE ORWELL *Animal Farm*

The low man goes on adding one to one,
 His hundred's soon hit:
This high man, aiming at a million
 Misses a unit.

ROBERT BROWNING *A Grammarian's Funeral*

PREVIEW In spite of the intuitive appeal of "schools without failures," "schools without tests," and other hypothetical situations in which everyone is highly motivated, absolutely dedicated, and deliriously happy, the nitty-gritty of classroom practice sometimes (perhaps frequently) requires assessment. This chapter describes the various methods by which student and *teacher* performance can be measured and evaluated, the reasons why assessment is important, and some of the abuses and misuses of assessment procedures.

■ *"Listen up, cows," the bear says. He feels like a missionary; he is an environmental crusader. "Listen up," he repeats. The cousset drums fall silent, the dancing stops. The last of the wild cows drags herself from the water. They stand on the floor of the valley below the bear's ledge.*

"Listen up. Pay attention. You there," he says to the brindle-faced wild cow. "Yes, you," he says as the cow pulls the cigar from her lips and raises her eyebrows as though to ask, "You mean me?"

"Pay attention," the bear repeats. He's terrific. What a teacher! Some of the cows shuffle their feet, as though anxious for the bear to continue. When the cow with the crooked horn slurps her whisky too noisily, the others glare at her. She looks embarrassed and puts her cup down. She looks toward the bear, but he can tell that her mind is not on the lesson, that she is still thinking about her whisky; she has that glazed look.

"We're going to play a game," the bear says, suddenly inspired. He has always known much about

the science of teaching, but at this very moment he learns something new about the art — something he can't quite put into words. A tremor of excitement rumbles through the group. The cow with the crooked horn stubs her cigar on the ground. Her eyes are no longer glazed; for the moment, she has forgotten about the whisky. Several of the cows whose tails are still intertwined from the dance now pull apart. They shuffle their feet, but it isn't the rhythms of the dance that move them; it is the voice of the teacher, the promise of his lesson.

"A wonderful game," the bear says. He has to think fast because if he doesn't, he will lose them. He has to think of a game before the wild cows go back to their whisky and their cigars.

"Line up," he says. It is a beginning. The bear doesn't yet know where he is going, but something will come to him. "Line up starting over there by the spruce." He points to his left, toward the tree against which the cows have constructed a temporary bar. On the bar are brown whisky jugs and a crock of water for those who like to cut their whisky. On the tree next to the mirror behind the bar, someone has nailed a styrofoam-cup dispenser. There are aerosol cans of hair spray on a shelf below the mirror.

"Start with the shortest. I want the shortest cow closest to the spruce tree. Yes, right up next to the bar," the bear says. "Put the second shortest cow . . . yes, stand next in line. And so on. . . . That's it."

There is much shuffling and jostling, much standing next to each other to gauge the top of the other's head, much arguing. The bear intervenes as necessary. "If you two are exactly the same height," he asks once, "what would be a fair way of deciding who should stand next in line?" He balances a coin on his nose. He is such a marvelous teacher.

Before we begin the game, I need to know a lot more about each of you," the bear says, the structure of the lesson suddenly unfolding in his mind. He recognizes this as a special pedagogical moment; he is filled with a wonderful feeling. He already has in mind the rudiments of a game that will lead the wild cows to a new environmental consciousness. It is a cooperative team game, with just enough interteam competition to pique the wild cows' interest.

Before the game begins, the bear must help the cows divide themselves into groups. For this task, he needs to know something of their individual abilities. He needs to measure their intelligence and their prior learning. He needs to evaluate their commitment, assess their interests and motivation, and judge their personalities. Quickly the bear decides what tests he will use to assess the wild cows. He's very excited; measurement and evaluation do that to him. He feels like such a pedagogue!!

The cow with the crooked horn stands in line. She is a short cow; as a result, she is very close to the bar. She's bored. "Enough of this crap," she finally mutters. She goes to the bar, pours herself a cup of whisky, and lights up a fresh cigar. One of the cousset drums draws her attention, and her rump begins to twitch rhythmically, and the air fills with the odor of methane gas.

The bear notices. "This is not yet an environmentally friendly cow," he thinks sardonically. "But by God I'll measure and evaluate her too!" ■

MEASUREMENT AND EVALUATION DISTINGUISHED

A statement such as, "The cow with the crooked horn is environmentally unfriendly," illustrates **evaluation**. The statement, "The brindle-face is 52 inches high," is an example of **measurement**. Measurement involves the use of an instrument (for example, a ruler or tape measure) to assess a specific *quantity*; evaluation is the formation of a judgment concerning certain *qualities*. In general, then, measuring is a more precise and more objective procedure; evaluating is less precise and more subjective.

Both measurement and evaluation are important parts of the instructional process. As we saw in Chapter 1, instruction can be described as a sequence of procedures conducted before teaching, during teaching, and after teaching (see Figure 14.1). In the before-teaching phase, measurement and evaluation may be involved in placing students, in selecting instructional procedures, and in determining student readiness. Plans for final assessment and evaluation should also be made at this stage. In the after-teaching phase, measurement and evaluation are used not only to determine the extent to which instructional goals have been met, but also to assess the effectiveness of instructional strategies and to reevaluate student placement and readiness. Measurement is being used when actual tests are used; it is essentially a quantitative process. Evaluation is being used when teachers make decisions concerning the adequacy of instructional procedures, the readiness of students, and the extent to which curriculum goals are being met; it is a more qualitative process.

Evaluation need not be based on measurement. Indeed, much teacher assessment of student behavior is not based on measurement. The countless value judgments made by teachers about the abilities of students, their motivation, their persistence, their pleasantness, and so on are often examples of evaluation without measurement. In this chapter the term *evaluation* is often used to include both subjective assessment and measurement with tests.

THE IMPORTANCE OF EVALUATION

Because evaluation is a central component of each stage of the teaching model presented in Figure 14.1, it might be expected that assessment procedures would occupy a significant portion of classroom time. This is in fact the case. Gullickson (1985) reports that an average of between 5 and 15 percent of class time is actually spent on tests. (In lower elementary grades, the percentage is closer to 5; in high school it is closer to 15.)

In addition to time spent actually writing, correcting, and going over tests, there is a tremendous range of other evaluative activities that fill school days: asking students questions; commenting on student responses and presentations; evaluating nontest performances in such subject areas as art, drama, music, and writing; informal observations of ongoing student work; correcting and grading homework assignments; evaluating written work; informal assessments of attitudes and efforts; and many more. In fact, the bulk of the teacher's evaluations, especially in lower elementary grades, is based on informal observation and on grading of assignments and performance, rather than on test results.

What kinds of impact do these evaluative procedures have on students? Profound ones. In fact, it is difficult to underestimate the influence of evaluation on student behavior. Ramsden (1988a) argues that students' beliefs about assessment are among the most important influences on learning. He explains that the types of assessments used determine what students study and how they learn. Sadly, our most common approaches to evaluation encourage a passive form of learning in which rote memorization of facts and formulas is heavily rewarded.

Put another way, there are two broad approaches to learning: a *surface approach* that emphasizes memorization of unrelated facts and a *deep approach* that involves a deliberate and active search for underlying principles and concepts and that attempts to discover relationships (Crooks, 1988). Because our tests emphasize the simple, surface components of curriculum content and largely ignore the more complex, deeper aspects of knowledge, the surface components are what students learn.

How do we change surface approaches to

The Instructional Process

Before Teaching

1. Establish goals 5, 6, 14*
2. Determine student readiness 6, 7, 8
3. Select instructional strategies; collect required materials 2, 3, 4, 5, 13
4. Plan for assessment and evaluation 14

Teaching

Implement instructional strategies 5, 9, 10, 11, 12, 13

After Teaching

1. Assess effectiveness of teaching strategies 14
2. Determine extent to which goals have been met 14
3. Reevaluate student readiness 7, 9, 14

*Chapters containing relevant information

Figure 14.1 A three-stage model of the teaching process.

deep ones? How do we get learners to pay attention to relationships and principles, and how do we get them to achieve understanding instead of memorization?

This text provides several possible answers. For example, there are programs whose express goals are to teach thinking, to develop cognitive strategies, to impart learning/thinking skills, or to develop metacognitive awareness. And there are cognitive learning theories, such as those described by Bruner and by Ausubel, that emphasize meaningfulness and comprehension while deemphasizing "meaningless rote learning." These theories provide a number of recommendations for helping students attend to the underlying structures of knowledge, to relationships, and to meaningfulness.

But perhaps, in Elton and Laurillard's (1979) words, "the quickest way to change student learning is to change the assessment system" (p. 100), because in the final analysis students try to learn what teachers test, not what teachers suggest is important. It is not sufficient to pay lip service to the importance of complex cognitive processes such as synthesizing or evaluating, or what Bruner calls "going beyond the information given." If teacher-made tests and final examinations ask students only to repeat what they have read in textbooks or heard in class, that is what students will learn to learn.

The point is clear: Teachers must evaluate students on the right things; that is, they must evaluate students on those things they consider most important — the things they want students to learn.

A second point should also be clear: Evaluation needs to be fair, consistent, and reliable. Whenever possible it should be based on the best measurements available, although often it will also result from informal observation.

There is much that an expert teacher should know about measurement. Read on. . . .

SCALES OF MEASUREMENT

A number of different ways of measuring — a number of different scales of measurement — are appropriate for measuring different things (see Table 14.1). The crudest and least informative scale of measurement is a **nominal scale**. As its label implies, this level of measurement simply names. The numbers on the backs of football players or descriptive categories such as *blue* and *red* or *house* and *barn* are examples of nominal measurement. They tell us nothing about amount, but only indicate the categories to which things belong.

At a more advanced level, **ordinal scales** permit us to rank, or order, individuals on the basis of the characteristics we measure. For example, tasting different beverages might allow us to rank them in terms of sweetness. The ranking (or ordinal scale) tells us nothing about absolute amount of sweetness, but does give us some information about relative amounts.

The third measurement scale, the **interval scale**, allows us to measure quantity in intervals that vary in fixed, predictable ways. We measure temperature using interval scales. We can therefore say that a change from 0 to 10 degrees is equivalent to a change from 10 to 20 degrees or to a change from 20 to 30 degrees. But what the interval scale does not permit us to do is to say that 20 degrees is twice as hot (or half as cold) as 10 degrees or that 30 degrees is three times as hot as 10 degrees. To be able to compare amounts in this way, we need to measure characteristics that conform to a **ratio scale**. A ratio scale has a true (rather than an arbitrary) zero. In a temperature scale, for example, the zero is completely arbitrary. It could have been set at any temperature — and is, in fact, set at different points on the Fahrenheit and the Celsius scales. Weight, age, and height, on the other hand, have exact, nonarbitrary zeros. And six feet *is* twice as tall as three feet.

Most of our measurement in psychology and education makes use of interval scales, although most of what we measure doesn't really fit this scale; that is, we assume that the difference between 60 and 70 percent on our tests is roughly equivalent to the difference between 40 and 50 percent. The emphasis should be on the word *roughly*. In most instances, we have little evidence to support this assumption of equivalency.

Table 14.1 Four scales of measurement

Scale	Characteristics and Functions	Example
Nominal	Names: places things in categories	Labeling reading groups "Giraffes," "Zebras," and "Goats"
Ordinal	Ranks: tells us about relative amount (more than/less than)	Being in first grade, second grade, third grade, and so on
Interval	Measures in equal intervals: has an arbitrary zero; permits precise measurement of change, but not comparison of absolute amounts	Most psychological and educational measurement; we *assume* that score intervals are equal
Ratio	Provides true zero and equal intervals: permits comparison of absolute amounts	Weight, height

Although most measurement in education uses an interval scale, virtually none of it is direct; that is, no instruments have yet been devised that measure knowledge directly, as a ruler measures length or a scale measures weight. Measurement in education is like estimating temperature: The measure is inferred from the observation that a column of mercury or alcohol rises or descends in a hollow glass tube; achievement is inferred from changes in behavior. Knowledge is not directly measurable, but we assume that some of its effects on behavior are.

MEASUREMENT AND EDUCATIONAL GOALS

The relationship between measurement in schools and educational goals is simple: Goals are what tell the teacher what behaviors need to be evaluated. It is difficult to imagine how teachers can assess the effectiveness of instructional procedures unless they know precisely what those procedures are intended to do. And before that, teachers need to know what outcomes they want if they are to select appro-

priate instructional procedures. A simple representation of the act of teaching comprises only three processes: specifying goals, implementing procedures to attain these goals, and evaluating the effectiveness of these procedures in terms of whether or not the goals were attained.*

School-Related Goals

Goals are desired outcomes. School-related goals include not only the specific instructional objectives of teachers but also the wider objectives of curricula, programs, principals, and communities. Questions relating to the wider objectives of education have traditionally been in the domains of philosophy, politics, and economics, rather than psychology, and such objectives are seldom evaluated directly in schools. Most classroom evaluation has to do with a teacher's general and specific objectives.

General Objectives. It is sometimes useful to begin the preparation of a unit or of an entire

---

*See Chapter 5 for more information about instructional objectives.

course by specifying in general terms what the final desired outcome of the instruction is. Such a statement may be of value in assessing the general effectiveness of the entire course or of a portion thereof. It is *not* likely to be of any real value, however, in determining the adequacy of specific instructional procedures or of particular lessons. For example, the general objectives of a unit in the natural sciences might include a statement such as this:

The students should be familiar with the flora and fauna of the Rocky Mountains and the adjoining foothills.

Although this statement of general objectives might serve as a guide for teachers, indicating to them that they need to prepare lessons about the flora and fauna of that area, it is not specific enough to serve as a *blueprint* for the construction of measuring instruments.

Specific Objectives. On the other hand, a specific instructional objective such as the following suggests means for evaluating the effectiveness of instructional procedures:

After the unit, the student should be able to recognize a lynx, a grizzly bear, a cougar, an elk, a mountain sheep, and a moose when presented with these animals.

An especially enterprising teacher can obtain bears, cougars, moose, lynx, elk, and sheep and use them both for instruction and for assessing the attainment of goals; a less enterprising teacher might settle for photographs or other visual aids.

A useful exercise in the preparation of any lesson is to list specific objectives at the very outset. Not only are these useful for evaluation, but they also often serve to clarify the teacher's thinking. And although this section deals only with highly specific behavioral objectives of the kind advocated by Mager (1962), recall that they are merely one of several forms that objectives can take. Eisner (1967), for example, advocates the use of expressive (affect-related)

objectives; Gronlund (1972) argues that in many cases instructors should begin with the statement of a general objective that can then be made more specific by listing examples of behaviors that reflect the general objective. Each of these approaches has merit (see Chapter 5), but specific behavioral objectives are more easily applied to testing.

Bloom's Taxonomy. Bloom et al. (1956) and Krathwohl, Bloom, and Masia (1964) have provided an exhaustive and useful list of cognitive and affective educational objectives. The usefulness of lists such as these (referred to as *taxonomies*) is that they can serve as guides in determining the goals for a lesson or course. The taxonomy of objectives for the cognitive domain, for example, describes a class of objectives, a list of educational objectives that correspond to this class, and test questions that illustrate it (see Table 14.2). The six hierarchical classes of objectives in that domain are, from the lowest to the highest level: **knowledge, comprehension, application, analysis, synthesis,** and **evaluation.** Each of these is broken down into subdivisions. You are referred to the handbook of objectives (Bloom et al., 1956) for a detailed consideration of Bloom's taxonomy of educational objectives.

In an earlier section we noted the importance of what teachers test — how what they test determines what and how students learn. We noted as well that schools tend to evaluate students on the basis of how many textbook- and teacher-presented facts they remember, rather than on the basis of how much they understand, how cleverly they generalize and extrapolate, or how elegantly they formulate hypotheses and generate new concepts. Research on Bloom's taxonomy corroborates this unhappy finding. Fleming and Chambers (1983) analyzed more than 8,800 questions used primarily in high-school tests. Nearly 80 percent dealt only with knowledge of facts and specifics — the lowest level in Bloom's taxonomy (see the box entitled "Remembering and Thinking").

Table 14.2   Bloom's cognitive domain, defined and illustrated

Class of Objectives	*Example*
1. Knowledge (items of factual information)	Who wrote *A Midsummer Night's Dream?*
2. Comprehension (understanding; obtaining meaning from communication)	What was the author trying to say?
3. Application (using information, principles, and the like to solve problems)	Given what you know about the authenticity of the first quarto and about weather conditions in England in the summer of 1594, when do you think the play was written?
4. Analysis (arriving at an understanding by looking at individual parts)	Find the most basic metaphors in Act I and explain their meaning.
5. Synthesis (arriving at an understanding by looking at larger structure or by combining individual elements)	Identify the four themes in *A Midsummer Night's Dream* and discuss how they contribute to the central action.
6. Evaluation (arriving at value judgments)	Do you agree with the statement that *A Midsummer Night's Dream* is Shakespeare's first undisputed masterpiece? Explain your answer.

Blueprints for Teacher-Made Tests

We should emphasize at the outset that a test — whether it is a teacher-made test or a standardized test — is not like other common measuring instruments, such as rulers, scales, and thermometers. Rulers measure whatever they measure *directly*; our psychological and educational instruments measure *indirectly*. In effect, a student's test performance consists of a sample of behaviors (selected from a large number of potential behaviors) that (we assume) represents some knowledge, ability, or attitude that we use as the basis for making inferences. The inferences we make about knowledge, ability, or other student characteristics are never based on direct measurement; they are simply inferences — educated bits of speculation based on nothing more than a sample of behavior. Hence, the question of precisely which behaviors to sample is very important.

As you probably know, the business of preparing tests, exams, and quizzes is frequently a pretty haphazard process. Teachers, who have a general idea of the sorts of things they want their students to learn, sit down near the end of the unit or term and fashion a compilation of questions that they hope will measure reasonably accurately some of the things they intended to teach. Some teachers are better than others at putting together appropriate questions. Many, however, might be helped considerably by learning more clearly the characteristics of good and bad test items (discussed later in this chapter) and by systematically attempting to blueprint their tests even before they begin to teach the relevant series of lessons.

A **test blueprint** is, in effect, a table of specifications for a test. It specifies the topics to be tested, the nature of the questions to be used, how many questions will relate to each topic, and the sorts of cognitive processes to be sampled. Test blueprints need not be developed only by the teacher; they can also involve the collaboration of students. Constructing the blueprint can do a great deal to clarify instructional goals, both for the teacher and for students. It can also contribute in important ways to the teacher's selection of instructional strategies and to the students' monitoring of their own learning processes.

Detailed test blueprints that take into consideration differences among possible learning outcomes can be based on systems such as Bloom's taxonomy. A typical test blueprint based on portions of this taxonomy takes the form of a table that lists all relevant topics down the side and all relevant domains across the top, and that specifies the number of items for each topic relating to each domain (see Table 14.3). However, most teachers and students might find it considerably easier and more useful to

use a classification that differentiates among learning outcomes that students can define and understand more easily. Popham (1981) suggests, for example, that items be divided simply in terms of whether they involve recall or go beyond recall.

There are a number of other ways to devise test blueprints, some of which are easier and more useful in certain subjects. In physical education classes, for example, in which Bloom's taxonomy and other similar classifications are not highly relevant, teachers might simply make a listing of the skills that students are expected to acquire. This list of skills, together with an indication of the criteria that will be used as evidence of skill mastery, serves as a test blueprint. Unfortunately, this kind of test blueprint in physical education classes is rare. Most often, teachers rely on informal, intuitive evaluation. And although there is clearly a need for

Remembering and Thinking

The six classes of objectives described by Bloom et al. (1956) fall into two broad classes: those that involve remembering and those that require thinking. Only the knowledge objectives fall into the first category (knowledge of specifics, knowledge of ways and means of dealing with specifics, and knowledge of the universals and abstractions in a field). All these objectives emphasize *remembering*.

Most teachers prefer to teach for *understanding* (comprehension, application, and so on) as well as for recall. Yet few know clearly the precise skills involved in such intellectual activities as comprehension, application, synthesis, analysis, or evaluation. The two most frequently confused skills are comprehension and application.

Comprehension is the lowest level of understanding, implying no more than the ability to apprehend the substance of what is being communicated without necessarily relating it to other material. It can be tested through items that require the students to translate (change from one form of communication to another, express in their own words), interpret (explain or summarize), or extrapolate (predict consequences or arrive at conclusions).

Application, on the other hand, requires that learners be able to use what they comprehend — that they abstract from one situation to another. Application cannot be tested simply by asking that students interpret or translate; they must also be required to abstract the material in order to see its implications.

Two final points should be made. The first is a simple appeal: Familiarize yourself with this taxonomy because of its implications both for teaching and for testing. The second is a reiteration of a very obvious point: Your instructional objectives (what you want of your students) are communicated very directly and very effectively to your students through your measurement devices. Even if you emphasize repeatedly that you want to teach for comprehension and other high-level skills, you will probably not be successful unless you construct achievement tests that reflect these objectives.

---

such evaluation, it is seldom as impartial as more formal evaluation. Nor does it serve nearly as well as a guide to instruction.

CHARACTERISTICS OF A GOOD MEASURING INSTRUMENT

Validity

It might seem platitudinous to say that a good test must be *valid* in the sense that it measures what it is intended to measure. Unfortunately, however, many tests do not measure what they are intended to measure, or they measure many other things as well and are therefore difficult to depend on. *Validity* is the most important characteristic of a measuring instrument. If a test does not measure what it purports to, then the scores derived from it are of no value whatsoever.

There are several different ways of measuring or estimating validity — several indexes of validity (see Figure 14.2). The first, **face validity**, is the extent to which the test appears to

Table 14.3 A simple test blueprint, based on Bloom's taxonomy, cognitive domain, for Chapter 4 of this text

Chapter 4 topics	Number of items by domain						
	Knowledge	Comprehension	Application	Analysis	Synthesis	Evaluation	
Cognition	4	3	3	2	3	1	
Bruner's theory	3	4	3	2	2	1	
Ausubel's theory	3	3	2	2	2	1	
Instruction	4	3	3	2	2	3	
Totals	14	13	11	8	9	6	61

measure what it is supposed to measure. This is probably the easiest type of validity to determine; if a test *looks* valid, then it at least has face validity. This type of validity is particularly important for teacher-made tests; students should be able to know just by looking at a test that they are in fact being tested on the appropriate things. In other words, a mathematics test that has face validity will consist of items that look like mathematics items; similar items would not find their way into an English exam — unless, of course, the teacher had, for some reason, undertaken to deceive the students in order to measure their spontaneous knowledge of mathematics. This possibility might seem a little remote, but there are other circumstances under which test makers very carefully avoid any semblance of face validity. Tests designed to measure some personality characteristics such as honesty or openness, for example, are likely to be highly invalid if they appear to measure what they are actually intended to measure. Because we know that dishonest people might very well lie to us, we are not likely to obtain an accurate measure of their honesty if we let them know that that is what we are interested in. Better to deceive them, lie to them, to determine what liars and scoundrels they really are.

Content validity, a second important index of the extent to which a test measures what it purports to measure, is assessed by analyzing the content of test items in relation to the objectives of the course, unit, or lesson. Content validity is perhaps the most crucial kind of validity for measurements of school achievement. A test with high content validity includes items that sample all important course objectives (both content and process objectives) in proportion to their importance. Thus if some of the objectives of an instructional sequence are the development of cognitive processes, then a relevant test will have content validity to the extent that it samples these processes. And if 40 percent of the course content (and, consequently, of the course objectives) deals with knowledge (rather than with comprehension, analysis, and so on), then 40 percent of the test items should assess knowledge.

Determining the content validity of a test is largely a matter of careful logical analysis. One of the great advantages of preparing a test blueprint of the kind described earlier is not only that it can guide instruction, but that it also should ensure content validity.

Note that tests and test items do not possess validity as a sort of intrinsic quality; that is, a test is not generally valid or generally invalid.

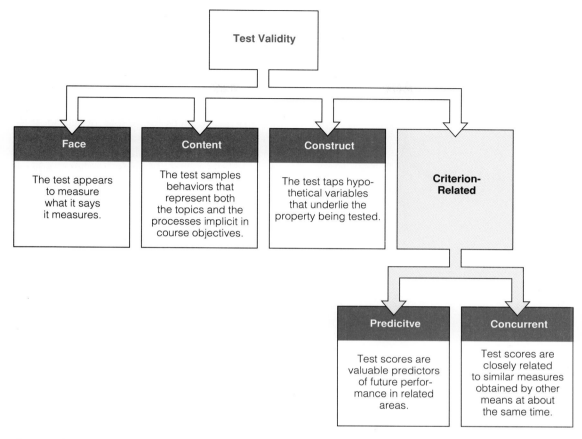

Figure 14.2 Types of test validity: determining that a test measures what it purports to measure.

Rather, it is valid for certain purposes and with certain individuals and invalid for others. For example, if the following item is intended to measure comprehension, then it does not have content validity:

> How many different kinds of validity are discussed in this chapter?
> a. 1
> b. 2
> c. 3
> d. 5
> e. 10

If, on the other hand, the item were intended to measure knowledge of specifics, then it would have content validity. And an item such as the following might have content validity with respect to measuring comprehension:

> Explain why face validity is important for teacher-constructed tests.

It is important to note, however, that this last item measures comprehension only if students have not been explicitly taught an appropriate answer; that is, it is possible to teach perform very poorly on these tests would not do well in sixth grade, and we might use this prediction as justification for having them fail fifth grade. The extent to which our predictions are accurate reflects **criterion-related validity**. One component of this form of validity, just described, is labeled **predictive validity** and is easily measured by looking at the relationship between performance on a test and subsequent performance. Thus, a college entrance examination designed to identify students whose chances of college success are high has predictive validity to the extent that its predictions are borne out.

Concurrent validity, a second aspect of criterion-related validity, is the relationship between a test and other measures of the same behaviors. For example, the most accurate way of measuring intelligence is to administer a time-consuming and expensive individual test; a second way is to administer a quick, inexpensive group test; a third, far less consistent approach is to have teachers informally assess intelligence on the basis of what they know of their students' achievement and effort. Teacher assessments are said to have concurrent validity to the extent that they correlate with the more formal measures. In the same way, the group test is said to have concurrent validity if it agrees well with measures obtained in other ways.

Reliability

A good measuring instrument must not only be *valid*; it must also be *reliable*. This means that the test should measure whatever it measures consistently. An intelligence test that yields a score of 170 for a student one week and a score of 80 the next week is probably somewhat unreliable (unless something has happened to the student during the week).

An instrument that is highly unreliable cannot be valid. Put another way, if a test measures what it purports to and that attribute does not fluctuate erratically, then the test will yield

principles, applications, analyses, and so on as *specifics*, so that questions of this sort require no more than recall of knowledge. What an item measures is not inherent in the item itself so much as in the *relationship* between the material as it has been taught to the student and what the item requires.

A third type, **construct validity**, is conceptually more difficult than either face or content validity. It is somewhat less relevant for teacher-constructed tests but highly relevant for many other psychological measures (personality and intelligence tests, for example). In essence, a construct is a hypothetical variable — an unobservable characteristic or quality, very often derived from theory. For example, a theory might specify that individuals who are highly intelligent should be reflective rather than impulsive. One way of determining the construct validity of a test designed to measure intelligence would then be to look at how well it correlates with measures of reflection and impulsivity. (See Chapter 9 for a discussion of correlation.)

One of the principal uses of tests is to predict future performance. Thus, we assume that all students who do well on year-end fifth-grade achievement tests will do reasonably well in sixth grade. We also predict that those who similar scores on different occasions. Hence, one way of assessing reliability is to correlate results obtained by giving the test twice or by giving two different forms of the same test. This is called **repeated-measures** or **parallel-forms reliability**. Another way, called **split-half reliability**, is to divide the test into halves and correlate the scores obtained on each half. If all items are intended to measure the same things, the scores on the halves should be similar.

A number of factors are involved in determining the reliability of a test. One is the stability of what is being measured. Clearly, if a characteristic fluctuates dramatically over time, then measurements of that characteristic will also fluctuate. However, most of the things we measure in psychology and education are not expected to fluctuate unpredictably; that is, although we expect change in many characteristics, we can often predict the nature of the change. Students are expected to read better, understand more clearly, solve more problems, and generally improve cognitively throughout the course of their schooling. Tests that are valid and reliable should reflect these changes.

A second factor that affects test reliability has to do with the test rather than with the trait being measured and is sometimes called **equivalence reliability** (Wiersma and Jurs, 1985). Simply defined, *equivalence reliability* refers to the extent to which different forms of a test (either parallel forms or split halves) yield consistent results.

A third important factor, particularly with respect to teacher-constructed, multiple-choice or true-false tests, is chance. As an example, consider a test consisting of twenty true-false items. The chance of getting any single item correct, if the student knows next to absolutely nothing, is one out of two. Hence, unless Lady Luck is looking pointedly in the other direction, the average score of a large class of hypothetical "know-nothings" should be around 50 percent. And some of the luckier individuals in this class may have astoundingly high scores. But a subsequent administration of this or of a parallel examination might lead to startlingly different results.

One way of increasing test reliability is obvious: Make tests longer. Of course, this does not mean that all short objective tests must be avoided. In the long run, the effects of chance tend to even out; one hundred very short tests, taken all together, make up one very long, sometimes very reliable test. The most important admonition is simply that the teacher should not place undue confidence in the results of only a handful of short tests, in which the effects of chance cannot easily be controlled.

Although a test cannot be valid without also being reliable, it can be highly reliable without being valid. Consider the following intelligence test:

Lefrançois's Dumb Scale of Intelligence

Instructions
Join the dot to the square with four *separate, parallel, but orthogonal* lines.*

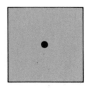

Scoring
Minimum score: 100
Add 50 for half a correct answer (i.e., two lines) _____
Add 25 for another half _____
Total (maximum 175) _____

Interpretation
If you scored:
100 — you are very bright
150 — you are a genius
175 — you are God

---

*PPC: "I don't think that's possible."
Author: "You score 100. Bravo!"

This intelligence test has been demonstrated to be extremely reliable (as well as extremely democratic). In other words, it is extremely consistent: Testees obtain the same scores repeatedly. Bright people usually score 100; geniuses, 150; and God, 175. Unfortunately, however, it is desperately invalid.

STANDARDIZED TESTS

A test is a collection of tasks (items or questions) assumed to be a representative sample of the behaviors that the tester wishes to assess. Given that human beings vary in countless ways, there are countless types of tests and countless examples of each type. A few examples of some *psychological* tests (creativity and intelligence) were given in Chapter 9. These tests are referred to as **standardized tests**. They are so called because they provide standards (also called *norms*) by which to judge the performance of individual students. Thus, intelligence tests are typically standardized in such a way that average performance is reflected in a score close to 100. In addition, the norms for intelligence tests tell us what distribution of scores we might expect for a large group.

A large collection of tests that are particularly important for classroom teachers are standardized achievement tests. These professionally developed tests are available for virtually every school subject and are designed to provide teachers, school administrators, and parents with information concerning the relative performance of individual students, classes, or schools. The indication of relative performance typically is derived by comparing the students' test results to the norms provided with the test. Hence, almost all standardized tests include the testing material itself and a manual that specifies the objectives of the test (what it is designed to measure), the age and grade levels for which it is appropriate, the samples on which it was standardized, and tables for converting the students' raw scores to

scores that can be compared directly with the test norms.

Many school jurisdictions make routine use of achievement tests. One study reports that students between first and fifth grades can expect to take an average of one and one-half standardized achievement tests a year (Levin, 1983). Unfortunately, teachers don't often use the results of these tests to modify their instructional procedures, although they might use them to make decisions about student placement.

Minimum-Competency Testing

There is an ongoing controversy concerning the use of standardized tests in schools. On the one hand, many educators feel that the tests are unfair, biased, unreliable, and often invalid—that they are excellent examples of "science and technology run amok" (Wigdor and Garner, 1982). On the other hand, many argue that in spite of their weaknesses, tests are more likely to be valid, reliable, objective, and fair than are other forms of evidence upon which teachers and educators base their judgments.

During the middle decades of this century, it seemed that the antitesting movement might become dominant. Increasing numbers of school jurisdictions began to abandon the use of standardized tests; their use seemed incompatible with the cry for equity (Linn, 1986). But the pendulum now seems to have swung in the opposite direction once more. One of the important reasons for this most recent swing was the publication of the report *A Nation at Risk* (National Commission on Excellence in Education, 1983). Among other things, the report put forth a cry for excellence, rather than simply for equity, and raised the frightening possibility that American schoolchildren might be seriously deficient in basic reading, writing, and arithmetic skills. The report lent support to the concept of **minimum-competency testing**, a general term for batteries of tests, often administered statewide, to determine whether students have achieved some minimum standard of competency. In fact, minimum-competency tests are now required in over half the states, and although they have been legally challenged on the grounds that they are unfair and discriminatory, challenges have typically been unsuccessful (Perkins, 1982). Whether their use will continue to proliferate is still unclear, however.

Uses of Standardized Tests

Linn (1986) describes five distinct and important uses for standardized tests in schools. The first is placement in special education programs. As we saw in Chapter 9, intelligence tests are widely used for this purpose. However, legal challenges of their fairness have often been successful, especially when it could be shown that a test was biased toward a certain group. These legal challenges have resulted in the modification of some tests to reduce their biases, the translation of tests into different languages, and the use of a variety of assessment procedures in addition to intelligence tests.

A second use of standardized tests is to certify student achievement. Minimum-competency tests are a clear example of this use, as are the variety of standardized entrance examinations used to decide whether or not to accept an applicant for a course of studies, and final examinations used to determine success or failure after a course of studies.

In addition to these two principal uses, standardized tests are being used in some jurisdictions to determine the competency of teachers, to evaluate schools (through the performance of students), and for instructional diagnosis.

Test Norms

To use and interpret standardized tests, it is important to know about the types of scores and norms that are used with them.

Among the various norms that are sometimes provided with standardized tests, **grade-equivalent scores** are the most common. Such norms allow teachers to convert a raw score on a test to a grade equivalent. For example, students who take a standardized reading test will typically have their scores expressed as a grade level: 3, 3.5, 5, and so on.

Several cautions are in order when interpreting grade-equivalent scores. First — and this applies to all standardized tests — it is extremely important to make sure that the test is suitable for the children and that the norms are appropriate. In the same way that intelligence tests are often biased against groups on whom they were not normed, so too achievement tests are often biased against students whose school curriculum is different from that of the norming population or whose social, language, and ethnic backgrounds are different.

Once you have determined that an achievement test is suitable and that grade-equivalent scores are therefore meaningful, it is then important to know precisely what their meaning is. A grade-equivalent reading score of 5 obtained by a fourth-grade student does not mean that the student should be in fifth grade. In fact, the raw test score (*raw* means the actual, untransformed score on the test) that corresponds to this grade-equivalent score is simply the *average* score of a large number of fifth-grade students. A few fifth-grade students will have scored much higher or much lower. Similarly, many of the fourth-grade students in the norming group will have raw scores as high as some of the fifth-grade pupils. Hence, an achievement test does not separate cleanly among different grade levels — it does not give us an absolutely accurate index of what grade level a student *should* be. Furthermore, achievement tests given at different times of the year can produce markedly different results. Bernard (1966) reports, for example, that those administered immediately after summer vacation often average a full half-grade lower than scores obtained the previous June.

Although most achievement tests designed for use in schools provide grade-equivalent scores, many also provide one or more of a variety of other types of norms, including age equivalents (and others, such as Z-scores, T-scores, percentiles, and stanines, explained in the box entitled "Norms and the Normal Distribution"). **Age-equivalent scores**, as the label implies, are norms expressed in terms of ages rather than grades. Such norms make provisions for converting raw scores to age equivalents that can be interpreted as meaning that a student is functioning at a level comparable to the *average* for a specific age group. Age-equivalent scores are more common for intelligence tests and other measures of ability or aptitude than they are for achievement tests. This is largely because it is more meaningful to say that a person is intellectually at the level of a four-year-old or a nine-year-old than to say that someone reads at a four-year-old or a nine-year-old level. When interpreting age-equivalent scores, observe the same cautions as when interpreting grade-equivalent scores. The most important caution is that these scores represent averages; hence there is a wide range of scores within most groups. In addition, because standardized tests are far from completely valid or completely reliable, we should be careful not to rely on them too heavily.

TEACHER-MADE TESTS

A large majority of the tests used in the classroom are made by classroom teachers, and some of these tests are highly representative of course objectives, are at an appropriate level of difficulty, and are used in reasonable and wise ways. Other tests are less well made.

Teacher-made tests can be used for a variety of purposes, only one of which is the assigning of grades. Other than this, a test can be used to determine whether students are ready to begin a unit of instruction, to indicate to the teacher how effective instructional procedures are, to identify learning difficulties, to determine what students know and what they don't know, to predict their probability of success on future learning tasks, and to motivate students to learn.

Teacher-made tests are almost always of the paper-and-pencil variety. Only occasionally can a sample of nonverbal behavior be used on a test. For example, in physical education, in art, in drama, and in some workshop courses, students are sometimes asked either to produce something or to perform. In most other courses they will be given an objective test or an essay test or both. An essay test requires a written response of some length for each question.

Objective tests, however, normally require very little writing, and the scoring procedure is highly uniform (hence objective). The four major types of objective test items are completion, matching, true-false, and multiple choice. Examples of each are given below:

1. *Completion*
   Test blueprints are often based on _____ taxonomy. Predictive and concurrent validity are two types of _____ validity.

2. *Matching*

   _____ Z-scores   1. mean = 50; standard deviation = 10

   _____ T-scores   2. mean = 0; standard deviation = 1

   _____ stanine   3. mean = 5; standard deviation = 2

3. *True-False*

   _____ a. A good achievement test should result in a grade-equivalent score of between 4 and 5 for an average fourth-grade class.

   _____ b. Content validity can be determined by making a careful, logical analysis of the relationship of test items to course objectives.

4. *Multiple choice*

The extent to which a test appears to measure what it is intended to measure defines:

a. content validity

b. face validity

c. construct validity

d. test reliability

e. criterion-related validity

Essay Versus Objective Tests

Objective tests of the kind just described and the more subjective essay tests can be used to measure almost any significant aspect of student behavior. However, some course objectives are more easily assessed with one type of test than with the other. Several of the major differences between essay and objective tests are given below. These differences can serve as a guide in deciding which to use in a given situation. Very often a mixture of both can be used to advantage.

1. It is far easier to tap higher-level processes (analysis, synthesis, and evaluation) with an essay examination, although it is possible to do the same thing with objective items. Essay examinations can be constructed to allow students to organize knowledge, to make inferences from it, to illustrate it, to apply it, and to extrapolate from it.

2. The content of essay examinations is often more limited than the content of the more objective tests. Because essay exams usually consist of fewer items, the range of abilities or of information sampled is necessarily reduced. The objective-question format, in contrast, permits coverage of more content per unit of testing time. Although a student's range of knowledge is often apparent in an essay test, the absence of that knowledge may not be so readily apparent.

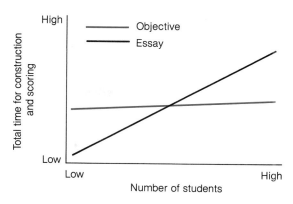

Figure 14.3   The relationship between class size and total time required for test construction and scoring for two types of test.

3. Essay examinations allow for more divergence. It is not unreasonable to expect that students who do not like to be restricted in their answers will prefer essays over more objective tests.

4. Constructing an essay test is considerably easier and less time-consuming than making up an objective examination. In fact, an entire test with an essay format can often be written in the same length of time it would take to write no more than two or three good multiple-choice items.

5. Scoring essay examinations requires considerably more time than scoring objective tests. This is especially true when tests can be scored electronically (as objective tests are in most universities and in an increasing number of schools). The total time involved in making and scoring a test is less for essay examinations than for objective tests if classes are small (twenty students or fewer, perhaps) but is considerably less for objective tests than for essay tests as the number of students increases (see Figure 14.3).

Norms and the Normal Distribution

If you were to throw 100 coins onto a table 1,000 times and record the number of heads and tails that came up, and if, in the interest of science, you were to keep track of the number of heads and tails on each of the 1,000 occasions, a figure representing your tallies would probably look very much like this (in which the "0" represents 50 heads and 50 tails and the scale on either side represents an increasing proportion of heads or tails):

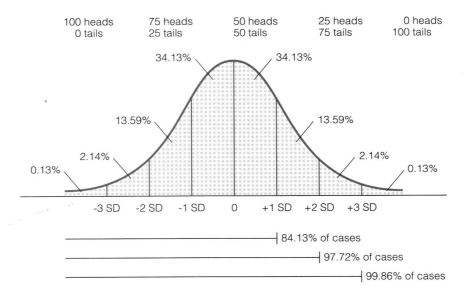

| 100 heads | 75 heads | 50 heads | 25 heads | 0 heads |
| 0 tails | 25 tails | 50 tails | 75 tails | 100 tails |

34.13% 34.13%

13.59% 13.59%

2.14% 2.14%

0.13% 0.13%

-3 SD -2 SD -1 SD 0 +1 SD +2 SD +3 SD

84.13% of cases

97.72% of cases

99.86% of cases

This is a **normal curve** — a mathematical abstraction to which the majority of the observations that concern us in the social sciences and in education conform. When we know that a set of observations, such as test scores, are normally distributed, we also know what a graphic representation of these scores would look like if we had enough of them. We know that most of the scores would cluster around the **mean** (arithmetic average) and that there would be fewer and fewer scores as we got farther and farther away from the mean.

Thus, if we knew the average, we might have some idea of what a score meant. But we would have an even better idea of its meaning if we also knew the **standard deviation** — an index of how scores are distributed around the mean. Knowing the standard deviation allows us to determine how unusual a score is, because we know that approximately 66 percent of all observations will fall within one standard deviation of the mean, and approximately 95 percent will fall within two standard deviations of the mean. Hence those who score more than two standard deviations above a mean will be in the top 2½ percent of the population.

It follows, then, that in order to interpret a test score (providing we can assume that a large collection of such scores would be normally distributed), we especially need to know the mean and the standard deviation. This is, in fact, what most manuals accompanying standardized tests tell us when they describe test norms.

Test norms can take a variety of forms, including age and grade equivalents, or simply means and standard deviations. They can also be expressed as **percentiles, Z-scores, T-scores, or stanines**.

Percentiles indicate the percentage of scores that fall below a given point. Thus, the seventy-fifth percentile is the point at or below which 75 percent of all observations fall. If a student scores at the fiftieth percentile on a standardized test, that student's score is exactly in the middle. Note that a score corresponding to the fortieth or the thirty-fifth percentile is *not* a failing score; it is simply the score at or below which 40 or 35 percent of the observations fall.

Z-scores, T-scores, and stanines are all standard scores with a predetermined mean and standard deviation. They are used to simplify interpretation of test results. Because raw scores on different tests vary a great deal, as do means and standard deviations, simply knowing that a person has a score of 112 or 23 or 1,115 is meaningless unless we know what the mean and standard deviation are for a comparable group on that test. But if these raw scores are transformed into one of the standard scores, they become meaningful.

Z-scores are standard scores whose mean is 0 and whose standard deviation is 1; T-scores have a mean of 50 and a standard deviation of 10; and a stanine score uses a mean of 5 and a standard deviation of 2. The meaning of these standard scores, relative to each other, is depicted in the figure below. As you can see, a T-score of 80 would be an extremely high score (three standard deviations about the mean is above the ninety-ninth percentile); the equivalent Z-score would be 3. There is no exactly equivalent stanine score because the highest score possible on this nine-point scale is 9, which is two standard deviations above the mean.

Converting raw test scores to one of these standard-score scales is usually extremely simple because virtually all tests that use them provide transformation tables. These tables typically allow you to read the standard-score equivalent directly once you know the student's raw score and age or grade. And if you can remember what the mean and standard deviation are for these standard scores, they will be meaningful. Otherwise, they are just numbers.

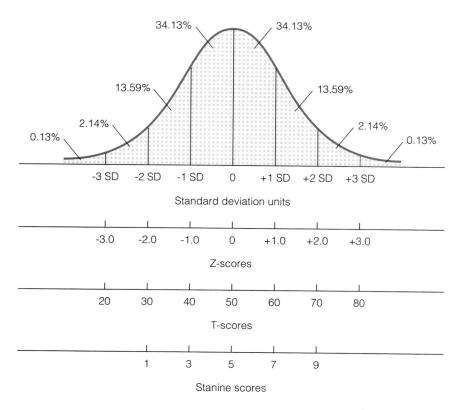

To Be Objective or Subjective?

The question is purely rhetorical. Not only does it have no answer, but it deserves none. Very few teachers will ever find themselves in situations in which they *must* always use either one form of test or the other. Some class situations, particularly those in which size is a factor, may lend themselves more readily to objective test formats; in other situations, essay formats may be better; and sometimes a combination of both may be desirable. The important point is that each has advantages and disadvantages. A good teacher should endeavor to develop the skills necessary for constructing good items in a variety of formats without becoming a passionate advocate of one over the other.

---

6. The reliability of essay examinations is much lower than that of objective tests, primarily because of the subjectivity involved in their scoring. Numerous studies attest to this fact. In one (Educational Testing Service, 1961), 300 essays were rated by fifty-three judges on a nine-point scale. Slightly over one-third of the papers received all possible grades; that is, each of these papers received the highest possible grade from at least one judge, the lowest possible grade from at least one other, and every other possible grade from at least one judge. Another 37 percent of the papers each received eight of the nine different grades; 23 percent received seven of the nine.

Other studies have found that a relatively poor paper that is read after an even poorer one will tend to be given a higher grade than if it is read after a very good paper, that some graders consistently give moderate marks whereas others give very high and very low marks, although the average grades given by each might be very similar; that knowledge of who wrote the paper tends to affects scores, sometimes beneficially and sometimes to the student's detriment; and that if the first few answers on an essay examination are particularly good, overall marks tend to be higher than if the first answers are poor.

There are a number of methods for increasing the scorer reliability of essay examinations, not the least of which is simply being aware of possible sources of unreliability. Some of the suggestions given below may be of value in this regard.

Suggestions for Constructing Tests

The advantages of a particular type of test can often be increased if its items are constructed carefully. By the same token, the disadvantages can also be made more severe through faulty item construction. Essay examinations, for example, are said to be better for measuring "higher" processes. Consider the following item:

> List the kinds of validity discussed in this chapter.

If the tester's intention is to sample analysis, synthesis, or evaluation, this item has no advantage over many objective items. However, an item such as the following might have an advantage:

Discuss similarities and differences among three of the different types of validity discussed in this chapter.

Several specific suggestions follow for the construction of essay tests and of multiple-choice tests, the most preferred among objective-item forms.

Essay Tests. The following suggestions are based in part on Gronlund (1968):

1. Essay questions should be geared toward sampling processes not easily assessed by objective items (for example, analysis, synthesis, or evaluation).

2. As for all tests, essay questions should relate directly to the desired outcomes of the learning procedure. This should be clearly understood by the students as well.

3. Questions should be specific if they are to be easily scorable. If the intention is to give marks for illustrations, the item should specify that an illustration is required.

4. A judicious sampling of desired behavior should make up the substance of the items.

5. If the examiner's intention is to sample high-level processes, sufficient time should be allowed for students to complete the questions.

6. The weighting of various questions, as well as the time that should be allotted to each, should be indicated for the student.

7. The questions should be worded so that the teacher's expectations are clear to both the student and the teacher.

There are ways of making the scoring more objective as well. One of these is to outline model answers before scoring the test (that is, write out an answer that would receive full points). Another is to score all answers for one item before going on to the next. The purpose of this is to increase uniformity of scoring. A third suggestion is simply that the scorer should intend to be objective. For example, if poor grammar in a language-arts test results in the loss of five points on one paper, grammar that is half as bad on another paper should result in the loss of two and a half points.

Multiple-Choice Items.

A multiple-choice item consists of a statement or series of statements (called the *stem*) and three to five alternatives, only one of which is the correct or best solution. The other alternatives are referred to as *distractors*. Each of the distractors is a response that will appear plausible if students do not know the answer. If students do know the correct answer, distractors should, of course, appear less plausible.

Below are a number of suggestions for writing multiple-choice items. Most of them are common sense (which makes them no less valid).

1. Both stems and alternatives should be clearly worded, unambiguous, grammatically correct, specific, and at the appropriate level of comprehension. In addition, stems should be clearly meaningful by themselves.

2. Double negatives are highly confusing and should be avoided. Single negatives are not recommended either.

3. The items should sample a representative portion of subject content, but they should not be taken verbatim from the textbook. This is defensible only when the intention clearly is to test memorization.

4. All distractors should be equally plausible so that answering correctly is not simply a matter of eliminating highly implausible distractors. Consider the following example of a poor item:

   10 + 12 + 18 =
   a. 2,146
   b. 7,568,482
   c. 40
   d. 1

5. Unintentional cues should be avoided. Ending the stem with *a* or *an* often provides a cue, for example.

6. Qualifying words such as *never, always, none, impossible,* and *absolutely* should be avoided in distractors (though not necessarily in stems). They are almost always associated with incorrect alternatives. Words such as *sometimes, frequently,* and *usually* are most often associated with correct alternatives. In stems both kinds of qualifiers tend to be ambiguous.

Reporting Test Results

Having constructed, administered, and scored a test, the teacher is faced with the responsibility of making the wisest possible use of the information derived from it. Obviously, some of these uses are separate from the actual reporting of test results to students or parents; they are concerned instead with instructional decisions that the teacher must make. Are the students ready to go to the next unit? Should they be allowed to study in the library again? Should educational television be used? Should a review be undertaken? Should the teacher look for another job?

Even if the test is primarily intended to let the teacher make decisions concerning questions such as those given above, results should also be reported to the students. The feedback that students receive about their learning can be of tremendous value in guiding future efforts. It can also be highly reinforcing in this achievement-oriented society.

Although raw scores can be reported directly to the student, they are of little or no value unless they are related to some scale about which value judgments can be made. A score of 40 on a test with a maximum possible score of 40 is different from a score of 40 on a test in which the ceiling is 80. The traditional way of giving meaning to these scores is to convert them either to a percentage or to a letter grade that has clearly defined (though arbitrary) significance. Advanced students should probably be given more information than simply a percentage or a letter grade. To begin with, it is useful to know precise areas of weakness as well

Table 14.4 Formulas for summarizing test scores

	Individual	Test Score	$\overline{X}$	$(X-\overline{X})$	$(X-\overline{X})^2$
Scores on Test	Bill	37	33	4	16
	Joan	36	33	3	9
	Evelyn	35	33	2	4
	Edna	35	33	2	4
	Bob	33	33	0	0
	Sam	33·	33	0	0
	John	33	33	0	0
	Rita	32	33	−1	1
	Phil	30	33	−3	9
	Guy	26	33	−7	49
	Sums (Σ)	330	330	0	92
	N = 10				

Formulas

$$\text{Mean }(\overline{X}) = \frac{\Sigma(\text{sum})\,X}{N\,(\text{number of scores})} = \frac{330}{10} = 33$$

$$\text{Mode} = 33 \text{ (most frequently occurring score)}$$

$$\text{Median} = 33 \text{ (fiftieth percentile)}$$

$$SD\begin{pmatrix}\text{standard}\\\text{deviation}\end{pmatrix} = \sqrt{\frac{\Sigma(X-\overline{X})^2}{N}} = \sqrt{\frac{92}{10}} = \sqrt{9.2} = 3.03$$

as strengths. In addition, even a percentage score is relatively useless unless the student has some knowledge about the scores obtained by other students. A simple way of giving a class this knowledge is to report both the *mean* (arithmetic average) and the range of scores (low and high scores).

The mean is called a measure of **central tendency,** because it indicates, in an approximate way, where the center of a distribution of scores is. There are two other common measures of central tendency: the **median** and the **mode.** The median is the exact midpoint of a distribution. It is the fiftieth percentile — the point above and below which 50 percent of all scores lie. The mode is simply the most frequently occurring score; as such, it is not

particularly valuable for educational and psychological testing. It is of considerable interest to shoe and clothing manufacturers, however, because they are not interested in manufacturing average or median sizes, but those that occur most frequently.

As we saw when discussing standard scores, a measure of central tendency is not nearly as valuable by itself as it is when combined with a measure of variability. And the most useful measure of variability for normally distributed observations is the standard deviation. If students are sufficiently sophisticated, the standard deviation might be reported as an important dimension of test scores. A formula for computing the standard deviation is presented in Table 14.4.

CRITERION-REFERENCED TESTING

There is a small kingdom hidden in the steamy jungles of South America. One of its borders is the Amazon, which describes a serpentine half-circle around most of the perimeter of this kingdom. Its other border consists of an impenetrable row of harsh mountains. The inhabitants of the kingdom are therefore trapped by the river on one side (they dare not try to cross it) and by the mountains on the other (although they can climb the mountains to their very tops, the other side presents an unbroken row of vertical cliffs attaining dizzying heights of no less than 8,000 feet at any location). In this kingdom there are numerous, very ferocious people-eating beasts. Fortunately, all are nocturnal. I say "fortunately" because, although the human inhabitants of the kingdom live on the mountainsides well beyond where their enemies can climb, they must descend the mountain every day to find food.

In this kingdom a test is given to all able-bodied men, women, and children each day of their lives. It is a simple test. Before nightfall, each must succeed in climbing the mountain to a point beyond the reach of their predators. Failure to do so is obvious to all, for the individual who fails simply does not answer roll call that evening. Success is equally obvious. This situation, however, is not parallel to the ordinary testing practices of most schools. Passing this test does not require that individuals be the first to reach safety; it doesn't even require that they be among the first 90 percent to do so. Indeed, they will have been just as successful if they are among the very last to reach the fire. They will be just as alive as the first (and perhaps less hungry).

Consider the situation in schools, where testing is of the traditional, **norm-referenced** variety. Assume that all students are expected to attain a certain level of performance in a variety of subjects, a level of performance that we will denote by the symbol X. In the course of the school year, teachers prepare a number of tests and determine, probably relatively accurately, that certain individuals usually do better than others on these tests. These students are, in effect, comparable to the people in the aforementioned kingdom who typically reach safety first. They are the students that the teacher can rightly assume have reached (or even gone beyond) X.

But in assessing student performance and reporting grades, teachers don't often ask themselves which students have reached X and which haven't. Instead, they compare each child to the average performance of all children and on that basis make judgments about the relative performance of students. Thus, in a very advanced class, students who have in fact reached X but who fall well below average performance are assigned mediocre marks. In a less advanced class, these same students might be assigned much higher grades. Norm-referenced tests are therefore tests in which the student's performance is judged and reported in terms of some standard or norm that is derived from typical student performance on the test. In other words, the results of such a test are based on comparisons among students (Haertel, 1985).

In a second alternative, students are not compared one to the other, but instead performance is judged only in relation to a criterion. In the example of the South American kingdom, the criterion is simply the ability to climb beyond the reach of predators; success is survival and failure is death.

Criterion-referenced testing can also be used in schools, and is in fact used extensively in mastery learning and other forms of individualized instruction. If teachers are able to specify what is involved in achieving X in terms of precise behavioral objectives, then they can judge whether a student has reached the criterion without having to compare the student to any other. Obviously, it is sometimes difficult and certainly very time-consuming to define X with directly measurable objectives. On the other hand, it is quite possible to define aspects of X in those terms, in which case criterion-referenced tests can be used. The teacher can decide, for example, that all fifth-grade students should be able to read a selected passage within five minutes and subsequently answer three questions about the content of the passage. This amounts quite simply to establishing a criterion. Students can then be tested to determine whether they have reached the criterion.

The principal difference between criterion-referenced tests and norm-referenced tests lies not in the nature of the tests themselves but in the use that the teacher makes of them. In criterion-referenced testing, the student's performance is compared to a criterion; in norm-referenced testing, an individual's performance is compared to that of other students. Individual differences are far less important in criterion-referenced testing. Indeed, the objective is to have all students succeed.

Literature on educational testing has sometimes been preoccupied with a minor controversy surrounding the relative merits of these two approaches to testing (see, for example, Popham, 1978; Shepard, 1979). Advocates of criterion-referenced testing point to the inherent justice of their approach. No student need consistently fail for performing less well than others after a fixed period of time. When students reach the criterion, they will have succeeded. Indeed, at that point, they will be as successful on that particular task as all other students. And students who have more to learn at the onset of instruction will not fail simply because they start at a different place and consequently lag behind others in the beginning. If they reach the mountain heights before the beasts, they will have succeeded. Criterion-referenced testing argues strongly for the individualization of instruction and of evaluation; it fosters cooperation rather than competition; it encourages students to work toward the goals of the system rather than against other students; and it forces teachers to make those goals explicit.

But criterion-referenced testing has certain limitations, as critics have been quick to point out. Although it is relatively simple to specify that after taking typing lessons for six weeks a student should be able to type thirty words per minute with no more than two errors, it is considerably more difficult to determine precisely what a student should know after sitting in a social studies class for six weeks. A criterion-referenced test is clearly appropriate in the first instance, but less so in the second. A second limitation is that some students can perform better than the criterion. Some educators fear that exclusive reliance on criterion-referenced testing may thwart student incentive.

An advantage of norm-referenced testing is that it provides both students and those who would counsel them with very valuable information concerning their likelihood of success in academic situations in which they will, in fact, be required to compete with others.

What should *you* do while the controversy rages around you? Very simply, use both types of test. There are situations in which norm-referenced tests are not only unavoidable, but also very useful. There are also many situations in which students will respond very favorably to the establishment of definite criteria for success and in which both their learning and your teaching will benefit as a result. This, as is so often the case, is no either-or matter; your decisions should be based on the fundamental purposes of your instructional procedures in specific situations.

THE ETHICS OF TESTING

Assessment, a comprehensive term for measurement and evaluation, is a fundamental part of the teaching/learning process. Its potential benefits to both teacher and learner are, as we have seen in this chapter, rather important. Deale (1975) suggests that teachers need to assess students for the following reasons: to determine whether what has been taught has also been learned, how well it has been learned, and by how many; to monitor the progress of individual students as well as of groups; to evaluate instructional materials and procedures; to amass and retain accurate records of student attainment; and to aid learning. For each of these purposes, teachers can use their own teacher-made tests or standardized tests complete with administration, scoring, and norming procedures.

Several important words of caution are appropriate at this point. With the increasing use of tests, particularly of the standardized variety, and with increasing concern for privacy, individual rights, and equality, some of the ethical issues implicit in the administration and use of tests have become matters of political and social concern. Tests are frequently seen as a threat, as a violation of privacy, and as unjust. Unfortunately, these concerns are not entirely unfounded. For example, personality tests can invade privacy when they probe into matters that would not ordinarily be publicly revealed; tests can be threatening when school placement, job opportunities — indeed, success and failure — depend upon their results; and they can be patently unjust when used for purposes for which they were not intended or with groups for whom they were not designed.

None of these observations is intended as justification for abandoning the use of teacher-made and standardized tests in the schools; rather, they are intended as an argument for the sane and restrained use of both tests and the results obtained therefrom.

It is reassuring to note that in the United States increasing concern with the ethics of testing and records has recently been reflected in a public law affecting all schools funded by the Office of Education. Among other things, this law (Public Law 93–380) grants parents of children under eighteen the right of access to education records kept by schools and relating to their own children, the right to challenge the accuracy and appropriateness of these records, the right to limit public access to these records and to receive a list of individuals and/or agencies that have been given access to them, and the right to be notified if and when the records are turned over to courts of law. All of these parental rights become the student's rights after the age of eighteen or after the student enters a post-secondary educational institution.

SOME CONCLUDING THOUGHTS ON EVALUATION

In most schools, far more emphasis is placed on the use of tests for grading (mastery learning's *summative evaluation*) than on their instructional roles in identifying strengths and weaknesses, in suggesting remediation, and so on (*formative evaluation*). This situation, suggests Crooks (1988), needs to be rectified. Evaluation needs to be used more often to provide students with *feedback* about their performance. This feedback should emphasize progress toward important educational goals and should occur in the course of learning, rather than only at the end of a unit.

Our evaluation procedures are often weak not only in terms of how test results are used, but, perhaps far more important, in terms of what we choose to evaluate. Crooks (1988) notes that although classroom evaluation has a profound effect on what students learn, many teachers spend little time and effort in either developing good assessment procedures or attempting to ensure that what they test is really what they want students to learn. As we saw, one of the results is that most classroom evaluation emphasizes the lowest-level cognitive objectives — specifically, knowledge of specifics. Accordingly, schools teach students to remember isolated facts rather than to understand, to look for relationships, and to go beyond the information given.

The solution? At least in part, the solution lies in changing evaluation procedures. If we want to teach students to think, to evaluate, to be critical, and to solve problems, then we need to stop loading our tests with items that ask for a simple regurgitation of text- and teacher-sanctioned facts. We can tell our students what our grand goals are, but unless our tests reflect what we say, our students will not believe us.

MAIN POINTS

1. *Measurement* is the use of an instrument (a ruler, a thermometer, a test) to gauge the quantity of a property or behavior. *Evaluation* is making a decision about quality, goodness, or appropriateness.

2. A teaching model can be represented in terms of goals, instructional strategies, and assessment. Educational goals are important in determining both strategies and assessment.

3. A tremendous amount of class time is spent with tests or other forms of evaluation. What teachers evaluate is very important in determining what students learn. Because most school tests tend to emphasize recollection of unrelated facts (surface learning) rather than understanding relationships and going beyond the information given (deep learning), that is what students learn.

4. Measurement can be *nominal* (categorical), *ordinal* (using ranks), *interval* (using equidistant scales but with an arbitrary zero point), or *ratio* (based on a true zero). Educational measurement at least pretends to be on an interval scale (usually); it is indirect rather than direct.

5. Goals or objectives can be very general or more specific. Specific goals are usually more amenable to testing. Bloom's taxonomy can be of value both in setting up educational objectives and in designing tests to determine the extent to which these goals have been obtained.

6. *Bloom's taxonomy* of cognitive educational objectives includes six classes of goals: knowledge (facts, specifics); comprehension (obtaining meaning from communication); application (using principles to solve problems); analysis (understanding by looking at parts); synthesis (understanding by combining individual parts); and evaluation (judging value).

7. A *test blueprint* is a table of specifications for a test. Ideally, it should be prepared before actual instruction, and it should specify topics or behaviors to be sampled as well as the number or proportion of items that will relate to each. Bloom's taxonomy or related classifications are often used to organize a test blueprint.

8. Good measuring instruments need to be valid (measure what they purport to measure) and reliable (measure consistently). A test cannot be valid without also being reliable; however, it can be reliable without being valid.

9. *Face validity* is the extent to which the test appears to measure what it says it measures; *content validity* is judged by analyzing test items to determine whether they sample appropriate content; *construct validity* depends on how well the test reflects underlying, hypothetical variables that are theoretically linked to what is being measured; and *criterion-related validity* reveals the extent to which the measure agrees with other current measures (*concurrent validity*) or how well the test predicts future performance in areas it measures (*predictive validity*).

10. Reliability can be measured by looking at correlations between repeated presentations of the same test (*repeated-measures reliability*), between different forms of the same test (*parallel-forms reliability*), or between halves of a single test (*split-half reliability*).

11. Standardized tests are professionally developed instruments that provide *norms* or

standards by which to judge individual performance. Common standardized tests include measures of intelligence, personality, and achievement.

12. Common uses of standardized tests are for special education placement; to certify student achievement; to judge the competency of teachers; to evaluate schools; and for instructional diagnosis.

13. Standardized achievement tests typically provide one or more of the following norms: *age-equivalent scores* (raw scores are transformed into a number representing the average age of norming subjects who obtained such scores); *grade-equivalent scores* (standard or transformed scores representing the grade level for which specific scores were average); or *percentiles* (representing the percentage of the norming population scoring *below* a given point). Sometimes they also provide tables for transforming scores to one of several *normally distributed* standard scores. These scores are meaningful because we always know what their means and standard deviations are: for example, *Z-scores* (mean = 0, standard deviation = 1), *T-scores* (mean = 50, standard deviation = 10), and *stanines* (mean = 5, standard deviation = 2).

14. Teacher-made tests are most often of the paper-and-pencil variety. They are either objective (true-false, completion, matching, or multiple choice) or essay type.

15. It is easier to tap higher-level processes with essay tests, although this can also be accomplished with objective tests (particularly of the multiple-choice variety); the content of essay examinations is often more limited than that of objective tests; essay examinations often allow for more divergence; essay examinations are less time-consuming to prepare but far more time-consuming to score; the reliability of essay examinations is considerably lower than that of objective examinations.

16. When constructing essay examinations, effort should be directed toward sampling processes that are not easily measured with objective tests, as well as toward measuring relevant course goals. Questions should be specific and clearly worded, sufficient time should be allowed for answering, and relative weightings of different questions should be clear.

17. Good multiple-choice items have clear, meaningful stems; distractors whose plausibility is approximately equal; and no double negatives, absolute qualifiers ("always," "never"), or other unintentional cues ("a," "an," singulars, plurals).

18. One way to give raw scores on achievement tests meaning is to convert them to percentage scores or letter grades. The average score, the range of scores, the class distribution, and the standard deviation are also useful for both teachers and students.

19. Measures of central tendency include the *mean* (arithmetic average), the *mode* (most frequently occurring score), and the *median* (fiftieth percentile; midpoint).

20. Schools have traditionally used norm-referenced tests—those in which student performance is judged in relation to the performance of other students. Criterion-referenced tests judge students by comparing their performance to a preestablished criterion rather than to the performance of other students. Both should be used in schools.

21. Caution should be exercised in the administration, interpretation, and use of tests. On occasion they represent a violation of privacy; at times they can also be highly unjust.

22. If we do not test what we say is important, students will not believe us.

SUGGESTED READINGS

Harris and Bell's book is a useful and practical discussion of measurement and evaluation. It reflects education's increasing concern with teaching students to learn rather than simply teaching them facts, and it discusses approaches compatible with goals that are cooperative and individual rather than competitive.

HARRIS, D., & BELL, C. (1986). *Evaluating and assessing for learning.* New York: Nichols (London: Kogan Page).

Among the many comprehensive measurement and evaluation books for teachers are the following:

HOPKINS, K. D., & STANLEY, J. C. (1981). *Educational and psychological measurement and evaluation* (6th ed.). Englewood Cliffs, N.J.: Prentice-Hall.

POPHAM, W. J. (1981). *Modern educational measurement.* Englewood Cliffs, N.J.: Prentice-Hall.

WIERSMA, W., & JURS, S. G. (1985). *Educational measurement and testing.* Boston: Allyn and Bacon.

Perhaps the best arguments for criterion-referenced testing as opposed to norm-referenced testing are put forward by advocates of mastery-learning approaches. A good example is the following:

BLOOM, B. S., MADAUS, G. F., & HASTINGS, J. T. (1981). *Evaluation to improve learning.* New York: McGraw-Hill.

Purring among suckling young has been reported in the black bear. Growling among adult bears has also been reported   (Ewer, 1973).

EPILOGUE AND
A GROWING FOOTNOTE

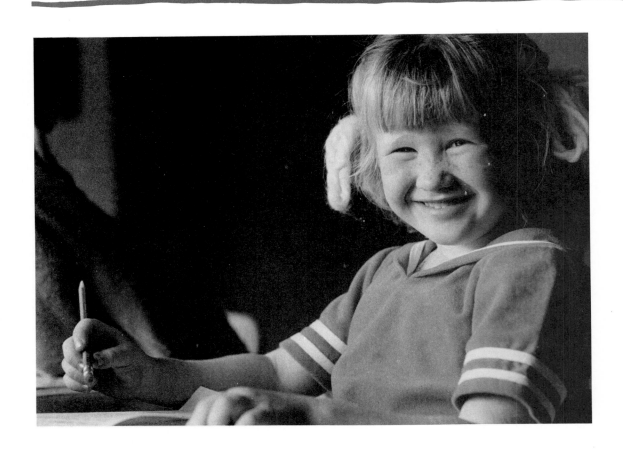

We have now come the full circle. And, in the manner of that wonderful design, we are ready to begin again. For it was somewhere near the beginning that you were given a word of caution; this same caution is equally fitting at the end. A science of humanity tends to dehumanize. It transforms living, breathing beings into *organisms*; it reduces our wonderfully complex behavior to stimuli and responses, and the activity of our mind to hypothetical structures that behave in a hypothetical fashion. At the beginning we said that students are more than all this. At the end we say again that they are much more. Psychology has only begun to understand; the last word has not been said or written. . . .

Yet something has been said in the pages of this text. On fourteen occasions, that something was reduced to a set of statements that were called Main Points. Here, in this epilogue, all those Main Points are reduced to a single, final, all-embracing Main Point. This, reader, is what this text has been all about:

A bear always faces the front. *

The relevance of this statement to teaching cannot easily be explained in anything shorter than a full-length book. Because the present book is now concluding, suffice it to say that a teacher should try to behave as sensibly as a bear who persistently faces the front of its footprints. Teaching has been described as an art and a science. The comment was made in Chapter 1 that, where science fails, art should be used. The point being made here is that both the art and the science partake heavily of common sense.

---

*In 1972 I had no doubt that this statement was entirely and absolutely true, but by 1975 I had realized that it is only a very stupid bear who does not occasionally look backward. Accordingly, the second edition loudly proclaimed: "A bear ~~always~~ usually faces the front." Truth is a precarious luxury. By 1979 the bear had been approached from the rear much more often, had become far wiser, and consequently spent a great deal of time facing backwards. Accordingly the title of the third edition announced with considerable assurance: "A bear ~~always usually~~ sometimes faces the front." How fickle truth. Perhaps more pertinent, how fickle bears. In 1982, with inflation rampant and the world situation tensing, we knew that the sagest of bears only very rarely faced the front. And a mere three years later, by 1985, it had finally happened. Confused by the awesome uncertainties of those years, though still moved by poetic visions of a peaceful and happy world, the bear looked boldly in all directions except, as the title page so unabashedly proclaimed, the front: "A bear ~~always usually sometimes rarely~~ never faces the front." But by 1988 things had again changed. In a cunning about-face, the bear began once more to face the front, only occasionally casting a furtive, sidelong glance in other directions.

Who said an old bear cannot learn new tricks? It is now 1991, and the bear has sniffed strong winds of change. His head has reeled from the stench of methane gases; he has seen dried-up streambeds; he knows the taste of dead clover. This bear has followed the spoor of wild cows across the forests; he has seen them playing cards, drinking whisky, and smoking cigars. He has heard them sing their Country songs.

He is not impressed; he intends to teach the wild cows better values. Even though the bear has become an environmental crusader, he will not, at this moment, commit himself to any single posture. Today, he looks in many directions; soon he will leap to the future.

GLOSSARY

This glossary defines the most important terms used in this text. In each case the meaning given corresponds to the usage in the text. For more complete definitions, the reader is advised to consult a standard psychological dictionary.

Acceleration   An approach in the education of the gifted. Acceleration programs attempt to move students through the conventional curriculum more rapidly than normal. See also *Enrichment.*

Accommodation   Modification of an activity or ability in the face of environmental demands. Piaget's description of development holds that assimilation and accommodation are the means by which individuals interact with and adapt to their world. See also *Assimilation.*

Adaptation   Changes in an organism in response to the environment. Such changes are assumed to facilitate interaction with that environment. Adaptation plays a central role in Piaget's theory. See also *Assimilation, Accommodation.*

Advance organizers   Introductory information that is given to learners to increase the ease with which they can understand, learn, and remember new material.

Affective learning   Changes in attitudes or emotions (affect) as a function of experience.

Age-equivalent scores   Standardized-test norms that allow users to convert raw scores to age equivalents. Such norms allow test users to interpret the subject's performance in terms of the average performance of a comparable group of children of a specified age.

Aggression   In human beings, a much-studied characteristic that is generally defined as the conscious and willful inflicting of pain on others.

Analysis   The process of breaking down into component parts. As an intellectual activity, it consists primarily of examining relationships among ideas in an attempt to understand them better. It is a relatively high-level intellectual skill in Bloom's taxonomy of educational objectives.

Anxiety   A feeling of apprehension, worry, tension, or nervousness.

Application   An educational objective described by Bloom. Consists primarily of the ability to use abstractions in concrete situations.

Arousal   A term with both physiological and psychological meanings. As a physiological concept, arousal refers to change in such physiological functions as heart rate, respiration rate, electrical activity in the cortex, and electrical conductivity of the skin. As a psychological concept, arousal refers to degree of alertness, awareness, vigilance, or wakefulness. Arousal varies from very low (coma or sleep) to very high (panic or high anxiety).

Assessment   The processes involved in measurement and evaluation; a judgmental process intimately involved in the teaching/learning process. See also *Evaluation, Measurement.*

Assimilation   The act of incorporating objects or aspects of objects into previously learned activities. To assimilate is, in a sense, to ingest or to use for something that is previously learned. See also *Accommodation.*

Associationistic   Describes a model of human memory based on the notion that items of information in memory are related (associated) with one another in a variety of ways having to do with content or meaning (rather than location).

Attitude   A prevailing and consistent tendency to react in a certain way. Attitudes can be described as positive or negative and are important motivational forces.

Attributes   Properties of objects or events that can vary from one object or event to another. See also *Values.*

Attribute-treatment interaction   The relationship between student characteristics (attributes), teaching methods (treatments), and outcomes. These relationships are sometimes very complex. Thus, a given treatment (instructional method, for example) may be more effective for students with certain attributes than for others with different attributes.

Autoinstructional device   Any instructional device that is effective in the absence of a teacher. Common examples are programmed textbooks and computers.

Aversive control   The control of human behavior, usually through the presentation of noxious (unpleasant) stimuli. This is in contrast to techniques of positive control, which generally use positive reinforcement.

Avoidance learning   A conditioning phenomenon usually involving aversive (unpleasant) stimulation, wherein the organism learns to avoid situations associated with specific unpleasant circumstances.

Bear (a literal bear)   A bob-tailed, omnivorous, quadrupedal mammal that walks on the soles of its feet inventing poetic images and humming wonderful love songs. See also *Bear* (*the metaphoric bear*).

Bear (the metaphoric bear)   Today's metaphoric bear is our hope for the future. He is everything that is inspiring and hopeful about teaching. He is commitment and sincerity, caring and compassion, wisdom and humility. He knows the science of teaching, and he understands its art as well. This bear is a fantastic teacher and—just as important—he is also an environmental crusader. But he still hums love songs as he follows the spoor of wild cows; he builds poems as he destroys their whisky stills and cleans their dance halls. And sometimes when he sniffs wild strawberries or when he finds a silver dewdrop on a rose petal, he dances a little jig and shouts "whoopee!" See also *Wild cow*.

Behavior   The activity of an organism. Behavior may be overt (visible) or covert (invisible or internal).

Behaviorism   A general term for theories of learning concerned primarily with the observable components of behavior (stimuli and responses).

Behavioristic theories   Learning theories whose primary emphasis is on stimuli and responses and the relationships between them. These theories are often called S-R theories.

Behavior management   Changes in the behavior of an individual; also refers to psychological theory and research concerned with the application of psychological principles in attempts to change behavior.

Behavior modification   See *Behavior management*.

Belief   The acceptance of an idea as being accurate or truthful. Beliefs are highly personal and, ideally, should not be an important part of scientific theory building. See also *Law, Model, Principle, Theory*.

Brainstorming   A technique popularized by Osborn and used in the production of creative solutions for problems. A brainstorming session usually involves a small group of people who are encouraged to produce a wide variety of ideas, which are evaluated later.

Branching program   Programmed material that, in contrast to a linear program, presents a variety of alternative routes through the material. Such programs typically make use of larger frames than do linear programs, and they frequently use multiple choices.

Capability   A capacity to do something. To be capable is to have the necessary knowledge and skills.

Categorization   The act of placing stimulus input into categories. According to Bruner, recognizing an object involves placing it in an appropriate category (categorizing it).

Category   A term used by Bruner to describe a grouping of related objects or events. In this sense a category is both a concept and a percept. Bruner also defines it as a rule for classifying things as equivalent. See also *Categorization, Coding system*.

Central tendency   The tendency for the majority of scores in a normal distribution to cluster around the center of the distribution. Measures of central tendency include the mean, the mode, and the median, all of which are at or near the center of their normal distributions. See also *Mean, Median, Mode*.

Chaining   The type of learning that involves the formation of links between stimulus-response bonds. Much human behavior that is describable in terms of S-R units is illustrative of chains because behavior is ordinarily so complex that it involves a large number of such S-R units.

Chains A term used by Gagné to signify the learning of related sequences of responses. A chain is a series of stimulus-response bonds in that each response in the sequence serves as a stimulus for the next response. Motor chains are involved in my typing of this material.

Chunking A memory process whereby related items are grouped together into more easily remembered "chunks" (for example, a prefix and four digits for a phone number, rather than seven unrelated numbers).

Circles of knowledge A generic term sometimes used to describe a variety of small-group learning approaches. These approaches stress face-to-face interaction, peer help, and rewards for cooperative, group activities rather than for individual activity. Such approaches are highly cooperative rather than competitive or individualistic.

Classical conditioning Also called *learning through stimulus substitution* because it involves the repeated pairing of two stimuli so that eventually a previously neutral (conditioned) stimulus comes to elicit the same response (conditioned response) that was previously elicited by the first stimulus (unconditioned stimulus). This was the type of conditioning first described by Pavlov.

Classification The act of grouping in terms of common properties. Classification involves abstracting the properties of objects or events and making judgments concerning how they are similar to or different from other objects or events. See *Categorization*.

Classroom management A comprehensive term for the variety of teacher actions designed to facilitate teaching and learning in the classroom. Classroom management includes disciplinary actions, as well as daily routines, seating arrangements, and scheduling of lessons.

Client-centered therapy Type of patient-counselor relationship in which the counselor (therapist or psychiatrist) is not directive in the sense of telling clients how they should behave, but rather attempts to allow patients to express themselves and discover within themselves ways of dealing with their own behavior. This therapeutic approach is generally contrasted with directive therapy. See also *Counseling, Directive therapy*.

Coding system A Brunerian concept; refers to a hierarchical arrangement of related categories.

Cognitive learning Learning concerned primarily with the acquisition of information, with the development of strategies for processing information, with decision-making processes, and with logical processes.

Cognitive strategy The processes involved in learning and remembering. Cognitive strategies include identifying problems, selecting approaches to their solution, monitoring progress in solving problems, and using feedback. Cognitive strategies are closely related to metacognition and metamemory. See also *Metacognition, Metamemory*.

Cognitive structure The organized totality of an individual's knowledge. See also *Knowledge*.

Cognitivism Theories of learning concerned primarily with such topics as perception, problem solving, information processing, and understanding.

Cohort A group of individuals born within the same specified period of time. For example, the cohort of the 1950s includes those born between January 1, 1950, and December 31, 1959, inclusive.

Combined schedule A combination of various types of *schedules of reinforcement*.

Communication The transmission of a message from one organism to another. Communication does not necessarily involve language because some nonhuman animals can communicate, usually through reflexive behaviors.

Comparative organizer A concept or idea that serves to facilitate the learning of new material by making use of the similarities and differences between the new material and previous learning.

Competence motivation White's phrase for our innate need to achieve competence and to feel competent. According to White, competence motivation has especially important adaptive value in a species that is born with little innate competence.

Comprehension The lowest level of understanding in Bloom's hierarchy of educational objectives; defined as the ability to apprehend the meaning of communication without necessarily being able to apply, analyze, or evaluate it.

Computer-assisted instruction (CAI) The use of computer facilities as autoinstructional devices. Computers may be used simply to present information or to present complex branching programs. Some advantages include their almost unlimited storage capacities, their retrieval ability, their problem-solving capacities, and their versatility of presentation modes.

Computer literacy The minimal skills required for interaction with computers. Thus, a person can be computer literate without knowing how a computer functions internally or even how to program it. Clearly, there are different degrees of computer literacy.

Concept A collection of perceptual experiences or ideas that are related by virtue of their possessing common properties.

Conceptualization See *Categorization*.

Concrete operations The third of Piaget's four major stages, lasting from age 7 or 8 to approximately age 11 or 12, and characterized largely by the child's ability to deal with concrete problems and objects, or objects and problems imagined in a concrete sense.

Concurrent validity See *Criterion-related validity*.

Conditioned response A response elicited by a conditioned stimulus. In some obvious ways a conditioned response resembles its corresponding unconditioned response. The two are not identical, however.

Conditioned stimulus A stimulus that, initially, does not elicit any response or that elicits a global, orienting response, but that, as a function of being paired with an unconditioned stimulus and its response, acquires the capability of eliciting that same response. For example, a stimulus that is always present at the time of a fear reaction may become a conditioned stimulus for fear.

Conditioning A type of learning that is described in terms of changing relationships between stimuli, between responses, or between both stimuli and responses. See also *Classical conditioning, Operant conditioning*.

Confluence model Zajonc's term for the hypothesis that the *intellectual climate* of the home, determined principally in terms of the numbers and ages of family members, contributes in important ways to the development of a child's intelligence. According to this model, children born into a relatively adult environment (first born and only

children, for example) should, *on average*, have an intellectual advantage over those born in a less adult environment (later-born children; children in large families; children in single-parent homes).

Connectionism A theory that explains learning as the formation of bonds (connections) between stimuli and responses. The term is attributed to E. L. Thorndike.

Conservation A Piagetian term for the realization that certain quantitative attributes of objects remain unchanged unless something is added to or taken away from them. Such characteristics of objects as mass, number, area, and volume are capable of being conserved.

Construct validity An estimate of test validity based on the extent to which test results agree with and reflect the theories that underlie the test.

Content A term used by Guilford to describe the content of a person's intellect. Intellectual activity (operations) involves content and results in products. See also *Operation, Product*.

Content validity Test validity determined by a careful analysis of the content of test items and a comparison of this content with course objectives.

Contiguity The occurrence of things both simultaneously and in the same space. Contiguity is frequently used to explain the occurrence of classical conditioning. It is assumed that the simultaneity of the unconditioned and the conditioned stimulus is sufficient to explain the formation of the link between the two.

Contingency A dependency relationship. An event is said to be contingent upon another when its occurrence is dependent upon the occurrence of the other.

Continuous reinforcement Reinforcement schedule in which every correct response is followed by a reinforcer.

Convergent thinking A term used by Guilford to describe the type of thinking that results in a single, correct solution for a problem. It is assumed that most conventional tests of intelligence measure convergent-thinking abilities rather than divergent-thinking abilities. See also *Divergent thinking*.

Correlation A statistical relationship between variables. See also *Variable*.

Correlative subsumption The type of learning that takes place when new information requires an extension of what was previously known and could not, therefore, have been derived directly from it. See also *Derivative subsumption.*

Counseling   The act of giving advice.

Creativity   Generally refers to the capacity of individuals to produce novel or original answers or products. The term *creative* is an adjective that may be used to describe people, products, or processes.

Criterial attribute   An attribute or characteristic of an object that is used in identifying it. For example, roundness is a criterial attribute for the category "circle."

Criterion-referenced test   Test in which the student is judged relative to a criterion rather than relative to the performance of other students. The teacher decides beforehand the specific performance expected and tests to see whether the student has reached this criterion.

Criterion-related validity   A measure of the extent to which predictions based on test results are accurate (predictive validity) and the extent to which the test agrees with other related measures (concurrent validity).

Critical period   A period in development during which exposure to appropriate experiences or stimuli will bring about specific learning much more easily than is the case at other times.

Crystallized abilities   Cattell's term for intellectual abilities that are highly dependent on experience (verbal and numerical abilities, for example). These abilities do not appear to decline significantly with advancing age. See also *Fluid abilities.*

Culture   The pattern of socially acceptable behaviors that characterizes a people or a social group. It includes all the attitudes and beliefs that the group has about the things it considers important.

Declarative knowledge   All the facts, information, and experiences that are part of what we know. See also *Procedural knowledge.*

Deferred imitation   The ability to imitate people or events in their absence. Deferred imitation is assumed to be crucial in the development of language abilities.

Derivative subsumption   The type of subsumption (or learning) that takes place when new material can be derived directly from what is already known. See also *Correlative subsumption.*

Desists   Teacher behaviors intended to make a student stop (desist from) some ongoing or impend-

ing misbehavior. Desists may take the form of threats, simple requests, orders, pleas, and so on.

Development   The growth, maturational, and learning processes from birth to maturity.

Differential reinforcement of successive approximations   The procedure of reinforcing only some responses and not others. Differential reinforcement is used in the shaping of complex behaviors. See also *Shaping.*

Direct reinforcement   The type of reinforcement that affects the individual in question directly rather than vicariously. See also *Vicarious reinforcement.*

Directive therapy   Type of counselor-client relationship in which the counselor takes the major responsibility for directing the client's behavior.

Discipline   The control aspects of teaching.

Discovery learning   The acquisition of new information or knowledge largely as a result of the learner's own efforts. Discovery learning is contrasted with expository or reception learning and is generally associated with Bruner, among others. See also *Reception learning.*

Discriminated stimulus   A stimulus that is perceived by the organism. In operant conditioning, the discriminated stimulus elicits the response.

Discrimination   Processes involved in learning that certain responses are appropriate in specific situations but inappropriate in other similar but discriminably different situations. Generalization is an opposite process. See also *Generalization.*

Disinhibition   The appearance of a suppressed behavior. See also *Inhibitory-disinhibitory effect.*

Disposition   An inclination or a tendency to do (or not to do) something; an aspect of motivation. See also *Motivation.*

Dissociability   A term used by Ausubel to indicate the ease with which material that is to be recalled can be separated (dissociated) from other related material that is also in memory.

Distance receptors   The senses that receive stimulation from a distance (for example, hearing and vision).

Divergent thinking   An expression used by Guilford to describe the type of thinking that results in the production of several different solutions for one problem. Divergent thinking is assumed to be closely related to creative behavior, and the term is used interchangeably with the term *creativity.* See also *Convergent thinking.*

Diversity of training   Bruner's expression relating to his belief that exposure to information under a wide range of circumstances is conducive to discovering relationships among concepts.

Drive   The tendency to behave that is brought about by an unsatisfied need.

Educational psychology   A science concerned primarily with the application of psychological knowledge (knowledge about human behavior) to problems of education.

Egocentrism   A way of functioning characterized by an inability to assume the point of view of others. A child's early thinking is largely egocentric.

Eidetic imagery   A particularly vivid type of visual image in memory. In many ways it is almost as though the individual were actually able to look at what is being remembered — hence the synonym "photographic memory."

Elicited response   A response brought about by a stimulus. The expression is synonymous with the term *respondent*.

Eliciting effect   Imitative behavior in which the observer does not copy the model's responses but simply behaves in a related manner. See also *Inhibitory-disinhibitory effect, Modeling effect*.

Emitted response   A response not elicited by a stimulus but simply emitted by the organism. An emitted response is, in fact, an operant.

Empower   To enable; to give power to. One of the most important goals of education is to empower students by providing them with both specific information and learning/thinking strategies, and by developing within them the feelings of personal power that come with the realization that one is competent and worthwhile.

Enactive   A term used by Bruner to describe young children's representation of their world. It refers specifically to the belief that children represent the world in terms of their personal actions. See also *Iconic, Symbolic*.

Encoding   A process whereby we derive meaning from the environment. To encode is to represent in another form. At a mental level, encoding involves the process of *abstracting* — representing as a concept or a meaning.

Enrichment   An approach in the education of gifted children. Enrichment involves providing students with additional and different school experiences, rather than simply moving them more rapidly through the conventional curriculum. See also *Acceleration*.

Environmentalism   The belief that whatever a child becomes is determined by experience (the environment) rather than by genetic makeup.

Equivalence reliability   An estimate of the consistency of a test based on the extent to which different forms of the test yield similar results. Common measures of equivalence reliability are provided by split-halves or parallel-forms approaches. See also *Parallel-forms reliability, Split-half reliability*.

Escape learning   A conditioning phenomenon whereby the organism learns means of escaping from a situation, usually following the presentation of aversive (unpleasant) stimulation. See also *Avoidance learning*.

Evaluation   In contrast to measurement, involves making a value judgment — deciding on the goodness or badness of performance; also denotes the highest-level intellectual skill in Bloom's taxonomy of educational objectives, in which it is defined as the ability to render judgments about the value of methods or materials for specific purposes, making use of external or internal criteria.

Exclusion   A time-out procedure whereby a child is not removed from the situation but is excluded from ongoing activities, often by being made to sit behind a screen, in a corner, or facing away from the class. See also *Isolation, Nonexclusion, Time-out*.

Exemplary model   A teacher.

Expectations   Anticipated behavior. Teacher expectations are particularly important because research tends to show that expectations significantly affect the behavior of some students.

Expository organizer   An idea or concept that serves as a description (exposition) of concepts that are relevant to new learning.

Expressive objectives   Instructional objectives that are concerned with the affective (emotional) components of learning rather than simply with content or performance.

Extinction   The cessation of a response as a function of the withdrawal of reinforcement.

Extinction rate   Time lapse between the cessation of a response following the withdrawal of reinforcement.

Extrinsic reinforcement   Reinforcement that comes from outside rather than from within — for example, high grades, praise, or money. See also *Intrinsic reinforcement*.

Face validity The extent to which a test appears to be measuring what it is intended to measure.

Fact Something that observation leads us to believe is true or real. Ideally, the observations that determine our facts are sufficiently objective and repeatable so as to provide us with some assurance that they accurately reflect the way things actually are.

Fatigue method A technique for breaking habits (described by Guthrie). The fatigue method involves forcing the appearance of the undesirable response over and over again until the individual is so tired that he or she can no longer respond. See also *Incompatible-stimuli method, Threshold method.*

Fixed schedule A type of intermittent schedule of reinforcement in which the reinforcement occurs at fixed intervals of time (an interval schedule) or after a specified number of trials (a ratio schedule).

Fluid abilities Cattell's term for intellectual abilities that seem to underlie much of our intelligent behavior and that are not highly affected by experience (for example, general reasoning, attention span, and memory for numbers). Fluid abilities are more likely to decline in old age. See also *Crystallized abilities.*

Forgetting The cessation of a response as a function of the passage of time; not to be confused with *extinction.*

Formal operations The last of Piaget's four major stages. It begins around age 11 or 12 and lasts until age 14 or 15. It is characterized by the child's increasing ability to use logical thought processes.

Formative evaluation Evaluation undertaken before and during instruction, designed primarily to assist the learner in identifying strengths and weaknesses. Formative evaluation is a fundamental part of the process of instruction.

Frames Units of information presented in programmed instruction. A frame not only presents information but also usually requires the student to make a response.

Fraternal twins Twins whose genetic origins are two different eggs. Such twins are as genetically dissimilar as nontwin siblings. See also *Identical twins.*

Gender roles Attitudes, personality characteristics, behavior, and other qualities associated with being male or female. Gender roles define masculinity and femininity.

Generalization The transference of a response from one stimulus to a similar stimulus (stimulus generalization), or the transference of a similar response for another response in the face of a single stimulus (response generalization). A child who responds with fear in a new situation that resembles an old, fear-producing situation is showing evidence of stimulus generalization.

Generalized reinforcer A stimulus that is not reinforcing prior to being paired with a primary reinforcer. Generalized reinforcers are stimuli that are present so often at the time of reinforcement that they come to be reinforcing for a wide variety of unrelated activities. Stimuli such as social prestige, praise, and money are generalized reinforcers for human behavior. See also *Primary reinforcer.*

Gordon technique A creativity-enhancing technique very similar to brainstorming except that an abstraction of a problem rather than a specific problem is presented.

Grade-equivalent scores Standardized-test norms that allow users to convert raw scores to grade equivalents — that is, that allow the user to conclude that the testee has performed at a level comparable to that of average children at a specified grade level.

Grammar Characteristic system of word forms and syntax of a language. See also *Syntax.*

Group test A type of test, usually used to measure intelligence, that may be given to large groups of subjects at one time. It is typically of the pencil-and-paper variety. See also *Individual test.*

Growth The physical aspects of development. It is somewhat similar in meaning to the term *maturation,* although it does not refer to the appearance of nonphysical capabilities.

Habit A customary way of responding in a given situation. Some behaviorists (for example, Guthrie) refer to all learning as involving the formation of habits.

Hardware The physical components of a computer, including monitors, controllers, drives, printers, and so on.

Hierarchy of classes An arrangement of concepts or classes in terms of their inclusiveness. At the top of the hierarchy is the concept (class) that is most inclusive (for example, *writing instruments*); below this highly inclusive concept are those that are included in it (for example, pens, typewriters, pencils, and so on).

Holistic education   A comprehensive term for educational approaches that attempt to remedy what is seen as traditional education's failure to educate the *whole* brain. Advocates of holistic education believe that the right hemisphere, thought to be associated with art, music, and emotion, is neglected by curricula that stress reason, logic, language, science, and mathematics (left-brain functions).

Holophrase   A sentence-like word uttered by young children early in the course of learning a language. A holophrase is a single word into which the child packs as much meaning as an adult would convey by using a much longer phrase.

Humanism   A term that describes the philosophical and psychological orientation that is primarily concerned with our humanity — that is, with our worth as individuals and with those processes that are considered to make us more human.

Iconic   A term that refers to a stage in the development of the child's representation of his or her world. The term is used by Bruner to describe an intermediate stage of development characterized by a representation of the world in terms of relatively concrete mental images. See also *Enactive, Symbolic*.

Identical twins   Twins whose genetic origin is one egg. Such twins are genetically identical. See also *Fraternal twins*.

Identity   A logical rule that specifies that certain activities leave objects or situations unchanged.

Imitation   The copying behavior of an organism. To imitate a person's behavior is simply to use that person's behavior as a pattern. Bandura and Walters describe three different effects of imitation. See also *Eliciting effect, Inhibitory-disinhibitory effect, Modeling effect*.

Imprinting   Unlearned, instinct-like behaviors that are not present at birth but that become part of an animal's repertoire after exposure to a suitable stimulus. Such exposure must ordinarily take place during what is referred to as a critical period. The "following" behavior of young ducks, geese, and chickens is an example.

Incompatible-stimuli method   A method for breaking habits (described by Guthrie). Involves presenting a stimulus that ordinarily brings about an undesirable reaction, but doing so at a time when the undesirable behavior is not likely to occur. See also *Fatigue method, Threshold method*.

Individual education plan (IEP)   An individualized instructional program tailored to a child's specific pattern of needs and abilities. IEPs may be used for gifted, learning-disabled, retarded, or average children.

Individual test   A test, usually used to measure intelligence, that can be given to only one individual at a time. See also *Group test*.

Individually guided education (IGE)   An individual approach to instruction based on the principle of ungraded schools. It makes use of teams of teachers, extensive in-service teacher training, individual programming for each student, home involvement, and the continual development of new curriculum material. Like IPI, it is also based on mastery learning.

Individually prescribed instruction (IPI)   A complex instructional system that involves reorganizing the entire curriculum for each subject (and over a wide range of grades) into a series of sequential units with clearly defined objectives and tests for each unit. Students progress at their own rate as they master each unit.

Inhibitory-disinhibitory effect   The type of imitative behavior that results either in the suppression (inhibition) or appearance (disinhibition) of previously acquired deviant behavior. See also *Eliciting effect, Modeling effect*.

Instinct   A complex, species-specific, relatively unmodifiable pattern of behaviors such as migration or nesting in some birds and animals. Less complex inherited behaviors are usually termed *reflexes*.

Instruction   The arrangement of external events in a learning situation in order to facilitate learning, retention, and transfer.

Instructional objective   The goal or intended result of instruction. Objectives may be short-range or long-range.

Intellectual skills   Gagné's term for the outcomes of the learning process. He describes seven such skills ranging from simple conditioned responses to abstract problem solving.

Intelligence   A property measured by intelligence tests; seems to refer primarily to the capacity of individuals to adjust to their environments.

Intelligence quotient (IQ)   A simple way of describing intelligence by assigning it a number that represents the ratio of mental to chronological age, multiplied by 100. Average IQ is therefore 100 and is based on a comparison between an individual's performance and that of comparable others.

Intermittent reinforcement A schedule of reinforcement that does not present a reinforcer for all correct responses. See also *Interval schedule, Ratio schedule.*

Interval scale A measurement scale that has no true zero but on which numerical indicators are arbitrarily set. Intervals between numbers are assumed to be equal in such a scale (a thermometer, for example).

Interval schedule An intermittent schedule of reinforcement that is based on the passage of time. See also *Fixed schedule, Random schedule.*

Intrinsic reinforcement Reinforcement that comes from within the individual rather than from the outside (satisfaction, for example). See also *Extrinsic reinforcement.*

Intuitive thinking One of the substages of preoperational thought, beginning around age 4 and lasting until age 7 or 8, marked by the child's ability to solve many problems intuitively and by the inability to respond correctly in the face of misleading perceptual features of problems.

Isolation A time-out procedure in which a child is removed from an area of reinforcement (typically the classroom, although sometimes the playground or other areas) and isolated in a different place. See also *Exclusion, Nonexclusion, Time-out.*

Jargon The unique, technical vocabulary of a discipline. The term implies that the vocabulary is not always essential.

Jargon shock My tongue was in my cheek in Chapter 8, but I'm glad you checked here. See *Jargon.*

Knowledge A generic term for the information, the ways of dealing with information, the ways of acquiring information, and so on that an individual possesses; also the lowest-level objective in Bloom's taxonomy of educational objectives.

Knowledge-acquisition components One of Sternberg's three facets of human intelligence, related to procedures used for learning new information (separating the important from the unimportant; associating items of information; comparing the new with the old). See also *Metacomponents, Performance components.*

Knowledge base The storehouse of concepts, information, associations, and procedures that we accumulate over time.

Knowledge of results Knowledge about the correctness or incorrectness of the student's response, provided for him or her in programmed instruction. Knowledge of results is usually immediate.

Language The use of arbitrary sounds in the transmission of messages from one individual or organism to another. Language should not be confused with communication. See also *Communication.*

Language immersion An approach to teaching a second language that involves placing the learner in an environment in which only the second language is used.

Lateralization A term that refers to the division of functions and capabilities between the two hemispheres of the brain.

Lateral thinking de Bono's term for a way of thinking that leads to creative solutions. See also *Vertical thinking.*

Law Statement whose accuracy is beyond reasonable doubt. See also *Belief, Principle.*

Law of effect A Thorndikean law of learning that states that it is the effect of a response that leads to its being learned (stamped in) or not learned (stamped out).

Law of multiple responses One of Thorndike's laws based on his observation that learning involves the emission of a variety of responses (multiple responses) until one (presumably an appropriate one) is reinforced. It is because of this law that Thorndike's theory is often referred to as a theory of trial-and-error learning.

Law of one-trial learning Guthrie's belief that the learning of a response requires a single pairing of that response with a stimulus.

Law of prepotency of elements A Thorndikean law of learning that states that people tend to respond to the most striking of the various elements that make up a stimulus situation.

Law of readiness A Thorndikean law of learning that takes into account the fact that certain types of learning are impossible or difficult unless the learner is ready. In this context, readiness refers to maturational level, previous learning, motivational factors, and other characteristics of the individual that relate to learning.

Law of response by analogy An analogy is typically an explanation, comparison, or illustration based on similarity. In Thorndike's system, response by analogy refers to responses that occur because of similarities between two situations. See also *Theory of identical elements*.

Law of set or attitude A Thorndikean law of learning that recognizes the fact that we are often predisposed to respond in certain ways as a result of our experiences and previously learned attitudes.

Learning Changes in behavior due to experience; does not include changes due to motivation, fatigue, or drugs.

Learning disability A depression in the ability to learn specific things (for example, reading or arithmetic), in which the learning difficulties are not related to mental retardation or emotional disturbance.

Learning style A unique and important learner variable manifested in differences in biological rhythms (morning versus evening people), perceptual strengths (visual versus auditory learners), sociological preference (large- versus small-group instruction), attention span (long or short), and a wealth of personality variables (dependence/independence, for example).

Learning theory Psychological theories concerned primarily with questions about how people learn, how they acquire information, and how they behave.

Learning/thinking strategy Processes involved in learning and thinking; another expression for *cognitive strategy*, introduced to emphasize that the strategies involved in cognition (knowing) are also involved in learning and thinking. See also *Cognitive strategy*.

Levels of processing An information-processing theory, attributed to Craik and Lockhart, maintaining that memory is a function of the level to which information is processed. At the lowest level, a stimulus is simply recognized as a physical event (and is available momentarily in short-term sensory memory); at a much deeper level, a stimulus is interpreted in terms of its meaning (and is available in long-term memory).

Linear program The presentation of programmed material in such a manner that all learners progress through the same material in the same order. Linear programs typically make no provision for individual differences in learning; the material,

however, is broken up into very small steps (frames).

Link system A memory system whereby items to be remembered are associated one with the other by means of a series of related visual images.

Loci system A mnemonic system whereby items to be remembered are associated with visual images of specific places.

Logo Seymour Papert's computer language, designed to be easily enough understood by young children to allow them to learn programming skills easily and painlessly as they might learn an exciting new game. The program uses a "turtle"—a small creature that can be instructed (that is, programmed) to move in different ways, tracing various geometric designs as it moves.

Long-term memory A type of memory whereby, with continued rehearsal and recoding of sensory input (processing in terms of meaning, for example), material will be available for recall over a long period of time.

Mainstreaming The practice of placing students in need of special services in regular classrooms rather than segregating them.

Mastery learning An instructional approach described by Bloom in which a learning sequence is analyzed into specific objectives, and progress requires that each learner master sequential objectives.

Mastery of specifics A Brunerian term for the learning of details. Mastery of relevant specifics is necessary for acquiring concepts and discovering relationships among them.

Maturation The process of normal physical and psychological development. Maturation is defined as occurring independently of particular experiences. See also *Development, Growth*.

Mean The arithmetic average of a set of scores. In distributions that are skewed (top- and bottom-heavy), the mean is not the best index of central tendency; that is, it is not necessarily at the middle of the distribution. See also *Central tendency, Median*.

Measurement The application of an instrument to gauge the quantity of something, as opposed to its quality. Assessing quality involves evaluation, not measurement.

Median The midpoint or fiftieth percentile of a distribution; the point at or below which 50 percent of all scores fall.

Memory The effects that experiences are assumed to have on the human mind. Refers to the storage of these effects. See also *Retention, Retrieval.*

Mentalism Sometimes used in a derogatory sense to describe an approach in psychology concerned largely with discovering, through a process of introspection, how people feel or react emotionally.

Mental retardation A significant general depression in the ability to learn, usually accompanied by deficits in adaptive behavior.

Mental structure See *Cognitive structure.*

Mentoring A one-to-one teaching/learning relationship in which the teacher (mentor) serves as a fundamentally important model with respect to values, beliefs, philosophies, religion, and attitudes, as well as a source of more mundane information.

Metacognition Knowledge about knowing. As we grow and learn, we develop notions of ourselves as learners. Accordingly, we develop strategies that recognize our limitations and that allow us to monitor our progress and to take advantage of our efforts. See also *Metamemory.*

Metacomponents One of Sternberg's three components of human intelligence. Metacomponents include the skills involved in planning, monitoring, and evaluating cognitive performance — in other words, the skills of metacognition. See also *Knowledge-acquisition components, Metacognition, Performance components.*

Metamemory The knowledge we develop about our own memory processes — our knowledge about how to remember, rather than simply our memories. See *Metacognition.*

Méthode clinique Piaget's experimental method. It involves an interview technique in which questions are determined largely by the subject's responses. Its flexibility distinguishes it from ordinary interview techniques.

Microcomputers Most modern home and business computers. They are termed *micro* because chip technology has resulted in a dramatic reduction in their size.

Minimum-competency testing A global term for the administration of batteries of tests designed to determine whether students, or teachers, have reached some minimum level of competency in basic areas such as language and mathematics.

Mode The most frequently occurring score(s) in a distribution.

Model A representation, usually abstract, of some phenomenon or system. Alternatively, a pattern for behavior that can be copied by someone.

Modeling effect The type of imitative behavior that involves the learning of a novel response. See also *Eliciting effect, Inhibitory-disinhibitory effect.*

Morphological analysis A creativity-enhancing technique, advanced by Arnold, involving the analysis of problems into their component parts and subsequent attempts to brainstorm each of these component parts.

Motivation The causes of behavior. Our motives are the reasons why we engage in some behaviors and not in others. They are what initiate behavior and what direct it.

Motor learning Learning that involves muscular coordination and physical skills. Such common activities as walking and driving a car involve motor learning.

Need Ordinarily refers to a lack or deficit in the human organism. Needs may be either unlearned (for example, the need for food or water) or learned (the need for money or prestige).

Need-drive theory A motivation theory that attempts to explain human behavior on the basis of the motivating properties of needs. Such theories typically assume that humans have certain learned and unlearned needs, which give rise to drives, which in turn are responsible for the occurrence of behavior. See also *Drive, Need.*

Need state Bruner's expression describing the arousal level of an organism.

Negative correlation The type of relationship that exists between two variables so that when one increases the other decreases.

Negative reinforcer A stimulus that has the effect of increasing the probability of occurrence of the response that precedes it. Negative reinforcement ordinarily takes the form of an unpleasant or noxious stimulus that is removed as a result of a specific response.

Neuron (nerve cell) An elongated cell that forms part of the nervous system. The main part of the neuron is the cell body; the elongated part is the axon.

Nominal scale A crude measurement scale that does no more than provide descriptive labels.

Nonexclusion The mildest form of time-out procedure; the child is not allowed to participate in ongoing activity but is required to observe.

Nonexecutive skills Sternberg's phrase for intellectual skills — the outcome of learning as it is ordinarily measured and observed in behavior. See also *Intellectual skills*.

Normal curve A mathematical function that can be represented in the form of a bell-shaped curve. A large number of naturally occurring events are normally distributed (chance events, for example). What this means, essentially, is that a vast majority of the events (or scores) cluster around the middle of the distribution (around the mean or median), with progressively fewer scores being farther and farther away from the average.

Norm-referenced test Test in which the student is competing against the performance of other students rather than in relation to some pre-established criterion of acceptable performance. See also *Criterion-referenced test*.

Object concept Piaget's expression for the child's understanding that the world is composed of objects that continue to exist apart from his or her perception of them.

Objective Adjective referring to research, theory, or experimental methods that deal with observable events. The implication is that objective observations are not affected by the observer.

Obliterative subsumption The incorporation of new material into preexisting cognitive structure such that the new material is eventually indistinguishable from what was already known (obliterated). In effect, obliterative subsumption results in forgetting.

Observational learning A term used synonymously with the expression *learning through imitation*. See also *Imitation*.

Operant The label used by Skinner to describe a response not elicited by any known or obvious stimulus. Most significant human behaviors appear to be of the operant variety. Such behaviors as writing a letter and going for a walk are operants because no known specific stimulus elicits them.

Operant conditioning A type of learning that involves an increase in the probability that a response will occur as a function of reinforcement. Most of the experimental work of Skinner investigates the principles of operant conditioning.

Operation (1) A Piagetian term that remains relatively nebulous but refers essentially to a thought process. An operation is an action that has been internalized in the sense that it can be "thought" and is reversible in the sense that it can be "unthought." (2) A term used by Guilford to describe major kinds of intellectual activity, such as remembering, evaluating, and divergent and convergent thinking. See also *Convergent thinking, Divergent thinking*.

Ordinal scale A scale of measurement that permits no more than simple ranking. An ordinal scale does not have a true zero, nor are the intervals between units on the scale necessarily equal. Using an ordinal scale, it is possible to say that A is greater than B and that B is greater than C, but never by how much.

Paradigm A model or pictorial representation of some phenomenon. For example, a paradigm for classical conditioning is:

$$UCS \rightarrow UCR$$
$$CS \rightarrow CR$$

Parallel-forms reliability A measure of test consistency (reliability) obtained by looking at the correlation between scores obtained by the same individual on two different but equivalent (parallel) forms of one test.

Penalty The type of punishment that involves losing or giving up something pleasant.

Percentile The point at or below which a specified percentage of scores fall. For example, the fiftieth percentile is the point at or below which 50 percent of all scores fall. A score of 50 percent is not necessarily at the fiftieth percentile.

Perception The translation of physical energies into neurological impulses — that is, stimuli into sensations — that can be interpreted by the individual.

Performance Actual behavior. The inference that learning has occurred is typically based on observed changes in performance.

Performance components One of Sternberg's three components of human intelligence. Performance components are the skills and processes actually used in carrying out intellectual tasks (reasoning, encoding, analyzing, remembering, and so on.) See also *Knowledge-acquisition components, Metacomponents*.

Personalized system of instruction (PSI) An instructional approach developed by Keller, based in part on Bloom's mastery learning, in which course material is broken down into small units, study is largely individual, a variety of study material is available, and progress depends on performance on unit tests.

Person-centered therapy   See *Client-centered therapy*.

Phenomenal field   The feelings, perceptions, and awareness that an individual has at any given moment.

Phenomenology   An approach primarily concerned with how individuals view their own world. Its basic assumption is that each individual perceives and reacts to the world in a unique manner, and that it is this phenomenological worldview that is of primary importance in understanding the individual's behavior. See also *Phenomenal field*.

Phonetic system   A particularly powerful mnemonic system that makes use of associations between numbers and letters combined to form words; visual images associated with these words are then linked with items to be remembered. Professional memorizers often use some variation of a phonetic system.

Phonology   The structure of speech sounds of a language.

Physiological needs   Basic biological needs, such as the need for food and water.

Placebo   A "sham" drug or treatment. As used in medicine, placebos often take the form of saline injections or sugar pills that have little physiological effect, but that can have powerful psychological effects.

Positive control   The control of human behavior, usually through the presentation of pleasant stimuli. This is in contrast to techniques of aversive control, which generally use negative reinforcement.

Positive correlation   The type of relationship that exists between two variables so that when one increases the other does likewise.

Positive reinforcer   A stimulus that increases the probability that a response will recur as a result of being added to a situation after the response has once occurred. Usually takes the form of a pleasant stimulus (reward) that results from a specific response.

Pragmatics   The implicit language rules that govern practical things such as when to speak and how to take turns in conversation.

Preconceptual thinking   The first substage in the period of preoperational thought, beginning around age 2 and lasting until age 4. It is so called because the child has not yet developed the ability to classify.

Predictive validity   See *Criterion-related validity*.

Premack principle   The recognition that behaviors that are chosen frequently by an individual (and that are therefore favored) may be used to reinforce other, less frequently chosen behaviors. (For example: "You can watch television when you have finished your homework.")

Preoperational thinking   The second of Piaget's four major stages, lasting from around age 2 to age 7 or 8. It consists of two substages: intuitive thinking and preconceptual thinking. See also *Intuitive thinking, Preconceptual thinking*.

Primary reinforcer   A stimulus that is reinforcing in the absence of any learning. Such stimuli as food and drink are primary reinforcers because, presumably, an organism does not have to learn that they are pleasant.

Principle   A statement relating to some uniformity or predictability. Principles are far more open to doubt than are laws but are more reliable than beliefs. See also *Belief, Law, Theory*.

Proactive inhibition   The interference of earlier learning with the retention of subsequent learning.

Procedural knowledge   Knowing how to do something; knowing procedures as well as facts (declarative knowledge). See also *Declarative knowledge*.

Processing   The intellectual or cognitive activities that occur as stimulus input is reacted to, analyzed, sorted, organized, and stored in memory or forgotten.

Product   A term used by Guilford to describe the result of applying an operation on content. A product may take the form of a response. See also *Content, Operation*.

Programmed instruction   An instructional procedure that makes use of the systematic presentation of information in small steps (frames), in the form of a textbook or some other device. Programs typically require learners to make responses and provide learners with immediate knowledge of results.

Prompts   Devices used in programmed instruction to ensure that the student will probably answer correctly. They may take a variety of forms.

Psychologial hedonism   The belief that humans act primarily to avoid pain and to obtain pleasure.

Psychological needs   Human needs other than those dealing with basic physical requirements such as food, sex, water, and temperature regulation (physiological needs). Psychological needs described by Maslow include the need to belong, to feel safe, to love and be loved, to maintain a high opinion of oneself, and to self-actualize. See also *Self-actualization*.

Psychology   The science that examines human behavior (and that of other animals as well).

Punishment   Involves either the presentation of an unpleasant stimulus or the withdrawal of a pleasant stimulus as a consequence of behavior. Punishment should not be confused with negative reinforcement.

Random schedule   (also called *variable schedule*) A type of intermittent schedule of reinforcement. It may be of either the interval or the ratio variety and is characterized by the presentation of rewards at random intervals or on random trials. Although both fixed and random schedules may be based on the same intervals or on the same ratios, one can predict when reward will occur under a fixed schedule, whereas it is impossible to do so under a random schedule.

Rate of learning   A measure of the amount of time required to learn a correct response, or, alternatively, a measure of the number of trials required prior to the emission of the correct response.

Ratio scale   A measurement scale in which there is a true zero and in which differences between units on the scale are equal. Educational and psychological measurements do not involve ratio scales, although we sometimes act as though they do — as, for example, when we assume that the difference between a percentage score of 78 and 79 is the same as that between 84 and 85. Weight is measured on a ratio scale.

Ratio schedule   An intermittent schedule of reinforcement that is based on a proportion of correct responses. See also *Fixed schedule, Random schedule*.

Reception learning   The type of learning that primarily involves instruction or tuition rather than the learner's own efforts. Teaching for reception learning often takes the form of expository or didactic methods; that is, the teacher structures the material and presents it to learners in relatively final form rather than asking them to discover that form. Reception learning is generally associated with Ausubel (among others).

Reciprocal determinism   Bandura's label for the recognition that even though environments affect individuals in important ways, individuals also affect environments by selecting and shaping them. Thus the influence (determinism) is two-way (reciprocal).

Reinforcement   The effect of a reinforcer; specifically, to increase the probability that a response will occur. See also *Negative reinforcer, Positive reinforcer, Reinforcer, Reward*.

Reinforcement menu   A list of activities, objects, or other consequences from which students can select reinforcers.

Reinforcer   A stimulus that causes reinforcement. See also *Reinforcement, Reward*.

Reliability   The consistency with which a test measures whatever it measures. A perfectly reliable test should yield the same scores on different occasions (for the same individual), providing what it measures has not changed. Most educational and psychological tests are severely limited in terms of reliability. See also *Validity*.

Relief   A common expression for negative reinforcement — the type of reinforcement that results when an unpleasant stimulus is removed as a consequence of behavior.

Remedial frame   A frame in a branching program to which students are referred when they make an incorrect response. The purpose of the remedial frame is to provide information required for a subsequent correct response.

Repeated-measures reliability   An estimate of the consistency (reliability) of a test based on the degree of agreement among scores obtained from different presentations of the same test.

Respondent   A term used by Skinner in contrast to the term *operant*. A respondent is a response that is elicited by a known, specific stimulus. Unconditioned responses are examples of respondents. See also *Unconditioned response*.

Response   Any organic, muscular, glandular, or psychic process that results from stimulation.

Response-cost   A mild form of punishment whereby tangible reinforcers that have been given for good behavior are taken away for misbehaviors. Response-cost systems are often used in systematic behavior-management programs.

Response rate   The number of responses emitted by an organism in a given period of time. Response rates for operant behaviors appear to be largely a function of the schedules of reinforcement used.

Retention   A term often used as a synonym for memory. See also *Retrieval*.

Retrieval   A term for the ability to bring items of information or impressions out of memory. It is often assumed that to forget is not to lose from memory but simply to lose the ability to retrieve from memory.

Retroactive inhibition   The interference of subsequently learned material with the retention of previously learned material.

Reversibility   A logical property manifested in the ability to reverse or undo activity in either an empirical or a conceptual sense. An idea is said to be reversible when a child realizes the logical consequences of an opposite action.

Reward   An object, stimulus, event, or outcome that is perceived as being pleasant and that may therefore be reinforcing.

Schedule of reinforcement   The time and frequency of presentation of reinforcement to organisms. See also *Continuous reinforcement, Intermittent reinforcement*.

Schema   (pl. *schemata*) The label used by Piaget to describe a unit in cognitive structure. A schema is, in one sense, an activity together with whatever structural connotations that activity has. In another sense, a schema may be thought of as an idea or a concept.

Science   An approach and an attitude toward knowledge that emphasizes objectivity, precision, and replicability.

Script   Term describing our knowledge of what goes with what and in what sequence. Scripts are a part of cognitive structure that deals with the routine and the predictable.

Self-actualization   The process or act of becoming oneself, of developing one's potentialities, of achieving an awareness of one's identity, of self-fulfillment. The term is central in humanistic psychology.

Self-efficacy   A term that refers to judgments we make about how efficacious (effective) we are in given situations. Judgments of self-efficacy are important in determining an individual's choice of activities and in influencing the amount of interest and effort expended.

Semantics   The meanings of the words of a language.

Sensorimotor intelligence   The first stage of development in Piaget's classification. It lasts from birth to approximately age 2 and is so called because children understand their world during that period primarily in terms of their activities in it and sensations of it.

Sensory memory   See *Short-term sensory storage*.

Seriation   The ordering of objects in terms of one or more properties. To seriate is to place in order.

Set   A predisposition to react to stimulation in a given manner.

Sex typing   The learning of behaviors appropriate to the gender of an individual in a given society; the acquisition of masculine and feminine gender roles. See also *Gender roles*.

Shaping   A technique whereby animals and people are taught to perform complex behaviors that were not previously in their repertoires. The technique involves reinforcing responses that become increasingly closer approximations to the desired behavior. Also called the method of successive approximations or the method of differential reinforcement of *successive approximations*. See also *Differential reinforcement of successive approximations*.

Short-term memory   Also called *primary* or *working memory*. A type of memory in which material is available for recall for a matter of seconds. Short-term memory involves primarily rehearsal rather than more in-depth processing. It defines our immediate consciousness.

Short-term sensory storage   Also called *sensory memory*. The phrase refers to the simple sensory recognition of such stimuli as a sound, a taste, or a sight.

Skinner box   Various experimental environments used by Skinner in his investigations of operant conditioning. The typical Skinner box is a cage-like structure equipped with a lever and a food tray attached to a food mechanism. It allows the investigator to study operants (for example, bar pressing) and the relationship between an operant and reinforcement.

Socialization   The complex process of learning both those behaviors that are appropriate within a given culture and those that are less appropriate. The primary agents of socialization are home, school, and peer groups.

Social learning   The acquisition of patterns of behavior that conform to social expectations; learning what is acceptable and what is not acceptable in a given culture.

Software   Computer instructions; programs.

SOMPA (System of Multicultural Pluralistic Assessment)   Mercer's battery of ten separate individual measures of medical status (hearing, vision, health), social functioning (school achievement), and ability, taking into account social and ethnic background. The SOMPA is designed to overcome the limitations of more conventional approaches to assessing ability among cultural and social minorities.

Split-half reliability   An index of test reliability (consistency) derived by arbitrarily dividing a test into parallel halves (odd and even numbered items, for example) and looking at the agreement between scores obtained by each individual on the two halves.

Standard deviation   A mathematical measure of the distribution of scores around their mean. In a normal distribution, approximately two-thirds of all scores fall within one standard deviation on either side of the mean, and almost 95 percent fall within two standard deviations of the mean.

Standardized tests   Professionally developed — rather than teacher-made — tests that provide the user with norms (standards), and which typically indicate the average or expected performance of groups of subjects of certain grades and/or ages. See also *Age-equivalent scores, Grade-equivalent scores.*

Standard language   The socially prestigious form of a society's dominant language; the form that is taught in schools and against which other dialects are judged for correctness.

Stanines   Standard scores that make use of a nine-point scale with a mean of 5 and a standard deviation of 2.

Stimulus   (pl. *stimuli*) Any change in the physical environment capable of exciting a sense organ.

Stimulus–response (S-R) theories   See *Behavioristic theories.*

Student-centered teaching   Rogers's expression for an approach to teaching based on a philosophy of self-discovered learning. The approach requires that the teacher genuinely care for students as individuals and that students be allowed to determine for themselves what is important in their lives.

Subsumer   The term used by Ausubel to describe a concept, an idea, or a combination of concepts or ideas that can serve to organize new information. Cognitive structure is therefore composed of subsumers.

Subsumption   Ausubel's term for the integration of new material or information with existing information. The term implies a process in which a new stimulus input becomes part of what is already in cognitive structure. See also *Correlative subsumption, Derivative subsumption, Obliterative subsumption.*

Summative evaluation   The type of evaluation that occurs at the end of an instructional sequence and that is designed primarily to provide a grade. See also *Formative evaluation.*

Superstitious schedule   A fixed-interval schedule of reinforcement in which the reward is not given after every correct response but rather after the passage of a specified period of time. It is so called because it leads to the learning of behaviors that are only accidentally related to the reinforcement.

Symbolic   The final stage in the development of a child's representation of his or her world. The term is used by Bruner and describes the representation of the world in terms of arbitrary symbols. Symbolic representation includes representation in terms of language as well as in terms of theoretical or hypothetical systems. See also *Enactive, Iconic.*

Symbolic model   A model other than a real-life person. Any pattern for behavior may be termed a symbolic model if it is not a person. For example, books, television, and written instructions can provide symbolic models.

Syntax   The arrangement of words to form sentences.

Synthesis   Putting together of parts in order to form a whole; complementary to analysis; a high-level intellectual ability in Bloom's taxonomy of educational objectives.

Task analysis   The process of analyzing what is to be learned in terms of a sequential series of related tasks. Essentially, task analysis provides the teacher with knowledge of important skills and knowledge that might be prerequisite for what is to be taught.

Technology of teaching   A Skinnerian phrase for the systematic application of the principles of behaviorism (especially of operant conditioning) to classroom practice.

Test anxiety A characteristic evident in a fear of taking tests and an expectation of poor performance. Evidence suggests that test anxiety can impair performance on tests.

Test blueprint A table of specifications for a teacher-made test. A good test blueprint provides information concerning the topics to be tested, the nature of the questions to be used, and the objectives (outcomes) to be assessed.

Theory A body of information pertaining to a specific topic, a method of acquiring and/or dealing with information, or a set of explanations for related phenomena.

Theory of identical elements A Thorndikean theory that holds that similar stimuli are related by virtue of the fact that two situations possess a number of identical elements, and these identical elements lead to transfer of responses from one situation to another.

Theory of trial-and-error learning See *Law of multiple responses*.

Third-force psychology A general expression for humanistic approaches to psychology such as those exemplified by the work of Carl Rogers and Abraham Maslow. The first two "forces" are psychoanalysis and behaviorism (S–R psychology).

Threshold method A means for breaking habits (described by Guthrie). It involves presenting a stimulus so faintly that the undesirable response is not elicited. Gradually the intensity of the stimulus is increased. See also *Fatigue method, Incompatible-stimuli method*.

Time-out A procedure in which students are removed from situations in which they might ordinarily be rewarded. Time-out procedures are widely used in classroom management. See also *Exclusion, Isolation, Nonexclusion*.

Tracking An instructional procedure that involves dividing the members of a classroom into groups according to their ability.

Transductive reasoning The type of reasoning that proceeds from particular to particular rather than from particular to general or from general to particular. One example of transductive reasoning is the following:

Cows give milk.

Goats give milk.

Therefore, goats are cows.

Transfer See *Generalization*.

Trial-and-error learning Thorndikean explanation for learning based on the idea that when placed in a problem situation, an individual will emit a number of responses but will eventually learn the correct one as a result of reinforcement. Trial-and-error explanations for learning are sometimes contrasted with insight explanations.

T-score A standardized score with a preset mean of 50 and a standard deviation of 10. A T-score of 70 is therefore quite high because 70 is two standard deviations above the mean, and only approximately 2.5 percent of all scores ordinarily fall beyond that point.

Unconditioned response A response that is elicited by an unconditioned stimulus.

Unconditioned stimulus A stimulus that elicits a response prior to learning. All stimuli that are capable of eliciting reflexive behaviors are examples of unconditioned stimuli. For example, food is an unconditioned stimulus for the response of salivation.

Validity The extent to which a test measures what it says it measures. For example, an intelligence test is valid to the extent that it measures intelligence and nothing else. Educational and psychological tests are limited by their frequently low validity. See also *Construct validity, Content validity, Criterion-related validity, Face validity, Reliability*.

Values Variations in a single attribute. For example, the attribute "sides of a coin" has two values: heads and tails.

Variable A property, measurement, or characteristic that is susceptible to variation. In psychological experimentation, qualities of human beings such as intelligence and creativity are considered variables.

Variable schedule See *Random schedule*.

Vertical thinking de Bono's term for thought processes that lead to correct, appropriate, and accepted solutions. This term is in contrast to lateral thinking, which leads to creative solutions. See also *Lateral thinking*.

Vicarious reinforcement Reinforcement that results from observing someone else being reinforced. In imitative behavior, observers frequently act as though they are being reinforced when in fact they are not being reinforced; rather, they are aware, or simply assume, that the model is being reinforced.

Wild cow (almost literal) A bovine creature found in both forested and nonforested regions of the world. Wild cows are particularly unrestrained creatures, given to a great variety of social and solitary diversions, including playing cards, smoking cigars, and drinking whisky. They also like to dance and to ice-skate, and some are quite wonderful surfers. Sadly, they do not fly nearly as well as pigs. See also *Wild cow (metaphoric)*.

Wild cow (metaphoric) Wild cows are a lot of the things that are wrong with this planet: starvation, pollution, illiteracy, preventable infant mortality, famine, terrorism, resource depletion, AIDS, murder, puny teacher salaries, and on and on. See also *Bear*.

"With-it-ness" Kounin's expression for a quality of teacher behavior manifested in the teacher's awareness of all the important things happening in a classroom. Teachers who are high in with-it-ness make more effective use of desists. See also *Desists*.

Working memory See *Short-term memory*.

Zone of proximal growth Vygotsky's phrase for the individual's current potential for further intellectual development. Conventional measures of intelligence assess current intellectual development rather than potential for future development. Vygotsky believed that the zone of proximal growth (future potential) might be assessed by further questioning and the use of hints and prompts while administering a conventional intelligence test.

Z-score A standardized score with a mean of 0 and a standard deviation of 1. Hence a Z-score of $+3$ is very high; one of -3 is very low.

BIBLIOGRAPHY

Adams, J. C., Jr. (1968). The relative effects of various testing atmospheres on spontaneous flexibility, a factor of divergent thinking. *Journal of Creative Behavior, 2,* 187–194.

Adamson, G. (1983, January). The coin with more than two sides. *ATA Magazine,* pp. 28–30.

Addison, R. M., & Homme, L. E. (1966). The reinforcing event (RE) menu. *Journal of the National Society for Programed Instruction, 5,* 8–9.

Ahsen, A. (1977a). *Psych eye: Self-analytic consciousness.* New York: Brandon House.

Ahsen, A. (1977b). Eidetics: An overview. *Journal of Mental Imagery, 1,* 5–38.

Alexander, P. A., & Judy, J. E. (1988). The interaction of domain-specific and strategic knowledge in academic performance. *Review of Educational Research, 58,* 375–404.

Alschuler, A. S. (1972). *Motivating achievement in high-school students: Education for human growth.* Englewood Cliffs, N.J.: Educational Technology Publications.

Altus, W. D. (1967). Birth order and its sequelae. *International Journal of Psychiatry, 3,* 23–42.

American Psychiatric Association (1980, March). *Diagnostic and statistical manual of mental disorders* (3rd ed.). Washington, D.C.: American Psychiatric Association.

Ames, R., & Ames, C. (Eds.). (1984). *Research on motivation in education (Vol. I): Student motivation.* New York: Academic Press.

Anastasi, A. (1958). Heredity, environment, and the question "how?" *Psychological Review, 65,* 197–208.

Anderson, C. W., & Smith, E. L. (1984). Children's preconceptions and content-area textbooks. In G. G. Duffy, L. R. Roehler, & J. Mason (Eds.), *Comprehension instruction: Perspectives and suggestions.* New York: Longman.

Anderson, H. H. (Ed.). (1959). *Creativity and its cultivation.* New York: Harper & Row.

Anderson, J. R. (1983). *The architecture of cognition.* Cambridge, Mass.: Harvard University Press.

Anderson, L. W., & Block, J. H. (1977). Mastery learning. In D. J. Treffinger, J. K. Davis, & R. E. Ripple (Eds.), *Handbook on teaching educational psychology.* New York: Academic Press.

Andrews, G. R., & Debus, R. L. (1978). Persistence and causal perception of failure: Modifying cognitive attributions. *Journal of Educational Psychology, 70,* 154–166.

Arlin, M. (1984). Time, equality, and mastery learning. *Review of Educational Research, 54,* 65–86.

Arlin, P. K. (1975). Cognitive development in adulthood: A fifth stage? *Developmental Psychology, 11,* 602–606.

Arnold, J. E. (1962). Useful creative techniques. In S. J. Parnes & H. F. Harding (Eds.), *A sourcebook for creative thinking.* New York: Scribner.

Aronfreed, J. (1968). Aversive control of socialization. In D. Levine (Ed.), *Nebraska Symposium on Motivation.* Lincoln: University of Nebraska Press.

Arter, J. A., & Jenkins, J. R. (1979). Differential diagnosis–Prescriptive teaching: A critical appraisal. *Review of Educational Research, 49,* 517–555.

Athey, I. J., & Rubadeau, D. O. (Eds.). (1970). *Educational implications of Piaget's theory.* Waltham, Mass.: Ginn-Blaisdell.

Atkinson, J. W., & Raynor, J. O. (1978). *Personality, motivation, and achievement.* New York: Wiley.

Atkinson, R. C., & Shiffrin, R. M. (1968). Human memory: A proposed system and its control processes. In K. W. Spence & J. T. Spence (Eds.), *The psychology of learning and motivation* (Vol. 2). New York: Academic Press.

Ausubel, D. P. (1958). *Theory and problems of child development.* New York: Grune & Stratton.

Ausubel, D. P. (1963). *The psychology of meaningful verbal learning.* New York: Grune & Stratton.

Ausubel, D. P. (1977). The facilitation of meaningful verbal learning in the classroom. *Educational Psychologist, 12,* 162–178.

Ausubel, D. P., & Robinson, F. G. (1969). *School learning: An introduction to educational psychology.* New York: Holt, Rinehart & Winston.

Axelrod, S., & Apsche, J. (Eds.). (1983). *The effects of punishment on human behavior.* New York: Academic Press.

Babad, E. Y. (1985). Some correlates of teachers' expectancy bias. *American Educational Research Journal, 22,* 175–183.

Bancroft, R. (1976). Special education: Legal aspects. In P. A. O'Donnell and R. H. Bradfield (Eds.), *Mainstreaming: Controversy and consensus.* San Rafael, Calif.: Academic Therapy Publications.

Bandura, A. (1962). Social learning through imitation. In N. R. Jones (Ed.), *Nebraska Symposium on Motivation.* Lincoln: University of Nebraska Press.

Bandura, A. (1969). *Principles of behavior modification.* New York: Holt, Rinehart & Winston.

Bandura, A. (1977). *Social learning theory.* Morristown, N.J.: General Learning Press.

Bandura, A. (1981). Self-referent thought: A developmental analysis of self-efficacy. In J. H. Flavell & L. Ross (Eds.), *Social cognitive development: Frontiers and possible futures.* Cambridge: Cambridge University Press.

Bandura, A. (1986). *Social foundations of thought and action: A social cognitive theory.* Englewood Cliffs, N.J.: Prentice-Hall.

Bandura, A., Ross, D., & Ross, S. (1963). Imitation of film mediated aggressive models. *Journal of Abnormal and Social Psychology, 66,* 3–11.

Bandura, A., & Walters, R. (1963). *Social learning and personality development.* New York: Holt, Rinehart & Winston.

Bangert, R. L., Kulik, J. A., & Kulik, C. C. (1983). Individualized systems of instruction in secondary schools. *Review of Educational Research, 53,* 143–158.

Baratz, J. D. (1969). A bi-dialectical task for determining language proficiency in economically disadvantaged Negro children. *Child Development, 40,* 889–901.

Bardwell, R. (1984). The development and motivational function of expectations. *American Educational Research Journal, 21,* 461–472.

Barnett, W. S., & Escobar, C. M. (1987). The economics of early educational intervention: A review. *Review of Educational Research, 57,* 387–414.

Barth, R. (1979). Home-based reinforcement of school behavior: A review and analysis. *Review of Educational Research, 49,* 436–458.

Basseches, M. (1984). *Dialectical thinking and adult development.* Norwood, N.J.: Ablex Publishing.

Beard, R. M. (1969). *An outline of Piaget's developmental psychology for students and teachers.* New York: Basic Books.

Bell-Gredler, M. E. (1986). *Learning and instruction: Theory into practice.* New York: Macmillan.

Bennett, N. (1976). *Teaching styles and pupil progress.* Cambridge, Mass.: Harvard University Press.

Berdine, W. H., & Blackhurst, A. E. (1985). *An introduction to special education* (2nd ed.). Boston: Little, Brown.

Berliner, D. C. (1983). Developing conceptions of classroom environments: Some light on the T in classroom studies of ATI. *Educational Psychologist, 18,* 1–13.

Berlyne, D. E. (1960). *Conflict, arousal and curiosity.* New York: McGraw-Hill.

Bernard, H. W. (1966). *Human development in western culture* (2nd ed.). Boston: Allyn and Bacon.

Bernard, L. L. (1924). *Instinct: A study in social psychology.* New York: Holt, Rinehart & Winston.

Bialystok, E. (1988). Levels of bilingualism and levels of linguistic awareness. *Developmental Psychology, 24,* 560–567.

Bijou, S. W., & Sturges, P. S. (1959). Positive reinforcers for experimental studies with children—Consumables and manipulatables. *Child Development, 30,* 151–170.

Blase, J. J., & Pajak, E. F. (1985). How discipline creates stress for teachers. *Canadian School Executive, 4,* 8–11.

Bloom, B. S. (Ed.). (1956). *Taxonomy of educational objectives: Handbook I: Cognitive domain.* New York: Longman, Green.

Bloom, B. S. (1964). *Stability and change in human characteristics.* New York: Wiley.

Bloom, B. S. (1976). *Human characteristics and school learning.* New York: McGraw-Hill.

Bloom, B. S. (1981). *All our children learning: A primer for parents, teachers, and other educators.* New York: McGraw-Hill.

Bloom, B. S. (1984). The 2 Sigma problem: The search for methods of group instruction as effective as one-to-one tutoring. *Educational Researcher, 13,* 4–15.

Bloom, B. S. (1987). A response to Slavin's mastery learning reconsidered. *Review of Educational Research, 57,* 507–508.

Bloom, B. S., Madaus, G. F., & Hastings, J. T. (1981). *Evaluation to improve learning.* New York: McGraw-Hill.

Bolles, R. C. (1974). Cognition and motivation: Some historical trends. In B. Weiner (Ed.), *Cognitive views of human motivation.* New York: Academic Press.

Borg, W. R. (Project Director). (1973). *Protocol materials.* University of Utah Protocol Project.

Boring, E. G. (1923). Intelligence as the tests test it. *New Republic, 35,* 35–37.

Borton, T. (1970). *Reach, touch, and teach: Student concerns and process education.* New York: McGraw-Hill.

Bossert, S. T. (1988). Cooperative activities in the classroom. In E. Z. Rothkopf (Ed.), *Review of research in education* (Vol. 15), Washington, D.C.: American Educational Research Association.

Bower, G. H. (1981). Mood and memory. *American Psychologist, 36,* 129–148.

Bradshaw, G. L., & Anderson, J. R. (1982). Elaborative encoding as an explanation of levels of processing. *Journal of Verbal Learning and Verbal Behavior, 21,* 165–174.

Brainerd, C. J., & Pressley, M. (Eds.). (1985). *Basic processes in memory development: Progress in cognitive development research.* New York: Springer-Verlag.

Brandon, P. R., Newton, B. J., & Hammond, O. W. (1987). Children's mathematics achievement in Hawaii: Sex differences favoring girls. *American Educational Research Journal, 24,* 437–461.

Bransford, J. D. (1979). *Human cognition: Learning, understanding and remembering.* Belmont, Calif.: Wadsworth.

Bransford, J. D., & Johnson, M. K. (1973). Consideration of some problems in comprehension. In W. G. Chase (Ed.), *Visual information processing* (pp. 383–438). New York: Academic Press.

Bransford, J., Sherwood, R., Vye, N., & Rieser, J. (1986). Teaching thinking and problem solving. *American Psychologist, 41,* 1078–1089.

Brantner, J. P., & Doherty, M. A. (1983). A review of timeout: A conceptual and methodological analysis. In S. Axelrod & J. Apsche (Eds.), *The effects of punishment on human behavior.* New York: Academic Press.

Braun, C. (1976). Teacher expectations: Socio-psychological dynamics. *Review of Educational Research, 46,* 185–213.

Bronfenbrenner, U. (1977). Is early intervention effective? In S. Cohen & T. J. Comiskey (Eds.), *Child development: Contemporary perspectives.* Itasca, Ill.: F. E. Peacock.

Brophy, J. E. (1981). Teacher praise: A functional analysis. *Review of Educational Research, 51* (1), 5–32.

Brophy, J. E. (1983). If only it were true: A response to Greer. *Educational Researcher, 12,* 10–12.

Brophy, J. E., & Evertson, C. M. (1974). *Process-product correlations in the Texas teacher effectiveness study: Final report.* Research Report No. 74-4. Austin, Tex.: Research and Development Center for Teacher Education, University of Texas.

Brophy, J. E., & Evertson, C. M. (1976). *Learning from teaching: A developmental perspective.* Boston: Allyn and Bacon.

Brophy, J. E., & Good, T. L. (1974). *Teacher-student relationships: Causes and consequences.* New York: Holt, Rinehart & Winston.

Bruch, C. B. (Ed.). (1981). *The faces and forms of creativity: Proceedings of the First National Conference on Creativity and the Gifted/Talented,* March 21–22, 1980, Houston, Texas. Ventura, Calif.: Ventura County Superintendent's Office.

Bruner, J. S. (1957a). On going beyond the information given. In *Contemporary approaches to cognition.* Cambridge, Mass.: Harvard University Press.

Bruner, J. S. (1957b). On perceptual readiness. *Psychological Review, 64,* 123–152.

Bruner, J. S. (1961a). The act of discovery. *Harvard Educational Review, 31,* 21–32.

Bruner, J. S. (1961b). *The process of education.* Cambridge, Mass.: Harvard University Press.

Bruner, J. S. (1966). *Toward a theory of instruction.* Cambridge, Mass.: Harvard University Press.

Bruner, J. S. (1973). Organization of early skilled action. *Child Development, 44,* 1–11.

Bruner, J. S. (1983). *Child's talk.* New York: Norton.

Bruner, J. S. (1985). Models of the learner. *Educational Researcher, 14,* 5–8.

Bruner, J. S., Goodnow, J. J., & Austin, G. A. (1956). *A study of thinking.* New York: Wiley.

Budoff, M., & Gottlieb, J. (1976). Special-class EMR children mainstreamed: A study of an aptitude (learning potential) × treatment interaction. *American Journal of Mental Deficiency, 81,* 1–11.

Burns, R. B. (1984). How time is used in elementary schools: The activity structure of classrooms. In L. W. Anderson (Ed.), *Time and school learning: Theory, research and practice.* London: Croom Helm.

Burns, R. B., & Anderson, L. W. (1987). The activity structure of lesson segments. *Curriculum Inquiry, 17,* 31–53.

Burt, C. L. (1958). The inheritance of mental ability. *American Psychologist, 13,* 1–15.

Calfee, R. (1981). Cognitive psychology and educational practice. In D. C. Berliner (Ed.), *Review of Research in Education* (Vol. 9). Washington, D.C.: American Educational Research Association.

Calfee, R. (1985). Computer literacy and book literacy: Parallels and contrasts. *Educational Researcher, 14,* 8–13.

Calfee, R., & Drum, P. (1986). Research on teaching reading. In M. C. Wittrock (Ed.), *Handbook of research on teaching* (3rd ed.). New York: Macmillan.

Cameron, A. W. (1956). *A guide to Eastern Canadian mammals.* Ottawa: Department of Northern Affairs and National Resources.

Carey, S. T. (1987). Reading comprehension in first and second languages of immersion and Francophone students. *Canadian Journal for Exceptional Children, 3,* 103–108.

Carment, O. W., & Miles, C. G. (1962). Resistance to extinction and rate of lever pulling as a function of percentage of reinforcement and number of acquisition trials. *Canadian Journal of Psychology, 64,* 249–252.

Carroll, J. B. (1963). A model of school learning. *Teachers College Record, 64,* 723–733.

Carroll, J. B. (1989). The Carroll model: A 25-year retrospective and prospective view. *Educational Researcher, 18* (1), 26–31.

Case, R. (1975). Gearing the demands of instruction to the developmental capacities of the learner. *Review of Educational Research, 45,* 59–87.

Case, R. (1985). *Intellectual development: A systematic reinterpretation.* New York: Academic Press.

Case, R., Haward, S., Lewis, M., & Hurst, P. (1988). Toward a neo-Piagetian theory of cognitive and emotional development. *Developmental Review, 8,* 1–51.

Cattell, R. B. (1971). *Abilities: Their structure, growth and action.* Boston: Houghton Mifflin.

Cermak, L. S., & Craik, F. I. (Eds.). (1979). *Levels of processing in human memory.* Hillsdale, N.J.: Erlbaum.

Chapman, J. W. (1988). Learning disabled children's self-concepts. *Review of Educational Research, 58,* 347–371.

Chi, M. T. H., & Glaser, R. (1980). The measurement of expertise: Analysis of the development of knowledge and skill as a basis for assessing achievement. In E. L. Baker & E. S. Quellmalz (Eds.), *Educational testing and evaluation: Design, analysis and policy.* Beverly Hills, Calif.: Sage.

Chomsky, N. (1957). *Syntactic structures.* The Hague: Mouton.

Chomsky, N. (1965). *Aspects of the theory of syntax.* Cambridge, Mass.: MIT Press.

Clarizio, H. F., & Yelon, S. L. (1974). Learning theory approaches to classroom management: Rationale and intervention techniques. In A. R. Brown & C. Avery (Eds.), *Modifying children's behavior: A book of readings.* Springfield, Ill.: Thomas.

Clark, B. (1983). *Growing up gifted: Developing the potential of children at home and at school* (2nd ed.). Columbus, Ohio: Merrill.

Clark, R. E. (1982). Antagonism between achievement and enjoyment in ATI studies. *Educational Psychology, 13,* 92–101.

Clawson, E. U., & Barnes, B. R. (1973). The effects of organizers on the learning of structured anthropology materials in the elementary grades. *Journal of Experimental Education, 42,* 11–15.

Coburn, P., Kelman, P., Roberts, N., Snyder, T. F. F., Watt, D. H., & Weiner, C. (1982). *Practical guide to computers in education.* Reading, Mass.: Addison-Wesley.

Cohen, D. K. (1972). Does IQ matter? *Current, 141,* 19–30.

Coladarci, A. P. (1956). The relevancy of educational psychology. *Educational Leadership, 13,* 489–492.

Colby, A., & Kohlberg, L. (1984). Invariant sequence and internal consistency in moral judgment stages. In W. M. Kurtines & J. L. Gewirtz (Eds.), *Morality, moral behavior, and moral development* (pp. 41–51). New York: Wiley.

Collins, W. A. (1983). Interpretation and inference in children's television viewing. In J. Bryant & D. R. Anderson (Eds.), *Children's understanding of television: Research on attention and comprehension.* New York: Academic Press.

Combs, A. W. (1965). *The professional education of teachers.* Boston: Allyn and Bacon.

Cook, T. D., Appleton, H., Conner, R. F., Shaffer, A., Tamkin, G., & Weber, S. J. (1975). *"Sesame Street" revisited.* New York: Russell Sage Foundation.

Coon, C. L. (1915). *North Carolina schools and academies.* Raleigh, N.C.: Edwards and Broughton.

Coopersmith, S. (1967). *The antecedents of self-esteem.* San Francisco: Freeman.

Copeland, W. D. (1987). Classroom management and student teachers' cognitive abilities: A relationship. *American Educational Research Journal, 24,* 219–236.

Corno, L., & Snow, R. E. (1986). Adapting teaching to individual differences among learners. In M. C. Wittrock (Ed.), *Handbook of research on teaching* (3rd ed.) (pp. 605–629). New York: Macmillan.

Côté, A. D. J. (1968). *Flexibility and conservation acceleration.* Unpublished Ph.D. dissertation, University of Alberta, Edmonton, Alberta, Canada.

Council for Exceptional Children. (1978). *The nation's commitment to the education of gifted and talented children and youth: Summary of findings from a 1977 survey of states and territories.* United States Office of Education, Office of Gifted and Talented. Reston, Va.: Council for Exceptional Children.

Craik, F. M., & Lockhart, R. S. (1972). Levels of processing: A framework for memory research. *Journal of Verbal Learning and Verbal Behavior, 11,* 671–684.

Cronbach, L. J., & Snow, R. E. (1977). *Aptitudes and Instructional Methods.* New York: Irvington.

Crooks, T. J. (1988). The impact of classroom evaluation practices on students. *Review of Educational Research, 58,* 438–481.

Crowder, N. A. (1961). Characteristics of branching programs. In D. P. Scannell (Ed.), *Conference on programed learning.* Lawrence: University of Kansas, Studies in Education.

Crowder, N. A. (1963). On the differences between linear and intrinsic programming. *Phi Delta Kappan, 44,* 250–254.

Cummins, J. (1986). Empowering minority students: A framework for intervention. *Harvard Educational Review, 56,* 18–36.

Cummins, J., & Swain, M. (1986). *Bilingualism in education: Aspects of theory, research and practice.* London: Taylor & Fry.

Dansereau, D. F. (1985). Learning strategy research. In J. W. Segal, S. F. Chipman, & R. Glaser (Eds.), *Thinking and learning skills* (pp. 1, 209–240). Hillsdale, N.J.: Erlbaum.

Dasen, P. R. (Ed.). (1977). *Piagetian psychology: Cross-cultural contributions.* New York: Gardner Press.

Deale, R. N. (1975). *Examinations bulletin 32: Assessment and testing in the secondary school.* London: Evans/Methuen.

Dean, C., & Whitlock, Q. (1983). *A handbook of computer based training.* London: Kogan Page.

Deaux, K. (1985). Sex and gender. *Annual Review of Psychology, 36,* 49–81.

de Bono, E. (1970). *Lateral thinking: A textbook of creativity.* London: Ward Lock Educational.

de Bono, E. (1976). *Teaching thinking.* London: Temple Smith.

de Charms, R. (1972). Personal causation training in the schools. *Journal of Applied Psychology, 2,* 95–113.

Dempter, F. N. (1985). Short-term memory development in childhood. In C. J. Brainerd & M. Pressley (Eds.), *Basic processes in memory development: Progress in cognitive development research.* New York: Springer-Verlag.

Dennison, G. (1969). *The lives of children: The Story of the First Street School.* New York: Random House (Vintage Books).

Derry, S. J., & Murphy, D. A. (1986). Designing systems that train learning ability: From theory to practice. *Review of Educational Research, 56,* 1–39.

Diaz, R. M. (1983). Thought and two languages: The impact of bilingualism on cognitive development. In E. W. Gordon (Ed.), *Review of Research in Education* (Vol. 10). Washington, D.C.: American Educational Research Association.

Doyle, W. (1979). Making managerial decisions in classrooms. In D. Duke (Ed.), *78th yearbook of the National Society for the Study of Education: Part 2. Classroom Management.* Chicago: University of Chicago Press.

Doyle, W. (1986). Classroom organization and management. In M. C. Wittrock (Ed.), *Handbook of research on teaching* (3rd ed.) (pp. 392–431). New York: Macmillan.

Drabman, R. S. (1976). Behavior modification in the classroom. In W. E. Craighead, A. E. Kazdin, & M. J. Mahoney (Eds.), *Behavior modification principles, issues, and applications*. Boston: Houghton Mifflin.

Dunn, L. M. (1968). Special education for the mildly retarded — Is much of it justifiable? *Exceptional Children, 35,* 5–22.

Dunn, R., & Griggs, S. A. (1988). *Learning styles: Quiet revolution in American secondary schools.* Reston, Va.: National Association of Secondary School Principals.

Durkin, K. (1985). *Television, sex roles and children: A developmental social psychological account.* Milton Keynes, Philadelphia: Open University Press.

Dweck, C. S. (1986). Motivational processes affecting learning. *American Psychologist, 41,* 1040–1048.

Edgerton, R. B. (1979). *Mental retardation.* Cambridge, Mass.: Harvard University Press.

Educational Testing Service. (1961). Judges disagree on qualities that characterize good writing. *ETS Development, 9,* 2.

Eisenberg-Berg, N. (1979). Development of children's prosocial moral judgment. *Developmental Psychology, 15,* 38–44.

Eisner, E. W. (1967). Educational objectives: Help or hindrance? *School Review, 75,* 250–260.

Eisner, E. W. (1982). An artistic approach to supervision. In T. J. Sergiovanni (Ed.), *Supervision of teaching* (ASCD 1982 Yearbook). Alexandria, Va.: Association for Supervision and Curriculum Development.

Elton, L. R. B., & Laurillard, D. M. (1979). Trends in research on student learning. *Studies in Higher Education, 4,* 87–102.

Engel, M. (1976). *Bear.* Toronto: McClelland and Stewart.

Ennis, R. H. (1976). An alternative to Piaget's conceptualization of logical competence. *Child Development, 47,* 903–919.

Ennis, R. H. (1978). Conceptualization of children's logical competence: Piaget's propositional logic and an alternative proposal. In L. S. Siegel & C. J. Brainerd (Eds.), *Alternatives to Piaget: Critical essays on the theory.* New York: Academic Press.

Epstein, H. T. (1978). Growth spurts during brain development: Implications for educational policy. In J. S. Chall & A. F. Minsky (Eds.), *Education and the brain.* Chicago: University of Chicago Press.

Erickson, F., & Mohatt, G. (1982). Cultural organization of participation structures in two classrooms of Indian students. In G. Spindler (Ed.), *Doing the ethnography of schooling.* New York: Holt, Rinehart & Winston.

Erlenmeyer-Kimling, L., & Jarvik, L. F. (1963). Genetics and intelligence: A review. *Science, 142,* 1477–1478.

Evertson, C. M., Anderson, L. M., & Brophy, J. E. (1978). *Texas junior high school study: Final report of process-outcome relationships.* Volume I, Research Report No. 4061. Austin: Research and Development Center for Teacher Education, University of Texas.

Ewer, R. F. (1973). *The carnivores.* Ithaca, N.Y.: Cornell University Press.

Feuerstein, R. (1979). *The dynamic assessment of retarded performers.* Baltimore: University Park Press.

Feuerstein, R. (1980). *Instrumental enrichment: An intervention program for cognitive modifiability.* Baltimore: University Park Press.

Fischer, K. W., & Silvern, L. (1985). Stages and individual differences in cognitive development. *Annual Review of Psychology, 36,* 613–648.

Fishkin, J., Keniston, K., & MacKinnon, C. (1973). Moral reasoning and political ideology. *Journal of Personality and Social Psychology, 27,* 109–119.

Flanders, N. A. (1970). *Analyzing teacher behavior.* Reading, Mass.: Addison-Wesley.

Flavell, J. H. (1985). *Cognitive development* (2nd ed.). Englewood Cliffs, N.J.: Prentice-Hall.

Fleming, M., & Chambers, B. (1983). Teacher-made tests: Windows on the classroom. In W. E. Hathaway (Ed.), *New directions for testing and measurement: Vol. 19. Testing in the schools.* San Francisco: Jossey-Bass.

Fodor, E. N. (1972). Delinquency and susceptibility to social influence among adolescents as a function of level of moral development. *Journal of Social Psychology, 86,* 257–260.

Fowler, H. (1965). *Curiosity and exploratory behavior.* New York: Macmillan.

Freeman, D. (1983). *Margaret Mead and Samoa.* Cambridge, Mass.: Harvard University Press.

Frick, W. B. (1971). *Humanistic psychology: Interviews with Maslow, Murphy, and Rogers.* Columbus, Ohio: Merrill.

Frisch, R. E., & Revelle, R. (1970). Height and weight at menarche and a hypothesis of critical body weights and adolescent events. *Science, 169,* 397.

Fuller, B., & Heyneman, S. P. (1989). Third world school quality: Current collapse, future potential. *Educational Researcher, 18,* 12–19.

Furth, H. G. (1970). *Piaget for teachers.* Englewood Cliffs, N.J.: Prentice-Hall.

Gabel, D. L., Kogan, M. H., & Sherwood, R. D. (1980). A summary of research in science education—1978. *Science Education, 64,* 429–568.

Gage, N. L. (1964). Theories of teaching. In E. R. Hilgard (Ed.), *Theories of learning and instruction: The sixty-third yearbook of the National Society for the Study of Education.* Chicago: University of Chicago Press.

Gagné, E. D. (1985). *The cognitive psychology of school learning.* Boston: Little, Brown.

Gagné, R. M. (1974). *Essentials of learning for instruction.* Hinsdale, Ill.: Dryden Press.

Gagné, R. M. (1977a). *The conditions of learning* (3rd ed.). New York: Holt, Rinehart & Winston.

Gagné, R. M. (1977b). Instructional programs. In M. H. Marx & M. E. Bunch (Eds.), *Fundamentals and applications of learning.* New York: Macmillan.

Gagné, R. M. (1985). *The conditions of learning* (4th ed.). New York: Holt, Rinehart & Winston.

Gagné, R. M., & Briggs, L. J. (1983). *Principles of instructional design* (3rd ed.). New York: Holt, Rinehart & Winston.

Gagné, R. M., & Dick, W. (1983). Instructional psychology. *Annual Review of Psychology, 34,* 261–295.

Gallagher, J. J. (1960). *Analysis of research on the education of gifted children.* State of Illinois: Office of the Superintendent of Public Instruction.

Galton, F. (1869). *Hereditary genius: An inquiry into its laws and consequences.* London: Macmillan.

Gardner, H. (1983). *Frames of mind: The theory of multiple intelligences.* New York: Basic Books.

Gelman, R. (1982). Basic numerical abilities. In R. J. Sternberg (Ed.), *Advances in the psychology of human intelligence* (Vol. 1). Hillsdale, N.J.: Erlbaum.

Gelman, R., Meck, E., & Merkin, S. (1986). Young children's numerical competence. *Cognitive Development, 1,* 1–29.

Genesee, F. (1983). Bilingual education of majority language children: The immersion experiments in review. *Applied Psycholinguistics, 4,* 1–46.

Genesee, F. (1985). Second language learning through immersion: A review of U.S. programs. *Review of Educational Research, 55,* 541–561.

Getzels, J. W., & Jackson, P. W. (1962). *Creativity and intelligence.* New York: Wiley.

Gilligan, C. (1982). *In a different voice: Psychological theory and women's development.* Cambridge, Mass.: Harvard University Press.

Gilligan, C., Kohlberg, L., Lerner, J., & Belenky, M. (1971). Moral reasoning about sexual dilemmas: The development of an interview and scoring system. *Technical Report of the President's Commission on Obscenity and Pornography* (Vol. 1). Washington, D.C.: U.S. Government Printing Office.

Ginsberg H., & Opper, S. (1979). *Piaget's theory of intellectual development* (2nd ed.). Englewood Cliffs, N.J.: Prentice-Hall.

Glaser, R., & Bassok, M. (1989). Learning theory and the study of instruction. In M. R. Rosenzweig & L. W. Porter (Eds.), *Annual review of psychology, 40,* 631–666.

Glass, A. L., Holyoak, K. J., & Santa, J. L. (1979). *Cognition.* Reading, Mass.: Addison-Wesley.

Glasser, W. (1969). *Schools without failure.* New York: Harper & Row.

Goldschmid, M. L., & Bentler, P. M. (1968). *Conservation concept diagnostic kit: Manual and keys.* San Diego, Calif.: Educational and Industrial Testing Service.

Goodenough, F. (1926). *Measurement of intelligence by drawings.* New York: Harcourt, Brace & World.

Gordon, T. (1974). *T.E.T.: Teacher effectiveness training.* New York: Peter H. Wyden.

Gordon, W. J. J. (1961). *Synectics: The development of creative capacity.* New York: Harper & Row.

Gould, S. J. (1981). *The mismeasure of man.* New York: Norton.

Gowin, D. B. (1981). *Educating.* Ithaca, N.Y.: Cornell University Press.

Grant, J. P. [Executive Director of the United Nation's Children's Fund (UNICEF)] (1986). *The state of the world's children: 1986.* New York: Oxford University Press.

Greene, J. C. (1985). Relationships among learning and attribution theory motivational variables. *American Educational Research Journal, 22,* 65–78.

Greenspoon, J. (1955). The reinforcing effect of two spoken sounds on the frequency of two responses. *American Journal of Psychology, 68,* 409–416.

Greer, R. D. (1983). Contingencies of the science and technology of teaching and prebehavioristic research practices in education. *Educational Researcher, 12,* 3–9.

Gregorc, A. F. (1982). *Gregorc style delineator: Development, technical and administrative manual.* Maynard, Mass.: Gabriel Systems.

Grippin, P. C., & Peters, S. C. (1984). *Learning theories and learning outcomes: The connection.* Lanham, Md.: University Press of America.

Gronlund, N. E. (1968). *Constructing achievement tests.* Englewood Cliffs, N.J.: Prentice-Hall.

Gronlund, N. E. (1972). *Stating behavioral objectives for classroom instruction.* New York: Macmillan.

Gronlund, N. E. (1975). *Determining accountability for classroom instruction.* Itasca, Ill.: F. E. Peacock.

Grossman, J. J. (Ed.). (1983). *Manual on terminology and classification in mental retardation, 1983 revision.* Washington, D.C.: American Association on Mental Deficiency.

Grotevant, H. D., Scarr, S., & Weinberg, R. A. (1977). Intellectual development in family constellations with adopted and natural children: A test of the Zajonc and Markus model. *Child Development, 48,* 1699–1703.

Guilford, J. P. (1950). Creativity. *American Psychologist, 5,* 444–454.

Guilford, J. P. (1959). Three faces of intellect. *American Psychologist, 14,* 469–479.

Guilford, J. P. (1962). Factors that aid and hinder creativity. *Teachers College Record, 63,* 380–392.

Guilford, J. P. (1967). *The nature of human intelligence.* New York: McGraw-Hill.

Gullickson, A. R. (1985). Student evaluation techniques and their relationship to grade and curriculum. *Journal of Educational Research, 79,* 96–100.

Gump, P. V. (1969). Intra-setting analysis: The third grade classroom as a special but instructive case. In E. Williams & H. Rausch (Eds.), *Naturalistic viewpoints in psychological research.* New York: Holt, Rinehart & Winston.

Guthrie, E. R. (1935). *The psychology of learning* (1st ed.). New York: Harper & Brothers.

Haddon, F. A., & Lytton, H. (1968). Teaching approach and the development of divergent thinking abilities in primary schools. *British Journal of Educational Psychology, 38,* 171–180.

Haefele, J. W. (1962). *Creativity and innovation.* New York: Reinhold.

Haertel, E. (1985). Construct validity and criterion-referenced testing. *Review of Educational Research, 55,* 23–46.

Hall, F. R., & Kelson, K. R. (1959). *The mammals of North America* (Vol. II). New York: Ronald Press.

Hallman, R. J. (1967). Techniques of creative teaching. *Journal of Creative Behavior, 1,* 325–330.

Haney, R. E., & Sorenson, J. S. (1977). *Individually guided science.* Reading, Mass.: Addison-Wesley.

Hargreaves, D. H., Hester, S. K., & Mellor, F. J. (1975). *Deviance in classrooms.* Boston: Routledge & Kegan Paul.

Harris, D. (1963). *Children's drawings as measures of intellectual maturity.* New York: Harcourt, Brace & World.

Harris, D., & Bell, C. (1986). *Evaluating and assessing for learning.* New York: Nichols (London: Kogan Page).

Hartshorne, H., & May, M. A. (1928–1930). *Studies in the nature of character: Studies in deceit* (Vol. 1), *Studies in self-control* (Vol. 2), *Studies in the organization of character* (Vol. 3). New York: Macmillan.

Hauser, R. M., & Sewell, W. H. (1985). Birth order and educational attainment in full sibships. *American Educational Research Journal, 22,* 1–23.

Haywood, H. C., & Switzky, H. N. (1986). The malleability of intelligence: Cognitive processes as a function of polygenic-experiential interaction. *School Psychology Review, 15,* 245–255.

Hebb, D. O. (1947). The effects of early experience on problem solving maturity. *American Psychologist, 2,* 306–307.

Hebb, D. O. (1955). Drive and the CNS (conceptual nervous system). *Psychological Review, 62,* 243–354.

Hebb, D. O. (1966). *A textbook of psychology* (2nd ed.). Philadelphia: Saunders.

Heckhausen, H., Schmalt, H., & Schneider, K. (1985). *Achievement motivation in perspective* (translated by M. Woodruff & R. Wicklund). New York: Academic Press.

Hembree, R. (1988). Correlates, causes, effects and treatment of test anxiety. *Review of Educational Research, 58,* 47–77.

Herbert, J. J., & Harsh, C. M. (1944). Observational learning by cats. *Journal of Comparative Psychology, 37,* 81–95.

Hewett, S. (1968). *The emotionally disturbed child in the classroom.* Boston: Allyn and Bacon.

Heyns, O. S. (1967, February 4). Treatment of the unborn. *Woman's Own*, p. 18.

Higbee, K. L. (1977). *Your memory: How it works and how to improve it.* Englewood Cliffs, N.J.: Prentice-Hall.

Hill, K. T., & Wigfield, A. (1984). Test anxiety: A major educational problem and what can be done about it. *Elementary School Journal, 85,* 105–126.

Hintzman, D. L., & Ludham, G. (1980). Differential forgetting of prototypes and old instances: Simulation by an exemplar-based classification model. *Memory and Cognition, 8,* 378–382.

Hoffman, M. L. (1970). Conscience, personality, and socialization techniques. *Human Development, 13,* 90–126.

Hoffman, M. L. (1976). Empathy, role-taking, guilt, and development of altruistic motives. In T. Lick (Ed.), *Moral development and behavior.* New York: Holt, Rinehart & Winston.

Hoge, R. D. (1988). Issues in the definition and measurement of the giftedness construct. *Educational Researcher, 17,* 12–66.

Holland, J. L., Magoon, T. M., & Spokane, A. R. (1981). Counseling psychology: Career interventions, research, and theory. In M. R. Rosenzweig & L. W. Porter (Eds.), *Annual review of psychology* (Vol. 32). Palo Alto, Calif.: Annual Reviews.

Holstein, C. B. (1976). Irreversible, stepwise sequence in the development of moral judgment: A longitudinal study of males and females. *Child Development, 47,* 51–61.

Holt, J. (1976). *Instead of education: Ways to help people do things better.* New York: Dutton.

Hopkins, K. D., & Stanley, J. C. (1981). *Educational and psychological measurement and evaluation* (6th ed.). Englewood Cliffs, N.J.: Prentice-Hall.

Horn, J. L. (1976). Human abilities: A review of research and theory in the early 1970s. In M. R. Rosenzweig & L. W. Porter (Eds.), *Annual review of psychology* (Vol. 27). Palo Alto, Calif.: Annual Reviews.

Horn, J. L., & Donaldson, G. (1980). Cognitive development in adulthood. In O. G. Brim, Jr., & J. Kagan (Eds.), *Constancy and change in human development.* Cambridge, Mass.: Harvard University Press.

Horner, M. (1969). Woman's will to fail. *Psychology Today, 3,* 36–38.

Horowitz, F. D., & O'Brien, M. (1986). Gifted and talented children: State of knowledge and directions for research. *American Psychologist, 41,* 1147–1152.

Horton, D. L., & Mills, C. B. (1984). Human learning and memory. *Annual Review of Psychology, 35,* 361–394.

Horwitz, R. A. (1979). Psychological effects of the open classroom. *Review of Educational Research, 49,* 71–86.

Humphreys, L. G. (1985). A conceptualization of intellectual giftedness. In F. D. Horowitz & M. O'Brien (Eds.), *The gifted and talented: Developmental perspectives* (pp. 331–360). Washington, D.C.: American Psychological Association.

Hunt, E. (1989). Cognitive science: Definition, status, and questions. *Annual Review of Psychology, 40,* 603–629.

Hunt, J. M. (1961). *Intelligence and experience.* New York: Ronald Press.

Intons-Peterson, M. J. (1988). *Gender concepts of Swedish and American youth.* Hillsdale, N.J.: Erlbaum.

Jacklin, C. N. (1989). Female and male: Issues of gender. *American Psychologist, 44,* 127–133.

James, W. (1890). *The principles of psychology.* New York: Holt, Rinehart & Winston.

Janos, P. M., & Robinson, N. M. (1985). Psychosocial development in intellectually gifted children. In F. D. Horowitz & M. O'Brien (Eds.), *The gifted and talented: Developmental perspectives* (pp. 149–195). Washington, D.C.: American Psychological Association.

Jensen, A. R. (1968). Social class, race and genetics: Implications for education. *American Educational Research Journal, 5,* 1–42.

Jensen, A. R. (1977). Cumulative deficit in IQ of blacks in the rural South. *Developmental Psychology, 13,* 184–191.

Johnson, D., & Johnson, R. (1975). *Learning together and alone.* Englewood Cliffs, N.J.: Prentice-Hall.

Johnson, D. W., Johnson, R. T., Holubec, E. J., & Roy, P. (1984). *Circles of learning: Cooperation in the classroom.* Alexandria, Va.: Association for Supervision and Curriculum Development.

Johnson, D. W., Maruyama, G., Johnson, R., Nelson, D., & Skon, L. (1981). Effects of cooperative, competitive and individualistic goal structures on achievement: A meta-analysis. *Psychological Bulletin, 89,* 47–62.

Justice, E. (1985). Categorization as a preferred memory strategy: Developmental changes during elementary school. *Developmental Psychology, 21,* 1105–1110.

Kaess, W., & Zeaman, D. (1960). Positive and negative knowledge of results on a Pressey-type punchboard. *Journal of Experimental Psychology, 60,* 12–17.

Kagan, D. M. (1988). Teaching as clinical problem solving: A critical examination of the analogy and its implications. *Review of Educational Research, 58,* 482–505.

Kalish, H. I. (1981). *From behavioral science to behavior modification.* New York: McGraw-Hill.

Kamii, C. (1972). A sketch of the Piaget-derived preschool curriculum developed by the Ypsilanti early education program. In S. J. Braun & E. Edwards (Eds.), *History and theory of early childhood education.* Worthington, Ohio: Charles A. Jones.

Kanchier, C. (1988). Maximizing potential of gifted and talented students through career education. *Agate, 2,* 6–13.

Kass, N., & Wilson, H. P. (1966). Resistance to extinction as a function of percentage of reinforcement, number of training trials, and conditioned reinforcement. *Journal of Experimental Psychology, 71,* 355–357.

Kaufman, K. F., & O'Leary, K. D. (1972). Reward, cost, and self-evaluation procedures with schizophrenic children. Unpublished manuscript, State University of New York. Cited in K. D. O'Leary & S. G. O'Leary. *Classroom management: The successful use of behavior modification.* New York: Pergamon Press.

Kavale, K., & Forness, S. (1985). *The science of learning disabilities.* San Diego, Calif.: College-Hill Press.

Kazdin, A. E., & Bootzin, R. R. (1972). The token economy: An evaluative review. *Journal of Applied Behavior Analysis, 5,* 343–372.

Kegan, R. (1982). *The evolving self: Problem and process in human development.* Cambridge, Mass.: Harvard University Press.

Keller, F. S. (1968). Good-bye teacher. . . . *Journal of Applied Behavior Analysis, 1,* 79–89.

Kellogg, W. N. (1968). Communication and language in the home-raised chimpanzee. *Science, 162,* 423–427.

Kelly, T. J., Bullock, L. M., & Dykes, M. K. (1977). Behavior disorders: Teachers' perceptions. *Exceptional Children, 43,* 316–318.

Kennedy, M. M. (1978). Findings from the follow-through planned variation study. *Educational Researcher.* Washington, D.C.: American Educational Research Association, 7, 3–11.

Kinsbourne, M., & Cook, J. (1971). Generalized and lateralized effects of concurrent verbalization on a unimanual skill. *Quarterly Journal of Experimental Psychology, 23,* 341–345.

Klausmeier, H. J., Rossmiller, R. A., and Saily, M. (1977). *Individually guided elementary education: Concepts and practices.* New York: Academic Press.

Koch, H. L. (1955). Some personality correlates of sex, sibling position, and sex of sibling among five- and six-year-old children. *Genetic Psychology Monographs, 52,* 3–50.

Koffka, K. (1935). *Principles of Gestalt psychology.* New York: Harcourt, Brace, & World.

Kogan, N. (1983). Stylistic variation in childhood and adolescence: Creativity, metaphor, and cognitive style. In P. H. Mussen (Ed.), *Handbook of child psychology* (4th ed.) (Vol. 3). *Cognitive Development* (J. H. Flavell & E. M. Markman, Eds.) (pp. 630–706). New York: Wiley.

Kohl, H. R. (1969). *The open classroom: A practical guide to a new way of teaching.* New York: Random House (Vintage Books).

Kohlberg, L. (1964). Development of moral character and moral ideology. In M. L. Hoffman & L. W. Hoffman (Eds.), *Review of child development research* (Vol. 1). New York: Russell Sage Foundation.

Kohlberg, L. (1971). Stages of moral development as a basis for moral education. In C. Beck, E. V. Sullivan, & B. Crittendon (Eds.), *Moral education: Interdisciplinary approaches.* Toronto: University of Toronto Press.

Kohlberg, L. (1980). *The meaning and measurement of moral development.* Worcester, Mass.: Clark University Press.

Kohlberg, L., & Candee, D. (1984). The relationship of moral judgment to moral action. In W. M. Kurtines & J. L. Gewirtz (Eds.), *Morality, moral behavior, and moral development* (pp. 52–73). New York: Wiley.

Kounin, J. S. (1970). *Discipline and classroom management.* New York: Holt, Rinehart & Winston.

Krathwohl, D. R., Bloom, B. S., & Masia, B. B. (1964). *Taxonomy of educational objectives, the classification of educational goals. Handbook II: Affective domain.* New York: McKay.

Krech, D., Rosenzweig, M., & Bennett, E. L. (1960). Effects of environmental complexity and training on brain chemistry. *Journal of Comparative and Physiological Psychology, 53,* 509–519.

Krech, D., Rosenzweig, M., & Bennett, E. L. (1962). Relations between brain chemistry and problem solving among rats raised in enriched and impoverished environments. *Journal of Comparative and Physiological Psychology, 55,* 801–807.

Krech, D., Rosenzweig, M., & Bennett, E. L. (1966). Environmental impoverishment, social isolation, and changes in brain chemistry and anatomy. *Physiology and Behavior, 1,* 99–104.

Kroth, R. L. (1985). *Communicating with parents of exceptional children: Improving parent-teacher relationships* (2nd ed.). Denver: Love Publishing.

Kulik, J. A., Kulik, C. C., & Cohen, P. A. (1979). A meta-analysis of outcome studies of Keller's Personalized System of Instruction. *American Psychologist, 34,* 307–318.

Kulik, J. A., Kulik, C. C., & Cohen, P. A. (1980). Effectiveness of computer-based college teaching: A meta-analysis of findings. *Review of Educational Research, 50,* 525–544.

Kurtines, W. M., & Gewirtz, J. L. (Eds.). (1987). *Moral development through social interaction.* New York: Wiley.

Labouvie-Vief, G. (1980). Beyond formal operations: Uses and limits of pure logic in life-span development. *Human Development, 23,* 141–161.

Labouvie-Vief, G. (1986). Modes of knowledge and the organization of development. In M. L. Commons, L. Kohlberg, F. A. Richards, & J. Sinnott (Eds.), *Beyond formal operations. 3: Models and methods in the study of adult and adolescent thought.* New York: Praeger.

Lambert, W. E. (1975). Culture and language as factors in learning and education. In A. Wolfgang (Ed.), *Education of immigrant students.* Toronto: Ontario Institute for Studies in Education.

Landry, R. (1987). Additive bilingualism, schooling, and special education: A minority group perspective. *Canadian Journal for Exceptional Children, 3,* 109–114.

Laurillard, D. (1988). Computers and the emancipation of students: Giving control to the learner. In P. Ramsden (Ed.), *Improving learning: New perspectives.* London: Kogan Page.

Lee, E. S. (1951). Negro intelligence and selective migration: A Philadelphia test of the Klineberg hypothesis. *American Sociological Review, 16,* 227–233.

Lefrançois, G. R. (1965). *Developing creativity in high school students.* Unpublished M. Ed. thesis, University of Saskatchewan, Saskatoon, Saskatchewan, Canada.

Lefrançois, G. R. (1966). *The acquisition of concepts of conservation.* Unpublished Ph.D. dissertation, University of Alberta, Edmonton, Alberta, Canada.

Lefrançois, G. R. (1968). A treatment hierarchy for the acceleration of conservation of substance. *Canadian Journal of Psychology, 22,* 277–284.

Lefrançois, G. R. (1982). *Psychological theories and human learning* (2nd ed.). Monterey, Calif.: Brooks/Cole.

Lefrançois, G. R. (1989). *Of children: An introduction to child development* (6th ed.). Belmont, Calif.: Wadsworth.

Lefrançois, G. R. (1990). *The lifespan* (3rd ed.). Belmont, Calif.: Wadsworth.

Leinhardt, B., & Greeno, J. G. (1986). The cognitive skill of teaching. *Journal of Educational Psychology, 78,* 75–95.

Lepper, M. R. (1981). Intrinsic and extrinsic motivation in children: Detrimental effects of superfluous social controls. In W. A. Collins (Ed.), *Aspects of the development of competence: The Minnesota Symposium on Child Psychology* (Vol. 14). Hillsdale, N.J.: Erlbaum.

Lepper, M. R., & Greene, D. (1975). Turning play into work: Effects of adult surveillance and extrinsic rewards on children's intrinsic motivation. *Journal of Personality and Social Psychology, 31,* 479–486.

Levin, B. (1983, March). Teachers and standardized achievement tests. *Canadian School Executive,* p. 11.

Levine, R. A. (1987). Women's schooling, patterns of fertility, and child survival. *Educational Researcher, 16,* 21–27.

Lewin, R. (1975, September). Starved brains. *Psychology Today,* pp. 29–33.

Linn, M. C. (1985). The cognitive consequences of programming instruction in classrooms. *Educational Researcher, 14,* 14–29.

Linn, R. L. (1986). Educational testing and assessment: Research needs and policy issues. *American Psychologist, 41,* 1153–1160.

Lockhead, J. (1985). New horizons in educational development. In E. W. Gordon (Ed.), *Review of research in education* (Vol. 12). Washington, D.C.: American Educational Research Association.

Loftus, E. F. (1979). *Eyewitness testimony*. Cambridge, Mass.: Harvard University Press.

Lorenz, K. (1952). *King Solomon's ring*. London: Methuen.

Lovell, K. (1968). *An introduction to human development*. London: Macmillan.

Lowe, L. L. (1983, January). Creative learning through fine arts. *ATA Magazine, 63,* 20–23.

Luria, A. R. (1968). *The mind of a mnemonist*. New York: Avon Books.

Lynch, E. W., Simms, B. H., von Hippel, C. S., & Shuchat, J. (1978). *Mainstreaming preschoolers: Children with mental retardation*. Washington, D.C.: Head Start Bureau: U.S. Government Printing Office.

Lynn, D. B. (1974). *The father: His role in child development*. Monterey, Calif.: Brooks/Cole.

Maccoby, E. E., & Jacklin, C. N. (1974). *The psychology of sex differences*. Palo Alto, Calif.: Stanford University Press.

MacKay, A. (1982). *Project Quest: Teaching strategies and pupil achievement*. Occasional Paper Series, Centre for Research in Teaching, Faculty of Education, University of Alberta, Edmonton, Alberta, Canada.

Macmillan, D. L., Keogh, B. K., & Jones, R. L. (1986). Special educational research on mildly handicapped learners. In M. C. Wittrock (Ed.), *Handbook of research on teaching* (3rd ed.) (pp. 686–724). New York: Macmillan.

Macmillan, D. L., & Meyers, C. E. (1979). Educational labeling of handicapped learners. In D. C. Berliner (Ed.), *Review of research in education* (Vol. 7). Washington, D.C.: American Educational Research Association.

Mager, R. F. (1962). *Preparing instructional objectives*. Palo Alto, Calif.: Fearon.

Maier, N. R. F. (1930). Reasoning in humans: I. On direction. *Journal of Comparative Psychology, 10,* 115–143.

Mandell, C. J., & Gold, V. (1984). *Teaching handicapped students*. St. Paul, Minn.: West.

Markle, S. M. (1964). *Good frames and bad: A grammar of frame writing*. New York: Wiley.

Markle, S. M. (1978). *Designs for instructional designers*. Champaign, Ill.: Stipes.

Markle, S. M., & Tiemann, P. W. (1974). Some principles of instructional design at higher cognitive levels. In R. Ulrich, T. Stachnik, & T. Mabry (Eds.), *Control of human behavior*. Glenview, Ill.: Scott, Foresman.

Marland, M. (1975). *The craft of the classroom: A survival guide to classroom management at the secondary school*. London: Heinemann Educational Books.

Marland, S. P. (1972). *Education of the gifted and talented*. Washington, D.C.: U.S. Government Printing Office.

Marquis, D. P. (1941). Learning in the neonate: The modification of behavior under three feeding schedules. *Journal of Experimental Psychology, 29,* 263–282.

Marshall, H., & Weinstein, R. (1984). Classroom factors affecting student's self-evaluations: An interactional model. *Review of Educational Research, 54,* 301–325.

Martin looks to close the gap in women's pay. (1989). *Edmonton Journal*, Friday, February 24, p. A1.

Marton, F., & Säljö, R. (1984). Approaches to learning. In F. Marton (and others) (Eds.), *The experience of learning*. Edinburgh: Scottish Academic Press.

Maslow, A. H. (1970). *Motivation and personality* (2nd ed.). New York: Harper & Row.

Matthews, L. H. (1969). *The Life of mammals* (Vol. I). New York: Universe Books.

Mayer, R. (1979). Can advance organizers influence meaningful learning? *Review of Educational Research, 49,* 371–383.

Mayer, R. E. (1981). *The promise of cognitive psychology*. San Francisco: Freeman.

Mayer, R. E. (1989). Models for understanding. *Review of Educational Research, 59,* 43–64.

McClelland, D. C. (1958). Risk taking in children with high and low need for achievement. In J. W. Atkinson (Ed.), *Motives in fantasy, action, and society*. Princeton, N.J.: Van Nostrand.

McClelland, D. C., Atkinson, J. W., Clark, R. A., & Lowell, E. L. (1953). *The achievement motive*. New York: Appleton-Century-Crofts.

McClelland, D. C., & Winter, D. G. (1969). *Motivating economic achievement*. New York: Free Press.

McCombs, B. L. (1982). Transitioning learning strategies research into practice: Focus on the student in technical training. *Journal of Instructional Development, 5,* 10–17.

McDougall, W. (1908). *An introduction to social psychology*. London: Methuen.

McKeachie, W. J. (1984). Does anxiety disrupt information processing or does poor information processing lead to anxiety? *International Review of Applied Psychology, 33,* 187–203.

McKeachie, W. J., Pintrich, P. R., & Lin, Y. G. (1985). Learning to learn. In F. d'Ydwelle (Ed.), *Cognition, information processing and motivation* (pp. 601–618). Amsterdam: Elsevier.

McMann, N., & Oliver, R. (1988). Problems in families with gifted children: Implications for counselors. *Journal of Counseling and Development, 66,* 275–278.

McPhail, P., Ungoed-Thomas, J. R., & Chapman, H. (1972). *Moral education in the secondary school*. London: Longmans.

Meacham, M. L., & Wiesen, A. E. (1969). *Changing classroom behavior: A manual for precision teaching*. Scranton, Penn.: International Textbook.

Mead, M. (1935). *Sex and temperament in three primitive societies*. New York: New American Library.

Means, V., Moore, J. W., Gagné, E., & Hauck, W. E. (1979). The interactive effects of consonant and dissonant teacher expectancy and feedback communication on student performance in a natural school setting. *American Educational Research Journal, 16,* 367–373.

Mednick, S. A. (1962). The associative basis of the creative process. *Psychological Review, 69,* 220–232.

Mercer, J. R. (1973). *Labeling the mentally retarded*. Berkeley: University of California Press.

Mercer, J. R. (1979). *System of Multicultural Pluralistic Assessment technical manual*. New York: Psychological Corporation.

Mercer, J. R., & Lewis, J. F. (1978). *System of Multicultural Pluralistic Assessment*. New York: Psychological Corporation.

Mercer, J. R., & Lewis, J. F. (1979). *System of Multicultural Pluralistic Assessment student assessment manual*. New York: Psychological Corporation.

Michael, J. (1967). *Management of behavioral consequences in education*. Inglewood, Calif.: Southwest Regional Laboratory for Educational Research and Development.

Milgram, S. (1963). Behavioral study of obedience. *Journal of Abnormal and Social Psychology, 67,* 371–378.

Miller, G. A. (1956). The magical number seven, plus or minus two: Some limits on our capacity for processing information. *Psychological Review, 63,* 81–97.

Mischel, W., & Baker, N. (1975). Cognitive appraisals and transformations in delay behavior. *Journal of Personality and Social Psychology, 31,* 254–261.

Mitchell, J. V., Jr. (Ed.). (1983). *Tests in print III: An index to tests, test reviews, and the literature on specific tests*. Lincoln, Neb.: Buros Institute of Mental Measurements, University of Nebraska Press.

Money, J., & Erhardt, A. A. (1972). *Man and woman, boy and girl: Differentiation and dimorphism of gender identity*. Baltimore: Johns Hopkins University Press.

Moore, K. D., & Hanley, P. E. (1982). An identification of elementary teacher needs. *American Educational Research Journal, 19,* 137–144.

Morsink, C. V. (1985). Learning disabilities. In W. H. Berdine & A. E. Blackhurst (Eds.), *An introduction to special education* (2nd ed.). Boston: Little, Brown.

Moynahan, E. O. (1973). The development of knowledge concerning the effects of categorization upon free recall. *Child Development, 44,* 238–245.

Mulcahy, R., Kofi, M., Peat, D., Andrews, J., & Clifford, L. (1986, Spring). Applying cognitive psychology in the classroom: A learning/thinking strategies instructional program. *Alberta Psychology.*

Mulcahy, R. F., Marfo, K., & Peat, D. (1985). *A strategies program for effective learning and thinking: A teacher's manual*. University of Alberta Cognitive Education Project, Edmonton.

Mulcahy, R. F., Peat, D., Andrews, J., Darko-Yeboah, J., & Marfo, K. (1990). Cognitive-based strategy instruction. In J. Biggs (Ed.), *Learning processes and teaching contexts*. Melbourne: Australian Council for Educational Research.

Murnane, R. J., Singer, J. D., & Willett, J. B. (1988). The career paths of teachers: Implications for teacher supply and methodological lessons for research. *Educational Researcher, 17,* 22–30.

Naglieri, J. A. (1988). *DAP; draw a person: A quantitative scoring system*. New York: Harcourt Brace Jovanovich.

Nagy, P., & Griffiths, A. K. (1982). Limitations of recent research relating Piaget's theory to adolescent thought. *Review of Educational Research, 52,* 513–556.

National Commission on Excellence in Education. (1983). *A nation at risk: The imperative for educational reform.* Washington, D.C.: U.S. Government Printing Office.

Nay, W. R., Schulman, J. A., Bailey, K. G., & Huntsinger, G. M. (1976). Territory and classroom management: An exploratory case study. *Behavior Therapy, 7,* 240–246.

Neisser, U. (1976). *Cognition and reality.* San Francisco: Freeman.

Newell, A., & Simon, H. A. (1972). *Human problem solving.* Englewood Cliffs, N.J.: Prentice-Hall.

Newman, H. H., Freeman, F. N., Holzinger, K. J. (1937). *Twins: A study of heredity and environment.* Chicago: The University of Chicago Press.

Nicholls, J. G. (1978). The development of the concepts of effort and ability, perception of academic attainment, and the understanding that difficult tasks require more ability. *Developmental Psychology, 49,* 800–814.

Nickerson, R. S. (1986). Why teach thinking? In J. B. Baron & R. J. Sternberg (Eds.), *Teaching thinking skills: Theory and practice.* New York: Freeman.

Nickerson, R. S. (1988). On improving thinking through instruction. In E. Z. Rothkopf (Ed.), *Review of research in education* (Vol. 15). Washington, D.C.: American Educational Research Association.

Nussbaum, J. (1979). Children's conception of the earth as a cosmic body: A cross age study. *Science Education, 63,* 83–93.

O'Banion, D. R., & Whaley, D. L. (1981). *Behavior contracting: Arranging contingencies of reinforcement.* New York: Springer.

Olds, J. (1956, October). Pleasure centers in the brain. *Scientific American.*

O'Leary, K. D., & Becker, W. C. (1967). Behavior modification of an adjustment class: A token reinforcement program. *Exceptional Children,* 637–642.

O'Leary, K. D., & Becker, W. C. (1968). The effects of a teacher's reprimands on children's behavior. *Journal of School Psychology, 7,* 8–11.

O'Leary, K. D., Kaufman, K. F., Kass, R. E., & Drabman, R. S. (1974). The effects of loud and soft reprimands on the behavior of disruptive students. In A. R. Brown & C. Avery (Eds.), *Modifying children's behavior: A book of readings.* Springfield, Ill.: Thomas.

Olson, D. R. (1985). Computers as tools of the intellect. *Educational Researcher, 14,* 5–7.

Osborn, A. (1957). *Applied imagination.* New York: Scribner.

Oser, F. K. (1986). Moral education and values education: The discourse perspective. In M. C. Wittrock (Ed.), *Handbook of research on teaching* (3rd ed.) (pp. 917–941). New York: Macmillan.

Page, E. B., & Grandon, G. M. (1979). Family configuration and mental ability: Two theories contrasted with U.S. data. *American Educational Research Journal, 16,* 257–272.

Pallas, A. M., Natriello, G., & McDill, E. L. (1989). The changing nature of the disadvantaged population: Current dimensions and future trends. *Educational Researcher, 18,* 16–22.

Palmares, U., & Logan, B. (1975). *A curriculum on conflict management.* Palo Alto, Calif.: Human Development Training Institute.

Papalia, D. F. (1972). The status of several conservative abilities across the life-span. *Human Development, 15,* 229–243.

Papert, S. (1980). *Mindstorms: Children, computers, and powerful ideas.* New York: Basic Books.

Papert, S. (1987). Computer criticism vs. technocentric thinking. *Educational Researcher, 16* (1), 22–30.

Parke, R. D. (1974). Rules, roles, and resistance to deviation: Recent advances in punishment, discipline, and self-control. In A. Pick (Ed.), *Minnesota Symposia on Child Psychology* (Vol. 8). Minneapolis: University of Minnesota Press.

Parloff, M. B., London, P., & Wolfe, B. (1986). Individual psychotherapy and behavior change. *Annual Review of Psychology, 37,* 321–349.

Parmelee, A. H., Jr., & Sigman, M. D. (1983). Perinatal brain development and behavior. In P. H. Mussen (Ed.), *Handbook of child psychology* (4th ed.) (Vol. 2). *Infancy and developmental psychobiology* (M. M. Haith & J. J. Campos, Eds.). New York: Wiley.

Parnes, S. J. (1962). Do you really understand brainstorming? In S. J. Parnes & H. F. Harding (Eds.), *A sourcebook for creative thinking.* New York: Scribner.

Parnes, S. J. (1967). *Creative behavior workbook.* New York: Scribner.

Parnes, S. J., & Harding, H. F. (Eds.). (1962). *A sourcebook for creative thinking.* New York: Scribner.

Parnes, S. J., Noller, R. B., & Biondi, A. M. (1977). *Guide to creative action* (rev. ed. of *Creative behavior guidebook*). New York: Scribner.

Parsons, J. B. (1983). The seductive computer: Can it be resisted? *ATA Magazine, 63,* 12–14.

Pazulinec, R., Meyerrose, M., & Sajwaj, T. (1983). Punishment via response cost. In S. Axelrod & J. Apsche (Eds.), *The effects of punishment on human behavior.* New York: Academic Press.

Peat, D., Mulcahy, R. F., & Darko-Yeboah, J. (1989). SPELT (Strategies Program for Effective Learning/Thinking): A description and analysis of instructional procedures. *Instructional Science, 18,* 95–118.

Perkins, M. R. (1982). Minimum competency testing: What? Why? Why not? *Educational Measurement Issues and Practice, 1,* 5–9.

Perry, R. (1966). *The world of the polar bear.* Seattle: University of Washington Press.

Peters, R. (1977). *The place of Kohlberg's theory in moral education.* Paper presented at the First International Conference on Moral Development and Moral Education, August 19–26, Leicester, England.

Peterson, P. L. (1977). Interactive effects of student anxiety, achievement orientation, and teacher behavior on student achievement and attitude. *Journal of Educational Psychology, 69,* 779–792.

Phillips, J. L. (1969). *The origins of intellect.* San Francisco: Freeman.

Piaget, J. (1932). *The moral judgment of the child.* London: Kegan Paul.

Piaget, J. (1957). *Logic and psychology.* New York: Basic Books.

Piaget, J. (1972). Intellectual development from adolescence to adulthood. *Human Development, 15,* 1–12.

Pinard, A., & Laurendeau, M. (1964). A scale of mental development based on the theory of Piaget: Description of a project (A. B. Givens, Trans.). *Journal of Research and Science Teaching, 2,* 253–260.

Pintrich, P. R., Cross, D. R., Kozma, R. B., & McKeachie, W. J. (1986). Instructional psychology. *Annual Review of Psychology, 37,* 611–651.

Popham, W. J. (1978). The case for criterion-referenced measurement. *Educational Research, 7,* 6–10.

Popham, W. J. (1981). *Modern educational measurement.* Englewood Cliffs, N.J.: Prentice-Hall.

Postman, N., & Weingartner, C. (1971). *The soft revolution.* New York: Delacorte Press.

Premack, D. (1965). Reinforcement theory. In D. Levine (Ed.), *Nebraska Symposium on Motivation.* Lincoln: University of Nebraska Press.

Purkey, W. W. (1984). *Inviting school success: A self-concept approach to teaching and learning* (2nd ed.). Belmont, Calif.: Wadsworth.

Ramsden, P. (Ed.). (1988a). *Improving learning: New perspectives.* London: Kogan Page.

Ramsden, P. (1988b). Studying learning: Improving teaching. In P. Ramsden (Ed.), *Improving learning: New perspectives.* London: Kogan Page.

Raphael, B. (1976). *The thinking computer: Mind inside matter.* San Francisco: Freeman.

Reese, H. W., & Overton, W. F. (1970). Models and theories of development. In L. R. Goulet & P. B. Baltes (Eds.), *Lifespan developmental psychology: research and theory.* New York: Academic Press.

Renzulli, J. S. (1977). *The enrichment triad model: A guide for developing defensible programs for the gifted and talented.* Mansfield Center, Conn.: Creative Learning Press.

Renzulli, J. S. (1986). The three-ring conception of giftedness: A developmental model for creative productivity. In R. J. Sternberg & J. E. Davidson (Eds.), *Conceptions of giftedness.* Cambridge: Cambridge University Press.

Renzulli, J. S., Reis, S. M., & Smith, L. H. (1981). *The revolving door identification model.* Mansfield Center, Conn.: Creative Learning Press.

Renzulli, J. S., & Smith, L. H. (1978). *The learning styles inventory: A measure of student preference for instructional techniques.* Mansfield Center, Conn.: Creative Learning Press.

Resnick, L. B. (1981). Instructional psychology. *Annual Review of Psychology, 32,* 659–704.

Rhoades, J., & McCabe, M. E. (1985). *Simple cooperation in the classroom.* Willits, Calif.: ITA Publications.

Riegel, K. F. (1973). Dialectic operations: The final period of cognitive development. *Human Development, 16,* 346–370.

Robin, A. L. (1976). Behavioral instruction in the college classroom. *Review of Educational Research, 46,* 313–354.

Rogers, C. R. (1951). *Client-centered therapy: Its current practice, implications and theory*. Boston: Houghton Mifflin.

Rogers, C. R. (1969). *Freedom to learn*. Columbus, Ohio: Merrill.

Rogers, C. R., & Skinner, B. F. (1956). Some issues concerning the control of human behavior: A symposium. *Science, 124*, 1057–1066.

Rolison, M. A., & Medway, F. J. (1985). Teachers' expectations and attributions for student achievement: Effects of label, performance pattern, and special education intervention. *American Educational Research Journal, 22*, 561–573.

Rosenshine, B., & Stevens, R. (1986). Teaching functions. In M. C. Wittrock (Ed.), *Handbook of research on teaching* (3rd ed.). New York: Macmillan.

Rosenthal, R. (1987). Pygmalion effects: Existence, magnitude, and social importance. A reply to Wineburg. *Educational Researcher, 16*, 37–41.

Rosenthal, R., & Jacobson, L. (1968a). *Pygmalion in the classroom: Teacher expectations and pupils' intellectual development*. New York: Holt, Rinehart & Winston.

Rosenthal, R., & Jacobson, L. (1968b). Teacher expectations for the disadvantaged. *Scientific American*, April.

Rosenzweig, M. R., & Leiman, A. L. (1982). *Physiological psychology*. Lexington, Mass.: Heath.

Ross, A. O. (1976). *Psychology aspects of learning disabilities and reading disorders*. New York: McGraw-Hill.

Ross, R. P. (1984). Classroom segments: The structuring of school time. In L. W. Anderson (Ed.), *Time and school learning: Theory, research and practice*. London: Croom Helm.

Ross, S. M., Rakow, E. A., & Bush, A. J. (1980). Instructional adaptation for self-managed learning systems. *Journal of Educational Psychology, 72*, 312–320.

Rubin, K. H., Attewell, P. W., Tierney, M. C., & Tumolo, P. (1973). Development of spatial egocentrism and conservation across the life-span. *Developmental Psychology, 9*, 432.

Russell, J. A., & Ward, L. M. (1982). Environmental psychology. In M. R. Rosenzweig & L. W. Porter (Eds.), *Annual review of psychology* (Vol. 33). Palo Alto, Calif.: Annual Reviews.

Ryan, K., & Cooper, J. M. (1988). *Those who can, teach* (5th ed.). Boston: Houghton Mifflin.

Salomon, G., & Gardner, H. (1986). The computer as educator: Lessons from television research. *Educational Researcher, 15*, 13–19.

Sarason, I. G. (1959). Intellectual and personality correlates of test anxiety. *Journal of Abnormal and Social Psychology, 59*, 272–275.

Sarason, I. G. (1961). Test anxiety and intellectual performance. *Journal of Educational Psychology, 52*, 201–206.

Sarason, I. G. (1972). Experimental approaches to test anxiety: Attention and the uses of information. In C. D. Spielberger (Ed.), *Anxiety: Current trends in theory and research* (Vol. II). New York: Academic Press.

Sarason, I. G. (1980). Introduction to the study of test anxiety. In I. G. Sarason (Ed.), *Test anxiety: Theory, research, and applications*. Hillsdale, N.J.: Erlbaum.

Satir, V. (1972). *Peoplemaking*. Palo Alto, Calif.: Science and Behavior Books.

Sattler, J. M. (1982). *Assessment of children's intelligence and special abilities* (2nd ed.). Boston: Allyn and Bacon.

Savell, J. M., Twohig, P. T., & Rachford, D. L. (1986). Empirical status of Feuerstein's "Instrumental Enrichment" (FIE) technique as a method of teaching thinking skills. *Review of Educational Research, 56*, 381–409.

Scanlon, R., Weinberger, J. A., & Weiler, J. (1970). IPI as a functioning model for the individualization of instruction. In C. M. Lindvall & R. C. Cox (Eds.), *Evaluation as a tool in curriculum development: The IPI evaluation program*. AERA Monograph Series No. 5. Chicago: Rand McNally.

Schank, R. C., & Abelson, R. P. (1977). *Scripts, plans, goals and understanding*. Hillsdale, N.J.: Erlbaum.

Schniedewind, N., & Davidson, E. (1988). *Cooperative learning, cooperative lives: A sourcebook of learning activities for building a peaceful world*. Dubuque, Iowa: Wm. C. Brown.

Schultz, D. P. (1964). *Panic behavior*. New York: Random House.

Schunk, D. H. (1984). Self-efficacy perspective on achievement behavior. *Educational Psychologist, 19*, 48–58.

Sears, R. R., Maccoby, E. P., & Lewin, H. (1957). *Patterns of child rearing*. Evanston, Ill.: Row, Peterson.

Semmel, M. I., Gottlieb, J., & Robinson, N. M. (1979). Mainstreaming: Perspectives on educating handicapped children in public school. In D. C. Berliner (Ed.), *Review of research in education* (Vol. 7) (pp. 223–281). Washington, D.C.: American Educational Research Association.

Seymour, D. (1971, November). Black children, black speech. *Commonweal, 19.*

Shapiro, A. K. (1960). A contribution to a history of the placebo effect. *Behavioral Science, 5,* 109–135.

Sharan, S., & Shachar, H. (1988). *Language and learning in the cooperative classroom.* New York: Springer-Verlag.

Shepard, L. A. (1979). Norm-referenced vs. criterion-referenced tests. *Educational Horizons, 58,* 26–32.

Shepard, L. A., & Kreitzer, A. E. (1987). The Texas teacher test. *Educational Researcher, 16,* 22–31.

Shepard, L. A., Smith, M. L., & Vojir, C. P. (1983). Characteristics of pupils identified as learning disabled. *American Educational Research Journal, 20,* 309–331.

Shepherd-Look, D. L. (1982). Sex differentiation and the development of sex roles. In B. B. Wolman and others (Eds.), *Handbook of developmental psychology.* Englewood Cliffs, N.J.: Prentice-Hall.

Shirley, M. (1933). *The first two years: A study of twenty-five babies.* Vol. II of *Intellectual Development. Institute of Child Welfare Monographs* (Series No. 7). Minneapolis: University of Minnesota Press.

Shuell, T. J. (1986). Cognitive conceptions of learning. *Review of Educational Research, 56,* 411–436.

Shulman, L. S. (1986). Paradigms and research programs in the study of teaching. In M. C. Wittrock (Ed.), *Handbook of research on teaching* (3rd ed.). New York: Macmillan.

Siegel, M. G. (1987). *Psychological testing from early childhood through adolescence: A developmental and psychodynamic approach.* Madison, Conn.: International Universities Press.

Siegler, R. S. (1989). Mechanisms of cognitive development. *Annual Review of Psychology, 40,* 353–379.

Silvernail, D. L. (1979). *Teaching styles as related to student achievement.* Washington, D.C.: National Education Association.

Simon, H. A. (1980). Cognitive science: The newest science of the artificial. *Cognitive Science, 4,* 33–46.

Simon, S. B., Howe, L. W., & Kirschenbaum, H. (1972). *Values clarification: A handbook of practical strategies for teachers and students.* New York: Hart.

Simpson, E. L., & Gray, M. A. (1976). *Humanistic education: An interpretation.* Cambridge, Mass.: Ballinger.

Skinner, B. F. (1948). *Walden II.* New York: Macmillan.

Skinner, B. F. (1953). *Science and human behavior.* New York: Macmillan.

Skinner, B. F. (1954). The science of learning and the art of teaching. *Harvard Educational Review, 24,* 86–97.

Skinner, B. F. (1955). *Transcripts of New York Academy of Science, 17.*

Skinner, B. F. (1961). *Cumulative record* (rev. ed.). New York: Appleton-Century-Crofts.

Skinner, B. F. (1965, October 16). Why teachers fail. *Saturday Review,* pp. 80–81, 98–102.

Skinner, B. F. (1968). *The technology of teaching.* New York: Appleton-Century-Crofts.

Skinner, B. F. (1971). *Beyond freedom and dignity.* New York: Knopf.

Slavin, R. E. (1980). Cooperative learning. *Review of Educational Research, 50,* 315–342.

Slavin, R. E. (1987). Mastery learning reconsidered. *Review of Educational Research, 57,* 175–213.

Slavin, R., Sharan, S., Kagan, S., Hertz-Lazarowitz, R., Webb, C., & Schmuck, R. (Eds.). (1985). *Learning to cooperate, cooperating to learn.* New York: Plenum.

Smedslund, J. (1961a). The acquisition of conservation of substance and weight in children. I. Introduction. *Scandinavian Journal of Psychology, 2,* 11–20.

Smedslund, J. (1961b). The acquisition of conservation of substance and weight in children. II. External reinforcement of conservation of weight and of operations of addition and subtraction. *Scandinavian Journal of Psychology, 2,* 71–84.

Smedslund, J. (1961c). The acquisition of conservation of substance and weight in children. III. Extension of conservation of weight acquired normally and by means of empirical controls on a balance scale. *Scandinavian Journal of Psychology, 2,* 85–87.

Smedslund, J. (1961d). The acquisition of conservation of substance and weight in children. IV. An attempt at extension of visual components of the weight concept. *Scandinavian Journal of Psychology, 2,* 153–155.

Smedslund, J. (1961e). The acquisition of conservation of substance and weight in children. V. Practice in conflict situations without external reinforcement. *Scandinavian Journal of Psychology, 2,* 156–160.

Snow, R. E. (1977). Research on aptitudes: A progress report. In L. S. Shulman (Ed.), *Review of research in education.* Vol. 4. Washington, D.C.: American Educational Research Association.

Snow, R. E., & Lohman, D. F. (1984). Toward a theory of cognitive aptitude for learning from instruction. *Journal of Educational Psychology, 76,* 347–376.

Solomon, D., Watson, M. S., Delucchi, K. L., Schaps, E., & Battistich, V. (1988). Enhancing children's prosocial behavior in the classroom. *American Educational Research Journal, 25,* 527–544.

Sonnier, I. L. (Ed.). (1985). *Methods and techniques of holistic education.* Springfield, Ill.: Thomas.

Soper, J. D. (1964). *The mammals of Alberta.* Edmonton, Alberta: Hamly Press.

Southern, H. N. (1964). *The handbook of British mammals.* Oxford: Blackwell Scientific Publications.

Spearman, C. E. (1927). *The abilities of man.* New York: Macmillan.

Stahl, L. (1983). Kids, careers, and computers. *Canadian School Executive, 3,* 17–19.

Stallings, J. A., & Stipek, D. (1986). Research on early childhood and elementary school teaching programs. In M. C. Wittrock (Ed.), *Handbook of research on teaching* (3rd ed.) (pp. 727–753). New York: Macmillan.

Standing, L. (1973). Learning 10,000 pictures. *Quarterly Journal of Experimental Psychology, 25,* 207–222.

Stanley, J. C. (1976). The case for extreme educational acceleration of intellectually brilliant youths. *Gifted Child Quarterly, 20,* 66–75.

Sternberg, R. J. (1983). Criteria for intellectual skills training. *Educational Researcher, 12,* 6–12.

Sternberg, R. J. (1984a). A contextualist view of the nature of intelligence. *International Journal of Psychology, 19,* 307–334.

Sternberg, R. J. (1984b). Mechanisms of cognitive development: A componential approach. In R. J. Sternberg (Ed.), *Mechanisms of cognitive development.* San Francisco: Freeman.

Sternberg, R. J. (1984c). What should intelligence tests test? Implications of a triarchic theory of intelligence for intelligence testing. *Educational Researcher, 13,* 5–15.

Sternberg, R. J. (1985). *Beyond IQ: A triarchic theory of human intelligence.* New York: Cambridge University Press.

Sternberg, R. J. (1986). *Intelligence applied: Understanding and increasing your intellectual skills.* New York: Harcourt Brace Jovanovich.

Stevens, S. H. (1984). *Classroom success for the learning disabled.* Winston-Salem, N.C.: John F. Blair.

Steward, A. J. (Ed.). (1982). *Motivation and society.* San Francisco: Jossey-Bass.

Stipek, D. J. (1988). *Motivation to learn: From theory to practice.* Englewood Cliffs, N.J.: Prentice-Hall.

Stodolsky, S. S. (1984). Frameworks for studying instructional processes in peer work-groups. In P. L. Peterson, L. C. Wilkinson, & M. Hallinan (Eds.), *The social context of instruction.* New York: Academic Press.

Sullivan, E. V. (1977). *A study of Kohlberg's structural theory of moral development: A critique of liberal social science ideology.* Unpublished manuscript, Ontario Institute for Studies in Education, Toronto, Ontario.

Sullivan, E. V., & Quarter, J. (1972). Psychological correlates of certain postconventional moral types: A perspective on hybrid types. *Journal of Personality, 40*(2), 149–161.

Suls, J., & Kalle, R. J. (1979). Children's moral judgments as a function of intention, damage, and an actor's physical harm. *Developmental Psychology, 15,* 93–94.

Swing, S. R., & Peterson, P. L. (1982). The relationship of student ability and small-group interaction to student achievement. *American Educational Research Journal, 19,* 259–274.

Tavris, C., & Baumgartner, A. I. (1983). How would your life be different if you'd been born a boy? *Redbook,* 99.

Taylor, C. W., & Holland, J. W. (1964). Development and application of tests of creativity. *Review of Educational Research, 33,* 91–102.

Terman, L. M., & Merrill, M. A. (1960). *Stanford-Binet intelligence scale.* Boston: Houghton Mifflin.

Terman, L. M., et al. (1925). *Genetic studies of genius. The mental and physical traits of a thousand gifted children* (Vol. 1). Stanford, Calif.: Stanford University Press.

Thomas, J. W. (1980). Agency and achievement: Self-management and self-regard. *Review of Educational Research, 50,* 213–240.

Thomas, R. M. (1985). *Comparing theories of child development* (2nd ed.). Belmont, Calif.: Wadsworth.

Thorndike, E. L. (1911). *Animal intelligence.* New York: Macmillan.

Thorndike, E. L. (1913). *The psychology of learning.* New York: Teachers College.

Thorndike, E. L. (1931). *Human learning.* New York: Appleton-Century-Crofts.

Thorndike, E. L. (1932). Reward and punishment in animal learning. *Comparative Psychology Monographs, 8* (No. 39).

Thorndike, E. L. (1933). A proof of the law of effect. *Science, 77,* 173–175.

Thorndike, E. L. (1935). *The psychology of wants, interests, and attitudes.* New York: Appleton-Century-Crofts.

Thorndike, E. L. (1949). *Selected writings from a connectionist's psychology.* New York: Appleton-Century-Crofts.

Thorndike, R. L., & Hagen, E. (1977). *Measurement and evaluation in psychology and education* (4th ed.). New York: Wiley.

Thorndike, R. L., Hagen, E., & Sattler, J. M. (1985). *Revised Stanford-Binet intelligence scale* (4th ed.). Boston, Mass.: Houghton Mifflin.

Thurstone, L. L. (1938). Primary mental abilities. *Psychometric Monographs.* Chicago: University of Chicago Press (No. 1).

Tittle, C. K. (1982). Career counseling in contemporary U.S. high schools: An addendum to Rehberg and Hotchkiss. *Educational Researcher, 11,* 12–18.

Tobias, S. (1982, January). Sexist equation. *Psychology Today,* pp. 14–17.

Toffler, A. (1970). *Future shock.* New York: Random House.

Toffler, A. (1980). *The third wave.* New York: Morrow.

Torrance, E. P. (1962). *Guiding creative talent.* Englewood Cliffs, N.J.: Prentice-Hall.

Torrance, E. P. (1966). *Torrance tests of creative thinking (Norms technical manual).* Princeton, N.J.: Personnel Press.

Torrance, E. P. (1974). *Torrance tests of creative thinking.* Lexington, Mass.: Ginn.

Torrance, E. P. (1984). *Mentor relationships: How they aid creative achievement, endure, change, and die.* Buffalo, N.Y.: Bearly Limited.

Torrance, E. P. (1986). Teaching creative and gifted learners. In M. C. Wittrock (Ed.), *Handbook of research on teaching* (3rd ed.) (pp. 630–647). New York: Macmillan.

Tryon, G. S. (1980). The measurement and treatment of text anxiety. *Review of Educational Research, 50,* 343–372.

Tryon, R. C. (1940). Genetic differences in maze learning in rats. *Yearbook of the National Society for Studies in Education, 39,* 111–119.

Tsang, M. C. (1988). Cost analysis for educational policymaking: A review of cost studies in education in developing countries. *Review of Educational Research, 58,* 181–230.

Turiel, F. (1974). Conflict in transition in adolescent moral development. *Child Development, 45,* 14–29.

Turner, R. L., & Denny, D. A. (1969, February). Teacher characteristics, teacher behavior, and changes in pupil creativity. *Elementary School Journal,* pp. 265–270.

Tyler, L. E. (1965). *The psychology of human differences* (3rd ed.). New York: Appleton-Century-Crofts.

Ukrainian famine survivors recall season in hell. (1983). *Edmonton Journal,* October 20, p. A1.

Ulrich, R. E., & Azrin, N. H. (1962). Reflexive fighting in response to aversive stimulation. *Journal of Experimental Analysis of Behavior, 5,* 511–521.

U.S. Bureau of the Census. (1988). *Statistical abstracts of the United States* (108th Edition), 1987. Washington, D.C.: U.S. Government Printing Office.

U.S. Department of Education. (1986). *What works: Research about teaching and learning.* Pueblo, Colo.: Consumer Information Center.

U.S. Department of Labor. (1988). *Employment and earnings* (G. P. Green & R. K. Epstein, Eds.), Vol. 35, No. 11, November, 1988. Washington, D.C.: Bureau of Labor Statistics.

U.S. Office of Education. (1977, August 23). Implementation of part B of the Education of the Handicapped Act. *Federal Register, 42,* 42474–42518.

Uzgiris, I. C., & Hunt, J. (1975). *Assessment in infancy: Ordinal scales of psychological development*. Urbana: University of Illinois Press.

Van Houten, R., & Doleys, D. M. (1983). Are social reprimands effective? In S. Axelrod & J. Apsche (Eds.), *The effects of punishment on human behavior*. New York: Academic Press.

Van Houten, R., Nau, P. A., MacKenzie-Keating, S., Sameoto, D., & Colavecchia, B. (1982). An analysis of some variables influencing the effectiveness of reprimands. *Journal of Applied Behavior Analysis, 15,* 65–83.

Velandia, W., Grandon, G. M., & Page, E. B. (1978). Family size, birth order, and intelligence in a large South American sample. *American Educational Research Journal, 15,* 399–416.

Vernon, P. E. (1969). *Intelligence and cultural environment*. London: Methuen.

Vygotsky, L. S. (1962). *Thought and language* (E. Hamsman and G. Vankan, Eds. and Trans.). Cambridge, Mass.: MIT Press.

Vygotsky, L. S. (1986). *Thought and language* (translated and revised by A. Kozulin). Cambridge, Mass.: MIT Press.

Waddington, C. H. (1975). *The evolution of an evolutionist*. Edinburgh: Edinburgh University Press.

Wagner, R. K., & Sternberg, R. J. (1984). Alternative conceptions of intelligence and their implications for education. *Review of Educational Research, 54,* 179–223.

Walberg, H. J. (1986). Syntheses of research on teaching. In M. C. Wittrock (Ed.), *Handbook of research on teaching* (3rd ed.). New York: Macmillan.

Walker, D. F., & Schaffarzick, J. (1974). Comparing curricula. *Review of Educational Research, 44,* 83–111.

Walker, H. (1979). *The acting-out child: Coping with classroom disruption*. Boston: Allyn and Bacon.

Wallach, M. A. (1985). Creativity testing and giftedness. In F. D. Horowitz & M. O'Brien (Eds.), *The gifted and talented: Developmental perspectives* (pp. 99–123). Washington, D.C.: American Psychological Association.

Wallach, M. A., & Kogan, N. (1965). *Modes of thinking in young children: A study of the creativity-intelligence distinction*. New York: Holt, Rinehart & Winston.

Walters, G. C., & Grusec, J. E. (1977). *Punishment*. San Francisco: Freeman.

Walters, R. H., & Llewellyn, T. E. (1963). Enhancement of punitiveness by visual and audiovisual displays. *Canadian Journal of Psychology, 17,* 244–255.

Walters, R. H., Llewellyn, T. E., & Acker, W. (1962). Enhancement of punitive behavior by audiovisual displays. *Science, 136,* 872–873.

Watson, J. B. (1913). Psychology as the behaviorist views it. *Psychological Review, 20,* 157–158.

Watson, J. B. (1916). The place of a conditioned reflex in psychology. *Psychological Review, 23,* 89–116.

Watson, J. B. (1930). *Behaviorism* (2nd ed.). Chicago: University of Chicago Press.

Weber, E. (1970). *Early childhood education: Perspectives on change*. Belmont, Calif.: Wadsworth.

Webster, S. W. (1968). *Discipline in the classroom: Basic principles and problems*. New York: Chandler.

Wechsler, D. (1958). *The measurement and appraisal of adult intelligence* (4th ed.). Baltimore: Williams & Wilkins.

Weikart, D. P., et al. (1969, September). *Ypsilanti-Carnegie infant education project: Progress report*. Ypsilanti, Mich.: Department of Research and Development, Ypsilanti Public Schools.

Weinberg, R. (1989). Intelligence and IQ. *American Psychologist, 44,* 98–104.

Weiner, B. (Ed.). (1974). *Cognitive views of human motivation*. New York: Academic Press.

Weiner, B. (1980a). *Human motivation*. New York: Holt, Rinehart & Winston.

Weiner, B. (1980b). The role of affect in rational (attributional) approaches to human motivation. *Educational Researcher, 9,* 4–11.

Weiner, B. (1984). Principles for a theory of student motivation and their application within an attributional framework. In R. Ames & C. Ames (Eds.), *Research on motivation in education* (Vol I): *Student motivation*. New York: Academic Press.

Weinstein, C. F., & Mayer, R. F. (1986). The teaching of learning strategies. In M. C. Wittrock (Ed.), *Handbook of research on teaching* (3rd ed.) (pp. 315–327). New York: Macmillan.

Wertsch, J. V. (1985). *Vygotsky and the social formation of mind*. Cambridge, Mass.: Harvard University Press.

West, L. (1988). Implications of recent research for improving secondary school science learning. In P. Ramsden (Ed.), *Improving learning: New perspectives*. London: Kogan Page.

West, L. W., & MacArthur, R. S. (1964). An evaluation of selected intelligence tests for two samples of Metis and Indian children. *Alberta Journal of Education Research, 10,* 17–27.

Whelan, R. J. (1978). *The emotionally disturbed.* In E. L. Meyen (Ed.), *Exceptional children and youth: An introduction.* Denver: Love Publishing.

White, M. A. (1975). Natural rates of teacher approval and disapproval in the classroom. *Journal of Applied Behavior Analysis, 8,* 367–372.

White, R. T., & Tisher, R. P. (1986). Research on natural sciences. In M. C. Wittrock (Ed.), *Handbook of research on teaching* (3rd ed.). New York: Macmillan.

White, R. W. (1959). Motivation reconsidered: The concept of competence. *Psychological Review, 66,* 297–333.

Whitener, E. M. (1989). A meta-analytic review of the effect on learning of the interaction between prior achievement and instructional support. *Review of Educational Research, 59,* 65–86.

Wielkiewicz, R. M. (1986). *Behavior management in the schools: Principles and procedures.* New York: Pergamon Press.

Wiersma, W., & Jurs, S. G. (1985). *Educational measurement and testing.* Boston: Allyn and Bacon.

Wigdor, A. K., & Garner, W. R. (Eds.). (1982). *Ability testing: Uses, consequences, and controversies, Part I: Report of the Committee.* Washington, D.C.: National Academy Press.

Williams, R. L., & Long, J. D. (1978). *Toward a self-managed lifestyle* (2nd ed.). Boston: Houghton Mifflin.

Wineburg, S. S. (1987). The self-fulfillment of the self-fulfilling prophecy: A critical appraisal. *Educational Researcher, 16,* 28–37.

Winick, M. (1976). *Malnutrition and brain development.* New York: Oxford University Press.

Winn, M. (1985). *The plug-in drug* (rev. ed.). New York: Viking.

Winsten, S. (1949). *Days with Bernard Shaw.* New York: Vanguard Press.

Wittrock, M. C. (1986). Students' thought processes. In M. C. Wittrock (Ed.), *Handbook of research on teaching* (3rd ed.) (pp. 297–314). New York: Macmillan.

Women's Bureau. (1982). *20 facts on women workers.* Washington, D.C.: U.S. Department of Labor.

Wood, B. S. (1981). *Children and communication: Verbal and nonverbal language development* (2nd ed.). Englewood Cliffs, N.J.: Prentice-Hall.

Woodward, J., Carnine, D., & Gersten, R. (1988). Teaching problem solving through computer simulations. *American Educational Research Journal, 25,* 72–86.

Zajonc, R. B. (1975, January). Birth order and intelligence: Dumber by the dozen. *Psychology Today,* pp. 37–43.

Zajonc, R. B. (1976). Family configuration and intelligence. *Science, 192,* 227–236.

Zajonc, R. B. (1986). The decline and rise of scholastic aptitude scores: A prediction derived from the confluence model. *American Psychologist, 41,* 862–867.

Zajonc, R., & Markus, G. B. (1975). Birth order and intellectual development. *Psychological Review, 82,* 74–88.

Zigler, E., & Muenchow, S. (1979). Mainstreaming: The proof is in the implementation. *American Psychologist, 34,* 993–996.

NAME INDEX

Davidson, E., 149
Deale, R. N., 389
Deaux, K., 195
de Bono, E., 262–63
Debus, R. L., 306
de Charms, R., 306
Dempter, F. N., 60
Dennison, G., 143, 146
Denny, D. A., 264
Derry, S. J., 127
Diaz, R. M., 172, 244
Dick, W., 69, 114, 360
Doherty, M. A., 333–34
Doleys, D. M., 332–33
Donaldson, G., 225
Doyle, W., 314, 315, 317, 318, 333
Drabman, R. S., 327
Drum, P., 104
Dunn, L. M., 278
Dunn, R., 146, 147–48, 342
Dweck, C. S., 286, 303–4, 308

Edgerton, R. B., 273
Eisenberg-Berg, N., 176
Eisner, E. W., 10, 112–13, 316, 370
Elton, L. R. B., 368
Engel, M., 79, 131, 155, 181
Ennis, R. H., 211
Epstein, H. T., 162
Erhardt, A. A., 195
Erickson, F., 317
Erikson, E., 166
Erlehmeyer-Kimling, L., 160
Escobar, C. M., 164
Evertson, C. M., 320
Ewer, R. F., 393

Feuerstein, R., 126, 127, 128, 215, 225, 230
Fischer, K. W., 211
Fishkin, J., 176
Flanders, N. A., 267
Flavell, J. H., 25, 68, 120, 123, 196, 197, 198, 210
Fleming, M., 370
Fodor, E. N., 177
Forness, S., 275
Freeman, D., 195
Freeman, F. N., 238
Freud, S., 73, 166
Frisch, R. E., 159
Fuller, B., 17
Furth, H. G., 212

Gabel, D. L., 98
Gage, N. L., 51
Gagné, E. D., 24, 58
Gagné, R. M., 25, 69, 83, 109, 110, 113–22, 123, 127, 211, 360
Gallagher, J. J., 244
Galton, F., 238
Gardner, H., 243, 352
Garner, W. R., 379
Gelman, R., 210
Genesee, F., 172
Gersten, R., 350–51
Getzels, J. W., 245
Gilligan, C., 176–77
Ginsberg, H., 212
Glaser, R., 60, 110, 118
Glass, A. L., 59
Glasser, W., 321
Goldschmid, M. L., 214
Good, T. L., 269
Goodenough, F., 235
Goodnow, J. J., 85, 86, 87
Gordon, T., 143, 144
Gordon, W. J. J., 260
Gottlieb, J., 278
Grandom, J. M., 238, 239
Grant, J. P., 16
Gray, M. A., 143
Greene, D., 326
Greene, J. G., 305
Greenspoon, J., 48
Greer, R. D., 49
Gregorc, A. F., 147
Griffiths, A. K., 212
Griggs, S. A., 146, 147–48, 342
Grippin, P. C., 8, 97, 102
Gronlund, N. E., 112–13, 370, 385
Grossman, J. J., 273
Grotevant, H. D., 239
Grusec, J. E., 324, 332
Guilford, J. P., 225, 242–44, 246–47
Gullickson, A. R., 367
Gump, P. V., 321
Guthrie, E. R., 29–33, 35, 50, 51

Haddon, F. A., 263
Haefele, J. W., 260, 261
Haertel, E., 388
Hagen, E., 231, 233
Hall, F. R., 55
Hallman, R. J., 264
Hammond, G. W., 195
Haney, R. E., 356
Hanley, P. E., 13, 17

Harding, J. F., 242
Hargreaves, D. H., 318
Harris, D., 235
Harsh, C. M., 187
Hartshorne, H., 177
Hauser, R. M., 239
Haywood, H. C., 125
Hebb, D. O., 168, 224, 225, 241, 290
Hembree, R., 294, 295
Herbert, J. J., 187
Hester, S. K., 318
Hewett, S., 327
Heyneman, S. P., 17
Heyns, O. S., 241
Higbee, K. L., 67, 75
Hill, K. T., 295
Hintzman, D. L., 68
Hoffman, M. L., 178, 324
Hoge, R. D., 243, 255
Holland, J. L., 194
Holstein, C. B., 176, 177
Holt, J., 143
Holyoak, K. J., 59
Holzinger, K. J., 240
Homme, L. E., 328
Horn, J. L., 225
Horner, M., 195
Horowitz, F. D., 256
Horton, D. L., 67
Howe, L. W., 144
Humphreys, L. G., 243
Hunt, E., 58, 59, 83
Hunt, J. M., 200, 214
Hurlock, 166

Inhelder, B., 196
Intons-Peterson, M. J., 194

Jacklin, C. N., 195
Jackson, P. W., 245
Jacobson, L., 268
James, W., 215
Janos, P. M., 256
Jarvik, L. E., 160
Jenkins, J. R., 278
Jensen, A. R., 237, 241
Johnson, D., 148, 149, 150, 335
Johnson, M. K., 83
Johnson, R., 150
Jones, R. L., 270, 278
Judy, J. E., 122–23, 124
Jurs, S. G., 377
Justice, E., 67

Pavlov, I., 25–26, 28, 35
Pazulinec, R., 334
Peat, D., 127, 128
Perkins, M. R., 379
Perry, R., 339, 363
Peters, R., 178
Peters, S. C., 8, 97, 102
Peterson, P. L., 359
Phillips, J. L., 212
Piaget, J., 164–65, 166, 173, 174,
    196–209, 210, 211, 212, 213,
    214, 225, 229
Pinard, A., 214
Pintrich, P. R., 295, 360
Popham, W. J., 372, 389
Postman, N., 143
Premack, D., 327
Purkey, W. W., 143

Quarter, J., 178

Rachford, D. L., 126
Rakow, F. A., 359
Ramsden, P., 104, 105, 367
Raphael, B., 76
Raynor, J. O., 304
Reese, H. W., 9
Reis, S. M., 256
Renzulli, J. S., 147, 255, 256
Resnick, L. B., 295, 359
Revelle, R., 159
Riegel, K. E., 211
Robin, A. L., 357
Robinson, F. G., 96, 101
Robinson, M. L., 278
Robinson, N. M., 256
Rogers, C. R., 137–41
Rolison, M. A., 269
Rosenshine, B., 122, 123–24
Rosenthal, R., 268, 269
Rosenzweig, M. R., 161, 241
Ross, A. O., 274
Ross, D., 188
Ross, R. P., 321
Ross, S. M., 188, 359
Rossmiller, R. A., 356
Rousseau, J., 139, 146
Rubadeau, D. O., 212
Rubin, K. H., 210
Russell, J. A., 195

Saily, M., 356
Sajwaj, T., 334
Säljö, R., 94
Salomon, G., 352

Santa, J. L., 59
Sarason, I. G., 294
Satir, V., 143
Sattler, J. M., 233, 234
Savell, J. M., 126
Scanlon, R., 356
Scarr, S., 239
Schaffarzik, J., 356
Schank, R. C., 84
Schniedwind, N., 149
Schultz, D. P., 291
Schunck, D. H., 300
Sears, R. R., 42, 331
Semmel, M. I., 278
Sewell, E. H., 239
Seymour, D., 172
Shachar, H., 150
Shapiro, A. K., 268
Sharan, S., 150
Shaw, G. B., 242
Shepard, L. A., 110–11, 275, 389
Shepard-Look, D. L., 195
Sherwood, R. D., 98
Shiffrin, R. M., 60
Shirley, M., 164
Shuell, T. J., 123
Shulman, L. S., 136
Siegler, R. S., 64
Sigman, N. D., 162
Silvern, L., 211
Silvernail, D. L., 267
Simon, H. A., 59, 60
Simon, S. B., 143, 144
Simpson, E. L., 143
Singer, J. D., 16
Skinner, B. F., 33, 35–37, 43, 44, 49,
    50, 52–53, 137–38, 140, 344
Slavin, R. E., 264, 356
Smedslund, J., 212
Smith, E. L., 104
Smith, L. H., 147, 256
Smith, M. L., 275
Snow, R. E., 93, 102, 358, 360
Solomon, D., 335–36
Sonnier, I. L., 162
Soper, J. D., 107
Sorenson, J. S., 356
Southern, H. N., 311
Spearman, C. E., 224
Spokane, A. R., 194
Stahl, L., 351
Stallings, J. A., 355
Standing, L., 73
Stanley, J. C., 256
Stein, M. I., 242, 243

Stern, C., 237
Sternberg, R. J., 120, 125, 127, 225,
    226–29
Stevens, R., 122, 123–24
Stipek, D. J., 296, 355
Stodolsky, S. S., 321
Sturges, P. S., 327
Sullivan, E. V., 178
Suls, J., 176
Swain, M., 173
Swing, S. R., 359
Switzky, H. N., 125

Tavris, C., 194
Terman, L. M., 166, 255
Thomas, J. W., 305
Thomas, R. M., 85
Thorndike, E. L., 33–35, 36, 41, 50,
    51, 231, 233, 314
Thurstone, L. L., 224
Tiemann, P. W., 344
Tisher, R. P., 98
Tittle, C. K., 194
Toffler, A., 346
Torrance, E. P., 244, 246, 256, 264
Tryon, G. S., 295
Tryon, R. C., 240
Tsang, M. C., 17
Turiel, F., 177
Turner, R. L., 264
Twohig, P. T., 126

Ulrich, R. E., 43
Ungoed-Thomas, J. P., 178
U.S. Department of Labor, 194
U.S. Office of Education, 271
Uzgiris, I. C., 214

Van Houten, 332–33
Velandia, W., 238
Vernon, P. E., 225
Vojir, C. P., 275
Vygotsky, L. S., 196, 214–16, 225,
    230

Waddington, C. H., 159
Wagner, R. K., 225
Walberg, H. J., 146
Walker, D. F., 356
Walker, H., 51
Wallach, M. A., 243, 245
Walters, G. C., 324, 332
Walters, R. H., 43, 185, 186, 188,
    189–90
Ward, L. M., 175

SUBJECT INDEX

TO THE OWNER OF THE BEAR:

I hope that you have enjoyed **Psychology for Teaching: A Bear** ~~Always Usually Sometimes Rarely Never Always Faces the Front~~ **Will Not Commit Himself Just Now, Seventh Edition.** Your comments are valuable to me as an author and educator. Would you care to share them?

School _____ Your instructor's name _____

1. What did you like *most* about The Bear? _____

2. What did you like *least* about it? _____

3. Were all the chapters of the book assigned for you to read? _____

   If not, which ones weren't? _____

4. How informative and helpful were the educational implications sections? _____

   In general, how practical did you find The Bear? _____

5. Did you use the Glossary, and how helpful was it? _____

6. How helpful were the illustrations? _____

7. Were any topics or concepts particularly difficult to understand? _____

8. Were there any topics on which you would have liked:
   More information? _____

   Less information? _____

9. Do you have any additional criticisms or suggestions to make? _____